THE COMPLETE
NEW ZEALAND GARDENER

A PRACTICAL GUIDE

THE COMPLETE
NEW ZEALAND GARDENER
A PRACTICAL GUIDE

GEOFF BRYANT & EION SCARROW

David Bateman

Published in 1995 by David Bateman Ltd,
Tarndale Grove, Albany Business Park, Bush Road, Albany,
North Shore City, Auckland, New Zealand

ISBN 1 86953 209 0

Design and production by Sally Hollis-McLeod and Derek Ward,
Moscow Design
Photographs by Geoff Bryant, Gil Hanly and Dick Roberts
Typeset by Typeset Graphics, Auckland
Printed in Hong Kong by Everbest Printing Co.

ACKNOWLEDGEMENTS

THE AUTHORS and publishers would like to thank the following people for their contribution to this book: designers Sally Hollis-McLeod and Derek Ward of Moscow Design; Gil Hanly and Dick Roberts for supplying extra photographs where needed; Mark Roman for his illustrations; Dianne and Kaye from Typeset Graphics for all their efforts.

And special thanks to all those gardeners that allowed their gardens to be photographed and reproduced, and the many people who provided their expertise and advice on the countless questions that arose in the course of writing this book.

More specifically, we would like especially to thank: Watkins Home & Garden Products Ltd for permission to use photographs of their new range of gardening tools that appear on pages 14-15; The New Zealand Consumers' Institute for permission to use tables from *Good Gardening with the New Zealand Consumers' Institute* (Bateman, 1993); Moira Ryan, author of *Organic Gardening: A New Zealand Growers Handbook* (Bateman, 1994), for allowing us to adapt the diagrams from her book that appear on pages 26, 27, 28 and 251; T.W. Walker, author of *The Vegetable Growers Handbook* (Bateman, 1992), for permission to use the tables that appear on pages 247 and 250; Janet Cheriton for her help with the captions; Richard Chambers for allowing us to adapt his original garden plans that appear on pages 35 and 39; Peter Russell of the Royal New Zealand Forest & Bird Protection Society, Christchurch office, for all his help in providing the information and tables used on pages 271-273.

Finally, thanks to the editorial team of Tracey Borgfeldt, Robert McKenzie, Kate Riggir and Janet Bateman.

Contents

SECTION THREE   CARING FOR YOUR GARDEN

INTRODUCTION

ALTHOUGH TODAY REGARDED primarily as a leisure activity, gardening has its origins in the tireless labour of primitive agriculture. Yet the appreciation of plants, as much for their beauty as for their functional attributes, must be an integral part of human nature, as almost every culture developed some form of ornamental gardening as soon as the pressures of subsistence living ceased to be an over-riding concern.

While we may tend to associate early gardening with the more familiar kitchen and 'physic' gardens of medieval Europe, the ancient Chinese and Persians tended purely ornamental gardens 2000 years before Europe's first efforts. Not only were they growing ornamentals, but they had already begun the process of selecting superior growth strains and had embarked on controlled propagation. In New Zealand, the pre-European Maori tended large gardens that included both functional and ornamental plants, and the continued survival of at least one species, *Clianthus puniceus* (kaka beak), may have been due to its cultivation in Maori gardens.

It has been said that gardening is the most popular hobby in New Zealand, and without doubt a huge amount of time, labour and money is invested in our gardens. New gardeners quickly learn that experience and knowledge are invaluable guides to successful gardening, and while it is perfectly possible to get ample enjoyment from your plants and garden without any great depth of knowledge, the more you know and understand your garden the greater and more reliable the rewards will be. But how do you gain that knowledge and experience?

With these points in mind, welcome to *The Complete New Zealand Gardener.* This book has something for all New Zealand gardeners and we would like to think that you will use it as your basic reference; the book you turn to first when those all too common gardening questions arise. It covers all of the main gardening topics and provides plenty of information to get the beginner started or motivate the more experienced.

The book is divided into three main sections, but before they begin there is a small chapter on botanical naming, the basic elements of which will help you to get the most out of this and other gardening books. The first section, 'Starting Out', looks at the important points to consider when starting a new garden or extensively modifying an existing garden – the right equipment, soil, climate and planning. Next, there are several chapters detailing the main plant groups, both ornamental and edible. The third and last section covers plant nutrition and composting, basic propagation, pruning, pest, disease and weed control, gardening under cover and includes a garden calendar to pull it all together. This is followed by a comprehensive index so that you can easily find your way around the book.

Beginners, particularly those with new gardens, will find the initial section very informative, and more experienced gardeners will find plenty to interest them there, too. But whether beginner or experienced, you will probably refer most often to the plant chapters. These are divided into groups based on plant type and provide detailed information on cultivation and maintenance as well as descriptions of hundreds of the most widely grown garden plants. Aspects such as propagation and pruning are covered within the chapters where applicable and information is cross-referenced with the later chapters that cover such topics in more detail.

The information, while concise, it thorough and, most importantly, it is written specifically for New Zealand gardeners. This means that in most cases you won't have to search for the plants we recommend and that all the information provided is genuinely relevant to New Zealand conditions and takes full account of our diverse range of climates and garden styles.

Of course no book can replace the skills gained by experience. However, *The Complete New Zealand Gardener* tells you all you need to know to get started properly and develop your gardening expertise. Also, while we acknowledge that a book of this type cannot be as detailed as a specialist plant guide, we think that you will be pleased with the thoroughness of the coverage, and we trust that it will enhance your enjoyment of plants and gardening.

STARTING OUT

BASIC BOTANICAL TERMS AND PLANT NAMES

FOR AS LONG AS people have been looking at plants they have been categorising them. First by their size and uses, and then by more precise methods, such as similarities in leaf and flower structure. By late Renaissance times, the increasing range of known plants, combined with the rise of scientific knowledge, demanded a standardised form of plant classification.

Swedish naturalist Carolus Linnaeus (1707–78) came up with the solution. He refined identification and classification so that any living creature could be classified by just two names. Hence his system, still in use today, is known as binomial (two names) nomenclature.

Binomial nomenclature is based on the concepts of genus and species. A genus, the first name, is a grouping of closely related living things that share certain characteristics. A species is a single type of plant or animal within a genus. A species must be genetically stable and capable of reproducing true to type sexually. Natural or artificial hybrids, mutants and selected forms are not regarded as new species.

The genera and species are in turn placed in wider groupings that are increasingly diverse until we return to the entire Kingdom of Living Things (see chart at right).

Some genera, *Rhododendron* included, are large, with many complex relationships, so some degree of subdividing within a genus is allowed. Our example, *R. impeditum*, is a typical small alpine rhododendron from Southern China and may be placed, with others of its type, in a division known as a subgenus, which may be further divided into sections and subsections. The initial letter of the genus name should be capitalised while the initial letter of the species name should be lower case. The whole botanical name should be italicised.

Natural hybrids or unusual forms may occur, and once a plant enters cultivation it is almost certain to be used in hybridisation or developed in some way. Hybrids and cultivated forms fail the first test of a species, they cannot

The system as it relates to one plant species, *Rhododendron impeditum*, is as follows.	
All Living Things	
PHYLUM	Plant Kingdom
DIVISION	Magnoliophyta
CLASS	Magnoliopsida
SUBCLASS	Dilleniidae
ORDER	Ericales
FAMILY	Ericaceae
GENUS	*Rhododendron*
SPECIES	*impeditum*

Above: *Pittosporum eugenioides* 'Variegatum'. A wealth of information is conveyed by plant names, if you know how to 'read' them. Below: Are you both talking about the same plant when you say, 'I'd like to plant some teasel'? It may be safer to use *Dipsacus fullonum*.

Rhododendron impeditum var. 'Blue Steel'. The 'var.' indicates that this is a naturally occuring variation of a species.

reproduce true to type from seed, so they must be classified in some other way. Three terms are commonly used to describe these plants; variety, cultivar and clone. Variety is the term commonly used to describe any hybrid or selected form but in botanical terms the definition is more precise. A variety is a naturally occurring variation of a species. This is normally expressed as the abbreviation 'var.', as in *Rhododendron impeditum* var. 'Blue Steel'. When cultivated it may also be known as a selected form.

Cultivar (a contraction of **cult**ivated **vari**ety) and clone (vegetative replicas of the original cultivar) are somewhat interchangeable terms, they refer to artificially produced hybrids and varieties. Names such as *Rhododendron* 'Unique' refer to cultivars, a plant produced by crossing two distinctly different parent plants and only capable of being perpetuated by vegetative reproduction. Cultivar, clone and variety names are not italicised.

Over the years certain conventions in plant naming have developed. If you know the basic rules and understand a little Latin it is often easy to work out the meaning of plant names, which may give you valuable hints with regard to coloration and habitat preferences. Most names describe some feature of the plant, commemorate a person significant in its history or describe where it was first discovered.

Names ending in **i, ae,** or **anum** usually refer to a significant person. *Rhododendron farrerae* was named after the wife of an officer of the East India Company, *Grevillea banksii* was named after Sir Joseph Banks. Names ending in **ensis** refer to a location, hence *sinensis* indicates a plant from China (Sino refers to China) and *canadensis* from Canada.

Names ending in **um**, such as *ferrugineum* (rust coloured), generally describe a characteristic. Yet other names describe colours, *alba* (white), *rosea* (pink), *rubra* (red) and *purpureum* (purple) are common examples. The suffix **ifera** means 'of', 'resembling', or 'used for', so we have *papyrifera*, used in paper making, and *tulipifera*, flowers resembling a tulip. The above are all examples of species names but genus names follow similar patterns.

The regularity with which plant names change is a source of constant confusion and frustrates many gardeners, but there are good reasons for it. Often it is because a botanical revision reveals that the relationships between genera and species were not quite as first thought, which necessitates a regrouping and some renaming.

The second instance in which plants are renamed is an application of the rule of precedence. In the 18th and 19th centuries, when many common plants were classified, botanists had limited opportunities to communicate with one another; there were no international telephone lines and computer networks back then. Consequently there were many instances where a plant had several names because it had been independently classified by different botanists. To eliminate this multiple naming it was decided that the first name given must stand; the first name has precedence over all others no matter how well known or widely used they may be.

In this book we have endeavoured to be as up to date as possible with our naming and have followed the conventions laid down in *The International Code for the Nomenclature of Cultivated Plants*. However, this is a gardening book not a botanical text, so we have in a very few cases opted to use older names for ease of recognition.

The study of plant names can be almost as fascinating as the plants themselves, but many people are put off by Latin – some names are larger than the plants – and the seemingly impenetrable mass of names. Try not to become disillusioned with gardening if you can't master plant naming, the most important thing is that you understand enough to find the information you need.

To help clarify the system and increase your gardening enjoyment, the following table lists some of the more commonly used parts of plant names and their meanings. Note that botanical Latin is not classical Latin; it includes many technical terms and words of Greek derivation.

THE MEANING OF NAMES

alba, albi, albo White.

anthum Referring to the anthers or more commonly the flower as a whole.

arbor Tree-like growth.

argentea (eum) Silver coloured.

atro A prefix meaning dark.

auriculata, auritum Having auriculate (shaped like the lobe of the ear) leaves, flowers, etc.

aureus (um) Golden coloured.

australis Southern, not necessarily from Australia, it is often used to refer to plants from southern Europe.

barbata (um), pogo Bearded, as in a seed or flower.

brachy, brevi Prefixes meaning short or abbreviated.

calo, calli Beautiful.

campo Bell shaped.

campy, campylo Bent.

capitata (um) Head-like, usually a reference to a flower form.

carpa (um) A reference to a fruit, as in brachycarpum, a short fruit.

cephala (um) The head, usually a reference to having flowers in clusters, or heads.

ceras, cerasti Cherry red coloration or resembling a cherry.

chamae, pseudo Prefixes meaning false, usually a reference to a plant of similar appearance, as in *Pseudopanax*, looking like *Panax*.

chion Snowy colour or texture.

ciliata (um), cilii Pertaining to cilia, hairs. Usually a reference to hairy stems or leaves.

cinerea Grey coloration.

citri, citrini Having a citrus (particularly lemon) scent.

clada (um) A reference to the twigs or branches.

cola, icola A suffix indicating the preferred habitat, as in alpicola (alpine), dumicola (thickets) and rupicola (rocks).

compacta (um) Having a compact growth habit.

complexa (um) Usually refers to a plant with a densely twiggy growth habit.

cornuta (um) Horned, usually a reference to flowers or seed pods.

cristata (um) Wavy or crinkled.

cuneata (um) Cuneate, or wedge shaped.

dendricola Of the trees. Usually a reference to an epiphytic growth habit.

dichro Two, a prefix indicating two distinct forms, flower colours or the like.

discolor Composed of, or found in, several colours.

edulis Edible.

fastigata (um) fastigiata (um) Upright growth habit.

ferruginea (um) Rust coloured.

fimbriata (um) Edged with minute hairs.

flexuosa (um) Flexible.

flora (um), flori A reference to a characteristic of the flowers, as in albiflorum, meaning white flowered.

folium A suffix indicating the foliage.

formosa (um) A descriptive term meaning beautiful.

fulgens Shining, usually a reference to foliage.

gigantea (um) Large growing.

glabra (um) Smooth or hairless.

glauca (um), caerulea (um), cyano Bluish coloured.

globula, globulata (um) Round or globe-like.

glutinosa (um) Sticky or covered in a sticky coating.

grande, grandi Large.

hirsuta (um) Hairy, usually a reference to foliage.

humilis Small or insignificant.

impedita (um), intricata (um) Tangled, generally a reference to a dense twiggy growth habit.

indumenta (um), tomentosa (um) The foliage has a felt- or hair-like covering.

insulare From an island.

lactea (um) Milky, usually a reference to colour.

lanata (um), lanigera (um) Woolly, used to describe heavily felted foliage.

laxi A prefix that indicates a drooping habit.

lepidi, lepido A prefix indicating a scaly covering, usually refers to foliage.

leuca, leuco White coloration.

longi Unusually long.

lutea (um) Yellow coloration.

macro, mega Large.

magnifica Magnificent or impressive.

maximum Largest.

meli, melia Honey-like.

micro, mucro Small.

minima, minimum Small and smallest.

nigra (um), nigro, nigrescens Black.

nivale, nivea (um) Snowy, in colour or texture.

nobilis Impressive or of noble stature.

obtusa (um) Blunt, usually a reference to leaf shape.

occidentale From the west.

odora, odorata (um) A reference to fragrance.

oides A suffix that usually means resembling, as in jasminoides, resembles jasmine.

olea, olei Leaves reminiscent of the olive (*Olea*).

orbic Round.

oreo Of the mountains.

orientale From the east.

ovata (um) Egg shaped.

pachy Thick, usually a reference to stolons or hairs.

paniculata (um) Flowers in sprays, or panicles.

para Similar to, as in *Parahebe*, similar to, or allied to *Hebe*.

parva, parvi small.

pauci Few or lacking.

pendula (um) Indicates a weeping growth habit.

penta, qinque Five, a reference to foliage or flower form.

phyta, phyton Suffixes that mean plant, as in macrophyton, large plant.

pilosa (um) Hairs, usually used as a suffix, as in rubropilosa, red haired.

pinnata (um) Resembling a feather.

poli, poly Many.

pubescens Covered in small hairs.

pumila (um) Small or of creeping growth habit.

punctata (um) Spotted.

purpurea (um) Distinct purple coloration.

quadri, tetra Four, a reference to foliage or flower form.

radicans Rooting, usually referring to plants that strike roots as they spread.

repens, prostrata Having a ground cover or very compact growth habit.

reticulata (um) Netted, or net-like, usually in reference to the venation of foliage.

rhoda, rhodo Rose coloured or rose-like.

rigida (um) Stiff.

ripense Found near rivers.

robusta Large, strong growing.

rosea, rosae, rosi Rose coloured or resembling a rose.

rubignosa (um), russata (um) A rusty red coloration.

rubra (um) Red coloration.

salici A prefix meaning willow-like.

sangui Blood, usually a reference to flower colour or, occasionally, sap colour.

scabra (um) Rough to touch.

schizo Split or found in two or more forms.

semi A prefix meaning partial.

sessile, sessili Strictly speaking this means directly attached and is often used to refer to leaves, but it is more commonly used to refer to plants that spread across the ground, striking roots as they grow.

setosa (um) Bristly.

sidero Iron, usually a reference to something being extremely hard (sideroxylon, iron-wood) or rust coloured.

spicifera (um) Spiky or bearing spikes.

spinulifera (um) Spiny or bearing spines.

splendida (um), splendens Splendid, impressive, usually a reference to vivid flowers.

spora (um) Seeds or a reference to some characteristic of the seeds, as in *Pittosporum*, sticky seeds.

squamata (um) A reference to scales, usually leaf scales.

stellata (um) Star shaped.

striata (um) Striped.

sub Beneath or less than.

sulfurea (um) Sulphur coloured.

supra Above or superior to.

sylvestris Of the forest.

telopea (um) Conspicuous, usually showy plants that can be seen at a distance.

tricha, tricho Hairy.

tuberculosa (um) Covered in small growths or nodules.

variegata (um) Having either variegated flowers or foliage.

vernalis Usually indicates spring flowering.

verrucosa (um) Covered in small wart-like growths.

vestita (um) Clothed or covered.

violacea (um) Violet or purple coloration.

virida, viridum, viridescens Green coloration.

viscida, viscidi Sticky or covered in a sticky coating.

vulgaris Common, usually used to indicate the first described or most common species of a genus.

xylon Wood, usually used as a descriptive suffix, as in leuco-xylon, white wood.

11

Starting Out

13

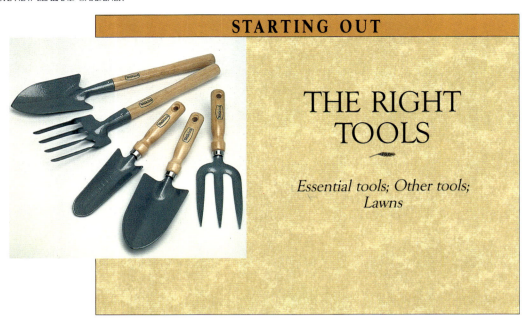

STARTING OUT

THE RIGHT TOOLS

Essential tools; Other tools; Lawns

TO ENJOY GARDENING, lessen your work load and do a good job, you need the right tools. You don't need to spend a fortune, but it is important that you have a good quality selection. The most important points to remember when buying tools are to avoid gimmicks and buy quality. Unusual tool designs make great promises of increased labour saving and greater efficiency, however, the common garden hand tools have changed little over the last 150 years, indicating they are a good design. Make sure you have a genuine use for unusual tools and that they are superior to those of a more conventional design.

Regardless of design, your tools should be the best quality that you can afford. Cheap tools are nearly always a false economy; not only do they deteriorate quickly, they are designed to be disposed of when worn rather than upgraded or repaired. Some companies do still make them like they used to – strong and reliable. Always choose heat-tempered steel over weak light alloys or castings. Buy steel-handled tools rather than those with rot-prone wooden handles and avoid anything that is chrome plated or covered in a thick layer of paint; it is usually there to hide poor workmanship and sloppy joins. Stainless steel is the longest lasting material and has the lowest maintenance requirements, but it is expensive. Also, look for tools that are easily dismantled for maintenance, that use commonly available components, have replaceable blades and a reliable supply of spare parts.

Good quality is usually expensive so don't ignore the maintenance of your tools. They will be in frequent use and in regular contact with moist plant tissue and soil, which leads to corrosion and dulled blades. Washing your tools after use, and wiping them with an oily rag once dry, will help prevent rust taking hold.

Any bladed tool will eventually need to be sharpened. Sharpening not only makes your blades more efficient it also makes them safer, as a sharp blade is less likely to slip or veer off line. It is no exaggeration to say that a well looked after quality tool will last a lifetime.

ESSENTIAL TOOLS

Some tools are absolutely indispensable, either because they have unique functions or because they are such labour savers that you simply can't afford to be without them.

Fork

Many gardeners use a spade when a fork would be a better option. When lifting perennials for division or harvesting crops such as potatoes, a fork is less damaging than a spade as it only causes damage when the tines actually penetrate a tuber or root. Forks are also useful for loosening soil that has already been dug over, breaking up large clods and incorporating compost materials.

Forks come in a range of handle sizes, tine lengths and weights, but the standard model suits most people and uses. A small border fork is a handy tool where working space is limited.

Hedging and pruning shears

These come in a variety of sizes and types, depending on their intended use. Standard hedging shears are only intended for light foliage trimming and removing branches less than 15 mm in diameter. Loppers and heavy-duty pruning shears will handle branches up to about 35 mm in diameter.

Hoe

Hoes are indispensable weeding tools. Regular use stops weed seedlings before they have a chance to become established and eliminates a lot of bending. The traditional push hoe is favoured for ornamental gardens but the chopping action of a Dutch hoe is useful between close rows, as in a vegetable garden.

Hoses

Regardless of how sophisticated an irrigation system you have, a garden hose is an essential piece of equipment. Top quality hoses are expensive but last well and are reasonably kink-free. When laying out your garden, bear in mind the position of the nearest taps and how far a hose may be required to reach. Any areas that may need occasional watering, such as flower beds, should be reasonably close to the water source, as the pressure loss within the hose will be considerable at distances over 30 m. Most domestic hoses are now a standard 15 mm in diameter, and virtually all modern hose fittings are designed to fit this size.

Rake

Whether levelling a seed bed, raking leaves or maintaining a gravel path, a rake is indispensable. A standard rake will be suitable for most tasks, but if you have a lot of deciduous trees a leaf rake may be a worthwhile investment. The back of the rake is almost as useful as the tines. Use it to break up clods and for final smoothing of seed beds and gravel pathways.

Saws

It may be possible to get by without a pruning saw, but most gardeners eventually need to trim a branch that is too heavy for secateurs or pruning shears. There are several styles of pruning saws, but the bow saw is usually the best compromise between durability, manoeuvrability and efficiency.

Secateurs

Secateurs are your basic pruning tool, and they are also extremely useful for plant propagation. A medium-sized pair will be suitable for most tasks. It is important to choose secateurs that are easily cleaned and lubricated, and that have replaceable blades.

Sharpening stone

Many tools have blades, so it is important that you have some way of sharpening them. Accurate blade sharpening is quite a skilled job that requires some practice. Grindstones are the best choice for sharpening, but they cut through metal very quickly and are not for the inexperienced; in most cases a good carborundum sharpening stone will suffice.

Honing guides are handy accessories that simplify the sharpening process by keeping the blade at the proper angle to the stone. However, they are only practical with small blades that can be removed for sharpening. How often you need to sharpen a blade depends on frequency of use and the quality of the blade. Generally you will know when the blade is becoming blunt.

Spade

The spade is perhaps the most important gardening implement, yet it is one that is often skimped on. Buy the best you can afford and it should last a lifetime. Steel handles are preferable to wooden ones, but they are not always readily available and can be quite expensive. The next best is the wooden handle sleeved into a long steel shaft.

Spades come in various sizes so take the time to find one that fits. There are special-purpose designs too, such as the narrow, tapered trenching spade and the small border spade.

Sprinklers

Garden sprinklers come in all shapes and sizes. All are simply ways of distributing water, but some are more efficient than others. Which works best for you depends on the design of your garden and your water pressure. For example, oscillating sprinklers can soak a large area but they require fairly high water pressure to keep them moving. Porous hoses will operate at very low pressures but they can only water a relatively small area. Look at the range of sprinklers at your garden centre to see which is best for your garden. In most cases the simple flat sprinkler is quite adequate.

Trowel and hand fork

These small hand tools are most useful for weeding and working with young plants. Some gardeners prefer to use a dibbler (really just a tapered stick) when setting out young plants, but a trowel is more versatile.

Hedging and pruning shears come in a variety of sizes and types. Heavy-duty loppers can handle branches up to 35 mm in diameter.

A spade and a fork are a gardener's basic tools. Buy the best quality you can afford.

Using long-handled edging shears adds that extra touch to a well-maintained lawn.

15

Watering can

For small gardens, a watering can is an effective substitute for more sophisticated spraying equipment. Watering cans may also be used for applying liquid fertilisers, and those with long nozzles are useful for reaching hard to get at places.

Wheelbarrow

Scarcely a day goes by in the garden when there isn't the need to move compost, weeds, large plants or some other bulky item. Look for a barrow that is solidly constructed from good materials. As the tray is always the first part to wear out, models with replaceable trays offer the best long-term economy.

OTHER TOOLS

These tools will make gardening easier, but they are not absolutely essential.

Bucket

Whether it is for mixing up sprays or just moving water, a bucket is often the easiest way. They are also handy for transporting small quantities of weeds or compost.

Shovel

Shovels are useful if you find that you have large amounts of excavation to carry out, otherwise a spade is usually just as effective.

Spraying equipment

Spraying equipment is not only used for applying insecticides or weedkillers, it is also very handy for liquid fertilisers and as a manual misting system for small seedlings and cuttings.

Today's spraying equipment is efficient and easy to use and maintain; unless you really have very little spraying to do, choose a modern pressurised sprayer. They eliminate the continual pumping required by a basic piston sprayer.

In most gardens a 5-litre portable model will do, but you may find a 10–15-litre knapsack more useful if you have fruit trees or large numbers of roses. Although they are the ulti-

Two forms of hand-pumped sprayers, suitable for small spraying jobs.

Although they can be unwieldy, reel mowers provide a level of finish unattainable with other types of mower.

mate in speed and convenience, few home gardeners need a motorised mist blower.

Marker lines

These are useful for all sorts of garden jobs: keeping straight seed rows, marking out lawns and setting plumb lines.

LAWNS

If you intend to have a lawn, you will also need the following lawn maintenance equipment.

Edging shears

Edging shears take the bending out of edge trimming and make it a quick and easy job. An edging wheel is the best method of trimming to a hard edge or mowing strip. Some motorised weed trimmers have edging attachments but they rarely do the job as neatly as hand shears.

Lawn mower

If you have only a small lawn, a hand mower is probably all you need, but most gardeners opt for a powered mower. Electric mowers are useful for small areas and modern models are safe and reliable. However, they are limited by their low motor power, short battery life or cable length.

Petrol or two-stroke mowers are best for heavy grass or large areas. Rotary mowers are effective on rough grass and are also suitable for most domestic lawns. These tough, dependable mowers, which have a flat blade that cuts with a scything action as it spins, are capable of cutting coarse grass and tackling rough, uneven areas. They require little maintenance and are relatively cheap to purchase and operate.

For a perfect lawn, the reel mower is the only choice. These mowers have a cutting cylinder with multiple blades and they also roll the lawn as they cut. Due to the way the blades and rollers lay the grass over after cutting, reel mowers create that striped effect that is typical of top-class sports fields and fine lawns. They are expensive to buy and operate, and are often large and difficult to handle, but they provide a level of finish that is simply not attainable with rotary or hand mowers.

Weed trimmer

Motorised weed trimmers, which may be electric or petrol powered, are very useful for cutting back rank growth. Although these are handy tools for large gardens or for clearing overgrown areas, most domestic gardens are too small and too regularly maintained to justify purchasing a weed trimmer.

ASSESSING YOUR SITE

Levels and natural features; Light; Existing trees; Weeds; Pests and diseases; Utilities; Soil – determining the pH; drainage, fertility

CREATING A GARDEN is an exciting challenge, with the potential to reward you with a lifetime of enjoyment. But the garden of your dreams won't happen overnight; it requires careful planning, hard work and knowledge of the essentials of gardening. Before you can even think about planting, you must thoroughly assess and prepare the site.

Whether you are developing a new garden or modifying an existing one, the basic groundwork is all important, and the more time spent on preparation, the better the results. This may require some expenditure that will not yield immediately visible benefits, but it will be money well spent! Skipping the initial preparation will only limit what you can achieve further down the track.

The following considerations are equally important for all gardens and gardeners, regardless of your climate, soil quality, and the types of plants and garden style you have your heart set on.

Whether you are buying a new section or an established house and garden, or altering your own garden, many of the considerations are the same: natural contours, exposure to wind and sun, light and soil. In an established garden you are surrounded by a myriad of clues indicating the nature of the garden, how well certain plants grow and how easy it would be to make changes. With a new section, by choosing carefully, you can avoid many of the worst garden problems.

If you are building from scratch, it is impor-

tant to remember that some construction processes can dramatically affect the section. The topsoil may be removed to make a more stable foundation, and it is very likely the soil will be compacted by machinery and builders. Levels, too, may be altered to suit building requirements.

Considerations such as views and exposure to the prevailing winds can be quickly assessed and are usually reflected in the price of the land. If you are completely new to an area it may be worthwhile viewing the site under various weather conditions, but your first impressions are often accurate. Nevertheless, you should fully investigate the site, paying special attention to the following points.

LEVELS AND NATURAL FEATURES

The natural contours of the garden or site have the greatest influence on house and garden design. Severely sloping land can be difficult to work with and may complicate garden maintenance; it also demands a higher level of fitness from the gardener. However, if the slopes can be modified, either by excavation or terracing, variations in level are one of the best ways of adding interest to a garden.

Small streams and natural rock features are easily incorporated into a garden design and can be a very important reason for purchasing a particular section. Sometimes it is better to buy a garden with the natural features you want and build a house to fit, rather than having to build the features into the garden.

Above: A section after a house has been removed. Are any of the trees worth keeping?
Right: It is often easier to find a section with the features you want and then build a house to fit, rather than extensively modify the land.

LIGHT

How much sun the site receives will affect the range of plants you can grow, and it may also determine how wet the soil is in winter, and how quickly it warms up in spring and dries out in summer. If you are building in an established area, the shade created by existing trees and buildings should be fairly apparent, but most new subdivisions are open, at least initially, and it can be hard to determine how further development will affect your section. If possible, find out the plans of those who will be building near you.

The site orientation will have a great influence on how much sun various parts of the garden receive. This can be difficult to assess with a bare section unless you know what the design of the house will be like and how it will be located. Sections that run north/south will experience greater variation in sun and shade between the front and back of the garden than those that run east/west. But until you have a clear idea of the design of the house, it is difficult to determine exactly where light and shade will fall. The design of the surrounding houses will also have some influence.

Also remember that the passage of the sun through various seasons will affect the site. Areas that receive high summer sun may be completely shaded in winter and, as the sun rises and sets further to the north in winter, even areas that receive low summer sun may be shaded in winter.

EXISTING TREES

Established trees and shrubs can be a considerable asset in a garden. If they are healthy and attractive they provide a ready-made framework on which to develop the garden further. Remember that they can often be transplanted if their position is unsuitable.

Although most new subdivisions are built on completely cleared ground, sometimes sections become available when a house has been demolished. Or they may be the last to be developed in an otherwise established area. Left unchecked, builders will almost invariably remove existing trees and large shrubs to make their job easier. If you want to preserve an existing shrub or tree, make sure the builders are aware of your wishes or that the plant is lifted carefully so that it can be replanted later.

WEEDS

A garden with serious weed problems should be immediately apparent, but you need to be wary of potential problems from more insidious weeds. Most weeds are dormant at certain times of the year and may not be obvious when you first view the garden. There is little you can do about this unless it is possible to see the garden over several months.

When you move into a new garden, it can be a pleasant surprise when unexpected spring bulbs appear. However, if they are accompanied by oxalis, cape tulip and couch grass your joy will not last; they rapidly spread through a garden and are very hard to eradicate once established. It is important to eliminate such weeds before they become well-established, otherwise you may well have a major task on your hands.

Most new sections in urban areas are thoroughly sprayed before construction begins and hence are relatively weed-free. However, in country districts, new houses are often surrounded by open fields that are full of potential nightmares, such as thistles, docks and oxalis. You will be able to control these weeds with hard work and selective weedkillers, but with a reservoir of seeds right on your doorstep it will be an ongoing problem. It may be worth remembering that while some rural sections look idyllic, the reality may be very different.

PESTS AND DISEASES

All established gardens have their share of pests and diseases, but very few of them are serious enough to be a reason not to buy. If the garden contains a good mix of plants and has a generally healthy appearance, there is unlikely to be much to worry about. However, if there are fruit trees on the site or extensive plantings of one type of plant, such as roses or rhododendrons, you need to make a more thorough examination.

Fruit trees, particularly apples and stone fruits, are prone to several serious fungal diseases, of which fireblight and silver-leaf are probably the most devastating. Large groups of similar plants in a small area speed the spread of pests and diseases and are likely to quickly deteriorate if affected. Look for signs of powdery mildew, black spot and rust on roses, and thrips, leaf-roller caterpillar, mildew and rust on rhododendrons.

These problems can be controlled if they are not too well-established, but it may be better to avoid them. See the Pests and Diseases chapter for details of identification and control.

UTILITIES

The siting of a house is often determined by the access to utilities, such as sewers and electrical supplies, and this can have a bearing on your garden design. You don't want to be in the position of having to destroy the appealing features of your site, such as large established trees, in order to lay a sewer line. Consider how the existing contours and features may be altered to accommodate such utilities.

SOIL

Good soil is a basic ingredient of a good garden. The ideal garden soil is well drained yet moisture-retentive, rich in humus, well aerated and teeming with beneficial microorganisms and the all-important earthworms. Few new sections have soil anything like this, and you can expect to have to put in a considerable amount of work to get the soil to this standard. Existing gardens can have their problems too, especially if the soil has been subject to chemical fertilisers and received no organic matter over the years.

Garden soil is composed of two parts: topsoil and subsoil. The topsoil layer is the layer

HOW TO IDENTIFY YOUR SOIL TYPE					
Rub soil between finger and thumb – is it →	Can it be rolled into a ball? →	Does it look polished when rubbed? →	Can it be rolled into a cylinder? →	Can the cylinder be bent into a ring?	SOIL TYPE – AND WHAT TO DO
gritty	no	no	no	no	SAND add organic matter, water regularly
gritty	yes	no	no	no	SANDY LOAM as above
gritty/sticky	yes	yes	yes	no	SANDY CLAY LOAM good garden soil if well drained
sticky	yes	yes	yes	no	CLAY LOAM requires digging and drainage
sticky	yes	yes	yes	yes	CLAY as above
smooth/silky	yes	slightly	yes	slightly	SILT add organic matter, green manure
dark, fibrous	yes	no	no	no	PEAT requires drainage

of well-aerated, well-drained soil that will support plant growth. Its depth depends on the structure of the soil. A loose-textured humus-filled topsoil will be deeper than a hard clay-based topsoil because it is better aerated. The subsoil starts at the limit of soil aeration. This anaerobic soil is often different in colour from the topsoil and sometimes smells unpleasant. It cannot support much plant life and is generally poorly drained.

The soil of a new section may alter considerably by the time the house is built. Removal of the topsoil is often considered an unscrupulous practice (an extra revenue source for the builder), but it is vital to ensure that the house is built on solid ground. Nevertheless, you paid for the topsoil and it should not be sold from under you. Make sure it is replaced once the house is completed.

In contrast, you may also have problems with a filled or reclaimed site. Such areas often have very poor, clay-based topsoil or a very thin layer of topsoil on a rubble foundation. This can lead to difficulties with stability, drainage and infertility that may be almost impossible to overcome. If you intend to build or develop a garden on a recently filled site, you must be sure of its stability and the nature and depth of the fill. Getting an independent geological assessment is an expensive option but it may be necessary for your peace of mind.

DETERMINING THE PH

Because of the variable amounts of minerals and organic matter in the soil, there will be variations in a soil's acidity. This means that any moisture will become either acid or alkaline as it filters through the soil. This will affect the range of plants you will be able to grow and how they will need to be cultivated. Acidity is measured on the pH (potential of Hydrogen) scale, which is a 14-point scale based around the neutral point of 7. As the pH becomes lower (7–0), so the acidity increases; as it becomes higher (7–14), the alkalinity increases. It is important to realise this is a logarithmic scale: 6 is ten times more acid than 7, 5 is ten times more acid than 6 and so on, therefore a pH of 4 is 100 times more acid than pH 6. The same applies on the alkaline side: pH 10 is 100 times more alkaline than pH 8.

The pH range that will support plant growth is from about 4.5 to 8.5, with progressively less choice of plants as you move in either direction away from neutral. Most ornamentals prefer slightly acid conditions (around 6–6.8) whereas vegetables generally do best in neutral to slightly alkaline soils (7–8). Woodland plants often prefer quite acid soils (5.5–6) as they have adapted to growing in soils with high levels of leaf mould, which tends to be acidic. Knowing your soil's pH and planting accordingly will ensure you avoid a lot of problems later on.

Many plants will only grow well within a narrow pH range and pH is also important in determining how efficiently soil nutrients will be able to be used. In general, trace element deficiencies will be more apparent on acid soils, but very few soils are so acid that the effect is noticeable unless the soil is regularly cropped. On the other hand, acid-soil plants will have difficulty taking up iron and magnesium if the soil becomes too alkaline. They will show all the signs (chlorosis and discoloured new growth) of deficiencies in these elements when, in fact, there may be ample present. It's just that at a higher pH these elements form compounds that are unavailable to plants.

A proper soil test is the only way to be absolutely sure of your soil's pH. However, you can get a fairly good indication by looking at the plants growing in it. The foliage of members of the erica family, such as rhododendrons, will have a yellow appearance in alkaline soil and such plants may not grow at all in very limey soils. Camellias, too, rarely look healthy in alkaline soil. Cabbages, on the other hand,

Right: Hortensia hydrangeas are an excellent indicator of soil pH: blue in acid soils and pink in alkaline soil.
Far right: Because of the acidic nature of the leaf litter they grow in, woodland plants are adapted to thrive on slightly acid soils.

Above left: A bare sloping site presents many challenges for the gardener, but with some soil modification and careful planting you can achieve a garden of rich variety and interest (above right).

will probably be thriving in such soils. The large-flowered hortensia hydrangeas are among the best indicators of soil pH. Their flowers tend towards blue with increasing soil acidity and pink in alkaline soil.

With cultivation, most garden soils become slightly acid unless lime is added. This is ideal because it is what most plants prefer and you can always add a little lime if necessary. The exceptions to this trend toward acidity are limestone-based soils or areas where the water supply is alkaline. If such conditions prevail, you're almost certain to find out very quickly. Limestone districts, such as Oamaru and Wai-kari, are generally well known and you will probably be informed of the nature of the soil early on. Alkaline water, which is usually described as hard, is less obvious. Common signs of hard water are soap that is difficult to lather and crusty white deposits on cooking utensils and in the pipes. This furring is due to high concentrations of dissolved calcium salts. Litmus paper will quickly indicate alkaline water by turning blue when dampened.

DRAINAGE

Drainage is another important issue for gardeners. Before starting your garden, dig several holes at least 50 cm deep in various parts of the section. Examine the subsoil – if it is very compacted clay there could be problems with drainage. Fill the holes with water and see how quickly they drain. If they are still holding water after three hours you will need to con-

sider additional drainage or deep cultivation to break up the clay layer. If the holes start to fill with water naturally, it indicates that the ground-water table is high. This is quite normal in winter or after heavy rain, but if these conditions don't apply it could mean serious drainage problems.

FERTILITY

Poor soil leads to poor plants, so general plant health is probably the best indicator of soil fertility. Look for such tell-tale signs as stunted growth, yellowing foliage, premature leaf drop and a generally tired appearance. Most soil fertility problems are easy to correct, either by improving the structure of the soil through the addition of compost or by using chemical fertilisers. Do, however, make sure that you are dealing with poor soil and not distorted growth that is the result of the use of long-term weed-killers. This is something that you need to be particularly wary of if topsoil has been brought in. Be suspicious if you see signs such as twisted and distorted tip-growth.

Now that you have looked at your new or existing garden, and have a good idea of its strengths and weaknesses, you need to assess one of the most important elements in developing a successful garden. It is something over which you have little control, but if you work with it rather than against it you can achieve incredible results. That element is, of course, the climate.

TABLE OF COMMON NATURALLY OCCURRING SOILS

SOIL TYPE	DESCRIPTION	ADVANTAGES
SAND	Very sandy soils contain over 80% beach or river sand. The soil is composed of large grains of finely crushed rock or shell.	Depending on the material from which it was formed, sand can be quite fertile. It is very free draining and easily cultivated. It can be modified with added humus, but this must be a continuing process, as the humus will tend to break down so that sand again predominates.
RIVER SILT	River silt is usually about a 50/50 mix of sand and very fine clay or mineral mud. Many riverine areas have a shingle base not far below the silty topsoil.	Silt is usually very fertile and capable of supporting most plants. It tends to be quite free draining as well as being easily worked and modified.
VOLCANIC	Volcanic soils are a combination of small stone particles, sand and a silty clay. They vary in composition depending on the nature of the original stone. Some volcanic soils are very gritty and close to sand, others are more clay-like.	Volcanic soils often have a very high mineral content and so can be very fertile.
SANDY LOAM	A loam soil with a high proportion (up to 30%) of coarse river sand. It may also include some decomposed turf or other fine organic matter, such as peat or sedge.	This is usually the best garden soil as it is the ideal combination of fertility and good drainage, with enough binding to ensure reasonably good moisture retention. It is also very easily modified to cater for plants with particular requirements.
LOAM	Loam is a mix of sand, silt, clay and decomposed organic matter. It is described as sand, silt or clay loam depending on which component predominates. Loam is often confused with leaf mould or humus.	Loam is more fertile than sandy soils and is not stiff and sticky like clay. It retains moisture well while also having good drainage and aeration.
CLAY LOAM	A loam soil with up to 35% clay. Many newly developed sections have a predominantly clay loam soil because the loamy topsoil has become mixed with a clay subsoil. Limestone soils tend towards a clay loam consistency but are usually very alkaline.	This type of soil holds moisture well while still being reasonably well drained, and offers a firm foundation for trees and shrubs.
CLAY	Pure clay is composed of very finely ground mineral deposits. It is readily identifiable as it forms an easily moulded pasty mud when wet and dries to a hardened crust. Water runs off flat clay surfaces and accumulates in any hollows.	Good for building foundations and laying paving.
PEAT	Soil formed over many years by the gradual filling of swamps and poorly drained areas. Organic matter accumulates faster than it decomposes and thus it is only slightly decomposed, locking up the nutrients, although forming a blackish-brown humus-rich soil.	Peat retains moisture and, provided the land is not low-lying, it drains well. Coarse peat does not compact and allows for easy root penetration. Peat retains warmth well in cool weather.

This table describes the most common natural soils. Existing gardens tend to have modified soil that is a composite of two or more of these soil types, but new sections will usually show a clear predominance of one soil type. The nature of the soil greatly affects the ease with which a garden can be developed and the rate at which larger plants, such as trees and shrubs, become established.

DISADVANTAGES	BEST PLANT CHOICE
Beach sands are often salty and may have a high lime content. Sand dries out quickly and can be difficult to moisten once dry. It tends to be very hot in summer and blows away in high winds.	Sandy soils are unsuitable for most plants other than those that are very drought tolerant. However, with some modification and regular attention they can be made to grow almost anything. Because it is so free draining, sand is a good base from which to start, but the work involved means that it is not an ideal first choice.
River silt dries out quickly and tends to form a crust once dry, although this is easily broken. The addition of coarser humus will break up the crust, prevent compaction and improve aeration. If too much clay is present, the soil can become compacted underneath and sandy on top, which leads to poor drainage and the sandy topsoil blowing away.	Most plants will grow well in river silt provided the soil is kept moist. Added humus is usually necessary to ensure good moisture levels and even aeration. Root vegetables do very well, as do annuals and fast-growing perennials, such as most daisies.
The soil may be too free draining and porous, which will make it difficult to wet thoroughly once it has dried. It will also dry out very quickly in summer. Finely ground volcanic soils will all become very clay-like in wet weather.	This depends entirely on the nature of the soil. Sandy volcanic soils are marvellous for root vegetables and can easily be modified with humus. Gritty soils tend to be too free draining for many plants unless they are well mulched. Clay-like volcanic soils are best suited to shallow-rooted plants and usually require additional humus to support trees and shrubs.
If the soil contains too much sand and the climate is very dry, excessive watering may be required. This is easily overcome by adding humus to the soil.	An excellent soil for most garden plants. Annuals, rockery plants and root vegetables thrive in sandy loam. Roses and leaf vegetables may prefer something slightly heavier, but the soil is easily modified to meet their requirements.
If the soil contains too much clay and the climate is very wet, poor drainage may be a problem. Add humus rather than sand to correct this problem. Sand may bind with the wet clay to form an impervious concrete-like layer.	Very good for leaf vegetables, fruit trees, roses and most large shrubs and trees. Acid-soil plants and root vegetables may require additional humus.
Clay loam can become poorly drained and badly aerated due to soil compaction. Careful attention to drainage will be required and the soil may require modification with added humus. Alkalinity can be a disadvantage with limestone-based soils.	Roses and most large trees and shrubs do well on clay loam as long as it is well drained. Root vegetables and plants with very fine roots, such as azaleas and ericas can find the soil difficult to penetrate and may require additional humus to loosen the soil. Alkaline limestone-based soils can lead to problems with ornamentals but are usually excellent for leafy vegetables. Rhododendrons and camellias will be very difficult to cultivate on limestone-based soils except in raised beds. Rockery plants may appreciate some additional fine grit to improve the drainage and aeration.
Pure clay is very unsuitable for most gardening because of its poor drainage and ease of compaction. Excessive run-off in wet weather is also likely to lead to severe problems. The topsoil can be modified, but its underlying clay base is likely to stunt the growth of large shrubs and trees.	Unless you are prepared to work hard to modify the soil, don't expect very much to thrive on clay. Most plants will make a start, but they soon run into problems with poor drainage and an inability to develop their root systems. Shallow-rooted, fast-growing annuals, such as portulaca, Californian poppy and many of the daisies will do well in summer. Native trees and shrubs can be ideal for clay-based soils, as many grow on them in their natural habitats. They can do extremely well with little or no soil modification.
Peat tends to be very acid and of low natural fertility. It can also become very wet and boggy if present in large quantities on low-lying land and can be difficult to work in winter.	Provided the drainage is good, peat is an ideal soil for acid-loving plants such as rhododendrons, camellias and ericas. Many vegetables grow well on peat if given some lime to counteract the natural acidity. Roses generally do very poorly on peat soils.

STARTING OUT

ASSESSING YOUR CLIMATE

Wind and salt spray – fences, walls, hedges, shelter belts; Sunlight and heat; Rainfall and humidity – irrigation; Frost; Neighbourhood

NO GARDENER CAN AFFORD to ignore the effects of the climate. Whatever style of garden you prefer, you must contend with the vagaries of the New Zealand weather; not just the havoc wrought by the occasional gale, but also the continual effects of wind, salt spray, sunlight, rain and temperature extremes. You must consider all of these factors, as well as your garden preferences, when designing a garden. A successful garden will blend with its environment rather than fight against it.

New Zealand covers a wide latitude range, with many variations in temperature and rainfall. Every district has its microclimates, where conditions are just that little bit more gentle or harsh than those of the surrounding area. One of the most common examples of this is the temperature difference between valleys and the surrounding hills. Valleys are nearly always cold at night because cold air drains to the lower levels. As a consequence, the hillsides are often surprisingly mild despite their higher altitude.

Many gardeners choose to push climatic limits, but attempting to grow marginal plants can be expensive and frustrating, and it can result in disaster during unusually extreme weather. A good understanding of the effects of climatic extremes – how they affect your small patch and how to deal with them – can make a great difference to the range of plants that you are able to grow.

WIND AND SALT SPRAY

Wind can dry out foliage, break off branches and may even entirely uproot a plant, but more serious in the long run are the general growth-retarding effects of strong winds. If a shrub's tender young growth is continually being damaged by strong drying winds or burnt by salt spray, it will take a long time for that plant to become established and it may never achieve its full potential.

Considering that New Zealand is surrounded by thousands of kilometres of open ocean, it is not surprising that we experience strong winds from time to time, and in some regions strong prevailing winds are the norm. These follow a fairly typical anticyclonic pattern: a predominant coastal breeze, northeasterly on the east coast and a more gentle northwesterly on the west coast, takes a westerly swing round to the southwest with the arrival of a cold front. As the front passes, the wind continues its anticlockwise movement until the predominant coastal breeze returns.

There are also regional variations in the wind. The best known is probably the 'nor'wester', which may affect the eastern parts of both islands and is particularly fierce in central and northern Canterbury. The nor'wester is a hot, dry wind that rapidly desiccates foliage, and it can be strong enough to break branches. In contrast, strong, cold, moist southerlies regularly sweep over the country and can also cause considerable damage, but as they tend to bring rain their drying effect is limited.

New Zealand has an extensive coastline and many of our major cities and towns are coastal. A constant salt-laden breeze off the sea can be

Your garden will be most successful
when you work with the climate rather
than against it. The coastal gardens
above and left show what can be
achieved when the right plants are
chosen for the right places.

taken for granted. For those of us not living on the waterfront, salt winds may have little effect, but if you live within a few hundred metres of the shore you will be well aware of the damaging long-term effects of a constant salty breeze. It doesn't just cause cars to rust and paint to peel, but also rapidly thins the ranks of weaker garden plants. The wind dries the foliage and the build up of salt burns tender new growth. Washing away the salt deposit will help, but most coastal gardeners soon accept there are some plants that just will not survive.

This is not necessarily a disadvantage. Knowing what you can't grow can make the path to a successful garden a lot simpler. Japanese maples and most rhododendrons may be off the menu, but in their place are a huge range of daisies, pelargoniums and members of the protea family. Many New Zealand natives also thrive in coastal conditions. Every climate has its compensations; coastal gardeners may have to put up with salt winds, but those same coastal breezes reduce the intensity of any frosts they may experience.

The effects of salt spray are purely coastal, but the coastal wind can continue for several miles inland. Offshore winds that are often strong and cold are a feature of most New Zealand cities, especially in spring. In some areas, particularly the eastern and southern

coasts of the South Island and around Wellington, these mistral-like, cold, drying spring winds can destroy new growth. The continual wind cycle dictates garden layouts over most of the country.

How can you compete against such an unyielding force of nature? The short answer is that you can't, but good plant selection and adequate shelter will help immeasurably. The provision of effective shelter will enable more tender plants to be successfully grown in otherwise exposed localities. However, shelter should be one of your first considerations regardless of your location. Ensuring your young plants get the best possible start is vital for the future success of your garden.

The best barrier against wind is a semipermeable screen. This can be natural or artificial, but the important point is that unless the area to be protected is small, it should not be a solid barrier. A solid windbreak directs the wind up and over the fence only to have it continue largely unabated on the other side. It also causes turbulence on the leeward side of the barrier and this can be much more damaging than the unobstructed wind itself. A semipermeable windbreak, such as windbreak cloth or a hedge, will break up the wind flow and considerably lessen its force without stopping it entirely.

Coastal breezes can be tempered by permeable barriers of trees and shrubs, protecting more tender plants.

verticals. Fibre-cement sheeting used on its own creates a very flat, two-dimensional fence; it looks best when restricted to short runs or when used in combination with palings or trellis. Pickets tend to be best suited to low fences or gates.

If only temporary shelter is required, or when appearances are not too important, windbreak cloth can be used, and it provides ample protection for most plants. This is only a temporary solution because sunlight and friction caused through rubbing against posts and wires quickly damage windbreak cloth. It is rare for such fences to last much over four years in exposed sites. One way of making windbreak cloth last longer is to attach it to wire-mesh fencing. This holds the cloth in place far better than strands of fencing wire and eliminates much of the damaging movement.

Wind is capable of showing up flaws in any construction and you should not underestimate its strength. A 1.8 m high paling fence will usually be sturdy enough if the post holes are 60 cm deep and the posts well rammed. However, it is preferable that the posts are set in concrete. Fences over 2 m high should have their supporting posts deep in the ground and preferably set in concrete. High windbreak fences must have their posts set in concrete and they should be well braced with wooden

It should be emphasised that all solid fences provide exactly the same degree of shelter. The only factor that can influence the protection provided by an impermeable barrier is its height. Large gardens will require higher fences or further windbreaks inside the fence line. The only way to reduce this need for increasingly higher fences is to break up the wind flow at low levels by using a semipermeable barrier.

FENCES

Almost all city houses, new or established, have existing boundary fences. These are often made from overlapping wooden palings and may be all the shelter a small city garden needs. Larger gardens, especially those in the country, will require greater protection and are often best divided into smaller gardens, each with their own wind breaks.

Plain paling fences can become very monotonous, but fortunately there are many variations you can use to add variety and colour while still providing shelter. A wire mesh or trellis fence can be used as a frame for growing a dense climber, such as *Tecomaria capensis*, that will eventually develop into a windbreak that is just as effective as any hedge. Latticed or louvred horizontal palings add interest, as does alternating horizontal palings with the

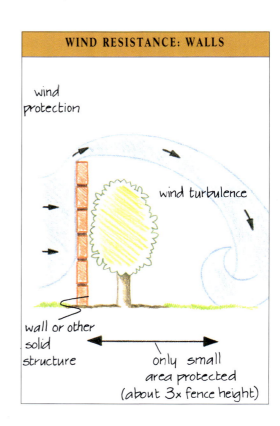

WIND RESISTANCE: WALLS

wind protection

wind turbulence

wall or other solid structure

only small area protected (about 3x fence height)

Above and above left are just two example of the different styles of walls and fencing available; many can be used to beautify the garden as well as protect it.

beams or steel pipes. When using windbreak cloth, follow the manufacturer's recommended spacing for wires and posts.

WALLS

Garden walls, which are usually made from stone, brick or concrete, are usually designed with their aesthetic qualities in mind rather than for the shelter they provide. Nevertheless, masonry will certainly stop the wind and it also retains considerable warmth after a sunny day. This extra warmth is often just enough to enable slightly tender plants to survive if they are grown close to or trained on to the wall.

Walls come in all manner of styles and designs and they can also be combined with fencing materials such as trellis, netting and lattice palings. However, walls are not as easily built as fences, and in most cases you would be well advised to hire a professional to do the brick or block laying, especially if you are looking at including gates or arches.

Place and use walls carefully; because they are solid structures they can create pockets of turbulence as the wind passes over them. Another reason for caution is that you may find you have created a wind tunnel rather than a sheltered garden.

HEDGES

A hedge can be an attractive garden feature as well as providing a superb windbreak. However, all too often hedges become untidy and start to die out in patches. Growing a good garden hedge requires careful planning and maintenance because, unlike a fence or wall, a hedge is a living, growing thing.

Preparation of the site to provide the right conditions for vigorous growth is of prime importance. Start by digging a trench at least 60 cm wide and deep. If this means digging into a hard clay pan or very poor subsoil, it may be best to also dispose of the subsoil.

Having dug the trench, check the drainage by running about 20 cm of water into it. If water still remains after three hours or if the

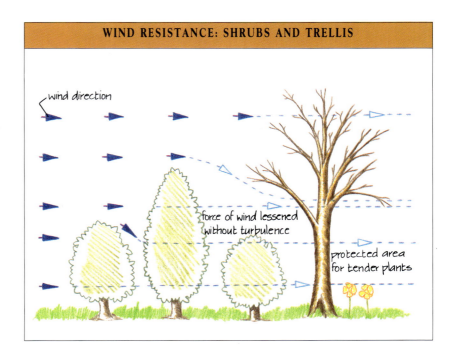

WIND RESISTANCE: SHRUBS AND TRELLIS

wind direction

force of wind lessened without turbulence

protected area for tender plants

Hedges make excellent wind breaks; they can be both practical and ornamental.
Top: A hedge of European copper beech, *Fagus sylvatica* 'Purpurea'.
Above: *Laurus nobilis* or bay laurel, here used as a hedge, is also a useful culinary herb.

trench has started to fill with groundwater, you may have to improve the drainage.

Once you are satisfied with the drainage, fill the trench with a blend of the soil that you removed and an equal amount of compost. This will ensure that the plants have plenty of room for root development and ample nutrients to get them started. Lightly firm the soil into place with your heel as you go, aiming just to eliminate air pockets.

Fill the trench so that the soil is slightly mounded on top and then soak it thoroughly. After a week or so, the soil level will have slumped slightly and you can now top it up and level off the trench. Give it another few days to settle and top up again if necessary. Moisten the soil again and you are ready to plant. Smaller ornamental hedges, such as box (*Buxus*) and lavender (*Lavandula*), don't require such elaborate preparation, but, as always, time spent in preparing the soil is never wasted.

Many plants are suitable for hedging; your choice will largely depend on the size of hedge required, the conditions it must withstand and the amount of maintenance you are prepared to put in. Dealing with salt-laden winds in seaside gardens can be difficult. It is usually better to stick to coastal natives, such as *Coprosma repens*, *Corokia*, akeake (*Dodonaea viscosa*), *Olearia*, pohutukawa (*Metrosideros excelsa*), ngaio (*Myoporum laetum*), *Pittosporum crassifolium*, *Griselinia littoralis* and karaka (*Corynocarpus laevigatus*). You can be sure that they will tolerate the conditions. Other plants suit-

able for hedging that do well in coastal areas include bottlebrushes (*Callistemon*), *Agonis*, *Escallonia*, *Feijoa*, *Grevillea*, *Hakea*, *Hibiscus*, *Nerium* and *Melaleuca*.

Hedges formed by using plants with fine branches and small, densely packed leaves are the easiest to maintain. They can be sheared off at any point and always look neat, whereas plants with large leaves and heavy branches must be cut back carefully if they are to avoid looking butchered. Conifers, such as macrocarpa (*Cupressus macrocarpa*), junipers (*Juniperus*), *Thuja* and yew (*Taxus*), are among the best in this respect.

Flowering and berry-bearing hedges can often be among the most ornamental features of a garden. The *Tecomaria* hedges that are so common around Wellington always look spectacular in late summer and heavy-flowering oleander (*Nerium*) hedges feature in many coastal gardens. When choosing plants for flowering hedges, you are really only limited by your imagination. Although some of the following are too small to provide much shelter, consider lavender (*Lavandula*), bottlebrush (*Callistemon*), *Cotoneaster*, *Hebe*, *Abelia*, *Agonis*, *Escallonia*, *Feijoa*, *Grevillea*, *Hakea*, *Hibiscus*, *Melaleuca* and *Viburnum*.

Many hedging plants have ornamental foliage and thus remain attractive throughout the year. Among the best are *Photinia*, *Phebalium* 'Illumination', *Elaeagnus* 'Maculata', *Euonymus japonicus* cultivars, *Viburnum tinus*, *Teucrium fruticans* and many cultivars of the

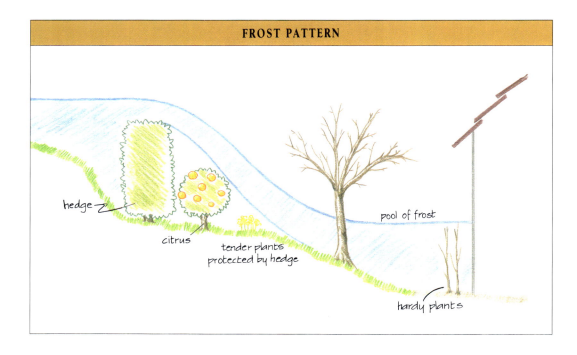

FROST PATTERN

hedge

citrus

tender plants protected by hedge

pool of frost

hardy plants

Above: A hedge has been used in this coastal garden to protect fruit trees from salt-laden winds.
Right: Hedges can also be used for delineating smaller areas within larger gardens.

native *Pittosporum tenuifolium*. Bay laurel (*Laurus nobilis*) also has attractive foliage and its leaves are an important culinary herb.

Hedges can also act as an impenetrable barrier to people and animals. Because of their thorns, plants such as holly (*Ilex*), *Pyracantha* and *Berberis* are not to be trifled with. This, of course, is a double-edged sword, because although intruders will find them unpleasant, they are equally unpleasant to trim.

When to trim is always something of a problem with hedges. In general, flowering hedges should be trimmed immediately after flowering. This will allow the maximum time before the next season's flowers develop. Foliage hedges should be pruned in spring and early autumn. As a rule you should not trim in late autumn or winter if it can be avoided, as this exposes the plants to frost damage when they are most vulnerable and regrowth will be slow. However, if you live in a frost-free area this is less important.

SHELTER BELTS

If you have a very large garden, hedges and fences may be too small to sufficiently cut down the wind. A shelter belt of quick-growing trees is the best solution. Remember, however, that as a rule, the faster a tree grows, the shorter its life. Trees such as *Acacia* and *Virgilia* will provide quick shelter, but after 15 years they will begin to die out and may look very unsightly. Slower-growing trees, such as macrocarpa (*Cupressus macrocarpa*) and *Thuja* are longer-lived alternatives. One exception to this rule is the Leyland cypress (x *Cupressocyparis leylandii*), but its great size precludes its use in all but the largest gardens.

In recent years many farm shelter trials have been undertaken, and as a result we are now seeing major changes. Many of these changes would be equally applicable to large gardens, so if you need to consider having a shelter belt, it may be wise to contact a farm advisory service for the latest information and advice.

In extremely exposed areas it may be impossible to establish shelter belts or hedging without first providing some artificial shelter. Even tough plants, such as Leyland cypress, *Olearia* and cherry laurel (*Prunus laurocerasus*), may suffer if not sheltered when young. In such circumstances some form of windbreak-cloth fence will be the quickest and simplest shelter to build. It may not last long if the site is really exposed, but it should be enough to get a shelter belt or hedge established.

SUNLIGHT AND HEAT

As a rule, sunlight and heat are closely linked; the sunnier the position, the hotter it is. The degree of shelter will also have some bearing on this. Under New Zealand conditions, damaging extremes of heat are rare except in extremely sheltered positions, especially where heat can be reflected off walls and trapped by glass. The north-facing wall of the house, directly under the eaves, is a problem area for many gardeners. This position rarely sees any rain and is a real heat trap. The best solution is to use heat-tolerant plants, such as gerberas and many other South African daisies.

All plants need sunlight to survive because they rely on photosynthesis to produce food for growth and photosynthesis depends on sunlight. Despite this, it is possible to have too much sunlight. Plants, like people, can become sunburnt and, as we are regularly told, New Zealand's ultraviolet levels are among the highest in the world.

Determining the light exposure a plant prefers can be rather difficult. Fortunately most plants provide some clues to help you. Silver-grey leaves usually indicate tolerance of strong sunlight as does purple or red foliage. Small leaves will generally tolerate more sun and heat than large leaves, and soft velvety leaves are more likely to burn than tough leathery ones. Succulent-leaved plants and cacti are also usually sun tolerant.

However, some commonly held beliefs are misleading. Not all palms prefer hot sunny situations – many are forest dwellers that do better with shade, at least when young. Also, fine needle-like leaves do not necessarily indicate sun tolerance, nor does bluish foliage. Not all rhododendrons prefer shade; some require at least a few hours direct sunlight per day.

Many choice garden plants prefer woodland conditions – cool, moist, humus-rich soil and dappled shade. Excessive sun and heat will damage, and may even kill, these plants. Most gardens have shady areas, such as the southern side of the house or boundary fences, but woodland plants generally prefer the dappled

shade of deciduous trees to the constant shade of overhanging buildings or other solid objects. Deciduous trees also provide the added benefit of an annual mulching of fallen leaves and additional light in winter when they are leafless.

For some plants, such as ferns, fuchsias and tender rhododendrons, it may be more practical to construct a purpose-built shadehouse. A common method is to build a wooden frame and cover it with shade cloth. The old-style lath house, which uses thin wooden strips to provide shade, is far more attractive than shade cloth and is more weather resistant in areas subject to snow. Unfortunately lath houses are usually more expensive to build.

RAINFALL AND HUMIDITY

When considering the effects of sun and heat it is important to bear in mind the tempering effect of humidity. Tropical rain forest areas experience more sun and heat than any New Zealand garden, but the effects are moderated by high rainfall and high humidity. With ample atmospheric moisture, plants are far more capable of withstanding heat.

If, on the other hand, you live in an area that is subject to hot, dry winds or prolonged periods without rain, even short bursts of hot weather will rapidly desiccate your garden. Providing adequate moisture during these times will minimise sun and wind damage and moderate their effects.

Some parts of New Zealand receive a very high rainfall. This leads to problems with soil scouring, and when combined with warm weather causes a greatly increased incidence of fungal diseases.

Continuous high humidity will also increase the incidence of fungal diseases. When combined with winters that are not cold enough to kill off overwintering disease spores, this can lead to serious ongoing problems. Rose growers in western and northern areas frequently despair over black spot and powdery mildew, while those in eastern and southern areas have far fewer problems.

Winter rainfall can be damaging to some mat-forming and cushion plants, too, particularly alpines. These small plants have often evolved to spend the winter under an insulating blanket of snow and when exposed to winter rains they break up and rot away. High summer humidity can also be damaging, but unseasonable warmth, humidity and rainfall is more likely to lead to problems.

Some plants need full sun, others require shading. Plants that thrive in shade, however, tend to prefer the dappled shade provided by trees and shrubs, as in the shady corner below.

IRRIGATION

To maintain a satisfactory supply of moisture during dry spells you will need some form of garden irrigation. There are now many automatic irrigation systems available to home gardeners. These often require the installation of underground supply lines, so it is wise to consider your irrigation needs before getting too advanced with garden construction.

Where once we were very liberal with garden watering, the availability of water for irrigation cannot always be guaranteed during times of drought and hence water should not be taken for granted. It therefore makes sense to be aware of the possibility of drought and water shortages when choosing plants and planning a watering system.

In most New Zealand cities up to one-third of the annual water consumption is used for garden irrigation, and this figure is considerably higher in summer. Yet this huge amount of water is often used very inefficiently: the Christchurch City Council's Water Services Unit estimates that up to 70% of the irrigation water used regularly misses its target or is lost to evaporation. Many home irrigation systems are sold on the promise of improved efficiency but this claim is not always true. Nearly all of these systems have some form of automation, which is essentially why we buy them, and it is how the system is controlled that ultimately determines how efficient it is.

Inexpensive systems use a simple timer control; this is inefficient because it fails to take account of rainfall, cloud cover and changes in temperature, all of which markedly influence the amount of water required. More advanced systems have a rain sensor that can override the timer. These come in two types. One simply shuts off the irrigation if rain is falling, which is of limited usefulness as it will come on even if a substantial downpour has just fallen immediately prior to the watering cycle. Also, this type of sensor has no way of determining how much rain has fallen. The more advanced sensor, which can assess soil moisture, should be considered almost essential. Without such a sensor or careful monitoring, any automated irrigation is almost certain to be wasteful and its operation ill-timed.

How the water is applied also greatly influences efficiency. The most common methods – sprinklers or fine jets – tend to be the least efficient because some of the spray almost always falls on barren ground such as pathways. In addition, strong winds can affect where the water falls and poor spacing of the sprinklers can lead to over-watering.

Drippers, soak hoses and other seepage-type systems are more efficient because they apply their water directly to the soil surface. However, they tend to be best suited to areas where the plants are grown in rows, such as vegetable gar-

Above left: Ground covers have been used as living mulches to conserve soil moisture in this striking subtropical garden.
Above: Close planting, shade and drought-tolerant plants mean that watering will not become a chore in this exotic garden.

While southern gardeners have to cope with frost, cold winters do have some benefits. There is the stunning autumn foliage and the striking forms of bare trunks and branches (top) and the delicate beauty of a frosted garden (above). If planned for, frosts need not be a problem.

dens and long narrow borders. Surprisingly, one of the most efficient forms of irrigation is hand watering. It enables you to direct water where it is most needed and the manual input required also ensures that watering is kept to a minimum.

Conserving soil moisture is also important – not having to apply water is the best way to save it. Regular use of compost will make your soil more moisture retentive and will allow the roots of your plants to spread more freely in their search for water. Mulches are a great help because they trap moisture and lessen the drying effects of the wind and sun on the soil's surface. Make sure that your mulches are permeable, however, as a mulch that acts as a thatch can prevent water from reaching the soil.

Even when hand watering, the temptation is often to water before it is really necessary. Check the soil moisture by scraping away the mulch. You'll be surprised at how often the soil can appear dry while still being quite moist underneath. When it is time to water, infrequent long soaks are more effective than regular surface sprays. Deep watering will encourage roots to seek moisture at lower soil levels, while surface watering keeps the roots near the surface where they are prone to drying out.

Efficient watering may enable you to keep growing plants with high moisture requirements, but it is far better to grow plants that are naturally drought resistant or that can cope with wide variations in available moisture. As mentioned earlier, co-operating with the climate is always preferable to attempting to overcome it. If you grow plants suited to your climate, your garden should also require less maintenance, as stressed plants that are not suited to the climate are more prone to diseases. However, grouping plants according to their moisture requirements will ensure that you don't have to entirely do without any moisture-demanding plants you really treasure.

COPING WITH FROST

Frost is one of the greatest killers of garden plants. Damage is caused not by the freezing of water inside the plant, but when it thaws – rapid thawing is much more injurious than slow thawing. Further damage may be caused if frosty nights are followed by clear sunny days, especially if the soil remains frozen during the day, resulting in the desiccation of the plant. Freezing of the soil can also lift the plant out of the ground and thus damage the root system. Very tender plants will be killed by even the lightest frosts, but hardier plants have evolved strategies that enable them to cope with frost. These include sap that will not freeze until well below 0°C and becoming dormant in winter by adopting a deciduous or herbaceous habit.

Most New Zealand gardens are located in coastal cities that rarely experience severe frost, that is below -4°C air temperature, but in the southern half of the South Island and the inland parts of both main islands, hard frosts limit the choice of plants that can be grown without protection. Although many tropical and subtropical plants are simply impossible to grow where repeated frosts occur, a little planning will greatly expand your plant choice.

A plant's condition as it approaches winter is a very important factor in determining its ability to withstand damaging frosts. If it is still in soft growth when the first hard frost hits, it is likely to suffer damage that will be more severe than if it had been properly hardened off. It will also be weakened and less able to survive the rest of the winter even if the conditions are somewhat milder than normal.

Properly preparing a tender plant for winter can go a long way towards ensuring its survival, and it is not just tender plants that will benefit.

Even otherwise hardy plants can be fatally damaged if frosted while in soft growth, either in autumn or by late frosts in spring. Stop applying growth-promoting fertilisers by the end of March and consider using a potassium-rich compound such as potash (potassium chloride) or a copper-based fungicide for additional hardening. Better still, try a combination of the two.

Move any tender plants under cover by the beginning of May and make sure that any temporary shelters are up by then. Cut down your irrigation as winter approaches, you should now find less need for it anyway, and this will reduce the amount of soft sappy growth. A dry autumn will harden plant growth and increase its frost resistance. If you have previously noticed any poorly drained areas, make sure that you have dealt with them before the onset of winter, as many plants are just as likely to rot because of poor drainage as freeze to death. This is particularly true of plants from areas with dry winters, such as gerberas and most cacti and succulents.

Overhanging eaves offer considerable protection from frost. Many tender climbers can be grown on walls with eaves and the climbers will themselves provide some protection for plants grown around them. Added protection in the form of simple wooden frames covered with frost cloth, hessian or plastic sheeting will provide adequate protection for many small plants up to about 1.8 m high. Temporary frames that can be removed after winter are particularly effective with citrus crops, as they not only prevent damage to the foliage but also stop the fruit becoming dry through repeated freezing.

One of the best ways of helping your plants through winter is to apply an insulating mulch. Bark chips, rotted sawdust, garden compost, leaf mould or rotted pine needles are all excellent choices. Mulching will help conserve moisture but, more importantly at this time of year, it will also help to insulate the surface roots of tender plants.

The roots are often more tender than the top growth and many otherwise hardy plants can be damaged if the soil freezes to any great depth. This is an important point to consider when deciding whether you wish to use large potted plants in your garden plan. A plant in a pot, growing out in the open, will need to be considerably hardier than a specimen planted in the garden, as the soil in its container may frequently be frozen solid.

Some other ways to cope with frost are:

- use larger hardy plants, shrubs or trees to provide shelter for tender plants.
- plant marginal plants and tender plants on slopes not in hollows.
- site tender plants where they are shaded from the morning sun to avoid problems with rapid thawing.

Remember, too, that very sheltered gardens are more likely to experience frosts than exposed ones.

Carrying out these simple tasks and carefully siting your more tender plants will greatly lessen the risks posed by hard frosts but, as with irrigation, it is better to co-operate with the climate. Many gardeners refuse to admit defeat, replanting tender specimens time after time only to lose them every winter. Certainly, try the odd piece of exotica, but bear in mind that eventually you will have to accept the dictates of nature.

However, there are advantages to cold weather and frosts. Conifers, roses and many other cool-climate plants are at their best in a climate that provides a distinct winter. Without that period of cold, they cannot become properly dormant and as a result tend to be rather short-lived and prone to disease. Frosts also kill many pests and diseases that would otherwise multiply at an alarming rate.

LOOK AROUND YOUR NEIGHBOURHOOD

Before you finally start serious planning and planting, take the time to look around your neighbourhood. This useful exercise familiarises you with your local soil and climate, and provides the type of first-hand information that no book can. An evening stroll can reveal many interesting plants that are thriving just where you least expected.

Parks and botanic gardens are also useful because they include a wide range of plants and many of them will be fully grown specimens. But you may find that unless they regularly make new plantings, their selection is quite different from that stocked by the local nurseries, which is where you'll most likely obtain your first plants.

Remember that your garden will have its own climatic variations. There will be small pockets that remain frost-free and others that never seem to thaw out. There will be hot, sunny areas that seldom see rain and cold, wet parts, too. Experience with your garden will teach you how you can best use these very small, localised microclimates to your advantage.

PLANNING YOUR GARDEN

Maintenance and use; Drawing a scale plan; Design elements; Structural elements; Plants and ornamental features

HAVING A GARDEN PLAN is vitally important if you are to avoid expensive, unsightly and inconvenient mistakes. However, a garden is not static, it is always changing and evolving, so a garden plan is not a blueprint that must be followed precisely; rather it is a checklist of ideas and suggestions. Above all, a garden plan requires thought to the future. Many gardens develop without such foresight; amenity items are located with little consideration as to how they will affect the garden, and plants are dotted around without fully thinking through how they will grow and develop. This approach can create problems, such as compost heaps located in full view of the house, and lead to an assortment of disparate styles.

A garden must be attractive, functional and, above all, enjoyable. To achieve this ideal demands some forward planning. Having considered the natural attributes of the site and the limits and opportunities created by your climate, you probably already have some ideas about the features you want to see in your garden and how these can be incorporated into the overall house and garden design, whether existing or new.

MAINTENANCE AND USE

Before getting too advanced with the planning, you should decide exactly what you want from your garden and the amount of time you are prepared to put in to maintenance and development. The most beautiful garden will not last long if it is not maintained, and the most

magnificent outdoor living and entertainment area is of little benefit if it is never used.

Be realistic about your dedication to gardening; you want to be able to enjoy your garden, not to feel that you always have to be working just to keep it under control. A garden that is too large and complicated will soon become a burden.

Likewise, be realistic about setting aside large parts of your garden for things like barbecue areas, swimming pools, tennis courts and children's play areas. Are they going to be used? And even if they are, how regularly and for how long? So often home owners will spend large amounts of time and money ripping up a perfectly satisfactory garden to install a barbecue area that is a maze of complicated fences, walls and decking only to find they spend far more time painting the fences than grilling steaks.

DRAWING A SCALE PLAN

As you go through the design and planning process, make a plan of your garden. This will help you to position things accurately and will highlight any impracticalities in your initial ideas.

Your plan doesn't need to be a masterpiece, but it should be drawn to scale, with the boundaries in their correct proportions, buildings accurately positioned, and any existing items, such as drives, paths, entrances, trees, fences and hedges, properly drawn. Also, you should note the position of north; this gives

SITE PLAN

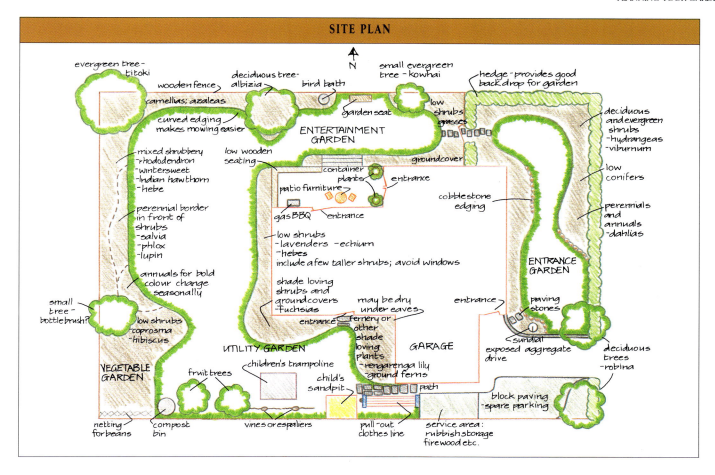

evergreen tree - titoki

wooden fence

camellias; azaleas

curved edging makes mowing easier

mixed shrubbery
-rhododendron
-wintersweet
-Indian hawthorn
-hebe

perennial border in front of shrubs
-salvia
-phlox
-lupin

annuals for bold colour change seasonally

small tree - bottlebrush?

low shrubs
-coprosma
-hibiscus

VEGETABLE GARDEN

netting for beans

compost bin

fruit trees

vines or espaliers

children's trampoline

child's sandpit

UTILITY GARDEN

deciduous tree - albizia

bird bath

garden seat

ENTERTAINMENT GARDEN

low wooden seating

container plants

patio furniture

gas BBQ

entrance

entrance

low shrubs
-lavenders -echium
-hebes
include a few taller shrubs; avoid windows

shade loving shrubs and groundcovers
-fuchsias

entrance

N

small evergreen tree - kowhai

low shrubs grasses

groundcover

may be dry under eaves

fernery or other shade loving plants
-rengarenga lily
-ground ferns

pull-out clothes line

GARAGE

path

hedge - provides good backdrop for garden

deciduous and evergreen shrubs
-hydrangeas
-viburnum

low conifers

cobblestone edging

perennials and annuals
-dahlias

ENTRANCE GARDEN

entrance

paving stones

sundial

exposed aggregate drive

deciduous trees
-robinia

block paving
-spare parking

service area:
rubbish storage
firewood etc.

---

garden centre staff or anyone else you may show the plan to some idea of the aspect of the section. Consider, too, any existing elements that you may wish to preserve and any unsightly objects you wish to hide.

If you have access to a home computer there are several relatively cheap garden design programs that make it easy to alter the design; mixing and matching plants and construction elements until you get it right. Sophisticated programs even allow the design to be projected forward over several growing seasons to see how the garden shapes up over time.

DO YOU NEED A LANDSCAPE GARDENER?

A simple plan combined with some common-sense and careful preparation is usually all that is needed to get started. But not all garden designs are straightforward. If you don't feel capable of doing the entire job, or just want a second opinion, it is a good idea to get professional advice.

A landscape gardener works in consultation with the garden owner to produce a plan that is best suited to the site, climate and the wishes of the owner. The plan produced can be a basic pattern for the owner to follow and modify as required, or it may be a detailed plan that the landscaper will put into action.

Getting a plan made up is only the first step. The section has to be laid out, the plants bought and planted and the garden tidied up afterwards. You can do all this yourself or you can hire a landscape gardener who will do all or any part of the job as you request.

If you intend to employ a professional, you need to be aware of the differences between landscape gardeners and landscape architects. Generally, landscape architects have formal qualifications and belong to a professional organisation. They usually produce work of a high standard but they are expensive and will often subcontract the actual construction work. On the other hand, anyone can set themselves up as a landscape gardener, and many do.

Whoever you choose, it pays to check their credentials. Ask for references and, if possible, inspect a few of their previous jobs. If the work appears satisfactory, and the owners seem satisfied, it's over to you. Many of the larger garden centres offer landscaping services and they can be a good place to start.

This small garden area combines many ornamental and practical elements, but through good design it avoids looking cluttered.

Climbers, such as the English ivy *Hedera helix* (above) can be used to disguise the sometimes harsh lines of fences and garages.

REMODELLING AN EXISTING GARDEN

Most of the topics discussed in this chapter apply as much to existing gardens as to new ones. The only real difference is that some of the features will already be present and others may have to be removed before alterations can be made.

Remodelling a garden can involve far more work than building a new one. Old plants have to be removed before new ones can be planted, tree stumps have to be lifted, and paths and patios may have to be altered. Don't rush into garden remodelling. You've lived with the garden this far, a little more time spent working out what you really need to change can save a lot of unnecessary labour later on.

A common problem when remodelling is that the new plants look completely out of proportion with the rest of the garden. Time will take care of this, but you may be better to buy slightly more advanced specimens; this will also lessen the risk of overplanting. Regardless of whether you are building a new garden or remodelling an old one, the work takes time and effort. It will also be several years before the full effect of your work becomes apparent. The worst thing that you can do is to attempt to rush everything just to see a quick result.

DESIGN ELEMENTS

By dividing your garden up into areas based on their use or features that you wish to highlight, you will develop a better idea of the space required for your plans and how functional considerations may affect the design.

Ornamental features and gardens are best kept separate from utility areas, but conflict can arise from this approach. For example, the clothesline needs to be near the laundry, but that may mean that it has to be passed on the way to the back lawn, or that the washing gets tangled up in the vegetable garden. Careful planning (and some compromise) can help you avoid this problem and others, such as the barbecue area that is situated right next to the compost heap.

Start by dividing the garden into areas based on use. This will highlight which areas are best for utilities, will simplify the laying out of paths and lawns, and will help you to spot potential clashes. Because initial impressions are usually the strongest, you should start the design process with the entrance to the garden. Most gardeners treat their entrance area as the showpiece of their garden. If the gardener has some particular area of interest this is where you will usually see his or her best plants: the beautifully maintained rose bed, the huge-flowered dahlias or massed annuals.

Entrances can be enhanced in many ways. Structural features, such as archways, pergolas, walls and fences, can be used to define as well as beautify the entrance. Small flower borders and potted trees or shrubs flanking the entrance

Two very different entrances (above and right), both reflecting the overall style of the house and garden, welcome visitors.

or a climber along the wall will soften the harsh lines of such structures, or a hedge can be used instead of a wall or fence. An unusual mailbox or a distinctive style of street number also contribute to the overall impression.

Next, consider any particular features that you may wish to have in your garden. Garden beds and small shrubs are easily accommodated, but large trees, ponds and patios demand careful siting and may impose restrictions by needing to be close to water or electrical supply lines.

Finally, look at how you can blend the functional and the ornamental. Trellises, hedges and other simple screening devices can be used to hide the rubbish bin, compost heaps or other unsavoury sights. Climbers can be used to cover the blank walls of the garage and tool shed.

Changes in level can be used to more clearly define the function of each part of the garden. These can be natural on a sloping site or artificial, as in patios and decks or steps that lead to an elevated area.

STRUCTURAL ELEMENTS

All gardens contain structural and utility elements. These hardware items are sometimes fixed, in which case the garden must be arranged around them. But often they can be altered to fit the garden or hidden from view. Most gardeners will want to include, or need

to take account of, some of the following items.

DRIVEWAYS AND PATHS

Grand driveways have always been a feature of large houses, and since the advent of the motor car the drive has come to dominate the entrance design of most houses. Drives and paths can create very rigid lines that do not blend well with the garden; anything that can be done to break away from straight lines will help. Pillars and arches with a grand sweeping curve of drive suit a large country estate but they are scarcely practical in a small garden, however there are other ways to break away from the straight drive that hugs the fence line.

The first step is to position the entrance more centrally, at least 2 m in from the boundary. This will eliminate the troublesome narrow border that is so often seen between the edge of the drive and the fence and allows for more variations in drive design.

Paths and paving should blend in with the rest of the garden. The approaches chosen above and right both seem an organic part of the design.

Curving the line of the drive also helps because it enables the side paths to be better integrated with the drive. They can be run off at tangents to the curve of the drive rather than at the rigid right angles that a straight driveway so often dictates.

Few modern houses are without driveways or entrance courtyards, and even those that do not have them will usually have main paths that are effectively pedestrian 'driveways'. Treat this path as you would a driveway. It is always a good idea to make it considerably wider than the side paths as this will naturally encourage any 'traffic' in the right direction.

Paths require careful siting to ensure that they divide the garden into the appropriate areas of operation while also providing the best access. A shortcut that is used in preference to a path means that the path is in the wrong place. Try taking a mental walk around your garden plan to check the layout of the paths, make sure they go to the places that you will visit most often. Wherever possible, avoid straight lines, but don't go overboard with curves either. Too many curves take the walker on a circuitous route and lead to shortcuts being used. Try to keep your main paths at least a metre wide; 75 cm is the minimum width for a one-person path.

GARAGE AND SHED

Often the garage is already sited by the time the garden is planned, but if not, try to incorporate it into the overall design instead of making it an ugly outhouse that will require camouflaging. (The same applies to garden tool sheds.) Often the area of driveway directly in front of the garage is used for car washing, so special attention should be paid to the drainage of this part of the garden.

SWIMMING POOLS, BARBECUES, DECKS AND PATIOS

These entertainment areas are usually directly linked to the house and the garden is built around them. Often they are not used regularly or they are used for other purposes. Try to make these features as multi-functional as possible because they do take up a lot of space. For example, a patio that is occasionally used as a barbecue area can be a good location for a hideaway clothes line.

As mentioned earlier, you should pay close attention to how often you will use these areas before committing yourself to their construction. This is especially true if you opt for more permanent structures, such as a brick patio, concrete or stone block barbecue area or an in-ground pool. These items are also likely to be a severe test of your do-it-yourself skills and some, especially an in-ground pool, will have to be professionally built.

Other points to consider with pools are the proximity of trees and the possibility of falling leaves and other debris; the pool surround, which should be paved as wet grass cuts up very quickly; and compliance with the fencing regulations.

COURTYARDS

As gardens have become smaller, it has become more common to have large paved areas that act as courtyards. A courtyard can be at the front of the dwelling, as a combined drive and courtyard; it can be a somewhat glorified patio and entertainment area; or it can be a genuine courtyard of the type often seen between groups of ownership flats.

Like all large areas of paving, courtyards pose problems with run off and a generally barren appearance. A well-laid courtyard should not develop puddles in wet weather and should not cause the surrounding garden to flood. Courtyards can be made more attractive with potted plants, and more sheltered and inviting by surrounding them with trellises covered in climbers and low hedges.

CLOTHESLINE

The main considerations here are what type of design you need, the location and how you will get to it. Fixed rotary designs offer the greatest convenience, but they tend to be the most difficult to fit into the garden. Although roll-away styles take some setting up each time they are used, they can be blended into the garden so that they are almost invisible when not in use.

A clothesline must be sited where there will be good air movement, not too much shading and it needs to be easily accessible from the laundry. You will either need a path that goes directly to the line or a line that can be strung across a patio.

WASTE STORAGE

All households create waste, and it soon piles up. Where you will keep the domestic rubbish prior to disposal is an important consideration. A waste area should be well screened so that it is not visible from the leisure areas within the

This patio has been separated and screened from the house and garden through the use of walls, hedges, trees and shrubs, providing a secluded sunny corner.

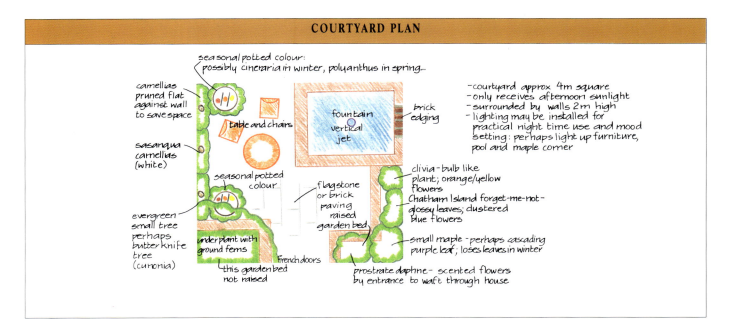

COURTYARD PLAN

- seasonal potted colour: possibly cineraria in winter, polyanthus in spring...
- camellias pruned flat against wall to save space
- table and chairs
- sasanqua camellias (white)
- seasonal potted colour
- evergreen small tree perhaps butter knife tree (cunonia)
- underplant with ground ferns
- this garden bed not raised
- flagstone or brick paving raised garden bed
- French doors
- fountain vertical jet
- brick edging
- courtyard approx 4m square
- only receives afternoon sunlight
- surrounded by walls 2m high
- lighting may be installed for practical night time use and mood setting: perhaps light up furniture, pool and maple corner
- clivia - bulb like plant; orange/yellow flowers
- Chatham Island forget-me-not - glossy leaves; dustered blue flowers
- small maple - perhaps cascading purple leaf; loses leaves in winter
- prostrate daphne - scented flowers by entrance to waft through house

Right: This formal hedge follows the gentle curve of the lawn as it disappears into the distance.

garden. It should also be protected from house-hold pets and any marauding neighbourhood animals.

COMPOST AREA

A good garden needs good compost. But you don't want the compost area to be highly visible, although it does need to be accessible, with enough room around it to comfortably manoeuvre a wheelbarrow. Once again, intelligent use of screening is the best way to disguise this very useful but often unattractive item.

LAWNS

A lawn could be considered an ornamental feature in its own right, as well as providing the perfect foil for many plants. It also has a utility role in providing access to garden beds and serving as a sportsground, playground, relaxation and entertainment area.

The details of laying a lawn are covered in a later chapter, but there are a few design points that should be discussed here. Unless it is the style you are looking for, it is usually best to avoid formal squares or rectangles of lawn; curves provide a more gentle, less austere effect and blend in better with the rounded forms of trees and shrubs. The arc created by a curve also leaves more room for planting at the corners of the garden.

Long narrow strips of grass tend to be walked on most at the centre and can become rutted tracks. Try extending the garden into the lawn at various points to break up the flow of traffic. This also reduces the alley-like look that often occurs when narrow lawns are flanked by garden borders.

CHILDREN'S PLAY AREA

Items such as swings, sandpits and games areas need not spoil the look of a garden but they are best sited away from your most precious rarities. Cricket balls and trilliums don't mix! Children grow up quickly, so build these facilities with a view to removing them later (the facilities, not the children).

GREENHOUSE

Although it can be very useful, a modern greenhouse is often not an attractive building. Yet, because it requires a position in the sun for maximum production and there is a need for easy access, the greenhouse will probably be out in the open and clearly visible. There is really no way round this; to screen the greenhouse would automatically reduce its effectiveness. All that you can do is choose the most attractive design. (See the chapter entitled 'Gardening under cover' later in the book.)

PLANTS AND ORNAMENTAL FEATURES

ORNAMENTAL TREES

Trees provide shade and add a vertical dimension to the garden, and because they have such a large impact on what can be grown or built around them, they should be the plants that you select first.

Trees are the tallest plants in the garden and they can be used to screen out unwanted

Left: Here, a sloping mixed border is contained by a stone wall, and sturdy steps at right lead to another level of the garden.

Above: Exuberant plantings and rustic steps, complemented by terracotta pots, create a cottage garden feel with a strong design element.

views or to screen you from unwanted viewers. Evergreens are best for screening and the more rapid-growing trees, such as acacias, eucalypts and *Virgilia*, are most commonly used. These trees tend to be short-lived but by the time they have to go, your later plantings should have grown sufficiently to replace them.

Deciduous trees are more often used as feature plantings. They are primarily grown for their flowers, as in the case of cherries or magnolias, or for their autumn foliage colour. They also provide shade in summer when it is needed while allowing in light in winter. Evergreen trees on the other hand, provide year-round shade, which may be useful in some instances but often causes problems.

Take care when siting trees that their roots will not interfere with sewers or other pipes and that they won't lift the surface of your drives and paths. Also, remember to allow for the leaf litter that is sure to accumulate; even the most beautiful tree can become a nuisance if you are continually having to remove debris. (See the trees chapter for more details on tree cultivation, selection and planting.)

MIXED SHRUBBERY

Almost all gardens include beds of mixed shrubs. They add height and form to the garden, and because they generally require little maintenance they are often used as fillers. There are so many different shrubs and they vary so widely in their flowers, foliage and growth habit that it is possible to create almost any effect on any scale.

When planning beds of shrubs, it is vitally important that you think ahead. You need to consider the variations in height and spread of the shrubs and grade the planting accordingly. It is very easy to underestimate the size of the plants when mature, and if you're not careful the shrubbery could develop into a jungle. (See the shrubs chapter for details on planning your shrubs and their selection and planting.)

DEDICATED SHRUBBERY

Enthusiasts for a particular type of plant, such as rhododendrons, roses and fuchsias, will often create beds dedicated to those plants alone. Keeping similar plants together makes it easier to cater for their requirements but may encourage host-specific pests and diseases and hasten their spread.

HERBACEOUS BORDER

A herbaceous border is similar to a shrubbery in layout but is composed of assorted perennials, sometimes in combination with shrubs and annuals, or collections of particular genera such as hostas, astilbes or *Phlox*. As few of these plants are evergreen, the herbaceous border is distinctly seasonal in habit.

Herbaceous borders tend to be long and relatively narrow. They are best used along driveways or for edging large lawns.

Flower and foliage colour, size and growth rates are important considerations when designing a herbaceous border. There are few areas of gardening where obtaining a pleasing blend of these elements is more important or

Flower beds don't have to be set in lawns: their beauty and fragrance can often be more easily enjoyed in raised beds. And any maintenance is easier on the back!

Perhaps our most stunning native climber, *Clematis paniculata*, set off to perfection on a framework of tree fern logs.

more difficult. For this reason, the herbaceous border is often considered the pinnacle of the gardener's art.

FLOWER BEDS

The everyday flower beds that are such a riot of colour in summer are made up of mixed annuals, biennials and heavy flowering, usually short-lived, perennials. Flower beds are easy to plant out and care for but they provide a relatively brief effect and require annual replanting. Indeed, for the best effect, they may need to be replanted up to three times a year.

For this reason, formal flower beds are not the extremely popular garden features they once were. Modern gardeners simply don't have the time for them. They opt instead to use annuals as colour accents among shrubs or in the herbaceous border. However, if you don't mind the labour involved, the formal flower bed is still the best way of providing solid blocks of colour.

MIXED BORDERS

Annuals, perennials and shrubs don't have to be segregated, nor do they have to be planted in large beds. The mixed border combines them all in a harmonious yet seemingly random blend. This style of planting, often described under the banner of cottage gardening, has become popular for its informal unstructured look and its apparent low maintenance. Unfortunately the low maintenance is only apparent, as weeds don't mind what style of garden they grow in. Nevertheless the mixed border is one of the best ways to create a natural-looking garden.

CLIMBERS

Bare fences often stand out starkly in new gardens and climbers may be used to soften the lines of fences and such utilitarian objects as sheds and garages. Or they may be grown on purpose-built structures, such as pergolas, archways and gazebos. Unfortunately many of the best climbers are frost-tender, so you will need to choose carefully. You will also need to take care when choosing a climber because some are very rampant growers and can quickly smother less vigorous plants or damage the structure they are growing on. (See the chapter on climbers for details of their care and maintenance.)

GROUND COVERS

At the other end of the scale are the ground covers. You may have a difficult slope that needs quick cover, or want to have a living mulch around your shrubs. Whatever the effect you require, there is a ground cover to suit. Many also have their own ornamental virtues, with wonderful foliage colour and fragrant flowers.

Many different types of plants can be used as ground covers, from the traditional grassed lawn to very prostrate shrubs, and some genera have species or cultivars that have a ground-covering habit. Any perennial that has a dense mat-forming habit will also do the job. But you

will need to take into account what you want your ground cover to do, especially as some can be quite vigorous and can easily overrun the garden if not contained.

PONDS

Water is always a restful feature in the garden and a pond can be an extremely beautiful addition to your design. The neighbourhood birds will also thank you: a garden pond attracts them from miles around. The activities of fish add interest to the garden and the odd frog or two doesn't go amiss.

WATER FEATURES

Water features, that is fountains, waterfalls and streams as distinct from static ponds, can be a simple way of adding movement in the garden. Waterfalls need to be carefully designed to avoid appearing contrived, but they and small streams can be used alone or combined with a pond to create a very pleasing natural effect.

Unless you have a natural stream in the garden, a recirculating pump is essential and this requires electricity to run. Small submersible pumps are the simplest to install but a fixed pump in an underground housing is less intrusive. Hardware shops, garden centres and pool specialists often stock garden pond and plumbing accessories and can advise you on design and hardware.

PLANTS IN CONTAINERS

Container plants can be used to provide quick colour and are very useful for areas where it would be difficult to have permanent plants. Patios, courtyards and outdoor entertaining areas are all enhanced by potted colour, while entrance ways and formal paths almost demand to be flanked with narrow upright shrubs in pots. Window boxes and planter troughs are a great way of livening up otherwise barren walls.

There really is no limit to what you can do with container plants, but do remember that they require regular watering and feeding, and repotting every year or two.

VEGETABLE GARDENS

In recent years the vegetable garden has often been sacrificed to make way for garden amenities and ornamental plants. However, vegetables are a satisfying and budget stretching form of gardening. Vegetable gardening is covered in detail in a later chapter, but when planning the layout of the garden it is important to realise that most vegetables require full sun. Wherever possible, the rows should run north/south to ensure the crop receives even light. Some crops, such as sweet corn, may be damaged by strong winds, and as crops should not regularly be grown in the same place, you will need to ensure that all parts of the vegetable garden are well sheltered if you are to safely rotate your crops.

FRUIT TREES, BUSHES AND VINES

As suburban gardens have become smaller, the

Containers are a great way to add variety to your garden. Not only are they ornamental in themselves, they allow you to grow plants with specialised requirements.
Shelter and shade are provided for this container plant, top left, and if necessary it can be moved.
Container gardens have high maintenance requirements. Plants need to be watered and fed more frequently, and their roots feel the extremes of temperature more than if they were in open ground.

Right: Herb and vegetable gardens can be as formal or as casual as you wish. Just remember to allow access for sowing, weeding and harvesting even in wet weather.

The ideal spot for a garden seat – a herb garden in a sunny corner!

home orchard has become less common. But newer fruit varieties, such as the 'Ballerina' apples and dwarf plums and nectarines, mean that enough fruit for a small family can be grown in a relatively small area. Fruit trees need sun and shelter from cold wind during the flowering to ripening period. They also need occasional attention to limit the impact of pests and diseases.

Currants, raspberries and gooseberries can be all be grown in home gardens. Grape vines are also a worthy addition to the backyard and can be grown on trellises and used as screens. (Also see the chapter on fruit and nut trees for more details.)

HERBS

Herbs can be used for all manner of purposes and herb enthusiasts may well opt to use a large part of their vegetable gardens for their favourite herbs. Most of us, however, concentrate on the culinary herbs and these are usually very easy-care plants. Many herbs are also ideal for growing in containers, and pots of culinary herbs can be a very useful and fragrant addition to a barbecue area. (See the herbs chapter later in the book.)

ARCHES, PERGOLAS AND CLIMBER FRAMES

Arches and pergolas can be ornamental features in themselves or they may have climbers trained over them or hanging baskets hung from them. Many designs incorporating trellises for climbers can be bought ready-made or as kitsets from hardware shops and garden

centres. Most of these are attractive enough that they don't have to be covered with climbers and some are large enough that they can also serve as car ports.

If the structure is to be largely hidden under a climber, it doesn't need to be very elaborate. Simple wooden or wire frames are perfectly adequate and need not be that strongly built if they can be attached to something sturdy that will take the weight of the climber.

Adding an arch is a good way of creating the feeling of entering a new area and is a technique that is often used to highlight a change in garden theme.

SEATS AND TABLES

A garden seat in the shade is the perfect place from which to enjoy your creation. There are hundreds of different styles of outdoor furniture, and enough choice that you should be able to find something that suits your taste. Avoid anything that is garishly coloured or gimmicky; plain wooden furniture is probably the least obtrusive and it lasts well provided it has been properly treated. Wrought iron also blends well with most gardens, although it is often painted white, which is very stark. An alternative to bought furniture is some sort of rustic seat. Stone is the traditional material, but almost anything can be used; manuka and driftwood being two increasingly popular alternative materials.

BIRD BATH AND FEEDING STATION

Some gardeners get upset when birds nibble

Rockeries are a great addition to any garden, and rockery plants have a delicate elegance that draws you down to enjoy them on their level.

If you have a damp corner in which nothing grows, exploit it by putting in a bog garden.

their crops, but birds add life to a garden and it would be a dull world without them. Providing them with food and water will encourage them into your garden; as will planting the right trees for nectar-feeding birds. The traditional bird bath on a pedestal doesn't always fit in well with a modern garden, so if you are planning to include a garden pond you may like to have a shallow area where the birds can drink and bathe.

Bird feeders can be suspended from trees or attached to posts, and many birds will be quite happy to feed on your back lawn without any elaborate feeding stations. Remember to leave a clear space around your bath or feeder. This allows the birds a good field of view. They are very wary of potential dangers and will not venture down, regardless of what you tempt them with, unless they feel secure. Dovecotes and nesting boxes can add further interest, but they are really best suited to large country gardens. Too much of this sort of furniture in a small city garden can become overwhelming.

OUTDOOR LIGHTING

Outdoor lighting can extend the time you spend in your garden, make it safer to navigate at night and help to deter intruders. Oil-, solar- and battery-powered garden lamps are available if you need portability, but mains electricity is usually the most convenient and easily controlled power source.

Spot lamps may be attached to the house and directed into the garden. However, this tends to make your garden feel like a floodlit football pitch; better that the lamps are situated *in* the garden.

Their effect is enhanced by keeping them low; the idea is to have the lamps illuminating the garden rather than dazzling the viewers, and this is best achieved by keeping the lamps below eye level or shielded from the direct field of view. Lamps on short stands or footlights directed back towards the plants provide ample light without being blindingly bright. They can be set to switch on automatically, either with a photosensitive switch or by using a movement detector.

Because electric lamps require permanent wiring, they are best installed at an early stage of garden development. However, digging a few small slit trenches for electric cables need not greatly disturb an established garden.

EXTRAS

Garden gnomes, boys with trays and ball-balancing seals have to be pretty cleverly used to avoid being crass. The same goes for wooden butterflies on trellises and 'Dunroamin' written across the front wall. Such things might have their place, but if added for a laugh the joke can quickly wear thin.

Garden statuary, ornamental urns, Japanese stone lanterns and drinking fountains are often more appropriate, although they still require restraint. Gardens are primarily about plants and people, so think carefully before including anything else.

A vibrant border of flowers and shrubs. Flower beds require careful planning to look this good year-round, but with outdoor lighting, you can enjoy them for longer when they are at their best.

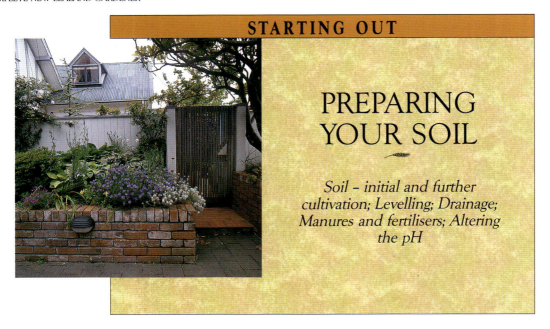

STARTING OUT

PREPARING YOUR SOIL

Soil – initial and further cultivation; Levelling; Drainage; Manures and fertilisers; Altering the pH

ONCE YOU HAVE ASSESSED your new or existing garden, and discovered its weaknesses and strengths, you will want to prepare it. All aspects of a garden can be modified to a greater or lesser extent, but with regard to site preparation, most of your efforts will be directed towards getting the soil in the best condition to support plants, levelling overly severe contours and improving the drainage.

SOIL

As mentioned in the chapter on assessing your garden, very few gardens start off with the ideal soil. Extensive modifications of the topsoil are nearly always necessary. How far you need to go will depend on the nature of the existing soil and the plants that you intend to grow. Sandy soil, for example, will need plenty of humus worked in if it is to support woodland plants, but will require little modification to grow marguerite daisies. Clearly, preparation and planning are interlinked topics, and it pays to consider your planting and layout options before going too far in preparation and perhaps doing a lot of unnecessary work. By the time you reach the stage of preparing the soil, you will probably have a good idea of where drives, pathways and patios are likely to be. These areas will still need to be levelled and surface drained, but the soil will not need modifying.

Before you attempt to make alterations to the soil, it is important to understand the nature of the soil, in your area. Study the table of natural soil types in the chapter Assessing your garden, to determine which soil most closely matches that in your garden.

INITIAL CULTIVATION

Most gardens, whether they are new or existing, have soil that has become compacted. This may be due to the heavy machinery used during building or it may be the natural compaction that occurs after a few years without cultivation. Whatever the reason, compaction badly affects drainage and aeration, so the first task is to break up the soil.

The two common ways of doing this are digging or rotary hoeing. Unless the area is

The first task on any new site is to break up the soil that has been compacted by heavy machinery.

The soil in vegetable gardens
needs to be regularly cultivated,
incorporating plenty of humus-
rich compost, to keep it in peak
condition.

very large, it is preferable to dig it over by hand. Although it is much slower, working with a spade cultivates more deeply, gives you more control and enables closer attention to be given to specific areas. Rotary hoes tend to be shallow cultivators that operate too quickly to give you much feel for the soil. Also, a rotary hoe capable of cultivating to a spade's depth is likely to be large and very unwieldy in a small garden, as well as being expensive to operate.

A garden spade is the normal tool for digging. However, a fork is better if the soil is wet or has a high clay content. Such soils are inclined to form large clods when turned and a fork is better at breaking up the soil.

Do not dig down below the topsoil and do not mix the topsoil with the subsoil. In most cases there will be distinct colour and texture differences between the two. If you have a very shallow topsoil (50–100 mm) it may be advisable to try and increase its depth with compost and mulch before cultivating. Do so by a technique called trenching (see the chapter on vegetables). The worst situation is to have a very shallow topsoil on a hard clay-like subsoil. This makes it very difficult to establish plants regardless of the quality of the topsoil. In this case, it is essential to try and break up the hard clay pan. The most labour-intensive method, and generally the most successful, is to remove the topsoil and dig over the subsoil while incorporating plenty of humus-rich compost. The topsoil should also be mixed with compost before returning it to the garden.

Improving heavy soils is never easy. Many products are sold as soil conditioners and most of them have some benefit. However, improving the soil is a continuous process and it would be foolish to expect any product to make an immediate miraculous difference. Lime or gypsum will break down clay and make it easier to work with, but the process is complicated by rather vague instructions regarding how much to use for specific soil types. The different brands vary widely in their suggested application rates, although they all agree that heavier soils require more. The best advice is to follow the instructions on the packet and see what happens. Apply lime or gypsum to freshly dug soil in late autumn or early winter and leave it to weather over winter. The material will wash into the soil with the winter rains and a spring cultivation will complete the distribution.

Some plants react badly to lime, so don't overdo it. Lime is very soluble and will leach into the subsoil quite quickly, but even so, if you plan to grow lime-sensitive plants it pays to err on the cautious side. Consider increasing the depth of topsoil by adding compost or growing sensitive plants in raised beds as alternatives to heavy liming.

FURTHER CULTIVATION

After the initial breaking up, the soil will need regular light cultivation to prevent weeds from becoming established and to keep the soil loose. Light forking over or regular hoeing will be sufficient.

Newly worked soils are nearly always full of weed seeds and this continued light cultivation is a vital part of weed control. Provided

Terracing allows you to utilise sloping parts of the garden, and can add real interest to the design.

you keep on top of the job you are unlikely to have any serious problems, but let the weeds set seed and your newly prepared garden will provide the ideal seed bed for reinfestation on a grand scale.

LEVELLING

Establishing levels and providing good drainage are related tasks. Most gardens have some variations in level, and even if they are only very slight they can lead to problems with puddling and soil being washed away.

If the slopes are gradual, a simple smoothing off may be all that is required, and this is most easily done immediately after the initial cultivation. Vigorous raking can eliminate slight humps and hollows, and these can be smoothed over by screeding the soil with a board attached to the head of a rake. Heavier boards and rollers can also be used on lawn areas, but be careful not to undo all your fine cultivating work by re-compacting the soil.

Severe slopes can be very difficult and tiring to work with. They can also lead to potentially dangerous run-off problems and slips. Terracing is usually the best option, and in all but the most basic cases, it is a job that requires professional contractors. They have the equipment and expertise to do the job quickly and easily. Also, building retaining walls above 50 cm high requires careful planning and is best left to those with experience. Poorly built retaining walls can turn a potentially dangerous slope into a disastrous slip just waiting to happen. Ambitious terracing jobs may require planning consent or building permits and this is another area where contractors can help.

DRAINAGE

Drainage serves three main purposes: it directs run-off water away from the house; eliminates poorly drained garden areas; and lessens the risk of any earth movement in sloping parts of the garden. Good drainage is vital for ensuring that your house is pleasant to live in and that your garden thrives. Poor drainage can lead to rotting and mildew in the house and is tolerated by very few plants.

The top 60 cm or so of soil can easily be altered, but the subsoil is largely permanent and unalterable and has a significant bearing on drainage. Clearly clay soils tend to hold too much water, whereas sandy soils often drain too freely. What is less apparent is the effect of a very heavy subsoil, often known as a clay pan or hard pan. Many parts of New Zealand have soil that is good for the top 60 cm, but below that you hit a hard clay layer. Plants that don't send down deep roots do well, but deeper-rooting plants often struggle when they hit the clay. Conversely, peaty soils, which can be marvellous to work with, are often saturated with water at lower levels. This can lead to root rots and may cause trees to become very shallow rooted, which can lead to stability problems.

The best time to install drains is while the house is being built or just after it has been completed. The roof will need to be on and the guttering installed before you can establish where the roofing drains will run. The builders will usually take care of this type of drainage, but if you work in with them it should be possible for these drains to also help drain wet areas in the garden.

Drives and pathways will also create run-off too, especially if they are sloping, and their position will need to be considered when installing drains. Surface drainage, such as edging gravel or small edging gutters, will remove much of this run-off, but subsurface water is a greater problem. The only solution is to remove it from the property by underground drains. These should always run to the lowest part of the property, where the water can be channelled into a stormwater drain.

If you do not have access to main stormwater drains, you will need to create a soak pit. A soak pit is simply a deep hole filled with coarse gravel or hard fill into which drainage water is piped and left to drain naturally. A soak pit is not practical in areas with a constantly high water table. Otherwise it works well enough, provided it is well below the level of the garden.

If your garden has areas that prove impossible or impractical to drain, you could consider turning these wet patches to your advantage by using them for bog gardens or ponds. However, if the poor drainage is caused by excessive run-off to a particular point in your garden, you may find that your garden is frequently scoured by run-off water and your pond silts up.

Trees pump up a huge amount of water from the soil and those that can tolerate very wet soil, such as swamp cypress (*Taxodium distichum*) and tupelo (*Nyssa sylvatica*), can be used to drain wet patches.

INSTALLING DRAINS

Most gardeners are capable of designing and creating a drainage system for gradual slopes, but severe grades and hillsides usually require an experienced drainlayer, and possibly even a surveyor.

Simple drainage systems are usually built around one or two main drains that are fed by smaller secondary drains if necessary. Generally, the main drains run with the slope of the land and the secondary drains run across and down the slope to intersect with the main drains at about a 45–60° angle.

Fortunately, with modern plastic drainage pipe this is no longer the tedious job that it was when clay field tiles were the only option. Perforated plastic drainage pipe, such as 'Agflow', comes in a variety of diameters and is easily cut, which greatly simplifies the joining of main and secondary drains.

The drains must have a gentle but constant fall of at least 10–15 cm per 30 m of pipe. Subsurface drains should rest level with the subsoil if possible and seldom need to be more than 60 cm deep. Often an inexperienced drainlayer will overestimate the fall and depth required, only to find the ditch getting deeper and deeper at an alarming rate. The best way around this is to measure the length of the drain and establish depths for each end. That sets the depth for each point along the ditch and enables you to check the depth as you progress with the digging.

The ditch-digging process is straightforward. As with digging over the ground, you have the choice of a quick mechanised method – a trenching machine – or a labour-intensive but cheap option – digging the ditches by hand. Either method works equally well, but digging ditches by hand soon loses its novelty.

Once the ditch is dug, and you are satisfied with its flow, it should be lined with coarse gravel to a depth of about 15 cm. The pipe is laid on the gravel bed and then covered with a further 15–30 cm of gravel. The gravel prevents

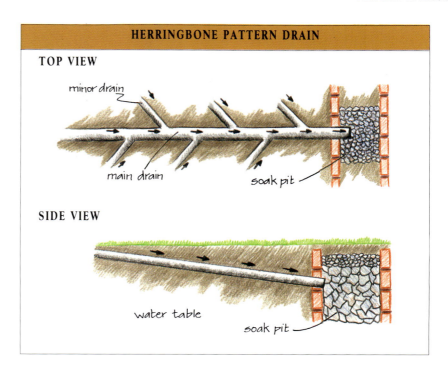

HERRINGBONE PATTERN DRAIN

TOP VIEW

minor drain

main drain

soak pit

SIDE VIEW

water table

soak pit

the pipe quickly becoming clogged with silt. This will happen anyway, but the gravel will considerably lengthen the silting period. If the main drainpipe runs to a stormwater drain, and both ends can be left open, blasting water through the pipe every few months will remove any silting.

Maintaining a constant fall over a long distance on undulating land is more complicated. Such drainage jobs are best left to the professionals, who will have surveying instruments to aid them with their calculations.

ALTERING ESTABLISHED DRAINAGE

Because drainage requires extensive digging, is messy and may necessitate the removal of established plants, it is better to take care of it before the garden is developed. Occasionally, however, nearby building developments and roading changes can alter the drainage patterns in established gardens.

If such problems are the result of the building activity of others, you may have some legal recourse with regard to correcting the problem. However, any time that an existing garden has to have its drainage altered, it is vital that great care is taken. Buried electricity and telephone cables, sewer pipes and existing drains are all potential hazards you must be aware of when digging drainage ditches. Hiring a professional drainage contractor is usually the safest option, and often turns out to be cheaper in the long run.

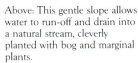
Above: This gentle slope allows water to run-off and drain into a natural stream, cleverly planted with bog and marginal plants.
Right: Natural water features or existing damp, boggy areas can be successfully incorporated into the overall garden design.

MANURES AND FERTILISERS

The next step is to incorporate plenty of humus-containing material. Humus is rotted vegetable and animal matter. It provides nutrients for the plants, opens up the soil to make it more easily penetrated by roots and also helps to retain moisture. Regularly adding humus is one of the best ways to maintain nutrient levels and conserve soil moisture in light, sandy soil or gritty, volcanic soil.

A common way of adding humus is to grow a bulky green crop, such as potatoes, or a nitrogen-storing legume, such as lupins or peas, to be dug in at the end of the season. If you have access to good compost, leaf mould or material high in humus, this can be dug in immediately, thus saving the time required to grow the cover crop. Don't be skimpy with the compost; it is impossible to have too much humus. (See the chapter on plant nutrition in Section 3: Caring for your garden.)

Next you need to add some fertiliser to ensure good levels of soil nutrients. Composting and plant nutrients are dealt with more fully in later chapters, but to briefly summarise there are three main ways of adding nutrients:

MANURES, which may be of animal origin, such as horse, cow and sheep manure, or green manures. These are a valuable source of nutrients, particularly nitrogen, and also add a considerable amount of humus.

FERTILISERS, either chemical or organic, liquid or powdered. These are usually formulated as general all-purpose fertilisers, but they may also be nutrient specific, and many include trace elements. All should be provided with an accurate chemical analysis.

MULCHING MATERIAL AND SOIL CONDITIONERS, such as pea straw, stable manure and seaweed, work well as mulches or may be dug in as a source of nutrients and humus.

ALTERING THE PH

Excessive acidity is easily corrected by adding lime, but altering highly alkaline soil is more difficult. Incorporating plenty of compost and using acid-based fertilisers will help, but lime is

Some plants prefer acid soils and others prefer more alkaline conditions. The natural woodland habitat of rhododendrons (above) means that they have adapted to slightly acidic soils. If you wish to grow plants with differing pH needs, containers (as used in the garden above left) provide an easy solution.

very soluble and will eventually seep back to neutralise any added acidity. Planting in raised beds filled with specially prepared soil offers the best long-term solution, because it keeps the plants above the level of the naturally alkaline soil and lime is unlikely to seep up into the raised bed.

Raised beds should have at least a 60 cm soil depth and should be wide enough to allow for a good root spread; a large rhododendron requires a bed at least 1 m wide. Raised beds can be made from treated timber or more permanent materials, such as bricks or concrete. Remember, however, that fresh mortar and concrete will release free lime and should be left to weather for several months before planting.

You will often be told that you should never add lime to plants that prefer acid soils, but there is an exception to this rule. In very acid soil, calcium can fall to dangerously low levels and all plants, even acid-soil plants, need calcium, so this problem requires treatment. Calcium is available as calcium sulphate, which will not raise the pH, but obviously this does not correct the underlying extreme acidity. The best solution is to use dolomite lime, which will slightly increase the pH, thereby freeing up calcium, and will also add some magnesium.

Dolomite lime (as opposed to hydrated lime) is largely composed of mineral dolomite, a natural form of limestone with quite a high proportion of magnesium. It is a more gentle form of lime that acid-soil plants will tolerate and the extra magnesium is also beneficial. Very few garden soils are acid enough that you would need to add dolomite lime to grow acid-soil plants, such as *Rhododendron* and *Kalmia*, but it may be necessary for potting mixes and composts.

RESULTS

You should now have an ideal soil; that is, a moisture-retentive, humus-rich, fertile, well-drained and aerated soil with a pH of around 6.5. This is the best canvas you can start with, and, once you have your garden plan, you can begin applying colour and texture to your design by using the huge range of plants available.

The Plants

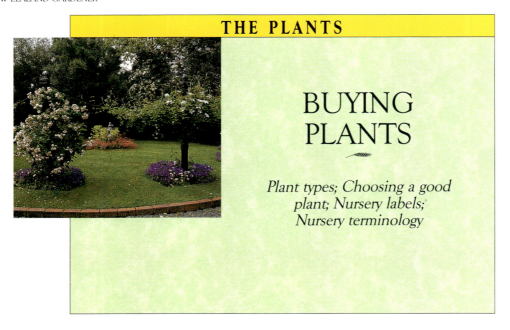

THE PLANTS

BUYING PLANTS

Plant types; Choosing a good plant; Nursery labels; Nursery terminology

Roses such as 'Viridiflora' (below) and 'Yellow Bird' (bottom) can be bought bare-rooted or in planter bags.

MANY GARDENERS ARE avid collectors and always interested in growing new plants. Consequently, modern gardens contain an enormous and ever-changing range of plants. Not only do we grow species from the world over, we have also produced hybrids by crossing species that would never have met naturally. We certainly can't complain of a lack of choice, but sometimes it is difficult to identify and choose the right plant.

Most gardeners buy their plants from garden centres and nurseries. However, beginning gardeners often find nurseries to be very confusing places; all those botanic names, hundreds of different types of plants and ill-defined nursery terms. The plant descriptions that follow will encourage you to visit your local nursery – knowing what you'll find there will help you to buy with your head rather than your heart.

PLANT TYPES

Nurseries sell many different types of plants and they are presented in various ways.

BEDDING PLANTS AND VEGETABLES

Bedding plants and vegetables are most commonly sold in plastic troughs holding from 3–12 plants, and they are sometimes available in boxes of up to 40 plants. Some vegetables, such as carrots, radishes and parsnips, are unsuitable for growing in troughs or transplanting and must be raised from seed sown in the garden.

BULBS, CORMS AND TUBERS

Bulbs may be purchased dry in loose packs, packed in moist sawdust or shredded newspaper, or growing in trays or pots. The packaging varies with the time of year. Gladioli, for example, are sold as loose bulbs in autumn and winter or as potted plants in spring and summer.

PERENNIALS

Perennials are usually sold in pots or plastic planter bags, although sometimes dormant perennials are sold packed in cardboard tubes or sealed plastic bags packed with moist sawdust or shredded newspaper. Buying what looks to be an empty pot can be disconcerting, but rest assured, something should develop. If not, return the plant to the nursery.

SHRUBS

In former years many shrubs were grown in open ground beds then lifted for sale. Now nearly all shrubs are raised in containers and potted on until ready for sale. The only common exception is roses, which are primarily still grown in open beds. They are sometimes sold bare-rooted, but it is increasingly common to pot roses for sale.

TREES

Trees are often still lifted from the open ground. Although some deciduous trees are sold bare-rooted when dormant, most are potted prior to being offered for sale. The trimming required to get them into the pots can cause damage that may not appear until well after the initial spring growth flush. When buying large potted deciduous trees it pays to wait until they have flowered and have reached the point where they are in leaf and making obvious growth.

CHOOSING A GOOD PLANT

Healthy plants usually stand out – they are the ones with the lush, unmarked foliage and the even well-branched shape. Avoid plants that are obviously diseased and those that have uneven growth. Also, as far as possible, make sure that the plant matches the description on the label, as it is not unknown for plants to be accidentally mislabelled.

You can expect the appearance of the plant to vary with the time of year. Deciduous plants will of course be bare of leaves in winter, but evergreens will also change appearance with the seasons. Their foliage may take on red or purple tones in winter and some degree of leaf drop can be expected, especially in spring.

It is common for one plant type to be sold in a variety of size grades and you can expect to pay considerably more for a large grade plant. Provided you are prepared to wait, small plants are sometimes a better buy, because they suffer less shock when transplanted and often establish better than large specimens. Nevertheless, large plants make an immediate impact and with careful attention to watering and staking there should be few difficulties in getting them established.

Generally, if there is any question about a plant's health or shape it is better to choose another one. The exception is the rare or unusual plant that you simply must have. Also, you may occasionally find a reasonably sound plant that has been in the pot too long and desperately needs planting out. If you can loosen the roots and provide plenty of water and feeding, such plants will usually recover quite quickly and should not be ignored, especially as they are often sold cheaply to save the nursery having to repot them.

NURSERY LABELS

Many gardeners get frustrated by inaccurate labelling. Flower colour, flowering season and general plant requirements are usually accurate, but hardiness and size are often suspect. The size on the label is supposedly the size that a reasonably mature plant can be kept to with moderate trimming. It is usually underestimated, often by as much as half. The hardiness, on the other hand, is usually overestimated. Unless the label states an actual degree of hardiness, i.e., hardy to -10°C, ask an assistant. Also, many labels have colour photographs that are liable to fade and may not present an accurate picture.

Becoming a good gardener requires experience, and nursery staff are often very experienced gardeners, so do ask questions. You'll generally find that they are friendly and willing to help, and they may well become your most valuable source of local gardening information.

Top: *Calycanthus floridus*

Camellia 'Bob's Tinsie' (middle) and *Rhododendron* 'Percy Wiseman' (bottom) are just two of the hundreds of varieties of rhododendrons and camellias available at any one time.

NURSERY TERMINOLOGY

All trades have their abbreviations, acronyms and special terms and the nursery business is no exception. The following are the most common.

FKV This stands for Free of any Known Virus, and refers to specially certified tissue-cultured plants that are free of known viral disease.

GRADE The grade is the size of the plant, which may be measured by container size, plant height or trunk girth.

HIGH HEALTH High health plants are propagated by conventional means using material from FKV plants. They are generally more vigorous than normal stock, although they are not certified virus-free.

OG This stands for Open Ground and refers to plants that have been raised in growing fields then lifted and offered for sale. OG plants are usually sold bare rooted (without soil); if potted after lifting they are called ex OG.

PB Planter Bag, the black polythene bags in which many nurseries grow their plants. They are graded from PB¼–PB150 according to their capacity in pints. Hard pots are usually measured by their capacity in litres, or their widest diameter in millimetres.

ROOT TRAINER Root trainers are multi-plant seedling containers that encourage straight root growth. They are made from moulded plastic in the form of a hinged book.

TUBE A tube is a small pot into which cuttings or seedlings are pricked out. Plants in tubes are sometimes called GOLs or growing-on-lines, which indicates that they are not intended for immediate sale but for growing on to a larger grade, but some small perennials and rockery plants are sold in tubes.

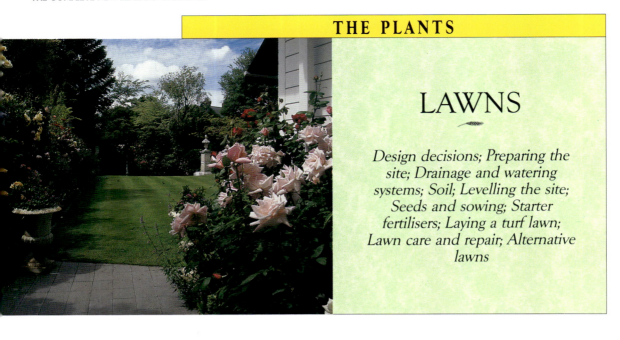

LAWNS

Design decisions; Preparing the site; Drainage and watering systems; Soil; Levelling the site; Seeds and sowing; Starter fertilisers; Laying a turf lawn; Lawn care and repair; Alternative lawns

LAWNS CONTRIBUTE to the character and atmosphere of a garden and help to unite the various elements. They create a sense of spaciousness and are the perfect foil to highlight flower beds, borders, trees and homes. In many gardens they simply provide a recreational area. In winter lawns bring viridity and life to what is often an empty-looking garden. Whatever its function, a well-maintained lawn is an attractive garden feature.

Often home owners strive to achieve a lawn of bowling-green quality. It can be done with the right preparation and maintenance, but it is better to first consider the time and money available and the functions of the lawn before striving for such an effect.

Once you have decided to incorporate a grass lawn into your garden, the next step is deciding where to put it. Take into consideration the aspect of your whole garden – how it lies with regard to the sun, whether it slopes or is flat, if it has to give access to other parts of the garden, will it be shaded by high trees or buildings, how much the children will play on it, the soil type, and the boundaries of your section.

DESIGN DECISIONS

If the site for your lawn is on a slope, it should not exceed 30 degrees. If it does maintenance is difficult (if not downright dangerous!), so

Below left: This superbly tended lawn unifies the garden design. Below right: Simple paving follows the gentle curve of the flower bed.

consider planting other types of ground cover plants. Remember that grass must have at least eight hours of sunlight per day to grow satisfactorily, and moss will thrive in areas that are too shady.

Designing the shape of your lawn and garden is the next important step. The shape should be one that appeals to you and your family and is practical within the area available. Good design is reflected in an attractive shape that is easy to maintain. Avoid the eye-catching lawn that is a nightmare to mow. A square or rectangle is the traditional and most labour-saving shape for a lawn, however a simple irregular outline is often more attractive. Avoid small, fussy curves or awkward corners at all costs; strive for gently flowing curves for ease of mowing.

If you are placing flower beds in your lawn, make them bold and try not to place them in the centre. The same rules apply to beds as to corners.

Paths should not lead directly onto a lawn. Excessive wear and compaction will be caused by heavy traffic where path and lawn meet. Instead, try running the path down the edge of the lawn. The level of the path should be lower than the lawn and a grass-free mowing strip should be maintained between them for tidiness and to make mowing easier. A mowing edge, such as a concrete strip, is a must and should extend all round your lawn. Maintenance of this strip is extra work, but it will keep your lawn looking immaculate.

PREPARING THE SITE

Good preparation of the site is essential for the future well-being of your lawn, and it should begin at least three months before the planned sowing or turfing dates. Having determined the size and shape of your lawn the next step is to mark out the lawn area. The easiest way of doing this is to use a long length of garden hose laid out into the desired shape, easing out sharp corners or accentuating a pleasing tree or shrub. When you are satisfied, push in small stakes every metre to mark the shape of the lawn's outer edges.

The first step if you have a new home is to clear away builder's rubble. Remove all rubbish completely, including rubble, bricks, discarded gravel and any other unwanted material, otherwise these objects will continue to appear in your lawn for years to come. If the new site is infested with weeds use a non-residual herbicide, such as glyphosate.

DRAINAGE AND WATERING SYSTEMS

Lawns, like the rest of your garden, require good drainage. If you are not sure about drainage systems, call in a qualified landscape designer or a professional greenkeeper. It will be money well spent. An expert will take levels and suggest drainage systems. Conversely, if you have very hot, dry summers an in-ground automatic watering system can be designed for your needs. Installing a watering system when you are laying your lawn is recommended.

There are many commercial lawn watering

Generous sweeps of lawn are easier to maintain than lawns with small fussy curves.

A mowing strip is essential for the well-defined lines in this formal garden setting.

Sturdy paving has been selected for this high-use area.

systems, either sprinklers or a permanent in-ground system with pop-up sprinkler heads. All of these systems have detailed instructions for their installation and operation.

SOIL

First establish the depth of the topsoil. Ideally there should be at least 15 cm. If there is less, you will need to buy sufficient top-quality soil from a reputable supplier.

Rotary hoeing by a specialist contractor would be the easiest and most practical way of preparing the soil. An experienced operator will also be able to level or contour your site, thus saving you many hours of back-breaking labour.

For clay soils, spread compost over the soil surface and lightly work it into the top 4 cm of soil. Sandy soils will require equal proportions of compost lightly worked into the top 12 cm to aid moisture retention.

Cultivating the soil several times prior to sowing will help control annual weeds, however for perennial weeds a non-residual weed-killer, such as glyphosate, will be required.

LEVELLING THE SITE

If doing it yourself, site levels are done by relating to nearby fixed levels such as home founda-tions, walls or paths. You don't need a perfectly level site – this can be difficult to achieve and a fall of no more than 30 degrees or 1:80 is quite acceptable and has the advantage of assisting drainage. Over larger areas a gentle natural slope or undulations can be visually pleasing.

Few lawns are truly level as most are done using human judgement. The ideal method is to use a spirit level, a straight-edged board about 2 m long and pegs.

Hammer in the master peg at a selected point, leaving 10 cm of the peg above the sur-face. Drive in the other pegs at 1.8 m intervals to form a grid system then establish the master peg at the required level. Working from this peg, adjust the other pegs to the correct level using the straight-edge and spirit level. Next, add or remove soil until the soil surface is at the desired level.

Where a slope is required, establish across-levels in the same manner. Down-slope levels can be established with pegs and a line, or more accurately with a spirit-level, using pairs of marked pegs at each site.

Now the basic levels are secured either dig over the area or, if it is a large area, use a rotary hoe. Hand-digging is good exercise and does not leave a hard pan underneath, which hap-pens when using a rotary hoe. Digging also improves soil texture, aeration and drainage, and reduces compaction.

Next firm the whole area. This is best done with a rake and by 'treading' it with your feet. If the area is large and there is access, a ride-on mower with rubber tyres is ideal. After each rolling the soil will have to be raked over to remove ridges and hollows. The final raking is done to procure a seed bed for the grass seed.

To reach this stage takes a lot of hard work and patience. Seed sowing is a simple and straightforward task, but carelessness at this stage can undo all your hard work. Selecting the right grass seed is crucial.

TYPES OF GRASS SEED

There is no such thing as the perfect seed mixture for every situation – the right one for you will depend on the type of lawn you want (luxury or utility grade) and the type of site you have (shady, sunny, clay or sandy). Quality grass seed is expensive, however your lawn will only be as good as the seed you sow.

A utility lawn is suitable as a playing area for children and other hard-wearing activities. This type of lawn will withstand moderate neglect and some bad management without serious deterioration and is more tolerant of poor-quality mowing than a luxury lawn. Utility grass seed is usually a mixture of rye grass and other broad-leaved turf grasses.

A luxury-grade lawn is a thick, closely knit turf of fine grasses. It is much less hard-wearing and requires a lot more upkeep. In New Zealand a mixture of Browntop and Chewings Fescue is commonly used, now mixed with the drought-tolerant Caliente rye grass. One such mixture is called Classic, which is an improvement on the popular Boston Green.

All grasses will grow in any type of soil, but in clay growth will be severely retarded. Such soils require the addition of compost to improve drainage. The new Caliente rye grass has proved more drought tolerant than older types of rye grass and is thus more suitable for sandy and volcanic soils.

The problem of growing lawn grasses in shady sites is currently being addressed in a series of trials in New Zealand. One mixture that is showing promise is called Jaguar, which contains species of fescue that are much broader leaved than any other lawn-grass species currently grown.

Buy sufficient seed to allow an application rate of 30–35 grams per square metre. Lower rates may mean that the lawn remains thin and sparse for an unnecessarily long time.

SOWING THE SEED

Choosing the right day for sowing is important; the weather should be fine and calm and the top of the soil should be dry with moist soil just below the surface. Delay sowing if mud is sticking to your boots.

First gently rake the surface soil in straight lines so that very shallow furrows are produced.

Seed may be sown either by hand or by a seed-sower. For hand sowing divide the grass seed into two equal portions. Sow half the seed by traversing the plot lengthways and the remaining half crossways. This method gives a more even coverage than a single application. Divide large areas into smaller sections or small plots marked out into square metres to facilitate accurate sowing. If using a seed drill or small centrifugal spreader, first ensure that it can be calibrated to apply grass seed at the required rate. Apply the seed in parallel strips using the previous run's wheel-track as a guide.

A park-like entranceway is created by using mature specimen trees set in a gently sloping lawn.

SOWING LAWN SEED

sow half the seed
widthwise

sow half the seed
lengthwise

One way to ensure even coverage is to
divide the lawn into metre-wide strips
using markers and string.

Again sow half the seed lengthways and the other half crossways.

After sowing, lightly rake over the seed bed to a depth of about 2 cm. The soil surface should have a fine tilth so that raking does not unevenly redistribute the seed. Do not use a roller, as this tends to flatten or cake the surface. If after a few days there has been no rainfall, irrigate gently but thoroughly with a garden sprinkler. Do not use a hose, a coarse sprinkler or a watering can as they may redistribute the seeds. Keeping the seed-bed damp will also help in stopping the birds dust-bathing.

The most suitable time for sowing seed is autumn; March in colder areas of the country and April in warmer areas. During this period soil temperatures are still high and moisture is usually plentiful, encouraging quick germination within 7–12 days and enabling the seedlings to become established before the first frosts.

STARTER FERTILISERS

Generally, most soils will benefit from a starter fertiliser, which usually contains nitrogen, phosphorus and potassium in a ratio of 1:2:1. In the early stages, young grass has a higher phosphorus requirement to assist in root development. Once established, less phosphorus but more nitrogen and potassium are needed. The starter fertiliser should be applied at a rate of 25–30 grams per square metre and raked in at sowing time.

After germination, when the young grass is about 4 cm high, lightly roll the surface on a dry day using a light roller or a rear-roller cylinder-mower with the front roller and blades lifted clear of the grass. Two or three days later, when the grass is growing vertically again, cut it with a sharp-bladed mower, removing no more than about one-third of the grass growth.

Use the lawn as little as possible during the first two months of growth. Feed it regularly according to seasonal requirements and irrigate as necessary. The object is to establish a grass coverage of sufficient density to prevent moss and weeds from becoming established.

LAYING A TURF LAWN

'Instant lawns' are quicker and easier than sowing your own but they are also more expensive. The same preparations are required as for sowing a grass lawn, and unless the area has been recently fertilised, apply a lawn fertiliser at 56 grams per square metre.

Standard turves, 30 x 90 cm, will be rolled up when delivered to you and laying should take place as soon as possible after delivery, as they can deteriorate quite quickly. Start laying with a single row along the side of the site closest to the stack of turves. Gently press

CONSTRUCTING A TAMPER

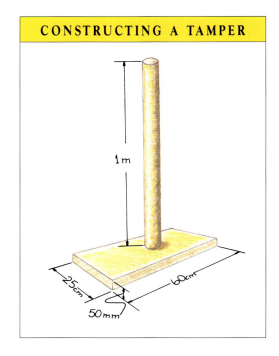

1 m

25 cm

60 cm

50 mm

down each row of turves with a tamper made from thick boards and a pole. Check the level with a board and spirit level. If there are bumps and hollows, never beat the turf down, but lift it and add or remove soil as necessary. Stand on a plank, never on the newly-laid turf or unturfed plot.

Trim edges with a half-moon edging iron. For curves, use a garden hose as your guide.

Fill in the cracks with a mixture composed of 1 part peat, 2 parts loam and 4 parts sand. Spread this sandy soil along the cracks and work it well into the turves with a yard-broom or the back of a rake. This will help the turves to knit together.

When growth begins in spring, cut the lawn with the blades set high. As the season progresses gradually lower the blades until a height of 2 cm is reached.

The new lawn is more susceptible to drought than established turf, so water thoroughly during prolonged dry spells. Regular feeding is also essential.

LAWN CARE

MOWING

When done correctly, mowing creates a vigorous high-quality turf. The secret is to keep the grass long enough to support the roots but short enough to be attractive and tidy. The recommended cutting height is at least 2 cm in spring and summer and at least 1 cm in winter. Mow often during rapid growth, but not too closely.

Only mow when the grass foliage is dry –

mowing wet turf is not only dangerous but can produce a ragged effect. The direction of mowing should be at right angles to the previous cut – this helps to keep the coarse grasses under control. Always mow in a constant forward direction and avoid pushing backwards and forwards. 'Wembley stripes' are produced with a mower fitted with a roller, the alternate stripes being mown in opposite directions.

Always pay attention to the safety and good maintenance of your mower.

TRIMMING AND TIDYING

Regular trimming of the lawn edges is crucial to the overall appearance of the lawn. There are many different tools suitable for this purpose, including lawn shears, motorised nylon-cord trimmers and small motorised edgers.

Lawns gather a great deal of debris during the year, such as fallen leaves and twigs, which must be removed for the sake of tidiness. The best tool for this purpose is a wire or plastic leaf rake.

AERATION

Aerating lawns is important to reduce compaction and improve gas exchange, water penetration and drainage. Compaction can be a problem where the lawn is heavily used and in heavy soils may seriously restrict water and oxygen uptake by the grass roots.

Two techniques help to overcome this problem: spiking, which consists of driving spikes into the soil to a depth of 7–8 cm, and pricking, which only breaks through the layer of

LAYING A TURF LAWN

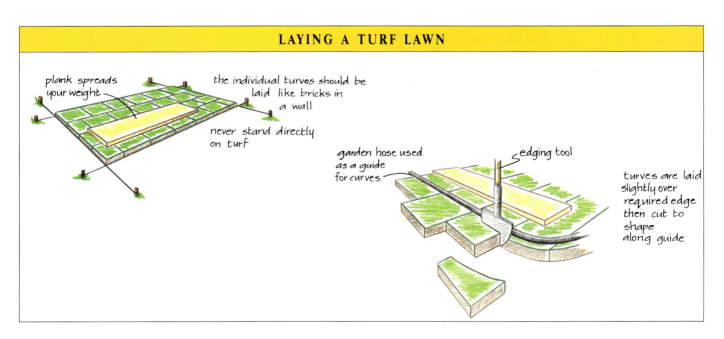

plank spreads your weight

the individual turves should be laid like bricks in a wall

never stand directly on turf

garden hose used as a guide for curves

edging tool

turves are laid slightly over required edge then cut to shape along guide

dead and decaying material that accumulates on the uppermost 2 cm of soil.

Only those areas showing symptoms of compaction, such as water-logging after rain, unusually rapid browning in dry weather, bare patches due to heavy traffic and poor grass vigour, require spiking. Spiking in February or March is the best time and choose a day when the soil is moist. There are many types of motorised spikers that can be hired. For small areas an ordinary garden fork is ideal.

Prick the entire lawn in summer if water applied in dry weather does not rapidly soak into the surface.

WATERING

Supplementary watering is essential during hot, dry periods to keep your lawn looking green and healthy. In New Zealand this is most likely to be necessary from January until the end of March. More frequent watering will be required for fine lawns and lawns on light soils.

Watering should begin when there is a loss of springiness in the grass. Further drying out of the top 10 cm of soil will lead to browning off, and in extreme cases the grass may die. However, the more drought-tolerant grasses are capable of sitting dormant until the rains return. Some weeds, such as clover and yarrow, are much more drought-resistant than grass and so will spread rapidly amidst weakened grass.

Encouraging deep and vigorous root systems increases drought resistance. Water the lawn thoroughly to a depth of around 10 cm. A light sprinkling with a hand-held hose will only encourage a shallow root system. The deeper the watering, the less frequent it will be necessary – once a week may prove sufficient. Early morning or evening is the best time to water. Never cut below 2 cm high and in very dry weather let the grass grow a little longer. Leave the clippings on the lawn in times of drought. Feeding regularly and applying a phosphate-containing fertiliser at least once a year will also promote healthy root systems.

FEEDING

Established lawns require regular feeding to remain in top condition. Neglect of feeding may lead to yellowing, patchiness, weed and moss encroachment, and reduced drought and disease resistance.

Like all plants, a range of nutrients is essential for grass growth, however nitrogen and phosphorus are the most important elements for grasses. Nitrogen is very important during the growing season (i.e., spring and summer) to promote a rich, green, vigorous turf. Phosphorus stimulates a healthy root system and promotes side-shooting in autumn. Potassium is required in smaller quantities but may increase drought and disease resistance.

A proprietary lawn fertiliser high in nitrogen is convenient for the home gardener. A slow-release formulation such as Floranid is even better. Apply it in spring and autumn and immediately water in well to avoid burning. Alternatively, a fertiliser higher in phosphorus and potassium and with only a little slow-acting nitrogen could be applied in autumn. A quick-acting source of nitrogen should not be applied in autumn as lush growth is not wanted in winter.

Nitrosol (liquid blood and bone) or sulphate of ammonia is an excellent summer booster; Nitrosol is preferable as it avoids the risk of burning.

When applying fertilisers, employ a similar procedure as for seed sowing to ensure even distribution, or use a fertiliser spreader.

LAWN PROBLEMS

WEEDS

The most troublesome weeds in established lawns are the low-growing perennials with creeping or rosette growth habits, such as daisy, clover, plantain, oxalis, yarrow, paspalum, hydrocotyle and Onehunga or prickle weed.

Regular mowing using the grass catcher, careful feeding and attention to water supplies will keep turf densely leaved and healthy, making it difficult for weeds to establish themselves. However, the appearance of weeds is unavoidable.

A number of lawn weedkillers are available. One of the better ones is a product called Proturf, which contains four different chemicals that will control a wide range of lawn weeds. It is best applied through a Lawnboy with Nitrosol added to the tank as a spreading agent as well as a foliar fertiliser.

Do not mow for at least seven days after treatment to allow translocation of the chemicals throughout the weed plants. Do not use the lawn clippings as a mulch around trees or shrubs and do not place in compost bins for at least two weeks. Avoid spraying in drought conditions, if rain is likely to fall within three hours of treatment, or when there is a heavy dew on the turf. Do not spray in windy weather in order to avoid spray drift.

Clumps of coarse grass do not respond to

lawn weedkillers. The recommended control method is to slash through the weed with a knife or edging iron before mowing.

Hand-weeding is an alternative to chemicals, as is the Speedy Weeder, which will root out quite large weeds.

Contrary to widespread opinion, the presence of moss in a lawn does not necessarily indicate the need for lime. Moss colonises lawns for various reasons. Excessive fertility or weakness of the turf due to attack by pests and diseases, lack of aeration, poor drainage and excessive shade will all result in weak sparse turf that allows moss to become established.

Preventative measures are the best means of control. Moss grows best in shady situations or poorly drained lawns, so prune back overhanging trees and improve drainage.

A product called Mossoff will kill lichens, moss, algae and liverworts. A repeat treatment may be necessary four weeks later. Within one month of treatment rake out dying moss patches, and apply a lawn fertiliser and reseed if necessary.

DISEASES

Several diseases can cause discoloration, weakening or death of large areas of turf. It is very important to determine as early as possible whether this is caused by a cultural problem or a disease.

Fairy rings are caused by certain soil-borne fungi. They appear as one or more bands of lush, dark green turf, which may be continuous or broken and have a strip of brown turf between them. During summer and autumn rings of spore-bearing toadstools or puff-balls appear if conditions are damp. To control single fairy rings first pierce the infected turf with a fork and thinly apply fine sand. Water the area with Citawet (10 ml per 10 l water) followed by Calirus (50 g in 20 l water per 10 m²) or a general fungus and mildew spray. A further treatment may be required 3–4 months later.

Fusarium patch is a common fungal disease of lawns. It is most prevalent in autumn and spring. It causes small patches of yellowing grass to about 30 cm across which may merge to form extensive brown areas. In moist weather the edges of the diseased areas may be covered with white or pale pink fluffy mould. Prevention is the best means of control. Avoid nitrogen-rich fertilisers in autumn or winter and spike the turf regularly. Control with Benlate applied at 3–6 g per 10 m² in sufficient water to thoroughly wet the turf. Repeat if needed at 10–14 day intervals.

Red thread attacks fine-leaved grasses and appears as irregular patches of bleached grass in late summer or autumn that later take on a pinkish tinge. In moist weather, small, red, needle-like growths on the grass leaves will be visible. Red thread does not kill the turf but it is unsightly until the bleached patches recover. Good lawn care is the secret. Feed your lawn every two months in spring and summer, spike the turf and avoid mowing too closely. Use Benlate for control.

Dollar spot is another disease that sometimes causes problems. It appears as straw-coloured or golden brown circular patches 2–5 cm across. Control is as for red thread.

PESTS

One of the worst pests from Auckland northwards is the black cricket. It will invade lawns during very hot, dry weather in large numbers, causing severe damage. To repel this insect keep lawns well watered throughout the dry months.

Possibly the worst pest of lawns is the grass grub. Populations can exceed 4000 per square metre! The adult beetle lays eggs 10–15 cm deep in the soil following the main flight period in November. The small grubs hatch after a few weeks and feed on the roots of grasses. Unfortunately the only chemical cure is a nasty organophosphate called Diazinon, which should be applied in late summer and autumn. Please be careful with this chemical. Always apply plenty of water to wash it into the soil and keep children and pets off the area for at least a week.

Porina caterpillars, which feed on the foliage, can also be a problem. Diazinon is also recommended for their control.

LAWN REPAIRS

Bare patches, broken edges, bumps and hollows all contribute to the patchy effect that spoils so many lawns, but such eyesores are easily repaired. The best time for renovations is autumn or spring when the weather is showery. Much of this work involves using replacement pieces of turf or the re-seeding of small areas. Turf can be sourced from a section of the lawn where its loss will hardly be noticed and the denuded area then built up and re-seeded.

BROKEN EDGES

Cut out a square of turf carrying the broken edge and move it forward, trimming it to line

The daisy *Bellis perennis* is a common lawn weed.

Lawn grass can be a lot more vigorous when wild clover is also growing in the lawn. Presumably this is because the clover fixes nitrogen in the soil, which is then used by the grass.

cut a
square
out of the lawn

using
a spade
or edging tool
to get a straight line

remove
broken edge

move
square
forward and
fill gap with soil.
Sow with new seed.

Popular alternatives to the more traditional grass include thyme (above) and *Isotoma fluviatalis* (right).

up with the rest of the lawn. Fill up the gap with either turf or soil that is then re-seeded.

BUMPS AND HOLLOWS

Bumps are regularly scalped by the mower and therefore tend to become bare. The turf should be removed with a spade or edging iron and the area levelled. Do not attempt to roll out bumps. If the bump is prominent and the soil is shallow, remove some subsoil and replace with topsoil. Firm the soil by treading, roll back the turf and firm it down after checking that the area is level. Fill in the cracks with sifted soil.

Depressions are usually caused by inadequate consolidation prior to sowing or the rotting of organic material below the surface. Small hollows can be gradually filled in by working sifted soil (no more than 1 cm deep at a time) into the turf at regular intervals. Deep hollows call for the same technique as bumps.

BARE PATCHES

Compaction and poor drainage are common reasons for the death of grass and may affect a large area of the lawn. Weed removal, under-tree drip, bitch urine burn, fertiliser overdosing and the scalping of bumps by the mower generally produce bare patches which are distinct in outline and limited in area. Excessive wear may be limited or widespread. Wherever possible, try to remedy the cause before carrying out the repair or the bare patch may quickly return.

There are two ways of repairing such areas.

The dead patch of turf can be removed and another piece of turf fitted in its place. Alternatively, the area can be re-seeded. For this method, prick the area with a hand fork and rake it over to remove debris and form a fine seed bed. Sow seed at 30 grams per square metre, cover with a thin layer of sifted soil and press down with a board. Protect from birds with crossed strands of cotton thread.

ALTERNATIVE LAWNS

For areas subjected to heavy wear, grass is the most reliable choice for a lawn. However, there are various alternatives, especially for sites that are difficult to mow or where lawn grasses do not grow well, or if you simply want a different look.

There are many plants for lawns that are more colourful than grass, sweet-smelling when walked on and require little or no mowing, but there are disadvantages too. Though low-growing, most do not form a smooth turf and are not as hard-wearing as grass, and in winter some may suffer frost damage. Also, weeding is a major problem, as most current weedkillers are unsuitable. Hand-weeding is the only option. An alternative lawn will also need to be bordered by paths, walls, etc., as regular edging may be ineffective.

The most popular alternative plant in New Zealand is Mercury Bay weed (*Dichondra micrantha*). In full sun or where it gets regular

foot traffic it will stay low and tight, but in the shade it may reach 12 cm high. It only tolerates light frosts. It can be grown from seed sown in summer, but plugs may be a better option. Dichondra lawns require similar preparation and maintenance to grass lawns and similar pests may attack both lawn types. Feeding well, to encourage luxuriant and dense growth, is the best means of weed control, but the weedkiller Dichondra Clean has been developed for dichondra lawns.

Chamomile (*Chamaemelum nobile*) lawns were popular in Elizabethan times. Non-flowering varieties, such as 'Treneague', are used and form dense carpets that smell of apples when walked on.

Creeping thymes are also commonly advocated, the best and easiest species being *Thymus serpyllum*, but to maintain a dense carpet may require periodic replacement.

Virtually any creeping plant with a dense, weed-suppressing habit can be used as a lawn substitute. However, most will take little or no foot traffic and are thus best for smaller areas,

e.g., beside paths, and where lawn grasses are unsatisfactory. Suitable plants would include *Acaena, Ajuga, Cotula, Dianthus, Fuchsia procumbens, Hedera, Leptinella, Ophiopogon, Parahebe, Pratia, Schizocentron* and *Scleranthus*, but there are many others. (Within other chapters in Section 2: The Plants, look for plants noted as ground covers, or that have a suitable spreading habit.)

There are numerous areas unsuitable for lawn grasses, e.g., in deep shade under trees, steep dry banks, poorly drained areas, and very sandy or stony soils. In addition to the host of creeping plants, numerous shrubs and perennials can be used for ground-covering purposes if planted *en masse*.

Wildflower meadows are another alternative. They are certainly more colourful and introduce a natural, informal look, but contrary to their appearance, they require a lot of preparation and maintenance to keep them free of undesirable weeds and they will inevitably look untidy for part of the year.

Above left: Mondo grass (*Ophiopogon*) makes an eye-catching ground cover.
Above right: Mercury Bay weed (*Dichondra micrantha*) is a very popular alternative lawn in New Zealand, as is *Cotula* (below).

THE PLANTS

ANNUALS AND PERENNIALS

Climate adaptability; Garden design; Annual bedding; Herbaceous borders; Cottage gardens; Woodland gardens; Bog gardens; Rockeries; Container growing; Care and cultivation; Obtaining plants

Above: Many perennials are hardy and tolerant of a wide range of conditions, as demonstrated in this closely planted southern garden.

Top: Iceland poppy (*Papaver nudicaule*)

WITH ANNUALS AND PERENNIALS you can have year-round colour. But annuals and perennials are not just a quick way to fill a garden with colour, they also possess a huge range of foliage forms, textures and growth habits. Although they may be scorned for being short-lived and sometimes untidy, they are relatively cheap, easily propagated, tough, adaptable, and, above all, versatile. Trees and shrubs are usually permanent, but they can become staid and uninteresting: annuals and perennials brighten the garden, introduce continuous variety, and make it easy for you to experiment until you have the effect you want. Marigolds are out if you want pastel shades, and impatiens are unsuitable for a dry garden, but whatever the design, there is such a wide range of annuals and perennials there is sure to be something that will fit the bill.

Before going too far we should define the terms annual, biennial and perennial. An annual is any plant that grows from seed to full maturity and dies within one growing season. Marigolds, ageratum and zinnias are typical annuals: they flower, set seed and die, all within a single year. Biennials, such as Canterbury bells and some foxgloves, complete the cycle over two years. Perennials are plants that live longer than two seasons, so, strictly speaking, shrubs and trees are perennials. However, this term usually refers only to plants that don't become woody.

There are several forms of perennial. Some, such as *Armeria,* are evergreen and don't have

a period of total dormancy, but very few flower continually. Herbaceous perennials generally have a period of dormancy, when they die back to a permanent rootstock. This is usually during winter, but those native to areas with hot dry summers may be dormant in summer or during periods of very low rainfall.

Some herbaceous perennials have roots or stems modified as food storage organs to improve their chances of surviving unfavourable conditions. These organs, which are known as rhizomes and tubers, can often be divided and grown on as new plants. They function in much the same way as bulbs and corms. Examples of tubers include dahlias and alstroemerias, whereas bearded irises are probably the most widely grown rhizomatous plants. Some plants, such as kikuyu grass, have specialised rhizomes known as stolons, which spread across the surface of the ground or just below the surface, taking root as they spread.

Some perennials are treated as annuals, either because they cease to be attractive as they age, or because they are incapable of surviving cold winters. Petunias and impatiens, for example, may live for several seasons if protected from frost, but they become leggy and untidy, so they are usually replaced annually. Others, such as *Gentiana corymbifera*, take several seasons to reach flowering age and then die after flowering; these plants are called monocarpic (once-seeding).

It is common for a genus to contain both annual and perennial species, such as the

An eye-catching combination of perennials *Scabiosa* 'Blue Butterfly', *Veronica teucrium* 'Royal Blue' and *Campanula persicifolia* 'Telham Beauty'.

This herbaceous border demonstrates the skilful use of annuals and perennials.

Lychnis viscaria 'Flora Plena' is a reliable performer in most New Zealand gardens.

annual and perennial cosmos, or species with differing growth habits, like the fibrous- and tuberous-rooted irises and begonias. Under garden conditions the differences between annuals, perennials, rhizomes, tubers, runners, corms and bulbs tend to become blurred. The important thing is how you use the plants, and with annuals and perennials you can give free rein to your imagination.

CLIMATE ADAPTABILITY

Annuals brighten any garden, and because they are only temporary plants, and always treated as such, they succeed everywhere. Gardeners in cold areas can briefly ignore the prospect of winter bleakness and inject a touch of 'tropical' colour into their gardens. The fact that annuals may be unable to reproduce successfully in your climte is unimportant. As long as they provide bright colour they will have served their purpose.

The climate adaptability of annuals is important when you want to plant for continuity. Most annuals are frost-tender and must be planted in spring, after the last frosts, with a view to summer and autumn flowering. However, many can be planted in the autumn and left to overwinter for spring flowering. These plants are known as hardy annuals because they can survive the winter cold. Pansies, sweet William and Iceland poppies are among the best known hardy annuals. With careful planning it is possible to have flowers in bloom almost year round.

Perennials vary greatly in their hardiness and adaptability. Most of the traditional garden perennials are hardy and very adaptable. However, those from southern Africa, Central and South America, and Australia tend to be less cold tolerant and may not be suited to frosty areas, especially where late frosts can be expected.

If you live in a colder climate, say the central North Island or from Canterbury southwards, it is still possible to grow these plants. Often the problem is not so much the cold but a combination of cold and wet conditions. Some plants, such as *Gerbera*, will tolerate quite hard frosts if they are kept dry but will rot if they are cold and wet. Most gardens have a few areas that are protected and remain dry in winter; these are the places to plant the South African daisies and the tender novelties like *Alonsoa*. Some tender perennials, such as heliotrope and the New Guinea butterfly impatiens, demand complete frost protection. They can be treated as annuals, otherwise you'll need to either grow them in containers, so they can be moved under cover for the winter, or propagate them in autumn and keep the small plants indoors until spring.

Annuals are also subject to all the normal

Right: This suburban garden uses dense plantings of shrubs and perennials to set off a display of roses.

The huge range of flower form, colour and size ensures there is always a suitable annual or perennial for whatever garden design you choose.
Top: *Campanula latifolia*.
Middle: *Anemone hepatica*.
Bottom: *Cleome spinosa*.

climatic considerations – wind, salt spray and summer heat – but they are remarkably resilient plants that carry on flowering under most conditions. Nurseries and garden centres stock a huge range of annuals and with careful planning there should be no shortage of choice wherever you live.

GARDEN DESIGN

Ideally you should have some idea of how you want your garden to look. If you're keen on having a cottage garden, perennials may make up the bulk of your planting; conversely if large rose beds are your preference you may need just a few annuals as fillers. Nevertheless every garden has a place for annuals and perennials and there are many ways to use them.

Think of annuals and the chances are you'll think of vivid flower beds. The massed plantings seen in botanic gardens and large private gardens are beyond most of us, but one or two beds devoted entirely to annuals do not look out of place, even in a small garden. Of course, lawns and flower beds go well together. A bowling green-like sward is offset to perfection by a bed of riotous colour and the flower beds are easy to view and walk around when surrounded by lawn.

Perennials are also often best grown in large beds. This not only enables you to make a bold impact by planting in colour groups, it also allows the various foliage forms to be

emphasised. The only disadvantage of large beds is that they can look very stark and bare in winter. Use hardy annuals, such as pansies, and the winter-flowering perennials like polyanthus for winter colour.

If your garden is too small for any of these grand schemes or you just want portable colour, annuals and perennials are great in containers too. Hanging baskets full of trailing lobelias, petunias and begonias may be something of a cliché but they're hard to beat for colour.

ANNUAL BEDDING

Fashionable gardeners may think annual flower beds vulgar, but most of us can't fail to be impressed by the effect of all that colour and diversity in such a small space. Planned massed bedding demands a considerable amount of time and effort for a fairly brief display and the effort must be repeated at least twice a year. This eventually loses its novelty for all but the most dedicated gardeners, and hence really impressive flower beds tend to be restricted to botanic or corporate gardens and private show gardens.

Making a good flower bed requires that the soil be worked to a fine tilth and regularly fertilised. Regular watering may also be necessary. The flower beds may need replanting up to three times a year to optimise the display. The main summer display is put in around late

Left: Plantings of *Convolvulus mauritanicus*, wallflowers, scabiosas and nasturtiums create a delightful tapestry of colour, screened from prevailing winds by mature trees.

Above: This mixed border shows skilful blending of colours accented with white.

As with many species, both *Anemone blanda* (top) and the double-flowered *Aquilegia* are treated as annuals or perennials depending on climate.

September to early October and may be removed as early as February. It is replaced by an autumn to early winter selection, which is removed in late May when the late winter to early spring selection is planted. In areas with cold winters only two plantings may be possible: mid October for the summer display and mid to late April for late winter to spring colour.

The bold display we expect from massed annuals allows the gardener to get away with some pretty shocking colour combinations. Beds composed of many clashing colours make an immediate impact, but they can be hard to live with. Careful colour planning and consideration of height will result in a bed that is just as colourful while being far more harmonious and relaxing on the eye.

Massed bedding doesn't have to be rigidly planned. The readily available wildflower seed mixes offer an easier alternative: just scatter the seed, rake it in lightly and wait. Provided the seed bed has been well prepared and you keep the weeds down, the plants will do the rest. The seed companies have done all the colour mixing and size gradation for you, although there is nothing to stop you making up your own seed mixtures and scattering them to the wind. Quite often the effects of such random sowing are better than anything you could have planned, which just goes to show that nature is still the best gardener.

Beds of annuals are not restricted to flowers.

Some very interesting effects can be created by foliage alone. Silverleaf, bloodleaf, *Coleus* and many other bedding plants don't need flowers to make an impact. Others, such as *Celosia* and the red-leaved bedding begonias, combine interesting foliage with bright flowers. Less ambitious gardeners can still grow flamboyant annuals without going to such great lengths. Incorporating annuals into a perennial border will help avoid the drab appearance that many perennials have late in the season. Annuals grown around shrubs achieve the same effect by extending the colour after the main spring floral display and they also act as a colourful ground cover that will smother out weeds.

A garden that combines annuals, perennials and shrubs, the 'mixed border', provides the maximum flower colour and foliage variation over the longer period. It is easy to plant out, develops quickly and grading the heights of the plants is simplified when you use annuals to fill in the gaps.

HERBACEOUS BORDERS

Herbaceous perennials blend well with other garden plants, especially annuals, but because they are regularly lifted and divided, it's often more convenient to cultivate them separately from other plants in large beds. Lifting the plants, dividing and composting is greatly simplified when there are no permanent shrubs or

Dense planting is always effective in the herbaceous border.

Below: The tall golden spires of *Solidago* are ideal for the back of the herbaceous border.

Careful planning has resulted in this relaxed, low-maintenance corner, where autumn tones predominate.

trees in the way. Because these perennial beds are often used as an edging to a lawn, driveway or wall, they are usually called herbaceous borders, even when they are not really borders.

The herbaceous border requires no special construction techniques, it is simply a large garden bed. It can be edged with a low hedge or some form of retainer, such as timber half-rounds or bricks, or it may just be cut from a lawn. The soil should be thoroughly prepared by digging in plenty of compost and applying supplementary fertilisers. Beds cut from lawns will benefit from a light dressing of lime, otherwise a general garden fertiliser will be adequate. Most large perennials are rapid growing and heavy feeding with fairly deep roots, so the deeper and more friable the soil, the better they grow. It is impossible to add too much compost, provided it is well rotted down.

The skill in developing a herbaceous border is in the planting. Done well it is the peak of garden excellence; done poorly it is just an assortment of mismatched plants. Decide on an overall theme before you begin. There should be some sense of direction or emphasis, such as planting within a restricted colour range; groups of compatible foliage, such as all silver-leaved plants; or plants with similar flower types, for example beds composed entirely of daisies. Remember to consider the varying heights of the plants. Obviously, if the

border is against a wall, the taller plants will need to go to the back, but you must also take care that the plants don't hide one another in a jumble of foliage. By varying the heights you can highlight particular plants or hide the less attractive parts of other plants.

This may seem a rather rigid way of planting, and indeed it can be. The best gardeners know when to break the rules with effects like brightly contrasting colours or foliage, and they know when to hold back too. Growing a successful herbaceous border demands that you know your plants and that you use that knowledge to its full effect.

COTTAGE GARDENS

The cottage garden aims to bring back fond reminiscences through natural randomness and plant associations. By planting simple flowers and rambling old-fashioned shrubs, particularly roses and other fragrant plants, it is possible to create a charming effect. A cottage garden should make you want to explore; it should be filled with interesting little novelties waiting to be found. Night-scented stocks, small pansies, cornflowers and larkspur are annuals that are perfect for the cottage look. Among the biennials and perennials, consider foxgloves, *Coreopsis*, *Scabiosa*, *Dianthus*, primulas, and peonies.

If your aim is to create a garden of memories, avoid using too many plants with large double flowers and vibrant colours. If the semi-wild look is what you are after, any colour is acceptable, but once again avoid flowers that look 'overdeveloped'. Cottage and wildflower

Above: *Campanula takesimana* and *Aquilegia* 'Nora Barlow' are classic plants for the cottage garden.

This happy abundance epitomises the cottage garden style.

The vibrant blue flowers of *Anchusa* 'Loddon Royalist' make it a striking accent plant for a floral border.

gardens should have a light, airy feel; single flowers on rather open bushes are more appropriate than compact bushes with large double blooms.

Cottage gardens and wildflower gardens are often promoted as an easy-care alternative, but don't be fooled, they require just as much planning as any other garden style and probably more maintenance. Planning a cottage garden depends largely on the layout of your site. Large open areas lend themselves to extensive beds and drifts of plants, and the wildflower seed mixes are very useful here. If large beds don't appeal, dividing a big garden into several small thematic gardens is a good way to maintain interest. Try to design the garden so there is always something new around every corner; the prospect of a pleasant surprise keeps people's attention and adds to your own pleasure. Compact gardens are usually better suited to small pockets of flowers and containers full of bright colour.

WOODLAND GARDENS

Recreating a natural effect is the prime aim of the woodland garden and the closely associated bog garden. However, such freedom doesn't mean you can ignore the rules: the natural look and the informality are only a deception. Creating a woodland requires just as much attention to detail as any other style, often more so because there is always the possibility of some plants running rampant and completely dominating the garden. The great paradox of gardening is that the more natural the effect, the more planning it requires. However,

making mistakes is one of the best ways to learn, so accept the occasional setback philosophically. Of course, to have a woodland garden you must first have trees. Very few woodlands are planned from scratch, rather they are developed to make use of the area under existing trees.

First appearances may suggest that foliage dominates in the woodland garden, but careful study will reveal a subtle blend of foliage and flowers and give you an idea of the plants' proportions. Novice gardeners are inclined to think that a woodland garden must be absolutely full of plants, when in reality a better understanding of plant sizes and growth forms enables the gardener to create an illusion of abundance with relatively few plants. In a well-designed garden there are really only a few main plants that immediately catch your eye, the bulk of the rest are fillers.

Another advantage of not cramming everything in is that you have room for the little treasures: those plants that you forget about for most of the year, then all of a sudden, much to your delight, they're there again. Flowers in the

Top left: Hostas, with their variety of leaf colour, are ideal for a shaded woodland garden. Top right: *Filipendula, Astilbe* and *Gunnera manicata* are excellent choices for bog gardens.

Trillium sessile (above left) and *Polygonatum* x *hybridum* (above right) thrive in a moist shaded environment.

Bergenia cordifolia has attractive foliage and flowers.

clump-forming plants are undemanding and often nearly evergreen, so they're attractive all year round. Small annuals, such as *Lobelia* and *Viscaria*, are not out of place in rockeries, but they must be used with discretion or they may overrun the choice plants.

CONTAINER GROWING

Many annuals and perennials make excellent container plants because they provide plenty of colour, yet don't take up a lot of room and don't have extensive root systems. Many, such as pelargoniums and *Portulaca*, are also drought-tolerant, which can be a life-saver when you forget to water.

Use window boxes and tubs planted with vivid annuals to brighten up dark areas in summer, then replace them with polyanthus and violas for winter colour. If you live in a cold area, but have a greenhouse, conservatory or covered patio, you can grow your tender perennials in containers and move them under cover for the winter.

Always use a good potting mix in your containers and remember to mix in some slow-release fertiliser. Add a wetting agent too, or you may find the mix very difficult to re-wet if it dries out completely. Your potting mix will probably contain fertilisers, but they leach out with regular watering. Container plants demand regular feeding and liquid fertilisers are usually the most convenient to apply. Don't be afraid to innovate and improvise: shocking colour combinations or novelty containers, such as boots and old commodes, add interest. The ways of using annuals and perennials in containers are endless.

woodland garden tend to be concentrated during spring, but there are enough late-flowering small perennials and shrubs to maintain interest. It is also acceptable to plant a few shade-loving summer annuals, such as impatiens and mimulus, to add a dash of colour. However, be discreet – tranquility is important in the woodland garden. Bog gardens and rockeries demand a similar approach.

BOG GARDENS

Woodland and bog gardens would be very bare places without perennials. Bog primroses, astilbes and irises beside a trickling stream make a perfect garden scene. These are the garden situations where foliage comes to the fore; the ferny fronds of the astilbes, the huge leaves of *Gunnera manicata* and *Rodgersia* species, the variety of colour and form in the hostas, and the dinner plate sized, glossy, deep green leaves of the Chatham Island forget-me-not. These plants continue to delight long after the spring flowers have gone.

ROCKERIES

Rockeries are the ideal place for many of the small alpine perennials, such as *Dianthus, Armeria* and *Aubrieta*. These little mat- or

CARE AND CULTIVATION

Annuals and perennials pack a lot of growth into a short period, consequently they often have high nutrient demands. Working in plenty of compost and supplementary fertiliser before planting gives the best results. Thorough preparation is preferable to trying to correct problems later; additional fertilisers, as a mulch or in organic, powdered chemical or liquid forms, can be used to keep the plants growing steadily, but they can't make up for inadequate preparation. Avoid using very high-nitrogen fertilisers or you may find that you get plenty of foliage but few flowers. A balanced fertiliser with a little extra potash is usually best. Some perennials, most notably the southern African daisies, prefer fairly poor soils, so yet again it pays to know your plants. You won't go far wrong with a well-worked friable soil with a little general fertiliser added before planting.

Regular watering is also important. It is no good having a rich soil if the plants are too wilted to use it. Watering annuals and perennials from above with sprinklers can damage the flowers and flatten the plants. It also causes puddling, which can lead to a hard crust developing on the soil surface. Perforated soak hoses and drip lines are preferable and more water-efficient. If you must use sprinklers, choose the finest mist you can get. Containers demand regular watering, often daily in summer, and hanging baskets dry out quickly.

Routine maintenance will keep your plants blooming longer. Remove any spent flowers and developing seed heads (unless you want the plants to self-sow), as once a plant sets seed it may cease flowering. Remove any damaged foliage or stems and stake tall plants, such as delphiniums. If obtaining large flowers is important, it pays to disbud plants like chrysanthemums, dahlias and tuberous begonias. This means removing the lateral flower buds to promote larger terminal buds. You will need to consult specialist publications for the precise methods for each genus.

Provided they are kept growing steadily, annuals and perennials are remarkably free of pests and diseases. Sure, they can fall foul of all the regular pests, such as aphids, mites and various caterpillars, but these problems can usually be traced back to the growing conditions. Established plants in good growing conditions can cope with minor pests and diseases, but those that are malnourished or suffering water stress may succumb. Young seedlings are far more vulnerable regardless of how good the conditions are. They are likely to be attacked by slugs, snails, cutworms, earwigs, slaters and birds, although losses from anything other than slugs and snails are seldom significant. See the pests and diseases chapter for control details. Seedlings are also prone to the fungal diseases known as damping off. Damping off rots the seed leaves and stems, causing the seedling to collapse. Good hygiene lessens the problem but damping off can occur at any time, so it is a good idea to regularly drench seedlings with a fungicide solution.

In early autumn you will need to remove the spent annuals and tidy up the dead growth on the perennials. If you intend to replant with overwintering hardy annuals remove the summer plants when they show noticeable signs of deterioration, otherwise leave them for some late colour. Getting your winter and spring annuals planted early ensures they are well-established before the cold weather arrives.

OBTAINING PLANTS

When first establishing a perennial garden you will probably buy all of your plants from a nursery or garden centre. However, by the end of the first season you will have quite a few large plants ready for dividing. Some perennials, such as peonies, will grow for many years without needing to be divided, but most need breaking up at least every three years. Many perennials may also be grown from cuttings. (Refer to the chapter on propagation for details.)

Annuals must be raised from seed – you can do this yourself or buy ready-to-plant seedling punnets from a garden centre. For small quantities, raising your own seedlings is seldom cheaper than buying seedlings, but if you have large beds to plant out, growing your own represents a considerable saving. If you need large quantities of seedlings it is best to find a nursery that will order for you from a commercial growers' seed catalogue. Not only is this cheaper, the commercial seed selection is usually better than garden centre stock in both range and quality.

Seed sowing and germination is usually very straightforward. In many cases the seed may be sown directly where it is to grow, although it is more common to sow in trays and then plant out. The only complication is timing: you don't want to sow too early as your seed may fail to germinate or the seedlings may be frost damaged; too late and they may not mature before cold stops their growth.

Bog gardens will be enhanced by the cultivation of *Salvia involucrata* (top) and *Iris sanguineum* (bottom).

POPULAR GARDEN ANNUALS AND PERENNIALS

THE RANGE OF ANNUALS and perennials is enormous, and it becomes larger with every passing season. No book of this size could cover all the genera and cultivars, and advances in plant breeding mean that information rapidly becomes outdated. The plants listed here are the ones you'll find in any garden centre. Many of them, particularly the annuals, are available in a wide range of hybrid and selected forms; this list includes only the most widely grown forms and is intended as a general outline only.

Each genus name is followed by an A, B, or P to indicate whether the plants are annual, biennial or perennial. Dimensions refer to height by width (e.g., 30 cm x 50 cm means 30 cm high x 50 cm wide).

ACANTHUS (P)

Bear's breeches (*A. mollis*) is a tough, adaptable plant mainly grown for its bold, deeply lobed, glossy foliage. Somewhat invasive, it should not be used in small gardens or narrow borders. It grows to 60 cm x 1.2 m with flower spikes up to 1.5 m high. Acanthus grows in full sun if moist, but is best in light shade. Propagate by seed, division or root cuttings. *A. spinosus* is similar, but has sharply lobed foliage.

ACHILLEA (P)

The yarrows come in a variety of styles and forms. One of the most popular cultivars, 'The Pearl', is scarcely identifiable as a form of yarrow, but most have the ferny foliage and flat flower heads of the well-known roadside weed. The 'Summer Pastels' series has become popular for summer bedding but most yarrows are used in perennial borders. They are easily grown in any sunny position. Sizes range from 24 x 40 cm for the 'Summer Pastels' up to 1.6 x 1.2 m for the larger cultivars, such as the *A. filipendula* forms. Propagate by seed or division.

ADONIS (A)

Adonis armuriensis has fern-like leaves that begin to unfurl from late July, and by mid August the first large, yellow, buttercup-like flowers start to open. *Adonis* is best in cool moist soil in light shade. It grows to 30 cm x 40 cm.

AETHIONEMA (P)

These perennial-like sub-shrubs have silvery grey foliage and heads of small pink flowers in late spring. They grow to about 20 cm x 30 cm and prefer well-drained gritty soil in the sun. Propagate the species by seed and hybrids by small cuttings or self-rooted layers.

AGAPANTHUS (P)

A genus of ten species from southern Africa. The common species, *A. praecox*, is a large clump-forming evergreen or deciduous plant with long strappy leaves and heads of 75 mm long lily-like flowers on tall stems. Typically the flowers are bright purplish-blue, but there are white and pink forms and some very dark purples, such as 'Stormcloud'. Late spring to early autumn is the main flowering season. Sizes range from the dwarf 'Peter Pan' at 50 cm x 50 cm to large forms that may reach 1.8 m x 1.8 m. The dwarf variegated cultivar 'Tinkerbell' is a superb small rockery plant. All agapanthus are tough adaptable plants that can be relied upon to make a good show under most conditions. They are best sited in a sunny position, but will tolerate semi-shade. Divide established clumps in early spring. Hardy to -7°C.

AGERATUM (A)

The blue ageratum is a very popular summer bedding plant. It forms 25 cm x 25 cm clumps with fluffy flowers of an unusual dusky-blue colour that blends effectively with many other bedding plants. Pink and white forms are also available.

AJUGA (P)

A. reptans is a tough ground cover that grows to about 10 cm x 60 cm with spikes of purplish-blue flowers.
Many different foliage forms are available. They grow in the sun or shade and most cultivars will spread rapidly if left unchecked. *A. genevensis* and *A. pyramidalis* are taller, non-invasive species, but have similar purplish-blue flowers. All are easily grown from cuttings or self-rooted layers.

ALCEA (B)

Hollyhocks have enjoyed a resurgence in popularity in recent years coinciding with the trend towards cottage gardens. They are available in almost any colour, but apart from the fancy double strains they are usually sold in mixed-colour packs. They are useful for adding height and colour at the back of a border and their sizes range from the 60 cm 'Majorette' through to the 1.8 m high 'Chater's Doubles'. Hollyhocks are easily grown in any sunny well-drained position, although they usually need staking to prevent wind damage and are often attacked by rust.

Miniature *Agapanthus*

ALCHEMILLA (P)

Lady's mantle (*A. mollis*) has unusual light green leaves and small loose spikes of yellowish-green flowers. It is usually about 50 cm x 80 cm, but may spread rapidly in loose soils. *A. alpina* is very like a quarter-sized *A. mollis*, and *A. glabra* is another attractive small species. After flowering they may become untidy, but in spring and early summer they are very appealing. The flowers last well when cut. Grow from seed or divisions.

ALONSOA (P)

Alonsoa warscewiczii grows to about 60 cm x 60 cm and is very showy in flower, but is short-lived and rather frost-tender. A clump-forming plant with small bright green leaves, the wiry stems are topped with heads of small flowers mainly in shades of pink and orange. Raise from seed (it often self-sows) or cuttings.

ALSTROEMERIA (P)

The Peruvian lilies are very popular and they are easily grown in most soils provided they receive about half a day's sun. The cut-flower hybrids are usually quite restrained growers. However, be wary of planting some species; *A. aurea* (syn. *A. aurantiaca*) and *A. psittacina* (syn. *A. pulchella*) in particular can be invasive in light soils. Most alstroemerias attain around 50 cm x 50 cm. Propagate by seed or division.

ANCHUSA (P)

Several species and forms are grown, ranging from small bedding varieties that are treated as annuals through to the larger *A. azurea* forms, such as

Antirrhinum 'Little Swee

'Loddon Royalist', which may reach 1.5 m high. Most anchusas have deep blue flowers. They are easily grown in any sunny position. Propagate by seed or division.

ANDROSACE (P)

One of the classic rockery genera, most species of which have light green or silvery grey foliage topped with small white or pink flowers in spring. They seldom grow larger than 10 cm x 30 cm and are best grown in sunny well-drained scree. Propagate by seed, cuttings or self-rooted layers.

ANEMONE (P)

The familiar bedding anemones, such as the 'St Brigid' strain, are the most fancy and gaudy forms, grown mainly for a bright splash of colour. There are many other species and hybrids that vary greatly in growth habit and flowering season. The wood anemones, such as A. nemorosa and A. blanda, are very attractive small plants that herald the arrival of spring with their purple, pink or white flowers. They form 15 cm x 40 cm clumps. The Japanese anemone, A. hupehensis (japonica), which has pink or white flowers on 1 m stems, blooms in late summer and autumn. It may become invasive in favoured locations. Most anemones prefer light shade and a soil high in humus. Propagate by seed or division.

ANTHEMIS (P)

Chamomiles are small mounding ground covers with masses of yellow daisy flowers in summer. A. nobilis is the species used for chamomile lawns. They are best grown in hot sunny positions. They are tough and adaptable, but intolerant of wet soil. Propagate by seed or cuttings; the non-flowering 'Treneague' must be vegetatively propagated.

ANTIRRHINUM (A)

Snapdragons may be grown year round in most areas. In mild climates they flower throughout the year, while where winters are cold they start to bloom with the first warm days. Antirrhinums

Alstroemeria 'Ligtu' hybrid

Anemone nemorosa

grow in most soils and will naturalise in cottage gardens. They are undemanding plants, but are often damaged by rust; new strains are rust-resistant. Snapdragons are available in various sizes, ranging from 'Floral Showers' and 'Pixie' at about 20 cm high to 'Madame Butterfly', which may reach 80 cm high. Some have the traditional 'snapping' flowers, but the doubles do not.

AQUILEGIA (P)

Most of the common aquilegias are hybrids of A. vulgaris, but there are some very attractive dwarf species, such as A. alpina and A. flabellata. Best in moist semi-shade with humus-enriched soil. The large forms grow to about 75 cm x 50 cm, while the dwarfs are 25 cm x 20 cm. Aquilegias are graceful plants and are available in many different colours; many are multi-coloured, often in pastel tones with very subtle shading. Propagated by seed or division, aquilegias often self-sow and unusual forms may pop up of their own accord.

ARCTOTIS (P)

These reliable, heavy-flowering perennial daisies are most at home in coastal conditions and can be seen in large drifts in many New Zealand seaside gardens. The colours are usually very bold, although some attractive creams and pastels are available. They are slightly frost-tender but will withstand considerable cold if kept dry. They grow to 20 cm x 50 cm. Plant *Arctotis* in light well-drained soil and full sun. They may be grown from seed, divisions or self-rooted layers.

ARGYRANTHEMUM (P)

The 'Marguerite daisies', formerly known as *Chrysanthemum frutescens*, now appear under the name *Argyranthemum*. They are somewhat frost-tender perennials that are easily grown in any sunny position. Marguerites are great coastal plants and can be seen growing wild in many areas, particularly Sumner, near Christchurch, where wild forms have hybridised with cut-flower varieties from nearby nurseries. There are many cultivars, ranging from dwarf bushes to large shrubs. Colours include many shades of pink, yellow, cream and white; and the flowers may be single, double or anemone form (crested). New cultivars are regularly introduced, 'California Gold' being one of the best recent introductions. They may be propagated by seed, but the best forms should be perpetuated by cuttings.

ARISARUM (A)

The mouse plant (A. proboscideum) is the best-known and most widely grown member of this genus of small *Arum* relatives from southern Europe. It is a little plant (12 cm x 50 cm) that is fascinating because the white and brown flowers resemble small mice disappearing into the clump of dark green foliage. It blooms in spring and early summer and is hardy and very easily grown in any moist humus-enriched soil in shade or partial shade. Be careful, as it may become slightly invasive. Friar's cowl (A. vulgare) is similar but is a larger, more tender plant and its flowers are usually held above the foliage,

which dies off quite quickly after the spring flowers finish.

ARMERIA (P)

A genus of clump-forming plants with tufted grassy foliage and pink or white chive-like flowers. They will grow in any position that gets a few hours sun. The most common species is A. maritima but several others, such as A. pseudoarmeria and A. latifolia, are widely grown. Dwarf forms are about 20 cm x 20 cm in flower, while larger forms may reach 40 cm x 30 cm. Propagate by seed or division.

ARTEMISIA (P)

There are many species of *Artemisia* and they are quite variable. Most are bulky upright bushes grown for their silver grey foliage but A. lactiflora is a rosette forming ground cover most notable for its white flowers while A. schmidtiana has fine, almost hair-like foliage. Most prefer to grow in hot sunny locations (A. lactiflora is an exception) and do best in a position where the foliage dries quickly after rain. Nearly evergreen but may become untidy over winter. Very hardy and tolerant of neglect. Sizes vary considerably with the species. Propagate by cuttings, the species may also be grown from seed.

ARTHROPODIUM (P)

The rengarenga lily (A. cirratum) is a native perennial often mass planted as a quick filler. It forms a clump up to 1.5 m wide with bold strap-like leaves and small white flowers on 60 cm stems. These adaptable plants are slightly frost-tender and new

Arthropodium cirratum

Astilbe chinensis

growth may be attacked by slugs and snails. Plant in light shade in a moist, humus-rich soil. Propagate by seed or division.

ARUM (P)

Many plants, especially *Zantedeschia aethiopica*, are commonly called arums, but *A. italicum* is the only true arum commonly grown. It forms a 25 cm x 80 cm deciduous clump and the arrowhead-shaped leaves often have cream coloured veins. The flower, which appears in spring, has a translucent white papery spathe with a creamy-yellow flower spike. The flowers are followed by conspicuous bright orange-red berries in heads of 30 or so. It is hardy and easily grown in any moist soil in shade or partial shade, but it may become somewhat invasive. Some of the other species, such as the black arum (*A. palaestinum*), are very striking but only rarely available.

ARUNCUS (P)

Goat's beard is a very hardy perennial that tolerates wet soil and looks much like a giant *Astilbe*. It may reach 2 m x 1.5 m or more and is very impressive in full bloom, although it is inclined to be untidy as it dies back. *A. dioicus* (*sylvester*) is the most common species. It has large sprays of very tiny creamy white flowers and fern-like foliage. Goat's beard may be grown from seed or divisions.

ARUNDO (P)

The giant reed, *A. donax*, is very effective beside ponds or slow-moving water courses. It is a huge grassy plant that develops into a large clump about 2.5 m x 2.5 m. The variegated foliage form is the more common. Giant reed needs very moist soil and is capable of growing in at least 100 mm of water. It prefers full sun or light shade and may be grown from seed or divisions.

ASPERULA (P)

Asperula gussonii has very small, somewhat silvery, leaves and heads of tiny light pink flowers in spring. It forms a dense cushion about 6 cm x 20 cm wide and prefers moist well-drained soil in the sun. Raise from seed, divisions or from small rooted pieces.

ASTELIA (P)

A native perennial often mistaken for flax (*Phormium*). Bold foliage plants for sun or light shade. Some also have attractive berry-like fruit in clusters. The best-known form is *A. chathamica* 'Silver Spear', which has metallic silver leaves of up to 1.2 m long. Trouble-free plants that should be more widely grown. Sizes vary considerably depending on the species. Propagate the species by seed and the hybrids by division.

ASTER (P)

The Michaelmas daisies are primarily autumn flowering, whereas the alpine asters flower from late winter to mid spring. Michaelmas daisies and the *A. novae-angliae*, *A.* x *frikartii* and *A.* x *dumosus* hybrids are rather prone to mildew in autumn, and gardeners in humid northern areas may find this difficult to combat. The low-growing *A. alpinus* is less susceptible to mildew. Asters range in size from ground covers through to plants that form 1.2 m x 1.2 m clumps. Plant in full sun and propagate by seed, division or cuttings. The annual asters are now classified under *Callistephus*.

ASTILBE (P)

Astilbes create a soft graceful effect with their fern-like leaves and feathery flower plumes. They come in many shades of red, pink, mauve and cream and vary from 30 cm to 1 m high. The common forms are hybrids of the *A.* x *arendsii* and *A.* x *hybrida* groups. Astilbes prefer a moist position in full sun or shade. Division is the quickest means of propagation.

AUBRIETA (P)

A. deltoide is a small spreading plant that covers itself in tiny pink, mauve, purple or white flowers in spring. It is best in full sun, but will tolerate partial shade. *Aubrieta* forms clumps about 15 cm x 50 cm. It is usually grown from seed but good forms can be perpetuated by division.

AURINIA (P)

The perennial *Alyssum*, of which *A. saxatile* is the best-known species, are now known by this name. Hardy easily grown plants that are most at home in a sunny rockery. *A. saxatile* has masses of tiny yellow flowers in spring and early summer. The other species are similar. Propagate by seed. Sometimes grown from divisions or self layered pieces.

AZOLLA (P)

The common floating fern, *A. rubra*, can be found in nearly every area of still water. It is composed of bright green overlapping scales that turn deep red in the sun. It carpets the surface of the water and is useful as a quick cover to provide some shade, but it must be thinned regularly or it will completely cover the pond. *Azolla* requires nothing more than still water to grow and is usually self-propagating.

BEGONIA (P)

The most commonly grown begonias are the bedding (*B. semperflorens*) forms, which are usually treated as annuals, and the tuberous (*B.* x *tuberhybrida*) forms.
Bedding begonias come in a wide range of colours and sizes, in both green and red leaved forms. The new strains are sun tolerant but prefer moist conditions. Mildew can be a problem late in the season or in humid areas. They are usually grown from seed, although fancy doubles may be propagated by cuttings.
Tuberous begonias come in a huge range of sizes and spectacular colours. The smaller-growing multiflora, or flamboy-ant, begonias are popular for massed plantings, whereas the larger forms may be grown in borders or pots. Trailing varieties for hanging baskets extend the range still further. They prefer a lightly shaded position and a moist humus-rich soil. Tuberous begonias may be grown from seed, divisions or cuttings. They are also somewhat prone to mildew, although newer strains are more resistant.

BELLIS (P)

Bellis perennis is a small daisy that is often treated as a winter and early spring-flowering annual. There are several bedding strains, which are available in pink shades and white. They are undemanding plants, but rather prone to rust. They are usually raised from seed, but fancy cultivars, such as 'Dresden China', may be propagated by division or cuttings. Other species, particularly *B. rotundifolia*, are occasionally sold by alpine specialists. Bellis daisies are best in cool, moist soil in sun or light shade and may be short-lived in northern gardens.

BERGENIA (P)

The common *B. cordifolia* is widely grown for its bold foliage and the heads of bright pink flowers that appear in early spring. It is very hardy and forms a 30 cm x 60 cm clump. Best in cool, moist, shady positions. It is usually propagated by division.

BRACHYCOME (A & P)

The perennial *B. multifida* is a very popular low grower that is hardy over much of the country. It produces masses of small pink, mauve or white daisy flowers from mid spring to early winter. The Swan River daisy (*B. iberidifolia*) is similar, but is an annual. Both species form 15 cm x 25 cm clumps. Plant them in a warm sunny position. Propagate by seed or cuttings. The native alpine species are sometimes available from specialists.

CALCEOLARIA (P)

C. herbeo hybrida has been extensively developed and is now a florists' speciality. It is generally treated as an annual. It grows to 20 cm x 25 cm and has pouch-shaped flowers in shades of red or yellow with contrasting markings.
C. integrifolia is larger and more shrubby and is reliably perennial. Both are best in a cool, moist, shady situation. Propagate by seed or cuttings.

CALENDULA (A)

The pot marigold forms 20 cm x 30 cm clumps of rather coarse foliage, but is valued in mild areas for its winter and early spring floral display. In cold winter regions they are grown as a summer annual. Many shades of cream through soft yellow to bright orange are available. They are easily grown in full sun or light shade.

CALLISTEPHUS (A)

The annual asters are now classified under this name. There are several strains of which the best known are the tall (80 cm) 'Giant Crego' and the dwarf (40 cm) 'Comet' series. The daisy-like flowers are large yet graceful. Available in shades of white, cream, pink, mauve and red. The china asters are superb cut flowers as well as being very attractive summer bedding plants. They need a sunny well-drained position.

CALTHA (P)

Caltha palustris is a hardy perennial bog plant with bright yellow buttercup flowers and kidney-shaped deep green leaves. It develops into a 30 cm x 40 cm clump. Double forms are available and there are also native species, such as the tiny white-flowered *C. obtusa*. They will grow in sun or shade and may be propagated from seed, cuttings or self-rooted layers.

CAMPANULA (B & P)

A large genus that covers a wide range of plants, all of which have the bell-shaped flowers that give the genus its name. Bellflowers range from tiny rockery species, such as the 8 cm x 15 cm *C. cochlearifolia* (*C. pusilla*), through to those that may reach 1.5 m or more, such as *C. lactiflora*. Canterbury bells (*C. medium*) is a biennial species often used in cottage gardens and for general bedding. The trailing species are particularly effective on stone walls or as rockery ground covers, and some also make good hanging basket specimens. The taller varieties with long stems are often excellent cut flowers. Bellflowers generally prefer a humus-rich moist soil and a position in semi-shade. The perennials are usually propagated by division, cuttings or self-rooted layers.

Calendula 'Touch of Red'

Centaurea macrocephala

CANNA (P)

The bold foliage and flowers of the canna lilies are a common garden feature. They are well known for vivid colours, but are now also available in a wide range of pastel shades. Cannas can grow to 2 m high, but dwarf forms that should not exceed 1 m are also available. Although hardy enough to be grown over most of the country, they do best in areas with consistently warm summers. Cannas prefer full sun and humus-rich soil. Propagate by division.

CATANANCHE (P)

Cupid's dart (*C. caerulea*) is a very apt common name for this hardy perennial. The pale blue tufted flowers resemble the flights of a dart, and the long stem, the point. A hardy perennial that looks very much like a cornflower. Easily grown in a sunny position, the flower stems reach about 60 cm high. A soil on the dry side is preferred. Propagate by seed or division of established clumps.

CELMISIA (P)

One of the most attractive native genera yet inclined to be tricky in cultivation. The foliage is usually a deep green with a silvery grey reverse. The flowers are large white daisies with prominent yellow stamens. Sizes range from minute alpines to large clump-forming perennials. A genuine scree soil that is well-drained on top but cool and moisture retentive below is the key to success. Generally unsuccessful in mild humid areas. Grow from seed.

CELOSIA (A)

Cockscomb is a showy annual that needs plenty of sun and warmth to produce good flowers. There are two main flower types: plume and crested forms. Plume flowers are feather-like, while the crested is a very unusual form in that the flower is twisted and recurved; both forms grow to about 45 cm x 20 cm. The colours are typically bright gold, orange or red, but new strains are available in many shades. The foliage is often a similar colour to the flower.

CENTAUREA (A & P)

The familiar annual blue cornflower (*C. cyanus*) is but one

Top: *Chrysanthemum* 'Shantung' cultivar
Above: *Cosmos atrosanguineus*

of over 500 species in this genus, which also includes some very impressive perennials. *C. macrocephala* is probably the best known, but *C. dealbata*, *C. argentea* and *C. montana* are also common. They cover a wide range of sizes from 20 cm to 1.5 m high. Flower colours include blue, yellow, white, pink and reddish shades. They are best in full sun with excellent drainage. Propagate by seed or division.

CHEIRANTHUS (B & P)

The wallflowers are useful for a splash of colour when little else is in flower. The biennial bedding forms will often flower in winter in mild areas, whereas the perennials often flower year-round. They are very easily grown in any moist soil in full sun or semi-shade. Propagate the biennials from seed and the perennials from cuttings. Biennials rarely exceed 40 cm x 30 cm, but perennials may reach 75 cm x 1 m.

CHRYSANTHEMUM (P)

The florists' chrysanthemums (*C. morifolium*, *C. indicum* and their hybrids) are available in a bewildering array of sizes, colours and flower forms. As with many large groups of

hybrids, chrysanthemums have been sub-divided into smaller groups based on flower type and growth habit. Specialist growers list them by categories, such as anemone, incurved and fantasy. Chrysanthemums extend the flowering season more than probably any other tall perennial: they often flower until early winter and can be forced into bloom out of season. However, getting the best out of them demands some attention to detail. Chrysanthemums are often damaged by chrysanthemum midge and powdery mildew. The midge larvae burrow into the leaf and produce small raised lumps that can be very disfiguring. A systemic insecticide is the only certain method of control. Regular pinching of the lateral flowers is also necessary to secure the largest blooms. Chrysanthemums strike easily from cuttings; autumn is the preferred time. The young plants may need to be wintered over under cover in cold areas and will need to be pinched back in mid spring and mid summer to produce strong stems and the best blooms.
Many of the plants formerly listed under *Chrysanthemum* have been transferred to other genera and in fact the plants covered here no longer belong in the genus. However, it will be some time before *Dendranthema* becomes a widely used name.

CLARKIA (A)

This genus of annuals now includes *Godetia* although you will find plants sold under both names. The larger azalea flowered forms of this genus are very useful for backgrounds or for mixing with other tall annuals and perennials. The plants and seed sold for producing bedding plants are mainly selections or hybrids of four species, *C. amoena*, *C. concinna*, *C. pulchella* and *C. unguiculata*. Grown as cool season annuals in mild areas and spring to summer annuals where winters are cold. Most forms reach 50-75 cm high x 30 cm wide. Plant in moist soil in sun or semi-shade. Propagate by seed.

CLEOME (A)

The spidery pink and white flowers of *C. spinosa* appeal as much for their novelty as their beauty. It is tall (up to 1.5 m) and shrubby and very effective as a background or centrepiece. Regular dead-heading is necessary to ensure a succession of bloom. It should be planted in full sun with a moist soil.

COLEUS (P)

The bold foliage colours of *Coleus* have an instant appeal. They are perennial in warm areas, but are generally treated as annuals. They are grown purely for the coloured foliage; the small purple flowers are insignificant and should be removed immediately they appear as they weaken the plant. Several strains are available with varying leaf patterns and sizes. Some can become quite large but should be kept trimmed to around 50 cm x 50 cm. Propagate from seed or cuttings, which strike extremely easily.

CONSOLIDA (A)

Larkspur (*C. ambigua*) grows to about 1.2 m x 30 cm and resembles a small delphinium. It is widely grown for its bold and long-lasting flowers, which are also excellent when cut or dried. Larkspur is now available in many shades of white, blue, pink and red. It grows best in full sun with a moist soil and should be sown in situ or planted out when very young, as the roots resent disturbance.

CONVALLARIA (P)

Lily-of-the-valley is famed for its perfume but can become very invasive and hard to eliminate. Nevertheless, there are far less attractive weeds. Grows in moist to wet soil and becomes particularly lush if well fed. Prefers full shade but sun tolerant if kept moist. The white, or occasionally pink, bell-shaped flowers appear in early spring followed by bright orange toxic berries. Very hardy. Propagate by seed or division.

COREOPSIS (A & P)

Coreopsis can be relied upon to provide colour despite poor soil

and neglect. The annual *C. tinctoria* is available in shades of yellow, bronze and red, but the perennials have bright golden-yellow flowers. They are easily grown in a light soil and a sunny position. The larger perennial species, such as *C. verticillata*, may grow to 1 m tall but most are considerably smaller. Propagate by seed or cuttings, and large clumps can be divided.

COSMOS (A)

The annual bedding hybrids, such as the 'Seashell' have large single flowers. They prefer a sunny position and light soil. The taller forms grow to 1 m high, but most are around 50 cm x 50 cm. The perennial black or chocolate cosmos (*C. atrosanguineus*) is also quite popular. It has very deep red flowers, grows to 60 cm x 1 m, and is propagated by cuttings or division.

COTULA (P)

Most gardeners will be familiar with this genus of perennial daisies through its use as a surface for bowling greens. The rockery species are all very compact clump-forming or slightly spreading plants. The most attractive species is the native *C. atrata*, which has fine ferny foliage and deep blackish-red flowers in summer. It grows to about 10 cm x 30 cm and is a natural scree plant that will grow in sun or very light shade. Propagate by seed, cuttings and natural layers or division.

CYPERUS (P)

Some of the *Cyperus* sedges, such as nut grass (*C. rotundus*), are extremely serious weeds. However, the ornamental species, such as papyrus (*C. papyrus*) and umbrella plant (*C. alternifolius*), are very useful marginal plants. They have strongly upright grassy stems and very prominent greenish-brown flower and seed heads on thickened stalks up to 1.5 m high or more. They will grow in up to 50 mm of water but require warm summer conditions to do well. Propagate by seed or division.

DAHLIA (P)

There are only a dozen or so *Dahlia* species but countless cultivars. The cultivars are divided into groups based on floral and growth characteristics. Specialist growers or books will provide details of these groups. Dahlias are available in a wide range of sizes. The smallest are the miniature cultivars, which grow to about 30 cm x 30 cm. The bedding dahlias, which are usually treated as annuals, grow to about 60 cm x 50 cm. The larger hybrids may exceed 1.5 m, and the tree dahlia (*D. imperialis*) can grow to 4 m or more. It has soft pink flowers and blooms in autumn.

The large tubers are best lifted in cold areas. Even in mild areas they should be lifted and divided every two or three years or the flower quality and quantity may suffer. Store the tubers in sand or sawdust in a dark frost-free place. They may be divided before replanting. Cuttings of the new spring growth strike quickly.

Dahlias are best planted in full sun or partial shade in a humus-rich soil. Pinching back and disbudding is necessary if show blooms are required. Dahlias are subject to caterpillars, thrips and powdery mildew, which almost always develops in autumn, but as the plants are nearing dormancy control is not always necessary.

DELPHINIUM (P)

Delphiniums are the ideal perennial – brilliant colours, quick growth, easy care and a very distinctive spire-like habit. Look at any good perennial border and you will see delphiniums; they are absolutely indispensable.

The most widely grown delphiniums are the 'Pacific Giant' hybrids, which grow up to 2 m high and cover a range of white, pink, mauve and blue shades. The 'Magic Fountains' are around 1.2 m high with similar colours. Many other hybrid selections are grown in Europe but are seldom seen here. A collection of *Delphinium* species, which are often very different from the hybrids, makes an interesting display.

Grow all delphiniums in full sun in a rich but free-draining soil. Mildew can be a problem in autumn and although the plants are nearing dormancy at this time it should be treated, as delphiniums are not fully deciduous and the disease may be carried over to the following season if left untreated.

DIANTHUS (B & P)

This genus includes the perennial border pinks and the carnations, as well as the biennial bedding plants and sweet William, which are both usually treated as annuals. They are often valued as much for their fragrance as the beauty of their flowers.

The many species and hybrid forms vary considerably. The tiny cushion pinks, which are so charming in rockeries, are no more than a few centimetres high, even when in flower. The florists' carnations, however, have flower stems up to 60 cm long (they often need staking), and in between are the border pinks and bedding dianthus, which grow into 20 cm x 30 cm mounds.

Dianthus is primarily spring- and early summer-flowering, although the fancy hybrid carnations are often forced into bloom out of season. All *Dianthus* grow best in full sun and a light or gritty soil and the larger carnations require regular feeding with dilute liquid fertiliser to keep them flowering well. Propagate the bedding varieties from seed, the perennials and hybrids from small cuttings (slips).

DIASCIA (A & P)

The two spurs found on the bright pink flowers of this southern African genus account for the name twinflower or twinspur. They are easily grown in any sunny position. The smaller perennial species are superb rockery plants that flower heavily over a long season and appear to be reliably hardy in all but the coldest or wettest areas. Propagate by seed or cuttings.

DICENTRA (P)

Most gardeners are familiar with the common pink bleeding heart (*D. spectabilis*) but there are many other species and hybrids. At 1 m x 1 m, *D. spectabilis* is the largest growing under our conditions. *D. eximea*, *D. cucullaria* and *D. formosa* are smaller species. All produce pink or white flowers. They are best grown in moist humus-rich soils in light shade, although most are sun tolerant provided they are kept moist. Some forms of *D. formosa*, particularly 'Bountiful', can become slightly invasive. Propagate by seed, cuttings or division.

DIGITALIS (B & P)

Foxgloves add height to a border but seldom need staking. *D. purpurea*, the common biennial foxglove, will grow almost anywhere but is best in a moist humus-enriched soil. It is sun tolerant if kept moist, otherwise very light shade is better. Most forms will grow to 1.5 m x 75 cm or more, but the 'Foxy' series is a dwarf annual, seed-raised strain that grows to about 1 m. Propagate by seed, basal cuttings or division.

DOROTHEANTHUS (A)

Commonly known as Livingstone daisies, these annual succulents always give a vivid display in hot dry positions. New strains come in a wide range of colours, the only shades missing seem to be blue and purple. They develop into 15 cm x 20 cm clumps and must be grown in full sun.

ECHINACEA (P)

Coneflowers are unusual, stiffly erect plants with pink or white daisy flowers on stems that can grow to 1.5 m or more. The petals of the common species, *E. purpurea*, hang down, giving it a very distinctive appearance. The seed heads may be used in dried arrangements. Coneflowers should be planted in full sun and a light, well-drained soil. Propagate by seed or division.

ECHINOPS (P)

To some people the *Echinops* species are just fancy thistles, but to others they are among the best garden perennials. There is some confusion over the naming of these plants: the species *E. exalatus* apparently includes the form commonly

Top: *Echinacea purpurea*
Above: *Dicentra formosa* 'Alba'

sold as *E. sphaerocephalus*, while *E. ritro* is a distinct species that includes the form sold as *E. ruthenica*. *E. exalatus* has white flowers whereas *E. ritro* has steel-blue to purple flowers. Both grow to about 80 cm x 1 m. They are easily grown in almost any soil in full sun or light shade. The flowers can be cut and used fresh or dried. Other thistle-like plants occasionally grown as perennials include the artichokes (*Cynara*), *Eryngium* and *Carlina*.

ECHIUM (A, B & P)

A genus that is renowned for its bright blue flowers. Pride of Madeira (*E. fastuosum*) is a 1.5 m x 1.5 m sub-shrub often found growing wild in coastal areas. Viper's bugloss (*E. vulgare*) is a small common wildflower and *E. wildprettii* produces 2 m spikes of deep pink flowers.

Echiums demand full sun and perfect drainage, with most species prefering a gravel or scree soil. Some are frost-tender but often recover even if cut back to ground level. Use them for their bold foliage or massed flowers. Propagate by seed or cuttings.

ELODEA (P)

E. canadensis is the least invasive of the three submerged aquatic plants commonly known as oxygen weed. The other two, Lagerosiphon major and Egeria densa, are now banned from sale because they have the potential to choke waterways. This is a twining plant that can quickly fill a pond, but it is useful in oxygenating the water. Elodea requires no special effort to grow but remember to keep it thinned. Any piece broken off can be used to start a new plant.

ERIGERON (B & P)

The spreading, white-flowered seaside daisy (E. karvinskianus) has proved to be something of a weed in mild gardens from Marlborough northwards, but where it behaves, it is a very useful ground cover. The other species have large daisy flowers in white, pink, lavender and purple shades. Some are deciduous, others evergreen. Plant in full sun or very light shade in a very free-draining soil. The upright species grow to about 50 cm x 30 cm. Propagate by seed, division or cuttings.

ESCHSCHOLZIA (P)

The California poppy (E. californica) is a common sight in all regions from spring to early winter. It is usually treated as an annual, but is hardy and naturalises in most areas. California poppies grow into a 30 cm x 30 cm clump and form thriving colonies in hot sunny positions on well-drained gritty soils. Most wild forms are orange or yellow but cultivated strains also come in white, cream, pink and red. Semi-doubles are available too. They are raised from seed.

EUPHORBIA (A & P)

This is one of the largest plant genera, comprising well over

1000 species. As might be expected of a genus this size, there is an enormous variation in size and flower types. The most common garden species are E. griffithii (including the hybrid 'Fire Glow'), E. myrsinites and E. characias (syn. E. wulfenii, E. veneta), all of which are hardy perennials. E. griffithii and E. myrsinites develop into 40 cm x 50 cm clumps, while E. characias may grow to 1.5 m x 1.5 m and is virtually evergreen. E. marginata (snow on the mountain) is a small annual, the variegated form of which is sometimes used as a bedding plant. While hardy euphorbias are capable of growing almost anywhere, they prefer full sun and a light well-drained soil. Propagate by seed, cuttings or division.

FELICIA (A & P)

The kingfisher daisies are natives of southern Africa. They are distinctive because of their blue flowers. The most widely grown is the relatively hardy perennial F. amelloides, which is available in several colours and a variegated form. Often treated as annuals where they are killed over winter, they are short-lived at best. Grow in full sun in a light well-drained soil. Easily propagated from seed or small cuttings. In some northern areas it can be slightly invasive.

FILIPENDULA (P)

These impressive, large, deciduous perennials are very hardy. Several species are grown but they are all similar – Astilbe-like with boldly cut foliage and plume-like flowers in shades of

Gaillardia grandiflora

white, cream, pink and mauve. Best in moist woodland conditions, and tolerant of the sun if kept moist over summer. Most species will grow to at least 2 m x 1.2 m and may become larger under ideal conditions. May be grown from seed, but division is more common.

GAILLARDIA (A & P)

These tough daisies usually have distinctive bicolour flowers in shades of yellow, red and bronze that last well when cut. They flower throughout summer and develop into 30 cm x 30 cm clumps. Gaillardias prefer a free-draining soil in full sun. Propagate by seed or division.

GAURA (P)

Gaura lindheimeri is a hardy herbaceous perennial with clusters of delicate white or pale pink flowers on stems up to 1.2 m high from mid spring to late autumn. It prefers a moist well-drained soil in full sun or light shade and may naturalise in some areas. Propagate by seed, division or basal cuttings in spring.

GAZANIA (P)

Gazanias are brightly coloured, tough, adaptable daisies for hot dry positions or any sunny place. They are frost tolerant if kept dry over winter, but may be grown as annuals in regions with very cold winters. The true species are seldom grown, most garden plants are selected hybrid strains. The new dwarf forms are ideal for pots and window boxes. Propagate by seed or division.

GENTIANA (P)

Most gentians are alpine plants and as such they have some fairly specific soil requirements. Some simply refuse to grow under garden conditions and those that do demand a genuine scree soil. This generally means a 50/50 mixture of fine shingle and potting mix or some other high humus material, which will ensure perfect drainage yet be moisture retentive. Gentians appreciate summer moisture but will rot if the crown is continually in wet soil. A sprinkle of fine gravel chips around the plant will keep the soil surface dry.

A selection of species and hybrids will provide flowers for most of the early spring to mid autumn period. Most gentians are low spreading plants but some, such as G. asclepidea, have an upright or arching habit. The Japanese gentian (G. rindo) is an upright grower that has become a popular cut flower in recent years. Grow from seed or division of established clumps. Some of the longer stemmed varieties may grow from cuttings.

GERANIUM (P)

Pelargoniums are often called geraniums, but the true geraniums (known as cranesbills) are quite different, although they belong to the same family. Most are small mounding or trailing plants with simple single flowers, but G. maderense is a large shrubby species growing to about 1.2 m x 1 m. Most cranesbills thrive in full sun in a light well-drained soil, although the more northerly species, such as *G. sylvaticum*, will tolerate light shade and prefer summer moisture. Some species, such as *G. pratense*, can become slightly invasive. The flowers may be white, various shades of pink, red, mauve or purple. The popular hybrid 'Johnson's Blue' is close to a true blue. Propagate by seed, cuttings, division or rooted layers. *Erodium* is a closely related genus.

GERBERA (P)

The common garden or florists' gerberas are hybrids of *G. jamesonii*. They come in a wide range of colours with single or double flowers and form 25 cm x 35 cm clumps with flower stems up to 40 cm high. The 'Black Heart' strain has flowers in bold colours with contrasting dark centres. They prefer full sun and a light well-drained soil. As with many southern African plants gerberas tolerate far more cold if kept dry over winter. Propagate by seed, which is inclined to damp off, or by dividing very well-established clumps.

GEUM (P)

These brightly coloured, trouble-free members of the rose family vary considerably in size. The small forms are good rockery plants, while the larger ones, such as the popular yellow double 'Lady Stratheden' and the red double 'Mrs Bradshaw', may reach 1 m high in flower and are often seen in perennial borders. They are easily grown in any sunny position but are very prone to aphid damage. Propagate from seed or divisions. The perennial potentillas are very similar.

GUNNERA (P)

The well-known 2 m x 2 m giant, rhubarb-like plant that is so often seen edging large ponds is usually *G. tinctoria* (syn. *G. chilensis*) or *G. manicata*. They are very tough and easy-going plants with a preference for rich soil that is near water or that remains moist throughout summer. Propagate by seed or division, but be careful when handling the plants as the spines are vicious.

GYPSOPHILA (A & P)

The annual *G. elegans* is sometimes used as a quick filler, but the perennial gypsophilas are far more widely grown, especially as cut flowers. The most popular white cultivars are 'Bristol Fairy' and 'Perfecta' while 'Flamingo' and 'Red Sea' are the best of the rather sprawling pink forms. These larger forms will grow to about 1 m x 1.2 m under ideal conditions. The prostrate *G. repens* forms excellent ground cover. Gypsophilas prefer a well-drained soil in full sun. Propagate by cuttings.

HACQUETIA (P)

Hacquetia epipactus is a hardy woodland perennial that can also be grown in shady rockeries. At only 8 cm high it is small enough that it could be overlooked but for its very early and unusual flowers. The first of the small yellow-centred bright green flowers appear in very early spring before the foliage. Propagate by seed or division.

HELIANTHUS (A & P)

The sunflower (*H. annuus*) is widely grown for its huge yellow flowers, impressive stature, and its seeds. This well-known annual may reach 3.5 m under ideal conditions, but there are several dwarf forms that are suitable for bedding. The perennial species grow to about 1-2 m and have bright golden-yellow flowers. The double forms are particularly bright and colourful. Sunflowers prefer full sun and a rich well-drained soil. Propagate the perennials by division or basal cuttings.

HELIANTHEMUM (P)

Small spreading sub-shrubs usually included with the perennials. Tough wiry stemmed and best in full sun. As the common name sun rose suggests they are most at home in rockeries. Hardy but may rot in cold wet winters. Many species and hybrids are available. Colours include white, various shades of yellow, bright pinks, orange and red. Specialist growers occasionally have double forms. Propagate the

species by seed or cuttings, the hybrids by cuttings.

HELICHRYSUM (A & P)

The everlasting daisy or strawflower (*H. bracteatum*) is an annual often grown for use as a dried flower. The genus covers a wide range of foliage types and sizes, but the bedding varieties are all around 35 cm high. *H. petiolatum* is mainly grown for its foliage as a ground cover. Strawflowers prefer a light well-drained soil in full sun. Propagate the perennials by cuttings.

HELIOTROPIUM (P)

Heliotrope or cherry pie (*H. arborescens*) is a tender perennial grown for its fragrant, bright purplish-blue or white flowers. It is treated as an annual in cold-winter areas but may become a medium-sized bush up to 1.2 m x 1 m if sheltered from frosts. Heliotrope prefers full sun or light shade with a moist humus-enriched soil. Propagate by seed or cuttings.

HELIPTERUM (P)

The *H. anthemoides* hybrids 'Paper Baby' and 'Paper Cascade' have become extremely popular. They are small perennial daisies that cover themselves with white papery flowers and are best grown in full sun and a light well-drained soil. They are short-lived but easily propagated by small cuttings. It has been suggested that *H. anthemoides* has the potential to be something of a weed in mild areas. The other common species, *H. roseum*, was formerly included in *Acroclinium*. This species is very similar to *Helichrysum bracteatum* and is used and grown in exactly the same way.

HELLEBORUS (P)

Hellebores are early flowering perennials with large buttercup-style flowers in white, pink, purple and green. There are numerous species and hybrids, particularly of *H. orientale*, ranging from 15 cm to 1 m high. Hellebores grow best in light shade, preferably under deciduous trees, in a rich moist soil with ample humus added.

Top: *Heuchera villosa*
Above: *Helleborus niger* 'White Magic'

Propagate by seed, which must be stratified, or division.

HEMEROCALLIS (P)

Day lilies are tuberous-rooted perennials that produce strong strappy leaves and masses of trumpet-shaped flowers, each of which lasts for only one day, hence the common name. The colour range now includes everything except blues and purples and there are some striking foliage colours that often contrast well with the flowers. They prefer to grow in full sun or very light shade and are not fussy about soil type, although they should have ample summer moisture. Propagate by division.

HEUCHERA (P)

Coral bells (*H. sanguineum*) is a clump-forming perennial with heads of small pinkish-red flowers on 30 cm stems. It is

Iris 'Prancing Pony'

Liatris spicata

often treated as an annual. Other species and forms, including some with very deep red foliage, are available. Plant *Heuchera* in full sun or partial shade in a well-drained soil. Propagate by seed or division.

HOSTA (P)

Hostas are among the best herbaceous perennials for a cool, moist, shaded situation. Although they are mainly grown for their foliage the spikes of white or lavender flowers should not be ignored. There are many species and a multitude of hybrids in a bewildering range of foliage colours, sizes and patterns. Hostas are hardy, undemanding plants, but care should be taken to prevent the new spring foliage from being damaged by slugs and snails. Propagate by division.

IBERIS (A, B & P)

Candytufts are small spreading plants that bear clusters of small white or pink flowers in spring or summer. In mild areas the perennials may flower almost year-round. Most candytufts form 20 cm x 30 cm clumps. The perennial *I. sempervirens* is probably the most common species and is frequently grown in rockeries or sunny perennial borders. They must have excellent drainage but are otherwise easily grown in any sunny position. Propagate by seed, rooted layers, or small cuttings.

IMPATIENS (P)

Water fuchsias or busy lizzies are often treated as annuals because they cannot tolerate frosts. There are many small seedling strains grown for summer bedding. They cover a wide range of colours and flower forms, including the very pretty rosebud doubles. These plants grow to about 30 cm x 40 cm. Some of the larger species, such as *I. sodenii*, may be medium sized shrubs in mild frost-free regions. Water fuchsias are best in light shade with a moist humus-enriched soil. Propagate the bedders and species by seed, the selected forms and hybrids by small cuttings. The sturdier-trunked forms commonly known as balsam will often self-sow and may become naturalised.

IRIS (P)

The most common of the herbaceous irises are the bearded forms, which come in a variety of sizes. As with other large hybrid groups there are divisions based on parentage, size, flower type and season. Consult a specialised reference book for the details of these divisions.
Plant bearded irises with the rhizomes at, or just below, the soil surface. They do best where they get plenty of summer sun. Good drainage is essential but even under ideal conditions fungal diseases, particularly ink spot (leaf spot) and powdery mildew, may cause problems,

particularly in humid northern gardens and in wet seasons elsewhere.
Clump-forming irises, such as *I. unguicularis*, *I. innominata* and *I. foetidissima*, are generally small (about 40 cm x 50 cm) and trouble free. They will grow in full sun or light shade and require little or no attention other than occasional summer watering. Larger perennial irises, such as *I. setosa*, *I. forrestii* and *I. wilsonii*, form clumps up to 75 cm x 1 m and can be used in perennial borders.
The bog irises, such as *I. sibirica*, *I. missouriensis* and the Japanese (*I. ensata*) hybrids, are also very easy-care plants. They can reach 2 m high and will grow in very wet conditions but do not need to be in water. Any position that does not become dry in summer will usually suffice. All herbaceous irises are propagated by division.

KNIPHOFIA (P)

The red hot pokers are not as widely grown as they used to be, but these clump-forming perennials are very effective for adding height. They are also one of the best plants for attracting nectar-feeding birds into a garden. The common orange-flowered species is *K. uvaria*, but several other species with flowers in various shades of orange, yellow and lime green are available. Sizes range from very small cultivars for rockeries through to those with 2 m high flower stems. Flowering time varies, with *K. uvaria* flowering from late winter onwards, depending on the local climate. *Kniphofia* will tolerate most soils but needs at least half a day's sun. Propagate by seed (it self-sows over much of the country) or division.

LATHYRUS (A & P)

The annual climbing sweet peas are available in a wide range of colour mixes and sizes. In mild areas autumn-sown seed may provide winter colour, but in most districts the main flower display is in spring and early summer. The perennials also vary in size and colour and generally flower from late winter to late spring. Among the more common species are *L. vernus* (purplish-blue to pink,

depending on the form), *L. grandiflora* (deep pink), *L. nervosus* (purplish blue) and *L. latifolius* 'Alba' (white). Sweet peas are usually best grown in full sun or light shade with a humus-enriched soil. Propagate by seed, which should be soaked before sowing. A light dressing of lime will boost the early season growth.

LAVATERA (A & P)

The annual mallows (*L. trimestris* forms) are now available in white and several shades of pink. They are superb long-flowering plants, but may become untidy as the season progresses. The perennial species may develop into subshrubs or even quite large bushes. The very popular 'Barnsley' may reach 2 m high, while most forms of *L. thuringiaca* are capable of growing to 1.2 m. Lavateras are easily grown in any sunny position in a light well-drained soil. Propagate the species by seed or cuttings, the hybrid by cuttings. The genera *Malva* and *Sidalcea* include very similar species.

LEMNA (P)

Like *Azolla rubra*, duckweed, *L. minor*, can be found on nearly every patch of still water. It is useful in ponds because the fish feed on the roots, which act as a mild laxative. It is a floating plant with minute leaves and insignificant flowers and is self-propagating.

LEONTOPODIUM (P)

Edelweiss (*L. alpinum*) is one of the most famous of the European alpine plants and is frequently grown in rockeries. It is low and spreading and grows to about 12 cm x 15 cm. Edelweiss has woolly, 25-mm long, silver-grey leaves and heads of the small cream flowers appear in summer surrounded by woolly bracts. It grows best in gritty well-drained soil in sun and is usually raised from seed.

LEUCANTHEMUM (P)

Shasta daisies are heavy-flowering plants invaluable as fillers for large herbaceous borders and as a source of cut flowers. They are considered to be hybrids between *L. maximum* and *L. lacustre*. Most shastas grow to about 1.5 m x 1.2 m and have white-petalled single flowers, although many cultivars are grown, including doubles, the yellow 'Cobham Gold' and the 50 cm x 50 cm dwarf 'Snow Lady'. They are easily grown in any sunny position. Propagate by seed, division or small basal cuttings.

LEUCOGENES (P)

The New Zealand edelweiss species resemble their European counterparts except that they have smaller, greyer leaves and slightly larger, brighter flowers. The flower heads are surrounded by woolly bracts like the true edelweiss. There are two species, South Island edelweiss (*L. grandiceps*) is smaller and more woolly than North Island edelweiss (*L. leontopodium*) and it is spreading rather than rosette-forming. Both grow to 10 cm x 20 cm and prefer a gritty well-drained soil in sun. They are usually short-lived in gardens but are easily raised from seed or self-rooted pieces.

LEWISIA (P)

This genus of semi-succulent rosette-forming perennials includes some of the most beautiful rockery plants. In spring and early summer they produce heads of very attractive starry white or pink flowers each of which is up to 15 mm across, depending on the species. They are very hardy but resent being wet during winter and are best grown in the crevices between rocks or in a very gritty yet moisture-retentive scree soil in sun or partial shade. The common species, *L. cotyledon*, is available in many hybrid forms. Propagate by seed or division.

LIATRIS (P)

Liatris spicata is the species commonly grown, although others are available from specialist perennial nurseries. It has spikes of bright pinkish-purple or white filamentous flowers carried on 60 cm stems, hence the common name gay feather. Grow in full sun in well-drained moisture-retentive soil. Propagate the species by seed,

the hybrids by division or basal cuttings in spring.

LIGULARIA (P)

This is a genus of perennials with bold foliage and bright golden yellow flowers. In some species the flowers are massed on spikes while in others they resemble daisies carried in large heads. *L. tussilaginea* 'Aureo Maculata' has tough leathery leaves with irregular yellow spotting that give it the common name leopard plant. It is best in cool moist positions and will grow around the edges of ponds. The size varies with the species, however, most are large bulky perennials at least 1 m x 1 m with flower spikes that may grow to 2 m high. Propagate the species by seed or division, and the hybrids and selected forms by division.

LIMONIUM (A & P)

Formerly known as statice, this genus is frequently planted for use as dried flowers. The perennial species vary in hardiness, with one of the most popular cut flower species, *L. caspea*, being among the more frost-tender. Other perennial species, such as *L. latifolia* and *L. tartarica*, are very hardy and excellent as cut flowers. Most of the perennials grow to about 1 m x 1 m, but the brightly coloured annuals rarely exceed 30 cm x 20 cm. All are best grown in full sun and a light well-drained soil. Seed is the usual method of propagation.

LIRIOPE AND OPHIOPOGON (P)

These two closely related perennial genera are also known by the common names lily turf and mondo grass. Will withstand considerable neglect yet remain neat and tidy. Small clumping plants with strappy leaves. Available in a range of foliage colours including *O. planiscapus* 'Nigrescens' ('Arabicas'), which has very deep bluish purple, almost black, foliage. The small white tinted mauve or purple flowers are followed by bluish purple berries. Easily grown in moist, humus enriched soil in sun or shade. Very hardy. Propagate the

species by seed, the selected forms by division.

LITHODORA (P)

Formerly classified as *Lithospermum*. One of the most widely planted perennial rockery ground covers. Most of the selected forms of *L. diffusa* have bright blue flowers but white and pink forms are available. Does best in well-drained soil in full sun but inclined to be short lived in mild areas. Regular trimming helps but expect to replace every few years. Propagate species by seed, the selected forms by small cuttings.

LOBELIA (A & P)

Most gardeners are familiar with the small annual *L. erinus*, which come in shades of blue white and pink. It is widely used in borders and the trailing forms are popular for hanging baskets. *L. cardinalis* is probably the most common of the perennial species. The intensely red flowers are borne on 1.2 m shoots in spring. Recently new Canadian hybrids of *L. cardinalis, L. fulgens* and *L. syphilitica* have been developed forming the group known as *L. x speciosa*. Other species and hybrids, such as *L. laxiflora* and *L. x gerardii* 'Vedrariensis' are also quite widely available. Annual lobelias will grow in almost any sunny position, but the perennials prefer a soil with added humus and ample summer moisture. Propagate by seed, division or basal cuttings taken in spring.

LOBULARIA (A)

The small border plants commonly known as alyssum (*L. maritimus*) are the most widely grown members of this genus and must rank among the most common of all garden plants. They are available in many shades of white, cream, apricot, pink and purple. Alyssum, which prefers full sun and a light well-drained soil, forms 12 cm x 30 cm mounds and frequently naturalises.

LUPINUS (B & P)

Wild lupins are troublesome weeds but the garden forms are undeniably spectacular. The garden strains, such as the 1.5 m high 'Russell' and the small biennial 'Minaretta', come in an impressive range of colours. While virtually foolproof, lupins prefer full sun and gritty well-drained soil. Specialist perennial growers will often have uncommon species, such as the bright blue Texas bluebonnet (*L. texensis*). Propagate by seed.

LYCHNIS (A & P)

A highly variable genus, the flowers of most species resemble *Phlox* or *Verbena*, but the foliage and size of the plants varies considerably. The many forms of *L. coronaria* have large pink or white flowers and silvery-grey foliage, whereas *L. chalcedonica* has large bright green leaves and heads of small orange flowers. The small annuals, which are sold as viscaria, are very similar to bedding dianthus. Most

Limonium roseum

Lobelia x superba

Mimulus 'Strawberries and Cream'

Monarda didyma 'Cambridge Scarlet'

Lychnis species and hybrids grow best in full sun, but L. chalcedonica prefers partial shade. The soil should be well-drained and humus enriched. Propagate by seed, division or basal cuttings.

LYSICHITON (P)

Skunk cabbage (L. camschatoensis and L. americanus) is a perennial for large-scale bog gardens. The flowers are arum-like with creamy yellow bract and protruding spathe. They have a slightly unpleasant smell but nothing like the common name may suggest. The large leaves are also arum-like. The two species grow to about 80 cm high and form a spreading clump. They do best in light shade and may be propagated by seed or division.

LYSIMACHIA (P)

Moneywort or creeping Jenny (L. nummularia) is a very adaptable hardy trailing plant with small rounded leaves and yellow buttercup flowers. The yellow-foliaged form is more common than the green. It may be used as a woodland ground cover and is also an effective marginal plant. It spreads to about 1.5 m wide and will tolerate most soils and conditions. Perennial nurseries stock other species not all of which tolerate boggy conditions. Propagate by seed, self-rooted layers or small cuttings.

MATTHIOLA (A & B)

The fragrance of stocks is one of the best-loved garden scents. This genus of annuals and biennials has been highly

refined in cultivation. The two main forms are the M. incana hybrids, which include the 'Brompton', 'Beauty of Nice' and 'East Lothian' and many other well-known biennials, and M. longipetala bicornis, the night-scented stock. A light well-drained, but fertile, soil with plenty of sunlight is best. Stocks have a reputation for diminishing vigour if they are repeatedly grown in the same place, so alternate them with other plants. In most areas stocks may be planted throughout the year.

MAZUS (P)

This genus of mat-forming ground covers includes some New Zealand species, but the star is M. reptans from the Himalayas. From early summer, it produces blue and yellow flowers that resemble small snapdragons. The native species, M. pumilo and M. radicans, have a similar growth habit but produce smaller white flowers with yellow or yellow and mauve markings. All grow to about 8 cm x 30 cm and prefer moist well-drained soil in sun or partial shade. Propagate by seed, self-layered pieces or small cuttings.

MECONOPSIS (P)

The Himalayan poppy (M. betonicifolia) and Welsh poppy (M. cambrica), unlike many of the poppies, do not relish hot dry locations, instead preferring a cool, moist, woodland situation. They are at their best with long, cool, moist spring conditions so do very well in coastal Otago and Southland. Hot dry winds shorten their lives in many eastern districts and the

Himalayan poppies in particular will struggle in mild northern gardens.
M. betonicifolia has bright blue flowers on 80 cm stems and the much easier to grow M. cambrica has bright yellow flowers on 40 cm stems. M. betonicifolia is often monocarpic (once-seeding) but the very similar M. grandis is reputed to be easier to grow and longer lasting. Specialists often have unusual species, including M. grandis, which has blue flowers on 1 m stems, and the golden-flowered M. villosa. Propagate by seed.

MESEMBRYANTHEMUM (P)

Although Mesembryanthemum is the best known genus of the plants commonly called ice plants, several others including Carpobrotus, Delosperma, and Cephalophyllum also have the same common name. All are low, spreading succulent plants with bright daisy-like flowers. They thrive in light soils and hot dry positions, and often naturalise in coastal gardens. Propagate by seed, rooted layers or cuttings.

MIMULUS (P)

This genus includes shrubby forms, small perennials, and seedling strains grown as annuals. The bedders, such as 'Calypso', are forms of M. hybridus (syn. M. tigrinus). They are invaluable for adding a touch of yellow and orange to cool shady areas. The small soft-stemmed perennials, such as M. cardinalis, are often grown in woodland areas. M. luteus and M. moschatus have become naturalised in some areas and can often be found near streams and other moist places. The

bushy M. longiflorus (Diplacus longiflorus) is often planted in large perennial borders or grown as a shrub. Mimulus prefers a cool, moist soil and some species are bog plants. A position in light shade is best. Propagate by seed, self-rooted layers or cuttings.

MONARDA (P)

Most of the garden forms of bergamot are derived from M. didyma and M. fistulosa, both of which develop into dense 80 cm x 1 m clumps. Dormant over winter, they send up strong shoots in spring. The heads of white, pink, purple or red flowers form at the tip of the shoots. Bergamot is easily grown in most soils in full sun or light shade. Propagate by seed, division or basal cuttings. This genus should not be confused with the citrus bergamot, or bouquet orange, which is used in perfumes and for flavouring Earl Grey tea.

MORISIA (P)

Morisia monantha is a rosette-forming ground cover with glossy deep green leaves and 15 mm in diameter bright yellow flowers in spring. It grows to about 7.5 cm x 20 cm and prefers well-drained gritty soil in sun. Propagate by seed or division.

MYOSOTIDIUM (P)

The Chatham Island forget-me-not is one of the most impressive native perennials. It is grown as much for its large glossy leaves as the heads of bright blue flowers. White and pink forms also occur. It may grow to 1 m x 1 m under ideal conditions. Despite its tropical appearance, it is reasonably frost hardy and easily grown in a moist, fertile, humus-rich soil in light shade. Some gardeners have difficulty in flowering the plants but regular feeding usually solves this problem. Slug and snail damage is common. Propagate by seed.

MYOSOTIS (A, B & P)

The common bedding forget-me-nots, available with blue, white or pink flowers, are forms of M. sylvatica. Other species, including the native *M. colensoi*, are often sold as rockery plants. The bedders, which develop into 15 cm x 30 cm clumps, are generally best in cool, moist, humus-enriched soils in light shade. The perennials vary in their soil requirements; some prefer a scree soil, whereas others are bog plants, but most need more exposure to sun. Mildew is a common problem throughout the year in humid areas and affects plants in most areas at some stage or other. Propagate by seed, division or basal cuttings.

MYRIOPHYLLUM (P)

A sub-surface genus that frequently projects above the water surface. Water milfoil has very fine feathery leaves arranged radially around long twining stems. It is an attractive plant that provides some oxygenation but it can get out of control. Parrot's feather (*M. aquatica*) is a vigorous species that is not for small ponds. Any piece broken off can be used to start new plants.

NELUMBO (P)

The sacred lotus (*N. nucifera*) is one of the classic water plants. It is hardy but requires warm summer conditions to do well and is only rarely successful in the South Island. The round leaves are up to 60 cm in diameter and are carried on stout stems that project up to 1.5 m above the water's surface. The flowers are similar to water lilies but are held well above the surface. They are followed by seed pods with conspicuous holes at the top. Many colour forms are available as are double-flowered cultivars. Propagate by seed or division.

NEMESIA (A & P)

The annual nemesias are very popular bedding plants. They are used for winter bedding in frost-free areas and summer bedding elsewhere. These small mounding plants (30 cm x 30 cm) bear masses of flowers but are very short-lived, needing to be replaced after three months or so. Most of the perennial species are now included in the genus *Diascia* and those that remain, such as

N. caerulea, are not readily available. Best grown in a light, well-drained, moisture-retentive soil in full sun.

NEPETA (P)

Catmint (*N. x faassenii*) develops into a 30 cm x 30 cm clump and is sometimes used as a low hedge, but its popularity with cats tends to lead to maintenance difficulties. It produces sprays of purplish-blue flowers that are carried above the foliage. Catnip (*N. cataria*) has similar flowers, but larger leaves and a more stiffly upright habit. Both species will grow in almost any soil in full sun. Propagate by seed or cuttings. *Lamium* and *Glechoma* are closely related genera.

NICOTIANA (P)

This genus includes the commercial tobacco (*N. tabacum*) and species commonly grown as annuals. The bedding strains of *N. alata*, such as the 'Flirtation' series, are mainly grown for floral colour, but some of the perennial species, such as *N. sylvestris*, have very fragrant evening-scented flowers. The sizes range from the small bedders at about 50-60 cm through to species that may reach 2 m or more. Flowering tobaccos prefer full sun or very light shade and a moist humus-enriched soil. Propagate by seed.

NIEREMBERGIA (P)

A genus of mainly small ground cover perennials. Usually grown in rockeries, pots or small borders. The most common are *N. repens* and *N. hippomanica violacea* (*caerulea*). These are both carpeting plants with flowers similar to the small *Campanula*. *N. scoparia* (*frutescens*) is a taller species. It may reach 1 m high x 60 cm wide and has purplish blue bell-shaped flowers. Grow in moist, well-drained, humus-enriched soil in sun or very light shade. Propagate by seed, self-rooted layers or small cuttings.

NIGELLA (A)

Love-in-a-mist (*N. damascena*) grows to 25 cm x 15 cm and makes a brief but very dainty and attractive display. It is

usually planted in late winter for a spring show and replaced in early summer. The flowers are typically a bright blue but the 'Persian Jewels' mix also includes white, pink and maroon shades. The leaves around the flowers are reduced to filaments that create a misty effect, hence the common name. It is easily grown in most soils in full sun or very light shade.

NYMPHAEA (P)

The water lily (*N. aquatica*) scarcely needs describing, as the floating leaves and cup-shaped flowers are seen in ornamental ponds throughout the country. Most of the plants grown in ponds are hybrids and there are two distinct types: tropical and hardy. The tropical forms can withstand most winters but they need warm summers to grow and flower well. The hardy varieties grow prolifically and flower reliably even in cool summers. Both forms come in a variety of flower colours and leaf sizes. Plant the roots in pots or directly into soil on the bottom of the pond. Water lilies may be raised from seed but as most plants are cultivars division is the usual method of propagation.

OENOTHERA (B & P)

Evening primroses have become popular in recent years for their essential oil, which is used in cosmetics and herbal medicines. *O. fruticosa* and *O. missouriensis* (syn. *O. macrocarpa*) are the most common species and the hybrid 'Pink Petticoats', developed from *O. speciosa*, has also been widely planted since its release. Several other species, such as the white *O. acaulis*, are occasionally available. Evening primroses grow best in a light well-drained soil in full sun. Propagate by seed, division or basal cuttings.

OSTEOSPERMUM (P)

The best known *Osteospermum* is the white form known as 'Starry Eyes', which has unusual crimped petals. Other hybrids tend to be more typically daisy-like and now come in a wide range of colours. These tough drought-tolerant plants will also

Top: *Papaver nudicaule* cultivars
Above: *Paeonia* 'Cora Stubbs'

withstand frosts of about -6°C provided they are grown in sun and kept dry over winter. Annual strains are also available. Propagate the species and annuals from seed, the hybrids by cuttings.

PAEONIA (P)

Peonies are indispensable in any large perennial border. Most of the plants grown in gardens are hybrids and a wide range of colours and flower forms is available. The biggest flowers are huge (over 20 cm across) and a few, such as 'Festiva Maxima', are fragrant.
Peonies need winter chilling to enable proper bud formation and many North Island coastal districts are not cold enough in winter to chill them adequately. Hot, dry winds can burn the flowers before they open, so shelter is necessary.
Peonies demand a rich, well-drained, humus-filled soil and ample moisture when actively growing. A position in full sun or very light shade is best. Propagate by division, which is difficult as the plants have very

Top: *Petunia* 'Celebrity Raspberry'
Above: *Phlox paniculata* 'Mother of Pearl'

strong woody roots that may have to be sawn up. They may not flower the first season after dividing but they generally re-establish quickly.

PAPAVER (A & P)

Poppies are among the most colourful and instantly recognisable garden plants. The Shirley poppy (*P. rhoeas*) is a popular annual available in single or double forms. The Iceland poppy (*P. nudicaule*) is a short-lived perennial usually grown as an annual for winter and spring colour. The alpine poppy (*P. burseri* syn. *P. alpinum*) is often grown in rockeries and frequently self-sows. These species will grow in most well-drained soils in full sun and are raised from seed. The oriental poppy (*P. orientale*) is a perennial most often grown in herbaceous borders. There are many cultivars in a wide range of colours. Propagate by root cuttings or division.

PARAHEBE (P)

Small wiry-stemmed native ground cover sub-shrubs often grown as perennials. Several species are in cultivation, all have similar growth habits. The massed flowers form on short stems and create a haze of bloom above the foliage. Colours include white, pink and mauve, often with contrasting markings. Easily grown on any moist soil in sun or light shade. Propagate by seed, self-rooted layers or cuttings, which strike quickly.

PELARGONIUM (P)

The true pelargoniums are spectacular plants that often have vividly coloured flowers. Four main forms are grown: the bedding forms, zonal hybrids, regal hybrids, and the climbing or ground cover ivy-leaved forms. Over the years a wealth of hybrids in all manner of colours, sizes and flower forms have been developed. Specialist growers can supply many fancy forms with strikingly patterned leaves, scented foliage or exceptionally large flowers. Pelargoniums grow best in full sun with a light well-drained soil and they do very well in containers. They are reasonably hardy provided they are kept dry over winter, but where the temperature regularly falls below -3°C, they may have to be treated as annuals. Pests and diseases can be troublesome, particularly white flies and looper caterpillars. Propagate by seed or cuttings.

PELTIPHYLLUM (P)

Peltiphyllum peltatum is a very distinctive marginal pond or bog plant. It is a fully deciduous perennial that starts into growth early in spring and the pink flower heads, which are carried on thick 50 cm high stems, appear before the foliage. The leaves that follow are rounded, up to 30 cm across and deeply lobed. It is at its best in humus-enriched soil with regular feeding. *Peltiphyllum* will grow in full sun but prefers shade during the middle of the day. Propagate by seed or division.

PENSTEMON (P)

The common border penstemons with their spikes of showy foxglove-like flowers are hybrids of *P.* x *gloxinioides*. They are hardy over much of the country but may be treated as annuals in very cold winter areas. Seedling strains and named hybrids are available. *P. barbatus* and *P. heterophyllus*, which include the 'blue penstemons' are also widely grown. Penstemons prefer a well-drained humus-enriched soil in full sun. Propagate by seed, division or basal cuttings.

PETUNIA (P)

The common garden petunias are highly refined hybrids developed from *P. nyctaginiflora* and *P. integrifolia*. They are tender short-lived perennials usually grown as annuals. There are many different hybrid strains in all colours and foliage forms. They are mainly small clump-forming plants about 15 cm x 35 cm, but some have longer stems and are used for hanging baskets. The 'Colour Wave' petunias are stronger growing and more reliably perennial. Petunias prefer a moist, humus-enriched soil in full sun.

PHLOX (A & P)

There are three main types of phlox: bedding, rock and border. Most prefer moist well-drained soil in full sun. Propagate the annuals by seed, the perennials by division or cuttings. The annual species (*P. drummondii*) is a small plant with the flowers clustered at the tip of 15 cm stems, seldom exceeding 12 cm high but may grow to about 15 cm x 25 cm. Usually sold as mixed colours including white, mauve and various pink shades.
Rock phlox are carpeting plants; they seldom exceed 12 cm but may grow to 1 m or more. The main species are *P. subulata, P. douglasii, P. divaricata* and *P. stolonifera* with many hybrid forms also grown. Most have small needle-like leaves and flowers close to the foliage, but *P. stolonifera* hybrids, such as 'Blue Ridge', have larger leaves and flowers on short stems. Border phlox are generally of *P. paniculata* parentage. They are typical herbaceous plants, almost deciduous over winter but starting into rapid growth in spring. The large terminal heads of white, pink, mauve or purple flowers are carried on heavily foliaged stems that may grow as high as 1.5 m. Many of the border phlox have a sweet honey scent.

PHYSOSTEGIA (P)

The obedient plant (*P. virginiana*) is similar to *Penstemon* in its general growth habit and flower. The common name derives from the flower, which stays in position if twisted on the stem. The usual colour is pinkish-purple but white forms are common. It grows to about 1.8 m x 1 m in flower. It prefers a moist well-drained soil in full sun or very light shade and may be invasive. Propagate by seed, division or small basal cuttings.

PLATYCODON (P)

The balloon flower (*P. grandiflorus*) is an attractive hardy perennial that gets its name from the large flower buds that open into 50 mm starry white, pink or blue flowers. Double forms are available but rare. It is a shrubby tuberous perennial that develops into a 1 m x 1 m clump. Easily grown in any well-drained soil in full sun, but may take a few years to get established. Propagate by seed or division. However, because the plants resent disturbance do not divide regularly.

POLEMONIUM (P)

Jacob's ladder (*P. caeruleum*) is a clump-forming perennial with bright green pinnate leaves and 60 cm flower spikes. The flowers are purplish-blue, but a white form is also available. *P. reptans* is a smaller spreading species with similar blue flowers. Jacob's ladder prefers cool, moist, well-drained soil in full sun or light shade. Propagate by seed, division or small basal cuttings.

POLYGONATUM (P)

Solomon's seal (*P. biflorum*) is a hardy tuberous woodlander with arching stems that bear many slightly scented, pendulous white flowers beneath the glaucous foliage. The foliage clump grows to about 1 m x 1 m, but may eventually spread to several metres wide. Dwarf forms are available and several species are sold under the name *P. multiflorum*, which may not be correct. Solomon's seal is easily grown in any cool, moist soil in shade or partial shade. Propagate by seed or division.

PONTEDERIA (P)

Pickerel weed (*P. cordata*) is an attractive pond plant that is only occasionally available. It grows in up to 30 cm of water and has pointed 25 cm x 15 cm leaves that push up through the surface on strong stems to a height of about 80 cm. In summer, spikes of purplish-blue flowers develop, and these too are carried on strong stems that usually extend just above the height of the foliage. Plant in full sun and propagate by seed or division.

PORTULACA (A)

Portulaca grandiflora is a widely grown summer bedding plant. It is a low spreader and has vividly coloured poppy-like flowers. It prefers a light, dry soil and is often sown directly on dry waste areas or shingle driveways for quick colour. Several seed strains are available; choose the new strains as their flowers will open on cloudy days, unlike the old strains that need sun.

PRATIA (P)

Both the native *P. angulata* and the Tasmanian *P. puberula* are small spreading ground covers. *P. angulata* has small white flowers in spring followed by bright red berries, while *P. puberula* has pale blue or white flowers and no noticeable fruit. Both thrive in cool moist soil in light shade and *P. puberula* can be somewhat invasive. Propagate from seed, self-rooted layers or division.

PRIMULA (P)

This is a large genus that includes around 600 species and, as with many large genera, the primroses are divided into groups with similar character-istics.
The first group are commonly

used for bedding. These tend to be short-lived perennials that are mainly grown for winter colour. Primroses are forms and hybrids of *P. vulgaris*. They are usually small plants with one flower per stem. Polyanthus are hybrids between *P. vulgaris* and the cowslip (*P. veris*). They have several primrose-like flowers per stem. The highly developed modern strains, such as 'Pacific Giant' and 'Ocean', are very heavy flowering. The slightly tender *P. malacoides* and *P. obconica* seedling strains are also used for winter colour in mild areas but are spring- and summer-flowering elsewhere. Candelabra primroses have tall flower spikes with the flowers in whorls at intervals up the stem. They grow in very wet soils or bogs and are deciduous. The largest is the giant cowslip (*P. florindae*), which has flower stems that may reach 1.2 m or more. There are also many species, such as *P. rosea* and the very small *P. warshnewskyana*, that are usually grown in rockeries or alpine houses. In general, most primroses grow best in partial shade with woodland conditions. They demand ample humus and often benefit from regular feeding. Polyanthus can be planted in sun for a winter colour display but they will suffer with the arrival of warmer weather.
Propagation varies with species: the true species are generally easily raised from seed, but many of the fancy forms are F1 hybrids and will not come true to type. Established clumps of the perennials may be divided or individual rosettes may be removed and treated much like cuttings.

PULMONARIA (P)

Lungwort is the unappealing common name for this genus of forget-me-not-like plants. The most common species are *P. angustifolia* and *P. saccharata*. *P. angustifolia* is a low spreading plant about 15-25 cm x 80 cm with small deep blue flowers opening from pink buds in spring. *P. saccharata* is slightly taller and has leaves with conspicuous white spots. The flowers are a purplish-pink or white. They are easily grown in a

cool, moist, humus-enriched soil in light shade. Raise from seed or divisions.

PULSATILLA (P)

The pasque flower (*P. vulgaris*) is most often grown in rockeries but is also suitable for borders and troughs. The general effect is that of a hairy anemone with a large simple flower. The colour range includes white, pink, purple and red. *Pulsatilla* prefers a moist gritty scree soil in sun or partial shade and can be short-lived in mild areas. Propagate by seed or division. Alpine specialists occasionally stock other species.

RAMONDA (P)

Ramonda myconii is a rosette-forming plant with deep green leaves covered in fine hairs. In mid to late spring it produces simple pale purple flowers on 12 cm stems that are held well above the foliage. Plant in moist, humus-enriched, well-drained soil in light shade and mulch with shingle chips to prevent the crown and rosettes becoming wet, which may cause rotting. Propagate by seed.

RANUNCULUS (P)

Although really corms, the common varieties, such as 'Tecolote Giants', are usually treated as perennials or bedding plants. These come in a huge range of colours and flower forms and are widely planted for late winter and spring displays. By staggering the planting time a good continuation of bloom can be achieved. They prefer a moist well-drained soil in full sun. The small buttercups, such as *R. ficaria*, are mat-forming plants far more suited to moist woodland conditions and some species are marginal bog plants. A few, such as *R. acris* and *R. sardous*, can become serious weeds in damp areas. Most buttercups prefer a moist soil in shade or partial shade. Propagate by division or self-rooted layers.

RAOULIA (P)

This native genus includes some classic-rockery plants, but they are not always easy to grow. They are composed of numerous tiny rosettes; some are prostrate,

Top: *Pulsatilla vulgaris* 'Alba'
Above: *Primula vulgaris*

spreading plants while others, such as *R. eximea*, form large hummocks. The hummock-forming species are known as vegetable sheep and can grow to over 50 cm x 2 m in their native habitat, but they are virtually impossible to cultivate. Most species have silvery grey foliage covered in fine hairs and very small yellow or white flowers, usually in early summer. Grow in moist scree soil in sun. The foliage will be damaged if moist for extended periods so good drainage and ventilation are essential. Propagate by seeds or divisions.

RODGERSIA (P)

A genus of hardy deciduous perennials for cool moist soil in sun or shade. Most are fairly large plants best suited to borders or around the edge of ponds or streams. The bold foliage, which may be up to 60 cm across, often develops vivid autumn colours and is as much an attraction as the *Astilbe*-like flowers. Several species are grown but none are common. Perennial specialists usually have *R. pinnata* and *R. podophylla*. Propagate by seed or division.

RUDBECKIA (P)

These large daisies with their

bold displays of bright yellow, gold or mahogany red flowers are very effective in large borders. *R. hirta* hybrids are short-lived, usually biennial, but *R. laciniata* forms are reliably perennial. Other species, such as *R. fulgida*, are also grown. Most have flower stems over 1.2 m, although 'Goldquelle' is reasonably compact. Rudbeckias prefer a light well-drained soil in full sun. Propagate by seed or division.

SALPIGLOSSIS [A]

Salpiglossis sinuata has sticky foliage and petunia-like flowers with interesting markings and patterns. It grows to about 50 cm high and prefers a rich soil in full sun, but may collapse if overwatered. Pinch back the young plants to make them bush out.

SALVIA [A & P]

This is an enormously variable genus. The flaming red flower bracts of the various forms of *S. splendens*, such as the 60 cm high 'Bonfire' and 40 cm high 'Blaze of Fire', are a feature of many bedding displays. The perennial *S. farinacea*, which is available in white, pink and blue, is also often used for bedding. Notable among the larger perennials are 'Pineapple Sage' [*S. elegans*, syn. *S. rutilans*], which has bright red flowers and pineapple-scented foliage, and *S. involucrata*, which has interestingly textured foliage and large pink flowers. The blue-flowered sages, especially *S. azurea* and *S. patens*, are widely grown in perennial borders. *S. azurea* grows up to 2 m high and flowers in late summer and autumn.

Sages are, in the main, sun lovers. Many are also drought tolerant, but all seem to do best in a moist well-drained soil. Propagate by seed, division or cuttings.

SAXIFRAGA [P]

Saxifraga is a large genus with over 300 species, that include many classic rockery plants. Most saxifrages are small rosette-forming plants with succulent foliage and heads of simple pink flowers on short stems in spring and summer. They prefer light well-drained soil in sun or light shade. Some species are inclined to rot if the centre of the rosette remains wet for long so a mulch of fine gravel chips is recommended. Propagate by seed, division or offsets.

SCABIOSA [A & P]

Scabiosa is often grown for use as a dried flower but is just as effective in the perennial border and the smaller species may be grown in rockeries. Dusky greyish-blue is the most common colour but white, cream and pink forms are also available. Most of the garden hybrids, including the widely grown 'Blue Mountain' and 'Blue Butterfly' have been derived from *S. caucasica*. They grow to about 50 cm x 30 cm and prefer full sun and a well-drained soil. Propagate by seed, division or basal cuttings. *Cephalaria* and *Knautia* are closely related genera.

SCHIZANTHUS [A]

Schizanthus pinnatus is known as the poor man's orchid because of its interestingly patterned, multi-coloured flowers. It is usually grown as a winter annual in mild frost-free areas and a summer annual elsewhere. Modern strains are very compact, about 25 cm x 20 cm, and heavy flowering. Plant *Schizanthus* in cool, moist, humus enriched soil. A sunny position is best in the winter, otherwise light shade is preferred.

SENECIO [P]

Cinerarias [*S.* x *hybridus*] are strikingly colourful daisies that are generally treated as winter annuals in mild areas and summer annuals or winter house plants elsewhere. Cinerarias grow to about 30 cm x 30 cm and prefer a moist humus-enriched soil and a shaded position. 'Silver Dust' and 'Silver Lace' are forms of *S. cineraria* that are grown mainly for their silver-grey foliage. They will grow in any well-drained soil in sun or very light shade. Propagate by seed.

SILENE [A & P]

The pink and white annual silenes are very colourful small bedding plants. They develop into densely foliaged 15 cm x 30 cm mounds and flower throughout the warmer months. This genus is closely related to *Dianthus* and *Lychnis* and many of the perennial species, such as *S. aculis*, bear a close resemblance to those genera. The soil preference is variable; some prefer moist peaty soil, whereas others are very drought tolerant. A position in sun or light shade suits most species. Propagate by seed or small cuttings. *Saponaria* is another closely related genus.

SOLDANELLA [P]

These charming little alpines are members of the primula family. They form rosettes of deep green, rounded, leathery leaves and in spring produce graceful heads of tiny fringed flowers on 15 cm stems. The smaller species, such as *S. minima* and *S. pusilla*, are the most appealing, but even the larger *S. montana* and *S. villosa* are irresistible. They demand a cool moist position with humus-enriched well-drained soil yet they resent excess winter moisture. They are genuine alpines and are often short-lived in mild areas. Soldanellas are usually raised from seed, but large clumps may be divided.

SOLEIROLIA [P]

Baby's tears [*S. soleirolii*] is a dense mat-forming plant with tiny bright green leaves. It looks very similar to Corsican mint [*M. requienii*] and can spread up to 1 m across. It may be blackened by hard frosts but usually shoots away in spring. It prefers a position in light shade with moist soil. Baby's tears will grow right up to the water's edge and it is very useful for softening the lines of stones and disguising concrete. It often self-sows and any small piece broken off can be used to start new plants.

SOLIDAGO [P]

Goldenrod is a genus of extremely hardy perennials. There are two species [*S. canadensis* and *S. brachystachys*] and several hybrids that are reasonably common. Most forms have feathery plumes of bright golden-yellow flowers in summer and grow to about 1.5 m x 1.5 m, but 'Baby Gold' is only about 60 cm x 60 cm. Goldenrod is best in a moist well-drained soil in full sun. Propagate by seed, division or small spring cuttings.

STACHYS [P]

Lamb's ear [*S. byzantina* [*lanata*]] is a perennial with silver grey leaves that are covered in a dense mat of hairs. Their shape and 'furriness' gives the plant its common name. The flower spikes, which bear small purple blooms, may be removed to keep the plant more compact. Grow in light well-drained soil in full sun. Very hardy but the foliage is damaged by heavy rain and frost. Propagate by seed, division or cuttings.

TAGETES [A]

The marigolds are among the most widely grown bedding plants. There is a large range of seedling strains, which generally fall into three categories: the French marigolds [*T. patula*], which are small compact plants around 30 cm x 30 cm; the African marigolds [*T. erecta*], which are large plants around 60 cm-1 m tall; and hybrids that fall in between. Less developed species, such as *T. tenuifolia*, are often used in wildflower seed mixes or used for informal plantings. Marigolds are easily grown in most well-drained soils in full sun.

TANACETUM [P]

The pyrethrum daisies [*T. coccineum*], which have ferny foliage and grow to about 60 cm high in flower, are available in white, pink and red shades, and single and double forms are grown. They are best grown in full sun and a light well-drained soil. Propagate by seed, division or small basal cuttings.

THALICTRUM [P]

Thalictrum is often planted for use as cut flowers. The foliage, which resembles maidenhair fern [*Adiantum*] or *Aquilegia*, is very delicate but the plants are tough and adaptable. The white pink, lavender or pale yellow flowers are small but carried in large heads well above the foliage creating the effect of a cloud of bloom. The most common species are *T. aquilegifolium* and *T. delavayi* (syn. *T. dipterocarpum*) and the sizes range from 30 cm to 1.8 m high. Thalictrums prefer a moist humus-enriched soil in partial shade. Propagate by seed or division.

TRILLIUM (P)

Trilliums are currently one of the most sought after and admired of the hardy North American woodland plants. Several species and hybrids are grown but they have never been common in gardens because they are slow to multiply and consequently expensive. The most readily available are *T. grandiflorum, T. luteum, T. nivale* and *T. sessile*. Trilliums come into growth in late winter and are in flower by early to mid spring. Each stem bears a whorl of three leaves and one flower, which has three sepals and three petals. The size ranges from dwarf species like the 10 cm high *T. nivale* through to *T. grandiflorum,* at around 60 cm tall. The larger species form substantial clumps with age. The smaller species tend to have white or pale pink flowers, but the larger ones are also available in shades of red and creamy yellow. The double-flowered forms of *T. grandiflorum* are spectacular.
Trilliums demand cool moist woodland conditions, humus-rich but well-drained soil, and a shady situation. The smaller species grow well in a scree soil in rockeries but they must have at least half a day's shade. Established clumps are easily divided in autumn, but larger species can only be divided every two to three years and seedlings take five or more years to flower.

TROPAEOLUM (P)

Nasturtiums are often grown as quick-spreading annuals, but in many areas these tuberous plants will live on as true perennials, sometimes becoming invasive. *T. majus* hybrids, which most commonly have bright yellow and orange flowers, are available in several sizes and styles. Some are small and

bushy, others climb, and the trailers are very good in hanging baskets. Other species, such as *T. speciosum*, are grown as perennial climbers. A well-drained humus-enriched soil in full sun or light shade is best. Propagate by seed, tubers or small cuttings.

TYPHA (P)

These aquatic grasses with long spear-like leaves and woody flower spikes topped with cylindrical brown heads are usually known as bulrushes or raupo. Large bulrushes are a feature of many natural ponds but they are often too bulky and invasive for garden ponds. However, they are impressive easy-care plants and the flower spikes dry well. They should be planted in full sun and will grow in up to 30 cm of water. Propagate by seed or division.

VERBASCUM (B & P)

Many of the sweet mulleins, particularly *V. thapsus*, are regarded as common roadside weeds, but the selected forms and hybrids are useful in large perennial borders or wild meadow gardens. *V. bombyciferum* and *V. blattaria* are the common cultivated species. They both have yellow flowers, but the hybrid strains come in a range of colours including some eye-catching purple shades. The larger species may reach 2 m high under ideal conditions, but 1.2 m is more usual. They prefer full sun and gritty, light, well-drained soil. Propagate by seed, or small basal cuttings taken in spring.

VERBENA (A & P)

Verbenas are excellent for providing a splash of colour in hot dry areas. The annual strains are generally sold in mixed colours but the perennials, which are short-lived, are sold as individually named cultivars. Perennial verbenas are ground covers that can spread to 1 m wide. Plant verbenas in full sun in a light well-drained soil. Mildew can be a problem in humid areas or in autumn in all areas. Propagate by seed, self-rooted layers, or small cuttings.

Trillium sessile 'Rubrum'

VERONICA (A & P)

The common *V. spicata* has spikes of light purple flowers in spring and is also available in white, pale pink and deep purplish blue varieties. The flower spikes may grow to 40 cm but the plant is little more than a ground cover. *V. teucrium* is a spreading ground cover with 15 cm high spikes of intensely blue flowers in spring. Veronicas prefer sun or light shade and a moist, well-drained, humus-enriched soil. Propagate by self-rooted layers, division of established clumps or small cuttings.

VIOLA (A, B & P)

This is a large genus with many species and countless garden forms. The common bedding violas and pansies are among the best-known garden plants. The hybrid seedling strains, such as 'Majestic Giants', 'Westland Giants', 'Ultima', 'Joker' and 'Imperial', are among the best hardy annuals. They come in every colour, thrive almost anywhere that's moist and may be planted year-round in all but the coldest areas. Plant violas in a sunny position in the winter, while in the summer they should be shaded from the hottest sun.
The perennial species are mainly small clumping plants, about 10 cm x 20 cm, that inhabit moist semi-shaded areas. Some, such as the sweet violet (*V. odorata*), are fragrant. Most have small flowers and deep green, heart-shaped leaves, but the 'Maggie Mott' forms resemble pansies. The original 'Maggie Mott' was one of a group of English hybrids derived from *V. cornuta* and other similar species, but in this country the

name has come to be synonymous with all the plants of this general style. Perennial violas prefer moist, well-drained, humus-enriched soil. Propagate by seed, self-rooted layers, or small cuttings.

XERONEMA (P)

The Poor Knights lily (*X. callistemon*) is one of the most impressive New Zealand natives, but it is too frost-tender for many areas. It has bold spear-shaped leaves and vivid red flowers reminiscent of a large 'toothbrush' grevillea. It forms a clump 80 cm x 1 m and prefers full sun and a well-drained but moisture-retentive soil. It is difficult to divide successfully, so it is usually grown from seed, which may take several years to reach flowering size.

ZAUSCHNERIA (P)

The Californian fuchsias are evergreen perennials or sub-shrubs. *Z. californica* and its form *latifolia* are the most common of the four species. It grows to 40 cm x 70 cm, has orange-red tubular flowers from early summer to autumn and prefers full sun and light well-drained soil. Propagate by seed, division or small cuttings.

ZINNIA (A)

These popular summer bedders demand a warm sunny position and are seldom successful where the summers are wet or cool. There are many seed strains in various sizes and colour mixes; the smallest are about 20 cm high, and the largest are up to 50 cm tall. Avoid overhead watering as it leads to mildew – soak the soil instead. Zinnias need full sun and a light well-drained soil.

THE PLANTS

FERNS

Cultivation; Growing ferns in containers; Fernhouses; Propagation; Popular ferns

THINK OF THE NATIVE bush and ferns immediately come to mind. They are one of its most dominant features – ranging from minute filmy ferns to huge tree ferns – but they are not widely grown in our gardens. Yet what they lack in the way of showy flowers is more than made up for by their graceful arching fronds. Ferns impart a coolness and a sense of calm to any garden area.

On the whole, ferns prefer shade. There are a few ground cover forms that do well in sunny rockeries, but most ferns are plants for moist, humid, shady corners. Excessive sun or very dry conditions will cause them to shrivel and die. But there is another very important reason why ferns do best in slightly wetter conditions: their reproductive cycle. Ferns evolved before the flowering plants and they produce spores rather than seeds.

CULTIVATION

Unless you know that a fern is sun-tolerant choose a shaded location. However, despite their preference for shade, ferns still require reasonably good light; too dark and they will become drawn and leggy. Shelter from wind is another important prerequisite, as fern fronds brown quickly when exposed to drying winds.

Ferns are primarily woodland plants so, not surprisingly, they prefer soil that is high in humus. It has been said before in this book and it applies to ferns too; you can't have too much humus. Work in plenty of compost, leaf mould or other high-humus materials to improve the texture of the soil, its moisture retention and drainage.

As with most woodland plants, ferns generally prefer slightly acid soils. There are a few species that come from limestone areas and these are consequently lime tolerant. Nevertheless, the occasional dose of dolomite lime is beneficial in preventing the soil becoming too acid and also for its value as a magnesium supplement.

GROWING FERNS IN CONTAINERS

Ferns may be grown in pots like any other container plant, but terrariums and bottle gardens are a popular way of growing ferns in containers. Ferns in pots often suffer from a lack of water, low humidity or both. A terrarium (the modern-day equivalent of the Wardian case) protects the tender fronds from low humidity and recycles the soil moisture. The high humidity and even temperature make it possible to grow even the extremely moisture-sensitive filmy ferns.

If you only intend to grow ferns in your terrarium, a fairly heavy potting mix is best, but if you want to grow other plants too ordinary potting mix will do. Terrariums and bottle gardens usually do not have drainage holes so the soil is built up in layers to compensate. A base layer of gravel ensures good drainage and this should be followed by a thin layer of horticultural charcoal, which filters impurities out of the water and absorbs most odours. You might also consider putting some fine wire mesh over the charcoal before adding the potting mix. This is optional, but it will stop the potting soil mixing with the lower layers, which could lessen their efficiency. Remember to leave enough room at the top of the container for the foliage to develop.

After planting, add enough water to lightly moisten the soil (don't saturate it) and close the container. Place your bottle garden or terrarium in a bright position out of direct sunlight. (Full sun through glass will cook your ferns in a few minutes.)

For the first few days after planting keep an eye on the moisture level. Condensation should appear on the sides overnight or in cold weather but disappear as the day warms up. Constant condensation is a sign that the soil is too wet; open the container and allow it to dry for a few days. Conversely, if there is no condensation add a touch more water.

If unnoticed, insect pests, particularly aphids, can easily get out of control in a terrarium. A mild combined insecticide/fungicide mixed in with the initial watering will help to prevent any problems developing.

PROPAGATION

Ferns are a type of perennial plant and many of them can be propagated in the time-honoured perennial method; division. You'll find that some ferns develop into easily divided clumps while others produce underground or surface rhizomes that can be separated from the parent plant.

Some ferns also produce small plantlets on the edge of the fronds. The most common example of this is the hen and chickens fern (*Asplenium bulbiferum*). Don't remove these from the frond, instead cut off the whole frond and pin it to the ground. Do this with wire hoops or by putting a very thin layer of soil over the frond. Within a few months the little plantlets will have roots and may be removed for growing on.

RAISING FERNS FROM SPORES

Growing ferns from spores is a very satisfying form of plant propagation. It is not difficult, but may take some time before the results become apparent.

Many ferns produce separate fertile and sterile fronds, the most common example of this habit is the *Blechnum* ferns. Their fertile fronds are very distinctive, they grow straight up from the crown and become covered in blackish

brown sporangia. As the sporangia mature they rupture, releasing the spores.

To collect the spores hold a paper bag under a ripe fertile frond and tap the frond on the bag to release the spores. An alternative is to pick a few ripe fertile fronds, put them in the bag, then shake it.

Some ferns do not have distinct fertile fronds. In which case you will need to examine the undersides of the fronds to detect the presence of ripe sporangia.

Having collected your spores the next step is to sow them. Fern spore does not remain viable for long and needs to be sown as soon as possible. The first point to note when sowing the spores is the need for constant moisture at the prothallus stage. This can be difficult to achieve with regular potting mixes as keeping them saturated tends to encourage algae, liverworts and mosses to proliferate, smothering the ferns before they have a chance to develop. One way around this problem is to sterilise the mix with boiling water, but it is not always successful.

I prefer to use a method that requires no potting mix and is clean and easy to use. Find

Ferns can be combined with other shade lovers, such as begonias and white anemones.

FERNHOUSES

Some fern houses are glazed and built along glasshouse lines and are suitable for very tender ferns. However, most fernhouses are built to grow hardy or slightly tender ferns, and more closely resemble shadehouses. Unlike the shadehouse, fernhouses often have solid walls with just the roof area open to the light. Wooden laths, tree fern trunks, palings and fibre-cement panels – typical fencing materials – are all suitable wall coverings.

The roof is constructed exactly like a shadehouse roof. The weight of shade-cloth used depends on what you intend to grow. For ferns only, a 50–75% cloth is best, but if you want to add a little colour by growing fuchsias or impatiens, a lighter cloth, say 30–50% will be required.

The ferns may be grown in containers on benches or planted out in the ground. The most common method is to lay a shingle or bark chip path around the house and plant the ferns in raised beds filled with a humus-rich compost. Natural-looking mounds and hollows will allow a range of ferns of various sizes to be grown.

Micro-jets at soil level combined with overhead misting together provide ample soil moisture and humidity: overhead watering alone often fails to penetrate the canopy of fronds while soil-level watering does not raise the humidity enough or wash the dust off the fronds.

an old, porous, unglazed, red clay brick. Scrub it clean using water and a very dilute bleach solution. Once clean, rinse it thoroughly to remove all traces of the bleach. Next, find a saucer or bowl; one that the brick can sit in. Fill the saucer with water and place the brick in it, wide side down. Leave it for a few hours and then check to see if the top surface of the brick is wet. (The moisture should be drawn up over the brick's porous surface by capillary action.) If the top of the brick is not wet you will need either more water in the saucer or a deeper saucer.

When you reach the stage where the brick stays wet, sow the spores on top of the brick. Cover the brick with a large plastic bag or some other clear cover. Keep the saucer and brick in a cool place and make sure the saucer is constantly topped with water.

Within a few weeks a green film will develop on the surface, this is the prothalli. If the moisture level is right, small ferns will soon develop. When they are large enough to handle they may be gently prised from the brick and grown on.

POPULAR FERNS

ADIANTUM

The maidenhair ferns are most commonly represented by the tropical and subtropical species grown as house plants (mainly *A. raddianum* forms). However, there are a number of hardy species that are quite suitable for growing outdoors.
Maidenhairs are at their best in cool moist shade. They are ideal for growing near small ponds or streams. The species commonly grown, *A. aethiopicum*, *A. cunninghamii* and *A. diaphanum*, all closely resemble the houseplant species in size and general habit. *A. formosum* is larger, with fronds up to 1 m long, while *A. hispidulum* is distinguished by the red coloration of the new fronds.

ASPLENIUM

The common hen and chickens fern (*A. bulbiferum*) is widely distributed throughout the country. It grows to 1 m x 1 m, is hardy to at least -5°C and is easily cultivated. This and the other common species, such as *A. flaccidum* and *A. lamprophyllum*, will tolerate some sun exposure if kept moist. Gardeners in mild frost-free areas may like to try the bird's nest fern (*A. nidus*), an Australian native.

ATHYRIUM

Not commonly grown, the *Athyrium* ferns are widely spread in the Pacific region. They have distinctly matt foliage that some find unattractive. They grow to about 30 cm x 60 cm, appear hardy and will tolerate partial exposure to sun. They are easily grown in any moist area.

BLECHNUM

The *Blechnum* ferns are among the most common in the bush and also some of the most widely cultivated. A distinguishing feature is the separate fertile and sterile fronds. The upright fertile fronds, covered in brown sporangia, emerge from the centre of the crown.
The species vary considerably in size and habit. *B. penna-marina* is a useful spreading ground cover that will grow in full sun, *B. capense* is very common and distinguished by its reddish new growth. *B. colensoi* may be seen as an epiphyte, while *B. fluviatile* may develop a small trunk with great age.
In general, these ferns pose no great difficulties in cultivation. All are hardy and most are sun-tolerant, but all do best in light shade.

CYATHEA

The silver fern (*C. dealbata*) is widely recognised as one of our national symbols. It is a tough and adaptable plant but the sheer size of this fern's crown – up to 5 m across – prevents it from being grown in many gardens. Of all the *Cyathea* species only *C. smithii* is really suitable for small gardens.

DAVALLIA

The tropical and subtropical species of rabbit's foot fern are often grown as houseplants, but they will survive outside in many areas. The native species (*D. tasmanii*) is seldom seen in gardens but it is not difficult to grow. It grows to about 15 cm x 45 cm wide and is frost-tender.

DICKSONIA

Of all the native tree ferns *D. squarrosa* is the most widely cultivated. It is tough and easy to grow and also withstands reasonably hard frosts and sun exposure if kept moist. Although it can reach 6 m high in the wild, it is unlikely to exceed 3 m in cultivation. In mild areas *D. lanata* is also a good garden subject.

DOODIA

These ferns are not widely grown but *D. media* has been used on occasion in hanging baskets. It is really better suited to a lightly shaded rockery where the reddish new fronds make an attractive display. This species grows to about 30 cm x 30 cm and is hardy to at least -3°C.

GLEICHENIA

The species most commonly

grown, *G. flabellata*, is an attractive fern but it is also frost-tender. Although sun-tolerant, it really needs a sheltered position in moist shade. It has arching 1 m long fronds and forms a clump up to 1.5 m across.

HYMENOPHYLLUM

The filmy ferns are for enthusiasts only; there are few gardens that would be suitable for them. With fronds that may be but a single cell thick they demand very high humidity of the type that only dense bush or a dedicated fernhouse can provide. They are, however, attractive and unusual plants. For the more casual gardener, a terrarium is the best way to grow filmy ferns.

HYPOLEPSIS

Although seldom cultivated, these ferns are graceful and easy to grow. They are hardy and reach to about 15 cm high but may spread up to 2 m across. The principal difficulty is that it is seldom sold in nurseries or garden centres. *H. tenuifolia*, which is not a native, is more commonly available than the native *H. distans*.

LASTREOPSIS

Although spread throughout much of New Zealand this genus has not been widely cultivated. They grow to about 40 cm x 1 m and are hardy to at least -5°C. Most species establish easily.

LEPTOPTERIS

These ferns, the best known of which is the Prince of Wales feather (*L. superba*), are impressive plants but difficult to grow. The fronds are up to 1 m long but only 15 cm wide. They are reasonably hardy, but like the filmy ferns they demand constant high humidity. They thrive in the bush of the South Island's West Coast but struggle in gardens. A fernhouse is the only option for most gardeners.

LOXSOMA

The common species (*L. cunninghamii*) grows to about 50 cm x 1 m and has very soft velvety fronds. Hard to come by, frost-tender and somewhat difficult to establish, it is a must for the serious collector.

MARATTIA

The para or king fern (*M. salicina*) grows to over 2 m high with a spread of up to 5 m. It is only for large gardens in relatively frost-free areas. Not difficult to cultivate, it has a strong root system and can be difficult to find room for.

NEPHROLEPIS

The Boston fern (*N. exalata*) sold in every garden centre throughout the country is the most common *Nephrolepis* in cultivation. The native (Kermadec Islands) *N. cordifolia* is very similar but is slightly larger and may reach 80 cm x 1 m. It requires a near frost-free climate to do well outside but is easily grown indoors.

OSMUNDA

The large deciduous royal fern (*O. regalis*) is a very hardy Northern Hemisphere fern. It is commonly grown in large gardens next to ponds or streams and thrives in near bog-like conditions. It is not really suitable for small gardens due to its large size (1.8 m x 2 m), rapid growth and heavy roots.

PELLAEA

The roundleaf or buttonleaf fern (*P. rotundifolia*) is a small spreading fern commonly sold as a houseplant but it is really better suited to a lightly shaded and rather dry rockery. It is hardy to about -5°C and grows to 30 cm x 50 cm, but tends to become rather untidy and is often short-lived.

PHYMATOSORUS

This is one of the most common native ferns, yet many gardeners find it hard to believe that the most common species (*P. diversifolius*) is in fact a fern. Its tough leathery leaf-like fronds and spreading or climbing epiphytic habit seem quite unfern-like. Nevertheless, it is a fern and a very easily cultivated and hardy one at that. Unfortunately the unusual growth habit of these ferns makes them rather difficult to fit into most gardens.

PLATYCERIUM

The subtropical epiphytic stag's horn fern (*P. bifucatum*) belongs to a genus from Australia and some of the Pacific islands. This is the hardiest species of the genus (-2°C) and has fronds up to 1 m long. It is most commonly seen grown on a slab of tree fern trunk. In recent years, this fern seems to have lost its novelty value and is now seldom grown. Its unusual form and habit do, however, add an extra dimension to a fern collection.

POLYPODIUM

The hare's foot fern (*P. aureum*) from Central America is most commonly seen as a houseplant. It has fronds up to 1 m long, and spreading rhizomes. It is hardy to about -2°C. Very similar to *Davallia* but larger growing.

POLYSTICHUM

The shield ferns are very common native plants. Sometimes seen in gardens, they are very hardy and easy to cultivate, though the fronds tend to be a little too leathery and bristly to create a luxuriant effect. *P. vestitum* will often develop a short trunk, up to 60 cm high, so that it effectively becomes a miniature tree fern.

PTERIS

The brake ferns are extremely easy to cultivate, although many gardeners feel that they are too coarse for garden use. The commonly sold *Pteris cretica* grows to about 80 cm x 1 m and is frost-tender. It is not a native but will grow outside in mild areas.

TRICHOMANES

Kidney ferns need cool moist shade and high humidity. They seldom exceed a few centimetres high and are hardy provided they are grown under trees. While not as demanding as filmy ferns or *Leptopteris*, they are, nevertheless, most at home in a fernhouse or terrarium.

From top to bottom:
Cyathea dealbata;
Phymatosorus diversifolius;
Polystichum vestitum var.
richardii;
Dicksonia squarrosa.

93

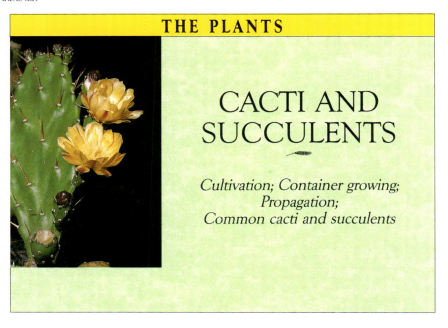

THE PLANTS

CACTI AND SUCCULENTS

*Cultivation; Container growing;
Propagation;
Common cacti and succulents*

Top: The flowers of cactus
Opuntia.
Above: *Agave attenuata* makes a
dramatic statement with its
flower spikes.

ONE LOOK AT A spine-encrusted cactus or a fleshy-leafed succulent tells you that these plants are tough survivors. No other group of plants is better suited to withstand the rigours of an arid environment. Succulent stems conserve and store moisture and the thorns of the cacti are an effective protection against browsing wildlife.

Cacti differ from succulents in several ways. The most obvious is that cacti do not have leaves whereas all succulents do. Cacti have spines that are generally arranged in geometric patterns whereas if succulents have any spines they are usually restricted to the leaf tips.

Cacti and succulents are undemanding plants that are more than capable of surviving neglect and when cared for they can be spectacular. Many cacti and succulents have large brightly coloured flowers; others have unusual foliage or a distinctive growth habit. Often newcomers to cacti and succulents think they all look the same but closer inspection reveals an enormous diversity of shapes, sizes, textures and colours.

Because of their very unusual and bold silhouettes and their immediate association with an arid environment, large cacti and succulents are often used as theme-setting plants in landscape designs. They blend extremely well with stark architecture, offering just enough of a natural look to soften harsh lines without totally disguising the building.

However you use them, cacti and succulents are very distinctive plants that usually provoke a 'love/hate' response and you can be sure that their use in your garden will generate some interesting reactions.

CULTIVATION

Many cacti and succulents come from high altitudes in southern Africa or the Andes, or from arid areas with very cold nights, consequently they can often endure quite hard frosts. What they cannot tolerate, however, is being cold and wet. Hardy cacti and succulents are far more likely to rot from excess moisture than die from the cold.

Cacti and succulents need regular water in summer and although they will grow in poor soil, they also appreciate light feeding with liquid fertilisers or very small doses of animal manures or chemical fertilisers. Do not water between early April and mid September unless conditions are extremely dry.

Cacti and succulents usually demand full sun and very few will tolerate prolonged periods in the shade without becoming soft and leggy. They also demand good ventilation because long periods of high humidity or moisture on the foliage or stems can lead to rotting. This may not be fatal but often causes patches of callus tissue to form when the damaged tissue dries.

Most gardens have an area that seldom sees any rain: a place that is protected from the prevailing wind and usually covered by overhanging eaves. This is the ideal site for a cactus and succulent garden. You could also plant them in raised beds filled with special coarse free-draining soil or create a dry rockery.

Cacti and succulents are very tolerant of extremes and provided you choose plants that are hardy enough for your climate and position them in full sun with free-draining soil you shouldn't have many problems.

CONTAINER GROWING

Each year thousands of cacti and succulents are sold as houseplants. They are an excellent choice because they are the plants best able to tolerate the sunny windowsills and low humidity found in so many houses. They will also survive for long periods even if you forget to water them and repotting is usually only necessary every two years. This should, however, not be taken as an excuse to neglect the plants, as they will do far better if given regular water in summer with an occasional dilute liquid fertiliser and the appropriate soil. Cacti and succulents are also excellent outdoor container plants. They thrive on hot patios and are an ideal choice for conservatories that get so hot in summer that little else will grow.

The most important part of container growing is getting the soil right. The potting mix should be porous and free-draining; many garden centres sell special cactus mix or you can make your own using ordinary potting mix as a base. To each part of potting mix by volume add one part of fine pumice and a third of a part of fine shingle chips. This will open up the mix and make it very free draining. You can vary this mix by using coarse bark chips or river sand and get very similar results. Once the plant is potted, top off the pot with a layer

of shingle chips. This will keep the rot-prone crown dry.

PROPAGATION

Cacti and succulents can be grown from seed but division and offsets are the most common propagation methods. Most cacti will bud and produce small offsets that can be removed and grown on as new plants. Succulents often produce offsets or they can be broken up into individual rosettes. Many succulents will also form natural layers as they grow and these can be lifted, divided and grown on. Some succulents can also be grown from leaf cuttings.

Top: A variegated cultivar of *Yucca gloriosa*.
Above: The winter buds of *Sedum spectabile*.

COMMON CACTI AND SUCCULENTS

The following plants can be grown outdoors in many parts of the country, particularly in drier eastern coastal areas from Gisborne to Christchurch and from Hamilton north. Most are commonly available from nurseries or specialist suppliers.

AEONIUM

This is a genus of rosette-forming succulents from the Mediterranean area and North Africa. Old plants often develop multiple trunks topped with several rosettes and may grow to over 1.2 m high depending on the species. The small starry yellow flowers are carried in large heads and many coloured-foliage and weirdly shaped forms are available. Most are hardy to at least -3°C.

AGAVE

A genus of succulents primarily from the southwestern United States and Mexico. They form large rosettes of broad strappy leaves that are often edged with sharp spines. The most impressive species is the century plant (*A. americana*), which when mature produces an enormous flower spike that may reach 10 m high. The rosette dies after the effort of flowering but its offsets continue to grow. The variegated species *A. victoriae-reginae* is very attractive when grown in large containers. Most species are hardy to at least -3°C. Some will withstand -8°C or lower.

ALOE

An African genus of rosette-forming plants with thickened fleshy leaves that are filled with a jelly-like pulp. The medicine plant (*A. barbadensis*, syn. *A. vera*) is the best-known member of the genus as the extract from its leaves is used in many medicines and cosmetics. The jelly is very soothing if applied to cuts and burns and appears to have natural antiseptic properties. Other species are more commonly grown as ornamentals and most have vivid orange-red flowers on multi-headed spikes that are usually about 60 cm high. Very few aloes tolerate temperatures much below -3°C with any regularity.

BEAUCARNEA

The pony tail or bottle palm (*B. recurvata*) from the southwestern United States and Mexico is a very distinctive succulent with a head of grassy leaves at the top of a round bulbous stem. The stem is a moisture reservoir that expands and contracts as its reserves vary. With great age the plant may grow to 2 m high with a base over 1 m in diameter but it is usually seen as a small to medium-sized pot plant. It needs water only when the base shows signs of starting to shrivel. This plant looks best on a pedestal, which allows its grassy foliage to droop to maximum effect. Hardy to -5°C once well established.

CARPOBROTUS

This African genus includes *C. edulis*, which is the most common ice plant found in coastal regions. It is a wide-spreading ground cover with fleshy succulent leaves and pink, yellow or white daisy-like flowers up to 75 mm across. It even grows well in pure sand and is hardy to about -5°C.

CEPHALOCEREUS

The old man cactus (*C. senilis*) from Mexico is so named because it is covered in fine white hair. Mature plants have deep pink flowers in spring. It is popular as a novelty houseplant and is also able to be grown outdoors where temperatures do not regularly drop below -3°C. Extremely old plants in the wild are up to 10 m high but unlikely to exceed 1.5 m high under New Zealand conditions.

CEROPEGIA

The string of hearts (*C. woodii*) is the best-known member of this southern African genus and is usually grown as a trailing or semi-climbing houseplant. Several other species more suited to outdoor or conservatory cultivation are available but relatively rarely grown. They have succulent foliage and/or stems and very unusual flowers that are designed to trap visiting insects until pollination is effected. All the species are tender and withstand little, if any, frost. They are semi-climbers that rarely exceed 1.8 m high x 1 m wide.

CRASSULA

This widespread genus of succulents includes many different forms from ground covers to large bushes. They have highly variable foliage but most species have clusters of tiny white, cream or pink flowers. The larger bushy species, such as *C. portulacea* (syn. *C. argentea*), which may be over 1 m high, are often grown as houseplants or in succulent gardens but the small species, such as *C. schmidtii*, are most at home growing in crevices and trailing over rocks. Grow in light well-drained soil in full sun. Most species are hardy to at least -3°C.

DROSANTHEMUM

This southern African genus of succulent trailing perennials with pink or purple daisy-like flowers is one of several genera known as ice plants. It is easily grown in any sunny well-drained position and often self-sows. It is a superb ground or bank cover in coastal areas and may cover many square metres. Hardy to about -5°C.

ECHEVERIA

This genus of rosette-forming succulents from Central and South America is available in a wide range of foliage colours and sizes. All have similar small yellow, orange or red flowers on wiry spikes that emerge from the side of the rosette. With great age most species can form large clumps. They are easily grown in any light well-drained soil and are usually hardy to about -5°C,

although some species are frost-tender.

ECHINOCACTUS

The infamous mother-in-law's chair (*E. grusonii*) from Mexico is a fearsome thing to have to handle. It is a globose cactus with a flat top and the whole plant is covered with very sharp, strongly built, yellowish spines but they are particularly densely packed on the upper surface. Large specimens are up to 1.2 m high x 80 cm diameter. It has small yellow flowers and is hardy to about -5°C once established but rots quickly in wet soil.

ECHINOPSIS

The Easter lily cacti from South America are globose to cylindrical plants that seldom exceed 20 cm high but may form small clumps. They have very large flowers for the size of the plant – up to 20 cm long. Species and cultivars with flowers in all shades of white, yellow, pink and red are available. They are hardy to about -3°C.

EPIPHYLLUM

Strictly a genus of epiphytic trailing or semi-climbing cacti from South America, but the name is also used to refer to crosses between this genus and related genera, such as *Aporocactus* and *Selenicereus*. The plants have flattened fleshy stems with very small soft spines in tufts and impressive flowers that are up to 20 cm wide and long. They are available in a wide colour range but red is by far the most common. Hardy to about -3°C but best with shelter. If growing in pots use a very coarse free-draining potting mix or an orchid mix.

EUPHORBIA

The best-known succulent, euphorbia is the crown of thorns (*E. milii*). It has strong succulent stems with vicious thorns and in periods of drought the plant resembles a cactus, but with moisture it sprouts small bright green leaves. The pairs of flat flower bracts may appear at any time and are usually bright red although other colours are occasionally

available. The plant may grow to 1.2 m high and can be used as a low climber. It is only hardy to very light and infrequent frosts. Other species display a range of strange growth habits, such as extremely stiff flattened stems or swollen roots that protrude above the ground.

FEROCACTUS

A southwestern United States and Mexican genus of globular to cylindrical cacti with very tough curved spines often with barbed tips. Should you feel so inclined the fleshy pulp of this genera is edible. The flowers, which are yellow with red centres, appear in spring. Most species rarely exceed 60 cm high and wide under New Zealand conditions. They are among the hardiest cacti: one species, *F. wislizenii*, will withstand -15°C or slightly lower.

GASTERIA

These clump-forming succulents from South Africa have broad fleshy leaves that are often attractively marked or coloured. One species, *G. verrucosa*, has leaves with prominent white warts, often in bands. The small yellow and red flowers are carried at the tip of wiry stems and appear in spring. They are hardy to about -5°C once established but must be kept dry in winter. *Haworthia* is a similar genus.

KALANCHOE

A genus of African succulents with enormously variable growth forms. Some are shrubby, others are ground covers. Some have small smooth leaves, others have large felted leaves. Most have brightly coloured flowers but the type of bloom varies. *K. blossfeldiana* is shrubby and has clusters of tiny flowers in very intense shades of pink, yellow and orange. *K. manginii*, which is usually grown in hanging baskets, has tubular orange flowers. Some species, such as *K. pinnata*, develop small plantlets along the edges of their leaves. Most kalanchoes will only tolerate very light frosts if any.

LITHOPS

The common name living

stones is an accurate description of these fascinating succulents from southern Africa. Each segment looks just like a small, rounded, split stone. These plants grow very slowly but may eventually form a small clump about 20 cm across. They occasionally produce a large yellow or white daisy-like flower from the fissure that runs across each 'stone'. Living stones are seldom grown outdoors, not because they are very tender, but because they are easily lost or covered with soil. They also rot very quickly if wet and should be watered only when absolutely necessary.

LOBIVIA

A genus of globose cacti from South America (the name is an anagram of Bolivia). They are mainly small plants that rarely exceed 15 cm high. Most species have brightly coloured flowers that can be nearly as large as the plant. Lobivias are generally only hardy to about -2°C. x *Lobiviopsis* is a hybrid between *Lobivia* and *Echinopsis*. It is stronger growing than *Lobivia* and produces its flowers in clusters.

MAMMILLARIA

These small globular or squat cylindrical cacti from South America are probably the most widely grown cacti. Many species are grown and they vary considerably in appearance although all are quite small (under 25 cm x 25 cm) and have their spine-bearing tubercles arranged in a spiral pattern. They usually produce offsets freely and quickly develop into small clumps. The small flowers vary in colour with the species and are available in cream, pale yellow, pink, orange and red. Many mammillarias are hardy to -5°C.

OPUNTIA

The prickly pear cacti from the United States and Mexico are instantly recognisable. They have an upright growth habit and are made up of flattened pads dotted with tufts of short spines. Large specimens can be as much as 4 m high. The flowers of the

edible fruited species, *O. ficus-indica*, are bright yellow and the fruit is yellow or red. This species is hardy to about -5°C once established and is easily grown outdoors in most areas. It was once a serious weed in the desert areas of Australia but is far more restrained in our climate.

PORTULACARIA

An African succulent often known as elephant's food, *P. afra* is a multi-branched bush with fleshy rounded leaves. It seldom gets above 1.5 m high under New Zealand conditions. It rarely produces its tiny pink flowers and is grown mainly for its form and foliage, variegated forms of which are available. It is very popular for bonsai. This species will not tolerate frost.

REBUTIA

A South American genus of small globose cacti that produce many offsets and develop into clumps. The prominent spine-bearing tubercles are arranged in a distinctive spiral pattern and the colourful flowers are often as large as the plant. The flowers are usually bright red or orange and appear intermittently. They are not widely grown outdoors but are hardy to at least -2°C.

SANSEVIERIA

Mother-in-law's tongue (*S. trifasciata*) is an African succulent with stiffly erect, spear-like, fleshy leaves that are up to 1.2 m long. The variegated forms are widely grown and frequently used in hotels and offices because they are capable of tolerating low humidity and reasonably long periods of low light levels. Many forms in a wide range of sizes and foliage patterns are available. *Sansevieria* is only hardy to about -2°C but where it can be grown outdoors it does well.

SCHLUMBERGERA

A South American genus of epiphytic cacti with flattened multi-jointed stems up to 50 cm long. They are grown mainly for the large flowers, which are usually deep pink, hose-in-hose and pendulous. Long nights are needed to initiate flowering, so

do not keep them in rooms where the lights are likely to be on for long periods at night in winter. They are natural trailers that are most often grown in hanging baskets. *Aporocactus* and *Rhipsalidopsis* have similar habits with cylindrical rather than flattened stems and red flowers.

SEDUM

This is a large and widespread genus of succulents and subshrubs, many of which are ground covers. The smaller species are usually mat or rosette forming and often have very fleshy rounded leaves, which gives them the common name of jelly beans. The larger species usually have similar foliage and their stems often form short trunks. The flowers, which appear in late summer or autumn, are most commonly white, pink or pinkish red. The individual flowers are tiny but are massed in heads that can be showy. One common species, the donkey's tail (*S. morganianum*) is a trailer with deep pink flowers. It is often grown in hanging baskets. Most sedums are hardy to about -5°C and grow well outdoors provided they are kept very dry over winter.

SEMPERVIVUM

Most species of this genus of rosette-forming succulents from Europe look similar to *Echeveria* but are considerably tougher and more adaptable. The foliage varies from tiny and almost triangular in *S. arachnoideum* to quite large and strappy in some forms of *S. tectorum*. Some species have leaf hairs that develop into a fine webbing over the foliage. The small flowers, which are usually cream or pink, are carried in heads on stocky stems and usually appear in late summer. Some species are commonly known as houseleeks because they were grown on the soil-covered roofs of alpine houses. Most species are very hardy (to at least -15°C) and can be grown throughout the country.

SENECIO

An enormously variable and widespread genus that includes

a few succulent species. The most common of these is *S. mandraliscae* (*Kleinia mandraliscae*), which is a wide-spreading ground cover with cylindrical blue-grey leaves. *S. serpens* is a similar but more upright species. Both are hardy to about -3°C. String of pearls (*S. rowleyanus*) has bead-like leaves on pendulous stems. German ivy (*S. mikanioides*) is a small climber with succulent ivy-like leaves that is often grown as a houseplant. Variegated German ivy is actually a different species, *S. macroglossus* 'Variegatus', but is very similar.

STAPELIA

The carrion plants are interesting, but with flowers that in some species smell like rotting meat they are not the ideal houseplants. A genus of about 100 succulent species from southern Africa, they have stout branching stems that are prominently ribbed. There are no distinct leaves, the green stems performing their function. The large star-shaped flowers, which appear irregularly, are reddish brown and creamy pink. The smell is intended to attract flies for pollination. Most species are hardy to about -3°C or slightly lower once established but are usually treated as greenhouse novelties and are seldom grown in gardens.

YUCCA

A genus of rosette or clump-forming near-succulent plants from North America. Although most species are not obviously succulent they are generally included in this group. Many species are grown. Some are ground covers but most develop into bushes or small trunked trees of at least 1.2 m high. The larger specimens resemble, and are related to, the native cabbage tree (*Cordyline australis*). The leaves are strappy and often glaucous and tipped with spines; variegated foliage forms are common. The bell-shaped flowers, which mainly appear in summer and autumn are usually cream and are carried on stems that can be over 1 m high. Most species are hardy to at least -10°C and can be grown outdoors in most areas.

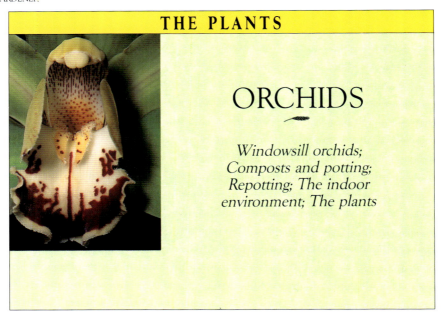

THE PLANTS

ORCHIDS

*Windowsill orchids;
Composts and potting;
Repotting; The indoor
environment; The plants*

Above: *Paphiopedilum insigne*
Top: The centre of a
Cymbidium.

ORCHIDS ARE AN extremely diverse and often spectacular group of plants found growing in a wide variety of situations. Terrestrial species grow in or near the ground, often in bogs or in leaf litter on the forest floor. Epiphytic species grow on trees or shrubs, drawing moisture and nourishment from the air and from humus collected in the angles of branches. In general, most orchids from temperate zones are terrestrial, whereas tropical species tend to be epiphytic.

While we tend to think of orchids as tender glasshouse specimens, there are thousands of species representing plants that can thrive in a wide range of environments. Some are suitable for growing in gardens in both warm and cool climates.

Many would-be growers in New Zealand are fortunate to live in areas where some exotic orchids can be treated as semi-hardy garden plants. An ideal position for many epiphytic orchids is to fasten them onto trees, where they will thrive. Even in those areas of New Zealand that experience frosts, situations will be found where orchids will grow well. Many terrestrial orchids fit into this category. They are often known as cool-growing orchids. Species from the following genera may be worth a try outdoors, especially in mild areas: *Coelgyne, Cymbidium, Dendrobium nobile, Epidendrum* and *Pleione.*

Other orchids prefer cool greenhouse or shadehouse conditions and some require the warmth and high humidity provided by a fully heated greenhouse. The home gardener without access to a heated greenhouse can still enjoy these spectacular plants, however, as many can be grown indoors.

WINDOWSILL ORCHIDS

In general, indoor orchids will thrive best on an east or west-facing windowsill from spring to autumn, but move them to one with a northerly aspect for the duller days of winter.

A narrow windowsill can be widened and if you are able to increase the sill to a minimum depth of about 30–38 cm there are polypropylene gravel trays available from most hardware stores that will conveniently fit in the area. Approximately 2.5 cm of water-retentive aggregate, such as perlite, pumice or vermiculite, should be placed in the bottom of the gravel tray and the pots placed on top. To maintain reasonable humidity this gravel tray should be kept perpetually moist but not waterlogged.

Be selective in the type of orchid you acquire. In the average home maintained at comfortable temperatures, cool-growing orchids are unlikely to flower well. Choose instead the warmth-loving genera that would not flourish in the cool greenhouse and select only those plants with a compact growth habit and a tidy root structure. Suitable genera include *Paphiopedilum, Phalaenopsis, Miltonia* and *Cattleya* – particularly the modern bigeneric hybrids with *Sophronitis* and *Laelia*, which are smaller-growing and freer-flowering plants.

COMPOSTS AND POTTING

However, or wherever, you decide to grow your orchids, you will need to provide the right growing medium (compost) and supply all their nutrient requirements, and as would be expected from such a diverse range of plants, these can vary enormously. Once you have decided on the type of orchids you wish to cultivate, reference to one of the many specialist books on orchids is advisable.

One good general rule is that it is important to use a growing medium that is closest to that which the orchid grows on in nature. For example, cymbidiums grow on branches, so a good medium is bark, in various sizes. Every cymbidium grower will have their own special combination of materials to create the right growing medium, including pine bark, sphagnum moss, pumice, small pieces of ponga fibre, polystyrene balls, etc. But as with cymbidiums, the ideal orchid compost is one which has a high air capacity, a high amount of easily available moisture and the ability to provide nutrients for the plant. Meet these requirements and you have a successful growing medium.

To measure the air capacity, or air-filled pore space, of the compost fill a container of the growing medium with water. Then drain the pot; the water which drains out will equate the volume of air now in the growing medium. This should ideally be not less than 30% of the total volume of the growing medium.

If you use fresh pine bark, be warned that it can contain toxic substances, such as tannin, and so should be stored in a moist heap for 3–6 weeks. Many growers will also add dolomite lime to reduce the acidity. (Note: The ideal pH for cymbidiums is slightly acid, pH 5.5–6.0.)

The growing medium for orchids is relatively inert, that is it does not in itself provide nutrients for the orchid. You will have to do this and there are many proprietary products available designed for both slow-release in the soil and liquid feeding. When and how much to feed will depend on the type of orchid you are growing and the time of year.

REPOTTING

Orchids generally should only be repotted when their roots fill their pot, when the growing medium has broken down, or gone sour, or when the plant's roots are rotting.

First, tidy up the orchid by removing dead leaf bracts, then check that the root system is sound. Live roots will be firm and a whitish colour, whereas dead roots are black and soft

Orchids are not just for greenhouses.

and spongy to the touch. If the plant is in good condition select a pot large enough to allow for two year's growth. The pot can be either clay or plastic but there must be ample drainage holes. Place a small amount of compost into the base of the pot and then place the plant in position and pour compost around the root ball. A few taps on the bench will ensure that the compost is packed correctly.

Apply firm finger pressure down the sides of the pot, then refill to within 2 cm of the top. If the compost is damp, no further water should be given until new growth is showing. Add any slow-release fertiliser at this stage.

THE INDOOR ENVIRONMENT

As with all plants grown in greenhouses, ventilation is important for orchids, even those that demand a very humid atmosphere. Regularly damp down the greenhouse right through the summer, especially on very hot days, and if the humidity falls too much when the ventilators are opened, use extra water around and over the plants.

In such an environment there will be no need to close the vents during much of the summer, both day or night, unless the weather turns really cool. During the winter, open the vents as often as possible without causing a drastic drop in temperature. Even in very cold weather a short period with the vents open, say for 30 minutes, will be sufficient to freshen the air inside the greenhouse and prevent a stagnant atmosphere, which is detrimental to all orchids.

Top: *Vanda* x *rothschildiana*
Above: *Cymbidium* cultivar

THE PLANTS

THERE ARE THOUSANDS OF species of orchids (some 25,000 is one estimate), plus thousands of hybrids created by plant breeders. These species are grouped into genera. The following genera have been selected as those that will provide an easy introduction for those new to growing orchids.

Cymbidium 'Crackerjack Rembrandt'

BRASSIA

The spider orchids flower from November to late March. Their cultivation is similar to *Cattleya* (below) and they grow well in slatted wooden baskets. The sweetly fragrant flowers are pale yellow-green with brownish-red, brown or blackish-brown markings.

CATTLEYA

The blooms of cattleyas are among the largest of the cultivated orchids. They are strong, robust plants and produce thick roots that can grow to extensive lengths. There are many hybrids with related genera, such as *Sophronitis* and *Laelia*. They flower in spring or autumn. Most are fragrant and the colour ranges from pristine white through delicate pinks, purple and yellow to vibrant reds, oranges and bronze. A warm greenhouse is best, but they will succeed in a warm sunny room. They require plenty of light, although not strong sunlight, and most have a resting period during winter. Divide plants after flowering.

COELOGYNE

Some species are warm growers, but others require cool summers, a rather dry winter, and will endure very low winter temperatures. Flower spikes appear with the new growth. The flowers are white to yellowish-green with yellow or darker markings. Most coelogynes grow well in wooden slatted baskets in an open well-drained mixture.

CYMBIDIUM

Cymbidiums are usually the first choice of orchid for beginners as they are easily grown and very rewarding. The modern hybrids are fairly large plants and can be grown in both cool and warm climates. They flower from July to November. Remove flower spikes after they have been open for about 6 weeks to allow the plant to produce new growth for the following year's flowering. Ideally they should have a night temperature of around 10°C, but they survive light frosts with some damage. Where autumn and winter night temperatures are above 15°C they are unlikely to flower. Cool night temperatures during summer are also important for flowering. An average daytime temperature in winter of around 15-18°C is adequate, but in summer keep the temperature below 28°C. Cymbidiums can be propagated by division when repotted. Always leave several bulbs and new growths to each division. Allow the medium to become partially dry before watering thoroughly and during winter very little water is needed. Feed cymbidiums with a liquid fertiliser every second watering when new growth starts after flowering, but as the leaves mature change to a fertiliser lower in nitrogen to ensure a good-quality flower spike is produced.

DENDROBIUM

The dendrobium has always been held in high esteem by orchid lovers. In dendrobiums the pseudobulbs have become elongated into canes up to 1 m or more long that often resemble bamboo, hence the popular name of bamboo orchids. Dendrobiums are epiphytic and many are deciduous, shedding their leaves after one season's growth and remaining dormant over winter. With the spring rains they cover themselves with flowers in a spectacular display. The flower colours are white (often suffused with pink or mauve), golden-yellow and shades of pink, cream and brown. Many have a delicate fragrance.

Dendrobiums are of two main types: the soft-caned or nobile type and the hard-caned or phalaenopsis type. The former require cooler conditions whereas the phalaenopsis type require more heat to do well. Both thrive on plenty of light and humidity.

Dendrobiums should be kept rather dry over winter and protected from frosts. From spring onwards they should be watered regularly and during summer aim to keep the compost continually moist. Every third or fourth watering add a liquid fertiliser.

A slight yellowing of the foliage indicates the cessation of growth for the season and when the terminal leaf can be seen at the top of the completed cane (in about April), gradually reduce the watering and feeding to nil over 4-5 weeks. It is important for the following season's flowering to expose the canes to brighter light over winter.

In summer the cool-growing types require a minimum night temperature of 12°C and up to 25°C during the day. The warmer-growing types should, if possible, be kept nearer to 18°C at night and with higher day temperatures – over 30°C for short periods will do them no harm. In winter a night temperature of 10°C will be fine for the cool-growing types with a daytime rise to about 16°C. The warmer-growing types require a night temperature of about 16°C with a correspondingly higher day temperature over winter. The higher the temperature, the higher the humidity should be.

Repotting is done in spring, ideally when the new growth is just visible at the base of the leading cane and before new roots appear. If the plant is flowering at the same time, delay repotting until immediately after flowering. Dendrobiums like to be potted in as small a pot as possible. They grow well attached to ponga slabs and hanging from the roof of the greenhouse. In the warmer parts of New Zealand many dendrobiums can be grown on tree trunks in this manner. Offshoots can be removed from the canes and grown on when they are about 3 cm long and have one completed bulb. The older leafless canes can be cut into pieces about 5 cm long, making the cuts between the nodes, and potted on a level with the compost. Within a few weeks new growth will appear, which can be potted singly when large enough.

A few desirable and easily grown species are *D. chrysotoxum*, *D. cunninghamii*, *D. densiflorum*, *D. infundibulum*, *D. kingianum*, *D. nobile*, *D. speciosum* and *D. wardianum*.

EPIDENDRUM

These very variable orchids are widely grown, with *E. radicans* the most popular species in New Zealand. This plant produces long reed-like stems up to 1 m high. In warmer regions it is popular as an outdoor tub plant but it is easily grown in the ground in a sunny frost-free situation. It produces dozens of 3 cm wide flowers that are typically orange-red with a distinctive 'cross' made from the column and lip, giving it its common name of the crucifix orchid. If happy, it will flower all year round.

HAEMARIA

Haemarias belong to a group of terrestrial orchids called the jewel orchids. They are equally attractive as foliage or flowering plants. The leaves are deep red underneath and may have pronounced red or yellow veins. The short brittle stems are usually red and may be erect or procumbent, the latter rooting readily at the nodes. A very hairy flower spike bears up to 12 white flowers with yellow anther caps. A good growing medium is a mixture of peat, perlite or pumice, and sandy soil with some compost added.

LAELIA

The laelias are closely related to the cattleyas and the two genera have been hybridised. Their cultivation is the same as for *Cattleya. L. purpurata* is the national flower of Brazil and is one of the easiest to grow. It grows 45 cm high and produces a spike of two to six flowers, each 13-18 cm in diameter. The flower colour is variable, ranging from white to purple with a frilled deep purple lip.

MILTONIA

These very beautiful flowering plants are commonly called pansy orchids. The majority have sweetly scented flowers that are long-lasting as a cut flower. They grow well in the warmest part of the greenhouse with plenty of humidity in summer. The flower spikes are produced in February and March with up to nine flowers on each spike. Quite often flowers will be produced at different times of the year.

ODONTOGLOSSUM

Odontoglossums are grown extensively as cut flowers. They are compact plants, usually requiring only a 10-12 cm pot. Most do not have a dormant period. The flowering season varies, but one or two spikes per season can be expected. A well grown plant will flower every 9 months. The flowers are up to 10 cm across with 10 or more on each spike. The flowers will last for six to eight weeks. A

suitable potting mixture is 60% pine bark, 30% sphagnum moss and 10% charcoal. All species are high-altitude plants and many endure severe frosts in their natural habitats. They love cool conditions, good light and excellent ventilation. During hot summer weather regular damping down of the floors and benches and a light overhead watering in the early morning is advisable to keep the humidity high. Although odontoglossums grow better in a cool greenhouse, some of the newer hybrids are very good houseplants, being more heat tolerant and adaptable.

PAPHIOPEDILUM

The slipper orchids are evergreen and mostly terrestrial in habit. The modern hybrids produce a single flower up to 15 cm across that lasts for up to 10 weeks. Most colours, with the exception of blue, are represented.
They require low light levels, which is one reason why they are so popular as indoor plants. The green-leaved types are cool-growing, whereas those with mottled leaves need a little warmth. They love humidity (about 60-70%), so damp down the benches and greenhouse paths in the early morning. Keep the potting mixture moist at all times, as they lack pseudobulbs and will suffer if the mix dries out. The frequency and amount of watering will vary but twice a week should be adequate.
In hot weather, misting the leaves several times a day will keep the plants in good condition. Careful watering in winter is essential. Always water in the early morning to allow leaves to dry before nightfall and make sure water does not lie in the centre of growths and thereby damage the flower buds. Feed regularly with a liquid fertiliser, starting in spring and increasing in summer to every second watering and easing off as autumn approaches to once a month during winter.
They do not like being pot-bound so repot them at least once a year after flowering. The plants can be carefully divided during repotting by gently prising them apart by hand.

Laeliocattleya 'Little Susan' x 'Sylvia Fry'

PHALAENOPSIS

The moth orchids are evergreen warm-growing orchids. The thick broad leaves are often attractively mottled in silver or grey. Their roots are also attractive, being flattened, silver-grey and extensive. Often these roots grow outside their pots and will adhere strongly to anything they touch, even glass. They love the heat and the warmer it is, the better they grow. They also like plenty of shade. They should be watered all year round, keeping the compost just evenly moist. Two or three flower spikes are produced each year; there is no strict flowering season. Often new flower buds will form on flowering stems that have finished flowering. The flowers are mainly in shades of white, pink and yellow and often striped or spotted in various shades.

PLEIONE

The pleiones are easily grown terrestrial orchids. The Himalayan species are better suited to an alpine house, but the others do well in a cool part of a greenhouse. In many areas of New Zealand they grow well outdoors. The flowers are mammoth for the size of the plant; some bear vivid purple blooms 10 cm across. They should be overwintered in a cool dry place and repotted in August. Keep them well-watered during the summer. Flower colours range from pure white to mauves, pinks and darkest purples.

VANDA

Vandas are evergreen epiphytic orchids that can attain heights of 2 m, but the average height is 1.2 m. Under ideal conditions they may bloom two or three times a year. Most vandas bloom in the winter, although some species come into flower in late summer or early autumn. A healthy plant can produce as many as three or four flower spikes.
Most should be grown in a warm greenhouse, doing best with a day temperature of 26°C. They can survive lower day temperatures if necessary but not for long periods. Night temperatures of around 15°C are required. Bright light or full sun is essential. The minimum humidity for them to grow well is about 50%.
Vandas resent being disturbed so repot them only when absolutely necessary. This is best done in spring as new growth is starting.
Vandas produce offshoots at various times of the year, usually in late autumn. When 5-7 cm long they can be cut from the parent plant and grown on, dusting the cut surfaces with charcoal. Older plants that are over 1 m high and becoming too large may be pruned by cutting off the top 30-40 cm of the parent plant. Dust both cut surfaces with charcoal and plant the cuttings.
Vandas need plenty of moisture all year, but always allow the mix to dry out before watering. Feed them every 14-18 days in spring and summer.

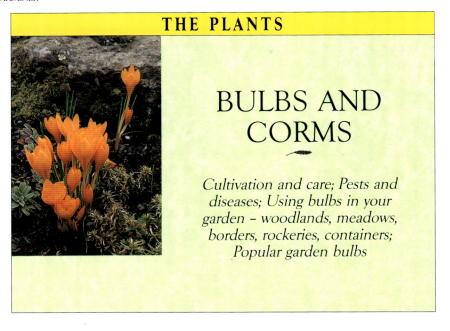

BULBS AND CORMS

Cultivation and care; Pests and diseases; Using bulbs in your garden – woodlands, meadows, borders, rockeries, containers; Popular garden bulbs

Above: *Crocus gargarious*
Below: Assorted bulbs and corms: *Anemone* (front left), *Gladiolus* (back left), *Narcissus* (back right) and *Lachenalia* (front right).

A HIGHLY VARIED GROUP of plants have evolved the ability to survive harsh climatic conditions by developing the food storage organs we call bulbs and corms. Their generally undemanding and versatile nature combined with the beauty of their flowers have made them indispensable in gardens.

To most of us, bulbs mean spring flowers. We often imagine large drifts of daffodils in park-like woodlands or formal beds of boldly coloured tulips. But there is much more to bulbs than the spring scene, glorious though it is. By planting a wide selection of bulbs you can have flowers throughout the year; a cheerful early spring display followed by the brilliant blue of irises, the vivid colours of gladioli in summer, and amaryllids and colchicums in the autumn. In mild areas, lachenalias will flower in winter and *Ipheion* and snowflakes are in bloom well before spring in most parts of the country.

Because they are dormant for much of the year, bulbs tend to have an element of surprise that is lacking in shrubs and perennials. The seemingly sudden appearance of daffodils, snowdrops and bluebells in spring is somehow more exciting than the flowering of trees and shrubs. Likewise, it is always a thrill to find *Amaryllis, Colchicum, Nerine* and *Schizostylis* bursting forth in autumn when all other plants are signalling the onset of winter.

Although they perform the same functions, bulbs and corms are anatomically quite distinct. True bulbs contain a complete miniature plant that remains dormant until favourable conditions return, whereas corms are simply modified stems. One means of distinguishing them is that the foliage and roots of bulbs arise from the basal plate, a flattened area at the base of the bulb; in corms, the foliage arises from growth eyes visible on the upper surface of the corm.

CULTIVATION AND CARE

Bulbs, perhaps more than any other group of temperate garden plants, will thrive with very little attention. However, such easy-care plants are likely to be neglected; just a little care and attention will ensure that your bulbs will continue to produce and look good for many years. Getting the best from your bulbs requires only that you prepare the soil correctly before you plant them, give them an occasional feed and deal with pests and diseases promptly.

Preparation of the soil is vital. As few bulbs will tolerate very wet conditions for prolonged periods, providing good drainage is usually the prime consideration. The addition of stone chips, coarse bark, pumice or perlite to the soil is the easiest means of improving drainage. A layer of such material beneath the bulbs will discourage rotting and allow their roots to spread quickly into the surrounding soil.

To avoid the risk of bulbs rotting while dormant, many can be lifted, dried off and stored in a cool dry place. However, amaryllids should be left in the ground as lifting can affect flowering for several years. Fleshy and scaly bulbs, such as lilies, fritillaries and callas, will shrivel up if lifted and dried off, so leave them in the ground. The decision to lift bulbs for storage depends upon climate, soil and your experience of local conditions. A good general rule is that unless there is a good reason to lift your bulbs, they usually do better left alone.

Some bulbs, most notably Asiatic lilies, prefer acidic conditions and grow well with rhododendrons and other acid-soil plants. Others, particularly tulips and irises with *I. tingitana* in their parentage, prefer slightly alkaline soils and do best with bone meal or dolomite lime added. Most bulbs, however, will grow well with a soil pH of around 6.5.

In general, bulbs have low nitrogen require-

Irises make a lovely addition to this floral focal point.

ments: phosphorus and potassium are the most important elements for bulbs to flower well. A complete bulb fertiliser is the best choice when feeding, but slow-release and liquid fertilisers that are low in nitrogen are equally suitable. Avoid nitrogen-rich fertilisers or you will get lush foliage with few flowers.

There are some spring-flowering bulbs which require cold winters for flower development, and this is an important consideration for gardeners in mild areas. Tulips are the best-

DIFFERENT TYPES OF BULBS

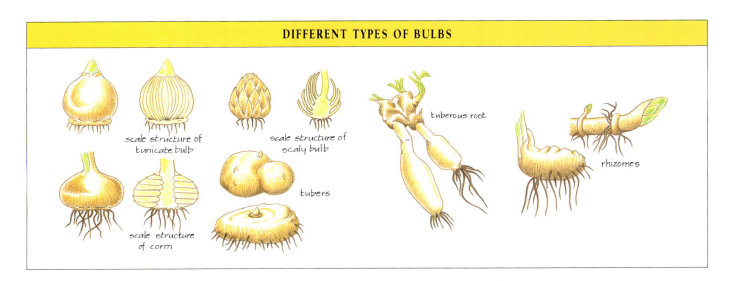

scale structure of tunicate bulb

scale structure of scaly bulb

tuberous root

rhizomes

tubers

scale structure of corm

Erythronium dens-canis, the dog-tooth violet.

Tulips are striking plants for spring flower beds (top), or, as with many bulbs, they are equally happy in a container (above).

known example. However, such bulbs can be grown for many years in mild areas if the bulbs are refrigerated (normally eight weeks is sufficient) prior to planting out each year.

PESTS AND DISEASES

If good drainage is provided, bulbs should not be greatly troubled by diseases other than viruses, which are incurable and often show up as yellow-flecked foliage or distorted flowers. Some viruses are relatively benign, but most gradually weaken the plant and may spread to healthy plants, so infected plants should be discarded. Most bulbs require dry conditions during dormancy and perfect drainage during the growing season: if they become too wet they soon rot. Bulbs that are forced into flower out of season may also rot if kept too wet.

However, if you restrict yourself to growing hardy bulbs outdoors, few diseases are likely to cause problems. The most troublesome pest is the narcissus bulb fly. The larvae burrow into the bulbs of daffodils and related plants and feed on the flesh. Bulbs will often continue to grow and flower despite fly damage, but they are usually stunted and distorted. Careful inspection and soaking in an insecticide solution before planting are the best ways to avoid this problem. Predator control offers the best prospect for organic control of narcissus bulb fly, and pyrethrum insecticides can be used as a drench. However, once they are in the garden, plants that are very prone to bulb fly have to be sprayed with a systemic insecticide during the growing season. Then, after the foliage has died, drench the soil with an insecticide.

Other burrowing pests, such as wireworms and millipedes, also damage bulbs, and slugs, snails and cutworms will feed on the foliage. Aphids are also common pests and frequently occur in large numbers on tulips. The damage caused by chewing and rasping pests can often be tolerated, but sucking insects, such as aphids, may spread viruses and should be kept under control.

USING BULBS IN YOUR GARDEN

There are many ways of using bulbs. They can be planted in large drifts under trees, massed in flower beds, used in a rockery or grown in pots. However you grow them, bulbs are primarily used to provide colour. Granted the leaves of trilliums and dog-tooth violets are attractive, and the spear-like foliage of the gladiolus is very distinctive, but were it not for the flowers it is very unlikely these plants would be widely grown.

The traditional situations for bulbs are formal beds, borders and woodland areas. However, as in all areas of gardening, don't be afraid to experiment. Many will adapt to a number of settings. Dwarf bulbs are superb in rockeries and can be used to create drifts of colour, and some southern African genera, such as *Lachenalia, Haemanthus, Scadoxus* and *Veltheimia*, are at home in succulent gardens. Where they may be marginal outdoors, bulbs can be grown in glasshouses and alpine houses.

BULB BOXES AND RAISED BEDS

Growing bulbs in raised beds eliminates the

risk of poor drainage and makes it easy to lift the bulbs without having to disturb other plants. Such beds are also natural focal points for a garden and are sure to attract attention. This is an advantage when the bulbs are flowering and looking their best, but it does mean that as they die off something has to be done to hide their untidy appearance. This is not so much of a problem with plants like gladioli, the planting of which can be staggered to provide a continuous display, but spring-flowering bulbs tend to finish within a few weeks of one another. The best solution is usually to plant fast-growing annuals, such as petunias, to hide the browning foliage.

Make your boxes at least 30 cm deep and build the soil up in layers. Use coarse gravel chips for the bottom layer to ensure good drainage. Next, add a layer of compost, potting mix or peat equal to about one-third of the box's depth. The bulbs should be planted in this layer; the neck of the bulb level with the top of the compost. Top off the box with 4–15 cm of gritty soil. The exact depth of this layer depends on the bulbs being grown; for example, gladioli should be planted at least 10 cm deep, while amaryllids prefer to be only partly buried.

WOODLANDS

Many bulbs do extremely well under woodland conditions and some may naturalise. Lightly foliaged deciduous trees, such as Japanese maples and dogwoods, are the best cover for woodland bulbs as their leaves provide a regular and natural mulch and only light shade. As long as the soil is not extremely acid or alkaline, establishing woodland bulbs requires little effort other than planting out and occasional light feeding.

This type of garden is often ultimately the most satisfying as it provides a cool natural setting, is appealing to gardeners and wildlife alike, and requires little maintenance once the initial weed problems have been brought under control.

The woodland bulbs, such as bluebells, trilliums and the wood anemones, don't have the flamboyance of hybrid tulips, gladioli and daffodils, rather, their charms are more subtle, and they tend to be longer flowering. Suitable spring-flowering bulbs include bluebells, trilliums, snowdrops, daffodils, erythroniums and grape hyacinths. For summer blooms, *Cardiocrinum* and some lilies are suitable; autumn-flowering bulbs include colchicums and autumn-flowering crocuses.

Nothing surpasses the bright welcoming colours of spring bulbs; always remember to plant plenty for a mass effect.

BULBS IN CONTAINERS

Almost all bulbs are well suited to container cultivation and growing them this way has several advantages.

- It enables tender bulbs to be grown under cover in cooler areas.
- They can be moved out of view after flowering, thus avoiding the problem of hiding them with other plants.
- Container growing is a good way of providing colour for paved areas, such as courtyards, or anywhere else that gardening in the soil is not practical. Small bulbs do well in window boxes.
- Fussier bulbs, such as *Haemanthus*, can be given the individual attention they require when grown in containers.
- The bulbs can be lifted or dried off without disturbing other plants.

By using containers, hardy bulbs can be potted and moved to a sheltered area for forcing into flower. Hyacinths, irises and the shorter varieties of daffodil make good subjects for forc-

Zantedeschia x *hybrida* 'Chromatella' is a striking bulb, both for its flowers and foliage.

Above: Bluebells (*Hyacinthoides*) in a woodland setting. Top right: Fritillaries are unusual and delicate plants. Left is *Fritillaria messanensis* var. *atlantica* and right *F. pontica* var. *substipetala*. Above right: *Crocus biflora*.

ing. Plant them in a bowl in early autumn and bury the container so that the rim is level with or just below the soil surface. Mound the soil over the container so the bulbs are slightly deeper than normal and make sure the container is clearly marked; they're easily lost in a crowded garden.

Lift the container in early winter and gently remove the excess soil to expose the growth shoots, which should be clearly visible. Place the container indoors in a bright position that remains at a steady cool temperature. As the flowers start to develop, the container may be moved to a warmer position, but excessive heat or lack of humidity shortens flower display.

For containers, use a mix similar to that described for boxes: a coarse base, a moisture-retentive middle layer and a free-draining top layer. Add a little bulb fertiliser so that the bulbs get a good start. Plant your bulbs so that each has room to expand as it grows. They need to be massed for greatest impact, but don't pack them in so tightly they have to compete for space, moisture and nutrients. Covering about half the available surface with bulbs is a good rule for most genera.

GARDEN MEADOWS

The typical picture-postcard scene of daffodils, bluebells, crocuses, snowdrops and other spring bulbs growing in grass in the shade of flowering cherry trees is not too hard to recre-

ate. Bulbs generally do well in such a situation and can be left undisturbed for years.

Treat these areas like a meadow, but don't attempt to mow the grass while the foliage of the bulbs is still green. It is important that the leaves are left to die off naturally because bulbs depend on their foliage to produce the reserves for the following season's growth. There should be no more than about 2 cm of green stem remaining when mowed.

Early-flowering bulbs, such as snowdrops and daffodils, generally dry off quickly after flowering, which will allow mowing by mid-December in most areas. Regardless of this, you should choose a fairly short grass, such as a variety of fescue, that won't overwhelm the bulbs or require too much mowing. You may also wish to have some autumn-flowering bulbs, such as *Colchicum* and *Sternbergia*, but you will be unable to mow from about late January onwards. By planting them in large clumps near the base of trees, or in other clearly defined areas, the bulbs should be obvious enough that you can mow around them.

FORMAL PLANTINGS

Only a few bulbs are suitable for massing in formal beds. Tulips are the traditional choice, but daffodils, irises, hyacinths and lilies are also bold enough to make stunning displays. Formal plantings of bulbs are costly, however, as a relatively large number of uniformly sized bulbs is required, and hence they are largely restricted to public displays.

BORDERS

Bulbs are eminently suitable for mixed and herbaceous borders, provided the soil is sufficiently well drained. In mixed borders, bulbs can be used as fillers to provide seasonal colour, however only those that can tolerate watering while dormant should be used, for example some fritillaries and lilies. Various bulbs, such as lilies and crown imperials, are commonly used in herbaceous borders, but they must accept rich soils and summer moisture.

ROCK GARDENS

Rockeries are the traditional setting for dwarf bulbs, but almost any bulb will thrive, as rock gardens are normally designed to provide maximum sunshine, excellent drainage, and are not subject to regular digging or rich soils. Bulbs that are intolerant of watering while dormant may do best in rockeries. Examples of rockery bulbs include *Chionodoxa*, *Rhodohypoxis*, rock tulips, *Erythronium*, *Fritillaria*, *Galanthus*, dwarf *Gladiolus*, *Ipheion*, dwarf *Iris*, dwarf *Narcissus*, *Crocus* and *Colchicum*.

POPULAR GARDEN BULBS

THE FOLLOWING IS A SELECTION of the most widely grown bulbous plants. This includes bulbs, tubers, corms and rhizomes if they are normally bought as a lifted bulb. Those that are bought ready-potted and treated as perennials are in the Annuals and Perennials chapter (see also Index). Each entry includes a brief description and guide to cultivation.

Propagation is also included where a specific method is applicable, but as all bulbs may be grown from seed this is not mentioned unless it is the usual method. All deciduous bulbs can be lifted and divided for propagation purposes when dormant. (See the chapter on propagation.)

A note on planting depth: most bulbs are quite happy planted at a depth equivalent to their height. For example, a 6 cm high hyacinth bulb should be planted around 6 cm deep. Major exceptions to this rule are noted under the individual plants.

ALLIUM

The ornamental onions are hardy and adaptable but lack the flamboyance we tend to associate with the other late spring- and summer-flowering bulbs. The tuft-like flowers are usually white or dusky shades of pink or blue, and are carried atop wiry stems. Size varies, but most form clumps about 20 cm x 20 cm. The foliage is usually fine and grassy, although some, such as *A. bodianum*, have · broad strappy leaves; these are attractive when young but are easily damaged and often become prematurely dry and brown at the tips. Grow in a light well-drained soil in full sun or very light shade. The smaller species, such as *A. carolinianum*, are suitable for rockeries. Some may require alpine house treatment.

AMARYLLIS

The sole species in this genus is the belladonna lily or naked ladies (*A. belladonna*), which is native to South Africa. It flowers in late summer and autumn. The 50-60 cm stems are topped by clusters of trumpet-shaped flowers that usually appear before the foliage develops. White forms and various shades of pink are available. *Amaryllis* should be planted with the neck of the bulb just above the soil surface in a light well-drained soil. Requires a warm dry summer to flower well, so position in full sun. Hardy to -15°C.

BABIANA

Several species of baboon flower are grown, of which *B. stricta* is the most common. In spring it produces 20-30 cm tall spikes of small cup-shaped flowers, which are usually purplish-blue, but white and yellow forms are occasionally available. It will eventually make a dense clump up to 30 cm in diameter. Of the other species, *B. rubrocyanea* is the most distinctive as its flowers have bright red centres. Baboon flowers thrive in a light well-drained soil in full sun.

CALOCHORTUS

This is a genus of some 60 species of bulbs, mostly natives of California. Some have pendulous flowers and are known as globe lilies, but the mariposa tulips have exquisitely marked, upward-facing, bowl-shaped flowers. Most are between 20-45 cm tall and slowly form small clumps. They need ample moisture during the growing and flowering period from spring to early summer, but once flowering is finished they should be dried off. Different species flower in spring or summer, and some are frost-tender, whereas others are extremely hardy. A spot in full sun or very light shade with light well-drained soil is best. Do not water after flowering. Propagate by offsets, but some species also form bulbils on their stems.

CAMASSIA

A very hardy American genus, of which the most common species are *C. cusickii*, *C. leichtlinii* and *C. quamash*. From late winter they form dense clumps up to 60 cm across of narrow, greyish-green, strappy leaves. In spring starry flowers are borne on spikes up to 1.2 m high. They may be white, creamy-yellow, pink or purplish-blue depending on the species. The named forms of *C. quamash* include the best of the blue shades and are often more compact plants. Grow in full sun or light shade in a moist humus-enriched soil. They can be grown in quite damp situations and are often treated almost as bog plants.

CARDIOCRINUM

The 3-4 m high giant Himalayan lily (*C. giganteum*) is one of the most impressive hardy bulbs you can grow, but it is unsuitable for small gardens. It has large, leathery, heart-shaped leaves that appear in spring, and the flower heads of mature plants develop at a startling rate, so that by mid December they are up to 4 m high. The cream trumpet-shaped flowers are strongly scented. The bulb dies after blooming but is replaced by several offsets that reach flowering size after 2-3 years. Well-established clumps will flower annually, but initially raising a few plants from seed (sow at 20°C) will help produce bulbs at various stages of maturity. *Cardiocrinum* should be grown in cool, moist, · woodland conditions in semi-shade and a humus-enriched soil. They are a perfect companion for rhododendrons and other shade-loving shrubs.

Amaryllis belladonna 'Alba'

Chionodoxa luciliae

Crocosmia masonorum

Colchicum speciosum

CHIONODOXA

Glory of the snow (C. luciliae) is a popular small spring-flowering bulb from the mountains of Turkey. The small, starry, blue flowers with white eyes are carried in clusters of about 6-10 blooms on 15 cm stems. It is very hardy and easily grown in any well-drained soil in full sun or very light shade. Other species, such as the pure blue C. sardensis, are occasionally available. They look superb when planted in drifts in rockeries or on gently sloping banks.

CLIVIA

C. miniata is a common outdoor plant in mild areas, but where temperatures regularly fall below -3°C it is a greenhouse or conservatory plant. C. miniata has 60 cm long, broad, strap-like leaves and 20 or more bright yellow and orange flowers clustered atop 50 cm stems. Flowering varies with the climate, but will occur between autumn and mid spring. The flowers and foliage are often damaged by slugs and snails. It is evergreen and requires a warm position with a moist well-drained soil. C. nobilis is similar but smaller,

with tubular flowers. It is better suited to cool climates but is still not very hardy. Divide clumps during winter and early spring.

COLCHICUM

Although commonly known as autumn crocuses, this genus is not closely related to the genus Crocus. Colchicum flowers in late summer and autumn, and the foliage appears in winter or spring. The flowers are usually white, pink or mauve, but they vary in size and shape; some are small and starry, others large and cup-shaped, and some have very fully double flowers, for example the violet-pink C. speciosum 'Waterlily'. They are easily grown in any moist well-drained soil in full sun or light shade.

CROCOSMIA

The best known of this late summer- and autumn-flowering South African genus is the bright orange-flowered montbretia (C. x crocosmiiflora). However, it is virtually a roadside weed in many areas and is now seldom cultivated in gardens. More widely grown are C. masonorum and C. paniculata, which are similar to montbretia but have larger flower stems (around 75 cm for C. masonorum and up to 1.2 m for C. paniculata). The flowers come in yellowish-orange to rusty-red shades, and well-established clumps with stems arching in all directions are very attractive. All forms do best in full sun or light shade in a moist well-drained soil, although they will tolerate considerable drought. They will self-sow if allowed to.

CROCUS

Although crocuses are considered to be one of the traditional spring flowers, there are also autumn- or early winter-blooming species. The foliage of all species is grass-like and the flowers goblet shaped. However, the range of flower colour and markings is vast. Most are about 10-15 cm high in flower and develop into small clumps. The best known species is C. vernus, but specialist growers list many species and hybrids. One of the most effective ways of growing crocuses is to naturalise them in lawns. For general garden use, plant them in full sun or light shade in a moist well-drained soil. In regions with mild wet winters and humid summers crocuses can be difficult, but in general they pose few problems.

DIERAMA

Lady's wand (D. pulcherrimum) is the most widely grown species of this southern African genus. It forms evergreen clumps of long narrow foliage and in flower is very distinctive. The flower stems are up to 2 m high and arch gracefully under the weight of the pendulous, bell-shaped, pale pink to purple flowers. The main flowering season is early to mid summer. The smaller, slightly earlier-flowering D. pendulum is occasionally available. It is a beautiful background plant for large rockeries. Both species are easily grown in any well-drained moist soil in full sun. They will self-sow if allowed to. Divide clumps during autumn and winter.

ERYTHRONIUM

The dog-tooth violets and trout lilies are among the most attractive spring-flowering bulbs and are very hardy. The foliage of some species is attractively marbled. Several species and hybrids are grown with flowers in various shades of cream, yellow and pink. Plant them in a moist humus-rich soil in shade or semi-shade. Most species are around 15 cm high in flower, but E. tuolumnense may reach 40 cm x 20 cm.

FREESIA

These popular cut flowers are widely grown for the beauty of the blooms and their fragrance. This southern African genus includes seven species, but the vast majority of garden plants are hybrids. F. lactea is the only true species that is at all commonly grown. The widely flared, trumpet-shaped flowers are clustered to one side of stems that may be 40 cm high. Hybrids are available in a wide range of colours and in single or double-flowered forms. Freesias are often forced into flower out of season by growing in greenhouses or very sheltered locations. Staggered planting will also extend the flowering season. Established plants are primarily spring-flowering, but fresh seed will bloom in approximately eight months from sowing. By regularly raising new plants from seed, flowers can be available year round in mild areas. Where temperatures fall below -7°C they require greenhouse conditions. Grow in a light well-drained soil in full sun.

FRITILLARIA

Fritillaries are beautiful plants, but they are not always easy to grow and are frequently difficult to obtain. The flowers appear in spring and are usually pendulous and bell-shaped. They are commonly in various shades of green, yellow, purple or brown and are often interestingly marked. They are difficult to describe, you really have to see one to understand their appeal.
Many are alpine plants and demand a scree soil: gritty and dry on top, well-drained but

moisture-retentive below. Any excessive moisture round the crown will lead to rot or fungal diseases and ultimately death. *F. meleagris* and *F. pontica* are the most common species and among the easiest to grow. The crown imperial (*F. imperialis*), which has yellow or orange flowers on strong 1 m high stems, is the largest of the genus and one of the most colourful. Most fritillaries are only available from specialists or as seeds.

GALANTHUS

The best-known member of this genus is *G. nivalis*, which grows only 10 cm high. Known as snowdrops, these plants are often confused with snowflakes (*Leucojum* spp.), but they are considerably smaller and with slightly glaucous foliage. The giant snowdrop, *G. elwesii*, grows to about 20 cm high and has strappy glaucous foliage. *G. byzantinus*, which is around 15 cm high, is also occasionally seen. The double form of *G. nivalis* is particularly charming but the pendulous flowers are so close to the ground that the effect is often lost, so it is best grown in a pot where it is more easily admired. True deciduous woodland conditions in a cool moist climate are best for snowdrops. Under such conditions they may naturalise.

GALTONIA

This is a small southern African genus of which the Cape hyacinth (*G. candicans*) is the

only one generally available. It is an attractive summer-flowering bulb that undisturbed may form a clump about 40 cm wide, but it should be divided before reaching this size or flowering will be reduced through overcrowding. The spikes of pendulous, white, tubular flowers may exceed 1.2 m high. A double-flowered form ('Moonbeam') and the light green-flowered species (*G. viridiflora*) are occasionally available from perennial specialists. Cape hyacinths prefer a light, well-drained, moist soil in full sun.

GLADIOLUS

Gladioli are among the best known of all garden bulbs. The common large-flowered garden varieties are hybrids of several species and have been grouped together as *G. x hortulanus*. Many colour forms and sizes are grown but all share the sword-like foliage and densely packed flower spikes. The true species are less readily identifiable and in many ways less brash and more endearing.

The *G. x hortulanus* hybrids are deciduous but some species are evergreen. The most common true species is the night-scented *G. tristis*. In spring and early summer it produces spikes of 2-6 sweetly fragrant, creamy-green, tubular flowers on wiry 50 cm stems. *G. papilio* (*G. purpureo-auratus*) is another common species that has more typically *Gladiolus*-like flowers, except they are pendant. Enthusiasts

grow many other species including the group formerly classified as *Acidanthera*. Plant *Gladiolus* in a light well-drained soil in full sun. They need ample moisture during the growing and flowering season, but can be dried off quickly after blooming. The true species vary in their precise requirements but most are not difficult to grow. Thrips can be a problem.

GLORIOSA

Only two species, *G. rothschildiana* and *G. superba*, are commonly grown. They are known as climbing lilies. These are impressive but tender plants that are really only suited to areas with mild winters and warm moist summers. They have bright red and yellow lily-like flowers in late spring. The petals of the flowers are very sharply recurved. These plants climb by means of their tendril-tipped leaves and may cover a considerable area. Grow them in a rich, moist, humus-enriched soil that is well-drained and does not lie wet over winter. The tuber is far more likely to rot in wet soil when dormant than to be killed by cold. Plant the tubers horizontally about 20 cm deep.

HAEMANTHUS

H. coccineus is the only species of this genus commonly grown. It is a very unusual and much admired plant with foliage that usually consists of two very long (up to 60 cm), broad, strappy leaves that spread across the ground. The flowers, which

Haemanthus coccineus

appear in autumn before the leaves, have large orange-red bracts that resemble a hellebore flower with a central mass of bright pink to flame-red stamens. The flowers are often called shaving brushes or paint brushes because of the brush-like nature of the massed stamens. The flower stem is 10-20 cm long and attractively mottled. This plant demands a well-drained humus-enriched soil in full sun or light shade and a warm dry summer. Because it needs excellent winter drainage, it is often grown in large pots. Plant with the neck of the bulb just above the soil.

HIPPEASTRUM

These showy large-flowered bulbs are commonly called amaryllis, but they do not belong to that genus. Most cultivated forms are hybrids, although you may occasionally see them sold as *H. vittatum*. The first flower stems appear in spring as the strappy agapanthus-like foliage begins to develop. The large trumpet-shaped blooms are carried on sturdy stems up to 75 cm high with usually two or three to a stem. The flowers come in shades of red, pink or white and are often bicoloured. Grow in a rich, moist, well-drained, humus-enriched soil in full sun or light shade and plant with at least the neck of the bulb above the soil surface. *Hippeastrum* hybrids are somewhat frost-tender and prone to winter rotting, so they are usually grown as house plants or lifted where winter temperatures fall below -4°C.

Galtonia candicans

Gladiolus recurvus 'Purpurea Auratum'

HYACINTHOIDES

The spring-flowering English bluebell, formerly known as *Scilla nonscripta* and *Endymion nonscriptus*, is now known as *Hyacinthoides nonscripta*. The closely related Spanish bluebell (*H. hispanica*) has also been transferred to this genus by a similar route. With any luck they have found a permanent home. These easily grown woodland bulbs naturalise well in a cool, moist but well-drained, humus-enriched soil in sun or dappled shade. They are most at home under deciduous trees. The flowers, which are carried on 20-30 cm stems, are not always blue; white, pink and various mauve shades are also available.

HYACINTHUS

The common garden hyacinths have mainly been derived from *H. orientalis*. Large-flowered florists' strains have been cultivated for over 400 years and are available in an enormous range of colours and forms, all of which share a similar general appearance. The densely massed flowers are borne in sturdy, upright spikes 30 cm high. Hyacinths are often forced into flower in winter but normally flower in early to mid spring. If you intend to raise hyacinths indoors for winter flowers, use only top-grade large bulbs as smaller ones often collapse before flowering. When growing outdoors, choose a site with cool, moist, well-drained, humus-enriched soil in sun or light shade. Plant the bulbs with their tops level with or just below the soil surface. Hyacinths are prone to damage by narcissus bulb fly, so check the bulbs for signs of damage before planting. They may be propagated by bulb scooping.

IPHEION

The single species in this genus, *I. uniflorum*, is a popular small evergreen or deciduous clump-forming bulb that often naturalises well. The pale lilac short-stemmed flowers are star-shaped and the foliage is grass-like, which leads to the common name star grass. It is an undemanding plant that will quickly form a 30 cm wide clump. In many areas it will flower through winter and well into spring, and may have occasional flowers through the year. It is easily grown in moist well-drained soil in full sun.

IRIS

The evergreen and rhizomatous members of this large genus are covered in the annuals and perennials chapter. The irises discussed here are all spring-flowering, form tunicate bulbs and may be lifted and stored dry. Most are also capable of being forced into flower out of season and are commonly grown for the cut-flower markets. The evergreen and rhizomatous irises require quite different treatment. The most common forms of bulbous iris are Dutch, English and Spanish hybrids, which are popular cut flowers as well as effective garden ornamentals. They all share *I. xiphium* in their parentage and most have long-stemmed (up to 45 cm) flowers. The flowers are predominantly bright blue or yellow, although there are some interesting mustard to orange-shaded cultivars.

Other widely grown bulbous irises include the very early *I. reticulata* hybrids, the almost *Narcissus*-like *I. histrioides*, and the yellow irises, *I. bucharica* and *I. danfordiae*. Of these, *I. reticulata* is the most popular. Its flowers, which are on 15 cm stems, appear only briefly in late winter or early spring, but they are so beautifully coloured and marked and the plants so easy to grow that most gardens seem to have a few.

All of these irises require similar treatment. They should be planted in moist well-drained soil in full sun or partial shade. If fungal diseases, such as mildew and foliage spotting, occur, spray or drench the bulbs with a systemic fungicide when lifted. Propagate by bulb scaling.

IXIA

This is a genus of hardy spring-flowering bulbs, the most common of which are hybrids of *I. maculata*. The starry flowers are borne on wiry stems up to 50 cm tall and usually only open on sunny days. Ixias come in many colours and the most unusual species (some think it the most attractive) is the so-called green ixia (*I. viridiflora*), although the colour is actually duck-egg blue with a black centre. The colour is very distinctive and the flower appears almost translucent, with a waxy texture that is most unusual. Ixias are easily grown in light well-drained soil in full sun.

LACHENALIA

Lachenalias are colourful and easily grown bulbs that flower in winter or early spring. The most widely grown species is *L. aloides*, which grows up to 35 cm high. Although sometimes forced into flower indoors over winter, it normally flowers in early spring. The tubular flowers are pendulous and the colours vary, but they are usually in yellow and orange shades with red and greenish tints. *L. bulbiferum* is another common species, growing to 45 cm tall and bearing flowers that have distinctive purple markings. *L. orchioides* (*L. glaucina*) has beautiful greenish lavender-blue flowers. Grow in light well-drained soil in full sun or very light shade.

Flowering is better if the plants have cool overnight temperatures, but shelter from all but light frosts is essential. Dry summer conditions are very important for ripening the bulbs. Well-ripened bulbs are less likely to rot in winter and they flower more heavily. Slugs and snails often damage the young foliage.

LEUCOJUM

Often mistaken for snowdrops, the early spring-flowering snowflake (*L. vernum*) and the later-flowering *L. aestivum* are ideal for areas with cold winters, but they nevertheless do well in mild winter areas too. The small white flowers are borne on 30 cm (*L. vernum*) or 50 cm (*L. aestivum*) stems and are dainty rather than flamboyant. A third species, *L. autumnale*, blooms in very late summer and autumn. Grow in moist, well-drained, humus-enriched soil in full sun or light shade. Snowflakes will naturalise in deciduous woodland areas.

Ipheion uniflorum

Iris xiphium form

LILIUM

The true lilies are magnificent plants that have been highly valued for centuries. With some 80 species and many more hybrids, this genus provides a diverse range of outstanding garden plants. They are very versatile but are particularly stunning when massed.

Lilies come in all sizes, from 20 cm dwarfs to 2 m giants, and in most shades except blues and purples. Some, such as *L. regale*, are strongly fragrant. There are a number of different flower forms to choose from, such as trumpets (e.g., *L. longiflorum*), bowl-shaped (e.g., Oriental hybrids), Turk's caps (e.g., *L. martagon*), and bell-shaped. Lilies are mainly summer- and early autumn-flowering and most are very hardy.

The planting depth depends on the type of bulb. The Madonna lily (*L. candidum*) and *L. martagon* are the only commonly grown lilies that produce roots from the bulb only. They should both be planted just below the surface. All other widely grown species and hybrids also produce stem roots above the bulbs and should be planted 15-20 cm deep. The bulbs should not be lifted and stored dry during dormancy.

Drainage and soil conditions are very important. Most lilies prefer a moist acidic soil with ample humus and excellent drainage. In areas inclined to lay wet, raised beds may be required. They dislike hot dry summers.

Lilies are subject to several fungal and viral diseases but when grown under favourable conditions they are generally trouble-free.

Most lilies are easily propagated from offsets and by bulb scaling, but some produce small bulbils in the leaf axils. Stem-rooting lilies can also be encouraged to form small bulblets in their leaf axils by allowing the stems to develop in spring, then disbudding them and burying the stems in shallow trenches. The flowers have to be sacrificed, but this method produces hundreds of small bulblets.

MUSCARI

Grape hyacinths are tough, adaptable plants that provide good colour and thrive on neglect, although to some gardeners they are somewhat weedy. Several species and forms are grown and all have a similar appearance, with grassy foliage and flower heads resembling miniature hyacinths. The blue and purple forms are the most popular, but white and pink forms are also available. Some are lightly scented. The flower spikes, which are up to 20 cm high, appear in late winter or very early spring. Most garden grape hyacinths are cultivars of the blue-flowered *M. armeniacum*. The white-flowered *M. botryoides* is a beautiful little species, although not widely available. Grape hyacinths are very easily grown in moist, well-drained, humus-enriched soil in full sun to moderate shade.

NARCISSUS

Daffodils have been popular garden plants for centuries. A wide array of species and hybrids are now grown, all of which are distinctive plants. Their distinctiveness comes from the unusual form of the flowers, which consist of an array of petals at the base of the flower (the perianth) and a trumpet- or cup-shaped centre (the corona). The large-flowered hybrid daffodils derived from *N. pseudonarcissus*, such as 'February Gold' and 'Emperor', are the best known but there are many other species and forms. The smallest common daffodils are the *N. bulbocodium*, or hoop petticoat, forms. These have grass-like leaves and flowers with a widely flared corona and greatly reduced perianth. The smallest species to resemble a traditional daffodil is *N. asturiensis*, which is a tiny miniature, but perfect in all the details. There are also double hybrids and unusually coloured hybrids. Collectors grow many species that are seldom available commercially.

The jonquils and paperwhites of New Zealand gardens form similar-sized clumps to the larger daffodils, but they have much smaller flowers, that often have sharply recurved petals. They are hybrids or forms of *N. tazetta*. The true jonquil (*N. jonquilla*) is not as widely grown. The poets' narcissus (*N. poeticus*) has a white perianth and a very small

A double form of *Narcissus pseudonarcissus*

corona that is creamy-yellow edged with orange. The form 'Actaea' has flowers that are about twice the size of those of the species.

Narcissus generally prefers cool, moist, well-drained, humus-enriched soil in full sun or dappled shade, but most are very adaptable. Plant bulbs of the large-growing forms up to 15 cm deep and the smaller forms about 7.5-10 cm deep. After flowering, the plants may be allowed to dry off. Smaller species, such as *N. bulbocodium* and *N. cyclamineus*, are well suited to rockeries.

All narcissus are subject to attack by narcissus bulb fly, which can be devastating. Carefully inspect bulbs for any sign of burrowing or hollowness. It is a wise precaution to soak new bulbs in a systemic insecticide for an hour or so before planting. They can be propagated by scaling.

NERINE

Nerines are among the best known of the autumn-flowering amaryllids. They are so common as to be almost a weed in some areas. Nevertheless, they are colourful and adaptable plants that bloom from mid to late summer to early winter, when most other bulbs are dormant. Some nerines flower before their strappy leaves develop, others flower with the foliage. Several species are grown. *N. bowdenii* is the common pink species but you may also see the orange-red *N. curvifolia* 'Fothergillii Major', the grassy-leaved, pink-flowered

Muscari botryoides

N. filifolia, and the belladonna-like, reddish-pink *N. sarniensis*. The white nerine seen occasionally is usually *N. flexuosa* 'Alba'; the typical pink form of this species does not appear to be in cultivation. All except *N. filifolia* have strappy leaves and flower stems up to 45 cm high.

Nerines are easily grown in any free-draining soil in full sun or light shade. Plant the neck of the bulb at or just above the soil level. *N. bowdenii* is the hardiest species, tolerating heavy frosts through its winter dormancy. The other species are rather frost-tender and summer dormant. Nerines can be propagated by scaling.

ORNITHOGALUM

Chincherinchee (*O. thyrsoides*)

is the best-known member of this widespread genus. Other common species include star of Bethlehem (*O. umbellatum*) and *O. arabicum*. These species produce spikes of white starry flowers. The large-flowered *O. reverchonii* has flower spikes up to 1 m high, but most other species seldom exceed 40 cm. In mild areas they may remain evergreen and can flower at any time, but in areas with cold winters they are deciduous and flower from mid spring. Plant in light well-drained soil in full sun or light shade.

OXALIS

Just the mention of this name is enough to send some gardeners running for the weedkiller, but not all *Oxalis* species are noxious weeds. In fact, among the 800 or so species there are many very attractive small plants well suited to rockeries and sunny banks. Of the bulbous species, the most widely grown are *O. adenophylla*, which has large pink flowers, *O. hirta*, with flowers in white or various pink shades, and *O. lobata*, which has bright yellow flowers. They are all spring flowering, forming small mats of clover-like foliage and seldom exceeding 10 cm high when in flower. Other common species include the very narrow leaved *O. laciniata* and the autumn- to winter-flowering *O. purpurea*. All are easily grown in any well-drained soil in full sun and are drought tolerant once established.

POLIANTHES

The tuberose (*P. tuberosa*), which is a Mexican native and the sole member of this genus, is a sought-after bulb famed for its fragrance and lasting ability as a cut flower. The 50 cm high spikes are produced in late summer and autumn. The very fragrant white flowers are lily-like and there may be 10 or more blooms per stem. The double form known as 'The Pearl' is the most widely grown cultivar. Plant it in moist well-drained soil in full sun and allow to dry off after flowering. Tuberose must be divided at least every two years or the clumps will become overcrowded, causing them to lose vigour and cease flowering.

Oxalis variabilis, pure white form

RHODOHYPOXIS

This genus of spring-flowering corms is most commonly represented by *R. baurii*, notable for its extremely free-flowering nature. This very charming little plant forms a small grassy clump with waxy star-shaped flowers on 10 cm stems. Several colours from white through many pink shades to red are available. *Rhodohypoxis* prefers gritty well-drained soil in full sun or partial shade and demands perfect winter drainage or the corms will rot. Greatest success is usually achieved by growing them in pots or rockeries.

ROMULEA

This genus of approximately 90 species of spring- and summer-flowering corms is widespread from Europe to South Africa. The best-known species are *R. bulbocodium*, from Europe and the Middle East, and *R. sabulosa*, from South Africa. The European species resemble crocuses, with grassy foliage and flared tubular pink flowers, but the South African species are more distinctive. *R. sabulosa* has fine grassy foliage and large deep pink flowers with dark centres on very short stems. When grown well, the flowers make a dense carpet. *R. bulbocodium* has bright yellow flowers. All species form clumps that can cover a considerable area (up to 1 m across), but they seldom exceed 15 cm high. Grow them in light well-drained soil in full sun.

ROSCOEA

These small bulbous plants seldom exceed 30 cm x 40 cm. The iris-like flowers usually

A white form of *Schizostylis coccinea*

appear with or just before the spear-shaped leaves. The deep pink flowered *R. humeana* is probably the best species. Plant in moist, well-drained, gritty soil with added humus in sun or dappled shade and propagate by seed or division.

SANDERSONIA

S. aurantiaca (golden lily-of-the-valley) is a beautiful winter-dormant tuberous plant related to *Gloriosa*. It is easily grown in most districts, but in areas that regularly experience frosts that freeze the top 5 cm of soil or that have very wet winters, it is advisable to lift the bulbs over winter. This plant is a scrambling semi-climber and it may grow to 1 m high if supported by surrounding shrubs. In early summer it produces branched stems bearing nodding, orange, lantern-shaped flowers that last well when cut. *Sandersonia* prefers moist well-drained soil in full sun and benefits from an occasional liquid feed when in growth. Plant the tubers with the prongs pointing downwards.

SCHIZOSTYLIS

The kaffir lily (*S. coccinea*) is an undemanding South African species that grows well in any

moisture-retentive but free-draining soil in full sun or light shade. It has naturalised in many parts of New Zealand and will self-sow if allowed to. It is evergreen but the foliage is not particularly attractive. The main reason for planting this in the garden is the late summer and autumn flower display. The flowers are star-shaped and carried on 50 cm tall spikes. Colours range from white through various pink shades to crimson. These plants are hardy to -15°C and prefer humus-rich soils and plenty of summer moisture. Regular division in spring is recommended for continued vigour.

SCILLA

The most commonly grown species are the late winter-flowering *S. siberica* and *S. tubergeniana*, and the spring-flowering *S. peruviana* and *S. hyacinthoides*. The flower colours range from white through cream and pink to various shades of blue and purple. The two early species are small plants that seldom exceed 10 cm high when in flower, *S. peruviana* has 30 cm tall stems and those of *S. hyacinthoides* can reach 60 cm high. All are easily grown in moist, well-

Tigridia pavonia, white form

drained, humus-enriched soil in full sun or light shade, but some species do best in a hot sunny situation. Most are quite hardy. Do not plant the bulbs deeply; just below the soil surface is fine for most species, but *S. hyacinthoides* should be planted with the neck of the bulb just above the surface.

SPARAXIS

Several species (*S. elegans*, *S. grandiflora* and *S. tricolor*) are grown and seem to interbreed regularly, but they are nearly always sold as *S. tricolor* regardless of their true origin. The starry flowers, which appear from mid spring, are carried on 30 cm tall spikes. The colourful flowers come in various shades from white through pink and orange to deep purplish-red with contrasting centres and markings. They are easily grown in light well-drained soil in full sun and often naturalise. They are hardy to -7°C.

TECOPHILEA

The Chilean blue crocus (*T. cyanocrocus*) is an alpine bulb with intensely blue crocus-like flowers in spring, and is so attractive that it has become

virtually extinct in the wild through over-collection. It prefers moist well-drained soil in sun or very light shade and should be dried off after flowering. Propagate by seed or division.

TIGRIDIA

Jockey's cap (*T. pavonia*) is a vigorous grower and its reproductive proclivity can lead to problems, but the flower form is unusual and effective if used with restraint. The pink, yellow and red flowers are carried on 35 cm stems and have three petals around a central 'saucer' or 'cap'. Each flower only remains open for one day, but there is a succession of bloom from late spring to mid autumn. Jockey's caps are hardy to -15°C and are easily grown in any light well-drained soil in full sun. The bulbs can be lifted over winter in cold or wet areas, and the clumps will need thinning every few years to keep them under control.

TRITONIA

This genus of South African corms is closely related to *Freesia* and is similar in general appearance, except that the flowers, which appear in late spring and early summer, are more densely bunched (on 40 cm stems) and very intensely coloured. The common species, *T. crocata*, is normally a brilliant orange, but several pastel shades, including soft yellow, pale pink and white, are available. Grow them in full sun and water well while in active growth, but dry off after flowering. They are hardy to -15°C.

TULIPA

Tulips have been prized as garden plants for several centuries and there is now a wide range of hybrids available. The most familiar are the showy large-flowered Darwin hybrids, most of which have vivid red, orange or golden yellow flowers. Enthusiasts grow many of the smaller species and hybrids. The best-known smaller forms are the so-called rock tulips. These hybrids of *T. greigii* and *T. kaufmanniana* are short-stemmed and compact. They

usually have red, orange or yellow flowers and often have attractively marked foliage. Tulip hybrids are available in virtually every colour and flower form. Among the more interesting are the doubles, the unusually shaped parrot tulips and the serrated-petalled fringed tulips. Many bicolour or multicolour forms are available. The hybrids are shown to perfection in massed plantings and other formal settings. Tulips prefer a position in full sun and the soil should be moist in spring and well-drained. Some prefer hot dry summers to ripen the bulbs, but if grown in a position that is too warm the bulbs may lose their vigour. Tulips need cool winters to flower well. In most parts of New Zealand they will receive enough natural chilling, but in very mild areas chilling for eight weeks in the refrigerator before planting will ensure good flowering. Tulips are prone to aphid attack and viral infection, so control of aphids is essential.

VALLOTA

The Scarborough lily (*V. speciosa* syn. *Cyrtanthus purpureus*) is the only member of this genus. It is one of the most admired summer- and early autumn-flowering bulbs. The large, bright-red, trumpet-shaped flowers are carried in clusters of 3-10 blooms atop 30 cm stems. Although resistant to drought and very adaptable to soils and competition with other plants, it is somewhat frost-tender. Evergreen in mild areas, it is semi-evergreen or deciduous elsewhere. Grow in full sun or very light shade in light well-drained soils. Divide established clumps in early summer.

WATSONIA

This is a variable genus, either spring- or summer-flowering, and deciduous or evergreen, depending on the species. Most species tend to be near evergreen and may eventually form clumps 60 cm x 2 m, but they are usually divided before becoming that large. The common spring-flowering species, *W. aletroides* has 60 cm stems with clusters of 4 cm long, tubular, salmon-pink flowers

that are easily distinguished from the bright pink trumpet-shaped blooms of the summer-flowering *W. beatricis*. Most species have flower stems in excess of 1 m high. Watsonias are easily grown in well-drained soil in full sun.

ZANTEDESCHIA

The most familiar species is the common white-flowered *Z. aethiopica*. It has very large, bright green, arrowhead-shaped leaves and forms clumps up to 2 m x 1.5 m. The white arum-like flowers are on sturdy 2 m high stems. 'Green Goddess' is a semi-dwarf form with green flowers. It prefers a rich moist soil and is evergreen and continuous flowering in most areas, but it may be cut back by severe frosts.
The smaller species, such as *Z. albomaculata*, *Z. elliotiana* and *Z. rehmannii*, are also occasionally seen. They are more seasonal than *Z. aethiopica*, being summer-flowering and deciduous in winter. Interbreeding has produced new hybrids that have rapidly supplanted the species in gardens. This has greatly extended the colour range so that all shades of yellow, orange, red and purple, and some very unusual combinations, are now available. Callas prefer a moist humus-enriched soil and a position in sun to moderate shade. They benefit from regular liquid feeding.

ZEPHYRANTHES

Some of the more familiar members of the genus, such as *Z. candida*, are now more correctly included in *Argyropsis*, although they are seldom listed under this name. Zephyr lilies have grass-like leaves about 30 cm long and cup-shaped flowers reminiscent of *Crocus*. Most have flower stems up to about 20 cm tall with one flower per stem. *Z. candida* has creamy-white flowers and those of *Z. grandiflora* are rosy-pink to purple. These two common species bloom over a long period, from mid summer to early winter, and may form sizeable clumps. Some species are evergreen, others deciduous. Hardy in most areas, they are easily grown in any sunny position with well-drained soil.

SHRUBS

Planning; Plant selection; Buying shrubs; Planting; Aftercare; Transplanting; Pruning and training; Camellias; Ericas and callunas; Fuchsias; The protea family; Rhododendrons and azaleas; Roses; Other popular garden shrubs

SHRUBS ARE USUALLY defined as any plant that develops permanent woody stems but which does not develop the main trunk (or trunks) that is the key feature of trees. This definition encompasses an enormous range of plants of all shapes and sizes.

While annuals and perennials provide large drifts of vivid colour and varying foliage, and trees may be more physically imposing, shrubs provide the permanent year-round framework for a garden. Trees can provide a canopy of foliage that no shrub can match and their flowers or foliage may be just as attractive, but in many situations their sheer size limits their potential. Shrubs, especially evergreens, do not suffer from such limitations. Their smaller size allows them to be used in places where trees would not fit, and, unlike many annuals and perennials, they provide year-round interest.

There is such a vast range of attractive and useful garden shrubs that the effects that can be created are virtually limitless. If your climate allows, there are many incredibly flamboyant tropical shrubs, or, at the other extreme, you may wish to replicate an alpine scene. Shrubs can provide a wealth of flowers or maintain interest with foliage alone. How you use them is entirely over to you, but there are many things you should consider before making your choice and you will need to know how to get the best out of them.

PLANNING

A well-chosen selection of shrubs combines all the features essential for a good garden: interesting and attractive foliage, beautiful and unusual flowers, year-round interest and ease of maintenance. But be careful when choosing shrubs, because the vast range available not only provides choice, it also leads to complications that can trip up the unwary or the uninformed.

Ultimately your choice of plants will be influenced by your personal likes and dislikes, the general nature of your garden and soil, and the climatic conditions. All of these things must be considered before you even begin to weigh up which of the myriad of species and cultivars best suits your needs.

Because shrubs are usually much smaller than trees, garden size is not such an issue, however, you must always remember that shrubs are long-term plants. Rather than planting for an immediate effect, you must consider how the plants will develop and what the garden will look like after a few years.

Most gardeners plant mixed shrubberies, often with room for annuals and perennials for seasonal colour, but you may prefer to devote your entire garden, or parts of it, to one group of plants. If you are going to opt for a 'one type' garden, the plants you choose must be capable of sustaining your interest throughout the year. Roses and rhododendrons are probably the most common choices. Roses generally do best on their own or in open beds with low-growing perennials, but rhododendrons and azaleas tend to look more at home as part of a larger woodland scene (both these

Top left: Shrubs feature strongly in the design of this sheltered garden.
Top right: Rhododendrons provide a colourful backdrop to the vigorous perennials in the foreground.

and other very popular genera are covered in greater detail within the shrub selection later in the chapter).

An alternative approach is to choose a theme: the Mediterranean look with lavenders, oleanders and silver-leaved shrubs; an alpine shrubbery; a dry-country garden with predominantly South African and Australian plants; or the New Zealand garden with an emphasis on native plants.

Whatever you choose, take the time to plan the layout of your shrubs so that they blend well with the other elements of your garden and try to get it right first time. Granted, many shrubs will tolerate transplanting, but this should always be looked on as a last resort.

EXPOSURE

There are shrubs for full sun, partial shade and full shade and many will tolerate a wide range of conditions. There are no hard-and-fast rules here, but generally plants that prefer shade, such as rhododendrons and fuchsias, will tolerate sunnier positions provided they are moist. However, plants that prefer sunny situations, such as most of the Australian natives, tend to suffer and become leggy if they are too shaded. If in doubt, it is generally better to err on the bright side when deciding on a site.

SOIL CONDITIONS

All plants have a preferred range of soil conditions outside which they will not grow well. Some prefer dry stony soils, but most do better in moist well-drained soil with plenty of addi-tional compost or leaf mould to provide the all-important humus.

Soil structure can be improved over time but the underlying pH is usually very difficult to alter. Most shrubs prefer a neutral to slightly acid soil, so avoid adding too much lime (which increases alkalinity) unless your soil is very acid. Neutral to moderately alkaline soils will benefit from mild acid fertilisers, but highly alkaline soil is often difficult to neutralise as lime is very soluble and tends to defeat most attempts at neutralisation.

If you have alkaline soil, especially if it is due to the presence of limestone, you will have to put up with a restricted choice of shrubs. There are ways to work around this, such as using raised beds of specially built-up soil and by avoiding planting acid-loving plants in low-lying parts of the garden where lime is likely to accumulate. However, it is usually better to accept your lot and stick to those plants that cope best. Don't be afraid to experiment, many plants will surprise you with their tolerance. Refer to the chapter on compost and plant nutrition for a detailed explanation of pH.

You can't beat flowering shrubs for the provision of solid blocks of colour.

Pyracantha 'Shawnee' produces a mass of rich golden berries.

CLIMATE

Shrubs vary enormously in their frost hardiness, some surviving -40°C while others are totally intolerant of frost. The limits imposed by your climate can't be ignored and may have the greatest influence on your choice of plants. Frost is probably the biggest killer, but don't underestimate the effects of wind, drought and coastal salt spray.

In the long run it is better to work within your climatic limitations than to constantly battle against them. However, gardeners are always willing to test the extremes of a plant's tolerance and it is amazing what can be grown in the most unlikely areas when shelter is provided. Covers made of light wooden stakes covered with hessian or frost cloth will provide some frost protection, as will siting your more tender plants against north-facing walls and under overhanging eaves. Windbreak fences and hedges will protect against the worst excesses of the wind and should be considered essential in many coastal areas and eastern districts that are prone to northwest winds. Very choice tender shrubs may be grown in containers and moved under cover for the winter.

PLANT SELECTION

What you choose to plant should reflect your personal preferences. However, even the most imaginative gardens have to obey a few rules and the following factors must always be considered.

PLANT SIZE

Shrubs vary in size from prostrate to 4 m high and more, but size is not just a matter of height. Many shrubs grow wider than they do tall and so you must consider the eventual spread of the plant as well as its potential to overshadow smaller plants. Failing to take account of the ultimate width of shrubs and packing everything in tightly for immediate effect is probably the most common reason for having to remodel a garden.

FOLIAGE RETENTION

Shrubs may be evergreen, deciduous or somewhere in between. Whether you choose evergreen or deciduous is largely a matter of personal preference and how it fits in with your garden. However, don't be fooled into thinking that by choosing evergreens only you'll escape the effects of winter. All plants, even evergreens, tend to look somewhat drab in the winter months. Rhododendrons with drooping leaves and tender plants with frost-damaged foliage can be just as unsightly as a mass of dead-looking sticks and may not hold half the promise of beauty come springtime.

Evergreen shrubs have the advantage of

year-round foliage. Yet this can become boring as they often lack the seasonal variation of deciduous shrubs. Plants like *Forsythia*, *Deutzia*, *Weigela* and the deciduous azaleas may look very dead in winter, but they more than make up for it in spring and often also provide a dash of foliage colour in auumn.

FOLIAGE TYPE

Flowers may be very pretty, but remember to consider the foliage when choosing your shrubs, as that is what you will be looking at for most of the year. Shrubs come in a huge range of foliage types and by planting a varying combination of leaf sizes, textures and colours it is possible to create year-round interest. Grouping plants with similar foliage can also be very effective. Try massing silver-leaved plants to create a hot dry look, or shrubs with large deep green leaves for a cool lush effect.

Plants evolve a particular type of foliage as a reflection of their natural environment. Large leaves generally indicate a high moisture requirement whereas needle-like or silver foliage usually indicate drought tolerance. Sometimes your climate will play a part in your foliage choice: coastal gardeners may find they have a predominance of shrubs with small silver or sage green leaves. This can be capitalised on by massing such plants together to highlight the colour or by planting something totally different for contrast.

FLOWERS AND FLOWERING SEASON

The flowers of most shrub genera come in a fairly narrow colour range. For example, there are many species and cultivars of *Viburnum*, but they all have white or pink flowers. Likewise, there are many daphnes, but the colour range is restricted to white, pink and mauve. Even those genera that are available in a wide range of hues may lack one or two significant colours. However, it is possible to select a shrub with flowers in just about any shade.

Flower shape and size are also enormously variable and can have just as much impact as colour. There are the filamentous flowers of the bottlebrushes, the pea-like blooms of *Polygala* and the huge flowers of the tropical *Hibiscus*. Some bear their blooms on weeping branches, others on strongly upright spikes.

Although spring and summer are the predominant flowering seasons, there are shrubs in flower in every season. Within the larger genera there is often a range of flowering seasons, so, for example, it is possible to have buddleias in bloom for up to eight months

A Japanese atmosphere is created by the lacquer-red foliage of *Enkianthus perulatus* combined with large moss- and lichen-covered boulders.

just by planting a selection of species and cultivars. Very early or very late flowers may be subject to weather damage, but they extend the period of interest.

FRAGRANCE

To some fragrance is all important, to others it matters little. If you choose to add fragrant shrubs to your garden site them so as to gain the maximum benefit. Some flowers are only scented in the evening and so are best planted near the house. Others are strongly scented and need to be in an open space to prevent them from becoming overpowering.

LIFESPAN

Shrubs are usually considered to be permanent plants, but they won't live indefinitely. In fact, relatively few shrubs have a garden lifespan of more than 15 years. By that time they have died of natural causes, become so overgrown and unsightly they've been removed, or they have outlived their welcome in some other way.

Rhododendrons and camellias are seldom replaced until they die, but most other shrubs are removed long before death occurs. The gardener may be acknowledging a mistake, but often it is just because the novelty of that particular plant has worn off. Don't be concerned about admitting such things, after all it's your garden and part of the fun lies in making changes.

BUYING SHRUBS

Make sure any plants you purchase are correctly labelled, well shaped and healthy. Avoid shrubs that are lopsided or have broken branches, those that have clearly just been potted or are obviously root bound. Diseased deciduous shrubs can be hard to identify when they have no leaves but make sure the twigs are firm yet pliable, not dry and brittle with shrivelled bark. Shrubs in leaf should have healthy unmarked leaves. A little frost damage or sunburn is acceptable but avoid plants with unidentifiable leaf spotting or discoloration.

To be sure of the colour, flowering shrubs are best bought in flower, but this isn't always possible. Try to at least see a good colour photograph of the flower, as nursery label descriptions are not always accurate. Likewise labels tend to quote sizes that are generally on the small side, so allow for a plant that grows somewhat larger than the stated size. In fairness to nurseries, plants grow as long as they are alive and they are subjected to widely varying growing conditions so it is very difficult to give an accurate size guide.

PLANTING

Perhaps one overriding cause of failure with shrubs is a lack of humus in the soil. Improving the structure of the soil is more important than raising its nutrient level, so

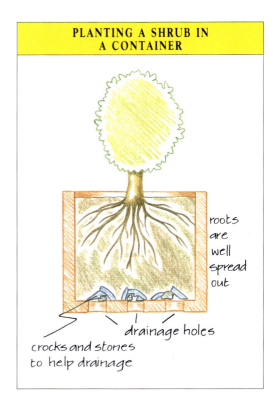

PLANTING A SHRUB IN A CONTAINER

roots are well spread out

drainage holes

crocks and stones to help drainage

take the time to work in plenty of compost before planting. You can always mulch and add fertilisers later, but miss the opportunity to add humus to the root zone before planting and it is gone forever.

With your ground thoroughly prepared and your shrubs in hand, it is time to plant them. The oft-repeated saying that it is no good putting a five-dollar plant in a one-dollar hole still holds true. Newly planted shrubs need loose soil in order to make quick root growth, so make sure you dig a hole that is at least twice the size of the plant's root ball.

Soak the shrub before you remove it from its container or the roots may adhere to the sides and suffer damage. Planter bags may be cut away or carefully eased off and most plants in hard pots come away quite easily if the pot is upended and given a firm rap on the rim. If the shrub is clearly pot bound (with roots spiralling or growing out the container's drainage holes), gently loosen up the root ball, otherwise just lightly work your fingers into the root ball to allow moisture to penetrate. Place the shrub in the hole so that the soil is at the same level up the plant's stem as it was in the container. Gently firm the plant into position with your heel as you replace the soil; don't ram the soil back into place or you'll undo all the work that went into loosening it up. Some gardeners like

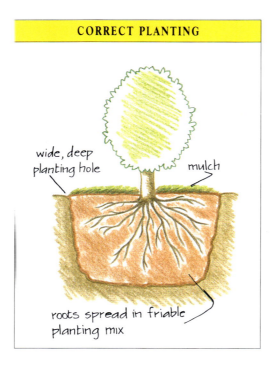

CORRECT PLANTING

wide, deep planting hole

mulch

roots spread in friable planting mix

to make a rim of soil around new plants to act as a reservoir when watering and this is a useful idea in dry areas.

You may like to apply a light dusting of general fertiliser to the soil after planting, but the most important thing is to water the plant if the soil is at all dry. Also, staking may be necessary with larger shrubs to prevent wind-rock.

AFTERCARE

WATERING

Water well during the first summer, but don't drown young plants. When watering plants that were raised in containers make sure that the root ball is actually getting wet. Sometimes when the original potting mix dries it is very hard to re-wet. You may think you are watering well when, in fact, the soil around the plant is getting wet but the all important root-ball remains dry. This is a very common reason for failure.

The only way to tell whether this has happened is to probe around the roots. Those closest to the main stem may be noticeably dry and the soil may be very dusty. However, you may have to lift the plant to check the roots. Don't be afraid to lift such plants because by this stage there's little additional damage that you can do and it may help solve the problem.

FEEDING

Any plant will gradually deplete the soil of nutrients and slowly decline unless given an occasional feeding. Feeding is most important with young, rapidly growing plants, but even very large shrubs, which are often left to look after themselves, will benefit from fertiliser.

Unless you know that a shrub has particular requirements, use a general-purpose fertiliser. Powdered fertilisers and animal manures are usually best applied in spring and early autumn and should be watered in well. Dilute liquid fertilisers can be used throughout the growing season. Do not continue to feed tender shrubs into autumn as frosts may damage any soft new growth.

MULCHING

Mulching around your shrubs in spring and autumn will help retain soil moisture and maintain a more even soil temperature while making weeding less of a struggle.

Larger shrubs with branches at ground level can be difficult to mulch around. Some of the lower branches can be removed, but sometimes large shrubs reach the size where mulching may have to stop.

Lavenders and lupins are natural companion plants for 'Iceberg' roses.

Apply mulches in spring while the soil is still damp. Many materials are suitable as mulches around shrubs, such as pea straw, leaves, bark, well-rotted compost, even stones and 'living' mulches (i.e., groundcover plants).

TRANSPLANTING

Some shrubs can be transplanted with ease whereas others are almost certain to die if

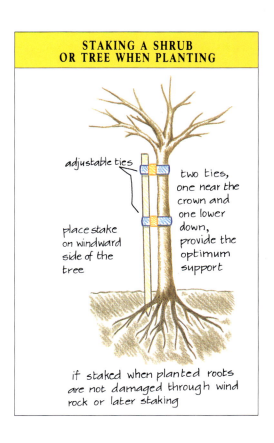

STAKING A SHRUB OR TREE WHEN PLANTING

adjustable ties

two ties, one near the crown and one lower down, provide the optimum support

place stake on windward side of the tree

if staked when planted roots are not damaged through wind rock or later staking

moved. Knowing which is which is a matter of experience, but as a general rule, relatively few plants from dry climates, such as South Africa and Australia, tolerate transplanting whereas those from moist regions, such as Japan and eastern North America, usually present no great difficulties. This is largely to do with their root systems: dry-country plants tend to have widespread roots and may have a deep tap root, whereas plants that get regular rainfall tend to have a more compact root system.

Preparation is the key to successful transplanting. Make sure that you have the hole dug and the soil prepared at the destination and that you have a large enough barrow or team of helpers to handle the move. Dig around the plant well away from the main stem beyond the shallow feeder roots and take as large a root ball as you can manage. The next step, lifting the plant, is fraught with difficulties. Don't underestimate the weight of a mature shrub with its ball of roots and soil or you may have a damaged back as well as a dead shrub. Sometimes the plant can be slid onto a sack or tarpaulin and dragged to its destination or you may be able manoeuvre a wheelbarrow under the shrub, but most often it requires a team effort to hoist the plant onto a barrow or trolley.

When you have reached the destination, reverse the process to plant the shrub. Once replanted the shrub will need regular watering until it is re-established. Very leafy shrubs may be pruned back to lessen the stress, but don't overdo it or you may reduce the plant's ability to photosynthesise.

PRUNING AND TRAINING

Most shrubs do not require any specialised pruning techniques, just trimming and shaping. When pruning endeavour to maintain a well-balanced branch structure. Remove any dead wood and strong-growing water shoots and thin out crowded central stems to allow better air circulation. Hardy shrubs are best cut back in late winter while they are still dormant, but tender shrubs should be left to show signs of spring growth before being pruned. If they are cut back in winter they may suffer more damage than they normally would and leaving pruning until growth starts also makes any dead branches more apparent.

Consider also the flowering period of the shrub: shrubs that bloom on the old wood should be pruned after flowering or all the flower buds will be removed; plants that set their flower buds in autumn should be pruned before mid summer.

HEDGES AND TOPIARY

Many densely foliaged shrubs are suitable for use as hedges. Fashions in hedging change; cherry laurel, privet and *Elaeagnus* used to be

TRANSPLANTING A SHRUB

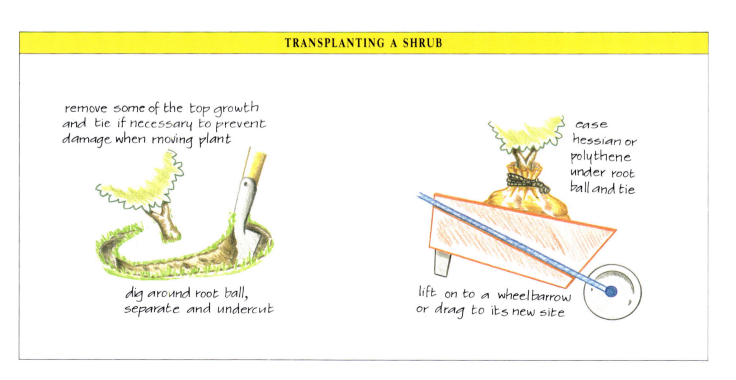

remove some of the top growth and tie if necessary to prevent damage when moving plant

dig around root ball, separate and undercut

ease hessian or polythene under root ball and tie

lift on to a wheelbarrow or drag to its new site

the most common, but *Abelia*, *Photinia* and lavender are now more popular. What you choose to hedge with largely depends on the height of hedge you require. Lavender and box are clearly best as low hedges, while *Photinia* and *Viburnum tinus* are much larger plants.

Do not skimp on the plants when hedging. Tighter spacing may be more expensive but you get results more quickly and it is far easier to gradually remove a few plants from a dense hedge than it is to fill in gaps – a hedge with gaps is among the most unsightly of garden features.

Hedge trimming is a chore, but the results are worthwhile. The frequency will depend greatly on the type of plant and where it is growing. An annual trimming may be sufficient for a box hedge in Dunedin, but the same plant may require three trimmings per year in Auckland.

Topiary, which is the art of trimming plants into shapes, is just hedging to a slightly more fanciful design. It requires more work and the range of suitable plants is restricted – box and yew being the best – but if you like the effect of topiary it may be worth the extra effort.

Many densely foliaged shrubs, such as *Pittosporum* cultivars (top left) and lavender (above), are suitable for use in hedging and topiary, as is the taller-growing ngaio (*Myoporum*) (top right), which has the added bonus of fragrant leaves.

121

CAMELLIAS

Camellias are native to Southeast Asia and over 4000 years ago the Chinese were using the leaves of Camellia sinensis for tea and extracting oil from the seeds of C. oleifera. As early as 600-900 A.D., ornamental camellias were highly developed and the plants were being traded between China and Japan.

CHOOSING AND PREPARING YOUR SITE

Camellias are easy to grow if a few important points are remembered: they will need pruning, they can grow up to 10 m high, they do not like lime soils (it should be neutral to acid, in the range of pH 5.5 to 7.0); and they do not like soil that dries out too much in summer. As they need good drainage, too, clay soils are generally not conducive to good camellia growing either. But camellias are by no means fussy plants. Most species and hybrids are hardy throughout the country, needing no protection except perhaps in very cold winter areas, and the summers here are not usually hot and dry enough to cause much damage, though dry, windy conditions on the east coasts of both islands may cause problems.

In their native habitat, camellias grow mostly on woodland and forest slopes, where the drainage is good, the shallow layer of soil is slightly acid, and ample humus is provided by the annual leaf-fall of the surrounding trees. If camellias are to succeed we need to recreate these conditions in our gardens.

PLANTING AND CARE

Camellias do best in sheltered positions in light shade or where they get only morning sun. This is not so much for the plant's sake as the flowers': the plants will tolerate exposed sunny sites but the flowers won't. If the shade is too dense, it will promote lank growth and reduce flowering, if it is too sunny, the flowers will burn and drop prematurely. Also, a site that is exposed to strong winds will dramatically shorten the life of any flowers but especially camellias.

Planting camellias can be fun and very rewarding if done correctly. Always dig a hole at least three times as large as the plant's rootball and at least twice as deep. Place two to three handfuls of bone-dust or bone-meal at the base of the hole and lightly fork this into the sub-soil.

Deep planting of camellias is fatal. They must be planted so that the soil level once planted is at the same level on the trunk as it was in the container. Also, sometimes you will notice when you remove the plant from the container that some roots might have grown around the rootball. If this is the case, with a sharp knife, cut through these roots from top to bottom, and new roots will soon grow from the cut ends.

Water the plant in well. You might like to add a liquid blood and bone fertiliser, such as Nitrosol, to give the plant a good boost. Finally, remove any plastic labels and write out another. This should be placed in the soil alongside the trunk.

Once your camellia is established, regular feeding, especially after flowering when the plant is coming into new growth, is part of its ongoing care. This helps to avoid chlorosis, to which camellias are sometimes subject. Likewise, regular mulches are also beneficial.

TRAINING CAMELLIAS

Besides their normal bushy habit, many camellias are suitable subjects for training. The most common forms are the standard and the espalier.

Standards can be created in two ways. The easiest is to select a young plant with a single straight stem and simply remove the lower foliage and any side shoots as they appear. Stake the main stem as it grows and, once it has reached the desired height, nip out the tip growth to induce the branching that will eventually form the head.

The process can be speeded up by grafting but the mechanics are not as simple. Select a vigorous upright plant that will rapidly produce the standard trunk, and graft your selected

Left: The soft pink flowers
of this camellia contrast well
with its glossy green leaves.
Top: *Camellia* 'Anticipation'
Above: *Camellia* 'Brian'

cultivar on at the desired height. Cleft grafts are the preferred method for camellias but I have found side wedge grafts to be successful. Grafting is the only practical way to produce a weeping standard. Espaliering is just a matter of selecting an appropriate plant and having the patience to wait long enough to see the results. There are several methods of training the branches to achieve the best coverage, but most camellias with thin pliable stems (primarily the Sasanquas) can be espaliered with very little effort. Remember though, camellias are not natural climbers, so espaliers need to be secured to the structure against which they are growing.

Camellias can make effective hedges, either tightly clipped or grown informally. As might be expected of a genus that contains the tea plant, camellias can withstand frequent trimming when actively growing.

PROPAGATION

Most camellias root from cuttings. The best time to take them is when the first growth stops and hardens before either extending into secondary growth or hopefully making flower buds. Depending on where you are in the country, this period can be from late November to early February. Also, this is when the sun's heat can be used in a small greenhouse to assist rooting. Some bottom heat may also improve strike rates. Take new tip growth cuttings that are about 10-15 cm long and follow the procedures outlined in the chapter on propagation.

FLOWER FORMS

Camellias are available in several different flower forms. The descriptions in this book are kept as simple as possible but occasionally the technical terms must be used. The terms single, semi-double and double are familiar and fairly self-explanatory, but most of the following terms are peculiar to camellia cultivation.

ANEMONE A style with large outer petals and massed small central petaloids.

PEONY (PAEONY) & INFORMAL DOUBLE Large outer petals and smaller loosely clustered central petals and petaloids. The more fully petalled flowers are known as full peony form.

ROSE FORM DOUBLE A double flower that opens fully to reveal the stamens, like a fully blown rose.

FORMAL DOUBLE This flower type has perfectly arranged concentric circles of neatly overlapping petals. Some have the petals in a very clearly defined spiral pattern.

There are also rules governing the terms used to describe the size of flowers, but as most non-specialist gardeners find these to be more confusing than useful they have not been strictly adhered to.

SPECIES AND CULTIVARS

There are hundreds of *Camellia* cultivars available in New Zealand, so the following selection of species and cultivars is necessarily brief and includes those most popular for garden use or that have interesting or unusual features. They are divided into hybrid groups.

SPECIES

The following are the most popular or influential of the species but they are not widely available in nurseries, most gardeners preferring the hybrids.

C. chrysantha (China) is the only true yellow camellia and although the bright yellow flowers are only about 60 mm diameter, it is not the size of the flowers but rather their potential for hybridising that has breeders so enthused. It is not generally available through garden centres.

C. fraterna (China) has white slight fragrant flowers with white stamens and prominent gold anthers.

C. granthamiana (Hong Kong) is very rare in the wild. The creamy white flowers appear early in the season and have massed golden stamens. Not totally hardy.

C. hiemalis (Japan) is not known in the wild and is probably a natural hybrid between *C. japonica* and *C. sasanqua*. It has pale pink flowers with golden stamens.

C. kissi (North East India to Southern China) has small white flowers that are usually fragrant.

C. lutchuensis (Southern Japan including Okinawa) has very fragrant white flowers with white stamens and white anthers. It is not always easy to grow and not totally hardy.

C. japonica (Japan, Eastern China and Korea) is the parent of a vast number of cultivars, and though the flower colour is variable, it is usually red. This easily grown camellia flowers mid season. There are several cultivated forms.

C. oleifera (Northern India, Southern China and South East Asia) has mildly fragrant small white flowers with yellow stamens and twisted petals.

C. pitardii (Southern China) has small white, pink or white flushed pink flowers.

C. reticulata (Southern China) is extensively used in hybridising and has mid pink flowers.

C. salicifolia (Hong Kong and Taiwan) has loose white flowers with white stamens that are mildly fragrant.

C. saluensis (Southern China) has white to mid pink flowers with small golden stamens. They may be single or semi-double.

C. sasanqua (Japan and Ryukyu Islands) has white to pale pink flowers with yellow stamens that are occasionally slightly fragrant. It flowers early.

C. sinensis (India to China and South East Asia), as the tea plant, is the most commercially important camellia. The white flowers (occasionally pale pink) have yellow stamens and appear early.

C. transnokensis (Taiwan) has clusters of very small white flowers with white stamens and golden anthers.

C. tsai (Southern China, Burma and Vietnam) has a slightly weeping growth habit and clusters of mildly fragrant small white flushed pink flowers. Not totally hardy.

SASANQUA AND HIEMALIS

A group of primarily early-flowering plants (autumn to late winter) that is made up of varieties and hybrids of three species; *C. sasanqua*, *C. hiemalis* and *C. vernalis*.

'Akebono' Single pink flowers. Excellent hedge or espalier.

'Bonanza' Medium to large semi-double red flowers over a long flowering season. Good in tubs.

'Bonsai Baby' Small red double flowers on a bush with a low, spreading growth habit.

'Chansonette' Large deep pink double flowers with slight ruffled petals. Suitable for training.

'Cotton Candy' Large soft pink semi-double flowers with slightly ruffled petals. Strong growing but inclined to be rather open and benefits from regular trimming to shape.

'Exquisite' Large very pale pink single flowers with ruffled and lobed petals. Well-suited to espaliering.

'Jennifer Susan' Soft mid pink loosely petalled semi-double flowers. Makes a good hedge or espalier.

'Kanjiro' (Often sold as 'Hiryu'.) Deep cerise pink single to semi-double flowers with lighter coloured centre.

'Mine No Yuki' Medium sized white to cream semi-double flowers with ruffled petals. Loose pendulous growth habit.

'Plantation Pink' Large mid pink single flowers. Strong growing and makes a quick hedge.

'Setsugekka' Large white semi-double with ruffled, slightly incurving petals. Strong growing upright bush.

'Showa No Sakae' Medium sized light to mid pink loose semi-double flowers. Weeping to horizontal growth habit; may be used in hanging baskets.

'Sparkling Burgundy' Small to medium sized deep pinkish red double flowers. Long flowering season. Vigorous grower. Suitable for most training styles.

'Yuletide' Small bright red single flowers with prominent golden stamens. Does well in tubs.

JAPONICA

The species forms and hybrids of *C. japonica* are among the most popular and widely grown camellias. Also included in this group are the Higo hybrids. These often ancient forms from Japan are not widely grown in New Zealand but a few are available. The following is a selection of the most popular Japonica hybrids.

'Ave Maria' Pale pink medium sized formal double.

'Bambino' Small coral pink anemone form with well-defined petaloid centre.

'Berenice Boddy' Medium sized light pink semi-double.

'Betty Sheffield Supreme' Large loose white or very pale pink double with petals edged in deep pink.

'Blood of China' Medium sized deep pinkish red semi-double to peony form. Often mildly scented.

'Bob Hope' Large blackish-red semi-double.

'Bob's Tinsie' Small deep red anemone form with a white centre.

'Brushfield's Yellow' Medium sized anemone form with white outer petals and creamy yellow petaloid centre.

'Can Can' Medium sized light pink peony form with deep cerise edged petals and veins.

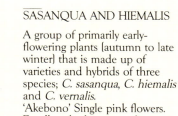

Camellia sasanqua 'Chansonette'

Camellia sasanqua 'Moonlight'

Camellia 'Shishi Gashira'

'Debutante' Medium sized light pink full peony form. Leaves may be a lighter green than most camellias.

'Desire' Medium sized light pink formal double with deeper coloured petal edges.

'Dolly Dyer' Small bright red anemone form with a densely packed petaloid centre.

'Elegans Supreme' Large deep pink anemone form with finely serrated petal edges. Large wavy edged leaves.

'Grand Slam' Large deep red semi-double or anemone form. Slightly fragrant.

'Guest of Honor' Large mid to deep pink loose semi-double to peony form. Heavy flowering.

'Guillio Nuccio' Very large deep coral pink semi-double with prominent stamens. The petals have wavy edges. Strong growing and very popular. Also available in a white and red variegated flower form.

'K. Sawada' Large white rose form or formal double.

'Kramer's Supreme' Large bright red full peony form.

'Laurie Bray' Medium to large light pink flowers that may be single or partially petaloid semi-double. Heavy flowering, tough and adaptable.

'Man Size' Small white anemone form.

'Margaret Davis' Medium sized informal double. White with petals edged deep pink to orange red.

'Mark Alan' Large deep purplish red semi-double or peony form.

'Midnight' Medium sized red semi-double to anemone form.

'Mrs D.W. Davis' Very large bright pink semi-double.

'Nuccio's Pearl' Medium sized very pale pink flushed mid pink formal double.

'Pink Pagoda' Medium to large mid pink formal double.

'Prima Ballerina' Medium to large semi-double. White washed with soft mid pink.

'Roger Hall' Medium sized bright red formal double.

'San Dimas' Medium to large deep red petaloid semi-double.

'Tiffany' Very large loose peony form. Soft mid pink with deeper tones.

RETICULATA

Reticulata hybrids are usually regarded as being less hardy than other camellias, but most survive New Zealand winters unscathed.

'Barbara Clark' Medium sized mid pink semi-double. Starts to flower early and continues over a long season.

'Brian' Medium sized deep pink semi-double.

'Buddha' Large deep pink semi-double flowers with wavy edged petals.

'Dr. Clifford Parks' Large bright red flowers. The form is very variable, from semi-double to peony to anemone form.

'Grand Jury' Large salmon pink peony form.

'Lasca Beauty' Very large light pink semi-double.

'Pavlova' Very large bright red semi-double. Good espalier.

'Phyl Doak' Medium to large pale pink semi-double.

'Sugar Dream' Medium sized mid pink anemone form.

'Valley M. Knudsen' Large deep pink semi-double to peony form

X WILLIAMSII

This group of hybrids results from fertilising *C. saluensis*, or a hybrid thereof, with pollen from *C. japonica*. This gives rise to an artificial species known as *C. x williamsii* to which all these hybrids belong regardless of their diverse appearance.

'Anticipation' Large deep pink peony form.

'Ballet Queen' Large salmon pink peony form.

'Debbie' Large bright mid pink semi-double to full peony form. One of the most popular cultivars.

'Donation' Large mid pink semi-double with darker veining.

'Dreamboat' A large formal double. The base colour is mid pink but has very subtle lavender and salmon pink shading.

'E.G. Waterhouse' Medium sized light pink formal double. Also available with a light pink and white variegated flower.

'Elsie Jury' Large deep pink full peony form. May be trained as an espalier.

'Jury's Yellow' Medium sized anemone form. White with creamy yellow petaloid centre. Starts early and flowers over a long season.

'Water Lily' Medium sized formal double. Bright light pink

with darker toning. The petals have distinctly rolled edges.

HYBRIDS

This catch-all group covers plants of indeterminate parentage and those that don't fit into any of the other groups.

'Baby Bear' Miniature light pink single. A small densely foliaged bush that is very popular for container growing.

'Baby Willow' Miniature white single. Very distinctive weeping growth. When grafted it makes a good weeping standard.

'Cinnamon Cindy' Miniature pale pink peony form. The central petaloids may be very pale pink. Espaliers well.

'Cornish Snow' Small white tinted pink single flowers. Very heavy flowering.

'Itty Bit' Miniature light pink anemone form. A densely foliaged, low, spreading bush.

'Jubilation' Large mid pink rose form double. Occasionally has darker flecked flowers.

'Mary Phoebe Taylor' Very large mid pink peony form.

'Nicky Crisp' Large lavender pink semi-double. Flowers early and continues over a long season.

'Night Rider' Small deep red semi-double.

'Quintessence' Miniature white single with conspicuous golden yellow anthers and white stamens. Mildly fragrant. Very popular as a container plant.

'Snippet' Small pale pink semi-double.

'Tiny Princess' Miniature semi-double to peony form. White to very pale pink with darker tints.

Camellia 'Betty Ridley'

Camellia 'Snippet'

ERICAS AND CALLUNAS
[HEATHS AND HEATHERS]

Heaths (Erica) and heathers (Calluna) are superb garden plants. They are suitable for a wide range of uses and generally require little maintenance.

Top: *Erica sessiflora*
Above: *Erica ventricosa*
'Globosa Rosea'
Below left: *Erica walkerii*
Below right: *Erica canaliculata*

Many ericas and callunas have very attractive and unusual flowers, but they are not only grown for their flowers. Some have brightly coloured winter foliage or vivid new spring growth, others are superb ground covers or rockery plants that would be well worth growing even if they never flowered.

The two genera are closely related and often look very similar with tiny narrow leaves and small bell-shaped flowers, but there are some important differences between and within the genera that have a considerable influence on their cultivation.

Erica is a genus of around 800 species but there is only one heather species: *Calluna vulgaris*. However, there are so many heather cultivars that at first it is hard to believe they are all derived from just one species. While a fairly variable lot as regards size and foliage, they are all hardy to at least -20°C. There are three main groups of ericas: those from northern Europe; those from southern European/North

Africa; and those from southern Africa.

The northern European species are all very hardy and tend to be ground covers or small shrubs. Those from southern Europe often grow into large shrubs and may be somewhat frost-tender where frosts are hard and regular, such as the inland parts of the South Island. The South African ericas range from tiny rounded bushes to large shrubs; some are hardy to around -8°C, but most are damaged if regularly exposed to temperatures below -4°C. They do very well in many North Island areas and are generally successful in mild coastal gardens further south.

Which heaths and heathers will grow best in your garden depends on the climate and soil conditions. Over much of the North Island and in mild areas of the South Island, the taller, tender *Erica* species are often used to provide winter flower colour. In very cold winter areas, such as Central Otago, the hardy heaths and heathers are used as ground covers and their spring and autumn flowers are a common sight. Ericas from drier regions will tolerate some drought and a fairly wide range of soil conditions, but callunas prefer moist, acid soil.

FLOWERS, FOLIAGE AND GROWTH HABIT

Undoubtedly the South African ericas have the most spectacular flowers. They tend to be tubular or globe-shaped and may be very brightly coloured, as in the orange-red *E. cerinthioides*, or very delicately shaded in pastel shades, such as the soft pink of *E. parkeri*. South African ericas vary in their flowering season, so by planting a selection of species it is possible to have flowers through most of the year.

The flowers of European ericas are very small when compared to most of the South African species, but they often make up for this with an abundance of bloom. Their tiny bell-shaped flowers are generally white or

shades of pink and a plant in full bloom may be absolutely smothered. They tend to bloom in autumn or spring, a few flower in winter.

Most callunas have flowers that are similar to those of European ericas, but a few cultivars, such as 'Alba Plena' and 'H.E. Beale', have double flowers, which make them appear to be very heavy blooming. The heathers mainly bloom in the late summer and autumn.

South African ericas usually have deep green foliage that shows little variation over the course of the year. European ericas and callunas, however, are available in a wide range of foliage colours including deep green, yellow, gold-tinted red and silver-grey. Many also intensify in colour in winter or have bright yellow or red spring growth.

Heaths and heathers vary enormously in size. Most northern European ericas and callunas are small, about 40 cm x 60 cm, but some of the southern European species are up to 4 m high. South African ericas range from about 40 cm x 40 cm to over 2 m high.

SOIL REQUIREMENTS

All the plants of the erica family (*Erica, Calluna, Rhododendron, Pieris, Kalmia*, etc.) have very fine, hair-like roots. These roots determine their soil requirements: fine roots cannot penetrate heavy soil, they rapidly rot in wet soils and desiccate quickly in dry soil; they are not able to grow to any great depth but may form a dense mat and cover a large area.

In the wild, ericaceous plants generally grow in three main environments: woodland with a soil composed of high-humus leaf mould; moist peat-based soils; or in moist alpine pockets of fairly new, gritty, mineral-based soils. All of these soils tend to be rather low in nutrients, moist, well aerated and are mildly to quite highly acidic. Ericas and callunas prefer soil in the range pH 5–6, although a few are moderately lime-tolerant.

Where many gardeners run into difficulties is in assuming that all plants with tiny needle-like leaves are tolerant of drought. Heaths and heathers need regular summer moisture. Some may be able to withstand short periods of drought, but in the main their root structure limits their tolerance. While moisture is important, good drainage is also vital. Prolonged periods in wet soil will inevitably lead to the drowning of the roots or root rot.

Heaths and heathers have relatively low nutrient requirements, but they will benefit from additional feeding. However, avoid concentrated chemical fertilisers because there's always a temptation to add just a little bit

more and that may cause severe, even fatal, damage to the very fine roots. Mild fertilisers, such as liquid blood and bone or slow-release pellets, are safe and just as effective.

None of these requirements are difficult to meet and they do not require the soil to be extensively modified. *Erica* roots do not go below about 50 cm so it is really only a matter of ensuring that the sub-soil drains well and providing added humus in the topsoil.

PRUNING

Ericas are not very long-lived plants; most are past their best by about 10 years old. However, careful pruning can prolong their useful life. Trim them back by about a third to a half, depending on size, after flowering. Hard cutting back will sometimes rejuvenate old plants, but replacement is usually the best option.

PROPAGATION

Erica and callunas are usually propagated from tiny summer and autumn tip cuttings taken from non-flowering stems or by removing self-layered pieces. (See the propagation chapter for details).

The species may be raised from their seed, which is very fine. Collect the seed by shaking dried seed heads over an envelope or paper bag. The seed usually germinates best on fine sphagnum moss or peat-based potting mix. It should not be covered with soil but the seed tray should have a glass cover and be kept in the shade at around 15–22°C.

Top: An *Erica* garden with flowering cherries.
Above: *Calluna* 'Wickwar Flame'
Below: *Calluna* 'H.E. Beale'
Bottom: *Erica glauca*

FUCHSIAS

Fuchsias are indispensable garden plants because they flower in shady positions and continue to bloom right through from late spring until early winter.

Fuchsias are popular as both standards and container plants.

It is hard to think of any other heavy flowering shrubs that are as easy to grow and provide such a beautiful display over such a long season as fuchsias. Grown as bushes, hedges, standards, ground covers, hanging baskets and climbers, fuchsias are available in a wide range of sizes and forms. Rather than attempt what could only be minimum coverage of species and cultivars, the following information is a general guide to fuchsias and their care.

Although they are best known for the striking deep pink colour, often called fuchsia pink, and combinations of red and purple, the fuchsia colour palette is wide. The range includes white, all shades of pink and mauve, purple, orange and red.

The flowers are followed by large reddish-purple berries that may be considered a curse or a feature, and while they can make a mess on paths and driveways, they are undeniably colourful. One of our native fuchsias, *F. procumbens*, is primarily grown for its large, bright red berries.

F. procumbens is also distinctive because of its prostrate habit and it is among the lowest growing of all fuchsias. Most fuchsias are rounded bushes that grow to about 1 m x 80 cm. At the other extreme are the tree-like species, of which the most common is the native *F. excorticata*. This species can grow to 12 m high.

CULTIVATION

As would be expected of plants most at home in dappled shade and woodland conditions, fuchsias prefer a loose, moist, humus-filled soil that is neutral to slightly acidic (pH 6.5–7). Work in plenty of high-humus compost before planting and water well in summer and your fuchsias should thrive. They also appreciate regular feeding and respond well to mild liquid fertilisers.

Provided they can be kept moist and sheltered from hot dry winds, fuchsias can also grow in reasonably sunny positions. You may lose a few of the summer flowers to sunburn, especially the darker blooms, but you will get flowers later in the autumn. The important point is that they must be kept moist.

Fuchsias are unusual in the way they react to winter cold. If exposed to frosts, they become deciduous; the foliage drops and the plant remains bare until spring. But in frost-free areas, fuchsias remain evergreen and may even flower year round. There are also some fuchsias that are genuinely frost tender and they may be killed over winter. Most fuchsias can withstand having the top growth killed off by frost provided the roots are well insulated and new shoots will soon develop as the weather warms in spring if the roots are healthy. The frosts of inland Canterbury and Otago may be too much for most fuchsias, but in less severe climates an insulating mulch layer will help the plants survive.

BUSHES AND HEDGES

Most hybrid fuchsias are naturally bushy and develop into plants that are about as wide as they are high. Young plants should be pinched back to encourage bushy growth, but once established bush fuchsias usually require little in the way of maintenance other than a light trimming and tidying once a year. Where fuchsias remain evergreen, prune in autumn or winter, otherwise leave any pruning until spring to lessen the risk of frost damage. Pruning as the new growth starts in spring also makes it easy to identify any branches that have been damaged over winter.

Some of the very densely foliaged fuchsias, particularly *F. magellanica* and its varieties, can be used for hedging. Usually a light annual pruning after winter is enough to maintain a good shape and does not affect the flowering too much. If the growth is very rapid, a summer pruning may also be necessary. It is not possible to create a dense, closely cropped hedge, but where an informal style is required fuchsias can be very effective.

CONTAINERS AND HANGING BASKETS

Fuchsias adapt well to container cultivation.

Use a good quality neutral to slightly acid potting mix and ensure that the plants do not become dry at any time. Regular feeding with liquid fertilisers or slow-release pellets will dramatically improve the foliage colour and flower yield.

Where regular winter frosts are likely, it is important that you either choose very hardy fuchsias or that the pots can be protected. Fuchsias react badly to having their roots frozen and if the soil in the pot freezes solid the plants may die. Some fuchsias, including the native *F. procumbens*, are natural trailers or ground covers. They can make useful ground covers but because the flowers tend to hang down much of the colour display is lost. For this reason, trailing fuchsias are more commonly grown in hanging baskets.

Fuchsias in hanging baskets dry out very quickly and demand regular watering. Even with the use of water-holding crystals in the potting mix, they may still need daily watering in summer. Trailing fuchsias are rapid growers, so regular pinching back and fortnightly feeding with a liquid fertiliser are also important.

STANDARDS

Fuchsias are seldom grafted so the usual method of producing a standard is to train and trim naturally upright bushes. To make your own standard, start with a single-stemmed cutting. Pinch out the lower leaves and any side growths and keep removing them as the stem grows. It will need staking and repeated tying, but eventually the stem may reach as high as 1 m. When the desired height is reached, pinch out the top to bush up the head of foliage.

Standards can be grown in garden beds, but as they only have one main stem it is important that they don't get frosted. Wrapping the stem with an insulating layer of carpet underlay or similar material will help protect against winter cold. However, gardeners in the South Island and central North Island usually find it less troublesome to grow their standard fuchsias in pots so that they can be moved under cover for the winter.

PROPAGATION

Most of the commonly grown fuchsias are hybrids, consequently they must propagated vegetatively. Soft or semi-ripe fuchsia cuttings, which may be taken at any time during the growing season, strike extremely easily and are a quick method of increasing plant numbers. Many gardeners strike their fuchsia cuttings in water but better root systems develop on plants struck in soil.

Above left: *Fuchsia thymifolia*
Above: *Fuchsia* 'Caroline'
Above right: *Fuchsia* 'Lye's Unique'

NATIVE FUCHSIAS

F. excorticata is one of the most common native shrubs. It may eventually become a tree up to 12 m high, but it can be kept trimmed to a large shrub. The flowers are small and may pass unnoticed. The tube and sepals open green but darken to a purplish red. The sepals often remain greenish cream at the base and have green tips. The corolla is deep purple. The dry peeling bark is very distinctive.

F. procumbens is the most popular of the native fuchsias. It is a wiry-stemmed sprawling ground cover that can be up to 2.5 m wide, although it is usually trimmed and is often grown in rockeries or hanging baskets. Its leaves are light to mid green and cordate to almost round, with slightly serrated edges. The flowers are upward facing and greenish yellow with no corolla. They are most notable for their red stamens and bright blue pollen. This is one of the few fuchsias grown primarily for its fruit; the berries that follow the flowers are up to 25 mm diameter. They are like small plums and are covered with a plum-like bloom. It is hardy in all but the coldest areas.

The berries of *Fuchsia procumbens*.

THE PROTEA FAMILY

*The protea family (Proteaceae) includes a wide range of
ground covers, trees and shrubs that often make superb
garden plants. While some of the species are frost-tender,
they are in all other respects remarkably resilient.*

Top: *Toronia toru*
Middle: *Hakea salicifolia*
Bottom: *Leucadendron tinctum*

Proteas (the term is often used collectively as
well as for the particular genus *Protea*) are a
variable group. Indeed, the family was named
after Proteus, a Greek god capable of changing
his shape at will. It includes some 60 genera
and 1400 species of Southern Hemisphere
plants, the bulk of which are native to southern Africa and Australia, with the remainder
coming from South America and many of the
Pacific islands, including two species (*Knightia
excelsa* and *Toronia toru*) from New Zealand.

There is an enormous variety of foliage
among the proteas. It is almost always evergreen, but may be needle-like, as with many
grevilleas; long, narrow and serrated; or rounded and leathery. Some genera, particularly
Leucadendron, include species with brightly
coloured foliage, the intensity of which varies
with the season.

Protea flowers are composed of clusters of
narrow tubes that are often curved. These 'spider' flowers are seen at their simplest in our
two native species and some of the grevilleas.
In many cases, what appears to be the flower is
actually a bract of brightly coloured leaves surrounding the true flowers. The flowering season also varies; many proteas and grevilleas
flower in winter, while leucospermums tend to
flower in summer. With careful selection it is
possible to have plants in flower all year round.
Some flowers contain large quantities of nectar
that many native birds, especially bellbirds and
tuis, relish.

Under New Zealand conditions the South
African and Australian Proteaceae tend to be
at their best in coastal or northern districts, but
they also do particularly well in the drier eastern areas from Gisborne to Banks Peninsula.
Inland, unseasonable early and late frosts often
kill all but the hardiest specimens. In these
areas, try the South American genera as they
tend to be hardier and prefer somewhat
damper conditions. For example, *Embothrium*
can withstand hard frosts and is grown over
most of the country. But where winter temperatures regularly drop to -6°C or lower, most
proteas require frost protection.

CULTIVATION

Other than a suitable climate, the key to success with proteas is establishing the right soil
conditions. The protea family is mainly adapted to mineral-based soils that drain very quickly and which often have low nutrient levels.
These soils tend to be moderately acid and are
often especially low in phosphates.

Good drainage is *absolutely essential*. Rich
loams and heavy clays do not make good protea soils. If you have a heavy soil do not try to
improve it by adding sand or shingle as this
will often make the problem worse; the soil
binds with the sand and shingle and sets like
concrete. Instead, add more humus. Proteas
will not appreciate a rich compost so the
humus used should be fairly low in nutrients –
natural leaf mould and rotted pine needles
work well. To avoid these materials compacting
down into a poor-draining thatch, incorporate
about 50% fine shingle grit by volume and
combine the mix with the existing soil.

Most proteaceous plants come from areas
with low rainfall or where the rains are strictly
seasonal. Many are coastal plants, although
most of the South African genera include
alpine or sub-alpine species. *Knightia* from
New Zealand and *Embothrium* from Chile are
exceptions; they usually occur away from the
coast, in areas where rainfall is quite high and
not seasonal. Nevertheless, they still demand
excellent drainage.

Although proteas are remarkably resilient
and not difficult to grow, there seems to be
some common myths regarding their cultivation. Like most myths these have some basis in
fact, but they can be misleading.

MYTH 1: Feeding proteas will kill them. This
is not strictly true. Proteas need nutrients just
like any other plant. It is not fertiliser that does

the damage but high phosphate levels and intense bursts of nutrients that lead to rapid growth. Avoid most general garden fertilisers, fresh animal manures and anything with added superphosphate.

Because proteas will tolerate poor soils, it is often easier not to feed them rather than risk damage, but you'll certainly get better results if you apply a slow-release low-phosphate fertiliser in late winter and mid summer. This will keep the plants growing slowly but steadily.

MYTH 2: Proteas need a hot sunny position. Although under New Zealand conditions most Proteaceae prefer full sun or something near to it, that doesn't necessarily mean the hottest, most baked position you can find. They can survive severe conditions once established, but extreme heat and drought will cause damage, especially to young plants. Shade from the hottest sun will prolong the flower display and, provided the drainage is good, occasional deep watering is also recommended.

The optimum time for planting depends on your climate. Autumn or winter is best in mild areas, as this is when moisture requirements are at their lowest, while spring is the preferred time if regular frosts are expected, as this allows the young plants to get well established before having to endure winter conditions.

Most proteaceous plants need occasional trimming and tidying. This may be to improve their growth habit or to remove old flowers or seed heads that have become dry and unsightly. How far to cut back varies with the genera, although as a rule only light pruning is recommended as there is a general reluctance among proteas to reshoot from bare wood. The best time to prune is usually immediately after flowering. In areas where there is the possibility of frost damage, it is advisable to leave pruning autumn and winter-flowering plants until spring.

Above: *Protea neriifolia*
Left: *Protea amplexicaulis*

PROPAGATION

Proteas can be frustratingly difficult plants to propagate. Fresh seed often germinates well only for the seedlings to collapse after a few weeks. This is usually due to a fungal disease that blackens the foliage and eventually kills the young seedlings. Regular fungicide applications are important. Prick out the young seedlings into a coarse, free-draining, unfertilised potting mix once they have their first true leaves.

Cultivars and selected forms must be propagated vegetatively. The usual method is firm semi-ripe cuttings in late summer and autumn. The success rate varies markedly; some cultivars, such as *Leucadendron* 'Safari Sunset', strike quite easily, while many others may be virtually impossible without professional equipment.

COMMON GENERA

Many of these plants are not widely available at garden centres, although specialist growers would consider them to be just the most common genera and are likely to stock others as well. All of the species and genera covered here are evergreen unless otherwise stated.

Top: *Grevillea* 'Robin Hood'
Above: *Hakea laurina*
Left: A colourful group of Proteaceae provide excellent winter colour in a well-drained position.

AULAX

This is a South African genus of small to medium sized shrubs, of which only *A. cancellata* is commonly sold ready-grown in garden centres. It grows to 1.5-2 m x 1 m and has fine needle-like leaves. In spring, female plants produce red-edged yellow flowers that develop into red seed cones. The catkin-like male flowers are yellow. It is hardy to about -5°C.

BANKSIA

An Australian genus of about 60 species, ranging in size from ground covers to medium sized trees. The flowering season is primarily from late winter to late spring and most species have cylindrical cone-like flower heads composed of densely packed filamentous styles radiating from a central core. Creamy yellow to light golden-yellow is the predominant colour range, although those of *B. coccinea* are red. Most species have narrow serrated leaves that are mid to deep green above and silvery grey on the undersides. Hardiness varies; some are quite frost-tender but others will tolerate -10°C.

DRYANDRA

An Australian genus of around 60 species of shrubs ranging in height from about 1-4 m. Most have mid to deep green leaves that are often very long and narrow with sharply toothed edges. The rounded flower heads, which appear from mid winter, are usually light to bright yellow. The most common species is *D. formosa*, which grows to about 3 m and is hardy to around -5°C once established. Dryandras will grow on extremely poor soil and generally react badly to most fertilisers.

EMBOTHRIUM

The Chilean fire bush (*E. coccineum*) is a small tree around 5 m x 2.5 m. It has 100 mm long, leathery, bright green leaves that may become somewhat sparse on older plants. In mid to late spring the tree turns vivid orange-red as the honeysuckle-like tubular flowers open – the flowering

Banksia integrifolia

Embothrium coccineum

Leucospermum cordifolium

season is brief but spectacular. Overall *Embothrium* requires more moisture than most Proteaceae but good drainage is still important.

GREVILLEA

With some 250 species, this is the largest of the Australian proteaceous genera. Most of the common garden species and cultivars are ground covers to medium sized shrubs (up to 3 m) with needle-like foliage. The more densely foliaged plants, especially *G. juniperina* and *G. rosmarinifolia*, are often used as hedging plants. These plants grow to at least 1.5 m high. Grevillea flowers are often described as 'spider flowers'. This refers to the styles of some species, which tend to radiate from the centre like a spider's legs. Some species have 'toothbrush' flowers: the styles are all on one side like the bristles of a toothbrush.

The species and hybrids vary enormously in hardiness. Some will stand little or no frost but others, such as *G. rosmarinifolia*, will tolerate frosts of -10°C or lower – all prefer full sun with good drainage.

HAKEA

This Australian genus includes about 130 species, few of which are widely cultivated. The most common is probably *H. laurina*,

the pincushion hakea. It grows to about 6 m x 4 m and mature shrubs have a slightly weeping habit. The name pincushion refers to the flowers, which are spherical, with numerous radiating styles. They appear in late autumn and early winter, opening cream and turning to orange and red as they age. This shrub is hardy to about -5°C once well established and is easily grown in most well-drained soils.

ISOPOGON

An Australian genus of 34 species of small to medium sized shrubs, most of which grow from 1-2 m high and about as wide. They have a preference for poor but well-drained soil and will quickly collapse if over-watered or overfed. Most species have narrow lanceolate leaves about 75 mm long and some, such as the common *I. anemonifolius*, have finely cut foliage reminiscent of Marguerite daisy or *Anemone* leaves.

The flower heads, which open in spring and early summer, are composed of a central cone from which radiate numerous styles. The flower colours are mainly white, yellow or pink. The two most widely grown species, *I. anemonifolius* and *I. anethifolius*, are hardy to about -5°C, but many species, such as *I. cuneatu* and the beautiful pink and yellow-flowered *I. latifolius*,

are damaged at temperatures below -2°C.

KNIGHTIA

The rewa rewa or New Zealand honeysuckle (*K. excelsa*) is the best known of the two native proteaceous species. In the wild it can grow to 25 m high but in gardens it is more restrained, and seldom exceeds 8 m x 3.5 m. Rewa rewa has semi-glossy, deep green to bronze-green, narrow, lanceolate to oblong leaves that are very tough and leathery. In summer it produces tubular honeysuckle-like flowers that develop from buds covered in a reddish brown tomentum. As the flowers open, the tomentum-covered sepals and the petals curl back to form a congested mass in the centre of the flower head. The flowers, which can smell unpleasant, are followed by conspicuous brown velvety seed pods. Rewa rewa is easily grown in moist well-drained soil in sun or partial shade and is hardy to about -5°C or slightly lower once established. It may be grown in any coastal area if protected when young.

LEUCADENDRON

Species of this genus are the most widely grown of the South African Proteaceae. Most are medium-sized shrubs around 1-2.5 m high. However, one of the best known species, the silver tree (*L. argenteum*), can grow to 10 m high.

Many species and cultivars are grown here, but probably the most widely planted is *L.* 'Safari Sunset'. Typical of the genus, it has narrow lanceolate leaves that are up to 100 mm long. The upward-facing foliage densely covers the narrow, upright branches and develops deep red tints at the flowering tips. Deep red leaf bracts enclose the flower cones. As the insignificant flowers near maturity, the bracts become intensely coloured. 'Safari Sunset' has red bracts but others develop cream, yellow, pink or orange tones. Leucadendrons generally develop their best colours from mid to late winter but 'Jester', a pink, cream and green variegated sport of 'Safari Sunset', is brightly coloured throughout the year. The species and hybrids vary considerably in hardiness, but most will tolerate frosts of at least -3°C provided they have good drainage and the humidity is not excessive. 'Safari Sunset' is hardy to about -8°C. In the North Island, leucadendrons generally thrive in all but the coldest central areas and they can be grown with varying degrees of success in all coastal areas of the South Island.

LEUCOSPERMUM

A South African genus of about 50 species, most of which are medium to large shrubs that grow to about 1.5-3 m high. Some have strongly upright growth habits, but most are dense and bushy.

The flowers are variously described as 'Catherine wheels', 'pincushions' and 'sky rockets', all of which refer to the numerous radiating styles. These are often incurved, creating a cupped effect. The flowers usually appear in late spring and continue for about two months. Most garden leucospermums are cultivars of *L. cordifolium* and are hardy to occasional frosts of about -5°C, but they resent wet or humid winter conditions, which can often lead to tip die back. Good drainage is also very important.

MIMETES

This South African genus includes 11 species, only one of which is widely grown. *M. cucullatus* has 40 mm long oblong leaves with small lobes at the tips that densely cover the branches like upward-facing scales. The small white flowers are enclosed within leaf bracts that change colour to a bright red as the flower buds mature. Mimetes may flower throughout the year but is usually at its best in late spring when the new growth appears, as this is also red. It grows to about 1.5 m x 1.5 m, is hardy to around -3°C, and prefers moist well-drained soil (it is not very drought tolerant).

PARANOMUS

The most common species of this 18 species genus, *P. reflexus*, is an undemanding 1.5 m x 1.8 m bush with bright yellow bottle-brush-like flower heads in winter and spring. The foliage is *Anemone*-like and very finely cut; the flower stems have small diamond-shaped leaves just below the flower heads. It is easily grown in any well-drained soil in full sun. Although the plant is hardy to about -5°C, the flowers are damaged by frosts over -2°C.

PROTEA

Protea is a genus of about 80 species that is confined to southern Africa and concentrated around the Cape of Good Hope. The species range in size from less than 50 cm high to over 4 m. Most commonly grown proteas are small to medium sized shrubs in the 1-2.5 m high range.

The best known species is *P. neriifolia*. It has narrow leaves up to 150 mm long that are covered with a fine tomentum when young. In autumn, winter and spring, upright, 125 mm long x 75 mm wide, goblet-shaped flowers are carried at the tips of the branches. They are composed of a woolly central cone surrounded by overlapping, upward-facing, petal-like, deep reddish-pink bracts tipped with a fringe of black hairs. Many forms with varying colours of bract and tip hairs are grown. The central cone, often with many incurving styles, is common to all *Protea* species but the arrangement of the bracts varies. Many have them arranged in a stellate or star-shaped fashion.

The foliage is also variable. It may be needle-like, lanceolate, oblong or rounded. It can be silvery grey, glaucous or bright green depending on the species and it may or may not be tomentose.

Likewise, hardiness varies considerably. Most species will tolerate at least -3°C with good drainage and low humidity but many are considerably tougher. *P. neriifolia* will withstand -5°C and *P. grandiceps* will often survive -10°C when well established. Proteas do well over most of the North Island and many species can be grown as far south as Christchurch with a little winter protection.

SERRURIA

Blushing bride (*S. florida*) is very popular with florists because its *Nigella*-like papery white bracts are very delicate and last well as cut flowers. The bracts, which are surrounded with finely cut lacy leaves, are produced freely in winter and spring. Blushing bride can be difficult to grow, because not only is it frost-tender (it tolerates only occasional exposure to -2°C), it must also have full sun and absolutely perfect drainage. It is one of a genus of 44 species from South Africa, of which the only other species commonly grown is *S. rosea*. It is a densely foliaged 70 cm x 90 cm bush with small pink bracts and is slightly hardier and definitely easier to grow than *S. florida*.

STENOCARPUS

The Queensland firewheel tree (*S. sinuata*) is a large tree (12 m x 8 m) that produces a magnificent display of orange to red flowers in summer. It has large, glossy, dark green leaves that are deeply lobed. The flowers are tubular and are carried in flattened clusters that radiate spoke-like from a central hub, hence the name firewheel tree. It is hardy to about -4°C once well established but is very tender when young and does best in moist well-drained soil in full sun.

TELOPEA

Natives of Australia, the waratah genus includes just four species. The New South Wales waratah (*T. speciosissima*), the one most commonly grown, has finely serrated oblong leaves that are up to 125 mm long with small notches or lobes at the tips. It develops into a large shrub or small tree up to 5 m x 5 m. The flowers, which are produced in spring and carried at the tips of the branches, are impressively large, bright red, and composed of numerous incurving styles surrounded by red foliage bracts. Several cultivars, such as the semi-dwarf 'Forest Fire' (2 m x 2 m) are available.

The Victorian waratah (*T. oreades*) is a similar plant with slightly lighter coloured leaves and flowers. Both of these species and their cultivars are hardy to around -8°C. Waratahs prefer moist well-drained soil in full sun and once established they require little care. But many die during the initial establishment period. This is possibly due to essential mycorrhiza failing to establish. These minute fungi form a symbiotic relationship with the plants' roots and are vital in the uptake of nutrients. It has been suggested that taking soil from an established waratah and putting it around new plants may help lessen these difficulties.

TORONIA

The sole species in this genus is the lesser known of our two native proteaceous species. Formerly listed as *Persoonia toru*, it is now known as *Toronia toru*. A small bushy tree that can grow to about 9 m x 5 m, it is usually far smaller in gardens. The narrow, lanceolate, olive green to bronze leaves are about 100 mm long but may grow to over 150 mm on mature trees in sheltered sites. The buff-coloured starry flowers, which appear in late winter and early spring, are carried in racemes and develop from golden brown felted buds. It is easily grown in any moist well-drained soil in full sun or partial shade and is hardy to about -8°C once established.

Toronia toru is a relatively unspectacular plant but its flowers are pleasantly honey-scented and it is interesting because it is one of our more unusual natives.

RHODODENDRONS AND AZALEAS

Rhododendrons can truly be said to have it all – colour, form and foliage – and in a bewildering variety. They range from minute plants scarcely a couple of centimetres high right through to forest giants; they are available in almost every flower colour.

Rhododendron is a large genus of at least 800 species. It ranges over most of the Northern Hemisphere, with just a few Southern Hemisphere representatives. Species exist in all climates and the wider family to which they belong, the Ericaceae, is distributed worldwide.

You will notice that this chapter is headed rhododendrons and azaleas, but they are really one and the same thing – all azaleas are rhododendrons.

SOIL

All the plants of the Ericacae family have very fine, hair-like roots. This enables rhododendrons to make the best use of the shallow soils in which many naturally grow, but in periods of drought the fine roots dry out quickly and if they become waterlogged they rot. Also, they can't penetrate heavy soil. This may make them

Rhododendrons thrive in southern gardens.

seem fussy plants but it all comes down to one thing, humus.

To grow good rhododendrons you should make the utmost effort to condition your soil before planting. It is virtually impossible to work in too much compost or other humus-containing material. Apart from insect damage or sunburn, nearly all rhododendron disorders can be traced back to some problem with the roots and ultimately the soil.

Many rhododendrons have evolved to grow under deciduous trees where they receive an annual dressing of fallen leaves and where the soil, over time, becomes composed almost entirely of leaf mould. This type of soil is not high in nutrients but it is extremely high in humus and is moisture-retentive yet well drained. It is not a deep soil; and even if it were, the tree roots would remove many of the nutrients from the lower levels. However, the soil that is there is loose and easily penetrated by fine roots, water and air. This sort of compost-based soil is usually acidic.

To get the best from your rhododendrons, you need to try to recreate these conditions in your garden. Start by working plenty of humus-rich compost into the soil; leaf mould and garden compost are ideal and the black thatch that you find under the surface layer of fallen pine needles is also very good. You could also add bark chips and very well-rotted sawdust; these don't contain much humus but they will open up the soil and improve the effectiveness of your compost.

When the soil has a loose, fluffy texture, a light dressing of acid plant fertiliser can be added and you are ready to plant.

SHADE

Rhododendrons are generally thought of as plants for shade and it is true that most of

.hem do prefer to be sheltered from the hottest sun. However, there are varying degrees of shade, and rhododendrons tend to prefer quite bright positions in light or dappled shade. Too shady and they will have difficulty forming flower buds and will become lank and leggy growers. The ideal position for large-leafed rhododendrons is a fairly open site under deciduous trees.

Deciduous azaleas, alpine rhododendrons and smaller-leafed forms prefer brighter sites and many will perform well in sunny positions. As a rule, the larger the leaf the more shade it will require, but when in doubt err on the brighter side, because, provided the soil conditions are good, most rhododendrons will tolerate some sun.

MULCHING AND NUTRITION

Mulching with compost or material such as rotted pine bark in spring and autumn will help to conserve moisture as well as insulating the surface roots from climatic extremes such as hot sun and ground-freezing cold. Avoid mounding excessive mulch up against the trunk or main stems of larger rhododendrons; it may cause a deterioration in the bark and lead to fungal or viral troubles.

Rhododendrons do not need to be heavily fed (mulching will often provide enough supplementary nutrients), but even under the best of conditions, plants may occasionally suffer from some nutrient deficiencies. When feeding rhododendrons it is best to use mild fertilisers; too strong and you'll burn the surface roots causing a browning of the leaf tips and edges. It is generally best to use mild organic fertilisers such as liquid blood and bone or sulphate-based (acidic) chemical fertilisers. These will ensure that the soil is not excessively 'sweetened', that is, made too alkaline. Incorporating some slow-release fertiliser granules or a mild acid fertiliser in with the twice yearly mulching will usually maintain adequate nutrient levels.

CONTAINER GROWING

Their dense root system makes rhododendrons, particularly evergreen azaleas, suited to container growing. Specimens not exceeding about 1.2 m high and wide after 10 years' growth are ideal.

By using a good quality potting mix (garden centres often have special rhododendron potting mix that is slightly more acidic than the standard mix) and regular applications of liquid blood and bone or other mild fertilisers, the plants should be able to remain in the container for up to two years before repotting

is necessary. When the time to repot does arrive, you have a choice: you can either move the plant up to a larger container or undertake some light root pruning and repot it in the same container. If you don't remove more than a third of the roots, you won't need to cut the foliage back, although it is a good opportunity to trim the plant if necessary.

PESTS AND DISEASES

Leaf roller caterpillars and thrips are the most common pests. Leaf rollers are usually restricted to small-leafed rhododendrons and ever-

Shade and a humus-enriched soil are ideal for rhododendrons, as shown in the gardens above, where they combine beautifully with shade-loving perennials.

Many rhododendron varieties create soft, flowing effects (top left and right). Deciduous azaleas, however, tend to have a more upright habit (above).

green azaleas but thrips may attack any of the forms. As both of these pests can be hard to get at, systemic insecticides usually give the best results.

The main fungal diseases are azalea leaf gall and mildew. Azalea leaf gall causes a very unsightly thickening and distorting of the new growth. The damaged leaf turns white as the fungal spores mature but eventually it blackens and dries. Fungicides will control the spread of the disease and you should also remove damaged leaves before they fall. Mildew is most common in the autumn and most fungicides are effective against mildew.

Die back and root-rot diseases, such as *Armillaria*, *Phomopsis* and *Phytophthora* rots, often cause problems with rhododendrons and are usually an indication that the drainage is poor. There is very little you can do, as once a plant shows signs of damage it is often too late to save it. Check your growing conditions to prevent a recurrence.

PRUNING AND TRIMMING

Rhododendrons seldom need regular pruning, just occasional trimming. Any trimming and shaping is best done immediately after flowering because this leaves the whole growing season for regrowth and limits the effect of pruning on the following season's flowering.

Unless you want the plants to set seed, you should remove the spent flower heads. This 'dead-heading' allows the plant to concentrate its energies on growth rather than seed production. It is also a good idea to pinchout the apical leaf-bud when dead-heading as this encourages strong lateral branching and dense growth.

PROPAGATION

Rhododendron species are often propagated by seed, but cultivars and selected forms must be propagated vegetatively. Cuttings are the most widely used method and layering is also popular. Some rhododendrons strike poorly from cuttings and these varieties used to be grafted, and often still are, but many are now being propagated by tissue culture.

RHODODENDRON SPECIES AND CULTIVARS

All of the species and cultivars listed here are hardy to at least -10°C, flower mid season (late September to early November) and are evergreen unless otherwise noted.

SPECIES

The following are some of the more popular or influential species.

R. arboreum (northern India to southern China)
An early-flowering upright small tree with medium-sized deep olive green leaves. It has bright red bell-shaped flowers in rounded trusses of 15-20 blooms. There are several forms including 'Album' (white) and 'Roseum' (deep pink) and it is a parent of many early-flowering red cultivars. 2.5 m x 1.8 m.

R. catawbiense (eastern United States)
A large bush with medium to large, glossy, deep green, oval leaves. It has white, pink or mauve flowers in trusses of up to 20 blooms. It is an important species that has frequently been used to add hardiness and heavy-flowering characteristics to cultivars. 2 m x 1.8 m.

R. ciliatum (eastern Himalayan region)
A small compact bush with glossy, rounded, bronze green leaves fringed with fine hairs, and widely flared white flushed pink flowers in loose clusters of up to 4 blooms. It often blooms early and has reddish-brown peeling bark that is very distinctive. 1 m x 1.2 m.

R. cinnabarinum (eastern Himalayan region)
A large upright bush with striking reddish brown peeling bark and aromatic bright to bronze green, medium-sized, glossy leaves. The waxy tubular flowers are deep brownish-red and are carried in clusters of up to 5 blooms. 2 m x 1.5 m

R. edgeworthii (eastern Himalayas, southern China and Burma)
A small bush with a rather open growth habit and medium-sized, oval, dark green leaves with a heavy covering of fine hairs on the undersides. The white flushed pink flowers are fragrant

and are carried in loose clusters of about 3 blooms. This species, which is the parent of many fragrant hybrids, is hardy to only -8°C. 1.2 m x 1.2 m.

R. forrestii (Tibet, southern China and Burma)
A low, spreading bush with rounded, deep green, glossy leaves. The waxy bright red flowers are carried singly or in pairs. 30 cm x 75 cm.

R. fortunei (eastern China)
A large bush or small tree with oval mid green leaves up to 200 mm long. The large, fragrant, pale pink flowers fade to white and are carried in trusses of up to 7 blooms. This species has everything – impressive foliage, fragrant flowers, great hardiness and vigour. 2.5 m x 2 m.

R. griersonianum (southern China and Burma)
A spreading bush that has been extensively used in hybridising. The narrow mid green leaves are up to 200 mm long and covered with fine hairs, and the flared bright orange-red flowers are carried in loose trusses of about 5 blooms. 1 m x 1.5 m.

R. japonicum (Japan)
Formerly known as R. molle (and it may yet revert to that name), this deciduous azalea has hairy oval leaves and yellow to orange red flowers in trusses of up to 12 blooms. This species, the 'Mollis Azalea', was very important in the development of many cultivars. 1.8 m x 2 m.

R. kiusianum (Japan)
A densely twiggy evergreen azalea with tiny oval leaves covered in fine hairs and small bright purple flowers in clusters of up to 5 blooms. This azalea becomes deciduous when exposed to extreme cold. Several colour forms are available, including white and pink. 60 cm x 1 m.

R. occidentale (western North America)
A large deciduous azalea that remains compact for many years. It has oval to oblong leaves that colour brilliantly in autumn and

Rhododendron lochae

Rhododendron javanicum

very fragrant white to cream flowers with pink and yellow markings in trusses of up to 12 blooms. Several forms are available of which the most common are 'Equisita' and 'Delicatissima'. 1.5 m x 1.5 m.

R. williamsianum (southern China)
A densely foliaged compact bush with very distinctive bright green leaves up to 50mm long and 50 mm bell-shaped flowers in clusters of 2 or 3 blooms. The colour ranges from light to deep pink. 45 cm x 60 cm.

R. yakushimanum (Yakushima Island off southern Japan)
A small, densely foliaged, mounding bush with very distinctive deep green, leathery leaves with rolled edges and a heavy covering of woolly white hairs on the undersides. The white to pale pink flowers open from deep pink buds and are carried in round trusses of up to 10 blooms. There are many cultivated forms and hybrids and these are often called 'yak' hybrids. 60 cm x 1 m.

VIREYA RHODODENDRONS

The tropical vireya rhododendrons have always enjoyed a

fairly limited popularity as greenhouse or frost-free garden plants. But, although tending to be rather straggly, they often have fragrant or very brightly coloured flowers. They are not seasonal and may flower at any time, with autumn being the most common.

Vireyas are not difficult to grow provided they are protected from frost. If you live in a mild frost-free climate you can treat vireyas much like any other rhododendron, otherwise an unheated greenhouse is usually all the protection required. Among the more common vireya species are R. aurigeranum (bright orange-yellow); R. jasminiflorum (honeysuckle-like, tubular, very fragrant, white); R. javanicum (orange); R. laetum (soft yellow to orange); R. lochae (bright red); and R. zoelleri (golden-yellow edged bright orange).

RHODODENDRON CULTIVARS

The following are just a few of the thousands of cultivars available. The parentage and breeding date are given because they are valuable clues to the

Rhododendron 'Virginia Richards'

Rhododendron 'Jingle Bells'

Rhododendron 'Loderi King George'

nature of a plant. As you grow more rhododendrons and learn more of their history you will be surprised at just how much information can be gleaned from a phrase such as 'a *griersonianum* hybrid raised in 1939'!

DWARF BUSHES
LESS THAN 1 M HIGH

'Brickdust' (*R. williamsianum* x 'Dido' 1959) Rounded bright green leaves and bell-shaped pinkish orange flowers; 'Curlew' (*R. ludlowii* x *R. fletcheranum* 1969) Small, oval, bronze green leaves and wide open bright yellow flowers that often appear early; 'Elisabeth Hobbie' ('Essex Scarlet' x *R. forrestii* var. *repens* 1945) Oblong very deep reddish-green leaves and blood red bell-shaped flowers; 'Ginny Gee' (*R. keiskei* x *R. racemosum* 1979) Small rounded leaves with very bright green new growth and masses of tiny pink and white flowers; 'Patty Bee' (*R. keiskei* 'Yaku Fairy' x *R. fletcheranum* 1978) Small oval leaves and soft yellow flowers in early spring; 'Scarlet Wonder' ('Essex Scarlet' x *R. forrestii* var. *repens* 1960) Deep green oblong leaves and small trusses of intense red bell-shaped flowers; 'Snow Lady' (*R. leucapsis* x *R. ciliatum* 1955) Mid green, slightly hairy, rounded leaves and very slightly fragrant pure white flowers in loose trusses in early spring.

MEDIUM SIZED BUSHES
1 M TO 1.8 M HIGH

'Blue Diamond' ('Intrifast' x *R. augustinii* 1935) Oblong deep green to slightly glaucous leaves with wide open lavender to mid blue flowers in small clusters; 'Bumble Bee' (*R. ponticum* hybrid) Narrow deep green leaves and conical trusses of purple flowers with a very dark blotch; 'Christmas Cheer' (*R. caucasicum* hybrid) Rounded mid green leaves and small trusses of pale pink and white flowers that open from deep pink buds in late winter or very early spring; 'Jingle Bells' ('Fabia' x 'Ole Olson' 1974) A densely foliaged bush with mid green leaves and loose clusters of orange flowers that fade to golden yellow; 'Lem's Cameo' ('Dido' x 'Anna' 1962) Oblong, deep bronze green leaves and reddish new growth and waxy apricot-pink flowers with lighter tones in trusses of up to 20 blooms; 'Nancy Evans' ('Hotei' x 'Lem's Cameo' 1983) Deep bronze green, leathery, oblong leaves and reddish new growth and bright golden-yellow-edged-orange flowers opening from orange buds in trusses of up to 20 blooms; 'Percy Wiseman' (*R. yakushimanum* x 'Fabia Tangerine' selfed 1971) Deep green slightly glossy leaves; cream flowers with pink edges and yellow markings in trusses of up to 15 blooms; 'Rubicon' ('Noyo Chief' x 'Kilimanjaro' 1979) Deep green oblong leaves and waxy deep blood red flowers in trusses of up to 18 flowers; 'Unique' (*R.*

campylocarpum hybrid 1934) Mid green, leathery, oblong leaves on a densely foliaged, neat, mounding bush with dome-shaped trusses opening light pink from deep pink buds and fading to cream; 'Virginia Richards' ((*R. wardii* x 'F.C. Puddle') x 'Mrs Betty Robertson' 1966) Oblong mid green glossy leaves with pink buds opening to orange-cream flowers with pink and yellow tones in trusses of up to 12 blooms; 'Winsome' ('Hummingbird' x *R. griersonianum* 1930) Mid green lanceolate leaves and masses of deep cerise flowers in loose clusters; 'Yellow Petticoats' ('Hotei' x ('Pink Petticoats' x *R. wardii*) 1983) Mid green oblong leaves and bright yellow slightly frilly flowers in trusses of up to 15 blooms.

LARGE BUSHES
OVER 1.8 M HIGH

'Anna-Rose Whitney' (*R. griersonianum* x 'Countess of Derby' 1954) Large, mid green, oblong leaves up to 200 mm long with clear deep pink flowers in rounded trusses of up to 12 blooms in late spring. (3 m x 3 m); 'Cornubia' (*R. arboreum* x 'Shilsonii' before 1912) Light to mid green oblong leaves and bright clear red flowers in rounded trusses in very early spring. One of the most widely planted early red cultivars. (3 m x 2 m); 'Fastuosum Flore Pleno' (*R. catawbiense* x *R. ponticum* before 1846) Large light to mid green oblong leaves and light purple semi-double flowers with

yellowish throat markings and purple spotting. The first of the still very few double flower rhododendron cultivars. (3 m x 2.5 m); 'Fragrantissimum' (*R. edgeworthii* x *R. formosum* 1868) An open, loosely structured bush with deep bronze green, slightly hairy, oval to lanceolate leaves and very fragrant, large, white-flushed-pink trumpet-shaped flowers in loose clusters. A slightly tender, often untidy bush but its fragrance keeps it popular and it espaliers well. (2 m x 2.5 m); 'Lem's Monarch' ('Anna' x 'Marinus Koster' 1971) Large mid green oblong leaves with pale pink or white flowers with deep pink edges in very large conical trusses of up to 20 blooms. 'Point Defiance' is from the same cross and is very similar in all respects. Both are superb plants. (2.5 m x 2 m); 'Loderi King George' (*R. griffithianum* x *R. fortunei* 1901) Slightly glaucous oblong leaves up to 200 mm long and mildly fragrant pale pink flowers opening from deep pink buds. One of a group of very similar, very impressive hybrids that will eventually grow to tree-like proportions. (3 m x 3 m); 'Mrs G.W. Leak' ('Coombe Royal' x 'Chevalier Felix de Sauvage' before 1934) Medium sized mid green leaves with very sticky new growth and light pink flowers with conspicuous darker throat blotches in trusses of up to 12 blooms. (2.5 m x 2 m); 'Pink Pearl' ('George Hardy' x 'Broughtonii' 1897) Mid green oblong leaves and light pink flowers with reddish spotting in large conical trusses opening from deep pink buds and fading to very pale pink. (3 m x 2 m); 'Purple Splendour' (*R. ponticum* hybrid before 1900) Deep green leaves that are quite long and narrow and deep purple flowers with a very dark blotch in rounded trusses. (2 m x 1.8 m); 'Sappho' (unknown before 1847) Deep green lanceolate leaves and white flowers with a striking blackish-purple blotch in conical trusses of up to 12 blooms. Inclined to be leggy but easily shaped if kept trimmed when young. (2 m x 1.8 m); 'Trude Webster' ('Countess of Derby' selfed 1961) Mid green oblong leaves up to 175 mm long with clear mid pink flowers in large conical trusses. A very impressive plant even when not in flower. (2 m x 2 m); 'Van Ness Sensation' ('Sir Charles Butler' x 'Halopeanum') Large mid green oblong leaves and mildly fragrant, waxy, light pink flowers with soft yellow tones in large trusses. (2 m x 1.8 m)

EVERGREEN AZALEAS

Evergreen azaleas are very heavy flowering and are often massed to provide solid blocks of colour. They show more variety in their flower forms than other rhododendrons, with flowers that may be single, semi-double or double. Many of them are hose-in-hose, a form in which the sepals develop into petals, thereby creating another row of petals. Although the largest of them may grow to over 2 m high and wide, evergreen azaleas are usually small plants, around 1 m x 1 m or less. They are divided into groups based on their parentage and understanding these groups is the key to success with evergreen azaleas. The main groups are Indica, Kurume, Kaempferi, Satsuki, Inter-group.

INDICA

Derived from *Rhododendron simsii*, which is only hardy to about -4°C, so it is not surprising that this group includes some slightly frost-tender hybrids. Most grow to about 75 cm x 1 m. Among the most widely available are 'Albert Elizabeth' (white edged deep pink, semi-double); 'Bride's Bouquet' (white, double);

'Comptesse de Kerchove' (soft orange-pink, double); 'Elsa Kaerger' (brick red, semi-double); 'Goyet' (bright red, double); 'Leopold Astrid' (white edged red, double); 'Little Girl' (soft pink); 'Mme. Alfred Sander' (deep pink, double); 'Red Wings' (pinkish red, single); 'Ripples' (deep pink, double); 'Rosa Belton' (white edged mauve, single); and 'Southern Aurora' (white suffused orange, double).

KURUME

Kurumes are dense, compact growers with small leaves and masses of small flowers early in the season. With great age they can become large plants but may be kept trimmed to about 1 m x 1 m if necessary. Most are hardy to about -12°C. Common cultivars include 'Christmas Cheer' (vivid cerise, single to hose-in-hose); 'Hino Crimson' (light red, single); 'Kirin' (mid pink, hose-in-hose); 'Kocho No Mai' (purple, single); and 'Ward's Ruby' (deep red, single).

KAEMPFERI

This group includes the hardiest hybrids. However, when exposed to very low temperatures, they will drop most of their foliage. Kaempferis vary in size but most are ultimately around 1.5 m x 1.5 m. Widely available cultivars include 'Elsie Lee' (lavender, double); 'Johanna' (bright red, single to semi-double); 'Lorna' (mid pink, hose-in-hose double); 'Purple Splendor' (purple, frilled hose-in-hose); and 'Vuyk's Scarlet' (bright red, single).

SATSUKI

Satsukis are usually less than 1 m high and are hardy to about -12°C. They have large single flowers with highly variable colouration. The very dwarf Gumpo Satsukis are often used as rockery plants. Nurseries sometimes stock 'Benigasa' (brick red, single); 'Fuji No Tsuki' (lavender, single); 'Gumpo' (various colours, single); 'Hitoya No Haru' (pink to lavender, single); and 'Shiko' (light purple, single).

INTER-GROUP

This is a catch-all group that includes hybrids produced by

Deciduous azaleas: (top left) 'Gibraltar'; (top right) 'Pink Delight', and (above left) 'Louis Williams'.
Above right: Azalea 'Ben Morrison'

breeding between the other groups and those raised from newly introduced species. Among the best are 'Ben Morrison' (white striped red, single); 'Betty Ann Voss' (light pink, single to semi-double); 'Frosted Orange' (orange with a white centre, single); 'Happy Days' (mid purple, double); 'Miss Suzie' (bright red, single); 'Sweetheart Supreme' (light pink, double); and 'Tenino' (purple, single).

DECIDUOUS AZALEAS

Deciduous azaleas offer flowers in vivid yellow and orange shades that are not often seen among the other rhododendrons, and many also develop bright red autumn foliage. They are divided into groups based on their parentage but these have less significance to gardeners than those of the evergreen azalea groups. Almost all deciduous azaleas have slightly hairy leaves, are very

hardy, bloom heavily from mid October and grow to be 1.8 m x 1.8 m bushes.
Look out for 'Anthony Koster' (yellow with an orange blotch); 'Carmen' yellow flushed pink flowers with deep gold throat markings); 'Cecile' (red with bright yellow markings); 'Gibraltar' (intense orange red); 'Ilam Gold' (yellow shaded and marked orange); 'Ilam Yellow Giant' (golden yellow); 'Melford Flame' (vivid orange red); 'Ming' (orange with yellow markings); and 'Red Rag' (bright orange red to red).

ROSES

Roses are without doubt the best known cultivated flower,
yet they are so versatile they should not be grown for their
flowers alone. Roses are also easy plants to cultivate, so be
adventurous!

Rosa foetida

The popular damask rose 'Omar
Khayyam'.

This book cannot attempt to cover all aspects of the rose in detail, so, as with the other larger and more popular groups of shrubs, we will briefly describe roses, present some options for their use in your garden and highlight specific cutlivation notes. As there are so many cultivars available to gardeners, we have only listed some of the most popular for you to try.

The style of flower widely recognised as being the typical rose, the pointed bud of the hybrid tea, is a relatively modern form. Beginning with species roses, roses have be hybridised into many different forms which are grouped under the following headings.

EARLY CULTIVARS

The early European garden roses were probably forms of *R. gallica*, a native of Europe. GALLICAS are usually compact plants with fragrant flowers in a variety of shades from white through pink to red (including bicolours) and in all forms from single to very full doubles. 'Charles de Mills', a deep wine-red double, with very distinctive flat circular flowers is currently among the most popular of the gallicas.

The DAMASK roses (*R. gallica* x *R. moschata* and *R. gallica* x *R. phoenicea*) and the bicolour form known as the yellow rose of Asia (thought to be a form of *R. kokanica* though usually listed as *R. foetida*) are generally regarded as the ancestors of most of the early European roses. They were extremely important in the development of the rose because of their fragrance, a tendency to produce double flowers and because their flowering season extends into autumn. These characteristics laid down the pattern for our expectations of roses.

Among the damasks most widely grown in modern gardens are 'Ispahan', a fragrant, soft mid pink double; 'Omar Khayyam', a strongly fragrant mid pink double; the original pink autumn damask, which is known as 'Quatre Saisons'; and 'Versicolor' or 'York and Lancaster', which has loosely double variable pink and white flowers.

Another species, *R. alba*, is also important in the development of the rose because it was crossed with the existing gallicas and damasks and produced very scented flowers – the ALBAS.

The CENTIFOLIA or cabbage roses were the next development. This exceptionally full double rose has at times been regarded as a species, although it is now thought to be a hybrid between the Autumn Damask and an Alba. They are usually compact bushes and their flowers are so fully double and heavy with petals that they often droop under their own weight. 'Cristata' ('Chapeau de Napoléon' or 'Crested Moss') is one of the most popular centifolias. It has fragrant, mid pink, double flowers, the buds of which are covered in fine tubercles or filaments known as moss.

MOSS ROSES are natural mutations that first occurred on damask and centifolia roses. They were very fashionable in the 18th and early 19th centuries and several hundred forms were raised. Some, such as very deep blackish-red-flowered 'Nuits de Young', are still grown today.

Other developments of the damask rose, such as the PORTLAND ROSES, tended to be obscured by major developments in the late 18th and early 19th centuries. At this time, roses, like many other large genera, saw an enormous change in their development as plant hunters started to send back material from China.

Perpetual flowering semi-dwarf bushes were cultivated in China well before the start of European rose breeding. The parent of many of these, *R. chinensis*, was introduced around 1752. CHINA ROSES, as these early hybrids are known, are still available. Among the most commonly grown are 'Cramoisi Supérieur', a small shrub with deep red semi-double to double flowers that is also available in a climbing form and 'Old Blush', a fragrant mid pink semi-double that was among the first introductions, again also available as a climber.

BOURBON ROSES, originated from a chance

Climbing roses are an important landscaping tool.

The climber 'Veilchenblau'

POPULAR CLIMBERS

'Albertine', fragrant soft pink double flowers; 'Birthday Present', strongly fragrant deep red double flowers; 'Compassion', fragrant apricot-pink double flowers; 'Dublin Bay', masses of bright red double flowers; 'Ena Harkness', fragrant deep red double flowers; 'Handel', white flushed and edged deep pink double flowers; 'New Dawn', fragrant pale pink loosely double flowers; 'Veilchenblau', fragrant semi-double greyish-purple flowers that have occasional white streaks; 'Wedding Day', massed fragrant white single flowers.

'Wedding Day', a sumptuous climbing rose.

natural hybridising between *R. chinensis* and an autumn damask, are long-blooming and strongly scented. 'Souvenir de la Malmaison' (pale pink, double) and 'Zephirine Drouhin' (deep pink, double) are the most popular.

NOISETTE ROSES were the first hybrid group to originate from the United States. They result from hybrids of *R. moschata* x 'Parson's Pink China'. They are generally strong growing bushes or climbers with clusters of fairly small flowers in pastel shades of yellow or pink. Among the most commonly available are: 'Alister Stella Gray', a light golden-yellow, fragrant double; 'Lamarque', fragrant double, pale yellow flowers that age to creamy white; and 'Mme Alfred Carrière', which has large white-blushed-pink double flowers.

TEA ROSES or tea-scented roses are another development of *R. chinensis*. These plants, which flower in shades of white, pink and yellow, are hybrids of *R. gigantea* x *R. chinensis*, a cross known as *R. x odorata*. They enjoyed a period of popularity around the 1830s, but the real significance of the tea rose to modern gardeners is that it was crossed with the other styles to produce the hybrid perpetual roses, which were the direct predecessors of the modern hybrid teas.

HYBRID PERPETUALS were by far the most popular garden roses of the 19th century. For about 70 years they enjoyed immense popularity, but they are now something of a novelty. Hybrid perpetuals often have very large strongly scented flowers but they are seldom tidy growers. Few nurseries stock many hybrid perpetuals, but you may see 'Général Jacqueminot', a fragrant, deep cerise-tinted-red double, and 'Prince Camille de Rohan', which has deep purplish-red, fragrant, double flowers.

MODERN ROSES

The hybrid perpetual roses were strong healthy plants that made the tea roses appear rather weak and spindly, but tea roses had beautifully shaped buds and flowers in shades of soft yellow that were lacking in the hybrid perpetuals. It was an obvious move to cross the two and in 1867 the first HYBRID TEA, 'La France', a soft pink double, appeared.

There are hundreds of hybrid tea roses to choose from and most of them are very heavy flowering and have large blooms on long stems that are ideal for picking. Which to choose is largely a matter of personal preference and what best suits your garden.

About the same time as the first hybrid teas were appearing, the POLYANTHA ROSES were introduced. These compact plants bear their small flowers in large clusters and were produced by crossing dwarf forms of *R. multiflora*

POPULAR FLORIBUNDAS

'Burma Star', slightly fragrant golden-yellow buds opening to soft buff double flowers; 'City of Belfast', bright red double flowers; 'Colour Break', unusual rusty orange-brown double flowers; 'Friesia', brilliant intense yellow fragrant double flowers; 'Iceberg', masses of semi-double white flowers. It is also available as a climber; 'Margaret Merril', strongly scented pure white semi-double to double flowers; 'Playboy', intense orange single to semi-double flowers with deep golden-yellow centres; 'Regensberg', pink-edged-and-reversed white semi-double flowers; 'Sexy Rexy', masses of light pink double flowers; 'Trumpeter' massed brilliant red double flowers; 'Westerland', fragrant soft orange semi-double flowers with golden yellow reverse.

The floribunda 'Iceberg' comes in shrub and climbing forms.

'Sexy Rexy'

A spring flowering of old-fashioned roses can be seen at right.

The English rose 'Mary Rose' with delphiniums.

with either a dwarf China or a small hybrid tea. Polyanthas have continued to be grown and new introductions appear occasionally. Some of the best are 'Cecile Brunner', which has small pale pink double flowers and is also available as a climber; 'Perle d'Or', a somewhat rangy grower with buff-pink double flowers; 'Strawberry Ice', which is a dense compact bush with white-edged-cerise double flowers; and 'The Fairy', a mid pink double that can be grown as a bush or miniature climber.

The polyanthas were very successful roses, but their flowers tended to be very small and poorly formed. The logical step was to cross polyanthas with hybrid teas and by so doing, the the first floribundas were produced. FLORIBUNDA ROSES are compact and heavy flowering, with several blooms per stem. As cut flowers they cannot compete with the hybrid teas but for sheer colour they are hard to beat.

CLIMBING ROSES

Climbing or strongly upright bushes have been common over the centuries of rose breeding, but the majority of garden climbers are really strongly upright bushes that are tied to fences, pillars or pergolas to create the effect of a climber. Ramblers are climbing roses that produce very strong growth from the base.

OTHER STYLES OF MODERN ROSES

MINIATURE ROSES are a style that can be traced back to the small China rose, *R. chinensis* 'Minima', particularly the form 'Roulettii'. This is an old form but it is only in recent years that miniatures have become very popular as new colours and styles have been produced by crossing the old forms with *R. wichuraiana* and some of the smaller floribundas. Not all miniature roses are small bushes. They all have small flowers but many bushes may reach 60-80 cm or more with time. Some forms are budded onto vigorous bush rootstocks to produce PATIO ROSES. Others are budded onto tall stems to produce miniature standards and weeping standards.

GROUND COVER ROSES are an increasingly important group that has been produced from a wide range of breeding stock. These include unusual species, such as *R. sempervirens*, *R. bracteata* and *R. californica*, as well as the more common *R. wichuraiana* and the various hybrid groups. Most are extremely vigorous plants capable of carpeting a wide area and many are similar in flower and foliage to miniature roses.

OLD ROSES AND MODERN ROSES

Although for many years hybrid teas and floribunda were the predominant rose types, old roses are now enjoying a revival. But what is an old rose? Much of the recent interest in old roses can be traced to the ENGLISH ROSES raised by David Austin. By crossing gallicas, damasks and centifolias among themselves, and with floribundas and hybrid teas, it has been possible to produce the flower form and scent of the old roses on compact vigorous bushes that flower throughout the season.

LANDSCAPING WITH ROSES

Roses are versatile plants that should not be grown for their flowers alone. There is now such a wide range of roses in all manner of colours, shapes and growth forms that they can be made to perform almost any landscaping function in any style of garden. The smaller types, particularly the miniatures, can be planted with other shrubs to provide splashes of colour and they also blend very well with perennials and annuals. They can also be used as informal hedges along pathways or for edging larger beds. Ground cover roses can be used to carpet sloping ground or for cascading over retaining walls. Climbers are most often used on fences but the more vigorous growers are perfectly capable of covering an unsightly shed or old tree and when grown over an entrance arch or French doors they provide a fragrant greeting for visitors to the garden or house. Roses of graduated heights are very effective for edging garden steps and for making a smooth transition between low borders and taller shrubs or trees. Strongly upright roses, such as 'Queen Elizabeth' can even be used for hedging.

Regardless of whether your garden is the height of formality or completely casual, roses should be an integral part. They lend themselves to formal planting in rows, large beds and carefully colour-coordinated borders or they can just be dotted about and left to look after themselves. There are also roses that can be used for specimen planting. Weeping miniature standards, for example, often look at their best when out in the open where their form is uncluttered by other plants.

CULTIVATION

Before you prepare the ground or plant your roses consider the practicalities involved. You will need to make sure that large growers do not overshadow smaller plants, that there is adequate ventilation between the plants and that there is easy access for pruning and spraying. As a rule you can reckon on a rose bush having a spread that it at least two-thirds of its height. This is important not just in working out the spacing but in ensuring that the roses do not encroach too far over paths or lawns.

Roses require a position that receives about six hours sun per day; is well ventilated without being exposed to strong winds; has slightly acid moisture-retentive yet well-drained soil; and which is free from any excessively competitive large shrubs and trees. Roses that are too shaded will tend to become drawn and flower poorly. They will also be more likely to suffer from fungal diseases. Roses in too windy a site will become damaged and their flowers will quickly burn, while poor ventilation is sure to lead to fungal diseases.

Ideally the planting site should be prepared well in advance. Roses are heavy feeders so incorporate as much organic matter and well-rotted manure as possible, but don't add strong chemical fertilisers at this stage. It is important that the roses establish well in their first season and too much top growth may stress the young root system and will almost certainly lead to the production of foliage at the expense of flowers. Also, long soft stems are very prone to wind damage. Stick to mild slow-acting fertilisers until the plants are firmly settled in.

PLANTING

Look at the main stem of the bush; you should be able to see a change in colour that shows the level at which the bush was planted in the field. This is the level it should be in your garden. If you bought bare-rooted plants, soak them in a bucket of water (possibly with dilute fungicide added) for several hours, this will ease them over their transplant shock.

Don't just dig a hole large enough to accommodate the plant. Make sure there is good depth and spread of loosened soil so the root system can quickly develop. Space the plants to allow enough room for easy access when pruning. Routinely stake standards and tall bushes to avoid damage from wind rock.

PRUNING

The main reasons for pruning are to promote strong new growth that rejuvenates the bush; to produce a well-shaped plant; to maintain plant health through improved ventilation, which reduces fungus problems; and to allow light to penetrate to the centre of the bush, thus promoting even growth.

'Charles Austin'

POPULAR ENGLISH ROSES

'Abraham Darby', fragrant apricot-pink tinted yellow double flowers; 'Charles Austin', fragrant soft buff-yellow double flowers; 'Constance Spry', strongly fragrant soft pink double flowers; 'Gertrude Jekyll', very fragrant bright pink double flowers; 'Graham Thomas', very fragrant deep yellow double flowers; 'Heritage', fragrant pale pink fully double flowers; 'Mary Rose', very fragrant deep pink double flowers; 'Othello', fragrant deep wine-red centifolia-style flowers.

'Mary Rose'

'Othello'

'Auckland Metro' – a classic hybrid tea rose.

POPULAR HYBRID TEAS

'Alexander', vivid vermilion orange double; 'Aotearoa NZ' very fragrant soft pink double flowers; 'Auckland Metro', slightly fragrant creamy white double flowers; 'Big Purple', large fragrant deep reddish-purple double flowers; 'Deep Secret', reddish foliage and very dark red fragrant double flowers; 'Double Delight', slightly fragrant cream-edged-carmine double flowers; 'Fragrant Cloud', strongly scented orange-red fading to coral double flowers; 'Gold Medal', deep golden-yellow buds that open to bright yellow double flowers; 'Ingrid Bergman', deep red double flowers that last well when cut; 'Loving Memory', large fragrant deep red double flowers on long stems; 'Peace', large and beautifully formed soft yellow-edged-pink slightly fragrant double flowers; 'Solitaire', slightly fragrant deep yellow-edged orange-pink double flowers; 'Whisky', fragrant soft orange-apricot semi-double to double flowers.

'Peace'

You can find all sorts of theories about how hard to cut back and why but it all comes down to the initial reasons for pruning; renewing vigour, maintaining health and shaping. Hard pruning tends to promote strong stems with fewer but better blooms while leaving longer stems promotes dense bushy growth with more but smaller blooms.

Consider the ultimate shape of the plant before you cut. Most bush roses are best grown in a vase shape: a clear centre with outward growing branches. The branches will tend to shoot from the bud immediately below a cut, so if the centre of the bush is to remain open you must cut to buds that face away from the centre of the bush. These are known as outward-facing buds.

When pruning bush roses, look for strong branches of the previous year's wood, these will normally have smooth reddish green bark. Having identified these main stems, completely remove any old, diseased or spindly branches. Then take out any overlapping branches, water-shoots and basal suckers so that just the main stems remain. Cut each main branch back to the first outward facing bud, then look at the shape of the bush.

Is it going to be the shape you want? If not, trim back to lower outward-facing buds. *Does it have too many main branches?* If so, thin out some of the branches, you really only need four or five main stems. *Is it still too tall?* If so, simply cut back to lower outward facing buds.

Repeat flowering climbers can be pruned in much the same manner as bushes, but you may wish to leave some inward-facing buds to fill out the structure. Also, when vigorous water-shoots are produced it is better to use them to fill out the plant's growth rather than cut them back. Once-flowering climbers and ramblers tend to flower on lateral growth off the old wood. You will almost certainly have to trim them to reduce their growth but cutting back too hard will severely reduce their flowering. The objective is to encourage side shoots, which will flower and can then be encouraged to grow out sideways to produce more flowering side shoots.

Always spray with a fungicide after pruning. You may well have disturbed fungal spores that will find an easy entry to the plant by way of the freshly cut stems. Also remove all pieces of debris. There is no point in leaving diseased material lying around to infect your plants.

Roses are normally pruned in winter because that is when the plants are dormant and the branch structure is most easily seen, but there is no reason why you shouldn't trim and thin in summer if you wish. Miniature and ground cover roses generally have masses of fine twiggy stems so careful trimming is impractical. With these types of roses summer pruning is usually the best option; just remove old or damaged wood and trim to shape.

PESTS AND DISEASES

Roses have an unfortunate reputation for being prone to pests and diseases. In reality they are not much more affected than any other plants, but the pests and diseases that attack roses spread rapidly and quickly become very obvious. The key is early control.

The number one pests are aphids. They can strike at any time from the first flush of spring growth till the last leaf falls in autumn, and in mild areas they may even carry on through winter. Aphids are easily killed, even soapy water or regular hosing off will control them, but because of their numbers, you can knock them back but you can't wipe them out.

In the long run fungal diseases are more likely to cause lasting damage than any insect pests. The most common rose diseases are mildew (powdery and downy), blackspot, rust and botrytis. Botrytis is only really a problem if you leave the old flowers to rot on the bush, in which case it may lead to die-back. Regular dead-heading eliminates this potential problem. Mildews lead to premature foliage drop and general debilitation; blackspot has a similar effect and is very unsightly.

Good ventilation and avoiding overcrowding will go a long way to preventing fungus problems, as will regular feeding, watering and soil conditioning. Healthy plants grown under good conditions are far less likely to suffer from pests and diseases and are more able to cope with them if they are attacked.

PROPAGATION

Most of the roses sold in garden centres and nurseries have been budded onto vigorous, disease-resistant, non-suckering rootstocks. Budding roses is not difficult but good rootstocks are not always generally available to the public. Roses can also be grown from cuttings, although some modern varieties do not grow well on their own roots and suckering varieties can become nuisances. Roses will grow from hardwood or semi-ripe cuttings. The propagation chapter gives details of these methods.

Growing roses from seed is generally restricted to species or raising new hybrids. The seed germinates well, but it must be stratified for 8-12 weeks before sowing.

OTHER POPULAR GARDEN SHRUBS

THE FOLLOWING IS A SELECTION of the most popular garden shrubs. The size of the shrub is given as height x width.

ABELIA

Frequently used for hedging, abelias are also effective as specimen shrubs. *A. x grandiflora* is the most widely grown, particularly the golden-bronze-leaved form 'Frances Mason', but *A. floribunda* and *A. schumannii* are also quite common. They are medium to large shrubs growing about 1.5 m x 1.2 m. The leaves often develop bronze tones in autumn. The white or pink tubular flowers, which are most abundant in early autumn, are attractive, as are the pink calyces that persist after the flowers have fallen. Evergreen in mild areas, but elsewhere semi-deciduous, abelias are easily grown in most sunny positions. *A. x grandiflora* and *A. schumannii* are considerably hardier than *A. floribunda*, which will only tolerate about -6°C. Propagate by semi-ripe cuttings. *A. x grandiflora* will also grow from open-ground hardwood cuttings taken in late autumn or winter.

ABIES

This coniferous genus includes a few compact dwarf forms that are excellent rockery plants. The best of these, *A. balsamea* 'Hudsonia' and 'Nana', develop into compact 30 cm globes with very fine, needle-like, deep green foliage. 'Hudsonia' has flattened stems, whereas those of 'Nana' have needles arranged radially around the stems. Grow in a cool moist soil in full sun with ample summer water and shelter from hot dry winds. Hardy to -25°C and may be propagated by semi-ripe summer cuttings.

ABUTILON

These vigorous shrubs prefer a loose open soil that allows unimpeded root development. In soils with a shallow hard clay pan they often collapse at an early age. They have large, multi-lobed leaves and *A. vitifolium*

has soft hairs on the foliage and stems. Hybrids must be propagated by semi-ripe cuttings. *A. darwinii* hybrids have pendulous, brightly coloured, 50 mm diameter, hibiscus-like flowers throughout the warmer months. They grow into large shrubs up to 2 m x 2 m. Although vigorous, they are often short-lived. They are evergreen in mild areas and semi-deciduous elsewhere and hardy to about -5°C. *A. megapotamicum* and its hybrids are rangy open shrubs or semi-climbers. The calyces of the red and yellow flowers often develop into bladder-like structures that almost enclose the petals, but some hybrids have flowers similar to the *A. darwinii* hybrids. They are hardy to about -10°C. *A. vitifolium* and its hybrids eventually become very large shrubs or small trees. Their white to soft pastel-pink and mauve flowers, which usually appear in spring, are more open than other species. They are hardy to -15°C and usually more difficult to propagate than the others.

ADENANDRA

A South African genus, of which two species, *A. fragrans* and *A. uniflora*, are commonly grown. Both are small shrubs (50 cm x 75 cm) with a preference for warm, sunny locations. They are easily grown in any well-drained soil, but are somewhat frost-tender. *A. fragrans* has starry, bright pink flowers that are scented and is hardy to about -3°C. *A. uniflora* has beautiful porcelain-like white starry flowers. It is easier to grow and will tolerate occasional -7°C frosts. Both species flower throughout the year with the main flowering in spring and early summer. Propagate from semi-ripe cuttings.

ALOYSIA

Formerly known as *Lippia*

Arctostaphylos nevadensis 'Woods Red'

citriodora, the lemon-scented verbena (*A. triphylla*) is a fairly hardy (to -12°C) deciduous to semi-evergreen shrub mainly grown for the citrus scent and herbal uses of its foliage. It grows to about 2 m x 2 m and is inclined to be a rangy and untidy plant. But the powerfully aromatic foliage makes up for this. Lemon verbena grows best in full sun in a rich well-drained soil with ample summer moisture. In summer and autumn this shrub has minute lavender flowers in loose heads. Propagate by open-ground hardwood cuttings over winter. Semi-ripe cuttings will strike with mist and bottom heat.

ANDROMEDA

Andromeda polifolia is an excellent small shrub (20 cm x 40 cm) for rockeries. It has narrow bluish-green 2 cm long evergreen foliage and white to pink lily-of-the-valley-like flowers

in mid spring. *Andromeda* prefer partial shade and moist acid soil with good drainage. Propagate by seed, layers or small tip cuttings.

ARCTOSTAPHYLOS

The best known member of this very hardy North American genus is the small ground cover *A. nevadensis*. It grows to about 15 cm x 1.2 m and has 10 mm long leathery leaves and in spring produces clusters of small, pink, bell-shaped flowers. It has very attractive cinnamon to reddish bark, which peels away to reveal a layer of bright orange-red new bark beneath. Prefers a moist well-drained soil in full sun or very light shade and is hardy to -15°C. Propagate by semi-ripe cuttings.

ASCLEPIAS

The best-known species of this genus is the swan plant (*A.*

Abutilon megapotamicum 'Variegatum'

Berries of *Aucuba japonica* 'Crotonoides'

Berberis 'Rosy Glow'

fruticosa), which is widely planted as a host for the caterpillar of the monarch butterfly. *A. tuberosa* is a far more attractive bush that is just as popular with the butterflies. Both are upright shrubs with willowy foliage and soft stems. They grow to about 1.8 m x 1 m and flower from late spring to autumn. *A. fruticosa* has small white flowers followed by large inflated bladder-like seed pods that give it the common name swan plant. It is evergreen but damaged by temperatures below -4°C. *A. tuberosa* has terminal heads of bright orange and yellow flowers and long cigar-shaped seed pods. It is very hardy but is deciduous in cold areas. Both prefer light well-drained soil in full sun. Propagate by semi-ripe cuttings

AUCUBA

The Japanese laurel (*A. japonica*)

Baeckia crenatifolia

is an evergreen shrub notable for its large evergreen leaves and ability to thrive in deep shade. Sexes are separate with female plants bearing bright red fruits from late winter. Many variegated forms are grown, the most common being 'Crotonoides' (female) and 'Mr Goldstrike' (male). Both may eventually reach 2 m x 1.8 m. Other forms such as 'Salicifolia', are grown for their foliage shape rather than colour. Grow in moist humus-enriched soil in shade. While sun tolerant, aucubas are inclined to burn in hot dry positions. They are hardy to about -15°C. Propagate by semi-ripe cuttings.

BAECKEA

The most common species in New Zealand is *B. virgata*, but *B. crenatifolia* is reasonably widely grown. Both species have minute leaves and small, starry, white flowers in spring, which are occasionally used for floral decoration. If left untrimmed these shrubs are inclined to become rangy, but they respond well to pruning. Both reach about 1.5 m x 1 m. They will tolerate -7°C for short periods. Grow them in light well-drained soil in full sun. Propagate by small semi-ripe tip cuttings.

BAUERA

An Australian genus of only three species, two of which, *B. sessiliflora* and *B. rubioides*, are quite common. Known as the river rose, these shrubs are densely clothed with small leaves and can be kept trimmed if a

neat bush is required. *Bauera* is mainly grown for its starry, white or pink flowers that appear from late spring. It prefers a moist humus-enriched soil in full sun or light shade. Both common species grow to 80 cm x 60 cm and are hardy to about -8°C. Propagate selected forms by small semi-ripe cuttings.

BEAUFORTIA

B. sparsa is a popular autumn-flowering Australian shrub. It is a small upright bush with wiry stems that seldom exceeds 1.5 m x 1 m under New Zealand conditions. The bright orange bottlebrush flowers always attract attention and appear when most other shrubs have finished blooming. Plant in moist well-drained soil in full sun. *B. sparsa* and *B. purpurea* are hardy to about -8°C and can be grown in most northern and coastal areas of New Zealand. Propagate by semi-ripe cuttings.

BERBERIS

Some species of *Berberis*, particularly *B. darwinii*, are regarded as weeds in some areas, but where their growth is less vigorous they are useful ornamental shrubs. There are evergreen and deciduous species and many hybrids. Some are grown for their clusters of small, bright yellow or orange flowers, others for their foliage or fruit, and some for their near impenetrable growth, which makes them ideal for hedging. Nearly all species have formidable thorns. Grow in cool, moist soil in full sun or light

shade. The coloured-foliage forms of *B. thunbergii*, such as 'Little Favourite' (purple) and 'Rosy Glow' (pink and purple), require full sun to produce the best colour. Most barberries grow to about 1.5 m x 1 m but some are considerably larger and several dwarf forms, such as *B. thunbergii* 'Aurea', are available. All are hardy to at least -12°C and most are considerably tougher. Propagate the hybrids by semi-ripe cuttings in summer.

BERZELIA

B. lanuginosa is a compact evergreen shrub with fine feathery foliage and minute creamy-white flowers in button-like heads. The flower stems last well when cut. In cultivation it rarely exceeds 1.5 m x 1 m. It is an undemanding plant that is easily grown in any light well-drained soil in full sun and able to withstand frosts of -4°C or more, although it prefers a mild climate. Propagate by small semi-ripe cuttings.

BORONIA

Justifiably one of the best-known spring-flowering shrubs, the very fragrant brown boronia (*B. megastigma*) is one of about 60 species. In recent years many other species and hybrids have become available. The colour range now includes a number of bicolour forms and many with vivid pink or mauve flowers, however *B. megastigma*, especially the form 'Heaven Scent', is the most fragrant species. It grows to about 1.2 m x 1.2 m and is hardy to -10°C.

Boronia denticulata

Boronia 'Southern Star'

Grow in moist well-drained soil in full sun or light shade. Other common species and hybrids include the vivid cerise-flowered red boronia (*B. heterophylla*), which can grow as high as 1.8 m. A smaller species, sold as *B. molloyae* (syn. *B. elatior*), is about half the size of the red boronia. The mauve-flowered *B. denticulata* and the pink *B. fraseri*, which is best known in its form 'Southern Star', have open starry flowers. *B. pinnata* and *B. muelleri* have starry pink flowers and *B. muelleri* is also available in a white form. *B. pilosa* has deep pink flowers, of which 'Rose Blossom' is a very distinctive double form.

Most boronias have very fine, almost needle-like foliage but *B. crenulata* has rounded leathery leaves and looks very like a *Crowea*. *B. fraseri* also has slightly broader leaves. Boronias should be pruned immediately after flowering to maintain the shape of the bush and prolong their notoriously short lives. Even so don't count on a lifespan of more than 5-7 years. *B. megastigma* tends to be the shortest lived, seldom lasting beyond 4-5 years. Propagate by semi-ripe cuttings.

BOUVARDIA

Most members of this genus are too tender for New Zealand gardens. However, a few species are reasonably hardy, of which the most widely grown is *B. longiflora*. This species has fragrant, jasmine-like, tubular, white flowers. The main flowering season is summer and autumn, but in mild climates it will bloom throughout the year. The bush is inclined to be rather untidy and is often best grown in hanging baskets or as a small climber. It usually grows to about 1.2 m x 80 cm and does best in rich moist soil in full sun or light shade. Shelter it from cold winds and temperatures below -3°C. Propagate by semi-ripe cuttings.

BRACHYGLOTTIS

The native rangiora (*B. repanda*) is a large evergreen shrub or small tree growing to about 4.5 m x 3 m. The broad, oblong, leathery leaves up to 30 cm long x 20 cm wide. The undersides of the leaves are covered. Purple ('Purpurea') and variegated ('Variegata') foliage forms are available. The small cream daisy-like flowers, which occur between late spring and early autumn, are borne in profusion. Grow in well-drained soil in full sun or light shade and shelter from strong winds, which will damage the large leaves. It is hardy to about -4°C. However, many of the other shrubby species are remarkably similar, bearing cream, yellow or orange daisy flowers and most having leaves with silvery-grey felted undersides.

The most commonly grown species are the New Zealand natives *B. compacta*, *B. greyi* and *B. monroi*. Clusters of light to bright yellow flowers appear from late spring. All can grow to 1.5 m x 1.2 m but *B. compacta* rarely exceeds 60 cm x 60 cm. They are hardy to about -10°C and are best grown in light well-drained soil in full sun. Most species make excellent coastal plants. Propagate by semi-ripe cuttings.

BRUNFELSIA

The commonly grown species, *B. pauciflora* (*B. calycina*) and *B. latifolia* are beautiful soft-stemmed shrubs with masses of widely flared, light mauve to deep purple flowers. They are very attractive plants but too frost-tender for all but nearly frost-free areas. In suitable gardens they may grow to 1.2 m x 1 m but they are more commonly grown in containers and kept severely trimmed. They may also be used as annuals. *B. pauciflora* 'Floribunda' is sometimes known as yesterday, today and tomorrow as the flowers change from purple to lavender to near white over three days. Grow in moist, well-drained soil in full sun or light shade and shelter from draughts and frost. Propagate by semi-ripe cuttings.

BUDDLEIA

These shrubs are widely planted because they grow quickly, flower over a long season, and attract butterflies and small nectar-feeding birds. They are often used as a quick hedge or screen. Most species and hybrids are large (around 2.5 m x 2 m) evergreen or deciduous shrubs. The foliage is greyish to deep olive-green and the minute flowers are carried in large tapering panicles. The flowering season varies and by growing a range of species it is possible to have blooms from mid-winter to mid-summer, at least in mild winter areas. *B. davidii* and its cultivated forms, which have flowers in white and numerous

Bouvardia longiflora

pink, lavender and purple shades, are the most common. *B. fallowiana* is similar to *B. davidii* but its foliage is covered with a heavy coating of white felt. 'Lochinch' is a hybrid between *B. davidii* and *B. fallowiana*, with inferior foliage to *B. fallowiana*, but its fragrant lavender flowers make it a better all-round choice.

B. globosa is an evergreen with unusual balls of light orange flowers in late winter to late spring depending on the climate. *B. alternifolia* is deciduous, has an attractive weeping growth habit and flowers very heavily. *B. colvilei* is an evergreen with panicles of large bell shaped pink to maroon flowers and new growth that is coated with a reddish brown felting. *B. asiatica* is hardy to -5°C and bears long weeping panicles of fragrant white flowers.

Buddleias flower on one-year-old wood so any pruning should be done immediately after flowering to ensure a good display in the following season. A few species are frost-tender, but most are hardy to -10–15°C and *B. alternifolia* can withstand -20°C. They grow best in moist humus-enriched soil in full sun or light shade and tolerate short periods of drought. Propagate by semi-ripe cuttings.

BUXUS

Box (*B. sempervirens*) is a small, densely foliaged evergreen shrub able to withstand regular heavy trimming making it extremely popular for hedging and topiary. Box hedging has been in use since Roman times. There are many forms of *B. sempervirens* ranging from 30 cm x 30 cm to 2 m x 1 m, as well as a cream variegated form. If you are planning a box hedge make sure you choose a variety of the appropriate size. Box is usually slow growing and does best in moist well-drained soil, but is drought tolerant and capable of growing in a wide range of soil types. Growth is more compact in full sun but it will withstand quite deep shade. Propagate by semi-ripe cuttings. Other species, such as the large-leaved *B. balearica* and the very small-leaved *B. microphylla*, are occasionally grown.

CAESALPINIA

In mild climates *C. gilliesii* is a medium-sized tree, but under New Zealand conditions it seldom exceeds 2.5 m x 1.8 m. It is an attractive, if somewhat thorny, plant with fern-like foliage and in summer it produces heads of yellow flowers with prominent scarlet stamens. It grows best in light well-drained soil in full sun, but shelter from strong wind and temperatures below -4°C are essential. It may be evergreen in very mild areas but elsewhere is semi-deciduous or deciduous. *C. pulcherrima* is a similar species with orange flowers and more distinctly deciduous. It will tolerate freezing back to ground level provided the spring and summer are warm enough to permit rapid regrowth. *C. pulcherrima* can be kept trimmed if a neater bush is required. Usually raised from seed, they can also be grown from semi-ripe cuttings in summer.

CALCEOLARIA

The shrubby *Calceolaria* species have similar flowers to the small bedding and perennial species, but are longer-lived and substantially larger plants. The most common species is *C. integrifolia*, which has yellow or reddish-bronze flowers. The pouch-shaped blooms are carried throughout the year in mild areas. It is evergreen but can become untidy over winter in cold areas. May grow to 1.5 m x 1.2 m but is usually kept trimmed. Grow it in cool, moist, humus-enriched soil in light shade. It is hardy to about -8°C. Propagate by semi-ripe cuttings.

CALLISTEMON

Only a few bottlebrushes are commonly grown in gardens, although specialist seed suppliers stock most species. The most common garden form is probably *C. citrinus* 'Splendens', a 2.2 m x 1.8 m evergreen shrub with bright red, filamentous, bottle-brush flowers in spring and autumn. Other species and hybrids produce white, yellow, green, orange or purple flowers. All but a few are large shrubs that can become untidy unless pruned to shape. 'Little John' is a

Callistemon 'Mauve Mist'

low-growing, spreading cultivar that is more compact than most other bottlebrushes, but is only hardy to about -4°C. Grow in light well-drained soil in full sun. Most species are hardy to about -8°C with a few able to tolerate -12°C although they may be badly damaged. Most hybrids strike freely from semi-ripe cuttings.

CALYCANTHUS

The Carolina allspice (*C. floridus*) and the closely related *C. occidentalis* both have strongly fragrant reddish flowers in early summer and large, deep green, rounded leaves. The general appearance is rather like a red-flowered magnolia. All parts of the plants are aromatic. *C. floridus* grows to about 2 m x 1.5 m and *C. occidentalis* may reach 4 m x 2.5 m. They prefer moist humus-enriched soil in full sun to moderate shade. They are hardy to about -15°C and can be grown in all but the coldest areas. Propagate by semi-ripe cuttings in summer.

CALYTRIX

The fringe myrtle (*C. tetragona* syn. *C. sullivanii*) is an upright shrub that grows to about 1.5 m x 1 m. The foliage is small, needle-like, and may become sparse with age. The flowers, which are small, white and starry, are carried in loose heads and a bush in full flower is attractive. It is not a spectacular shrub but is often used for informal hedging or other utility plantings. It should be grown in light well-

drained soil in full sun and is hardy to about -10°C. The pink-flowered *C. alpestris* is also quite common. Similar species are occasionally grown. Raise from semi-ripe cuttings.

CANTUA

These evergreen to semi-deciduous shrubs are mainly grown for their very attractive and conspicuous pendulous tubular flowers. The most common species is the sacred flower of the Incas (*C. buxifolia*). It is an open upright bush (2 m x 1.2 m) and is rather undistinguished save for its spectacular bright pink flowers. It is the kind of plant that remains unnoticed until spring, when it blooms and everyone wants to know what it is. It is best grown in mild areas, as it will not tolerate temperatures below -3°C with any regularity. Grow it in light well-drained soil in full sun or light shade. Propagate by semi-ripe cuttings. Other species occasionally seen include *C. bicolor*, which has yellow and red flowers, and the very attractive *C. tomentosa*, which has larger leaves and masses of pinkish-orange flowers.

CARMICHAELIA

This genus of blooms is not often seen in gardens, but native enthusiasts grow four New Zealand species: *C. cunninghamii*, *C. grandiflora*, *C. odorata* and *C. williamsii*. These are all wiry-stemmed shrubs that grow to about 1.8 m x 1.5 m and are leafless for most of the year. The flattened, photosynthetic stems are very distinctive. They bear small sweet pea-like flowers in dense clusters from late November or early December. *C. cunninghamii* has white flowers; those of *C. grandiflora* are purplish or lilac and are very fragrant; *C. odorata* retains its foliage longer than the other species and has strongly scented, pink and white flowers; and *C. williamsii* has creamy-yellow flowers veined with purple over a long season. All are drought tolerant once established, but they do far better in moist well-drained soil. Unlike most brooms, *Carmichaelia* species seem to prefer light shade rather than the full heat of the sun. They can be grown from cuttings, which may be difficult to strike.

CASSINIA

This genus includes several New Zealand representatives. They are not highly regarded as garden plants but one species, *C. fulvida*, is sometimes grown in gardens or amenity plantings. It is a distinctive 1.8 m x 1.5 m shrub with minute greenish-gold foliage, which gives it the common name golden cottonwood. The tiny creamy white flowers, which most commonly appear in spring, are massed in small heads but are not particularly spectacular. However, it is hardy to -15°C and will grow in exposed windswept positions. It tolerates most conditions, but is best in light well-drained soil in full sun. Raise from semi-ripe cuttings.

CEANOTHUS

This large North American genus is one of the best for providing plants that are hardy, evergreen and heavy flowering. Most species have bright blue flowers but there are now hybrids in white and many shades of pink and blue. The flowers are minute but massed in heads up to 50 mm in diameter. *C. papillosus* 'Roweanus' is a large shrub or small tree with masses of deep blue flowers in spring. Other species vary in size from ground covers, such as some *C. gloriosus* and *C. griseus* forms, to medium-sized trees, such as

Calycanthus floridus

Cantua buxifolia

C. thyrsiflorus. All are hardy under most New Zealand conditions. Grow in light well-drained soil in full sun. Excessive moisture and humidity can lead to fungal problems and rotting. Propagate by semi-ripe tip cuttings.

CEDRUS

The large cedars have given rise to a few dwarf and ground-cover forms. The best known of these is the dwarf Himalayan cedar (*C. deodara* 'Nana'), which has deep green needles that are yellowish-green when young. It grows very slowly to 1 m x 2.5 m. There are also two ground-cover forms of the cedar of Lebanon (*C. libani*); both 'Nana' and 'Sargentii' have deep green needles and spread slowly to form a 1.5 m wide carpet that mounds slightly at the centre. Cedars prefer moist well-drained soil and a position in sun. Propagate by semi-ripe cuttings in summer.

CERATOPETALUM

The New South Wales or Sydney Christmas bush (*C. gummiferum*) is an evergreen shrub noted for the way its flower calyces intensify in colour as they mature. The starry 15 mm calyces are at first cream and change through pink to a

vibrant red. They are at their most intense in late December hence the name Christmas bush. The true petals are insignificant. With time this plant can develop into a small tree up to 5 m x 3 m, but it is usually trimmed to encourage new growth and more flowers. Plant in cool, moist, humus-enriched soil in full sun or very light shade. It is hardy to about -4°C and may be grown in southern areas if sheltered when young. Propagate by semi-ripe cuttings.

CERATOSTIGMA

Chinese plumbago (*C. willmottianum*) is a deciduous shrub with intense, deep blue, phlox-like flowers in summer. It may grow to 1.2 m x 1 m, but is often treated as a perennial and cut back to near ground level each year to encourage new flowering shoots and dense foliage. The 50 mm long leaves are deep green to bronze-green. It is able to grow in a wide range of soils and is tolerant of light shade, although it does best in full sun. Hardy to -15°C, it will recover even when frosted back to ground level. Propagate by semi-ripe cuttings. *C. griffithii* and *C. plumbaginoides* are similar species that are lower

growing and somewhat later flowering.

CESTRUM

The night-scented jasmine (*C. nocturnum*) is a soft-stemmed evergreen shrub with small, unspectacular flowers in late spring and summer that are very sweetly scented at night. These are followed by white berries. Unfortunately this 2.5 m x 1.8 m bush is very frost-tender. Other species, such as *C. aurantiacum* and *C. elegans*, have more spectacular (though unscented) flowers and fruit but are also frost-tender. *C.* 'Newellii' is considerably hardier and will tolerate frosts of about -6°C without excessive damage. It has bright red unscented flowers and will grow to 2 m x 1.2 m. *Cestrum* grows best in sunny sheltered positions with rich, moist, well-drained soil. Propagate by semi-ripe cuttings.

CHAENOMELES

The flowering quinces (*C.* x *superba*) are deciduous shrubs that flower in winter and early spring. They have an untidy sprawling habit and vicious thorns, but are popular for winter display. Generally known as japonicas, they are the result of hybridising *C. japonica*, *C.*

Chamaecyparis pisifera 'Filifera Aurea'

Clianthus puniceus

leaves are an attractive mid-green shade ('Sundance' is a golden-foliaged form) and the clustered, starry, white flowers have a mild spicy scent. The whole bush is aromatic. *Choisya* may grow to about 2 m x 2 m but is usually trimmed quite heavily and can be used for loose informal hedges. It flowers most heavily around mid spring but carries some bloom throughout the year in most areas. Easily grown in almost any soil in full sun or light shade, but it benefits from regular feeding and occasional deep watering. Propagate by semi-ripe cuttings.

cathayensis and *C. speciosa*. The true *C. japonica* is a very compact bush that seldom exceeds 1 m x 1 m.
New hybrids with more compact growth and larger, less garish flowers have been introduced in recent years. Many of these flower later than the older forms. Most flowering quinces can grow to 4 m x 3 m but are usually trimmed to far smaller dimensions. They may be used for hedging and espaliering as well as general garden use. They are extremely hardy and will withstand any New Zealand conditions. Propagate by semi-ripe cuttings in late summer or hardwood cuttings in winter.

CHAMAECYPARIS

There are countless small cultivars of *Chamaecyparis* that are suitable as general garden shrubs or rockery specimens. Most are forms of *C. lawsoniana*, *C. obtusa* and *C. pisifera* and tend to be small rounded bushes or ground covers. Among the best small forms of *C. lawsoniana* are 'Ellwood's Gold', light yellowish-gold foliage that darkens as it ages and a pyramidal habit to about 1.5 x 45 cm; 'Fletcheri', deep bluish-green foliage and forms a broad-based pyramid 1.2 m x 1.5 m; 'Fletcher's White' with patches of cream foliage; 'Green Globe', forming deep olive-green mounds; 'Minima' a 60 cm x 60 cm mound of slightly yellowish-green foliage.
C. obtusa 'Nana' has deep bronze-green foliage and eventually reaches about 1.5 m x 1.5 m but is very slow growing.

Among the dwarf cultivars of *C. pisifera* are 'Compacta Variegata', which forms a 20 cm x 40 cm mat of bright green flecked with light yellow; 'Filifera Aurea' has bright yellow foliage and thread-like stems and eventually grows to about 2 m x 3 m; and 'Snow', a very slow-growing cultivar that eventually reaches 1.8 m x 1.2 m and has bright bluish green foliage heavily flecked with cream. There are many more cultivars with new ones constantly being released. They are all hardy to at least -20°C and are at their best in cool, moist, well-drained soil in full sun or partial shade. Propagate by semi-ripe cuttings. Red spider mite can be a problem in hot dry positions.

CHAMAELAUCIUM

The Geraldton waxflower (*C. uncinatum*) is an evergreen Australian shrub that does best in mild areas without excessive humidity; it is best suited to the North Island's east coast, Nelson and coastal Marlborough. The dark green foliage is needle-like and inclined to be sparse, but the plant is grown for the flowers, which are small and starry and borne in sprays of eight to twelve flowers; they are long lasting when cut. There are several forms with flowers in white and various pink and red shades. Large plants, which may grow to 2 m x 3 m, develop gnarled trunks that are full of character. Plant in light, very well-drained soil in full sun. It is hardy to about -6°C. Propagate the selected forms by small semi-ripe cuttings.

CHIMONANTHUS

Wintersweet (*C. praecox*) is mainly grown for its scented flowers. It is a deciduous shrub or small tree growing to about 4 m x 2 m with sparse foliage and relatively insignificant flowers, however the scent and its winter-flowering habit have ensured its continued popularity. The 150 mm long individual leaves are easily damaged and fall early so the overall effect is untidy. The waxy, light yellow, purple-blotched flowers appear from late winter and have a powerful spicy fragrance. 'Grandiflora' has large flowers and larger leaves, and the flowers of 'Luteus' are a pure bright yellow with no purple markings.
Plant them in cool, moist, humus-enriched soil in full sun or light shade. *Chimonanthus* is very hardy (to -25°C) and needs at least a few frosts to ripen the wood and flower well, so it may not be suitable for mild northern areas. Usually propagated by seed, which takes several years to reach flowering age, but the selected forms are grown from layers or grafted.

CHOISYA

Mexican orange blossom (*C. ternata*) is one of the most widely planted evergreen shrubs. Its chief attributes are its bright green foliage, good display of scented white flowers, hardiness and tolerance of neglect. Its only drawbacks are its susceptibility to leaf-roller caterpillars and scale insects. The glossy trifoliate

CHORDOSPARTIUM

C. stevensonii is a broom native to the Kaikoura region and very rare in the wild although quite extensively cultivated. It is leafless and wiry stemmed but has some redeeming features. The first is its graceful weeping habit (it grows to about 3.5 m x 3 m) and the second is its magnificent display of highly scented, lavender to purple flowers. The flowers are small but carried in huge numbers for a few weeks from early December. As with most New Zealand brooms, it prefers moist well-drained soil and is not as drought or heat tolerant as the European brooms. Hardy to at least -10°C and easily grown in most gardens. Raise from seed, which should be soaked for several hours before sowing. It may be grown from semi-ripe cuttings but they can be difficult to strike.

CHORIZEMA

The flame peas are an Australian genus of which the most widely grown is *C. cordata*. It is an open spreading shrub that grows to about 80 cm x 1.2 m with heart-shaped foliage. When grown among other shrubs it will behave as a small semi-climber. It has small, bright purple and orange, sweet pea-like flowers throughout the warmer seasons. *C. ilicifolia* has red and yellow flowers, and *C. varia* has yellow and purple flowers with red veins. All do best in light well-drained soil in full sun or light shade. They are hardy to about -5°C, but are best sheltered from frost. Raise from semi-ripe cuttings.

CISTUS

One of the classic genera for hot dry conditions. Most *Cistus* species are native to the Mediterranean area and the Iberian Peninsula. They bear flowers, primarily in spring and early summer, that resemble single roses; the colour is usually white or pink, often with contrasting blotches. The foliage is usually light green or greyish-green and sticky. The plants have an aromatic, sticky, resinous sap and can be very combustible in hot dry weather. Many species and hybrids are grown, ranging from ground covers, such as *C. salvifolius*, to large (1.8 m x 1.2 m) shrubs, such as *C. ladanifer* and *C. laurifolius*. Plant them in light well-drained soil in full sun and trim to shape after flowering. Most species are hardy to -10°C and rarely pose any problems under New Zealand conditions. Propagate from semi-ripe cuttings.

CLERODENDRUM

Most species are too tender for New Zealand gardens but three – *C. bungei*, *C. trichotomum* var. *fargesii* and *C. ugandense* – are reasonably hardy. *C. trichotomum* is the hardiest and should withstand at least -15°C. All are deciduous (semi-evergreen in mild areas) and eventually grow to at least 1.8 m x 1.2 m, but *C. trichotomum* may reach 3.5 m x 2.5 m. They have large rounded leaves and unusual butterfly wing-shaped flowers with conspicuous protruding anthers. They usually bloom in spring and the flower colour varies with the species but is generally lavender-pink to purplish-blue. *C. bungei* has very fragrant rosy-red flowers. The bright blue or purple berries that follow are also attractive. Grow them in cool, moist, humus-enriched soil in full sun or light shade. Propagate by semi-ripe cuttings in autumn. Some of the subtropical species, such as the fragrant *C. philippinum* or the bright red-flowered *C. speciosissimum*.

CLETHRA

The lily-of-the-valley tree (*C.

arborea) is the best-known species, but the sweet pepper bush (*C. alnifolia*) is also sometimes seen. *C. arborea* is an evergreen large shrub or small tree generally growing around 3.5 m x 2 m but it may reach 6 m x 3 m. It has large, deep green, laurel-like foliage and from mid summer it bears masses of mildly fragrant, white, lily-of-the-valley-like flowers in large panicles. It is not entirely hardy but will withstand occasional frosts of -6°C. *C. alnifolia* is a very hardy deciduous shrub that grows to about 3 m x 1.8 m. Its foliage, which does not appear till late spring, is similar to *C. arborea* as are its flowers, which differ in that they are borne on upright spikes not drooping panicles. Pink forms of *C. alnifolia* are available but rare. *Clethra* does best in cool, moist, humus-enriched soil in full sun or light shade. Water well in summer. Raise from semi-ripe cuttings.

CLIANTHUS

The kaka beak (*C. puniceus*) is a New Zealand native that is now very rare in the wild, and it has been suggested that it was only through cultivation in Maori gardens that it survived to the present day. It is a very attractive evergreen shrub with ferny foliage and a spreading habit; mature specimens are about 1.5 m x 2.5 m. From spring to early summer it provides a display of its large, long-keeled, sweet pea-like flowers. The species has red flowers but pink and white forms exist. 'Kaka King' is a new, larger, heavy-flowering cultivar. Although it is an undemanding plant, it tends to be short-lived and is prone to a leaf miner and witches' brooms which are caused by the action of minute mites. Treat *C. puniceus* as a temporary plant and, if you tolerate the problems rather than trying to beat them, you'll find it has a lot to offer. Grow in moist well-drained soil in full sun or light shade. It is hardy to about -10°C. Propagate the selected forms from semi-ripe cuttings.

COLEONEMA

A South African genus closely

Clerodendrum trichotomum

related to *Diosma*. *C. album*, which is often sold as *Diosma ericoides*, grows to about 1.5 m x 1 m and has small needle-like leaves and tiny, white, starry flowers in spring. As with all *Coleonema*, the bush is spicily aromatic. *C. pulchrum* is very similar to *C. album* but has slightly softer foliage and pink flowers. Several forms are cultivated with white or deeper pink flowers. 'Sunset Gold' is a very popular form with bright yellow foliage and light pink flowers in spring. It is more compact than the species, usually growing as a spreading flat-topped bush and may reach 70 cm x 1.5 m. All *Coleonema* forms withstand regular trimming. Plant them in light, but moist, well-drained soil in full sun. 'Sunset Gold' in particular must be grown in the sun to maintain the foliage colour. They are hardy to around -8°C. Propagate by semi-ripe cuttings.

CONVOLVULUS

Two shrubby species, both non-invasive, are grown in gardens. *C. cneorum* is a low compact bush (60 cm x 1.2 m) with bright silvery leaves and large white flowers in late spring and summer. It is easily grown in any light well-drained soil in full sun and makes a very effective ground cover for dry banks. *C. mauritanicus* is more of a true ground cover. It will only reach 15 cm high but may spread to 1.2 m wide. It has lavender to purple flowers and soft green, rounded leaves. It too is an

excellent ground cover for dry banks or large rockeries. Both are hardy to -8°C. *C. mauritanicus* will often shoot from the rootstock if frosted to ground level. Propagate by semi-ripe cuttings.

COPROSMA

This genus of evergreen shrubs and ground covers ranges from prostrate alpine species, such as *C. atropurpurea*, to large shrubs or small trees, such as *C. robusta*. A wide range of hybrids and cultivars are grown. The flowers are generally insignificant but are often followed by attractive berries, however, many of the garden forms do not set fruit.
C. x *kirkii* is a wide-spreading ground cover that may grow to 40 cm x 2.5 m. It has strong wiry stems clothed with tiny, deep olive-green leaves. *C. repens* is an upright shrub that may reach 2.5 m x 2 m. It is common in coastal areas and is grown for its large, extremely glossy, rounded leaves, which give it the common name of mirror plant. There are many coloured foliage forms, such as 'Silver Queen', which has white edged leaves. *C. repens* is slightly frost-tender, but it is an excellent coastal plant able to tolerate the harshest salt winds. Numerous hybrids with variegated foliage are also useful garden plants. Grow coprosmas in moist, well-drained soil in full sun or very light shade. Cultivars should be propagated by semi-ripe cuttings.

Cotoneaster 'Cornubia'

Crinodendron hookerianum

COROKIA

This endemic genus contains only three species of evergreen shrubs, but there are numerous hybrids and cultivars. They are grown for their deep bronze-green to purple foliage and their yellow, orange or red berries. Their scented, small, yellow flowers can also be attractive in spring. *C. macrocarpa* is the most attractive species and in late winter and early autumn it carries a heavy crop of orange to red berries. Many of the garden forms are hybrids. There are several bronze-leaved forms, such as 'Bronze Knight' and 'Bronze Lady', and others, such as 'Red Wonder' and 'Yellow Wonder', have been selected primarily for their fruit.
They are all tough and adaptable and will become large bushes up to 3 m x 2.5 m if left untrimmed. Corokias withstand regular trimming and may be used for hedging. They also tolerate salt spray and are very effective coastal plants. Corokias perform best in moist well-drained soil in full sun or very light shade. They are very hardy and are drought tolerant once established. Propagate selected forms by semi-ripe cuttings.

CORREA

These evergreen shrubs bear pendulous tubular flowers and are known as Australian fuchsias. Commonly grown species include *C. alba* (white to pale pink flowers), *C. pulchella* (pink to red flowers), and *C. reflexa* (pale pink flowers). There are also several hybrids with white,

creamy yellow, pink or red flowers. The best known of these is *C.* 'Mannii', which has 25 mm long red flowers. Australian fuchsias are not showy, the flowers often being hidden in the foliage, but they are undemanding with a subtle charm and are good for coastal gardens. Most grow to about 80 cm x 1 m. *C. alba* tolerates regular trimming and is occasionally used for low hedging. Grow them in light well-drained soil in full sun. They are hardy to about -10°C. Propagate by small semi-ripe tip cuttings.

COTINUS

The smoke bush (*C. coggygria*) is the better known of the two species in this northern hemisphere genus. It is grown both for its massed clusters of minute greyish flowers, which appear as a smoky haze in spring, and for its foliage, particularly the intense yellow to orange-red and purple autumn colour. Several purple-leaved forms, such as 'Royal Purple', are colourful throughout the growing season. The other species, *C. obovatus*, has more intense autumn colour, but is not as widely grown as it lacks the range of summer-coloured foliage forms. Both species are large deciduous shrubs or small trees that may reach 5 m x 4 m. They will withstand pruning if necessary. Grow them in moist, well-drained soil and full sun is essential for good autumn colour. Established plants often produce suckers, which may be removed with attached roots

and grown on, otherwise propagate by layers.

COTONEASTER

A genus of evergreen and deciduous shrubs, all of which are hardy to at least -15°C and many will tolerate -25°C. They range from spreading ground covers to large shrubs and are grown for their foliage, flowers and berries. The berries (usually bright red) are the most conspicuous feature of most species, but the foliage and flowers (massed, small, white stars in spring) should not be overlooked. The foliage ranges from the small rounded leaves of *C. congestus* to the longer willow-like foliage of *C. henryanus*. Some deciduous species, such as *C. adpressus*, develop good yellow and orange autumn foliage colours. There are many adaptable low, spreading species, such as *C. dammeri*, useful as ground covers, grafted onto upright stocks as weeping standards, or espaliered. There are also bushes, such as the heavily-berried *C. lacteus* and *C. conspicuus*, and very large species, such as *C. salicifolius*, which can grow to 5 m x 5 m. With their diversity and adaptability to training, cotoneasters are among the most versatile of ornamental shrubs. They will grow in any well-drained soil in full sun or light shade and are drought tolerant once established. Propagate by semi-ripe cuttings; most deciduous species will also grow from hardwood cuttings taken in winter.

CRINODENDRON

These shrubs are best grown in cool, moist, acid soil in a cool, damp climate. They do very well in coastal Otago, Southland and isolated areas further north, but hot dry winds are detrimental in many parts of the country. The best-known species is *C. hookerianum*. It is a beautiful large evergreen shrub or small tree with waxy, red, bell-shaped flowers in spring. The pendent flowers resemble fuchsia buds. Their matt, waxy texture is unusual and is as appealing as their colour. *C. patagua*, which has white flowers, is less common but easier to grow. Both are hardy to -10°C. Propagate from semi-ripe cuttings.

CROTALARIA

Most members of this large genus are too tender for New Zealand gardens but several species will grow well in mild, nearly frost-free areas from Napier northwards and given shelter will often survive further south. They are all similar soft-wooded, large, evergreen shrubs (2.5 m x 1.5 m) with deep green rounded leaves that are usually slightly felted. The large, sweet pea-like flowers are bright yellow (hence the common name canary bird flower) and slightly scented. They appear in summer and autumn and are very conspicuous. All are hardy to about -3°C but withstand harder frosts if they occur very occasionally. The best known species, *C. agatiflora*, has the largest flowers. They grow in most soils in full sun or light shade but good drainage is important, and they are drought tolerant once established. Easily raised from softwood or semi-ripe cuttings.

CROWEA

This Australian genus contains some very attractive and easily grown small shrubs. Some are a little frost-tender, but most will tolerate -8°C and can be grown over much of the country. The two most common species, C. exalata and C. saligna, are typical of the genus. They are compact evergreen shrubs about 80 cm x 60 cm with narrow mid-green leaves and masses of small, starry, pink flowers. They flower most heavily in late spring but are seldom without a bloom. Several cultivars, such as the deep pink flowered 'Festival', are available. 'Bindelong Compact' is a very small plant (30 cm x 40 cm) well suited to rockeries. They are easily grown in light, but moist, well-drained soil in full sun or very light shade. Propagate from small semi-ripe cuttings.

CRYPTOMERIA

Several dwarf forms of the Japanese cedar (C. japonica) exist and they look very unlike the typical form. Their needles are short and stiff and arranged radially around the stems, unlike the flattened sprays of the species, however, they do become rich purplish-brown in winter. The best-known dwarf cultivars are 'Globosa Nana', which grows into a bulky shrub about 3 m x 3 m and 'Vilmoriniana', which is a tiny rockery dwarf that rarely exceeds 50 cm x 50 cm. Japanese cedars are hardy to about -20°C and prefer cool moist conditions. Propagate by semi-ripe cuttings.

CUPHEA

Most species are very frost-tender, but several are grown in mild areas and treated as annuals where they are killed over winter. The two most common species are C. ignea and C. hyssopifolia. They are both small, rounded, evergreen shrubs that seldom exceed 75 cm x 75 cm. C. ignea is commonly known as the cigar or cigarette plant because of its unusual flowers. These are orange with a black and white tip that resembles the ash at the end of a cigar. The flowers are small and tubular but carried in great numbers. C. hyssopifolia produces minute starry flowers that are white, pink or purple in great numbers. 'Rob's Mauve' is an attractive heavy-flowering cultivar. Both species flower throughout the year and prefer moist well-drained soil in full sun or very light shade. They can be grown from small tip cuttings but often self-sow.

CYTISUS

Because some brooms are invasive weeds, the ornamental species are often overlooked by New Zealand gardeners. This genus includes some excellent garden plants, ranging from the beautiful cream-flowered ground cover, C. x kewensis, to the tree-like silver-leaved C. battandieri (syn. Argyrocytisus battandieri). Many species are virtually leafless but C. battandieri is an exception and is grown primarily for its foliage, which is large, trifoliate and silvery grey. Most Cytisus species have the bright yellow flowers in spring that so typify the wild broom (C. scoparius), but there are hybrids with white, orange, pink and red flowers and most are fragrant. The shrubby forms grow to about 2.5 m x 2 m, but may be trimmed after flowering if necessary. Grow them in light well-drained soil in full sun. All are hardy to at least -10°C. Propagate hybrids from semi-ripe cuttings.

DABOECIA

Many gardeners regard Daboecia as a form of Erica, but it is a distinct genus. The species seen most often is the Irish heath (D. cantabrica), a compact (35 cm x 50 cm), hardy (to -15°C), evergreen shrub with small deep green leaves and small bell-shaped flowers. It blooms most heavily in spring but usually has a few flowers throughout the year; white, deep pink and pinkish-purple forms are available. D. azorica is a similar species with slightly larger leaves. It grows well in most areas despite being a little more tender than D. cantabrica. Plant them in a sunny position with cool, moist, humus-enriched, well-drained acid soil. Daboecia is a superb rockery plants that often self-sows. Grow cultivars from small tip cuttings or layers.

DAPHNE

This genus includes many choice garden specimens. The best known is D. odora, particularly the form 'Leucanthe', famous for the strength of its perfume. It is an evergreen bush bearing clusters of small, starry, pale pink flowers, from late winter. It is not always easily grown as it is quite particular about soil conditions and is slightly frost-tender in cold winter areas. It prefers a cool, moist, humus-enriched, well-drained, acid soil in full sun or light shade. Work in plenty of compost or similar organic matter. Feed regularly with liquid fertilisers and give an occasional side dressing of acid fertiliser. Kept healthy D. odora may grow to 1.8 m x 1.2 m but it is not long-lived. Expect to have to replace your plant every 8-10 years. Virus-free plants, propagated by tissue culture, are now available and are vastly superior.

Other species look very different from D. odora. The most widely grown is D. x burkwoodii, a hybrid between D. cneorum and D. caucasica. It is a twiggy, densely foliaged, evergreen or semi-evergreen bush with masses of small, fragrant, pink flowers in spring. A variegated form is more widely grown. The rock daphne (D. cneorum) grows to about 20 cm x 60 cm and is not an easy plant to succeed with, although it is definitely worth trying. The form 'Eximea' is sturdier growing than the species. The exquisite dwarf D. arbuscula is a much sought-after rockery species with leathery deep green leaves and bright pink flowers. It grows to about 15 cm x 25 cm.

The deciduous species are quite distinct. When in leaf, the most common species, D. mezereum, could be mistaken for D. x burkwoodii. It flowers in early spring before the foliage develops and both white and pink-flowered forms are available. Connoisseurs regard D. genkwa as the most desirable deciduous species. It also flowers before the foliage develops. The flowers are lavender and quite large. They are only slightly fragrant but more showy than most other species. The new growth is covered in fine down, which combined with the coppery colour is very attractive. Most hybrids and cultivars will strike, often with difficulty, from semi-ripe cuttings, however D. genkwa is usually grown from root cuttings.

DEUTZIA

These are among the heaviest-flowering garden shrubs. Several species and many cultivars are available. They are all deciduous with small, starry, white or pink flowers in densely packed heads Double-flowered forms, such as D. scabra 'Candidissima', are popular. They range from very small bushes, such D. crenata 'Nikko' (60 cm x 60 cm),

Crowea saligna 'Alba'

Daphne arbuscula

Deutzia 'Rosalin'

through to large shrubs, such as *D. corymbosa* (up to 3 m x 2 m), however most are around 1.5 m x 1.2 m. Grows in most soils and is best in full sun or very light shade. All are very hardy, tolerating at least -15°C. Propagate from semi-ripe cuttings in summer and autumn or hardwood over winter.

DODONAEA

The native akeake (*D. viscosa*) is extensively grown in New Zealand. It is a densely foliaged, evergreen shrub growing up to 4 m x 3 m. The typical form has bright green leaves and light green flower bracts, 'Purpurea' has deep reddish-purple leaves and pink to red flower bracts. This species is easily grown in any light well-drained soil in full sun or very light shade and is hardy to about -10°C with some damage. It is ideal for coastal gardens. Propagate semi-ripe

cuttings. 'Purpurea' is reasonably true to type from seed but good-coloured forms should be propagated vegetatively.

DRIMYS

The most widely grown species is the South American *D. winteri*. It is an evergreen shrub with attractive foliage but the plant is grown mainly for its small, starry, white flowers, which appear from mid spring. They have a jasmine-like perfume and are carried in large heads. With time it may grow to 5 m x 3 m but is usually trimmed to shape. Hardy to at least -10°C, it grows best in a cool climate with moist, humus-enriched, well-drained soil and a position in full sun or light shade. Propagate by semi-ripe cuttings or by seed if available. The Australasian species *D. aromatica* is similar in general appearance but its flowers are not as fragrant,

although the foliage is aromatic when crushed. It tolerates a wider climate range than *D. winteri* and is drought tolerant once established.

EDGEWORTHIA

The yellow daphne (*E. chrysantha*) is a singularly unusual deciduous shrub. In late winter, before the foliage develops, it produces tiny, sweetly scented, trumpet-shaped flowers that are yellow in bud but open cream and fade to white. They are densely packed in rounded heads at the branch tips. It is difficult to convey the unusual appearance of the plant when in flower; somehow the flowers don't match the growth habit. It is hardy to -15°C and prefers cool, moist, humus-enriched, well-drained acid soil in full sun or light shade. Propagate from fresh seed or softwood cuttings taken in late spring or early summer.

ELAEAGNUS

Elaeagnus pungens is a tough, adaptable evergreen that was once one of the most popular hedging shrubs. Its decline in popularity is hard to understand; there are more interesting plants but few as undemanding. *E. pungens* grows to 5 m x 3 m and, as would be expected, tolerates regular trimming. Several variegated forms are grown, the most common of which is the golden-edged 'Maculata'. This species is hardy to about -15°C. Russian olive (*E. angustifolia*) and *E. multiflora* are 2.5 m x 2 m deciduous shrubs. *E. angustifolia*, which may eventually become a small tree, has willow-like foliage and bark that peels freely. It has small, creamy-green fragrant flowers followed by small olive-like fruit. It is extremely hardy and will withstand temperatures as low as -35°C. *E. multiflora* has silvery leaves and reddish-brown new growth and is hardy to -20°C. It also has greenish-cream fragrant flowers but the fruits are small, red, edible berries that are very popular with birds. *Elaeagnus* is easily grown in almost any soil and any position except deep shade. Propagate by semi-ripe cuttings

in late summer or hardwood cuttings over winter.

ENKIANTHUS

An Asian genus of deciduous shrubs and small trees belonging to the erica family, although this relationship is not readily apparent except when in flower. One of its main attractions is the vibrant autumn colour. One bush can take on a huge variety of orange, red and yellow tones. The best species for autumn colour is *E. perulatus*. *E. cernus* also has good autumn colour but is mainly grown for its white or deep pinkish-red flowers. The most common species is *E. campanulatus*, which is a large shrub or small tree that grows to about 3.5 m x 1.8 m. The foliage is oval and clustered at the end of the fine twiggy side-shoots. The small, light pink, lily-of-the-valley-like flowers, which appear in spring, are carried in small pendulous clusters. *E. campanulatus* var. *palibinii* has larger leaves and deep pink flowers. *Enkianthus* does best in a cool moist climate and demands moist, acid, humus-enriched soil. It is an ideal companion for azaleas and rhododendrons in a woodland garden. Propagate cultivars by layers as cuttings can be difficult to strike without mist.

EPACRIS

This Australasian genus occupies the niche filled by ericas and callunas in other parts of the world. The New Zealand

Dodonaea viscosa

species are seldom grown, except by alpine or native plant enthusiasts, but two Australian species are common in New Zealand gardens. *E. longiflora* and *E. impressa* are small to medium-sized spreading shrubs with wiry stems, and small leaves and tubular flowers. The red, white or deep cerise-pink flowers of *E. impressa* appear in late winter. *E. longiflora* blooms in spring and summer and has red flowers tipped with white. Both species can grow to 1.5 m x 1.5 m if left untrimmed but they are usually clipped back to keep them tidy. Both are hardy to about -5°C but are best grown in mild coastal gardens. Occasionally seen are *E. purpurascens*, with reddish-purple tubular flowers, and *E. pauciflora*, a New Zealand native with white starry flowers.

ERIOSTEMON

The Australian wax flower (*E. myoporoides*) is a useful and adaptable small evergreen shrub growing to about 1.5 m x 1.5 m but may be trimmed to shape. It is seldom without a smattering of its small, starry, white flowers and is completely covered in mid spring. The whole plant is aromatic. Wax flower is hardy to about -10°C and is easily grown in any moist well-drained soil in full sun and does well in most areas. Other species, such as the needle-leaved, mauve-flowered *E. nodiflora* may occasionally be seen. Propagate by semi-ripe cuttings.

Erythrina crista-galli

ERYTHRINA

The coral trees are tropical or subtropical leguminous shrubs or small trees. They are usually deciduous although a few are semi-evergreen. Coral trees are primarily grown for their flowers, which are usually bright red, pea-like and extremely showy. Vicious thorns are a common feature. Most species are somewhat frost-tender, but *E. crista-galli* is reasonably tough; in cold winters it may die back to the ground but it usually reshoots from the rootstock. In mild areas where winter damage is uncommon, *E. crista-galli* is occasionally used for hedging, its thorns making it virtually impenetrable. If not cut back by frost or human intervention it may grow to 6 m x 5 m. It is summer-flowering and remains semi-evergreen to about -3°C but is capable of withstanding -10°C. *E. caffra* is a briefly deciduous species flowering in late winter or early spring before the foliage appears. It seldom grows larger than 5 m x 4 m in New Zealand. It is hardy to about -3°C. *Erythrina* grows best in light, yet moist, well-drained soil in full sun and needs heat to flower well. Propagate cultivars from semi-ripe cuttings.

ESCALLONIA

A genus of useful hardy evergreens, many of which are well suited to New Zealand gardens. However, only a few species and hybrids are grown, with *E. x langleyensis* 'Apple Blossom' being by far the most popular. This is a densely foliaged evergreen shrub that may grow to 2.5 m x 2 m with small pink and white flowers clustered at the tips of the branches. 'Apple Blossom' flowers throughout the year in mild areas, but is essentially spring and summer blooming, and is hardy to -15°C. It may be trimmed severely and is often used for hedging. Other hybrids, such as 'Field's Scarlet', may occasionally be seen. *E. x exoniensis* is also reasonably common; it has white flowers with a pink tinge and is one of the best for hedging, growing up to 3.5 m high. Propagate from semi-ripe cuttings.

Elaeagnus pungens 'Maculata'

Enkianthus perulatus

EUONYMUS

This Northern Hemisphere genus of about 170 species includes a large range of evergreen and deciduous trees, shrubs and sub-shrubs. The common deciduous species is the spindle tree (*E. europaeus*), which bears unusual three-lobed pink fruit from late summer, but otherwise this multi-trunked large shrub or small tree (about 3.5 m x 2.5 m) is untidy and ungainly. It is also somewhat invasive. *E. japonicus* is a large (3.5 m x 2.5 m) evergreen shrub primarily grown for its foliage, of which there are several variegated forms. The smaller species, such as the attractively variegated *E. fortunei* 'Emerald 'n' Gold' (1.2 m x 1.2 m), are colourful foliage plants. The flowers and berries are seldom showy, instead they are grown for their tough evergreen foliage and ease of cultivation. They can

also be used for hedging. *Euonymus* grows in most soils in positions from full sun to quite deep shade. Ample summer moisture will produce better foliage but the genus is generally drought tolerant once established. Most species are hardy to at least -15°C and *E. europaeus* will withstand -25°C. Propagate by semi-ripe cuttings.

EUPHORBIA

An enormous and variable genus containing a number of shrubby species. Many of these are frost-tender but a few are very hardy. Two familiar species are crown of thorns (*E. milii*) and poinsettia (*E. pulcherrima*); both are tender and often grown as house plants, but in frost-free areas with warm summers they may be grown outdoors. The most common hardy species is *E. characias* (syn. *E. veneta, E. wulfenii*), which grows to about

1.5 m x 1.2 m. Each branch is densely covered with bluish-green foliage and ends in a terminal head of yellowish-green flower bracts which are usually present year round. Easily grown in most soils in full sun or light shade and may be grown from semi-ripe cuttings.

EURYOPS

Three species of this African shrub daisy genus are common in New Zealand gardens, particularly coastal gardens where they often flower year round and tolerate strong winds and salt spray. The species most widely grown is *E. pectinatus* (some authorities suggest it is actually *E. abrotanifolius*). It is a densely foliaged, compact bush to about 1.5 m x 1.2 m. Bright yellow daisy flowers are borne throughout the year with the greatest abundance of bloom in late winter and spring. The fern-like foliage is silvery grey and slightly downy. *E. tenuissimus* is very similar but has very bright green foliage. The third common species, *E. acraeus*, is a small mounding bush about 50 cm x 1 m with 40 mm long, narrow, slightly toothed, bright silvery-grey leaves. The plant is covered in bright yellow flowers in late spring or early summer. These species are hardy to about -6°C and will withstand greater cold if kept dry over winter. Propagate from semi-ripe cuttings.

FATSIA

This genus contains only one species, *F. japonica*, which is one of the most widely grown house-plants and also makes an excellent garden specimen. The large palmate leaves may be up to 400 mm across and add a lush tropical effect despite being hardy to at least -10°C. Grown primarily for its foliage, this is an adaptable plant capable of growing in full sun if kept moist, but is most at home in deep, rich, moisture-retentive soil in light shade. A mature plant may be 5 m x 3.5 m. A variegated-leaved form is available but inclined to revert to green. The autumn flower heads are not insignificant but attract flies and so are best removed. Although easily raised from cuttings, these are large and unwieldy so propagation from seed is preferred.
Fatshedera lizei is a bigeneric hybrid between *F. japonica* and ivy (*Hedera helix*). It is a sprawling semi-climbing plant with leaves like a miniature *F. japonica*. Variegated forms are common but unstable. Usually grown as a houseplant, it will withstand -8°C. Propagate from semi-ripe cuttings.

FORSYTHIA

One of the most widely grown spring-flowering shrubs. Several species and many hybrids are grown. All have yellow flowers but vary in their ultimate size, flower size and colour, and earliness of flowering. The most common species are the upright *F.* x *intermedia* (2.5 m x 2 m) and the weeping *F. suspensa* (2.5 m x 2.5 m). The very strongly upright *F. viridissima*, which grows to 3.5 m high, is still grown but is more commonly used in hybridising rather than as a garden plant in its own right. Among the most distinctive hybrids are the very small 'Bronxensis' (60 cm x 60 cm); 'Arnold Dwarf' (1 m x 1.5 m); 'Karl Sax', which has large deep golden-yellow flowers and is late blooming; 'Lynwood', an upright grower with weather-tolerant flowers; and 'Beatrix Farrand', a large-flowered hybrid that grows to 2.5 m high. Purple-foliaged forms, such as 'Atrocaulis' are occasionally available. *Forsythia* will tolerate -20°C and grows in almost any well-drained soil in full sun or light shade. Propagate from hardwood cuttings in winter or semi-ripe cuttings in winter.

GARDENIA

These evergreen shrubs are hardier than is generally believed, but unless the climatic conditions are just right they often fail to bloom satisfactorily. *G. augusta* is an open shrub growing to 1.8 m x 1.8 m with bright green, leathery leaves and intensely fragrant, white, rosebud-like double flowers. 'Radicans' is a compact form that grows to 50 cm x 1 m, and 'Professor Pucci' is a large-flowered form that grows to 1 m x 1 m. *G. augusta* is primarily summer flowering and requires even night temperatures, regular water and humus-rich soil for good blooming. It is hardy to about -5°C for brief periods. Grow in full sun or light shade. *G. thunbergia* is a larger (2 m x 2.5 m) species with long, very deep green leaves and fragrant, white, single flowers from late winter or early spring. Less frost tolerant than *G. augusta*.

GARRYA

The tassel tree (*G. elliptica*) is a hardy (-15°C) evergreen shrub or small tree with deep green, 60 mm long, oval leaves and minute creamy yellow flowers in long tassels, which begin to develop in autumn and mature during winter. The male plants have the longest tassels; the form 'James Roof' is usually regarded as the best. If male and female plants are grown, the female may produce purplish berries from late winter. A mature specimen can be up to 5 m x 4 m but the plant remains shrubby for many years. It is easily grown in any moist well-drained soil in sun or very light shade. May be raised from seed but vegetative propagation by cuttings or grafting is the only way to be sure of the sex.

GAULTHERIA

A large genus of evergreen shrubs and ground covers. The native mountain snowberry (*G. depressa*) is an excellent rockery plant that grows to about 10 cm x 30 cm. It has tiny rounded leaves and small white flowers in spring that are followed by white berries in late summer and autumn. Snowberry is easily grown in moist, humus-enriched, well-drained soil in sun or light shade. It is usually propagated by semi-ripe cuttings. *Pertnettya* is a genus that includes some very similar species.

GREWIA

This principally tropical genus includes one species that is an attractive and easily grown plant for mild areas. *G. occidentalis* is a compact evergreen bush that grows to about 1.5 m x 1 m. The lavender-pink flowers resemble miniature passionfruit blooms and may be seen throughout the year with the main flowering season from spring to autumn. It is hardy to about -5°C with some damage and where the climate is suitable it may be used for hedging. *Grewia* prefers a moist, humus-enriched, well-drained soil in full sun or very light shade. Propagate by semi-ripe cuttings.

GRISELINIA

Only the two New Zealand species are cultivated in local gardens. *G. littoralis* is an evergreen shrub that normally grows to about 2.5 m x 1.5 m in cultivation. It is grown for its foliage, which is oval, bright

Euryops tenuissimus

Forsythia 'Beatrix Farrand'

green or boldly variegated, and very leathery. The leaves are often damaged by leaf-roller caterpillars. *G. lucida* is a more attractive species with larger foliage that is seemingly less prone to insect damage. Both species thrive in rich moist soils but are adaptable and drought tolerant once established. *G. littoralis* is a coastal plant that is very salt tolerant. *G. littoralis* is hardy to about -10°C and *G. lucida* to -5°C. Propagate cultivars by semi-ripe cuttings.

HAMAMELIS

The witch hazels are hardy deciduous shrubs and small trees valued for their fragrant winter flowers, which have narrow petals and are best described as spidery. The most popular species, *H. mollis*, has spicily scented, bright yellow flowers from mid winter. It may grow to 5 m x 3 m but is usually much smaller. *H. japonica* and *H. virginiana* are similar species. *H. virginiana* is spring flowering but its flowers tend be hidden among the foliage, however it is useful as a grafting stock. There are several excellent hybrids such as the brownish-orange-flowered 'Jelena' and the large-flowered 'Arnold Promise'. All species and hybrids are hardy to at least -20°C although the flowers may be damaged by very severe frosts. Grow in moist, humus-enriched, well-drained soil in full sun or light shade. Propagate the hybrids by semi-ripe cuttings in summer, but some may have to be grafted on *H. virginiana* stock.

HEBE

Worldwide, these are probably the most widely grown New Zealand natives. They are often more appreciated overseas than at home but many species and hybrids can be found in local gardens. The showiest flowers belong to *H. speciosa* and its selected forms, while the hardiest plants are the whipcord species. *Hebe* species range from minute ground covers to small trees, and from broadleaf forms to the conifer-like whipcords. They vary considerably in their hardiness and soil requirements. Most prefer moist well-drained soil in sun or very light shade. They are often badly damaged

Clockwise from top left: *Grewia occidentalis*; *Griselinia littoralis* 'Variegata'; *Hebe* 'Pamela Joy'; *Hebe* 'Wiri Joy'

by leaf-roller caterpillars. Propagate from semi-ripe cuttings. which strike easily except for some of the alpine species. The following are just a few from the huge range.
H. albicans is a spreading bush (60 cm x 1 m) with greyish-green leaves and short white flower spikes in summer. 'Boulder Lake' is a prostrate form.
H. x *andersonii* 'Andersonii Variegata', is probably the most boldly variegated hebe. The leaves are brightly edged and suffused with creamy white. The 100 mm long flowers spikes are lavender blue and produced in summer. It grows to about 1.5 m x 1.5 m.
H. armstrongii is a whipcord species that is now rare in the wild. It forms a rounded shrub (50 cm x 80 cm) and has bright golden-yellow stems and very small, tightly appressed leaves. Small white flower heads appear in early summer.
H. diosmifolia is a popular species that develops into a flat-topped spreading bush about 60 cm x 1.2 m and produces 60 mm spikes of pale mauve flowers in summer. Many of the new 'Wiri' hybrids show the influence of this species.
H. x *franciscana* 'Blue Gem' is a very showy shrub growing about

1.5 m x 1.5 m with 70 mm spikes of intense purplish-blue flowers in summer. It is very tough and tolerates coastal conditions. 'Waireka' is a variegated cultivar of similar parentage .
H. 'Inspiration' is a *H. diosmifolia* x *H. speciosa* hybrid growing to 80 cm x 1.2 cm with heads of bright purplish-pink flowers in winter and early summer.
H. 'McEwanii' A neat and distinctive bush (50 cm x 30 cm) that does well in rockeries. It has small greyish-green leaves, and upright reddish stems. Small heads of mauve flowers in summer.
H. odora (*H. buxifolia*) is a neat bush (80 cm x 1.2 cm) that responds well to trimming. It has glossy bright green leaves and heads of white flowers in late spring and early summer.
H. speciosa is a delightful long-flowering species growing to 1.2 m x 1.5 m. The bright pink, 125 mm long flower spikes are produced from late spring to autumn. It is not completely hardy but tolerates coastal conditions.
H. topiaria forms a dense rounded shrub about 80 cm x 80 cm with greyish-green foliage. The small heads of white flowers appear in summer.

HIBISCUS

There are two types of shrubby *Hibiscus*: the frost-tender subtropical hybrids derived from *H. rosa-sinensis*, and the hardy deciduous forms. These two groups are very different and many gardeners find it hard to believe they are related until they see the flowers.
The subtropicals are common from Gisborne north. The large flowers are available in vivid yellow, orange and red, pastel pinks and white. In favoured areas they will flower throughout the year and in mild areas they are easily grown, but frosts below -2°C are damaging and often fatal. Plant them in moist, well-drained, humus-enriched soil in full sun or very light shade and feed regularly. Propagate from semi-ripe cuttings in summer or early autumn.
The hardy deciduous species are just as spectacular but many gardeners find their bare winter branches untidy and unattractive. The most common species are the wine-red or purple-flowered rose of Sharon (*H. syriacus*) and the double white form of *H. mutabilis*. Many hybrids are available in Europe and North America, some with flowers up to 200 mm in diameter, but they are seldom

Top: *Hibiscus rosa-sinensis* hybrid
Above: *Kalmia latifolia* 'Pink Frost'

seen here. Deciduous forms may either be left to grow as large shrubs or cut back almost to ground level in spring, which encourages strongly upright growth. They are hardy to around -15°C and are able to reshoot from the rootstock even if frosted to ground level. Plant them in fairly light, well-drained soil in full sun. Hybrids should be propagated from semi-ripe cuttings or by dividing large established clumps in late winter or early spring.

HYDRANGEA

The well-known hortensia hybrids are derived from *H. macrophylla*, a Japanese species. They have large serrated leaves up to 150 mm across and large mop-headed flower clusters that can be as much as 300 mm in diameter. Regular feeding can produce huge flower heads. The lacecap hydrangeas, which are derived from *H. serrata*, have small sterile flowers in the centre of the head and larger flowers around the edge. The flowers of both groups change colour with the soil pH: pink in alkaline soils, blue in acid. To acidify soil add sulphur or any sulphur-based compound, such as iron sulphate; to make your soil more alkaline add hydrated lime. These hydrangeas develop into large bushes (1.8 m x 1.8 m) and mainly flower in summer.

HYDRANGEA COLOUR BY SOIL TYPE

CULTIVAR	ACID SOIL	ALKALINE SOIL
'Altona'	Deep blue	Light red
'Blue Prince'	Deep bright blue	Deep pink
'Holstein'	Bright blue	Mid pink
'Red Star'	Deep blue	Bright red
'Tosca'	Light blue	Salmon pink

There are many other hydrangeas, such as the tree-like *H. paniculata*, most of which are large deciduous shrubs that grow to around 1.8 m high, but there are also low-spreading or semi-climbing species. *H. paniculata* has off-white flowers that age to pink in lilac-like flower heads. *H. quercifolia* has rather plain white flowers but attractive foliage that develops brilliant red tones in autumn. *H. arborescens* is only a medium-sized shrub, but is often shaped like a miniature tree and has white, tinted pink, flower heads. *H. aspera* has very large leaves and flat, pink or white flower heads. The cream-flowered climbing hydrangea (*H. petiolaris*) was renamed *H. anomala* and may now be removed from the genus. All grow well in moist, humus-enriched, well-drained soil in dappled shade. They are hardy to about -15°C. Propagate from open-ground cuttings in winter or semi-ripe cuttings in summer.

HYPERICUM

This genus includes many evergreen and semi-deciduous shrubs. Some are little more than weeds but others are very useful and attractive plants. All have bright yellow, buttercup-like flowers in spring and summer and some also have colourful red fruit. Most shrubby species have rounded glaucous or deep green leaves resembling those of the deciduous honeysuckles. The rockery species often have small greyish-green leaves and tend to be low growing. *H. x moserianum* 'Tricolor' grows to 1 m x 1.2 m and has brightly variegated foliage in white, cream and pink shades. The most common species are the creeping *H. calycinum*, which may spread several metres wide and is often used in amenity plantings such as road islands, and the shrubby (up to 1.8 m x 1.8 m) *H. leschenaultii*. They are easily grown in full sun to quite deep shade in any soil that does not dry out entirely. Most species are hardy to at least -15°C and are propagated from semi-ripe cuttings.

INDIGOFERA

This leguminous genus contains many hardy species, such as *I. decora* and *I. cytisoides*, but those grown locally tend to be slightly frost-tender, although they will often shoot from the rootstock if cut to the ground by frost. Those commonly grown are *I. heterantha* (*gerardiana*) and *I. lindleyana*. Both have attractive pinnate leaves up to 200 mm long and pink, sweetpea-like flowers in 100-150 mm long racemes during summer. The ultimate size depends on winter frosts. In mild areas they become medium sized-shrubs up to 1.5 m x 1.2 m, but if cut to the ground they will rarely grow larger than 60 cm x 80 cm in one season. They will withstand occasional -4°C frosts without any great damage but repeated freezing to this level will cause the tops to die back. Easily grown in any light, yet moist, soil in full sun. Propagate from suckers or semi-ripe cuttings.

IOCHROMA

Three species are quite common in mild, nearly frost-free, areas. All three are soft-stemmed shrubs that grow to about 2.5 m x 2 m. They have large rounded leaves that taper to a point and pendulous clusters of long

Lacecap hydrangea, from *Hydrangea serrata*

trumpet-shaped flowers. *I. cyaneum* has deep purple flowers, *I. fuchsioides* has orange and yellow flowers, and those of *I. grandiflora* are mauve to purple. They will flower throughout the year climate permitting. Although best in frost-free areas they may tolerate -2°C with a dry autumn. Grow them in moist, humus-enriched, well-drained soil in full sun or very light shade. Semi-ripe cuttings strike well.

JACOBINIA

J. pauciflora, particularly the cultivar 'Firefly', is frequently seen in mild areas and may self-sow in suitable climates. It is a dense twiggy shrub that grows to about 1 m x 1 m. The orange and yellow tubular flowers are small (20 mm long) but carried in abundance, often throughout the year, but most heavily from spring to autumn. It is easily grown in any well-drained soil in full sun. Frosts below -3°C are likely to cause damage, although the rootstock often reshoots if defoliated. Propagate from small semi-ripe tip cuttings.

JOVELLANA

Closely allied to *Calceolaria*, this lesser-known genus contains two native species. One of these, *J. sinclairii*, is an attractive soft-stemmed shrub that grows to about 40 cm x 30 cm. The small, white, purple-spotted, pouch-shaped flowers are produced in loose sprays in summer. Grow it in moist, humus-enriched, well-drained soil in light shade. It is hardy to about -6°C. Propagate by semi-ripe tip cuttings. *J. violacea* is a

similar species from South America that is larger growing and more twiggy. Its flowers are lavender with darker spotting.

JUNIPERUS

The junipers are an enormously variable group of conifers. Some species are trees, but the majority are bushy or spreading. Many cultivars have been developed including dwarf forms suitable for rockeries. *J. chinensis* typically has an upright pyramidal growth habit and may reach 20 m high. However, among the many smaller cultivars are 'Aurea', which has yellow foliage and grows to 6 m; 'Japonica' is a spreading bush about 4 m x 4 m; 'Pyramidalis' has glaucous foliage and eventually reaches 4 m high; and 'Stricta' has silvery-blue foliage and forms a dense mound up to 3 m x 2 m. Several cultivars of *J. communis* are very popular; 'Compressa' has slightly glaucous foliage and a narrow upright habit to 1 m high and is perfect for rockeries or tubs; 'Depressa Aurea' is a ground cover with golden-brown foliage and spreads to 1.5 m wide; 'Depressed Star' is similar, but has pale yellowish-green foliage and grows to 2 m wide; 'Repanda' is a very low ground cover with bright green foliage and may eventually spread to 3 m wide.
The shore juniper (*J. conferta*) has silvery-grey needle-like foliage that is quite sharp and unpleasant to handle. It is a spreading ground cover that may grow to 30 cm x 3 m.
J. horizontalis and its hybrids are very glaucous-foliaged ground covers that often develop purple

tones in winter. They usually spread up to 3 m wide. 'Bar Harbor' and 'Douglasii' are the best-known cultivars.
J. x media hybrids cover a wide range of growth forms. They include 'Blue Cloud', a glaucous ground cover; 'Pfitzeriana Aurea' has golden foliage and tiered branches and grows to 1 m x 2.5 m; 'Pfitzeriana Glauca' is similar but has bluish foliage; 'Plumosa Aurea' is a golden-foliaged shrub with cascading branches that grows to 1 m x 2 m.
J. procumbens is a ground cover with glaucous foliage that may grow up to 60 cm x 5 m. 'Blue Danube' is the best-known cultivar of *J. sabina*; it has glaucous foliage and spreads to about 2 m wide.
J. virginiana has produced many blue-foliaged cultivars: the most widely grown is 'Glauca', a pyramidal large shrub or small tree that grows to 3.5 m x 2.5 m. Junipers are very tough and adaptable; they are generally hardy to at least -20°C and will grow in almost any position except deep shade. They are at their best in moist, well-drained soil, but are drought tolerant once established. Propagate by semi-ripe cuttings; the ground covers may be layered.

KALMIA

Grown well this genus includes some of the most beautiful members of the erica family. The mountain laurel (*K. latifolia*) not only has beautiful flowers, it is also extremely hardy, withstanding temperatures down to -30°C. The flowers, which appear in mid-spring, resemble small cake decoration flowers when in bud. The colour range extends from white through to lavender and red. The species may grow to 1.8 m x 1.2 m, but a dwarf form called 'Elf' grows to about 60 cm x 60 cm. The other common species, *K. angustifolia*, has similar, if smaller, flower heads. It is a smaller shrub that grows to about 60 cm x 60 cm and is equally hardy. *Kalmia* should be planted in moist, humus-enriched, acid soil. This genus demands perfect drainage; most failures can be put down to poor drainage or a shallow clay pan. Dig the ground over

Iochroma grandiflora

thoroughly before planting and add plenty of compost, or plant in raised beds. Layering is probably the most reliable form of vegetative propagation, but *K. angustifolia* strikes well from small tip cuttings.

KERRIA

This genus contains only a single species, *K. japonica*, which is an upright, multi-stemmed, deciduous shrub. A mature plant is up to 2.5 m x 1.8 m. The golden-yellow flowers are borne in spring on the tall arching canes. The double-flowered 'Pleniflora' is more usually grown. *Kerria* prefers a moist, humus-enriched, well-drained soil in full sun or light shade. It is hardy to -20°C and may be grown from open-ground cuttings in winter, semi-ripe tip cuttings, basal suckers or the division of well-established clumps.

KUNZEA

This genus is primarily Australian but now also includes the native kanuka (*K. ericoides*). The species most commonly cultivated are *K. ambigua*, *K. baxteri* and *K. parvifolia*. All are upright, finely twigged bushes with tiny bright green leaves and grow to about 2 m x 1.2 m. *K. baxteri* has bright red bottle-brush flowers but the other species have small, starry, filamentous flowers. Those of *K. ambigua* are pink to lavender and *K. parvifolia* has mauve to purple flowers. All are hardy to about -5°C and easily grown in

Hortensia hybrid, from *Hydrangea macrophylla*

Kunzea baxteri

Leptospermum scoparium
'Crimson Glory'

light well-drained soil in full sun. Propagate by semi-ripe cuttings.

LANTANA

In the tropics and subtropics *L. camara* is a noxious weed and in northern areas of New Zealand yellow, yellow-pink and pink-flowered forms are becoming a serious problem. It has been hybridised with the hardier mauve-flowered *L. monte-vidensis* to produce a range of very attractive heavy-flowering cultivars with compact heads of verbena-like flowers. A vast range of colours is now available and many of the flowers change colour as they open. Lantanas are easily grown in any light well-drained soil in full sun. In mild areas the plants will frequently self-sow but selected forms should be raised from tip cuttings. They are hardy to about -4°C or lower with some damage and may be treated as an annual or greenhouse plant in cold winter areas.

LAVANDULA

Lavenders are evergreen aromatic subshrubs that are currently very popular plants with many new cultivars introduced and old ones revived. English Lavender (*L. angustifolia*) is often sold as *L. spica* or *L. spicata*. It has small flowers in clusters at intervals along the stems. Several dwarfs, such as 'Munstead', are available as are pink and white-flowered forms. It is the lavender most

often used for hedging. Italian or Spanish lavender (*L. stoechas*) and the serrated-leaved French lavender (*L. dentata*) grow to about 1.2 m x 1 m. Their flowers are crowded at the ends of the stems with conspicuous large bracts at the very top – these are sometimes known as 'ears' and are most developed in the rabbit ears lavender (*L. stoechas* sp. *pedunculata*). The above species have silver-grey leaves. Woolly lavender (*L. lanata*) has stems covered in a silver felting and green lavender (*L. viridis*) has light green leaves and white to pale green flowers. All lavenders are aromatic, but green lavender smells more of turpentine than the typical fragrance. They also vary markedly in size depending on species and cultivar; some forms of the English lavender only grow around 30 cm high, but *L. dentata* 'Allardii' can grow to 1.8 m high. The main flowering period is late spring but many lavenders flower throughout the warmer months. All relish light well-drained soil in full sun. Most are hardy to about -10°C or lower if kept dry over winter. Propagate from semi-ripe cuttings. They frequently self-sow.

LEONOTIS

Lion's ear or lion's tail (*L. leonurus*) is a soft-wooded evergreen shrub that is hardy to about -5°C. It has 80 mm long, soft, mid-green leaves on 1.5 m upright stems. The felted, bright orange, tubular flowers are about

50 mm long and carried in clusters at the tips of the stems. In mild climates lion's ear flowers for most of the year. Where cut back by winter frosts, it is at its best in the autumn. Although it needs occasional trimming and shaping to keep it tidy, lion's ear can be spectacular if well cared for. Plant in light well-drained soil in full sun. Usually grown from semi-ripe tip cuttings.

LEPIDOTHAMNUS

The pygmy pine (*L. laxifolius*) is a subalpine species, formerly included in the genus *Dacrydium*, rarely seen in gardens. It has very short bronze-green to bluish-green needles, wiry stems and a trailing growth habit. The foliage develops purple tones in winter. With great age it can develop into a 3 m wide carpet. It is hardy to at least -15°C and should be grown in cool moist soil in full sun or partial shade. Propagate by semi-ripe cuttings or layering.

LEPTOSPERMUM

Forms of the native manuka or tea tree (*L. scoparium*), however several Australian species are also quite common. All are evergreen shrubs with small leaves and small starry flowers that are very colourful in spring or early summer. In milder climates many will also flower throughout winter. Cultivated forms are available in white, red and many pink shades with either single or double flowers. *L. scoparium* cultivars range in size from very small dwarf shrubs (30 cm x 30 cm) to small trees (3 m x 1.8 m). They are often badly damaged by manuka scale and this frequently leads to sooty mould, which is ultimately fatal unless treated (see the pests and diseases chapter).
The Australian species, such as *L. citrinum*, *L. laevigatum* and *L. rotundifolium*, are less affected by sooty mould. Most have fairly simple white flowers, but they tolerate coastal conditions and are more drought resistant than the manukas. 'Copperglow' is a hybrid that has attractive glossy bronze foliage.
Leptospermum is a fairly hardy genus but some Australian species may be damaged at -5°C, and even *L. scoparium* is

affected below -10°C unless well hardened in autumn. Grow in moist, humus-enriched, well-drained soil in full sun. Propagate from small tip cuttings.

LESCHENAULTIA

Many members of this Australian genus do not grow well in cultivation. Of those that do, by far the most common is *L. biloba*. It is a low-spreading evergreen shrub (60 cm x 1 m) with almost needle-like, deep green leaves. It has intensely vivid, pure blue flowers in terminal clusters from spring to early summer. This shrub demands a light, perfectly drained, moist soil. It will tolerate -5°C but resents being wet over winter. A north-facing wall that seldom sees winter rain is best. Propagate by small tip cuttings. *L. formosa* and *L. macrantha* are also occasionally grown. These shrubs are similar to *L. biloba* when not in flower, but have white, pink, yellow, orange or red flowers depending on the cultivar. The orange and red bicoloured form of *L. formosa* is the most commonly grown.

LEUCOTHOE

L. fontanesiana is a low-growing to medium-sized (1.2 m x 1.2 m) evergreen shrub. It has deep green pointed leaves up to 150 mm long, but a multi-coloured variegated form known as 'Gerard's Rainbow' or 'Rainbow' is more widely grown. The small, creamy-white, lily-of-the-valley-like flowers, which appear in spring, are carried in pendulous racemes beneath the arching stems. *Leucothoe* is hardy to -20°C and easily grown in any moist, well-drained, humus-enriched soil in full sun or light shade. 'Rainbow' is usually grown from semi-ripe cuttings or basal suckers. Seed is the best means of obtaining the less common species, such as *L. axillaris* and the erect-flowered *L. davisiae*.

LUCULIA

This Asian genus includes several fragrant winter-flowering evergreen shrubs. However, they are notoriously frost-tender. *L. gratissima*, the most common species, is a large sprawling shrub about 1.5 m x 1.8 m. It has 100 mm long, heavily ribbed, deep green leaves that take on bronze tones in autumn and winter or when grown in full sun. The strongly scented, small, pink flowers are produced in 200 mm diameter terminal clusters. It is hardy to about -2°C but should be given frost-free conditions as the flowers will be damaged by frosts even if the plant survives. *L. grandiflora* (*L. tsetensis*) is a similar species with larger white to very pale pink flower heads. Grow both in rich, moist, humus-filled soil in full sun or light shade. Grow cultivars from semi-ripe cuttings.

MAHONIA

A genus of hardy evergreen shrubs, most of which have large pinnate leaves composed of holly-like leaflets. Bright yellow flower spikes appear in mid winter, followed in spring by bluish-black berries. The fruit and foliage give the plant its common name of holly grape. Most species produce cane-like stems and spread by runners to form large clumps. An established clump of *M. lomariifolia* may be up to 2.5 m x 2 m and *M. aquifolium* grows to about 1.5 m x 2 m. *M. repens* is a rarely available species that grows to about 80 cm x 2 m and is an excellent ground cover for exposed banks. Most species are hardy to at least -15°C, however, *M. lomariifolia* withstands about -10°C only. Many species, especially *M. aquifolium*, develop bright red and orange foliage tones in winter. Mahonias will tolerate most conditions but are best grown in moist humus-enriched soil in full sun or light shade. Cultivars can be grown from semi-ripe cuttings, which can be difficult to handle.

MALVAVISCUS

Under New Zealand conditions these small evergreen trees seldom exceed 2.5 m x 2 m. Although not common, *M. arboreus* grows well in any nearly frost-free climate. It has 125 mm long, light to mid-green leaves that are serrated and slightly glossy when mature. The 25-50 mm long flowers appear

throughout the warmer months and resemble *Hibiscus* or *Abutilon* buds that are not fully open. They are usually carried in pairs at the tips of the branches. Under ideal conditions the effect is spectacular, but the flowers are easily damaged by very hot sun or low humidity and the plant is only hardy to about -2°C. Prefers moist, humus-enriched, well-drained soil in dappled shade. Propagate by semi-ripe cuttings. *M. arboreus* var. *mexicana* (syn. *M. grandiflorus*) is a similar but smaller species.

MIMULUS (DIPLACUS)

Most *Mimulus* species are annuals or perennials, but *M. aurantiacus* (*M. glutinosus*), is a soft-wooded evergreen shrub. The similarity between this 1.2 m x 1 m bush and the moisture-loving bog perennials is only evident when the orange or red 25 mm diameter flowers appear in spring. The narrow deep green leaves are quite sticky, which makes taking cuttings, the usual method of propagation, rather unpleasant. It is easily grown in most well-drained soils in full sun or light shade and is hardy to around -10°C. *M. longiflorus* is a similar but less hardy species with flowers in many shades from cream to deep red. Hybrids between *M. aurantiacus* and *M. longiflorus* are occasionally seen.

MURRAYA

M. paniculata (*M. exotica*) is a Malaysian native sometimes grown in frost-free areas. It is a densely foliaged evergreen that grows to about 2.5 m x 2 m and has glossy pinnate leaves. From spring to late autumn it produces clusters of very fragrant creamy-white flowers that resemble orange blossom in shape and scent and together with the jasmine-like foliage give the plant the common name orange jessamine. It is a very attractive plant, but is damaged by even the lightest frosts. It grows best in moist, humus-rich soil in full sun or very light shade. Propagate by semi-ripe cuttings.

MYOPORUM

The ngaio (*M. laetum*) is a

Lavandula angustifolia 'Rosea'

Mahonia lomariifolia

widespread and well-known native coastal plant. It has 100 mm long glossy leaves and small white flowers in spring and summer that are followed by purple berries. With time it becomes a small tree, however it is usually grown for hedging and kept trimmed to about 2.5 m high. In some areas it may self-sow and spread, but it is easily controlled. The very similar Australian species *M. insulare* and *M. tetrandrum* have to some extent replaced *M. laetum* as they are more drought tolerant. All three are frost-tender when young but will withstand -8°C once established. They grow best in moist well-drained soil in full sun or light shade. *M. parvifolium* is an Australian prostrate species that grows to about 20 cm x 1.5 m, striking roots as it spreads. It has an abundance of small white flowers in spring followed by purple berries. It is drought resistant and not fussy about soil

type, although it prefers ample summer moisture. It is hardy to around -8°C. All species are very easily grown from semi-ripe cuttings.

MYRTUS

This genus of over 100 species now includes the native plants formerly listed as *Lophomyrtus*. The only commonly grown exotic species is the true myrtle (*M. communis*). This is a small (1 m x 1 m) evergreen shrub with small deep green pointed leaves and starry cream flowers in spring followed by blackish-purple berries. It is hardy to about -15°C. A dwarf, cream-edged, variegated form ('Compacta Variegata') is more widely grown. Numerous hybrids between the native species *M. bullata* and *M. obcordata* are widely grown. The main attraction is their rounded, puckered and usually colourful leaves. The small creamy flowers generally appear in summer and are followed by berries that may be red to purplish in colour. Attractive cultivars include 'Kathryn', which has deep reddish-purple leaves; 'Gloriosa' has cream and pink leaves; and those of 'Traversii' are cream and green. Sizes range from very dwarf rockery forms, such as 'Pixie', to large shrubs up to 3 m x 2 m. Most are hardy to about -12°C and prefer moist, humus-enriched, well-drained soil in full sun or light shade. Propagate by semi-ripe cuttings.

NANDINA

This genus contains only one species, however several forms are cultivated. The species, *N. domestica*, is often called heavenly bamboo because of its bamboo-like canes. The pinnate foliage is carried on stiffly upright stems (up to 1.8 m) and creates an attractive lacy effect. The foliage colours brilliantly during winter with many shades of yellow, orange, red and purple. In spring terminal clusters of white flowers appear, followed by bright red berries if the plants are grouped (they are not self-fertile). However, 'Richmond' is a self-fertile form that fruits reliably without other plants for pollination. *N. domestica* eventually forms a clump about 1.5 m across, but it has none of the invasive tendencies of the true bamboos. 'Pygmaea' is a very dwarf, densely-foliaged cultivar that grows to about 30 cm x 50 cm and is widely grown in rockeries. Nandinas prefer moist, humus-enriched, well-drained soil in full sun. They will grow in shade but the best foliage colours are obtained in full sun. Propagate by semi-ripe tip cuttings, which are hard to work with, or by removing basal offshoots.

NERIUM

Oleander (*N. oleander*) is a large (2.2 m x 1.8 m) evergreen shrub most at home in areas with hot dry summers. The leaves are olive to mid-green, up to 150 mm long and quite leathery. The plant is mainly grown for its phlox-like flowers, which are massed in dense clusters. These appear throughout the warmer months, particularly in late summer and autumn. Many

flower colours are available, but bright pink 'Doctor Golfin' and the apricot-pink 'Monsieur Belaguier' (often sold as 'Punctatum) are by far the most common. 'Splendens Variegata' is a golden-yellow variegated-leaved form. Although not very frost tolerant (-8°C), oleanders are otherwise extremely tough and adaptable. They will withstand drought, poor drainage, the most terrible soils, extreme heat and salt. Oleander is, however, very prone to attack by scale insects, which may lead to sooty mould. For the best flower display grow them in light well-drained soil in full sun and give an occasional deep watering in summer. Propagate by firm semi-ripe cuttings in late summer.

NOTOSPARTIUM

This genus of New Zealand brooms includes only three species, of which *N. carmichaeliae* is occasionally seen in gardens. As with many brooms this plant is virtually leafless but its bright green weeping stems form interesting patterns. The plant only flowers for about four weeks in December but it is a spectacular display. The pink flowers are tiny but are carried in large numbers and are pleasantly scented. This shrub grows to about 2.5 m x 1.8 m and is hardy to at least -10°C. Grow it in moist well-drained soil in full sun or light

shade. It is usually raised from seed. The other species, *N. glabrescens* and *N. torulosum*, are similar and may be available from native plant specialists.

OLEARIA

The species grown locally are all natives with the exception the Tasmanian *O. phlogopappa*. It is a variable genus with sizes ranging from small shrubs, such as *O. cymbifolia* (1 m x 1 m) to small trees, such as the very narrow-leaved *O. lineata* (5 m x 4 m) and a variety of leaf forms. The small daisy flowers are usually white or cream and carried in large clusters in spring. *O. phlogopappa* is also available in pink and bluish-purple forms. Several species are used for hedging. For many years *O. paniculata* was the most widely grown but in recent years it has been supplanted by *O. traversii*, which is better able to withstand coastal conditions and continuous wind. Grow them in moist well-drained soil in full sun or light shade. Most species are hardy to at least -10°C. They can be grown from semi-ripe cuttings. Specialist seed houses sometimes stock uncommon species, such as the incense plant (*O. moschata*), which has scented wood.

OSMANTHUS

O. delavayi is a large evergreen shrub (2.2 m x 1.8 m) with small

blackish-green serrated leaves and clusters of tiny, trumpet-shaped, white flowers that are powerfully fragrant. It is primarily spring flowering but has occasional flowers in summer and autumn. *O. fragrans* is a very similar but larger species that may grow to 3.5 m x 2.5 m. *O. heterophyllus* is distinguished by its holly-like foliage; a variegated form is popular. All may produce small blackish-purple berries after flowering. They are easily grown in any cool, moist, humus-enriched, well-drained soil in full sun or light shade and are hardy to at least -10°C. Propagate by semi-ripe cuttings. *Osmanthus* x *burkwoodii* is a hybrid between *O. delavayi* and *O. decora*. It is very similar to *O. delavayi* but has slightly larger leaves and is more shade and drought tolerant. It grows to about 1.8 m x 1.5 m and is hardy to -10°C.

OXYPETALUM (TWEEDIA)

O. caeruleum is a small (80 cm x 1 m), but rangy, evergreen shrub with greyish-green felted leaves and stems. It is an untidy grower that is redeemed by its attractive pale blue flowers, which are carried in small terminal clusters throughout the warmer seasons and last well when cut. They are followed by prominent kapok-filled seed capsules. Grows best in light well-drained soil in full sun and is hardy to -5°C or slightly lower

Pachystegia insignis

Nandina domestica 'Richmond'

Philadelphus coronarius

if kept dry over winter. Propagate by semi-ripe cuttings. White and pink-flowered forms are occasionally available, but they are more frost-tender.

PACHYSTEGIA

The Marlborough rock daisy (*P. insignis*) is one of our finest native shrubs and now occupies a genus of its own. It is a tough evergreen shrub, that grows to about 1.2 m x 1.2 m with attractive foliage and flowers. It is a coastal plant but does well in inland gardens. The large (15 cm long x 10 cm wide) leathery leaves are a glossy deep green and covered with white felt below. Large daisy flowers, white with yellow centres, are produced from early summer followed by globose seed heads. *P. minor* is smaller in all respects

and grows to about 30 cm x 30 cm. The Marlborough rock daisy prefers light, yet moist, well-drained soil in full sun and is hardy to about -10°C. Propagate from semi-ripe cuttings or from seed, which may self-sow.

PAEONIA

The tree peonies have similar flowers to herbaceous peonies, but develop into large deciduous shrubs. The yellow-flowered *P. lutea* and the red-flowered *P. delavayi* are far more common than the very large-flowered *P. suffruticosa*, which tends to occur in pink shades, and its hybrids. This is not because they are superior plants but primarily because *P. suffruticosa* hybrids are among the most expensive garden plants due to propagation difficulties. The name tree peony is

something of a misnomer; they are essentially large shrubs (up to 3 m x 2.5 m), although very old specimens may develop tree-like proportions. The foliage is more finely cut and a lighter colour than that of the herbaceous plants. It begins to develop in early spring and can become very dense if the bushes are pruned after they flower in spring. Do not prune in winter as they flower on the old wood. These shrubs demand a moist, humus-rich soil to be at their best but they are not difficult to grow. A position in full sun or very light shade is ideal. They are hardy to at least -15°C and probably capable of withstanding -20°C. *P. lutea* and *P. delavayi* often self-sow, but the better *P. suffruticosa* hybrids usually have to be root grafted, which explains the extremely high prices asked for them. A batch of seedlings will often produce good plants but they will take several years to flower.

PENTACHONDRA

Pentachondra pumila is a prostrate native alpine shrub with tiny leaves and small white flowers in spring. The flowers are followed by berries 8 mm in diameter that are large and conspicuous on the plant. *P. pumila* is self-sterile, so at least two plants are needed to produce berries. It prefers moist gritty soil in sun or very light shade and is easily grown from cuttings or natural layers.

PERNETTYA

The most common species in

gardens is *P. mucronata*. It is a compact (1 m x 80 cm) evergreen shrub with very small, deep green, glossy leaves and tiny white flowers along its wiry branches. It blooms in spring and early summer, but the main feature is the berries that follow in autumn. These are up to 15 mm in diameter and usually a shade of purplish-pink. 'Bell's Seedling' has large pink berries; 'Davis Hybrid' is white; and 'Mother of Pearl' is pale pink. *P. mucronata* is easily grown in moist, humus-enriched, well-drained soil in full sun or light shade and is hardy to -15°C. Raise cultivars from semi-ripe cuttings.

PHAENOCOMA

The only species in this genus, *P. prolifera*, is a spreading, succulent-leaved, daisy-like subshrub growing to 50 cm x 1 m. The leaves, which are little more than small knobs protruding from the stems, are light green to silvery grey, as are the stems. The main feature is the mass display of 40 mm diameter pink everlasting daisies. It is at its peak in early spring but the odd flower is produced throughout the year. Grow it in light well-drained soil in full sun. It is hardy to -4°C or slightly lower if kept dry over winter and may be raised from small semi-ripe cuttings.

PHILADELPHUS

Relatively few mock oranges are grown in New Zealand gardens. The most widely grown is the double-flowered *P. virginalis*

Phylica pubescens

'Virginal'. It is a large (3 m x 1.8 m) deciduous shrub with 50 mm wide, very fragrant, white, semi-double to double flowers. Most hybrids and species have single flowers. 'Belle Etoile' is a smaller but very upright hybrid, usually about 1.8 m x 1 m. 'Frosty Morn' is a compact shrub that should not exceed 1.5 m x 1.2 m. *P. mexicanus* is an evergreen species that is only hardy to -6°C whereas the deciduous mock oranges will tolerate -25°C. Plant them in cool, moist, humus-enriched soil in full sun or light shade and prune to shape immediately after flowering. Propagate from open-ground hardwood cuttings over winter or semi-ripe tip cuttings in summer.

PHOTINIA

The most widely grown plant in this genus is *P. fraseri* 'Red Robin'. It is so common as to be almost a suburban cliché. It is a very useful bulk filler or hedging plant but is rather susceptible to scale insects and leaf-roller caterpillars. The larger species, such as *P. serrulata*, may become trees up to 10 m x 8 m, but most are bulky shrubs that grow to about 4 m x 3 m. All have large (100 mm long x 50 mm wide) deep green, serrated leaves with bright red new growth. In spring the clusters of small white flowers are a feature of some species, such as *P. serrulata* and *P. villosa*. Grow them in moist, humus-enriched, well-drained soil in full sun. Photinias will grow in semi-shade but much of the foliage colour will be lost. All

species are hardy to at least -12°C. Regular trimming will encourage plenty of bright new growth. Propagate hybrids by semi-ripe cuttings.

PHYLICA

The flannel flower or flannel bush (*P. plumosa*) is a 60 cm x 1 m evergreen shrub that is totally covered in fine downy hairs. The narrow deep green 20 mm long leaves have rolled back edges and although they are soft, they protrude straight out from the branches giving the bush a bristly appearance. The flowers have hairy bracts and resemble hairy cream daisies. They appear from early winter and are good cut flowers. *P. plumosa* is at its best in areas that do not experience heavy winter rains, which ruin the flower heads, or severe frosts, as it is hardy to only -4°C. Grow it in light well-drained soil in full sun. Propagate from semi-ripe cuttings or it may self-sow.

PICEA

The dwarf spruces, which are mainly forms of *P. abies*, are the best small conifers for rockeries and large tubs. They have very small needles and tightly congested growth and all grow extremely slowly. The best known are 'Globosa Nana', which grows to about 1 m x 1m and has branches that curve downwards at the tips and 'Pygmaea', which has slightly glaucous foliage and will not exceed 50 cm x 30 cm. Spruces prefer cool, moist, well-drained soil and should be watered well

in summer. Propagate by semi-ripe cuttings.

PIERIS

A genus of evergreen shrubs, all similar in general appearance but varying in size and flowering season. They have leathery, deep green leaves often with bright red new growth. The massed terminal heads of white, cream or pink lily-of-the-valley-like flowers appear from mid-winter to mid-spring depending on the species or cultivar. The flowers are occasionally very lightly scented. Sizes range from the very small 'Pygmaea' and the variegated-foliage hybrids, which seldom exceed 60 cm x 60 cm, to the large shrubby forms of *P. japonica*, which may reach 3.5 m x 2 m. The colour of the new growth varies; 'Forest Flame' probably has the brightest colour. The most intensely coloured flowers are the pink blooms of 'Flamingo'. All are hardy to at least -15°C and prefer cool, moist, humus-rich, well-drained soil that is slightly acidic. Grow from small semi-ripe cuttings.

PIMELEA

P. ferruginea 'Bonne Petite' is a 50 cm x 60 cm evergreen bush with upright branches clothed in small, bright green, fleshy leaves. In late winter and spring it develops 75 mm wide terminal clusters of small bright pink flowers. It is easily grown in any well-drained soil in full sun and -8°C with some damage. Of the New Zealand species the most widely grown is *P. prostrata*. It is a wiry-stemmed spreading ground cover that grows to about 10 cm x 80 cm. The small greyish-green leaves are only 10 mm long but densely cover the branches. In spring clusters of tiny, slightly fragrant, white flowers appear. It is frequently grown in rockeries. It grows best in moist well-drained soil in full sun and is hardy to about -10°C or possibly lower. Propagate pimeleas by semi-ripe cuttings, but the ground covers sometimes form natural layers.

PISONIA

The parapara or bird plant (*P. brunoniana*) is a rare evergreen

shrub native to New Zealand. It has large ovate leaves somewhat like those of the rubber tree (*Ficus elastica*). The variegated-foliaged form is a stunning plant, but as it is only hardy to about -1°C it can be grown outdoors only in mild areas. The flowers are insignificant. The common name comes from an unfortunate tendency for small birds to adhere to the sticky fruit and seed coating. Grow it in moist, well-drained, humus-enriched soil in light shade. Propagate from cuttings.

PITTOSPORUM

Next to *Hebe* this is the genus for which the New Zealand flora is best known internationally. The New Zealand species are primarily grown for their foliage, whereas the Australian and Asian species, particularly *P. undulatum* and *P. tobira*, also have attractive and fragrant white flowers. The New Zealand species also have fragrant flowers, but they are often purplish-red and rather inconspicuous. The most widely grown native species are *P. eugenioides* and *P. crassifolium*. Both are evergreen shrubs or small trees that grow to at least 3 m x 2 m. *P. eugenioides* has 50-100 mm long leaves that are usually light olive green, but there is a variegated form with cream margins. *P. tenuifolium* has 50 mm long, pale green leaves with wavy margins. It is suitable for hedging and the foliage is often used in floral decorations. Many foliage forms of *P. tenuifolium* are now available. Some of the best are: 'Deborah', which has light green leaves with a yellow to gold edge and often develops pink tones in winter. 'Irene Paterson', a dwarf (1.5 m x 1 m) with leaves that are almost entirely creamy white. It is slow-growing and prone to sunburn. 'James Stirling' (2.5 m x 1.5 m), similar to the species but the foliage is slightly greyer and the growth is very dense. It is an excellent hedging cultivar. 'Limelight', a dense bush to about 2.5 m x 2 m with bright green, somewhat leathery leaves. It is one of the best cultivars. 'Sunburst' (2.5 m x 1.5 m), probably the most striking of the large cultivars, producing leaves with deep green edges and yellow centres.

'Garnettii', a hybrid bearing leaves with irregular cream and green variegations. The foliage develops pink tones in cold weather. It grows to about 2.5 m x 1.5 m.

P. crassifolium and *P. ralphii* have deep green leathery leaves up to 75 mm long and may grow to 3.5 m x 2 m. In late spring they produce fragrant, deep burgundy-coloured flowers. The foliage of *P. ralphii* 'Variegatum' is among the most attractive of any variegated plant. Most native species are hardy to at least -8°C but some exotic species are quite frost-tender. Young plants of *P. undulatum*, for example, are usually killed by frosts below -3°C. Plant them in moist well-drained soil in full sun or light shade. Propagate cultivars by semi-ripe cuttings.

PLUMERIA

The true frangipani (*P. rubra*) is a small deciduous tree that in New Zealand gardens rarely exceeds 2.5 m x 1.5 m. It has short, stout branches and leathery, 250 mm long, velvety leaves. The main attraction is the overpowering fragrance of its waxy yellow 50 mm diameter flowers. Pink, and pink and yellow bicolour forms also exist but are rare. It is hardy to perhaps -2°C but is definitely best grown in frost-free areas. Frangipani prefers soil that is moist and well-drained during the growing season and dry in winter. Propagate by semi-ripe cuttings 150-200 mm long.

POLYGALA

P. myrtifolia is a slightly tender South African shrub that grows to about 2 m x 1.5 m. The leaves develop purplish tints in winter. It bears clusters of magenta pea-shaped flowers throughout the year and is one of the most valuable shrubs for providing a continuous display. It grows well in any well-drained soil in full sun but is damaged by frosts below -4°C. *P. chamaebuxus* is a very hardy rockery ground cover from the European Alps that grows to about 15 cm x 80 cm. It has pinkish-red and yellow flowers

Pieris japonica

Pittosporum crassifolium 'Variegata'

primarily in spring, with occasional flowers in summer and autumn. It is hardy to at least -15°C and is best grown in gritty, yet moist, well-drained soil in full sun. Propagate both species by semi-ripe cuttings.

POMADERRIS

The golden tainui (*P. kumeraho*) is a native species commonly grown in local gardens. It is a densely foliaged shrub growing to about 2.5 m x 1.5 m with leaves that are prominently veined with a silvery undersurface. In late winter and spring the bush is smothered in clusters of tiny golden-yellow flowers. Unfortunately this species is neither very hardy (to -4°C) nor long-lived, requiring replacement every five years or so. It tolerates most soils but is best in light, gritty, well-drained soil in full sun. It is usually grown from seed. Another native species, *P. apetala*, was once popular for coastal hedging but is now seldom grown. It is considerably larger and may grow to 6 m x 3 m.

POTENTILLA

Most of the shrubby potentillas grown in New Zealand gardens are deciduous hybrids derived from *P. fruticosa* and are valued for their profuse flower display. They are low mounding, densely branched bushes that grow to

about 80 cm x 1 m and are capable of withstanding -25°C. The foliage is similar to a very finely cut briar rose leaf and the flowers, which are carried at the end of short side shoots, resemble small single roses. They smother the bush in late spring and continue intermittently through summer and autumn. Cultivars are available in most colours, although red and yellow predominate. Some of the best are 'Tangerine' (light orange); 'Elizabeth' and 'Goldfinger' (bright yellow); 'Red Ace' (bright red); 'Princess' (bright pink); and 'Mount Everest' (white). Semi-double forms, such as 'Snowflake' (white), are occasionally available. Potentillas are best grown in light well-drained soil in full sun. Propagate by semi-ripe cuttings or self-rooted layers.

PROSTANTHERA

Australian mint bushes range in size from small rockery dwarfs, such as the red-flowered *P. aspathaloides*, to large shrubs that may grow to 2.5 m x 1.5 m. All are evergreen with aromatic foliage, but they vary in their foliage type and flower colour. *P. rotundifolia* and the very similar *P. incisa* bear masses of small bright purple flowers in spring and small deep green leaves and grow to about 1.5 m x 1.2 m. *P. ovalifolia* has similar flowers with slightly larger oval leaves and can

grow to over 2 m high; there is also a variegated form. *P. cuneata*, sometimes called the alpine mint bush, has a dense covering of small deep green leaves and masses of white flowers in spring. It grows to 80 cm x 1.2 m. *P.* 'Ballerina' is a strongly upright bush with narrow leaves and white and mauve flowers in spring. Most larger mint bushes are easily grown in any well-drained soil in full sun or very light shade but are prone to scale insects and sooty mould. The susceptible alpine species require gritty scree soil. The larger forms should be cut back after flowering each year. Most mint bushes are hardy to about -10°C and will grow in all but the coldest areas. Propagate by semi-ripe cutting.

PSEUDOPANAX

The native species are the only ones commonly seen in local gardens. They are primarily foliage plants and many species are notable for the differences between their juvenile and adult foliage. Lancewoods (*P. crassifolius*) and *P. ferox* are very narrow upright plants when young and have long narrow leaves with saw-toothed edges. As they mature they develop into round-headed small tree with variable, roughly maple-leaf-shaped foliage. At all stages the leaves are dark bronze-green and

Pseudopanax arboreus

leathery. Other species, such as the five finger (*P. arboreus*) have broad palmate leaves at all stages of their growth. The larger species develop into small trees up to 10 m high, but most of the shrubby forms are around 3 m x 1.5 m. Numerous foliage cultivars, such as the yellow-variegated 'Gold Splash' and the assorted bronze-leaved *P. lessonii* hybrids, are available. *Pseudopanax* does best in deep, moist, humus-enriched, well-drained soil in full sun or light shade. Most species are hardy to about -10°C but the new growth is very tender. Propagate by semi-ripe cuttings.

PSEUDOWINTERA

A genus of three species native to New Zealand, two of which, *P. colorata* and *P. axillaris*, are very similar. Both are evergreen shrubs that grow to about 2 m x 1.2 m in gardens. Their attraction is the multicoloured foliage. The leathery leaves are a light greenish-cream shade with red, purple or orange markings and blotches and silvery undersides. Both species are easily grown in moist well-drained soil in full sun or light shade and they are hardy (to -12°C) and colourful throughout the year. Good forms should be perpetuated by semi-ripe cuttings. The third

species, *P. traversii*, is a small shrub about 90 cm x 90 cm with smaller leaves and a dense wiry habit. The stems have attractively patterned bark.

PSORALEA

P. pinnata is an evergreen shrub that grows to about 3 m x 2 m and has bright green needle-like foliage that is soft and pliable and densely clothes the branches. Bright blue and white, sweet pea-like flowers are carried in terminal clusters in spring. It is hardy to around -4°C and does best in mild coastal areas. Easily grown in any light well-drained soil in full sun, it self-sows in favourable climates, or grows from semi-ripe cuttings.

PUNICA

The pomegranate (*P. granatum*) is a summer-flowering deciduous shrub. The fruit sets irregularly in New Zealand gardens but it is widely grown as an ornamental. There are two main forms, a large upright shrub (2.5 m x 1.5 m) and a dense mounding dwarf (50 cm x 50 cm, that are identical except for the size difference. The foliage turns bright yellow before dropping in autumn. From late spring bright orange, fully double flowers are produced. A

rare white form, 'Alba Plena', is occasionally available. Pomegranates may be grown in any light well-drained soil in full sun and are hardy to about -15°C. Propagate by hardwood cuttings in winter or semi-ripe cuttings in summer.

PYRACANTHA

The bright red, orange or yellow berries of *Pyracantha* are always a feature of autumn and winter. Several species are grown but most garden forms, such as 'Brilliant' (red), 'Mojave' (orange) and 'Shawnee' (yellow), are hybrids of *P. coccinea* and *P. rogersiana*. They are thorny evergreen shrubs that grow to about 3 m x 2 m but are usually kept trimmed to shape. In late spring the plants are smothered in small, white, scented flowers. Some people loathe the scent, others find it appealing. Two large species, *P. angustifolia* (orange) and *P. crenulata* (red), are sometimes used as espaliers. They grow to about 4 m x 4 m but are easily trimmed and trained. *Pyracantha* thrives in any moist well-drained soil in full sun or very light shade and is hardy to at least -15°C. They frequently self-sow, however hybrids should be propagated by semi-ripe cuttings or hardwood cuttings in late autumn.

REINWARDTIA

The sole species in this genus, *R. indica*, is a tender shrub useful for providing winter colour in nearly frost-free areas. The leaves, which resemble those of citrus, are about 75 mm long. The widely flared, bright yellow, trumpet-shaped flowers appear from mid winter to early spring. Under ideal conditions the plant may grow to 1.5 m x 1 m but is usually under 1 m high. Hardy to -2°C, it grows best if protected from frosts. Plant in moist well-drained soil in full sun or light shade. Propagate by semi-ripe cuttings.

RHABDOTHAMNUS

The New Zealand native *R. solandri* is a rather open growing finely branched shrub that may reach 1.8 m x 1.2 m. The 20 mm long flowers are bell-shaped, slightly pendulous, and are orange-red with conspicuous reddish-purple stripes in the throat. *R. solandri* prefers moist well-drained soil in shade or partial shade. It is hardy to only -4°C, but as it is usually grown under the cover of trees this is no great problem. Propagate from semi-ripe cuttings.

RHAPHIOLEPSIS

Indian hawthorn is a genus of hardy evergreen shrubs, two species of which are grown in New Zealand gardens. Both *R. indica* and *R. umbellata* have deep green, leathery, slightly felted, leaves about 50-70 mm long. In spring they produce clusters of small white to light pink starry flowers followed by deep blackish-purple berries. *R. umbellata* may grow to 3.5 m x 2.5 m but *R. indica* seldom exceeds 1.8 m x 1.2 m. Several hybrids and cultivars with heavier crops of larger and brighter pink flowers are grown. Among the best are 'Ballerina' and 'Enchantress'. They are all hardy to at least -10°C and easily grown in any moist well-drained soil in full sun or very light shade. Propagate by semi-ripe cuttings.

RONDELETIA

This genus includes several beautiful evergreen shrubs that resemble some *Viburnum* species but unfortunately lack their hardiness. Two species are grown in mild New Zealand gardens. The more common and hardier of the two is *R. amoena*, which is a large, rather open, shrub that may grow to 3 m x 1.8 m. It has pointed oval leaves that are light green with bronze tones, about 120 mm long x 60 mm wide and light yellow-centred, salmon-pink, tubular flowers in ball-shaped clusters from late winter. It is hardy to -5°C with some damage. *R. odorata* is smaller (1.2 m x 80 cm) with slightly felted leaves and orange-red fragrant flowers. It is hardy to -2°C and is best sheltered from frost. Both grow well in any moist well-drained soil in full sun. Trim to shape when young. Propagate by semi-ripe cuttings.

ROSMARINUS

Rosemary (*R. officianalis*) is one of the classic herbs and is also a very useful ornamental. There are two growth forms: the spreading ground cover and the upright bush. The foliage of all cultivars is deep green, very narrow and strongly aromatic, but the flower colour varies from very pale lavender to deep purple. Upright forms grow to about 1.8 m x 1 m and prostrate forms to about 40 cm x 2.5 m. Grow rosemary in light well-drained soil in full sun and clip regularly to keep the plants compact. It is hardy to -12°C, or lower if kept dry in winter. Grow from semi-ripe tip cuttings.

RUSSELIA

When not in flower it would be easy to confuse this green-stemmed, near leafless, weeping shrub with broom, but nobody would make that mistake when the bush is covered in its bright red, 25 mm long, pendulous, tubular flowers. The common species, *R. equisetiformis*, is a small to medium-sized (up to 1.2 m x 1 m) shrub with pendulous branches that flowers from mid spring to autumn. It is very useful in frost-free and coastal areas but is only hardy to -2°C. Grow it in light well-drained soil in full sun; it does well in hanging baskets and is a good conservatory plant. Grow from semi-ripe cuttings.

Rosmarinus officianalis 'Lockwood de Forest'

SANTOLINA

Cotton lavender (*S. chamae-cyparissus*) is a common small evergreen often used for a coloured foliage accent. The very reduced leaves and stems are silvery grey. The bush forms a dense mound up to 1 m x 1 m that must be trimmed or it will collapse under its own weight; with regular trimming it may be used as a small hedge. The flower heads, which appear in summer, are bright yellow balls carried on long stems. It grows best in a light well-drained soil in full sun and is hardy to -15°C. Propagate by semi-ripe cuttings.

SARCOCOCCA

S. ruscifolia is a hardy evergreen bush with 25 mm long, dark green, pointed leaves and small, white, slightly scented flowers in spring followed by bright red berries throughout winter. It is usually under 1.2 m but may grow to 1.5 m x 1.2 m. Although not a spectacular shrub, it is one of the few plants that grows well in dry and shaded positions. It prefers a moist well-drained soil in partial shade but will tolerate almost any situation. It is hardy to at least -10°C and is usually grown from seed.

SERISSA

This genus includes just one species, *S. foetida*, which is a soft-stemmed shrub with tiny leaves and small, starry, white flowers that cover the bush in spring and early summer. It grows to about 60 cm x 60 cm and is sometimes grown as a low hedge in mild areas. The variegated form sometimes known as 'Snowflake' is widely grown, as is the double-flowered 'Flora Plena'. *Serissa* is easily grown in any well-drained soil in full sun but is only hardy to around -3°C. Propagate by semi-ripe cuttings.

SESBANIA

S. tripetii is a medium-sized evergreen shrub that grows to about 2 m x 1.2 m. It has long pinnate leaves and from late winter it produces racemes of deep red, sweet pea-like flowers. A well-established bush in full flower is a spectacular sight. However, it is short-lived and often dies before achieving its full potential. Light soil with perfect drainage is essential and a position in full sun is best for maximum flower production. *S. tripetii* is hardy to about -4°C or perhaps slightly lower if kept dry over winter. Propagate by semi-ripe cuttings.

SKIMMIA

Two species of these hardy, evergreen, berrying shrubs are readily available. *S. japonica*, which grows to about 1.5 m x 1.8 m, has 100 mm long, glossy, deep green, leathery leaves. In spring terminal panicles of slightly fragrant creamy-white flowers develop followed by clusters of bright red berries that last well into winter. Sexes are separate and so both male and female plants are required for fruiting. *S. japonica* sp. *reevesiana* is a self-fertile species that sets good crops of dark red berries. It has somewhat glaucous foliage and is a much smaller plant (60 cm x 1 m). Both species are hardy to -15°C and grow best in moist, humus-enriched, well-drained soil in light to moderate shade. Grow from semi-ripe cuttings.

SPIRAEA

A genus of deciduous shrubs, the most widely planted of which is *S. japonica* and its various forms. Most cultivars, such as the popular golden-leaved 'Anthony Waterer', grows to about 1.2 m x 1 m and have terminal heads of tiny deep pink flowers in late spring and early summer. The serrated foliage is about 50 mm long and in full sun it may develop reddish tones that intensify in autumn. Also commonly grown are *S. cantoniensis*, which has 2 m arching stems and white flowers; the double form of *S. prunifolia*, which has *Gypsophila*-like flowers and the hybrid *S. x vanhouttei*, which has glaucous foliage and white flowers. All are hardy to at least -20°C and prefer moist well-drained soil in full sun. Severe pruning encourages fresh new growth; cut back the tall forms immediately after flowering, but trim the summer-flowering shrubs, such as 'Anthony Waterer' in winter. Propagate by open-ground hardwood cuttings in winter or semi-ripe cuttings in summer.

STREPTOSOLEN

Although frost-tender, the marmalade bush (*S. jamesonii*) is worth trying in mild areas. It is a large, loosely branched, evergreen shrub that grows to about 2 m x 1.8 m. It has ribbed leaves and clusters of verbena-like flowers that are usually bright orange, but may be any shade from yellow to light red. In suitable climates it flowers almost year round. Plant in light well-drained soil in full sun and water well in summer. It is hardy to about -2°C and is usually propagated by semi-ripe cuttings.

SYMPHORICARPOS

The snow berry (*S. albus*) is a deciduous shrub with honeysuckle-like leaves and small pink flowers in spring, but is primarily grown for its white berries that stand out so clearly in winter when the branches are bare. It grows to about 1.8 m x 1.2 m, is very hardy (to -30°C) and is easily grown in any moist well-drained soil in full sun or light shade. Propagate from open-ground hardwood cuttings in winter. Other species, such as the ground cover *S. mollis*, are occasionally available.

SYRINGA

Lilacs are one of the classic spring-flowering deciduous shrubs. Several species are grown but the hybrids are more popular. Most lilacs grow to about 2.5 m x 1.8 m. The

foliage sometimes colours well in autumn but lilacs are primarily grown for their upright panicles of highly fragrant flowers. The flowers appear from early October to mid-November and range in colour from white and pale yellow to all shades of pink, mauve and purple. Most of the common garden forms were raised in France in the late 1800s to early 1900s but new forms appear from time to time. Some of the best are: 'Charles Joly' (deep purplish-lavender, late flowering); 'Esther Staley' (deep pinkish-lavender); 'Firmament' (lavender-blue, early flowering); 'Marechal Foch' (deep wine-purple, early flowering and a vigorous grower to 3 m or more); 'Mme Felix' (white, early flowering); 'Primrose' (light primrose-yellow, late flowering). Several species are quite different from the common hybrids. *S. reflexa* grows to 4 m high and has pendulous panicles of deep lavender flowers; *S. microphylla* has small leaves, loose clusters of lavender flowers and grows to about 2 m high; and *S. patula* is a twiggy bush about 1 m x 1 m with pink to lavender flowers. Lilacs prefer moist, humus-enriched, well-drained soil in full sun or light shade. Most species and hybrids are hardy to at least -20°C and do best where the winters are cold because they require at least a few frosts to flower well. Lilacs will sometimes strike from hardwood or semi-ripe cuttings, but most cultivars are grafted. Established plants frequently produce suckers and if the plants are not grafted these may be used for propagation, but they should be removed in any case or they may spread. Any pruning should be done immediately after flowering or the following year's blooming may be reduced.

TETRAPANAX

The rice-paper plant (*T. papyrifer*) is a large, woody-stemmed, evergreen plant with extremely bold ornamental foliage. The overall effect is that of a very large and heavily felted aralia (*Fatsia japonica*), to which it is closely related. The broad palmate leaves are up to 60 cm across with the undersides and stems densely coated in thick

beige felt. Some people develop a form of dermatitis through contact with the felt. Large clusters of creamy white flowers develop in autumn followed by small blackish berries. A mature specimen may be 5 m x 4 m, but plants are usually pruned in late winter to keep them compact. As this plant spreads by underground runners, it can be somewhat invasive. Grow in moist well-drained soil in full sun to moderate shade and water well in summer. Given adequate watering, it does well in coastal areas. It is hardy to -5°C and usually reshoots from the roots if badly frosted. Propagate from suckers or cuttings which are unwieldy and unpleasant to handle.

TEUCRIUM

T. fruticans is an evergreen that grows to 2.5 m x 2 m. It has silvery-grey leaves on thin white stems and light mauve to purple flowers throughout the year, but mainly in summer. The flowers resemble those of *Lobelia* with a large lower lip. It is hardy to -10°C and is easily grown in any light well-drained soil in full sun. Because *T. fruticans* withstands regular trimming and salt-laden winds, it is frequently grown as a coastal windbreak or low hedge. *T. chamaedrys* is a smaller plant (50 cm x 50 cm) with light green leaves and bright pink flowers and is sometimes used for low hedging in herb gardens. Both species are propagated by semi-ripe cuttings.

THRYPTOMENE

T. calycina and *T. saxicola* are both small to medium-sized (1.5 m x 1.2 m), evergreen, wiry-stemmed shrubs with tiny leaves. *T. calycina* has an abundance of tiny, starry, white flowers all along the branches in late winter and spring. *T. saxicola* has slightly larger light pink flowers. Both are hardy to about -6°C and prefer light well-drained soil in full sun. They make good cut flowers and as they require regular light trimming, this is a good way to keep them compact. Propagate by semi-ripe cuttings.

THUJA

This genus of conifers contains a number of widely grown dwarf

cultivars. Most are forms of *T. occidentalis* and by far the best known is 'Rheingold', a mounding golden-foliaged bush that grows to 1.5 m x 1.5 m. 'Ericoides' is a very interesting cultivar growing to about 1.5 m x 1.5 m with erica-like foliage that develops deep reddish-purple tones in winter. There are also several very upright cultivars, such as 'Pyramidalis Compacta', which grows to 3 m x 80 cm. *Thuja orientalis* (now correctly *Platycladus orientalis*) has also produced some good cultivars, of which 'Rosedalis' is probably the most widely grown. It is an upright bush that grows to about 1.5 m x 80 cm. It is a juvenile-foliaged form with the needles changing colour with the season, from creamy-white in spring, green in summer, to glaucous purple in winter. Thujas are tough and adaptable plants that will thrive in most conditions. They prefer moist, well-drained soil with regular summer water and are hardy to at least -20°C. They are among the easiest conifers to propagate and strike easily from semi-ripe cuttings.

TIBOUCHINA (LASIANDRA)

Several species are grown but the most common is *T. urvilleana* (*T. semidicandra*). This is a 4 m x 2.5 m evergreen with bright green, 125 mm long, velvety leaves and 75 mm wide bright purple flowers that appear sporadically throughout the year but most profusely in summer and autumn. Only hardy to about -3°C, it is otherwise easily grown in any moist well-drained soil in full sun or very light shade. Propagate from semi-ripe cuttings. Other species are occasionally grown, of which the most distinctive is *T. scandens*. This is a semi-climbing shrub with leaves and flowers similar to those of *T. urvilleana* only smaller. It can be grown on a wall for added frost protection.

UGNI

Formerly known as *Myrtus ugni*, the Chilean cranberry (*U. molinae*) is a hardy 1.2 m x 80 cm evergreen shrub with a dense twiggy growth habit. In spring it produces small, starry, cream flowers followed by deep red, 15 mm diameter, edible fruit. It should not be confused

with the true cranberries
(*Vaccinum* spp.) but has similar
uses. It is hardy to -10°C or
slightly lower and should be
grown in moist, humus-
enriched, well-drained soil in full
sun or very light shade.
Propagate by semi-ripe cuttings.

VACCINUM

Dwarf cranberries, such a *V.
delavayii*, are excellent rockery
plants. They are evergreen
shrubs that grow to about
40 cm x 60 cm. The leaves are
about 10 mm long, rounded
and leathery and the small white
or pale pink flowers are followed
by attractive red or blackish-blue
berries. Cranberries prefer moist,
humus-enriched, well-drained
soil in sun or light shade.
Propagate by semi-ripe cuttings.

VIBURNUM

This is a large genus of
evergreen and deciduous ground
covers, shrubs and small trees.
They are so variable in size,
foliage type and flowering habit
it would be quite possible to
have an interesting garden of
viburnums alone. The following
are the best known garden
forms.
V. x *bodnantense* is a deciduous
much-branched shrub growing
to 2.5 m x 1.5 m with 75 mm
long leaves. It produces small
rounded clusters of very fragrant
white flowers with a faint pink
tint from late winter to early
spring. It is hardy to -20°C.
V. x *burkwoodii* is an equally
hardy semi-evergreen growing to
3 m x 2.5 m. The 75 mm long
leaves have greyish felt
underneath. Loose white and
pink ball-shaped flower clusters
are produced in spring and are
very fragrant.
V. carlesii is deciduous and
grows to about 1.8 m x 1.5 m.
The leaves are up to 100 mm
long with hairy undersides. Ball-
shaped flower clusters, pink in
bud opening to white, appear in
spring and are very fragrant. It is
hardy to -20°C.
V. davidii is an evergreen species
often massed as a large-scale
ground cover. It will grow to
about 1 m x 1.2 m. It has glossy,
heavily veined, leathery leaves up
to 140 mm long. Small clusters
of white flowers are borne in
mid spring followed by blue-
black berries. It is hardy to -15°C.

Thryptomene calycina

V. japonica is an evergreen and
remains small for many years
and may be used as a ground
cover. It grows to about 1.5 m x
1.5 m and is hardy to -15°C.
The deep green, glossy leaves are
up to 120 mm long. It has
bronze-coloured new growth.
Loose clusters of white flowers
appear in late spring followed by
a few red berries. Known as the
snowball tree because of its large
flower heads
V. opulus is a large deciduous
species growing to 5 m x 3.5 m
with large, three-lobed, maple-
like leaves that redden in
autumn. It produces large
rounded heads of white flowers
in spring followed by red berries.
There is a sterile form that does
not fruit. This species is hardy to
-20°C. A distinctive deciduous
species with tiered branches is *V.
plicatum*. It grows to about 3 m
x 3 m and is hardy to -20°C. It
has serrated, hazel-like leaves
and flattened clusters of white
flowers in spring. Very attractive
pink-flowered forms are also
available. An evergreen species
often used for hedging is *V.
tinus*. Untrimmed it will grow to
about 3 m x 2.5 m and is hardy
to -15°C. The leathery olive-
green leaves are up to 120 mm
long. A variegated form is
common. Loose clusters of white
flowers are produced in late
winter and spring. *V. triloba* is
among the best of all berrying

shrubs for colour and quantity
of fruit. It is deciduous, grows to
about 2 m x 2 m, and is hardy
to -20°C. The three-lobed
maple-like leaves often turn
bright red in autumn. Flat heads
of white flowers are borne in
spring with large clusters of very
bright red berries in late summer
to autumn.
Many others are readily available.
Viburnums are best grown in
moist, humus-enriched, well-
drained soil in full sun or light
shade, but *V. davidii* and *V.
japonica* will tolerate quite deep
shade if used as a ground cover
under trees. Propagate hybrids by
semi-ripe cuttings.

WEIGELA

This is one of the few deciduous
genera that remains as popular
as it has ever been. A few
months without leaves matters
little when you are rewarded
with such a magnificent spring
and early summer flower display.
The foliage colour in autumn is
not to be underestimated either.
Garden forms are hybrids
derived from *W. florida*, which
has pointed leaves about
100 mm long with finely
serrated edges and clusters of 25
mm long, funnel-shaped flowers
in spring. The most widely
grown form is undoubtedly *W.
florida* 'Appleblossom'
('Variegata'), which by virtue of its

bold cream and green foliage
continues to be attractive after
its pale pink flowers have fallen.
Most other cultivars, such as 'Eva
Rathke', have deep pinkish-red
flowers and grow to about 2 m x
1.5 m, but several dwarf forms,
such as 'Minuet' (1 m x 1 m), are
available. All grow best in moist,
humus-enriched, well-drained
soil in full sun and are hardy to
-20°C. Propagate from semi-ripe
tip cuttings.

WESTRINGIA

Australian rosemary (*W.
fruticosa*) is the only species to
be widely grown in New
Zealand. It is a 1.2 m x 80 cm
evergreen bush with narrow
leaves that resemble those of the
common rosemary. The small,
deeply lobed flowers are white
with mauve markings and are
most abundant in spring
although some flowers are
produced in most seasons. A
cream-edged variegated form is
widely grown. It is an excellent
coastal plant as well as being
hardy enough (to -10°C) to be
grown inland. It grows in any
well-drained soil in full sun or
light shade and is usually
propagated from semi-ripe
cuttings. Specialist seed suppliers
sometimes offer other species,
such as the mauve-flowered *W.
rubiaefolia*.

CLIMBERS AND TWINERS

Site and plant selection; Supports for climbers; Soil preparation and planting; Aftercare; Pruning and training; Popular climbers

Above: The common hop,
Humulus lupulus.
Top: One of New Zealand's
most impressive native plants,
Clematis paniculata.

CLIMBING PLANTS ARE AN important addition to any garden, helping to provide vertical interest, shade, privacy and a background to other plantings. They are especially useful in small gardens, courtyards, and wherever else space is limited. A variety of plants, including annuals, perennials and shrubs, have a climbing habit, all of which require a permanent means of support. Different climbers have different means of attaching themselves to a support and this influences the type of support structure that is most suitable. Some climbers produce aerial roots from the stems (e.g., the English ivy *Hedera helix*) and others produce adhesive pads or sucker discs, such as the Virginia creepers (*Parthenocissus* spp.). There are also many climbers with twining stems, such as wisterias and morning glories, and these tend to be the most vigorous climbers. Others, such as sweet peas and passion flowers, have tendrils to cling to their support. Serving a similar function are the twining leaf stalks of *Clematis* spp. and the tendril-tipped leaves of *Gloriosa*.

Also classified with climbers are numerous plants with long arching stems that require training and tying to cover walls and fences, such as the so-called climbing or rambling roses and bougainvilleas. If left to grow in the open, such plants form an untidy and sprawling bush resembling a wild blackberry. A number of shrubs with long weak branches, such as *Cavendishia acuminata*, also lend themselves to training up walls and fences.

SITE AND PLANT SELECTION

Boundary fences, sheds, patios, arches, pergolas, trees and old stumps can all be transformed through the use of climbers. However, before selecting a plant, careful consideration should be given to the following points:
- The soil type.
- The area to be covered, both vertically and horizontally.
- Whether the site is sunny or shady.
- The kind of support needed.
- The weight of individual creeping plants.

In addition, decide whether you want the climber to be:
- Deciduous or evergreen.
- Slow or fast growing.
- Grown for leaf colour, flowers, fruits, berries or fragrance.
- Hardy, wind tolerant or frost-tender.

The walls of our homes or boundary fences provide ideal positions for climbing plants. Tender climbers planted alongside a north-facing concrete, brick or stone wall will survive in colder climates because of stored heat in these types of wall. But before finally deciding on position, especially if it is alongside a house, give a little thought to the vigour and final height or length of each plant. In most cases it is undesirable to have climbers growing too high; it becomes difficult to prune and tie in new growth, or they may grow over windows

Above left: Climbers can be used to soften and beautify garages, car ports and sheds. Above right: In a sheltered outdoor living area, climbers add to the subtropical feel of a lush garden.

A cascading wall of colour (left) and a climbing rose (right) enfold a quiet garden corner.

and into gutters. Also, plants with very strong root systems can damage foundations if they are planted against a wall.

The weight of individual creepers is also very important, especially if you plan to grow them over pergolas or archways, and you should seek advice if in doubt. Some climbers, such as the cup of gold vine (*Solandra guttata*) and the Staunton vine (*Stauntonia hexaphylla*) are strong growing and produce a dense heavy mass of intertwining stems. Being evergreen, they will need constant pruning and thinning out to keep them under control.

Most climbers will do best if the foliage is in full sun or light shade and they have a cool shaded root-run. The latter is essential for some climbers, such as clematis, which are sensitive to hot dry summers. Planting on a south-facing wall, planting low-growing plants around their base, and regular watering in summer will be beneficial. However, some climbers, such as bougainvilleas, will thrive in hot dry situations.

There are climbers suitable for all climates. At one extreme are the many tender tropical vines that will only survive outdoors in frost-free northern areas. In all other districts they must be given protection over winter or treated as annuals. At the other extreme are the frost-hardy, usually deciduous climbers suitable for colder areas, such as the deciduous clematis and *Jasminum nudiflorum*.

Don't forget that many climbers are suitable for growing in containers on patios, in courtyards or indoors. In fact, through the restriction of the root system and regular pruning, strong-growing climbers can be restrained. Suitable climbers for containers include *Beaumontia*, *Bougainvillea*, *Dipladenia* and various ivies. In colder districts many tender species can be successfully grown in containers outdoors and then moved under cover in winter. Several other climbers are popular houseplants, examples include *Hoya*, *Monstera* and *Philodendron*.

Many climbers are grown for their flowers; most shades are available and they come in a staggering variety of forms and sizes. Many have haunting fragrances that waft through the spring and summer air. Others have distinctive foliage and attractive or edible fruits.

It should be pointed out that in New Zealand some formerly popular climbers are proving to be noxious weeds, invading our native forests and smothering or strangling native trees to death. These troublesome climbers include *Jasminum polyanthum* and *Solanum jasminoides* 'Grandiflora' and they should be avoided by gardeners.

171

Many climbers, such as this beautiful *Mandevilla splendens* 'Alice du Pont', are very vigorous, especially in warmer climates, so be sure to provide a strong support for them to grow up and over.

SUPPORTS FOR CLIMBERS

When selecting a plant it is imperative to consider the type of support it will need, or select a climber with a means of attachment most suited to the support you have in mind. Twining vines, for example, are unable to cling to bare walls. In such situations they will require something to twine around, such as netting or trellis. Growing them over arches, pergolas or gazebos may be a better option. Climbers with sucker discs or aerial roots are much more appropriate for stone or timber walls as they are able to cling directly to the wall surface.

There are many climbers that do not possess a natural means of supporting themselves, such as the kiwifruit vine, climbing roses and the Australian bluebell creeper (*Sollya fusiformis*). These will have to be secured to the support with plastic ties or twine. These ties will have to be inspected every three months and loosened or removed completely if they are strangling stems.

GROWING CLIMBERS ON TREES

A natural way of growing climbers is to plant them at the base of established trees, where they use their host tree to climb to the light.

GROWING A CLIMBER AROUND A POLE

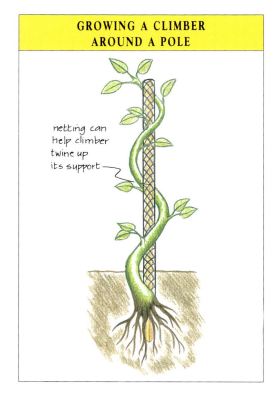

netting can help climber twine up its support

Careful selection can create some beautiful combinations of flowers, foliage and fragrance. By planting several different climbers in the same site, an on-going display of flowers and different foliage forms can be achieved. It is true the climbers may eventually kill their host tree, but it will take many years and in many cases hundreds of years.

An alternative is to place a tall ponga log upright in the ground and plant several smaller-growing climbers, such as hybrid *Clematis*, at its base. This makes a wonderful focal point.

FREE-STANDING TRELLIS OR WOOD

It is not advisable to grow vigorous climbers, such as wisterias, on wooden trellises because of their rapid growth rate. Eventually their thick woody stems will either crush or break open the trellis. Slower-growing climbers, such as *Clematis cirrhosa* or *C. alpina*, *Clytostoma callistegiodes*, *Hardenbergia violacea* and *Gelsemium sempervirens*, would be more suitable as they do not produce heavy stems nor grow as strongly.

BRICK OR CONCRETE WALLS

One of the most common methods for growing climbers on brick or concrete walls is to use strong plastic netting suspended from above and secured to pegs in the ground. If you wish to do this, keep this type of support

PLANTING A CLIMBER TO GROW UP A TREE

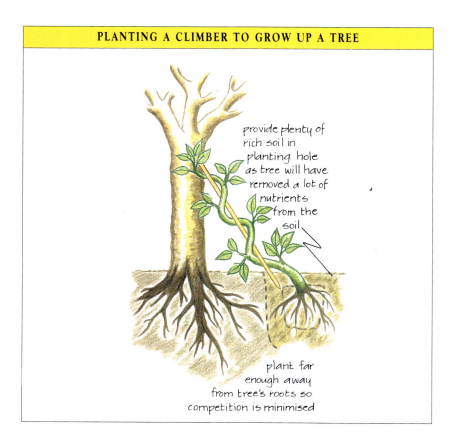

provide plenty of rich soil in planting hole as tree will have removed a lot of nutrients from the soil

plant far enough away from tree's roots so competition is minimised

about 6 cm away from the wall. Another good tip is to make allowances for taking down the support, with the climber attached, for painting or maintenance behind the plant.

Another support system is to fix galvanised wires horizontally (or vertically for twining climbers) to the wall 20–30 cm apart, held in position at regular intervals by hooked or eyelet-holed metal pins driven into the wall. Strong galvanised hooks can also be used. This type of support will work well with gazebos and pergolas. Trellis sections fixed onto walls by using wall plugs, screws or nails work well too.

Always remember when dealing with vigorous climbers that their stems should be kept well clear of any gutters or overhead wires from electricity or telephone lines. The annual growth can easily be disentangled and removed, but with age the main stems of wisteria, for example, can be 5 cm or more thick and can easily crush downpipes or gutters if allowed to grow behind them.

SOIL PREPARATION AND PLANTING

In their natural habitats most climbing plants grow with their roots in leaf-litter on the forest floor, where it is cool and usually shady. This can be replicated in the garden by using existing established trees. However, competing roots from existing trees can be a nuisance, so compensate for this with regular foliar feeding of liquid blood and bone. Using smaller annuals and perennials around the climber or a good mulch will replicate the leaf-litter effect and ensure a cool root-run.

For plants that are to be grown on boundary fences where other plants are growing, or on existing trees, new soil or special preparations will be needed to rejuvenate the soil as the existing tree's roots will have exhausted all the nutrients around the trunk. The easiest approach is to add a quantity of rich compost to the planting hole.

The soil alongside homes, garages, sheds and so forth may be very poor and it can become extremely dry under the eaves. Special preparations may thus be needed, such as taking out a trench at least 60 cm deep and refilling it with a mixture containing a high proportion of pure compost. Installing an irrigation system in this situation will overcome any watering problems.

Regardless of the size of the plant, the best planting site is a hole 60 cm x 60 cm square and at least 80 cm deep, filled with good topsoil and compost. Also ensure that the drain-

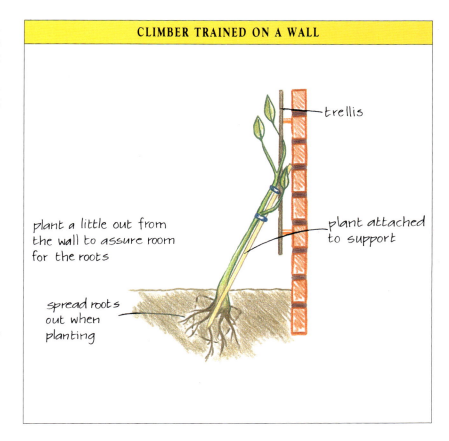

CLIMBER TRAINED ON A WALL

trellis

plant a little out from the wall to assure room for the roots

plant attached to support

spread roots out when planting

age is perfect.

If planting in a container, providing enough water can be a problem. It is a wise gardener who, when assembling all the ingredients for potting up a climber into a container, passes a length of 4 mm microtubing from the top of the potting mixture right through the drainage hole, just in case a complete watering system needs to be installed at a later date.

There are various supports suitable for climbers. The trellis makes an attractive support for *Trachelospermum jasminoides* (below left) and the wires will be quickly covered by *Clematis* 'Allanah' as it twines around the tree fern logs (below right).

Walls can be enhanced by the addition of a suitable climber as shown by the examples above. They can be chosen mainly for their colour, *Podranea rica soliana* (left); foliage, English ivy *Hedera helix* (middle); habit, *Wisteria sinensis* 'Alba' (right), or all three.

When buying plants check that no large roots are growing through the bottom drainage holes of the container. The plants should not have leaves that look yellow and starved. Prior to planting, undo any ties if a support system holds the plant upright in the container and always remove any labels. If the plant has become tangled with itself in the container, do not try and untangle the stems as this could do more damage than if they are left alone. When the plant is removed from its container, try to disturb the roots as little as possible. However, if any roots are running around the root-ball, cut through them with a very sharp knife on at least three sides. From these cut roots, new roots will be produced that will soon penetrate into the new soil mixture.

When planting, ensure the stem or trunk is no deeper than it was in the container. The original soil level will be clearly visible on the stem. The exception to this rule is *Clematis*, which should be planted several centimetres deeper.

To ensure a well-structured plant, select a few good, strong, evenly spaced leaders to secure to the support, rather than leaving the plant a tangled jungle of stems. The number and spacing of the leaders you choose will depend on the type of climber and its support. At this stage planning will produce a better looking plant and make subsequent pruning easier.

Once you have planted your climber, secure the chosen leaders to a strong stake or some other means of support, such as a little piece of manuka or some such piece of twiggy material (when the plant attaches itself to its permanent support do not forget to release any ties

before they strangle the stems). Some plastic netting anchored with some No. 8 fencing wire may help to prevent your new plant from being blown about by the wind and help it to attach itself quickly to its support.

Immediately after planting, water it in well with liquid blood and bone to give the plant ready access to nutrients. Then place a deep mulch around the plant; if the soil is in full sun place some flat rocks over the planting site to keep the soil cool.

AFTERCARE

All climbers will need regular feeding (at least once every two months) to keep them healthy and to optimise flower or fruit production. Any organic manure, such as blood and bone, fish meal, bone meal or dust, can be used to replenish the soil's nutrient levels, especially if plants are competing for nutrients with long-established host trees. Avoid using fast-acting nitrogenous fertilisers, especially on strong-growing rampant climbers. Every August apply a heavy mulch of compost, peat, or well-rotted manure at least 20 cm deep around each climber and extending at least 1 m out from the stem to condition the soil, feed the plants and help keep the roots cool over summer.

Once plants are established there should be no need for supplementary watering as most climbing plants have very effective root systems. However, watering may be crucial for plants growing alongside buildings, where they are warmed by the sun and sheltered from any rainfall. It would be advisable to install a permanent watering system for these plants.

PRUNING AND TRAINING

Climbing plants tend to require more maintenance than most other trees and shrubs. This will include the annual checking of support systems, the tying in of all new growth, the constant removal of old wood and pruning to contain the plant's size within its allotted area.

The time to prune depends on the time of year that the plant flowers and the type of growth. Climbers can be divided roughly into two groups: those that flower on the current season's shoots, generally from midsummer into autumn, and those that flower from late August to December on shoots produced the previous year. Pruning of the first group consists of cutting back the shoots that have flowered to a dormant bud near the ground level if possible. This should be done in August, or the first week in September, to give the plant the longest possible period for growing before flowering later in the year. The *Clematis* x *jackmanii* hybrids and bougainvilleas are examples of this type of climber. The second group should be pruned immediately after flowering, cutting back the strong growths which have just flowered to encourage new shoots. Sufficient young shoots should be left as they will bear the following year's flowers. *Clematis montana* and jasmines are examples of this type of climber.

Some climbers are not strong growing and require little or no pruning, except when they have reached their allotted space.

Climbers can provide large blocks of colour. In mild climates many climbers, for example, *Campsis grandiflora* (top left), and *Bougainvillea* 'Scarlett O'Hara' (background top right) and *Pandorea jasminoides* (left top right) have mass blooms of vivid tones, in cooler areas (left), the autumn foliage of Boston ivy performs a similar function.

For vines grown for their foliage or autumn colour the time of pruning is less important.

Winter is the best time for deciduous climbers and early spring for evergreens, with possibly a second pruning in January to thin out redundant or overcrowded branches.

All climbers benefit from the removal of old unproductive wood and any diseased branches should be removed.

POPULAR CLIMBERS

THE FOLLOWING ARE ALL popular garden specimens, but note the hardiness ratings and sizes. Slightly frost-tender climbers will often succeed in sheltered positions and large growers can be trimmed, but these two factors are important when making your choice of climber. Don't underestimate your winter climate, or overestimate your dedication to pruning!

AKEBIA

A. quinata is an evergreen, strong-growing, twining creeper from Japan and China with soft, green, clover-like leaves. In spring it produces sweetly scented clusters of small, cup-shaped, purplish-chocolate flowers. When mature and if the summer is hot enough, this plant will produce sausage-shaped, greyish-violet, edible fruits in autumn. Very hardy but deciduous below -10°C. Frequent heavy pruning is essential; it will grow to 3 m x 6 m. Grow from semi-ripe cuttings or layer in early spring. Seed should be sown in late spring.

ALLAMANDA

Golden trumpet (*A. cathartica*) is a robust tropical vine with whorled, leathery, glossy leaves up to 12 cm long and large, wax-like, funnel-shaped, golden-yellow flowers 6-8 cm across. It is very frost-tender, but one of the best summer-flowering climbers. Being strong growing it should be pruned heavily after each flowering. It will grow to at least 6 m. *A. violacea* is a less vigorous grower with deep reddish-purple flowers that fade to rosy purple. It blooms in winter but is very frost-tender. Propagate by softwood cuttings in spring and summer.

ALOE

A. tenuior is a delightful South African semi-climber seldom exceeding 2 m in height that is ideal for container growing. Terminal spikes of pinkish tubular flowers appear in autumn and will continue to appear through winter in frost-free areas. Propagate by offsets which are freely produced.

AMPELOPSIS

A. brevipedunculata (syn. *Vitis heterophylla*) is a luxuriant hardy vigorous-growing twiner with deeply lobed and bristly leaves. In autumn this vine produces berries that change colour with age from pale lilac-blue to turquoise-blue and then to violet-blue. Sometimes pinkish-mauve berries with metallic tones will also appear in the same cluster. Plant in full sun or partial shade with room to spread and a strong support. Propagate from cuttings in November and December.

ANTIGON

Coral vine, *A. leptopus*, is a tender evergreen climber that will behave as a deciduous perennial in cold winter areas if its roots are protected from freezing. The leaves are dark green and heart shaped with wavy edges. The small heart-shaped pink flowers, which appear throughout summer, are carried in clustered racemes that form into long trailing sprays. It thrives in a hot spot but requires ample summer moisture. It may grow to 7 m or more high and 12 m wide in a mild climate if left unchecked. Raise from seed, semi-ripe cuttings or division.

ARAUJIA

A. sericofera, often known as the cruel plant, moth plant or bladder flower, is a half-hardy strong-growing evergreen twining vine. Moths seeking nectar are caught by their proboscises in the centre of the flower and killed, hence its common names. It has heavy triangular leaves and produces a prolonged display of sweetly scented, bell-shaped, 2 cm wide, pure white flowers that are pink in bud.
It can smother other plants it climbs on or over and careful husbandry is needed with this plant to keep it within bounds, as there is deep concern that if it escaped into our native forests it could prove disastrous. It is very easily grown from seed and will grow to at least 7 m.

ARISTOLOCHIA

Dutchman's pipe (*A. gigantea*) is a strong-growing climber that is very frost-tender, but it can be grown as an annual in colder areas. It gets its common name from the fact that the flower, which is downy purple, resembles a smoking pipe. The heart-shaped leaves are downy and pointed. The flowers appear in summer. It needs good drainage but is otherwise easily grown in sun or shade. It will grow to 6 m in mild areas. Propagate from softwood cuttings in summer.

BAUHINIA

This is a spectacular heavy-flowering climber. The leaves are oval to lanceolate and deep green to glaucous with a prominent mid-rib. The star-shaped pink flowers are massed in large racemes that can totally cover the plant. Most species will only tolerate very light frosts, but *B. variegata* (*purpurea*) will withstand -4°C once established. *B. punctata* (*galpinii*) is also quite hardy. It has orange to red flowers. All grow to about 4 m x 4 m and should be planted in a warm sheltered position in light well-drained soil. Usually raised from seed, but may also be grown from semi-ripe cuttings.

BEAUMONTIA

The herald's trumpet or Nepal trumpet flower (*B. grandiflora*) is a magnificent strong-growing creeper. It is ideal for a semi-tropical climate but needs heavy pruning immediately after flowering. It is also suitable for growing in large pots. The 20 cm leaves are attractive, but it is grown for the stunning 10 cm wide, white, trumpet-shaped flowers, which are produced during spring and summer. It grows to at least 3-4 m, reaching 6 m in certain areas. Plant in a moist, humus-enriched, well-drained soil. Usually grown from cuttings.

BERBERIDOPSIS

The Chilean coral vine or coral berry (*B. corallina*) is an evergreen climber that does well even in cool temperatures. It is hardy to -6°C, but the new growth is very soft. Its very attractive heart-shaped, dark green leaves are accompanied by large terminal racemes of pendent, waxy, deep coral-red flowers during summer and autumn. It must have a lime-free soil and it needs to be tied in as it is not self-supporting. It makes a wonderful tub or patio plant. It will grow about 4-5 m. It may be raised from spring-sown seed, or semi-ripe cuttings. These cuttings are hard to strike and require bottom heat.

BIGNONIA

This genus used to include a wide range of trumpet-flowered climbers, but most have now been reclassified. Related genera include *Campsis*, *Clytostome*, *Distictis*, *Macfedyena*, *Panndorea* and *Pyrostegia*.

BILLARDIERA

The purple apple berry (*B. longiflora*) is a lovely evergreen Australian. It is a slower-growing, non-rampant twining plant that is ideal for containers. It may reach 3-4 m tall and is hardy to -8°C. It has small, narrow, dark green leaves up to 5 cm long and bell-shaped, creamy-white, blue-tipped flowers in spring. They are followed in autumn by long, shining, deep purple-blue berries which hang singly from slender stems. This plant requires a cool moist soil, but once established will tolerate extremely dry conditions and will grow well in semi-shade. Propagate by seed or semi-ripe cuttings taken in autumn.

BOMAREA

Often known as climbing alstroemeria, the foliage and flower heads are very similar to *Altsroemeria* but the flowers are smaller, more clustered and have less flaring trumpets. Several species are grown and many more remain to be isolated. It is evergreen in mild areas but the foliage dies back below -2°C. It will reshoot from rootstock, provided it is well insulated. It grows to 3 m x 2 m and is best in light well-drained soil in full sun. *Bomarea* may be raised

from seed or careful division in early spring.

BOUGAINVILLEA

These spectacular evergreen to deciduous scrambling climbers hail from tropical and subtropical South and Central America. Unfortunately some species can be very frost-tender, but in frost-free areas such as the Bay of Plenty, coastal Taranaki and from Auckland northwards, these plants, once established, can withstand very dry conditions. *B. glabra* hybrids are the most hardy and will withstand up to -6°C in a protected position, though they will lose their foliage in very cold weather. *B. peruviana* and *B. spectabilis*, and their hybrids, are more frost-tender and require overhead protection if temperatures are likely to drop below -2°C.

The showy 'petals' of these plants are actually three bracts that surround the small, central, tubular flowers, which appear on the current year's growth. Bougainvilleas usually produce long watershoots under normal conditions and these should be pruned back as they appear. Since bougainvilleas are not self attaching, the branches require tying in to their support.

There are many named varieties in all shades, of which some have beautifully variegated foliage and are less vigorous. Some are semi-dwarf and make ideal container plants. Bougainvilleas can also be trained into weeping standards, however left unpruned they may grow 10-12 m. When pruning, beware of the strong thorns that protect these plants.

Plant in light yet moist well-drained soil in full sun. Container plants should be kept nearly dry over winter and often bloom better if slightly root bound. Do not overfeed *Bougainvillea*, as it leads to production of foliage rather than flowers. Propagate by cuttings of firm yet green wood; layering may also be successful.

Clematis orientalis

Bougainvillea 'Scarlett O'Hara'

Campsis grandiflora

CAMPSIS

The trumpet vine (*C. grandiflora*) is a hardy (-10°C) deciduous climber from China and Japan that climbs by aerial roots and so can cling to most surfaces. It will grow as high as 10 m. Related to the bignonias, it is still often wrongly named *Bignonia* or *Tecoma*. The terminal clusters of showy 8 cm wide scarlet flowers appear during summer and late autumn. If necessary, prune in late winter. Two other popular species are *C. radicans* from Eastern North America, with slightly smaller more orange flowers, hardy to -20°C, and the pinkish red *C.* x *tagliabuana* 'Madame Galen'. All are easily grown in any well-drained soil in full sun, though in rich moist soil suckering can be a problem. Species may be raised from seed, but the hybrids are usually grown from semi-ripe cuttings or winter hardwood cuttings.

CAVENDISHIA

C. acuminata is a little-known member of the erica family that should be grown more widely. While it can be grown as a shrub, it does need support and can be trained on a support system to grow about 2 m high. The leaves are rich deep green and new growths are burnished coppery-red. The pendulous clusters of tubular, waxy, bright red, green-tipped flowers, appear in late summer and autumn. It must have a lime-free soil with plenty of compost or peat added. Propagation is semi-ripe cuttings taken in summer.

CELASTRUS

C. orbiculatus and *C. scandens* are strong-growing creepers that are deciduous and hardy (-30°C). Both have small, highly decorative yellow and red fruits in winter. Remove old fruiting wood after the crop has fallen. The leaves turn yellow before dropping. Grow in moist well-drained soil in sun or light semi-shade. They will reach at least 2-3 m. Usually raised from seed, but may be grown from root cuttings.

CLEMATIS

There is no cultivated genus of climbers to equal *Clematis*. This very useful and extensive group of plants provides some of the most beautiful effects one could wish for in a garden. There are over 250 species, both evergreen and deciduous, and with careful choice a display of flowers can be had from August through to May. *Clematis* will vary in height, depending on the situation, but the average height would be 4 m, though some reach much higher than this. The many hybrids now available produce flowers from 5-15 cm across and in colours ranging from pure white to deep burgundy-red and purple. *Clematis* are wonderful for planting at the base of trees.

Preparing the planting site is probably the most important part of growing *Clematis*. Dig a hole at least 80 cm square and at least 90 cm deep, then back-fill with a mixture of good compost, top-soil and bone meal. Select a position where the soil surface will remain cool and moist. All *Clematis* love an annual dressing of lime (100 g/m^2). They are hearty feeders so feed them regularly during the growing season, with the first application in early August and then every three weeks with organic fertilisers such as blood and bone or liquid blood and bone.

Clematis species are propagated by seed when available, which often germinates better with a period of stratification. Hybrids and selected forms are usually grown from semi-ripe cuttings, which strike easily but are very prone to damping off and clematis wilt. Good hygiene and regular fungicide are essential. There are hundreds of cultivars and species from which to choose, most are very hardy

Hardenbergia violacea 'Alba'

though a few are slightly frost-tender. The following list is just a few of the many available in New Zealand.

C. alpina is a hardy deciduous creeper with very attractive leaves and a summer display of nodding, satiny-blue, 5 cm wide flowers. It does not need pruning.

C. armandii is a very hardy, evergreen, strong-growing species with a breathtaking combination of dark green leaves and pure white flowers in spring that are heavily scented. It needs pruning after flowering to keep it to a manageable height.

C. cirrhosa is well worth growing as it blooms during July and August and is evergreen and very hardy. The coarsely-toothed leaves are three lobed and shining green. The nodding clusters of 5 cm wide, cupped, creamy flowers are downy on the outside. It is not strong growing and so is ideal for growing in large containers. *C. macropetala* is not well known but is very attractive and easily grown. The handsome, deciduous, fern-like foliage is composed of nine toothed leaflets. The drooping 8 cm wide flowers consist of many staminoides surrounded by four rich bluish-violet petals. It is another excellent species for growing in containers.

C. orientalis is a deciduous species with soft green leaves and orange-yellow flowers in autumn.

C. paniculata is the most spectacular of the nine native species. In late spring it produces a dazzling display of pure white starry flowers. *C. paniculata* x *C. forsteri* 'Purity' is an impressive slightly later-flowering form. It is excellent for growing up trees and will reach 5 m in just two years. It flowers profusely up to mid-November.

C. texensis is a deciduous semi-woody climber that produces solitary, urn-shaped, carmine-red, nodding flowers. As they open, the ends of the petals reflex. Since it is not strong growing it makes an ideal container plant. It needs help to climb as it is not self-twining.

C. montana is a very hardy, strong-growing species that will soon cover tree stumps and will eventually reach at least 6 m high. 'Alba' produces pure white flowers about 7 cm wide that appear in early spring. 'Rubens' is among the most popular of all clematis and is perhaps the easiest to grow. This cultivar flowers in early spring and the soft rosy pink flowers appear just before the coppery-bronze foliage. Quite often a second flowering surprises the gardener in December.

A host of large-flowered deciduous hybrids are also readily available.

'Belle of Woking' produces lovely silvery-mauve double flowers through the summer. It is not a strong-growing climber and grows to about 2 m. 'Henryii' has very large, pure white, sometimes creamy white, flowers up to 20 cm across from early spring through summer. *C.* x *jackmanii* 'Superba' is the most sought after of all the large-flowered clematis. Its rich deep violet-blue to reddish-purple flowers are produced in late summer and autumn. 'Nellie Moser' is the best known of all clematis, bearing pale mauve-pink flowers with a carmine bar through each petal in early spring and summer. 'Ville de Lyons' is the only truly red-flowered clematis and grows to about 2.5 m high. 'Will Goodwin' produces clear soft lavender flowers up to 20 cm across in late summer.

CLYTOSTOMA

Argentine trumpet vine, *C. callisteigioides,* has dark glossy-green leaves which end in tendrils by which the plant clings to its support. Although native to northern Argentina and southern Brazil this climber will withstand frosts to -7°C, and may reshoot from the roots if the foliage is killed. It will grow to about 3 m high, though can be slow to establish in colder districts. The 8 cm wide, trumpet-shaped flowers are soft lavender-violet and marked yellow and purple in the throat and appear from late spring to December. Propagate from semi-ripe cuttings.

DIPLADENIA

D. sanderi is a tender evergreen climber that has become popular in recent years as a container plant. It produces racemes of 8 cm wide, funnel-shaped flowers with wavy edges. The flowers are a lovely shade of warm pink, and are produced nearly all year round if grown in a frost-free situation. It makes an excellent indoor plant in a bright sunny position. It grows about 2 m high and may need tying to a stake. Propagation is by semi-ripe cuttings.

DISTICTIS

Formerly known as *Phaedranthus buccinatorius* and *Bignonia cherere,* Mexican blood flower (*D. buccinatoria*) is an evergreen vine that climbs by means of tendrils. It has pairs of long deep green leaves and can grow to 4 m. From late spring it produces heads of 10 cm long red trumpet-shaped flowers with yellow lobe tips and centres. Hardy to about -4°C or slightly lower with protection. Grow in moist well-drained soil in full sun. Usually grown from semi-ripe cuttings.

DOLICHOS

The Australian pea (*D. lignosus*) is a fairly hardy (-5°C) evergreen twiner that is native to South Africa, but gets its common name because of its prevalence in Australia. It has trifoliate leaves composed of unusual deep green triangular leaflets that are up to 5 cm wide. From late spring to autumn it produces erect racemes of small white to deep pink sweet-pea-like flowers. These are followed by seed pods that burst when ripe. It grows best in light well-drained soil in full sun and may reach 4 m or more. Usually raised from seed.

GELSEMIUM

The Carolina jasmine (*G. sempervirens*) is a twining evergreen climber that comes into flower in late winter and often continues well into summer. In mild districts, it can be used as a ground cover. Contrasting well with the shining dark green leaves, the tubular, deep-yellow, trumpet-shaped flowers are sweetly scented. It is quite hardy (-8°C) and will withstand heavy frosts if planted in a sheltered sunny position against a brick or concrete wall. It grows to 3 m. Semi-ripe cuttings will root easily.

HARDENBERGIA

This genus is highly valued for its magnificent winter flower display. The two common species, *H. comptoniana* and *H. violacea,* are hardy to -6°C once established. Both are strong growing evergreen twiners with deep green leaves. They produce masses of small, violet-blue or pink, pea-shaped flowers in late winter and not being strong growers they are ideal for growing in containers, eventually reaching 3 m. Easily grown in any well-drained soil, propagate by seed or semi-ripe cuttings.

HEDERA

The common ivy (*H. helix*) is well known and while attractive and easy to grow can be invasive in certain circumstances. It will grow in almost any soil type and is an excellent ground cover if kept to its allotted space. Many growers graft hederas onto a special rootstock and keep them clipped in a ball. In many parts of the world, including New Zealand, *H. helix* is employed as a ground cover in high erosion areas on steep banks, and once established it is quite drought-tolerant. Another widely grown species is *H. canariensis*, which although damaged by hard frosts usually recovers in spring. There are dozens of varieties grown in New Zealand, many of them having very attractive variegated foliage. Some ivies also make delightful indoor plants and are ideal for hanging baskets. Usually grown from semi-ripe cuttings.

HIBBERTIA

This evergreen Australian genus includes species that vary considerably in size. The two common species, *H. scandens* and *H. stellaris,* are quite different from one another. *H. scandens* is a strong growing twining climber with 10 cm long deep green leathery leaves that have a conspicuous red-tinted central vein. Throughout summer it produces bright yellow buttercup or single rose-like flowers. It is hardy to about -4°C and grows to around 3 m. It does best in rich moist well-drained soil in full sun. *H. stellaris* is a small-leafed spreading ground cover or small climber. It has bright yellow buttercup flowers and is hardy to -6°C, spreading to 2 m wide. It is very effective in hanging baskets. Both species can be raised from seed or semi-ripe cuttings.

HOYA

Wax flower (*H. carnosa*) is a twining climber that grows to about 3 m. It has mid green leathery lanceolate leaves about 10 cm long and from late winter produces pendulous round heads of fragrant, starry, pale pink flowers. The individual flowers are around 1 cm in diameter, while the flower heads can be up to 10 cm across. Don't remove spent flower heads as new flowers will form on the same bud next year. *H.*

carnosa is hardy to about -2°C but can be grown in colder areas with overhead protection. It is a superb plant for covered patios. *Hoya* grows best in light well-drained soil in light shade and does well in containers, often flowering better if somewhat root bound. The small trailing species *H. bella* is too tender to grow outdoors except in very mild areas. It has small leaves and creamy white flowers and will grow as a low climber to 1 m, but is usually grown in hanging baskets. *Hoya* can be raised from seed or semi-ripe cuttings.

HYDRANGEA

The climbing hydrangea, *H. anomala* (*H. petiolaris* [*scandens*]), is a deciduous climber with aerial roots that deserves to be grown more widely. It loves a cold wall on which to grow, so find a south-facing situation and you will be pleasantly surprised. It is hardy to -30°C. Its dull-white flowers appear in late spring through summer. It will attain a height in excess of 10 m if the wall is high enough, however with no support the plant will remain a tight bushy shrub. It grows well in shady sites. Propagation is by seed sown in spring or semi-ripe cuttings

IPOMOEA

The morning glories are well known for their large trumpet-shaped flowers that open in the morning and close in the evening and which are produced throughout the warmer months. Many of the perennial climbing species are rampant in warmer areas but in colder districts are usually cut back by frosts, which helps to restrain them. There are, however, numerous attractive annual climbers that are not at all invasive. The climbing species are all twining plants.
I. acuminata (syn. *I. learii*) is a perennial species with intense blue flowers about 9 cm across. It can be extremely invasive and must be kept within bounds. In some parts of New Zealand it has escaped from our gardens and has become a real nuisance. *I. lobata* (syn. *Mina lobata*) is a showy and popular annual

climber that provides a long flowering display. Sow the seed in late October and the plants will be flowering within two months. It will continue flowering until the frosts cut it down. The flowers form on slender racemes and are thin and tubular, at first crimson, changing to orange, then yellow and finally white. This plant loves the sun. It will grow to around 2 m high and does well in containers.
The moonflower (*I. bonanox*, syn. *Calonyction bonanox*) is an exquisite perennial species with large 15 cm wide, fragrant, white flowers that open in the evening and close the following morning. Unfortunately it is extremely frost-tender and is usually treated as an annual. All species are propagated by seed sown in spring.

JASMINUM

A genus of evergreen and deciduous twining climbers best known for the half-hardy, white-flowered, sweetly scented species widely grown in warmer areas. The frost-hardy species unfortunately lack the characteristic fragrance. Some species require tying in to the support.
The Azores jasmine (*J. azoricum*) has deep green glossy foliage and clusters of starry, 3 cm long, sweetly perfumed, pure white flowers that are produced all year round in milder districts. It is hardy to -5°C.
J. mesnyi (syn. *J. primulinum*) requires some form of support. It has deep green trifoliate leaves and in late winter and early spring smothers itself in 3 cm wide, primula-like, bright yellow flowers that are fluted at the edges. It is quick growing to 3 m high and will withstand 5°C frosts.
Winter jasmine (*J. nudiflorum*) is a very hardy deciduous species and as it is semi-climbing is often grown against a wall. It is valued for its 2-3 cm yellow flowers during the depths of winter when it is leafless. It never fails to flower no matter how cold the weather.
J. polyanthum is an invasive climber that will quickly cover a large area. It has beautiful fern-like foliage and comes into flower in late August. The

Ipomoea 'Pearly Gates'

Hoya carnosa

Kennedia nigricans

Kennedia rubicunda

sweetly scented flowers are pink in bud and open to pure white, giving the whole plant a pinkish tinge. It will grow in excess of 12 m and in warmer climates can become a real pest. It needs heavy pruning after flowering. There are moves to classify this jasmine as a noxious weed. It is reasonably hardy but some frosts will destroy the flower buds. A beautifully variegated golden-yellow foliaged form is available. All jasminums are propagated by cuttings, either soft tip cuttings in summer or mature lateral cuttings taken in autumn.

KENNEDIA

The coral pea (*K. coccinea*) is a vigorous twiner from south-western Australia that produces young growths which are silky and downy. The small pea-shaped flowers are a light salmon-scarlet with a purple-edged yellow spot and appear in spring. This evergreen climber makes an ideal container plant and is hardy to -5°C. In western Australia it grows under the taller forest trees in semi-shade in very arid conditions. They grow to 3 m and some plants may spread for several metres. *K. nigricans* has bold, evergreen, shiny leaves and one-sided racemes of deep purple-black flowers with a conspicuous yellow blotch in the centre of each flower. It must have a very hot situation in sandy soil to grow successfully, and will withstand severe drought conditions. It will not survive any frosts unless grown in containers in a frost-free position. *K. rubicunda* has attractive bean-like evergreen foliage that is brownish in colour and the dull-red 4 cm long flowers are produced in

spring. This species is also frost-tender and will spread to 3 m across. All species can be grown from seed or semi-ripe cuttings.

LAPAGERIA

The sole member of this genus is the aristocratic Chilean bell flower (*L. rosea*). Any gardener who sees its beautiful blooms immediately wants a plant. This species must have a cool root run and rich well-drained soil with plenty of compost. A southern aspect in full shade is ideal. It is hardy to about -10°C with some damage. The plant grows from a crown which sends up more new growths each spring, and slugs and snails feast on them if baits are not spread out. With a backdrop of dark, glossy green foliage, in spring these plants come into their own with beautiful, waxy, rose-red flowers 7-8 cm long and 5 cm wide at the mouth. It is very difficult to propagate, and seed, if available, is slow to germinate. *L. rosea* 'Albiflora' is a pure white form that is highly sought after but hard to obtain.

LATHYRUS

The perennial sweet peas are a variable lot. They range from small rockery ground covers to rampant climbers. The annual species (*L. odorata*) is available in several strains and they are reliable plants for quick colour and a ready supply of sweetly scented cut flowers. The blue Argentine pea (*L. pubescens*) is

probably the best known species, *H. comptoniana* and *H. violacea*, are hardy to -6°C once established. Both are strong growing evergreen twiners with deep green leaves. They produce masses of small, violet-blue or pink, pea-shaped flowers in late winter and not being strong growers they are ideal for growing in containers, eventually reaching 3 m. Easily grown in any well-drained soil, propagate by seed or semi-ripe cuttings.

LONICERA

Honeysuckle is a genus of evergreen and deciduous shrubs and climbers, most of which are very hardy. The most distinctive species is the giant Burmese honeysuckle, *L. hildebrandtiana*, but it is also the most frost-tender, although hardy to -6°C once established. This strong-growing evergreen climber with glossy green leaves produces clusters of highly perfumed, 16 cm long, tubular, creamy-white flowers throughout summer. In a warm position it will reach 12 m or more but in most gardens can be kept to 4-5 m. It is difficult to propagate but may be raised from seed or reasonably firm cuttings.
L. x 'Tellmaniana' is a hybrid honeysuckle and one of the most brilliant. The flowers form a terminal cluster of up to 12 blooms of yellowish-coppery-orange flushed red at the tips and with a deeper toning inside. It must be grown in virtually complete shade. It is evergreen and hardy to -10°C and has been known to grow at least 10 m in height.
The hardier species (-15°C) have smaller leaves and flowers but are easier to grow and more adaptable. Some, such as *L. caprifolium*, flower in a mass in spring while other species flower less prolifically over a longer season. The gold net honeysuckle, *L. japonica* 'Aureo reticulata' is a cultivar grown primarily for its yellow-veined foliage.
Some honeysuckles are very prone to aphid damage. These are difficult to keep clean and are probably best avoided. Most will grow best in cool, moist, well-drained soil in semi-shade and are easily grown from semi-ripe cuttings.

MANDEVILLA

The two commonly grown species of this genus are very different from one another. *M. splendens* 'Alice du Pont' is a delightful evergreen hybrid bred with 15 cm long glossy green leaves contrasting nicely with the bright, tubular, soft pink flowers, which are produced for many months. It is frost-tender (-2°C), but will survive colder conditions with overhead protection. It makes an ideal subject for container growing, reaching 2-3 m in height, and likes a rich, moist, humus-enriched, well-drained soil in sun or partial shade. Propagate by semi-ripe cuttings.
The Chilean jasmine *M. laxa* (syn. *M. suaveolens*) is an easily grown deciduous twining climber. Its oblong, pointed, deep-green foliage highlights the pure white, heavily scented flowers that are produced throughout summer. The 30 cm long seed pods are very popular with floral artists. It is hardy to around -6°C and will reshoot if frosted to ground level. It grows to about 5 m and does best in moist, humus-enriched, well-drained soil. Raise from seed or semi-ripe cuttings. Old plants can be cut to the ground and divided.

MANETTIA

This genus includes about 30 species but only one, *M. bicolor*, is commonly cultivated. It is a frost-tender soft-wooded twiner often used as a conservatory plant. It has deep green lanceolate leaves and tubular bright orange red flowers with yellow lobes. It dies back if exposed to temperatures below -2°C, but provided the rootstock is well insulated the plant will reshoot in spring. Grows to about 2 m and prefers a moist well-drained soil in sun or partial shade. May be raised from seed or cuttings.

METROSIDEROS

This genus includes a few climbers, of which the climbing rata vine (*M. carminea*) is the best known. It has distinctive juvenile and adult growth phases. If propagated vegetatively from the adult growth the resultant plants remain bushy and do not climb. This technique has been used to produce some interesting bushy forms, such as variegated 'Carousel', which is often used as a container plant.

Seedling plants climb vigorously when young by means of aerial roots. As with all members of this genus, the flowers have reduced petals and the enlarged stamens are the most showy part of the flower. *M. carminea* and *M. albiflora* both flower in spring and have scarlet and white flowers respectively. *M. fulgens* is an autumn-flowering species with orange-red flowers, but the form *M. fulgens* 'Aurata' has yellow flowers. Most species are rather frost-tender but *M. carminea* is hardy to -5°C. They require a cool root run and a moist well-drained soil. Propagate by seed or semi-ripe cuttings in summer, but remember that cuttings taken from mature plants will form a low-growing shrub instead of climbing.

MUTISIA

Three species of this South American genus are grown. All are evergreen semi-twiners. *M. clematis* and *M. oligodon* have tomentose pinnate leaves but those of *M. decurrens* are long and narrow, without tomentum. *M. clematis* may grow to 6 m but the others are considerably smaller. They have 12 cm wide daisy-like flowers during spring and summer. *M. clematis* has bright red flowers that are reminiscent of *Clematis* or *Dahlia. M. decurrens* has orange flower while those of *M. oligodon* are pink and yellow stamen. *M. oligodon* is the hardiest species and is capable of withstanding -15°C. The others withstand -5 to -10°C and will reshoot from the roots if they are well insulated. Grow in moist well-drained soil in sun or partial shade. They may be raised from seed, cuttings or self-struck basal suckers.

PANDOREA

This Australian genus includes some spectacular climbers that are among the best of the near-hardy evergreens. Two species and several cultivars are grown. They are vigorous twiners that can grow up to 8 m high and

wide. Both species (*P. jasminoides* and *P. pandorana*) have similar dark green leathery pinnate leaves. The leaves are about 20 cm long and composed of 5-9, 4 cm long leaflets.

The wonga wonga vine (*P. pandorana*) is the hardier species. It will tolerate -8°C with minor damage. In spring it has massed clusters of small bell-shaped cream flowers with purple spotted throats. Golden yellow ('Golden Showers') and pinkish red ('Ruby Heart') forms are available.

The bower of beauty (*P. jasminoides*) has heads of widely flared pink trumpet-shaped flowers that are about 5 cm wide. The species has white flowers with deep pink throats. The common cultivated form 'Rosea Superba' has light pink flowers with darker throats. A pure white form is also available. Hardy to about -4°C.

Grow all in rich, moist, well-drained soil in sun or very light shade. They usually flower better in sun but the foliage is better with light shade. The species may be grown from seed but the cultivated forms are propagated by semi-ripe cuttings.

PARTHENOCISSUS

This genus comprises about ten species of deciduous woody vines with brilliantly coloured foliage in autumn. They are often seen covering large buildings or walls. All are very hardy and deciduous. The silver vein creeper (*P. henryana*) is a delightful plant with soft olive-green, deeply lobed leaves with a touch of copper and which are beautifully marked with pink and white midribs and veins. In addition it is self-clinging and the leaves, which have more pronounced markings when the plant is grown in shade, turn rich shades of red in autumn. Dainty bluish berries that birds love to eat are an additional attraction. Hardy to -20°C and grows to about 4 m.

The Boston or Japanese ivy (*P. tricuspidata* 'Veitchii') is the well-known self-clinging plant often seen growing on brick or concrete walls. The large leaves are deep green and shiny underneath, and the small, rounded, blue-black fruits

Passiflora 'Eynsford Gem'

appear in clusters in autumn. The autumn leaf colour is stunning, with a riot of brilliant red shades before leaf-fall. It is very hardy (-35°C) and will grow up very tall buildings. Cuttings of firm young shoots can be rooted in summer and branches layered in summer will soon form roots.

PASSIFLORA

There are over 400 species of passion flowers found growing in the warmer regions of the world, in particular Africa and America. Most species will not tolerate more than -3°C, and some are totally intolerant of frost. Many species have the characteristic flower – with long petals and exserted stamens and style – but the fruits of only

Above: *Lonicera* 'Dropmore Scarlet'

Left: *Lapageria rosea*

eleven of these, as far as can be ascertained, are of any significance here. The most important is *P. edulis*, a native of Brazil, and its variety *P. e. flavicarpa*, the golden or Hawaiian passion fruit.

A number of other species are grown purely for ornamental purposes. *P. antioquiensis* is a strong-growing climber attaining 6 m or more. It bears rosy-red to scarlet-red flowers followed by long, banana-shaped, yellow-skinned fruits with orange fleshy seeds of delicious flavour. *P. coccinea*, from tropical South America, is one of the most brilliantly coloured species. The rich scarlet flowers of this frost-tender climber appear through the winter months. It is strong-growing in a warm, moist climate, but will withstand only light frosts. It may grow to 10 m or more in height. *P. caerulea* is a hardier species (-10°C) and may grow to 5 m in moist well-drained soil in full sun.

The seed of many species is available from specialists and plants can also be grown from semi-ripe cuttings.

PERESKIA

P. aculeata is an unusual member of the cactus family that not only looks great as a climber but makes an excellent basket plant. A very interesting foliage plant, it produces true leaves instead of spines, and these leaves are brilliantly coloured if grown in full sun. It requires tying in when grown as a climber and may grow to 2 m or more. Take short side-shoot cuttings in summer to propagate this fascinating plant.

PETREA

The purple wreath or sandpaper plant (*P. volubilis*) is a tender (-4°C) evergreen climber from Mexico that is best grown in light well-drained soil in full sun. Its leaves are deep green, narrow and 7-10 cm long. In full bloom, in late spring, it is a sight never to be forgotten. The long arching sprays carry massed racemes of hundreds of small violet-blue flowers. It will grow to 3 m in height. It is easily grown from cuttings taken in summer.

PHAESOLUS

The snail flower (*P. caracalla*) is a vigorous evergreen twiner that becomes deciduous when exposed to temperatures below -2°C. It will withstand occasional -5°C frosts, and if the roots are well insulated the plant will reshoot from the rootstock. It is neater when cut back to ground level each year anyway. From mid spring it produces unusual, fragrant, twisted and curled flowers that reflect its common name. The flowers are followed by bean-like seed pods. It grows best in moist well-drained soil in full sun. *Phaseolus* may be treated as an annual and raised from seed each year, or grown from semi-ripe cuttings, which strike easily.

PODRANEA

The Port St John creeper (*P. ricasoliana*) is a rather frost-tender (-3°C) evergreen twiner that can withstand being frosted to ground level provided the rootstock is well insulated. In near frost-free areas it can grow to 6 m, and may grow 4 m or more in one season. It has 15 cm long, deep green, pinnate leaves composed of about 7-9 leaflets. From early summer to mid autumn it produces trusses of widely flared pink trumpets that are up to 10 cm long and 7 cm wide. The flowers are followed by small seed pods. Plant in moist well-drained soil in full sun. Raise from seed, which often self-sows, or semi-ripe cuttings.

PYROSTEGIA

The flame vine (*P. venusta*) is a Brazilian native. Although it is quite hardy (-5°C) once established, it needs protection when young and never becomes tough enough to withstand repeated heavy frosts. It is an evergreen twiner that can reach 10 m in mild areas. It has mid green 7 cm long leaves and the flowers are intense reddish orange and narrow with widely flared trumpets. They are carried in clusters of 15-20 flowers. Depending on the climate, it starts to bloom from early winter to mid spring and the display lasts for several months. Grow in moist well-drained soil in full sun. It may be raised from seed but is usually propagated by semi-ripe cuttings.

QUISQUALIS

Rangoon creeper (*Q. indica*) is a very frost-tender evergreen climber that requires warm summer conditions to perform well. It is a quick grower, reaching 4 m, that prefers a rich, moist, well-drained soil. A position in full sun sheltered from cold winds will give the best results. It has deep green compound leaves and unusual long, tubular, starry flowers. The clusters of sweetly scented pendulous flowers appear from mid summer. It can be treated as an annual where it would not survive the winter and is usually grown from semi-ripe cuttings.

RHODOCHITON

Purple bells (*R. volubile*) is an interesting, evergreen climber with very tender heart-shaped leaves and unusual bell-shaped flowers with dark blood-red calyces and long, tubular, purple-black corollas. In New Zealand it is grown successfully as an indoor plant as it only grows about 1.8 m in height, and as such it will flower all year round. Grown from seed in spring.

ROSA

For information about the climbing roses, see the entry for roses in the shrubs chapter.

SCHIZOPHRAGMA

Sometimes called climbing hydrangea, *S. hydrangeoides* is closely related to *Hydrangea* and looks very similar. It is deciduous and climbs by means of self-clinging aerial roots. It will behave as a ground cover if there is nothing to climb over. Preferring a cool, moist, well-drained soil in light shade, it can reach 4 m high and 8 m wide. It has roughly heart-shaped leaves about the size and shape of poplar leaves. The typically hydrangea-like flower heads are white tinted pink and have small fertile, and larger sterile, florets. It is hardy to -20°C and usually grown from semi-ripe summer cuttings or winter hardwood cuttings.

SOLANDRA

The cup of gold vine (*S. guttata*) requires a hot climate and is only hardy to -3°C (but can withstand occasional frosts to -6°C with overhead protection). It has 20 cm wide, leathery, evergreen, shiny leaves, and huge chalice-shaped flowers up to 25 cm across. These flowers are cream in bud, golden yellow when fully open and age to orange. It makes an excellent creeper near the coast because it will tolerate salt-laden winds. If the summer is very hot and dry you will be rewarded with a better flower display the next season. It can grow to 15 m and should be pruned heavily after flowering. Grow in cool, moist, well-drained soil in full sun, shade the root zone if possible and provide ample water in summer. It is difficult to propagate, but may be raised from seed or grown from semi-ripe cuttings.

SOLANUM

Potato vine (*S. jasminoides*) is a reasonably hardy (-6°C) evergreen twiner. A strong grower that can reach 4 m, it has deep green lanceolate leaves. The flowers, which are clustered in large racemes, are white with yellow stamens, just like the flowers of the potato. It grows well in almost any well-drained soil in sun or light shade. Usually grown from semi-ripe cuttings.
Several other species are grown. *S. crispum* is purple flowered but otherwise very similar, except that it is much stronger growing. Costa Rican nightshade (*S. wendlandii*) also has purple flowers, but it is less hardy and has sharply barbed stems.

STAUNTONIA

From China and Japan, the Staunton vine, *S. hexaphylla*, is a hardy (-12°C) evergreen creeper with shiny, deep green, leathery leaves. In early spring it produces clusters of fragrant, bell-shaped, white flowers tinged violet. The female plants produce 8 cm long, very sweet fruits in an unusual shade of soft purple. It will grow to about 6 m. It prefers a cool, moist, humus-enriched, well-drained soil in light shade but will tolerate sun provided it does not dry out. Propagate from seed sown in early spring.

STEPHANOTIS

The most heavily scented of all climbing plants, *S. floribunda* is grown for its pure white waxy flowers which are used in bridal bouquets. It is also attractive when not in flower as the foliage is composed of paired 10 cm long waxy deep green leaves. It is very frost-tender, but grows well indoors or in a greenhouse, where it may be forced into flower throughout the year. Does best with a cool, moist root zone and the foliage in filtered sunlight. The sun rapidly burns the flowers. It may reach 3 m and layering is the easiest method of propagation.

TECOMANTHE

T. speciosa is a New Zealand native of which only one specimen was found, growing on one of the Three Kings Islands off the northern coast in 1945. It is a strong-growing, frost-tender (-3°C), twining climber. The tubular flowers are creamy-yellow and borne in early winter, and the leaves are a glossy deep green. It will grow to about 6 m. Grow in moist, humus-enriched, well-drained soil in sun or light shade. Propagation by cuttings in summer.
T. venusta is a rare plant from New Guinea that should be grown more. It loves the semi-shade and if grown in this situation will produce clusters of tubular scarlet flowers in late winter. It is very tender and will grow to about 3 m.

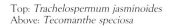

Top: *Trachelospermum jasminoides*
Above: *Tecomanthe speciosa*

Top: *Thunbergia alata*
Above: *Pandorea jasminoides* 'Rosea Superba'

THUNBERGIA

Black-eyed Susan (*T. alata*) is a well-known twining climber with triangular, light green leaves and bright orange, widely flared flowers with a black centre. If grown from seed a variation in flower colour can be expected. It is evergreen and frost-tender and grows to about 2 m high. Propagate from seed in spring and semi-ripe cuttings in summer.

The golden glory creeper (*T. gregorii*, syn. *T. gibsonii*) produces bright orange 5 cm wide flowers over nine months each year. Like *T. alata* it is very frost-tender. It grows well in a container as its height seldom exceeds 2 m. The blue sky flower (*T. grandiflora*) is a strong-growing climber that must have a frost-free growing area. The lush green leaves are a perfect foil for the 7 cm wide, trumpet-shaped flowers of pale blue. It grows to 3-4 m. *T. mysorensis* is a spectacular creeper, that produces metre-long racemes of asymmetrical, tubular yellow flowers with purple throats. It flowers from October to January or February. It will grow to about 6 m high and is frost-tender. All require moist warm conditions to do well and are easily raised from seed. They will also grow from semi-ripe cuttings.

TRACHELOSPERMUM

T. jasminoides has tough, leathery, oval leaves about 7 cm long. In early summer it produces 2 cm wide, sweetly scented, starry white flowers. This twining climber can grow to 7 m, but is usually smaller. Hardy to about -10°C, it is easily grown in any moist well-drained soil in sun or light shade. May be raised from seed but usually grown from semi-ripe cuttings. *T. asiaticum* is a similar but slightly hardier species. It has smaller leaves and 2 cm wide creamy yellow flowers.

TROPAEOLOM

The nasturtiums are among the easiest plants to grow and very effective as quick fillers or back covers. The common garden nasturtium (*T. majus*) comes in dwarf and climbing forms. It has round greyish green leaves and vivid yellow or orange trumpet-shaped flowers. It is a herbaceous perennial that is hardy to -10°C provided the roots are well insulated. It also self-sows freely. Other species vary in leaf and flower type. Red and yellow are the predominant colours. Most are hardy to at least -10°C and are easily grown in any well-drained soil in sun. May be raised from seed or division.

VITIS

A number of relatives of the grape vine (*Vitis vinifera*) are grown solely for their ornamental value. One such species is *V. coignetiae*, a very hardy deciduous vine that produces a most brilliant display of orange, scarlet, and deepest crimson tones before the leaves fall in the autumn. The fruit varies in size, edibility and degree of ornament. It will grow to 15 m or more and is hardy to at least -20°C. Grow in well-drained soil in full sun. The best foliage forms are cutting grown from either semi-ripe summer or winter hardwood cuttings. *V. armuriensis* is another popular species that is similar in growth habit and cultivation requirements.

WISTERIA

There are two main species and one less commonly grown species from this genus of rampant-growing, deciduous, twining climbers. Most wisterias seen in gardens are derived from Japanese wisteria (*W. floribunda*) or Chinese wisteria (*W. sinensis*). The silky wisteria (*W. venusta*), which has broad silky leaves and white to very pale lavender flowers, is far less common. However, the purple form, Violacea, is one of the most fragrant cultivars and well worth growing.

Both common species have pinnate leaves and long pendulous racemes of white, pale pink, lavender or purple flowers. Double flowered forms are available in both species. *W. x formosa* is a cross between the two common species and it has very narrow racemes and drooping foliage. On exposed sites it is better to avoid the cultivars with long racemes as they are easily damaged by strong winds.

Wisterias all need very strong support systems and pruning depends on how you want the plant to grow. During the growing season, many long runners are produced. If you are happy with the amount of top growth present, let the runners grow through summer but cut them out in winter. If you would like more top growth, remove the runners as they appear. If the framework of your climber is sparse, train some of the runners upward to fill out the structure. Wisterias are spur-pruned each year in both winter and summer. In summer, after flowering has finished, prune back the long runners to 40 cm from the main branches. In mid winter shorten all the laterals back further to within two or three buds, so creating spurs which will spring flush with flowers. Select new growths to train and tie into place as replacements. Wisterias can be trained into weeping standards and the easy way to accomplish this is to train a young vine up a strong stake to a height of at least 2 m. When the leading shoot reaches this height, pinch out its growing tip to encourage laterals to grow. Allow only four or five laterals to develop at the top of the plant. Remove all other laterals as they appear and keep pinching back the new laterals as they grow at the top. Within one growing season a well-formed head will exist.

Wisterias are hardy to at least -15°C and are easily grown in any moist well-drained soil in sun or partial shade. The species and some colour forms may be raised from seed, which should be soaked before sowing, but most cultivars must be vegetatively propagated.

TREES

Choosing – practical and ornamental considerations; Native trees; Planting; Maintenance and care; Popular ornamental trees

Conifers provide a variety of foliage forms and colours.

TREES ARE A VITAL part of garden design, providing height, shade, a buffer against wind and noise, a playground for children and a home for garden wildlife. But just as importantly, at least as far as gardeners are concerned, trees define a garden by setting the tone for all other plantings. Just as the nature of a European woodland is determined by the light shade provided by a canopy of deciduous trees, and the New Zealand rainforest by its dense cover of lush evergreen foliage, so the style of your garden will be markedly influenced by the choice of trees.

Most trees grow to at least 5 m high x 3 m wide, but the dividing line between trees and shrubs is not always clear. The traditional definition is that a tree is a large perennial plant with a single woody trunk and a crown of foliage, but don't let that limit the way you use trees and large shrubs. Large shrubs can be trained into a tree-like form with a single trunk if that suits your design and trees can be trained into multi-trunked forms for hedging or use as a windbreak. The only real limitation is your imagination.

Trees may be evergreen or deciduous, broad-leaved or coniferous, tall and narrow like a poplar or as squat and wide as a crabapple. They may race to 10 m high within a few years or take many years to reach 2 m high. There are trees with all manner of foliage types and colours and those with unusual forms, such as palms and tree ferns, but ultimately size is the most important considera-

tion when deciding which trees to plant. Most gardens need at least one tree, but as city gardens become smaller it is increasingly difficult to find trees that are suitable. If you live on a multi-hectare block in the country your selection of suitable trees is enormous, but move to a 50 m^2 suburban garden and it dwindles to but a few. However, the difficulty is not the limited choice, rather the failure to acknowledge the limitation. So many people with small gardens plant trees that will rapidly outgrow the site and cast the whole garden in deep shade. How often do you see trees that have outgrown the space allocated to them or that have been heavily pruned to make them fit? Don't attempt to grow a tree unless you are sure you can cope with its size.

Despite their importance, trees are often an afterthought in home gardens. The lawn is sown, the favourite shrubs and perennials are planted, then the trees are positioned to provide shade or to block undesirable views. This is absolutely the wrong way to plant a garden. The trees should be planted first, especially as they are usually much longer-lived than most other garden plants.

PRACTICAL CONSIDERATIONS

Trees are generally permanent and, more than any other non-edible garden plants, they are usually required to perform functions other than being purely ornamental. These functions differ from providing shelter and soil stabilisa-

Above: Both *Malus* and *Prunus* species are widely appreciated for their voluptuous spring display.
Left: Deciduous trees allow early spring sunshine to warm the garden.

tion on rural blocks, to giving privacy and reducing noise on a suburban section, and perhaps attracting native birds, to giving shade and a focal point to a city garden or courtyard. Whatever your requirements, take time to choose the right trees and make sure you base your choices on the right criteria.

Before visiting a nursery you should know the general dimensions of the trees you want (spread as well as height) and what functions they are to perform. Wide-spreading trees cast more shade than narrow, upright trees, which are better suited to use as windbreaks or for privacy. Deciduous trees are just as effective at providing summer shade, but they let in light in winter, while evergreens provide a better year-round windbreak. Fast-growing trees give quick results, but slower growers, such as kauri, can be used in smaller gardens because of the time it takes for them to reach their towering ultimate heights.

Equally importantly, any plant you choose must be able to survive in your climate and soil. Frost, wind tolerance and rainfall are the main climatic concerns, and drainage, depth, humus content and pH are the most important soil considerations. The climate will also influence the rate of growth. Some trees are naturally fast growers, but generally the more favourable the climate, the quicker the growth.

The position and nature of the planting site plays a vital part in tree selection. When siting trees, bear in mind the layout of household drains and sewers. Removing tree roots from a blocked sewer is not one of life's most pleasant jobs, and it is not just a matter of cleaning out the plumbing, it usually also means removing the tree. You can save a lot of work and heartache by keeping trees away from pipework. The same point can be made for above-ground structures. If planting near a house, garage or overhead lines, think about the ultimate size of the tree, as it will be expensive and heartbreaking to remove a mature tree that is threatening to push the garage over or break up the concrete driveway.

The aspect and the angle of the sun, which varies with the season, determine how much shade a tree will cast. Any large tree will provide a considerable amount of shade throughout the year, but when the sun is at its lowest in winter, a wide-spreading tree can shade an entire city garden.

Dense, heavily foliaged trees provide the best privacy but they have little else in their favour, in smaller gardens especially. They cast too much shade, are less effective as windbreaks than more permeable trees and it is very difficult to grow other plants under them. The ideal shade tree has a wide canopy of lacy open foliage – it protects from the heat of the midday summer sun but allows the breeze and the low-angled sunlight of morning and evening to penetrate. And, if the tree is deciduous, it allows winter sun into the garden. The silk tree (*Albizia julibrissin*) and the various forms of *Gleditsia* are excellent shade trees for small gardens.

BASIC TREE SHAPES

Conical

Rounded

Flat topped

Columnar

Spreading

Weeping

NATIVE TREES

Many of New Zealand's native trees are valued and cultivated widely overseas, yet for many years we have undervalued and exploited them. It is true that many of our native trees are too large for small gardens (though some slow growers can be grown for years in a suburban garden without becoming a problem), but only a minority are presently common in cultivation. Apart from the cabbage tree, kowhai and pohutukawa, few native trees could be called common garden plants, yet many have great value both ornamentally and ecologically.

Among the smaller native trees are several with attractive flowers, such as hinau (*Elaeocarpus dentatus*), kamahi (*Weinmannia racemosa*), lacebark (*Hoheria populnea*) and the scented cream panicles of the marbleleaf (*Carpodetus serratus*). Native trees often have very distinctive growth habits. The graceful weeping rimu (*Dacrydium cupressinum*), the palm-like cabbage tree (*Cordyline* species) and the heavy-set totara (*Podocarpus totara*) are instantly recognisable.

Almost all native trees are evergreens and many have bold foliage. Pukanui (*Meryta sinclairii*), puriri (*Vitex lucens*) and taraire (*Beilschmiedia tarairi*) all have very large glossy leaves that add an almost tropical touch to the garden.

Native trees enhance the survival prospects for native wildlife; not just birds, but lizards and insects too. Nectar-bearing trees, such as pohutukawa (*Metrosideros excelsa*), or those with berries, such as tawa (*Beilschmiedia tawa*), are particularly valuable food sources. Natives also provide nesting sites, and are hosts to insects that birds and lizards feed on.

The warm, vibrant tones of deciduous trees bring welcome colour to the autumn garden, as shown by the three gardens at right and far right.

ORNAMENTAL CONSIDERATIONS

Whether used as a focal point in mixed plantings or as a specimen tree in a lawn, given the choice, most gardeners will opt for evergreens over deciduous plants, the advantage of year-round foliage nearly always being decisive. However, deciduous trees have plenty to offer, not just in terms of their superiority as shade and compost providers, but as ornamental plants too.

Think of deciduous trees and the first thing that comes to mind is autumn foliage and the vivid tones of yellow, orange and red; but the bright green of the new spring growth should not be underestimated. There is also a wide range of summer foliage colours among the deciduous trees – the bright yellow of *Robinia* 'Frisia', the deep blackish-red of the copper beeches (*Fagus sylvatica*), and the silvery-grey of the weeping silver pear (*Pyrus salicifolia*).

Conifers are generally thought of as being evergreen trees with needle-like foliage, but a few, such as the larches (*Larix* spp.), are deciduous. Most develop into large trees but there are a few very dwarf species and others that don't really match our usual ideas of coniferous appearance. The best known of the 'non-coniferous' conifers is the ginkgo, which is so distinctive it is placed in a separate family and order by itself. It has broad, leaf-like cladophylls that in no way resemble needles and to all intents and purposes it looks like a broad-leaved tree. Other conifers with an unusual appearance include our native celery pines (*Phyllocladus* spp.), which also have broad cladophylls.

The bark of a tree can be very attractive too. The paper bark maple (*Acer griseum*) and silver birch (*Betula pendula*) have very distinctive bark, but few trees can match the eucalypts. This large Australian family shows an enormous variation in bark texture, colour and the degree to which it peels. Some species shed their bark entirely to reveal stark white trunks, others shed flakes of bark to create a multi-coloured effect, and some retain their bark, which may become a deep reddish-brown. However, unlike fallen leaves, which all gardeners know make the best compost, large pieces of bark take a long time to break down and can become a fire hazard.

All broad-leaved trees flower, although not all are particularly colourful. The flowering cherries (*Prunus*), dogwoods (*Cornus*), and the large magnolias are often planted for their flowers but as far as most other temperate climate trees are concerned, flowers are often a secondary consideration.

In contrast, many tropical and subtropical trees have very spectacular flowers. The large Proteaceae family which includes the Queensland firewheel tree (*Stenocarpus sinuatus*), the tree banksias, and the larger grevilleas, are extremely colourful, but few can match the brilliant crimson blooms of our own pohutukawa (*Metrosideros excelsa*). Among the hardier trees the acacias and Judas tree (*Cercis siliquastrum*) are very colourful and distinctive.

In milder regions, by choosing carefully, it is

possible to have different trees in flower year round. But where winters are colder this becomes more difficult as the choice of trees becomes more restricted.

Foliage colour, bark texture and flowers all contribute to the attractiveness of a tree, but size and form are generally more important. Don't allow the beauty of a tree's flowers and foliage to cloud your judgement when it comes to choosing the right one, because even the most beautiful tree is a liability if it becomes too large.

PLANTING

Having chosen a suitable site and tree you must ensure that whatever you plant thrives. There's a hackneyed old saying that says you shouldn't plant a five dollar tree in a one dollar hole. Apart from the need to update it to take account of inflation, that old saying is perfectly true. As with just about every aspect of gardening, the more time you put into preparation the better the results. When you've taken great care to plant the right tree in the right place, why rush to plant it?

The roots of a tree spread far more widely and deeply than those of a shrub. It is not possible to incorporate enough compost and fertiliser to keep a tree happy for its entire life, so the best you can do is give it a good start. Dig over the soil to about 30 cm below the depth of the new tree's root ball and to at least 50 cm greater diameter that its current root spread. This will allow the tree to establish

new roots quickly, which will help to boost its growth and stabilise it. Dig in plenty of fine compost to improve the soil texture and increase its moisture retention. If you live in an area with a hard clay subsoil, use a crowbar or a pick to break up the clay or you may find that your trees start to suffer from poor drainage and impeded root development once their roots strike the subsoil.

Remove the tree from its container and plant to the same depth as it was in the container. If the surface roots are showing you may plant it a little deeper, but take care that you don't bury the union point of grafted or budded trees. Hammer in a stout stake before finally firming the tree into place, taking care not to damage the roots. The ground around the tree will need to be trodden down somewhat to firm up the tree, but don't overdo it; it's better to firmly stake the tree and keep the soil loose than it is to compact down all that soil you laboriously loosened up. In very dry areas, or where the tree must fend for itself, it is often a good idea to make a small ridge of soil around the drip-line of the tree. This ensures that any moisture dripping from the foliage is channelled back to the roots.

It is usually best to let the tree become established before applying fertiliser, otherwise an overly compact root system may develop because there is no need for new roots to spread and seek out soil nutrients. Making the tree stable should be your first consideration, and although staking helps, encouraging a quick root spread is the best way. When fer-

Metrosideros excelsa 'Variegata'

tilisers are eventually used, they should be applied just outside the drip-line and watered in well to encourage the roots to spread downwards and outwards.

Modern nursery practice dictates that most plants are now grown in containers, but large deciduous trees are the exception, with the majority still being lifted from the open ground. This is usually done in winter when the trees are dormant. Ideally the nursery will pot the trees after lifting, but if you buy a bare-rooted deciduous tree it must be planted immediately. Once established in a large container, trees lifted from the open ground may be treated just like any other container-grown plant. They may be planted out at any time, provided the soil is in a suitable condition to work and the weather is not exceptionally hot or cold.

MAINTENANCE AND CARE

Maintenance is most important during the first two years after final planting. Trimming to shape, loosening ties and restaking, fertilising and watering are all necessary to ensure your trees get the best start. Once established, trees can largely look after themselves.

PRUNING

Unless you intend to train a tree to a specific shape or style of growth, the pruning of young trees is generally just a matter of removing any damaged branches and those that are likely to head off at strange angles. Garden trees often look better if they're allowed to develop naturally. Just aim to maintain a clean trunk with good canopy development; there's no need to train it into a perfectly straight-trunked forestry specimen.

If planted in the right place, established trees rarely need pruning unless they have been damaged in some way. If a large tree has to be trimmed, it's a job best left to professional tree surgeons. Very few gardeners have the necessary ladders and climbing equipment to scale a large tree, let alone to correctly trim it. Likewise, felling a tree, especially in a built-up area, demands experience.

TREES IN CONTAINERS

Of course, you don't have to plant your tree out in the garden, trees can be grown in containers permanently. Half barrels, large boxes made from treated timber and concrete troughs and tubs are all suitable containers for trees.

Large trees demand large pots and these can be very heavy and unwieldy. They also have considerable watering and feeding demands and are usually treated as temporary container plants that are transplanted to the garden when they become too large to be comfortably repotted. Though in the case of slow-growing trees, this can take several years.

Trees usually have deep root systems, so urn-shaped pots that are much deeper than they are wide allow for the best root development. This is an important consideration if you intend to eventually plant the tree in your garden; a tree with a poorly developed root system will be prone to wind damage in later life.

Use a good quality potting mix – most garden centres stock specialised tree and tub mixes – and feed regularly. Regular watering is vitally important, too, because a tree with a large head of leaves can pump up a huge volume of water. Potted trees are usually the first container plants to show signs of moisture stress.

Meyer lemons are excellent subjects for containers.

STAKING

A young, newly planted tree with a large head of foliage will very likely be damaged by the wind, either by directly damaging the super-structure or by causing the tree to rock, which may weaken the tree at ground level or damage the roots. Young trees must be firmly staked, but staking can also cause problems. Young trees have soft bark that is easily damaged if it continually rubs against a stake or against the ties that hold the tree to the stake, and as the tree grows its trunk and branches increase in diameter, which can cause the stake and ties to cut into the bark.

Use ties made of a soft material that breaks down with time and regularly check that the ties are still slightly loose and the stake is not cutting into the trunk. The new foam-rubber tree ties are excellent and can be adjusted as the tree grows, but strips of old cloth are just as good and they are biodegradable. In most cases the stake can be removed after two years, often sooner, but don't underestimate the strength of the wind.

FEEDING AND WATERING

Young trees will establish more quickly if fed and watered, but as mentioned earlier this is better kept at a subsistence level in order to encourage good root development. Established trees will also benefit from feeding, especially if their roots are at all confined. Use a general garden fertiliser and water it in well.

The soft lines and gentle colours of *Prunus subhirtella* 'Rosea'.

PESTS AND DISEASES

Young trees are usually vigorous growers that are not greatly troubled by pests and diseases. If problems do occur they can be treated as you would treat a large shrub. However, large established trees can be more difficult to treat; they are often too tall to safely get to the top of and effective coverage with sprays is all but impossible with domestic gardening equipment. Controlling pests and diseases in large trees is usually an area for professionals who have the necessary equipment and expertise. No tree is worth covering yourself in pesticide or breaking your neck for. That said, most trees are worth the effort of saving.

POPULAR ORNAMENTAL TREES

THE FOLLOWING LIST includes some of the more common garden trees. The height and width given indicate the tree's mature height in metres under average garden conditions in New Zealand; of course 'average' New Zealand conditions are hard to estimate, so where necessary I have erred on the high side as there is nothing worse than having to prune or even remove a tree that has grown larger than expected. A mature tree is one that is about 30-40 years old; extremely old trees may be considerably larger. The rate of growth is indicated by the figure following the mature height and width, e.g., (4) indicating the height in metres of the tree at 5 years of age.

ABIES

This genus includes some very large trees, but most of the garden forms are among the more compact evergreen conifers (30 m x 15 m (2.5)). They are superb plants for high-altitude gardens with all species, except perhaps *A. delavayi*, hardy throughout New Zealand (to -20°C). They are conical in habit and have short, flattened needles arranged around or along the top of the branches. Many, especially *A. concolor*, have glaucous foliage. The cones, which are often tinted purplish-blue and dripping with resin, sit erect on the branches rather than hanging from them. Firs prefer a cool moist soil with ample summer water and rarely do well in hot and dry or very windy areas. The species may be raised from seed sown at 15°C, selected forms and hybrids are raised from cuttings in summer.

ACACIA

A genus of about 1000 species mainly found in Australia and Africa. Those in New Zealand gardens are virtually all Australian species. These broadleaf evergreens have three main foliage types: the sickle-shaped leaf, typified by *A. floribunda* and *A. longifolia*; the fine ferny leaf, such as that of *A. cardiophylla*; and the small triangular leaves seen in a few species, such as *A. cultriformis* and *A. pravissima*. They have a round-headed upright habit and all of the commonly grown species bear fluffy yellow flowers, often in great abundance. The flowering season ranges from mid winter to summer depending on the species. Acacias are colourful, easy-care plants best grown in a light well-drained soil in full sun. They grow to 6 m x 6 m (4) and are hardy to -8°C. Raise from seed sown at 18°C.

ACER

The maples are deciduous trees with a round-headed weeping habit that include a wide range of species from temperate regions of the northern hemisphere. *A. platanoides* has interesting tassel-like flowers but most maples are grown for their form and foliage. The style of

Acacia baileyana

Acer platanoides 'Drummondii'

leaf varies but the typical palmate maple leaf, as depicted on the Canadian flag, is common to most species. The leaf size ranges from less than 25 mm across to over 150 mm. The new spring growth often goes through several colour phases as it matures and many species and cultivars provide superb autumn colour. The most common garden species are the Japanese maple (A. palmatum), the Norway maple (A. platanoides), and the box elder (A. negundo). The many forms of A. palmatum are probably the best suited to small domestic gardens. However, they are prone to wind burn. Some species, such as A. griseum, have interesting peeling bark. Hardy to -25°C, they grow to 10 m x 6 m (3). Species are raised from seed sown at 18°C, selected forms are grafted onto species stock.

Aesculus carnea

AESCULUS

The horse chestnuts are not for small gardens. Both common species, A. carnea and A. hippocastanum, are deciduous trees with spreading habits that will grow to at least 15 m x 10 m (3.5). They have deep green, fan-shaped leaves up to 200 mm across. A. carnea (particularly the form 'Briotii') has upright spikes of pink flowers in spring and is the more attractive of the two species when blooming. However, it is less widely planted than the white-flowered A. hippocastanum, which has proved to be tougher and more adaptable. Both species have 50-75 mm diameter fruits enclosed in spiny capsules that can be messy. Horse chestnuts are most at home in park-like settings where they have the room to develop into stately specimen trees. They are best grown in deep moist soils. Hardy to -25°C. Species are propagated by stratified seed sown at 18°C, selected forms are budded or grafted.

AGATHIS

This genus of columnar conifers includes about 15 species native to the Pacific region. The best known species is A. australis, the New Zealand kauri. Several species, such as the Queensland kauri (A. robusta) are or have been important timber trees. Mature kauri are now relatively rare in the wild, although it is widely planted in parks and large gardens. Ancient trees are

enormous, with huge trunks and crowns, but garden specimens are unlikely to exceed 8 m until many years after planting, after five years they are still only 2 m. The narrow, lanceolate, bronze green leathery leaves are up to 100 mm long on young trees but only 40 mm long on fnature trees. The almost spherical cones are about 70 mm diameter. Although naturally restricted to the northern part of the North Island (generally hardy to only -8°C), A. australis will grow as far south as Dunedin, although it is very slow growing in southern areas. Kauris prefer a moist, humus-enriched, well-drained soil and ample summer water. Raise from seed sown at 20°C.

AGONIS

An Australian genus of about 12 evergreen species. The best known tree-sized species (8 m x 5 m (4)) is the willow myrtle (A. flexuosa). In general appearance it resembles a weeping eucalyptus. It is a broad-headed tree with 125 mm long, pendulous willow-like leaves and small, scented creamy-white flowers in clusters in early summer. The flowers are showy but the tree is mainly grown for its graceful growth habit. Apart from being somewhat frost-tender (-4°C) it is easily grown in any sunny well-drained position. It is usually raised from seed sown at about 20°C. The very attractive variegated form is only rarely seen because it is difficult to propagate.

AILANTHUS

Tree of heaven (A. altissima) is a very rapid-growing, spreading, deciduous tree with deep bronze-green, pinnate leaves that are up to 600 mm long. The unspectacular greenish-cream flowers, which appear in late spring, are followed in autumn by russet-coloured winged fruit that are useful in dried arrangements. It is a tough, adaptable tree that tolerates drought, heat and air pollution once established and also has good autumn colour. Ailanthus will grow well in any deep moist soil, reaching 15 m x 10 m (7), and is hardy to -25°C. It may be raised from stratified seed sown at 20°C or from root cuttings.

ALBIZIA

The silk tree (A. julibrissin) is an excellent shade or lawn tree. It grows to 7 m x 8 m (4.5) and has a flat-topped spreading habit. The large bipinnate leaves composed of many tiny leaflets filter the sun well; they also rot down or blow away quickly when they fall in autumn. In summer it produces fluffy, ball-shaped, pale yellow and pink flowers. The form 'Rosea' has deep pink flowers. It thrives in a light well-drained soil and is usually raised from seed sown at 22°C. It is hardy to -12°C. Selected forms are sometimes propagated by semi-hardwood cuttings in autumn or by grafting.
A. lophantha is an evergreen species that closely resembles an acacia. It has bright, slightly glaucous, green pinnate leaves

and 100 mm long, fluffy yellow bottlebrush flowers. It grows rapidly to 7 m x 4 m and can become invasive as it self-sows freely. It is hardy to about -4°C.

ALECTRYON

The titoki or New Zealand oak (*A. excelsus*) is the only commonly grown species. This evergreen is a densely foliaged spreading tree with glossy, mid-green, pinnate leaves up to 300 mm long. It grows to 6 m x 4 m (2) and is hardy to only -4°C. The clusters of tiny flowers, which appear in late spring, are followed by brown seed capsules that split open to reveal a large black seed surrounded by a bright red fleshy pulp. The new growth, flower buds and seed pods are covered in a fine brown indumentum. Plant in a cool, moist, well-drained soil. It is usually propagated by seed, which should be soaked and sown at 20°C.

ALNUS

Alders are ideal for poorly drained areas but being deciduous and spreading they can be a little too untidy for carefully maintained gardens. The common *A. glutinosa* may reach 30 m with great age, though generally alders reach 15 m x 8 m (3). The leaves are about 75 mm long, deep green and coarsely toothed. In spring, large woody catkins form, which can be messy when they fall. It is a rapidly growing tree that tolerates very wet, even salty soil. *A. rhombifolia* has large toothed, nearly palmate, leaves that are deep green above and silvery-grey on the underside. *A. cordata*, the Italian alder, has 100 mm long, heart-shaped leaves. It is less upright than other alders and forms a good canopy. *A. incana* has slightly tomentose stems and leaves and is available in a yellow-leaved form, 'Aurea'. All are hardy to at least -15°C. Apart from the selected foliage forms, which are grafted, alders are usually raised from seed sown at 18°C.

ARAUCARIA

This southern hemisphere genus of conifers is most commonly represented by the monkey puzzle tree (*A. araucana*), the

Norfolk Island pine (*A. heterophylla*) and the bunya bunya (*A. bidwillii*). All are ultimately too large for small gardens at 15 m x 6 m (2), but they are slow growing and attractive when young. They have deep green spiny foliage arranged radially around the branches and all develop large cones with edible nuts. These trees are very stiffly upright with a symmetrical branch structure that, in young trees, is almost perfect. *A. bidwillii* and *A. heterophylla* are superb coastal trees but *A. araucana* is best sheltered from salt winds. It is hardy to about -15°C, *A. bidwillii* to about -10°C once established, and *A. heterophylla* to -4°C. They prefer a moist well-drained soil, but will tolerate drought once established. Propagate by seed sown at 20°C.

ARBUTUS

The evergreen strawberry tree (*A. unedo*) is so called because of its prominent warty red fruit that follow the spring and summer-borne clusters of lily-of-the-valley-like flowers. The rounded, dark green, red-stemmed leaves are about 60 mm long and finely serrated. The reddish-brown bark is attractive also, especially when wet. The spreading tree needs to be shaped when young to produce a neat tree. It grows to 8 m x 6 m (2) and is hardy to -15°C. It is also tolerant of coastal conditions and alkaline soil, which is unusual for an ericaceous plant. Grow in a moist, well-drained, humus-enriched soil in sun or light shade. Raise from seed sown at 18°C.

AZARA

The vanilla tree (*A. microphylla*) is a rather open-growing, spreading, evergreen tree that grows to 8 m x 5 m (2.5). It has tiny, rounded, deep bronze green leaves and, in spring, clusters of small, fluffy yellow flowers that are strongly vanilla scented. It is easily grown in most well-drained soils. A very attractive golden cream variegated form exists but is only rarely available. Hardy to -15°C and propagated by seed sown at

Albizia julibrissin 'Rosea'

Alectryon excelsus

18°C or by semi-ripe cuttings. *A. lanceolata* is a similarly sized species with larger lanceolate leaves and larger flower clusters that are not as highly scented as those of *A. microphylla*, nor is the tree as hardy. Other species, such as the somewhat tender (-4°C) but highly fragrant *A. dentata*, are seldom seen outside large public gardens.

BEILSCHMIEDIA

This southern hemisphere genus includes two New Zealand natives; tawa (*B. tawa*) and taraire (*B. tarairi*), both of which are cultivated. They are both very upright evergreen trees growing to 8 m x 4 m (2.5) with a dense foliage canopy. Taraire has rounded leathery leaves up to 140 mm long that are deep green above and whitish below. Tawa has 100 mm long narrow leaves that are also whitish on the underside. The new growth of both species is covered in a fine brown indumentum. Both species have insignificant spring flowers that are followed by 30 mm long fleshy berries; those of taraire are black, and tawa has red fruit. *Beilschmiedia* are a

little frost-tender (-4°C) and prefer a moist well-drained soil. Propagate by seed sown at 20°C.

BETULA

So extensively planted that it is virtually an urban cliché, the silver birch (*B. pendula*) and its close relatives are, nevertheless, attractive trees. Most of the species are very similar (weeping, deciduous and 10 m x 6 m (3.5)), differing only in leaf size and minor growing details. *B. pendula* is the most common and typical. It has 75 mm long, finely serrated, pendulous, pointed oval leaves and peeling silvery bark. The spring flower catkins shed profusely and can be a nuisance. Other species, such as *B. albosinensis*, *B. nigra*, *B. maximowicziana* and *B. papyrifera*, vary in bark colour and leaf size but they are similar in general appearance. Birches grow in almost any soil and tolerate the most severe frosts (-30°C). However, they are rather prone to aphid damage, which can lead to sooty mould. Raised from seed sown at 15°C, but selected forms are sometimes grafted.

Brachychiton gregorii

Cedrus atlantica 'Glauca'

BRACHYCHITON

The Illawarra flame tree (*B. acerifolius*) is an upright deciduous tree that grows to 10 m x 5 m (2) and is hardy to only -4°C. It has 200 mm wide leaves that are somewhat maple-like, although glossy and quite leathery. The deep red flowers are 25 mm across and carried in large panicles that are extremely showy. The vivid flowers are made all the more conspicuous as the leaves around the flower heads fall just before blooming starts. It flowers in early to mid summer. The boat-shaped seed capsules that follow can be dried for use as floral decorations. Several other species are grown; the most distinctive is the kurrajong (*B. populneus*), which is upright with poplar-like leaves and growth habit. It is hardier than *B. acerifolius* but its white flowers are not nearly as spectacular. Propagate by seed sown at 22°C.

CASSIA

A genus of over 500 species of tender (-3°C) evergreen shrubs and trees, many of which have been reclassified as *Senna*, but they are likely to be known as *Cassia* for many years. The most common species is *C. corymbosa*, particularly the form 'John Ball'. It has a spreading habit and bright green pinnate leaves that are up to 150 mm long and composed of leaflets with prominent midribs. Yellow buttercup-like flowers in large clusters appear from about the middle of March. Grow in a

light well-drained soil in full sun. It grows to 4 m x 4 m (2.5). Most other species have a similar appearance but vary slightly in size, leaf shape and flowering season. *C. tomentosa* is a shrubby winter-flowering species that may self-sow and become invasive. Except for 'John Ball', which is grown from cuttings, cassias are usually raised from seed sown at 22°C.

CATALPA

The Indian beans are large (10 m x 8 m (3.5)), upright, deciduous trees that are surprisingly showy for such hardy plants (-25°C). The two common species, *C. bignonioides* and *C. speciosa*, have pointed oval leaves that may be up to 250 mm across. Heads of white, yellow and purple trumpet-shaped flowers appear in summer and are held well above the foliage. The flowers are followed by prominent seed pods. The yellow-leaved form of *C. bignonioides*, known as 'Aurea', is an impressive tree even when not in flower. A purple-leaved hybrid is also occasionally sold. Plant in a moist well-drained soil. Indian beans may be raised from seed sown at 20°C, but the selected forms are grafted or budded.

CEDRUS

The cedars are a genus of evergreen conifers that reach a height of 15 m x 12 m (2). Many magnificent specimens of the Atlas Mountain cedar (*C.*

libani ssp. *atlantica*), the Himalayan cedar (*C. deodara*) and the cedar of Lebanon (*C. libani*) grace our larger parks and gardens, but the fourth species, the Cyprus cedar (*C. brevifolia*) remains rare. Cedars have wide spreading drooping branches that are densely clothed with clusters of fine needles. There are several selected foliage forms, the best known of which is the blue Atlas cedar (*C. libani* ssp. *atlantica* 'Glauca'). Cedars have resinous egg-shaped cones that are held erect on top of the branches. The cones are quite a feature when young and green but lose their appeal as they age to dry brown husks. Cedars prefer a moist well-drained soil, although they are drought tolerant once established. Hardy to -20°C. The species may be raised from seed sown at 18°C, but selected forms are usually raised from cuttings in autumn or occasionally grafted.

CERCIS

Judas tree (*C. siliquastrum*) and Chinese redbud (*C. chinensis*) are deciduous, spreading trees that grow to 8 m x 5 m (2) and have similar foliage and flowers. Both have distinctive light bronze-green heart-shaped leaves that are about 100 mm long and the flower clusters, which seem to sprout from every twig in spring, are an unusual shade of purplish-pink, followed by bean-like seed pods. White-flowered forms are also available. The foliage often colours well in the autumn. These trees are easily grown in most reasonably well-drained soils. Hardy to -25°C.
Other species seen occasionally are the very hardy Eastern redbud (*C. canadensis*) and the glaucous-leaved Western redbud (*C. occidentalis*). All may be raised from stratified and soaked seed sown at 20°C. The selected forms of *C. canadensis* are usually budded but white forms of *C. siliquastrum* will come true to type if hand pollinated.

CHAMAECYPARIS

The most common species of this genus of conifers is the Lawson cypress (*C. lawsoniana*). The true species has somewhat drooping fan-like sprays of bright green foliage and reaches

10 m x 5 m (2), but it is available in an enormous range of cultivated forms that include ground covers, rockery dwarf, columnar shrubs, and trees. It also comes in a wide range of foliage types and colours. The other common species, *C. nootkatensis*, *C. obtusa*, *C. pisifera* and *C. thyoides*, are not quite as variable but have, nevertheless, been developed into many widely differing forms. All are extremely tough plants (hardy to -25°C) that do well in a cool, moist, well-drained soil. They are reasonably drought-tolerant once established but are not at their best in hot dry areas. Except for farm shelter belts, the true species are seldom grown. Most garden specimens are cultivars propagated by summer or autumn cuttings.

CINNAMOMUM

The camphor tree (*C. camphora*) has a spreading habit and grows to 12 m x 10 m (1.8) and has bright yellowish-green to pink new growth and clusters of fragrant, small, yellow flowers. The flower clusters appear in late spring and are followed by tiny blackish fruits. The leaves are about 125 mm long and deep glossy green when mature. Although classed as an evergreen, there is significant leaf fall in late winter and early spring. A sturdy strong-growing tree that is hardy to -6°C, it has heavy branches and a dense root system that limits how close it can be positioned to paths, driveways or buildings. The bark is very attractive, especially when wet, and is also very aromatic. It is the source of camphor and camphor-wood. It is best grown in a moist well-drained soil with ample summer moisture. Propagate by semi-ripe autumn cuttings or seed sown at 20°C. The Nepal camphor tree, *C. glanduliferum*, has larger leaves, a more upright growth habit, and is more frost-tender.

CORDYLINE

The native cabbage tree (*C. australis*) is an upright evergreen that is very widely grown. Young trees usually have only one trunk topped with a head of long sword-shaped leaves. As they mature basal shoots and new trunks often develop to create a

Cornus alternifolia 'Argentea'

Catalpa bignonioides

clump of trunks. The basal shoots are sometimes removed from garden specimens, which leads to greater branching higher up and a tree-like shape. It grows to 6 m x 3 m (1.8) and is hardy to -15°C. The fragrant, small, white flowers, which open from late spring, are massed on panicles up to 1 m long and are followed by small white berries. Several selected foliage forms, including the beautiful variegated 'Albertii', are available. Other species occasionally grown in domestic gardens include the mountain cabbage tree (*C. indivisa*), which has much wider, somewhat glaucous, leaves with prominent ribbing. It is an attractive plant but demands moist soil and high humidity to be at its best. *C. banksii* is a multi-trunked shrub that flowers very heavily. *C. stricta* and *C. terminalis* are frost-tender Polynesian species: *C. stricta* has lavender flowers and *C. terminalis* comes in many boldly variegated forms, which are often grown as houseplants. Most species prefer a moist soil and are quite tolerant of poor drainage. Usually grown from seed sown at 18-20°C, although selected forms are propagated vegetatively either by suckers or by using sections of the young stems as cuttings.

CORNUS

Dogwoods are spreading deciduous trees with simple but bold spring flowers, good autumn foliage colour, and some have brightly coloured winter stems. They grow to 6 m x 5 m (1.8). *C.·controversa, C. florida* and *C. kousa* usually have the best flowers, and *C. nuttallii* provides brilliant autumn colour. *C. alternifolia* has a graceful tiered growth habit but insignificant flowers. *C. stolonifera* has bright red winter twigs and *C. capitata* is evergreen with unusual fruit. Most species have simple, pointed, oval leaves about 125 mm long and there are some attractive variegated forms. The flowers have four leathery petals and are usually white when first opening but become tinted with pink as they age. The flowers are often followed by large round fruits that are seen at their best on *C. kousa* and *C. capitata*. Most dogwoods are very hardy (-20°C) but *C. capitata* is often damaged at -6°C when young. They do best when planted in a moist, humus-enriched, well-drained soil in sun or light shade. The species may be raised from stratified seed sown at 20°C; hybrids and selected forms are grafted or grown from suckers or semi-ripe summer to early autumn cuttings.

CRATAEGUS

Hawthorns have become uncommon because of a general move away from deciduous plants, together with their thorns and high susceptibility to fireblight and pear slug. Some people also object to the smell of the flowers. Nevertheless, there are many attractive species and hybrids. Generally spreading and 6 m x 5 m (2), they vary in leaf size, flower colour, and the colour and size of the fruit.

English hawthorn (*C. laevigata*, syn. *C. oxyacantha*) has 50 mm long, three-lobed leaves and small, white to pale pink flowers that are followed by bright red fruit. Many selected forms of this species, and the very similar *C. monogyna*, have been produced with white, pink and red flowers in both single or double forms. The doubles do not set much fruit but are more attractive when in flower. Other common species include the glossy-leaved *C. phaenopyrum* and *C. crus-galli*, which is also noted for its autumn colour. Hawthorns are tough adaptable plants that will grow in most conditions but are best suited to areas with cold winters (hardy to -25°C). The species may be raised from stratified seed sown at 18°C, but selected forms are usually grafted onto species stock.

CRYPTOMERIA

The Japanese cedar (*C. japonica*) is a large evergreen pyramidal tree (20 m x 8 m (2.5)) with horizontal branches that droop at the tips. The soft needle-like foliage is bright mid-green in summer turning to rich purplish-brown in winter. The cultivated forms range from tiny rockery dwarfs to large shrubs. Their foliage often differs from the parent species, with varying size and density of needles. The species has small reddish-brown cones, but many of the cultivated forms appear to be sterile. Japanese cedars are best grown in a cool, moist, well-drained soil. Hardy to -20°C. The species may be raised from stratified seed sown at 18°C; the selected forms are usually grown from cuttings.

x CUPRESSOCYPARIS

Leyland cypress (*C. leylandii*) is a bi-generic hybrid between *Chamaecyparis nootkatensis* and *Cupressus macrocarpa*. Early

Crataegus diffusum

examples are now over 30 m tall, but as it has only been in existence for about 100 years its absolute size is unknown. Assume a size of at least 20 m x 8 m (3). Because it is so rapid growing, extremely hardy (-25°C), and tolerant of most soil conditions, including periods of poor drainage, it has become a popular conical evergreen for shelter belts. Leyland cypress will withstand regular hard trimming and has also been grown as a timber tree. The foliage is typically cupressoid and composed of flattened sprays. Several forms with varying foliage and growth habit have been selected. 'Leighton Green' is the best known. It has very bright green foliage and a somewhat more open branch structure. Propagate from heeled cuttings, which may be taken at any time.

CUPRESSUS

The conifer Monterey cypress (C. macrocarpa) covers thousands of kilometres of the New Zealand countryside as hedgerows and windbreaks. It is columnar and spreading and reaches 15 m x 12 m (3). It has sprays of deep green foliage composed of flattened whippy stems clothed in tiny scale-like leaves. Many selected forms have been developed so that a huge range of sizes and foliage types is now available. These range from tiny dome-shaped rockery plants through to large trees. The golden forms of C. macrocarpa are among the best and brightest yellow-foliaged conifers.

The pencil cypresses (C. sempervirens forms), particularly the very narrow forms 'Stricta' and 'Gracilis' and the yellow-foliaged 'Swaine's Gold', are popular for flanking entrance ways and avenues. They add a stark upright element that is useful for breaking a predominantly horizontal design. Although hardy, C. sempervirens is a poor choice for areas that experience regular snowfalls: the weight of the snow bends the branches outwards and destroys the shape.

Other species commonly grown include C. arizonica and its variety var. glabra. Their tendency towards glaucous foliage has enabled the development of blue conifers that are very tolerant of drought and poor soil. C. hialaica var. darjeelingensis (syn. C. cashmeriana) and C. funebris are large species with drooping foliage sprays on horizontal branches that move gracefully in the breeze.

Most species have small, resinous, spherical cones of about 40 mm diameter. C. cashmeriana is not reliably hardy below -12°C but the other species tolerate -15 to -20°C. The species may be raised from stratified seed sown at 18°C, but the cultivated forms must be propagated vegetatively, usually by cuttings.

DACRYDIUM

Rimu (D. cupressinum) is a graceful native conifer with a silhouette that is impossible to mistake for any other tree,

especially when young. Until it reaches about 10 m high, the rimu has a weeping conical habit, but as it matures it develops into a columnar tree of 15 m x 5 (1.8). The branches are clothed in very short, stiff, bronze-green needles, which are green in spring and summer turning to reddish-brown in autumn and winter. The bright red drupes with protruding black seeds are unusual, but seldom occur in large enough numbers to be a feature.

There are several other cultivated species: D. bidwillii (syn. Halocarpus bidwillii) resembles a very small D. cupressinum, growing to about 2.5 m high. The Huon pine (D. franklinii syn. Lagarostrobus franklinii) is a Tasmanian native that is similar to D. cupressinum. Rimus are hardy to about -15°C and they are best in a cool but humid climate with a moist, humus-enriched, well-drained soil. They are usually propagated by stratified seed sown at 18°C; small cuttings will strike roots, but they are not very reliable.

ELAEOCARPUS

Two species of these spreading evergreens are seen in gardens: the Australian blueberry ash (E. cyaneus syn. E. reticulatus) and the hinau (E. dentatus), a New Zealand native. Both have deep green leathery leaves that are about 100 mm long with serrated edges and bear racemes of small, pendulous, creamy white flowers. Those of E. cyaneus are finely fringed at the edges. Both species have small purplish-blue berries. E. dentatus is the taller of the two species (8 m x 5 m (2)) and it will also withstand more frost (-8°C). Both trees appreciate a moist, humus-enriched, well-drained soil in full sun to moderate shade with ample summer moisture. Raise from seed sown at 18°C or semi-ripe cuttings.

ENTELEA

Whau (E. arborescens) is a spreading native evergreen with light green, heart-shaped to three-lobed leaves that can be up to 200 mm across. In late spring it produces massed clusters of white anemone-like flowers, which are followed by bristly seed capsules. It is easily

grown in any moist well-drained soil in full sun or light shade provided it is sheltered from frost (-2°C). It reaches 5 m x 3.5 m (3.5). Whau becomes untidy with age and if pruned its pithy stems tend to die back. However, as it grows very quickly and is easily propagated from spring-sown seed there is no difficulty in establishing new plants.

EUCALYPTUS

This large genus of over 600 species is almost exclusively Australian and is the characteristic feature of that country's flora. The typical gum tree has peeling bark and sickle-shaped, glaucous-green, leathery leaves somewhere between 75 mm and 150 mm long. The fluffy filamentous flowers, which may be any shade of white, cream, pink, yellow, orange or red, vary in size and season of production. Some, such as E. ficifolia, put on a truly magnificent floral display whereas others have insignificant flowers.

Eucalypts range in size from the snow gum (E. pauciflora ssp. niphophila) at around 6 m to giants, such as E. globulus, which may exceed 60 m. Although most species eventually develop the familiar sickle-shaped leaves, some have juvenile leaves that envelop the stem, such as the silver dollar gum (E. polyanthemos). Gums also vary in their hardiness; some are almost totally intolerant of frost, whereas others can withstand -15°C.

Many gardeners reject eucalypts because of their rapid growth, leaf and bark litter, and potentially large size. However, they are among the most attractive and easy-care evergreen trees available. Plant them in a light well-drained soil in full sun and water well in summer until established. Eucalypts are attacked by a wide range of pests, such as scale, tortoise beetles, weevils and leaf-roller caterpillars but in most cases they outgrow the problems. Raise from seed sown at around 20°C. Specialist suppliers offer a huge range of species.

EUCRYPHIA

This genus is composed of several large upright evergreen

Entelea arborescens

shrubs or small trees native to Chile and Australia (8 m x 3.5 m (2)). The species most widely grown is *E. cordifolia*, a Chilean native. The other Chilean species, *E. glutinosa*, is rarely seen in gardens but has been crossed with *E. cordifolia* to produce the hybrid *E.* x *nymansensis*. The three Australian species, *E. milliganii*, *E. moorei* and *E. lucida*, are rarely seen. All species have similar anemone-like white flowers that appear in spring but they vary in foliage and size. *E. cordifolia* has 75 mm long, deep green, serrated-edged oval leaves with silvery undersides. *E. glutinosa* has mid-green serrated-edged pinnate leaves composed of five leaflets. *E. moorei* has mid-green, smooth edged pinnate leaves composed of seven leaflets, whereas the other two Australian species have small oval leaves. *E.* x *nymansensis* has foliage with the colour of *E. cordifolia* and the form of *E. glutinosa*, and has larger flowers than any of the species. As with many choice Chilean plants it grows best in a cool moist climate, such as that of coastal Otago or Southland. They are generally hardy to -12°C. The species may be raised from seed sown at 18°C, but the hybrids are propagated by semi-ripe cuttings.

FAGUS

The European beech (*F. sylvatica*) is a large wide-spreading deciduous tree that is unsuitable for small gardens as it reaches 12 m x 10 m (2.5). The true species is seldom seen, but several cultivated forms are grown. All except the cut-leaved 'Laciniata' have similar 100 mm long, deeply ribbed, rounded leaves. However, the foliage colour varies considerably from golden, variegated and tricolour-variegated forms to the purple and blackish-purple forms, such as 'Riversii', that are commonly known as copper beeches. There is also a very upright-growing variety called 'Fastigiata'. These easily grown trees tolerate most soils, although they seldom grow well in coastal conditions, and are hardy to -30°C. The species and some of the purple-leaved forms may be raised from stratified seed sown at 18°C; the best selected forms are usually

grafted. Other species, such as the larger-leaved American beech (*F. grandifolia*), are occasionally seen in parks and larger gardens.

FICUS

Many of the evergreen *Ficus* species that are often used as houseplants are hardy enough to be grown outdoors in mild areas. Of these the toughest are *F. elastica* (-3°C), *F. macrophylla* (-3°C), *F. rubignosa* (-4°C) and *F. benjamina* (-2°C). However, even if these species survive the winter they require warm summer conditions to grow well. All of these species will eventually become large, wide-spreading trees (7 m x 5 m (2.5)) with rounded leathery leaves that are often very large and glossy. The common edible fig (*F. carica*) is hardy to about -10°C. It is a deciduous tree that is often espaliered. Valued for its edible fruit and its boldly lobed palmate leaves, it grows well in most areas provided it gets as much sun as possible. Good fruit can only be expected in areas with reliably warm summers. Grow in a moist well-drained soil in full sun. The species may be raised from seed sown at 22°C, semi-ripe cuttings, or aerial layers.

FRAXINUS

The ashes are a hardy (-20°C) northern hemisphere genus of some 65 species of shrubs and trees. The common *F. angustifolia* is a broad-headed deciduous tree that is frequently used as a street tree. It has 200 mm long pinnate leaves usually made up of seven leaflets. In spring the plant is covered in panicles of tiny, fragrant, white flowers. In autumn the foliage develops rich purple and gold tones. Several forms, the most common of which is the claret ash, 'Raywoodii', have been selected for their autumn foliage colour. It reaches approximately 12 m x 7 m (3.5). The European ash (*F. excelsior*) is also widely grown. It has slightly larger leaves composed of seven to eleven leaflets that develop little or no autumn colour. However, the form 'Aurea' and the pendulous 'Aurea Pendula' have bright yellow autumn leaves. *F.*

Euchryphia cordifolia

Eucalyptus leucoxylon 'Rosea'

Eucalyptus ficifolia form

excelsior is available in several growth forms: upright, round-headed and pendulous. The third common species is the manna ash (*F. ornus*). This species has a dense foliage cover, large flower heads and colours well in the autumn. *F. sieboldiana* (syn. *F. mariesii*) is similar. The species may be raised from stratified seed sown at 18°C, but selected forms are usually grafted onto *F. excelsior* stocks. Specialist seed suppliers stock many species including the near-evergreen *F. uhdei*.

GINKGO

The maidenhair tree (*G. biloba*) is the sole survivor of a group of plants that once dominated much of the earth's surface.

Hardy to -25°C, it reaches 15 m x 10 m (3). Its light to mid-green leaves are shaped like the individual pinna of a maidenhair fern frond and give the tree an appearance quite unlike that of any other conifer. In autumn the leaves turn a bright yellow before falling and this is one of the tree's main attractions. Forms selected for better colour are occasionally available. Female trees bear soft round fruit that have an unpleasant smell when squashed, so if possible plant only male trees. The ginkgo will grow in most soils and conditions but is best with ample summer moisture. It may be raised from stratified seed sown at 22°C, but the only way to be sure of getting a male plant is to graft or take cutting material from a tree of known sex.

HOHERIA

This New Zealand genus includes some of the few native deciduous trees. They are commonly known as ribbonwoods or lacebarks because of the fine filigree of bark that underlies the surface bark. The most common species is the evergreen *H. populnea*. When young it is a very upright tree, but as it ages it becomes more round-headed and reaches 12 m x 4 m (3). It has 75-125 mm long, quite heavily veined, pointed, elliptical leaves with serrated edges and is hardy to -10°C. 'Variegata' is a form with leaves that have a large central yellow blotch, 'Alba Variegata' has a broad white margin to the leaves, 'Osbornei' has a purple reverse to the leaf and flowers with purple stamens, and 'Purpurea' has leaves with deep purple undersides. All of the varieties produce massed small clusters of 2 cm diameter white flowers in late summer and early

autumn. Other evergreen species grown include *H. sexstylosa*, which is very similar to *H. populnea*, and *H. angustifolia*, a 6 m high species that has very narrow leaves and small flowers. The two deciduous species, *H. lyallii* and *H. glabrata*, are similar to one another. *H. lyallii* grows to about 7 m while *H. glabrata* is a little taller at 9 m. The leaves are similar to those of *H. populnea* but are covered in fine hairs. *H. glabrata* has somewhat glaucous leaves. Both species flower in summer and are hardy to at least -15°C. All species grow best in a moist, humus-enriched, well-drained soil in sun or light shade. They may be raised from seed sown at 18°C, but the selected forms must be propagated vegetatively.

HYMENOSPORUM

The Australian frangipani (*H. flavum*) is more closely related to *Pittosporum* than the true frangipani (*Plumeria rubra*). It is an evergreen spreading tree that grows to 8 m x 5 m (3). It has 125 mm long, glossy, deep green, pointed, elliptical leaves that tend to be clustered at the ends of the branches. The terminal clusters of deep yellow, flared trumpet to stellate flowers have a sweet scent. They may occur at any time of the year but are most abundant in spring and early summer. Australian frangipani requires a moist well-drained soil and a position in

full sun or very light shade. Hardy to -6°C. Usually raised from seed sown at 22°C or by semi-ripe cuttings.

ILEX

The common holly (*I. aquifolium*) is widely recognised as a symbol of Christmas.The true species is seldom grown, except as hedging. However, selected forms or hybrids, such as *I. x altaclerensis*, with varying foliage shapes and colours and various berry colours, are planted. Only female plants set fruit, which is an advantage in some cases as the fruit can be messy. If desired, self-fertile plants are available. Sizes vary, but most hollies are large shrubs or small trees (6 m x 4 m (2)) and hardy to -15°C. Several other species are also grown. Some, such as *I. cornuta*, are very similar to *I. aquifolium* but others, such as *I. crenata*, have small, smooth, rounded leaves and are excellent low hedging plants. Plant holly in a moist well-drained soil with full sun to moderate shade. The species may be raised from stratified seed sown at 18°C, but hybrids and selected forms are grown from semi-ripe cuttings.

JACARANDA

Only one species of this genus is widely grown. *J. mimosifolia* is a common spreading tree in milder areas, reaching 12 m x 8 m (3), and is sometimes used as a street tree. It is a semi-evergreen or deciduous tree that is almost totally frost-tender when young, but tolerates -5°C once well established. The very finely divided, fern-like, bipinnate leaves may be up to 300 mm long. Jacaranda is mainly grown for its spectacular clusters of bright purplish-blue trumpet-shaped flowers; these may appear in spring in very mild areas, although summer is the main flowering season. White and pink flowered forms are occasionally available. This tree needs warm temperatures to flower well. Jacaranda does best in a moist well-drained soil in full sun. Usually raised from seed, which should be soaked, and sown at 24°C.

KOELREUTERIA

The golden-rain tree (*K.*

paniculata) is by far the most common species of this genus although the Chinese flame tree (*K. bipinnata*) is also grown. Both are spreading and deciduous and have pinnate leaves that may be as much as 50 cm long. The foliage tends to be among the last to fall in autumn and often turns a bright yellow before dropping. In summer, both species have large terminal heads of yellow flowers that are followed by clusters of papery seed capsules. Those of *K. paniculata* are usually a light brown but the capsules of *K. bipinnata* take on many shades of pink orange and red, hence the name flame tree. *Koelreuteria* will grow to 10 m x 7 m (2.5) in most soils and can withstand high alkalinity, as well as being very heat- and drought-tolerant once established. It is hardy to -15°C. Usually grown from stratified seed, which should be soaked, and sown at 20°C.

LABURNUM

These well-known deciduous spring-flowering trees are now somewhat unpopular because of their untidy appearance after flowering. The true species are rarely seen, most garden specimens are hybrids between *L. alpinum* and *L. anagyroides*. They reach 7 m x 4 m (3) and are very hardy (-30°C). The soft green trifoliate leaves are attractive when young but tend to brown quickly and fall very early. *Laburnum* is commonly known as the golden chain tree because of the long pendulous racemes of yellow sweet pea-like flowers that appear in spring. These flowers are followed by long seed pods, which are best removed as they are untidy and a drain on the plant. They are also full of extremely poisonous seeds. Laburnums are easily grown in almost any moist well-drained soil. As most of the garden forms are hybrids they are usually propagated vegetatively by open-ground hardwood cuttings in winter.

LAGERSTROEMIA

The crepe myrtle (*L. indica*) is a beautiful heavy-flowering small tree 6 m x 4 m (2) that needs consistent summer heat to flower well. Although deciduous,

Koelreuteria paniculata

it is not particularly hardy, being damaged at about -6°C. The simple, glossy, deep-green, oval leaves are about 60 mm long and are usually carried in groups of three. The 150-300 mm long terminal flower clusters, which appear in summer, are composed of many 30 mm wide frilly flowers. There are many colour forms in shades of white, cream, pink, mauve and red; there are also dwarf forms suitable for tub cultivation. Grow in a well-drained soil in full sun and water well in summer. Usually grown from semi-ripe cuttings under mist or by hardwood cutings in winter.

LAGUNARIA

The Queensland hibiscus (L. patersonii) is not a true hibiscus but does belong to the same family. Quick growing when young, this upright evergreen slows considerably after reaching 4 m, eventually attaining 8 m x 3.5 m (2.5). It has mid-green, leathery, oval leaves about 75 mm long with silvery-grey undersides. The 40-50 mm diameter mid-pink mallow-like flowers are followed by five-sectioned seed pods that contain irritant hairs. Remove the pods before they ripen unless you want to collect the seed. Queensland hibiscus is easily grown in most well-drained soils and is a good coastal tree. Hardy to -3°C. It is usually raised from seed sown at 20°C but will also grow from semi-ripe autumn cuttings.

LARIX

The larch (L. decidua) is one of the few deciduous conifers. It has a conical habit and reaches 15 m x 5 m (3). The bright to deep green needles grow in whorls along the stems and in autumn they become a bright yellow before slowly turning brown and falling. The squat cylindrical cones mature quickly and are usually seen fully open. This extremely hardy tree (-35°C) needs a climate with a distinct winter and grows well in high altitude areas. Larches do best in a cool, moist, well-drained soil. The genus includes around a dozen species and several hybrids but only one, the hybrid L. x marschlinsii, is at all common. It is a quick-growing,

somewhat glaucous tree with a profusion of warm brown cones and a slightly weeping, open growth habit. Other species are available from specialist seed suppliers. The species are raised from stratified seed sown at 18°C; selected forms should be grafted.

LAURUS

The evergreen, upright bay laurel (L. nobilis) does double duty as a classic culinary herb and a first-rate garden specimen. It is not the only species of the genus but is by far the most common. While ultimately a large tree (7 m x 3.5 m (2)), it is able to be comfortably kept to 5 m x 2 m by regular trimming. The deep-pointed oval leaves are up to 100 mm long with wavy edges. They are, of course, very aromatic when crushed. The small yellow flowers, which appear in mid-spring, are relatively insignificant and are followed by small blackish berries. However, this is primarily a foliage tree and often used as a tub or topiary specimen. It may also be used for hedging. Laurel performs best in a moist well-drained soil but will withstand drought. Hardy to -10°C. It is usually propagated by semi-ripe cuttings in late summer or autumn cuttings.

LIBOCEDRUS

This genus includes two New Zealand conifers. They are not widely grown in gardens but are quite frequently planted in parks and reserves. The best known is L. bidwillii, which is a columnar subalpine tree with light green cupressoid foliage carried in fern-like sprays or plumes. L. plumosa is a similar but larger species with larger foliage sprays. Both reach about 8 m x 2.5 m (1.8) and are hardy to -12°C. The New Zealand cedars prefer a cool moist soil and semi-shade when young. They may be raised from seed sown at 18°C or by semi-ripe cuttings in early autumn cuttings.

LIQUIDAMBAR

L. styraciflua is among the most spectacular of all autumn-foliage trees. It reaches 12 m x 4 m (2.5) and has an upright habit. It could easily be mistaken for a

Magnolia grandiflora

maple as the leaves have the typical maple leaf shape. In autumn they develop magnificent yellow, orange, red and purple tones before falling. In mild areas it may be almost evergreen. However, variegated and other coloured-leaved forms are available. Liquidambars also have very distinctive corky bark. The flowers are insignificant but the fruit that follows in autumn is conspicuous if not particularly attractive. Grow in a sunny position with a moist well-drained soil. Hardy to -25°C. Forms selected for superior foliage colour are grown from hardwood cuttings in winter, grafted or budded, however most seedlings will colour well. Other species grown include L. formosana, which generally does not colour as well in autumn, and L. orientalis, which is a smaller tree with smaller leaves.

LIRIODENDRON

The spreading deciduous tulip tree (L. tulipifera) belongs to a genus of two species that is closely related to Magnolia. It is very hardy at -30°C and eventually grows to 12 m x 8 m (1.8). The leaves are an unusual shape, deeply lobed with a notch where the leaf tip would normally be. They are about 125-150 mm long and light green turning to bright yellow in autumn. There is a variegated form with a broad cream margin called 'Aureo Marginatum'. The tulip-like, yellowish-green, orange-based flowers appear in late spring. Viewed off the tree they are attractive but are usually so far up in the branches they

are all but invisible. The tulip tree is easily grown in any moist well-drained soil. Selected forms, such as the columnar 'Arnold', are budded or grafted. Seed, which should be stratified and sown at 20°C, is not popular as seedlings do not flower reliably until they are at least 10 years old, while vegetatively propagated plants flower at 3-4 years old.

MAGNOLIA

This genus includes deciduous, semi-deciduous and evergreen trees and shrubs generally with spreading habits. Most of the deciduous species have the large cup-shaped flowers typified by the best-known forms M. x soulangiana. They have simple, leathery, oval leaves that may be up to 200 mm long or larger in the case of M. macrophylla, which has 300-600 mm long leaves. Those of the evergreen M. grandiflora are a glossy olive-green on top with rust-coloured felting below. Forms such as 'Ferruginea' have very heavy indumentum. Some of the smaller species, such as M. stellata, are large shrubs but many magnolias become substantial trees (12 m x 8 m (2.5)). M. campbellii may grow to 20 m x 12 m. It is also one of the earliest to flower, usually starting in mid to late August. Except for the unusual yellow-flowered M. acuminata and its hybrids, there is not a wide range of flower colours, only white, pink, mauve and purple shades. However, the flowers are often very large. Those of the New Zealand hybrid 'Mark Jury'

Malus 'Oporto'

Malus 'Floribunda'

are up to 200 mm across and those of *M. macrophylla* may be up to 300 mm in diameter. Of course, flowers that size need protection from the elements and may not be practical for many gardens. The flowers of most species appear in spring and early summer but *M. grandiflora* is less seasonal in its flowering and may even have a few flowers in winter in very mild areas. A few species, such as *M. tripetala*, have reasonably attractive seed heads. Some magnolia flowers are perfumed, which can vary from a slight scent to a very heavy fragrance. The most common scented magnolias are *M. grandiflora*, *M. denudata* (syn. *M. heptapeta*) and *M. sieboldii*.

Plant magnolias in a moist, humus-enriched well-drained soil in full sun or very light shade. They are hardy to -20°C. By careful pruning to shape when young, it is possible to produce a wide-spreading shrub-like growth, or a single-trunked tree as desired. The species may be raised from seed but they will not bloom for several years. The exact length of time varies with the species; *M.* x *loebneri* will flower in three years from seed but *M. campbellii* may take 20 years. Hybrids and selected forms are grown by budding, grafting or cuttings taken in summer and autumn.

MALUS

Crab apples are attractive, flat-topped, heavy-flowering small to medium-sized deciduous trees – 7 m x 7 m (2). However, they are perhaps too wide spreading and untidy, in terms of leaf and fruit drop, for small gardens. The leaves are elliptical, about 75 mm long, and virtually identical to the common fruiting apples and subject to the same diseases, such as leaf curl, mildew, etc. In spring the trees are covered with blossom. The flowers are followed by the conspicuous small apples that remain well into winter. Many species and hybrid forms are grown overseas but relatively few are available here. There is a good range of flower colours but most have red fruit. Among the best are the ever-popular 'Jack Humm', which has long-lasting bright red fruit, *M. ioensis* 'Plena', which has large, semi-double, pink and white blooms, and 'Oporto', which has deep pinkish-crimson flowers and purple foliage. Grow crab apples in a moist well-drained soil in full sun. They are hardy to -30°C. The species may be raised from stratified seed sown at 18°C, but hybrids are usually grafted.

MAYTENUS

The Chilean mayten (*M. boaria*) is an attractive evergreen tree that resembles a small weeping willow. When mature it is a handsome broad-headed tree, approximately 8 m x 6 m (2.5), with drooping branches that are densely clothed in small, bright green, finely toothed, lanceolate leaves. When young it is more upright and narrow. The flowers and fruit are insignificant. It is easily grown in most well-drained soils and may be raised from seed sown at 18°C. However, it is usually grown from semi-ripe cuttings in summer and autumn. Maytens can self-sow and may become invasive in untended areas, but they are not difficult to control. Hardy to -15°C.

MELALEUCA

This Australian genus includes about 140 species of evergreen shrubs and trees. Most have tiny, often appressed, needle-like or elliptical leaves. The flowers are similar to those of the closely related bottlebrush (*Callistemon* spp.) but are usually smaller. They are often followed by woody seed capsules that surround the stem in the same way that those of *Callistemon* do. There are species in almost every flower colour, but cream, yellow, pinkish-mauve and red predominate. Generally reaching 8 m x 5 m (2) and of a weeping habit, many species benefit from regular pruning to shape, but others look better thinned to expose their branch structure. Most are extremely adaptable, withstanding drought, alkalinity, high salt content, low fertility, and occasional waterlogging. They also tolerate coastal conditions, but relatively few are hardy below -6°C. Best grown in a light, yet moist, well-drained soil in full sun. Melaleucas are usually raised from seed sown at around 20°C, but they are also easily propagated by semi-ripe tip cuttings in summer and autumn.

MELIA

The bead tree (*M. azedarach*) is deciduous with a weeping habit and grows to 8 m x 4 m (2). It has finely cut, luxuriant, deep green, bipinnate leaves that may be up to 600 mm long. In early summer it develops terminal panicles of fragrant lilac flowers. The fruit that follows is a hard 12 mm diameter yellow berry. If left untouched by birds, they will remain on the tree after the leaves have fallen. The foliage develops little autumn colour. It is a hardy tree (-10°C), but it requires shelter from the wind to protect the large leaves from damage. Plant it in any well-drained soil. It is usually raised from seed sown at 20°C, and established plants may self-sow.

METASEQUOIA

The dawn redwood (*M. glyptostroboides*), rediscovered in China in 1945 after being thought extinct, is the sole surviving species of a very ancient genus that once dominated the world's forests. It is a columnar conifer 15 m x 6 m (2.5) with fine, light green,

75 mm long, pinnate leaves composed of narrow straight-sided leaflets. Although the foliage reddens in autumn before falling, it does not develop the intense colour of the swamp cypress (*Taxodium distichum*), which it superficially resembles. Grown for its bright green new growth, rugged red bark and graceful growth habit, this is a tree for large gardens. It is hardy to -20°C. Dawn redwood is usually raised from stratified seed sown at 20°C, but can also be grown from semi-ripe summer cuttings.

MERYTA

The foliage of the evergreen puka or pukanui (*Meryta sinclairii*) is among the most spectacular of any of our native plants. It has large, deep green, leathery, oval leaves, that may be up to 350 mm long, on a tree 6 m x 3.5 m (2). A cream variegated form is occasionally available. The panicles of greenish-white spring and early summer flowers and the blackish fruit that follows are conspicuous but not particularly attractive. However, this is primarily a foliage tree. Very frost-tender when young, it can withstand light frosts once established (-2°C). In colder areas it makes a good houseplant. Outdoors, plant it in a moist, humus-enriched, well-drained soil in light to moderate shade. It will grow in full sun but the foliage tends to look bleached. It is usually raised from seed sown at 20°C, but the variegated form must be grown from semi-ripe cuttings in summer or autumn.

METROSIDEROS

The pohutukawa (*M. excelsa*) is the best-known member of this South Pacific genus of evergreen trees, shrubs and vines. It reaches 8 m x 8 m (2) and from mid November it becomes a very conspicuous feature of many of our coastal gardens as its clusters of intense deep red, filamentous flowers begin to open. The rounded leaves are a glossy mid-green on young plants, but mature trees have deep green leathery leaves with white indumentum. Old trees often develop aerial roots on the trunk and branches. Various flower colours and leaf forms are available. Except for being frost-tender (-3°C), especially when young, this is an easily grown tree. It tolerates most soils and is well suited to coastal conditions. Several other species are also grown. Those from the Kermadec Islands, Tahiti and other Pacific islands tend to be too frost-tender to be grown outdoors in many areas but they are very effective tub plants for frost-free conservatories. The southern rata (*M. umbellata*) and the northern rata (*M. robusta*) are far tougher plants and have similar flowers to the pohutukawa, but they seldom do well in gardens. Both species are hardy to at least -10°C so they are worth trying in areas too cold to grow *M. excelsa*. They grow very slowly and may take many years to flower from seed. All *Metrosideros* species grow well from seed sown at around 20°C. However, selected forms must be propagated vegetatively, usually by semi-ripe cuttings in summer or autumn, or by removing pieces with aerial roots from mature plants.

MICHELIA

This genus of upright evergreens is closely related to *Magnolia* and the two common species, *M. doltsopa* and *M. figo*, could easily be mistaken for small-flowered magnolias. Both have mid-green, leathery, oval leaves about 100-150 mm long. *M. doltsopa* is the larger of the two species, sometimes reaching 10 m high and 3 m in width, while *M. figo* rarely exceeds 5 m. Both species flower in spring. *M. figo* is known as the port wine magnolia because of the fruity scent of its cream, purple-flushed, 75 mm diameter cup-shaped flowers. *M. doltsopa* has larger (125-175 mm diameter) but similarly shaped creamy white flowers that have a delicate scent. Several hybrid forms have become available in recent years. Grow in a moist, humus-enriched, well-drained soil in sun or light shade. Frost protection may be necessary for young plants, but once established both are hardy to -8°C. The species may be raised from seed sown at 20°C or by semi-ripe cuttings. Hybrids must be propagated vegetatively.

Melaleuca armillaris

Specialist seed suppliers sometimes stock less common species.

NOTHOFAGUS

Because of their large ultimate size (15 m x 8 m (2) plus) southern beeches are seldom grown in domestic gardens, but they are sometimes seen in large parks and reserves. The genus includes about 20 species of evergreen and deciduous trees native to the temperate regions of South America (primarily Chile), Australia and New Zealand. Most of the plants seen locally are New Zealand natives. The three main species, of which all are evergreen, are red beech (*N. fusca*), silver beech (*N. menziesii*) and black beech (*N. solandri*). The fourth native species, *N. truncata*, is very similar to *N. fusca*. All develop into large trees with rounded canopies, although they may be rather columnar when young. Most have small rounded leaves with serrated edges, but *N. solandri* has tiny smooth-edged leaves. *N. fusca* is probably the best choice as a garden specimen because of its bronze foliage tones. All species are subject to attacks by scale insects and aphids, which lead to sooty mould. Grow them in a cool moist soil. They are hardy to -15°C and are usually raised from seed sown at around 15°C, but selected forms can be propagated from semi-ripe tip cuttings taken in late summer and autumn. The Australian beeches are rarely grown, but in recent years there has been some interest in the Chilean species.

NYSSA

The spreading deciduous tupelo

Metrosideros excelsa 'Variegata'

Metrosideros umbellata

Picea pungens

Podocarpus totara 'Aurea'

PHEBALIUM

Although this genus of evergreen shrubs and trees includes a New Zealand native, *P. nudum*, the species commonly grown in gardens, *P. squameum*, is Australian. It is a columnar tree that grows to 5 m x 1.5 m (2.5) and is hardy to -8°C. The 75 mm long narrow leaves are deep green on the upper surfaces and light green to silvery-grey underneath. The yellow and green variegated form known as 'Illumination' is very popular. The small, starry, cream flowers, which appear in early summer, are conspicuous but not particularly showy. *Phebalium* is most commonly grown as a hedging or screening plant because its very narrow upright habit reduces the need for trimming. It is easily grown in most light, well-drained, slightly acid soils in full sun. It is usually grown from semi-ripe tip cuttings, which may be taken throughout the year.

PHYLLOCLADUS

A Pacific genus of conifers with three New Zealand species: *P. aspleniifolius* var. *alpinus*, *P. glaucus* and *P. trichomanoides*. They are commonly known as celery pines because the cladophylls are crowded at the tip of the branches, much like the leaves at the top of a celery stalk. Alternatively they are known by the name toa toa. Approximately 8 m x 3 m (1.8), they have stiff branches with terminal whorls of cladophylls that resemble oak leaves. *P. aspleniifolious* var. *alpinus* and *P. trichomanoides* have light olive-green foliage, while the new foliage of *P. glaucus* is a stunning bluish-green, which turns to olive as the foliage matures. All are hardy to -15°C and should be planted in a moist well-drained soil. Usually raised from seed sown at 18°C but will grow from semi-ripe tip cuttings in autumn.

PICEA

Spruce is a genus of about 30 species of trees and shrubs. This conifer is the model for the traditional Christmas tree: upright and pyramidal with symmetrical horizontal branches clothed in short needles

---

(*N. sylvatica*) is grown primarily for its magnificent autumn colours and its ability to grow in very poorly drained conditions that would kill many other plants. It will reach 12 m x 6 m (1.8) and has a twisted and contorted stem and branch structure that is clothed from spring to autumn in simple, slightly glossy, rhomboidal, mid-green, 100 mm long leaves. In autumn the foliage develops intense fiery orange, red and yellow tones before falling. The spring flowers are inconspicuous but are followed in late summer and autumn by small, blackish, olive-like fruits. It is hardy to -25°C and easily grown in most soils. Usually raised from stratified seed sown at 20°C. *N. aquatica* is a similar species that tolerates very wet conditions and will even grow in a few centimetres of water.

OLEA

The olive (*O. europaea*) is one of the world's most important commercial crops, while at the same time being a beautiful flat-topped evergreen specimen reaching 8 m x 10 m (2). Old trees, and they can live to a great age, develop twisted and contorted branches of magnificent character. The 75 mm long narrow leaves are deep green and leathery with silvery-grey undersides that are often seen to great effect as the branches droop when wet with rain. The small panicles of tiny white flowers that appear in late spring are insignificant, but they are, of course, followed by the bright green fruit, which turns black late in the season just before dropping.

Olives are beautiful trees but they do create a litter problem. Fallen leaves and fruit can range from a nuisance to a constant chore. For this reason, they are best located away from paths and driveways. In recent years much work has gone into selecting superior fruiting strains and even non-fruiting forms are sometimes available. Hardy to -12°C, plant them in a light, yet moist, well-drained soil. They may be raised from seed sown at 20°C, but most plants are grown from semi-ripe cuttings in summer and autumn.

PAULOWNIA

This is a Chinese genus of about half a dozen very quick-growing deciduous trees. *P. tomentosa* is the species generally grown as a garden specimen (12 m x 8 m (4)). It is probably the hardiest of the genus, tolerating temperatures down to -15°C or even lower if protected when young. It is a strongly branched tree with large (up to 300 mm long) leaves that are heart-shaped, tapering to a point at the tip, deep green on the upper surfaces and light green underneath with some felting. As it is impossible to keep a tree of this size out of the wind, it is inevitable that the foliage will suffer some damage. The flowers open in spring from furry brown buds that are carried right through winter and late frosts may damage the developing buds. The flowers are spectacular purplish-blue trumpets. They are followed by rounded seed capsules that hang on well into winter. Trees often carry the seed capsules and the following season's buds at the same time. Plant in a moist, well-drained soil. Usually raised from stratified seed sown at 22°C.

arranged radially along the branches. The commonly grown *P. abies*, *P. glauca* and *P. pungens* match this image quite closely, but there are many hybrids and cultivated forms. These range from minute rockery dwarfs to 30 m high trees. The best known tree-sized *Picea* cultivars are the blue forms of *P. pungens*, the best known of which is 'Kosteri'. It is beautiful steel-blue and perfectly symmetrical when grown well, although few perfect specimens exist and most eventually suffer some damage that spoils the shape. Spruces prefer a cool, moist, well-drained soil with ample summer moisture. They are hardy to -25°C and the species may be raised from stratified seed sown at 18°C, but the selected forms must be propagated vegetatively. Most are grown from semi-ripe cuttings in summer and autumn, although the best forms of blue spruce are usually grafted.

PINUS

Perhaps because *Pinus radiata* covers vast areas of the countryside and is one of New Zealand's main products, pines are nowadays seldom considered for their ornamental merit. Nevertheless, greater use could be made of these trees, especially the smaller species (12 m x 5 m (3)). Pines vary widely in the size and arrangement of their needles and the size of their cones. Some, such as *P. coulteri*, have large cones, whereas those of other species such as *P. mugo*, are quite insignificant. Pines also vary in their growing requirements; some are very cold hardy and extremely drought tolerant, but others are frost-tender or demand regular moisture. There are not many selected forms of *Pinus* except for the very small cultivars of *P. mugo* and a few glaucous and golden-foliaged forms. The species most likely to be seen in domestic gardens is the Mexican weeping pine (*P. patula*). It has very long drooping needles that are bright grass-green when young. It is only hardy to about -10°C, making it one of the more frost-tender pines. *P. wallichiana* has a similar appearance when young and is hardier, however it will become a very large tree. The Italian stone pine (*P. pinea*) is an

attractive round-headed tree that remains compact for many years. Most pines will grow in any well-drained soil. Garden pines are generally grown from seed, which should be sown at about 18°C. Selected forms are either grown from semi-ripe cuttings in autumn or grafted.

PLAGIANTHUS

The ribbonwood (*P. regius*), so called because of its tough stringy bark, is one of the few native deciduous trees and the only species of its genus in general cultivation. It ultimately becomes a large tree but remains bushy for many years at about 8 m x 5 m (2.5). The foliage of young trees is small and round, whereas the foliage of adult trees is bronze-green, lanceolate and about 60 mm long with serrated edges. The small creamy flowers appear from late spring and are carried in panicles about 200 mm long. Ribbonwood will grow in any moist well-drained soil and is hardy to -15°C. It is usually raised from seed sown at 18°C or by semi-ripe cuttings in autumn.

PLATANUS

The London plane tree (*P. x acerifolia*, syn. *P. hybrida*) is a spreading deciduous tree often seen in large parks, especially those in cities, as it is very tolerant of air pollution. It is not considered to be a natural species but a hybrid between *P. orientalis* and the American sycamore (*P. occidentalis*). Although the London plane is far more widely grown, the Arizona sycamore (*P. wrightii*) is often considered to be superior because of its neat shape and bright white bark. All are large deciduous trees (15 m x 12 m (2.5)) with three to five lobed, roughly maple-shaped, palmate leaves that may be up to 250 mm across. All species have peeling bark that often develops interesting patterns. They are hardy to -25°C and easily grown in any well-drained soil and may be propagated by stratified seed sown at 18°C or by open-ground hardwood cuttings in winter.

PODOCARPUS

The totara (*P. totara*) is one of

the few native conifers to be widely grown in domestic gardens. At over 20 m high and very solidly built, the species is far too large for anything but parks and reserves, but it has popular smaller and slow growing forms, such as the golden-foliaged 'Aurea'. It has small, needle-like, bright golden-yellow leaves and deeply fissured reddish-brown bark. *P. hallii* is similar to *P. totara* but tends to grow at higher altitudes in the wild and is slightly smaller. Other species, not necessarily native, are also cultivated. Of these, *P. macrophyllus* from China and Japan is the most distinctive. It has deep green, 150 mm long, strap-like leaves and grows slowly to about 9 m high. The form 'Maki' has the largest and best-coloured foliage. Most species have conspicuous red berry-like fruit with a single seed. This often leads to them being confused with yews (*Taxus*), which have similar fruit. Podocarps prefer a cool, moist, well-drained soil with ample humus and are generally hardy to -15°C. The species may be raised from seed sown at 20°C, but the selected forms are usually grown from semi-ripe summer and autumn tip cuttings or, very rarely, grafted.

POPULUS

Poplars are generally too large for domestic gardens but they are a feature of shelter belts in country areas. The common columnar Lombardy poplar (*P. nigra* 'Italica') at 15 m x 4 m (3) is the variety most widely grown. Its bright green leaves are

somewhat heart-shaped and turn bright yellow before falling. The flowers and fruit are insignificant. The other common species, white poplar (*P. alba*) is something of a weed unless grafted onto non-suckering stock. It has too many bad points to be recommended, so it might be better to opt for *P. x canescens*, which is similar but less aggressive. However, it is not as widely available. Poplars are easily grown in most soils and are hardy to -25°C, but the poplar rust fungus can be a serious problem with some species. Species and non-suckering forms are generally raised from open-ground hardwood cuttings in winter, while selected suckering forms are usually grafted onto *P. yunnanensis* stock. All poplars have strong aggressive roots so don't plant them where they might cause damage to paths, drives, sewerage or other pipes.

PRUNUS

The ornamental *Prunus* – flowering cherries, apricots, plums, peaches and almonds – are among the most common ornamental deciduous trees. Several species and many hybrids are grown and they range in size from the very dwarf almonds, such as the *P. glandulosa* forms, which are suitable for small gardens and containers, through to large spreading trees, such as *P. sargentii*, which may grow to 18 m x 12 m. Always heavy flowering, they vary in flower colour, size, style and season and growth habit.

Plagianthus regius

Clockwise from top left: *Prunus* 'Ko Fugen', *Prunus* 'Ukon', *Prunus gladulosa* form, *Prunus* 'Shidare Sakura'

Among the most popular are the weeping and horizontal standards. These are genetically low, spreading plants that have been grafted onto upright standards from 1-2.5 m high. The standard trunk doesn't grow any higher than the point at which it is grafted but the branches arch up and spread out to make a substantial plant. Flower colours are mainly white and various shades of pink. There are also a few very deep pink, bordering on red, cultivars and some with orange tints. The flowers may be single, semi-double or fully double; often a double-flowered form will also carry some single flowers. Many of the ornamental forms are sterile and do not bear fruit, but some develop small, usually inedible, fruit after flowering. The trees are generally very frost hardy (-15°C), but some of the very early flowering forms, such as *P. subhirtella* 'Autumnalis', may suffer flower or bud damage from hard frosts.

This genus is easily grown, although subject to several pests and diseases, the worst of which is silver leaf, a disease that seriously debilitates plants and may eventually kill them. See the section on fruit trees for details on the identification and control of *Prunus* pests and diseases. Plant them in a moist well-drained soil. As most plants are hybrids or selected forms they are generally budded or grafted. The species may be raised from stratified seed sown at 18°C.

PYRUS

Pears are seldom grown as ornamentals but one non-fruiting species, the weeping silver pear (*P. salicifolia* 'Pendula'), and one inedible species (*P. calleryana*) are grown for the beauty of their foliage. The silver pear is an upright deciduous tree that grows to 8 m but the weeping-foliaged form 'Pendula' is grafted on a standard stem or trained to produce a small weeping tree. It has 75-100 mm long, narrow, willow-like leaves that are covered in soft silvery hairs. In spring, small white flowers appear.

P. calleryana also has white flowers, usually very early in spring. They are followed by small inedible fruits. This tree, which grows to about 9 m x 5 m, is grown for its autumn foliage display. It has 75 mm long, glossy, dark, oval leaves with wavy edges. In autumn the foliage develops fiery orange and red tones. Both species are easily grown in well-drained soils, but they are inclined to be damaged by wind when young and are best staked. They are hardy to -20°C. The species may be raised from stratified seed sown at 18°C but 'Pendula' and other selected forms must be propagated vegetatively, usually by grafting. Specialist seed suppliers offer other species, such as *P. ussuriensis*, which also colours well in autumn and has small, yellow, inedible fruit.

QUERCUS

The oaks are a large genus of about 500 species of evergreen and deciduous trees spread over much of the temperate northern hemisphere. The cork oak (*Q. suber*) is an evergreen species that is the source of cork and thus a valuable commercial tree, but most species are grown as ornamentals. The common English oak (*Q. robur*) is a large deciduous tree (20 m x 10 (2.5)) with dark green deeply lobed, 100 mm long leaves that tend to stay on the tree after they brown off in autumn. It usually sets large crops of rounded acorns. Scarlet oak (*Q. coccinea*) is another large deciduous species. It is widely planted for its vivid red autumn foliage colour. Many other deciduous species are grown but few of the potentially very useful American evergreen species are readily available. Specialist suppliers sometimes stock seed of the canyon live oak (*Q. chrysolepis*) and the holly-leaved *Q. wislizenii*, which are well worth trying. Most species are hardy to at least -15°C, often lower. They are generally easily grown in any well-drained soil and usually raised from stratified seed (acorns) sown at around 20°C.

RHUS

The sumach or wax tree (*R. succedeana*, recently renamed *Toxicodendron*) is a low flat-topped tree that has some of the most vividly coloured autumn foliage of any deciduous tree. It is often seen as a large multi-trunked shrub but it is best trained to one or two main stems by pruning to shape when young. It can reach 8 m x 8 m (2.5) and is hardy to -25°C. The leaves are pinnate, about 40-50 cm long, and composed of 15-30 leaflets. The new spring growth is covered with a fine hair that can cause a contact dermatitis. In summer the leaves are deep green, but in autumn they change to orange then intense red and purplish-crimson shades. The small spring flowers develop into large, reddish, cone-shaped seed heads that are very waxy. They can supposedly be used as candles simply by threading a wick through them. The plant suckers very freely and can become invasive and difficult to remove once established.

R. typhina is a very similar species. Both are easily grown in any moist well-drained soil. Plant in full sun to get the best autumn foliage colours. They are usually grown from root cuttings or suckers but may be raised from stratified seed sown at 18°C. Specialist suppliers often stock seed of less common species, such as the evergreen and drought-tolerant *R. lancea*.

ROBINIA

R. pseudoacacia 'Frisia' (10 m x 6 (2.5)) is the most commonly planted member of this deciduous genus of spreading trees and has become enormously popular over the last decade. It has bright golden-yellow, 200 mm long, pinnate leaves composed of about 14 rounded leaflets. The white flower clusters are not insignificant but are seldom seen on this form. In common with most *Robinia* species, it has vicious thorns that are seldom seen until you have to extract them from your flesh. The green-leaved typical form of *R. pseudoacacia* has regular early summer crops of fragrant white flowers followed by bean-like seed pods. A selected form of another species, *R. hispida*, has recently been promoted as the pink wisteria tree. It has long racemes of pink flowers and grows to about 4 m. Many interesting small forms of *Robinia*, such as 'Mop Top' and 'Lace Lady', are now widely grown and make excellent tub specimens. All are easily grown in a well-drained soil but have brittle branches that are easily damaged by wind, so stake them well when young. They are hardy to -25°C. The species may be raised from stratified and soaked seed sown at 18°C; selected forms and hybrids are usually budded or grafted.

SALIX

Willows are very attractive but they need room to grow as they reach at least 10 m x 8 m (3). This deciduous genus includes about 300 species of trees and shrubs, the most widely cultivated of which is *S. matsudana*, commonly seen used as a quick-growing shelterbelt. The shelter forms are not grown as ornamentals but the tortured or corkscrew willow (*S. matsudana* 'Tortuosa') is an interesting cultivar. It has twisted and contorted branches that are, of course, most obvious in the winter when the tree is leafless. The weeping willow (*S. babylonica*) is a feature of many parks and gardens. It is a graceful tree with long weeping branches covered in bright green foliage, but has high water demands and a strong fibrous root system. The common pussy willow (*S. caprea*) is generally seen growing wild along riverbanks. Its fluffy catkins are attractive in early spring but its untidy growth and invasive habits rule it out for all but the largest gardens.
The tree-sized willows will all grow to at least 8 m but there are some small species. *S.*

purpurea is the best known of these. In its darkest forms the catkins are an intense reddish purple. The leaves are glaucous, often with a hint of purple on the reverse. It grows to about 5 m x 3 m. Willows will grow in any soil that never entirely dries out and are hardy to -25°C. They are usually raised from open-ground hardwood cuttings in winter.

SCHEFFLERA

There are two common species: Queensland umbrella tree (*S. actinophylla*), which is often grown as a houseplant, and the New Zealand native *S. digitata*, often seen in the wild. Both species are spreading in habit and reach approximately 7 m x 4 m (2.5). They have deep green digitate leaves composed of around 5-12 leaflets. The leaves of *S. actinophylla* are very large, with leaflets up to 300 mm long. The leaflets of *S. digitata* rarely exceed 200 mm long and are dull dark green, in contrast to the glossy bronze-green of *S. actinophylla*. Neither is very hardy, but *S. digitata* will withstand -3°C once established. *S. actinophylla* is unlikely to survive -2°C without damage. The greenish-yellow, becoming red, flowers appear in spring. They are not particularly attractive but are carried in large conspicuous panicles. The flowers are followed by reddish-brown berries. They grow best in a moist humus-enriched soil in full sun or light shade. Propagate by seed sown at 20°C or by semi-ripe cuttings, which may be taken whenever the new growth is reasonably firm.

SCHINUS

Two species of this evergreen genus are commonly cultivated. Both are South American natives and both are known as the pepper tree. *S. molle* var. *ariera* (syn. *S. ariera*) is a graceful, weeping, spreading tree from Peru that grows to 10 m x 8 m (2.5). It has bright green, finely divided, pinnate leaves and very deeply fissured corky bark. The drooping panicles of tiny cream flowers that appear in summer are not a major feature but they are followed by small green berries that redden as they ripen.

These add interest to the tree in winter. Easily grown and hardy to -6°C, it may even be slightly invasive in some areas.
S. terebinthifolius is a Brazilian species commonly called the Brazilian pepper tree. It has larger bronze-green leaves composed of fewer leaflets than *S. molle*. Its fruit is also slightly larger, but at 8 m x 6 m it is ultimately a smaller tree. Both species are reasonably hardy if protected from frost when young. These trees tolerate most soils but require good drainage. They may be raised from seed sown at 22°C or by semi-ripe cuttings in summer and autumn.

SEQUOIADENDRON

The giant sequoia or big tree (*S. giganteum*) is usually regarded as the world's largest tree. It may grow to 115 m high with a trunk up to 10 m in diameter. It is a very straight conical tree with deep green, slightly prickly, cupressoid foliage. It has a stoutly buttressed trunk with deeply fissured reddish-brown bark. Obviously, it is far too large for most gardens, but there is a very slow-growing narrow form called 'Pendulum' (only 2.5 m after 5 years) which has weeping branches and is useful for adding height with very little width. This makes an interesting specimen but it requires careful staking and training to do well. It prefers to grow in a cool, moist, well-drained soil, although it is drought tolerant when established. It is hardy to -20°C. As a selected form, 'Pendulum' must be propagated from semi-ripe cuttings taken in late summer or autumn.

SOPHORA

A widespread genus of evergreen and deciduous trees and shrubs. Most common in New Zealand gardens are the native species collectively known as kowhai. The three native species are the North Island kowhai (*S. tetraptera*), the South Island kowhai (*S. microphylla*), which both reach approximately 8 m x 5 (2.5), and *S. prostrata*, which is usually a densely foliaged shrub about 2 m x 1.8 m. The two tree-sized species have a weeping habit and are evergreen for most of the year but often

Robinia pseudoacacia 'Frisia'

drop most or all of their leaves as flowering begins in late winter or early spring. Both have pinnate leaves and yellow flowers that are very attractive to nectar-feeding birds. However, they differ in leaf size and flower colour and size. The leaves of *S. tetraptera* are olive green and can be quite stiff and leathery, which tends to make the leaves curl slightly, and are composed of large leaflets. This species has pendulous clusters of large bright yellow flowers. *S. microphylla* has very small, deep green leaflets and smaller flowers, but there are more blooms per cluster and they tend to be a golden, rather than bright, yellow. The flowers of both species are followed by brown, bean-like seed pods. Kowhai is best grown in a moist well-drained soil in full sun and is hardy to -10°C. The species are usually raised from soaked seed sown at 18°C.
Several exotic species are also grown, of which *S. japonica* is the most common. It is a deciduous species with 200 mm long, light green, pinnate leaves and cream, or occasionally pale pink, flowers in 200-300 mm long terminal panicles. It may grow to 15 m x 12 m but is often grafted onto 2 m standards to produce a small weeping tree. It is hardy to at least -25°C. *S. secundiflora* is a rare North American species with fragrant lavender-blue flowers. It is evergreen, hardy to -6°C and grows to 8 m high.

Tamarix parviflora

Schinus molle

SORBUS

The bright orange berries of the deciduous mountain ash or rowan (*S. aucuparia*) are a common sight in autumn and make it the most widely recognised member of this northern hemisphere genus. Most species have pinnate leaves and terminal clusters of small creamy-white flowers in spring. The flowers, which are often rather unpleasantly scented, are followed by showy berries, the colour of which varies with the species. Mountain ash has orange berries, *S. americana* has white berries, while those of *S. hupehensis* are white tinted pink. These trees grow to 8 m x 3.5 (2.5). The smaller-growing (up to 4 m x 1.8 m) *S. vilmorinii* is available in pink, yellow or red-berried forms. Some species, most notably *S. discolor*, have attractive autumn foliage but most show little autumn coloration.

Rowans are hardy to -25°C and easily grown in any well-drained soil. They are most at home in areas with distinct winters. The species may be raised from stratified seed sown at 15°C, but the selected forms are usually layered or grafted.

STYRAX

These small (7 m x 4 m (2)) deciduous trees have a neat growth habit and an attractive spring floral display. The most common species, *S. japonicum*, grows to about 7 m and has deep green, pointed, heart-shaped leaves and slightly drooping racemes of small, bell-shaped, white flowers. *S. obassia* is a similar but taller species (to 10 m high) that has fragrant flowers. Both prefer a cool, moist, well-drained soil and cool, moist summer conditions. They are hardy to -20°C. They blend well with rhododendrons, camellias and fuchsias. They are usually raised from stratified seed sown at 18°C but may also be grown from hardwood cuttings in winter and semi-ripe cuttings in late summer or autumn.

TAMARIX

This genus includes about 80 species of shrubs and trees, most of which are deciduous. Many are untidy rangy growers, but among the rest are some of the best flowering trees for coastal conditions. They are small trees at 6 m x 3 m (2.5) and hardy to -20°C. Tamarisks have tiny appressed leaves that are reminiscent of heather (*Calluna*) and carried on slender branches and wiry twigs. *T. aphylla* has silvery-grey leaves and is primarily grown as a foliage plant. In late spring and early summer, depending on the species, plumes of minute pink flowers develop at the ends of the branches. *T. chinensis* is usually regarded as the best flowering species. Tamarisks prefer a light well-drained soil in full sun. They are able to tolerate the full blast of coastal salt winds but are neater and heavier flowering if cared for with regular water and occasional trimming. They may be raised from seed sown at 18°C but are usually propagated by open-ground hardwood cuttings in winter.

TAXODIUM

The swamp cypress (*T. distichum*) is the best known species of this ancient genus of deciduous conifers. It is an attractive large conical tree (15 m x 6 m (3)) that is well known for its ability to grow in as much as 80 cm of water. It develops special breathing roots that emerge from the water's surface some distance from the main trunk. These 'knees' are a prominent feature. However, the tree is mainly grown for its graceful light structure, rugged bark and beautiful rusty red autumn foliage colour. The fine pinnate leaves develop the colour quite early yet remain on the tree until early winter. Swamp cypress will grow in moist garden soil and, of course, it is not fussy about drainage. It is hardy to -25°C. Raise from stratified seed sown at 22°C.

TAXUS

The yew (*T. baccata*) has been cultivated for over 1000 years, during which time it has mainly been used for hedging and topiary. It is very large spreading shrub or multi-trunked tree (12 m x 10 m (2.5)) with a dense covering of blackish-green, slightly glossy, leathery, 25 mm long, needle-like leaves. In spring the strobili are quite obvious. These are followed by bright red berry-like fruits that contain one seed.

Not surprisingly for a tree that has been in cultivation for so long, there are many cultivated forms. The best known is the columnar 'Fastigiata'. This is often used for flanking entrances or driveways or for making narrow hedges. All forms of *T. baccata* will withstand severe trimming and are excellent hedging plants. Golden-foliaged, variegated and dwarf cultivars are also quite widely grown. Other species are seen occasionally, but *T. baccata* is by far the most common.

Yews prefer a moist well-drained soil and a position in full sun. They are very hardy (-30°C). The species may be raised from stratified seed sown at 18°C, but the cultivars are usually grown from semi-ripe cuttings in summer and autumn tip.

THUJA

Because it is commonly planted for farm shelter, *T. plicata* is probably the most widely grown member of this genus of conical conifers. However, none of the true species are much used in domestic gardens. Most garden forms are cultivars of *T. occidentalis* or *T. plicata*. Both of these species have small scale-like leaves and fan-shaped foliage sprays with small spherical cones that are very resinous. The garden cultivars are usually rockery dwarfs or shrubs. The best known of the larger cultivars is the variegated *T. plicata* 'Zebrina', which grows to about 2.5 m x 1.5 m. Thujas

Taxus baccata

are very hardy (-30°C) and will grow in any well-drained soil. The species may be raised from stratified seed sown at 18°C; the cultivars are usually propagated by semi-ripe cuttings in summer and autumn.

TILIA

The lime or linden tree (*T. x vulgaris*) is a large, spreading, deciduous tree (15 m x 10 m (2.5)) widely used for avenue planting. The leaves are about 75-100 mm long, light to mid-green, heart-shaped and deeply veined with a prominent point. They develop golden-yellow to orange tones in autumn. The small cream flowers, which appear in late spring, are scented and very attractive to bees. They are followed by clusters of small brown seed capsules. The linden is hardy to -25°C and is easily grown in any moist well-drained soil, although it is too large for small gardens. The species is usually raised from stratified seed sown at 18°C, while the selected forms grafted.
Other species, such as the smaller-leaved *T. cordata* and the upright growing American linden (*T. americana*) are seldom sold in garden centres. However, seed of these and other species is available from specialist seed suppliers.

ULMUS

The recent threat of Dutch elm disease has raised the question of whether it is worth the risk of planting these spreading trees. There are many magnificent elms throughout the country but it may only be a matter of time before they succumb. Several species of these large (15 m x 10 m (2.5)) trees are grown. Most species have 75-100 mm long, deep green, deeply veined, rounded leaves with serrated edges. The most widely planted are *U. glabra* and *U. procera* and two cultivars dominate the local plantings: the golden elm (*U. procera* 'Louis van Houtte') and the wide-spreading weeping Camperdown elm (*U. glabra* 'Camperdown'). At the full mature size all elms are too large for small gardens, but they make magnificent specimens for large lawns or parks. Elms are primarily deciduous, however

Weinmannia racemosa

the evergreen *U. parvifolia* may occasionally be seen. It has smaller leaves (60 mm long) and interesting peeling bark rather like the London plane, but is less hardy, tolerating only about -8°C until well established. All species have early spring flowers with conspicuous bracts but they are rarely considered a feature. The papery seeds can make a mess and elms are notorious for suckering, but they are impressive stately trees. They are very hardy (-30°C) and easily grown in any moist well-drained soil. The species may be raised from stratified seed sown at 18°C; the selected forms are usually grafted.

VIRGILIA

Although they provide a good display of spring and early summer flowers, care should be taken when planting these evergreen South African natives. In many areas they self-sow freely and may become weeds. The two species *V. oraboides* (syn. *V. capensis*) and *V. divaricata* are considered by some authorities variants of the same species. *V. oraboides* is slightly larger growing with lighter-coloured flowers, but there is not much to choose between them, both reaching approximately 10 m x 8 m (4). They have deep green, somewhat leathery, pinnate leaves composed of many small leaflets. The underside of the leaves is light green to slightly

silvery. From spring to early summer pendulous clusters of pink to mauve sweet pea-like flowers appear. A tree in full flower is quite spectacular but the display doesn't last long. Virgilias are easily grown in any light well-drained soil and are hardy to -6°C. They are often best used as quick-growing temporary shelter as trees over 15 years old often become very untidy and open. They are usually grown from seed, which should be soaked and sown at 18°C.

VITEX

The puriri (*V. lucens*) is one of the few New Zealand native trees with pinkish-red flowers. The flowers, which are carried in panicles, are most often seen in late winter, although they may occur at any time. The flowers are followed by bright red 20 mm long berries. The foliage of the puriri is very handsome. The leaves are a lustrous, glossy green, digitate and composed of three to five broad leathery leaflets that are up to 125 mm long. Puriri is a very impressive tree at 15 m x 10 m (2.5) and, fittingly, it is host to one of our most impressive insects: the puriri moth. The caterpillars of this large moth can often be found on trees in the wild, but they do little damage. Puriri does best in a humus-enriched, moist, well-drained soil and should be shaded and protected from wind

and frost when young, though when mature it is hardy to -4°C. It is usually raised from seed sown at 20°C, but may also be propagated by semi-ripe cuttings whenever these are available.

WEINMANNIA

Kamahi (*W. racemosa*) is a very attractive upright flowering evergreen that could be far more widely grown in New Zealand gardens. It reaches 15 m x 6 m (2.5) and has elliptical, deep bronze-green, serrated-edged leaves that can be up to 100 mm long, although they are more commonly around 75 mm. Young trees have leaves composed of three leaflets, but in adult trees the leaves are single bladed. In summer, the tree produces masses of 150 mm long, narrow, creamy-white bottlebrush-like flower heads. The massed flowers often swarm with bees as they are heavy with nectar and pollen. The flowers are followed by 20 mm diameter red berry-like fruits. There is a purple-leaved form that is occasionally available. Kamahi prefers a moist, slightly acid soil and is easily grown in most areas, being hardy to -15°C. It can be propagated by seed sown at 18°C or by semi-ripe cuttings in summer and autumn.
The towai (*W. silvicola*) is a similar species that occurs in the north of the North Island, although it appears to be hardy well outside its natural range.

THE PLANTS

PALMS AND CYCADS

Siting; Growing in containers;
Propagation; Popular palms

Most palms have panicles of small yellow flowers similar to those of the Chinese fan palm, *Trachycarpus fortunei*, shown here.

EVERYBODY RECOGNISES palm trees, they are the universal symbol of the tropics. But many are hardy enough for our temperate climate gardens. Until recently, New Zealand gardeners have had only a very limited number of palms to choose from, but in the last five years the range has grown enormously as nurseries have been encouraged by gardeners eager to experiment.

Nevertheless, palms are, on the whole, slightly tender plants. Those that will tolerate regular frosts of -6°C or more are few in number. The best known are *Phoenix canariensis* and *Trachycarpus fortunei,* but you should also consider *Jubaea chilensis, Chamaerops humilis, Butia capitata, Washingtonia robusta* and *Brahea armata*. If your minimum temperature does not crop below -2°C, or if you are in a frost-free area, the range of suitable plants increases considerably.

Palms often grow well in coastal conditions but benefit from occasional wash downs to remove any salt-spray deposits. They are not prone to any unusual pests and diseases; frost damage is likely to be the biggest problem.

There are two main styles of palms; the fan and the feather. The names refer to the layout of the fronds. Fan palms have the leaflets of the frond arranged just like a hand-operated fan. The most widely grown fan palm is *Trachycarpus fortunei*, the Chinese fan palm. Feather palms have the leaflets of their fronds arranged along a rigid midrib. The most commonly grown feather palm is *Phoenix canari-*

ensis, the Canary Island date palm.

Palms are extremely important plants to the world's economy. The true date palm, *Phoenix dactylifera*, is rarely seen in New Zealand but it is the most common commercially grown palm. The coconut, *Cocos nucifera*, is not far behind. Possibly more significant than fruit crops is the use of palms for shelter.

SITING

Although palms are associated with sun and sand most species appreciate light shade when young. Shelter from wind is important if the fronds are to look their best, but as the plants can become quite large they will eventually have to tolerate exposure to sun and wind.

When siting a palm remember to take into account the spread of the crown. This is not so significant with a mature plant as the crown is usually well above most obstructions. The problem is adolescent plants, which tend to have much the same spread as adults without the height. They take up a considerable area until the trunk begins to develop.

Palms generally do best in a rich, moist, well-drained soil. They have fairly strong roots that anchor them firmly and the roots of many palms can withstand a considerable amount of abuse, which enables the trees to be safely transplanted at almost any size.

GROWING IN CONTAINERS

Palms make superb container plants, both

indoors and outdoors. They are undemanding and tolerant of neglect. In cold areas it is often best to keep young palms in containers until well established, as they can be moved under cover for winter. Once they have a spread of over 1.5 m or so they should be hardy enough to plant out, but if it is not inconvenient it is better to wait as long as possible.

PROPAGATION

Palms are nearly always propagated by seed. They usually have only one growing point, so vegetative propagation is not practical.

Occasionally suckers form at the base of established plants and may be carefully removed for growing on but this is not a reliable method of propagation.

Palm seed varies greatly in its ease of germination. The most common problem is very hard seed coats. No amount of scarification or soaking will soften the toughest of them. Sometimes acid treatment is resorted to but patience is the usual method. Some, such as *Butia capitata*, may take upwards of a year in the soil before germination but eventually, with the right combination of moisture, temperature and time, they sprout.

Many palms and cycads make ideal container plants; the dramatic *Cycas revoluta* (above left) is no exception.

Above right: Bromeliads combine well here with cycads and palms to create a dynamic courtyard garden.

POPULAR PALMS

DO NOT EXPECT to find all of the species listed at your local garden centre; many of these palms are only available as seed from specialist nurseries. Unless otherwise stated, all of these palms have panicles of small yellow flowers.

ARCHONTOPHOENIX

The king palm (*A. alexandrae*) is a prominent feature in many tropical and subtropical areas but it is too tender for all but the very far north. *Archontophoenix cunning-hamiana* is a better bet but it still requires a near frost-free climate with warm summers. It is a feather palm with long arching fronds. It can reach 20 m high but rarely exceeds 7 m in New Zealand gardens. The flowers are

followed by masses of small red berry-like fruit. *A. cunninghamiana* may be grown indoors but it needs high light and humidity levels. The seeds germinate easily.

ARENGA

Two species of this genera are suitable for growing outdoors in mild areas. Both are feather palms with broad leaves that have silvery undersides. *A. pinnata* requires near frost-free

conditions but *A. engleri* from Taiwan will tolerate infrequent light frosts. Both species have interesting flowering habits and fruit. *A. pinnata* is monocarpic; it dies after flowering although it takes at least ten years to reach maturity. *A. engleri* survives to flower again but the leaf stem beside the flower stalk dies. Both species have fruit with extremely caustic pulp. They are unlikely to exceed 3.5 m high under New Zealand conditions, but *A. pinnata* may reach 18 m in its native Southeast Asia. *A. pinnata* seed germinates quickly and easily but *A. engleri* is erratic and may take several months to sprout. They are not usually grown indoors.

BRAHEA

These fan palms are becoming more common in New Zealand

gardens. Both of the common species, Mexican blue palm (*B. armata*) and Guadeloupe palm (*B. edulis*), are reasonably hardy and adaptable plants. *B. armata* has beautiful finely divided glaucous fronds. It is the hardier of the two, and will withstand -8°C once established. It has a stocky trunk for many years but may eventually reach 12 m high. *B. edulis* is tender when young but withstands -6°C once the trunk is over 10-15 cm in diameter. It grows slowly to about 15 m high. Both species are tolerant of drought and low humidity. *B. armata* has 12 mm diameter brown fruit, while *B. edulis* has edible 18 mm diameter blackish fruit. Grow both in full sun. The germination of *B. armata* seed is very erratic and may take up to year. *B. edulis* is less tricky but still not very reliable. High light requirements make *Brahea* unsuitable for indoor cultivation.

BUTIA

The pindo palm or jelly palm (*B. capitata*) from Brazil is a hardy feather palm with long drooping olive to bluish green fronds. It will withstand -10°C once established and deserves to be more extensively grown. It grows to about 7 m high and the flowers are followed by yellow to red 25 mm diameter pulpy fruit. Grow in full sun. Seed germination is highly variable, it is unlikely to take less than two months and may be a year or more. High light requirements mean this palm is not very suitable for growing indoors.

CARYOTA

The fishtail palm (*C. mitis*) is often grown as a houseplant and is unlikely to grow well outdoors except in the very far north. *Caryota urens* has slightly lower heat requirements but will not tolerate any frost. It has very dark green, slightly arching fronds. All *Caryota* palms have intricately cut bipinnate feather fronds. Most species grow to large sizes (over 18 m high) in the tropics but are unlikely to exceed 8 m high under New Zealand conditions. They have fruit with caustic pulp that should not be handled with bare hands. The seed germinates easily. *Caryota* palms grow well indoors but they prefer warmth and high humidity.

CHAMAEROPS

The Mediterranean fan palm (*C. humilis*) is a bushy fan palm that is usually multi-trunked and will not exceed 6 m high. The trunks take many years to form and are seldom seen in gardens. Most plants grow to about 1.5 m high x 5 m wide. The fronds are tipped with sharp spines. It is a very hardy palm that tolerates -15°C and is tolerant of low humidity and drought. Grow in full sun. The seed germinates well and takes about six weeks to sprout. High light requirements and sharp spines make it unsuitable for indoor use.

COCOS

The coconut palm (*C. nucifera*) is one of the most important commercial crops. It is essentially a tropical palm but will grow outdoors in the frost-free areas of the far north. It is a large feather palm that often develops a leaning trunk. It may grow to 30 m high in the tropics but rarely exceeds 8 m in gardens. The fruit will not develop to its normal size in our climate but becomes large enough to be a conversation piece. Coconuts germinate well but take at least three months to sprout. They need consistent warmth and the whole nut must be planted, do not strip away the husk. May be grown indoors but resents cold draughts.

CYCAS

The cycads are very similar in appearance to palms but they are not closely related. Cycads

Chamaerops humilis

are ancient plants more closely allied to the conifers but their appearance dictates that this is the appropriate place to include them. The sago palm (*C. revoluta*) is the best known and most widely grown. Its feather fronds are deep green and leathery. It is *very* slow growing but attractive and unusual at all stages. It may grow to 3 m high with multiple trunks and is hardy to about -8°C once established. As it will tolerate low light it is well suited to growing indoors. Other genera are becoming more common as these plants develop a following. Among the most likely to be seen are *Ceratozamia*, *Dioon* and *Zamia*.

HOWEA

These palms are very popular indoors but capable of growing outdoors in frost-free areas. They were formerly classified as *Kentia* and are still widely known by that name. Two species (*H. belmoreana* and *H. forsterana*) are grown, both are natives of Lord Howe Island. They are feather palms with deep green gracefully arching fronds and narrow trunks. *H. belmoreana* grows to about 7 m high and *H. forsterana* to about 15 m high, but both are unlikely to reach these sizes in New Zealand gardens. They have brown olive-sized fruit that takes two years to ripen. Only very fresh seed will germinate and even then it is erratic. Both species need shade when young, which is why they perform well indoors.

JUBAEA

The Chilean wine palm (*J. chilensis*) is a hardy (-8°C) feather palm that should be more widely grown. It has deep green arching fronds and a very distinctive trunk. The trunk becomes greatly enlarged, rather like a baobab tree, so that when mature it may be up 2 m diameter. Within the trunk is a large reserve of sap, which may be tapped and fermented into an alcoholic drink, hence the name wine palm. This palm can grow to 20 m high or more but it takes many years to get above 10 m. The 40 mm diameter fruit is yellow and the seed it

contains germinates easily but takes about four months to sprout. May be grown indoors but has high light requirements.

LIVISTONA

These fan palms are native to Southeast Asia and Australia. Two species, *L. australis* and *L. chinensis*, are suitable for growing outdoors in mild areas and they are very similar to one another. Both have deep green spiny fronds with leaflets that droop and fray at the tips. They have quite solidly built trunks that grow to about 12-15 m high. Under New Zealand conditions it takes many years for them to reach 10 m. Both species are hardy to about -5°C when well-established. *L. australis* has 18 mm diameter reddish fruit and *L. chinensis* has 25 mm diameter green fruit. The seed of both species germinates easily and quickly. May be grown as houseplants but they have high light requirements.

PHOENIX

The Canary Island date palm is by far the most common feather palm grown in New Zealand gardens. It has deep green arching fronds and a trunk studded with the bases of old fronds. When young, the trunk tends to be quite bulbous but as it gains height it becomes more tree-like. A mature tree may be up to 18 m high and have a very solid trunk. The fruit is about 40 mm in diameter and yellowish orange. *Phoenix dactylifera* is the true date palm of commerce that is such a well-known symbol of North Africa and the Middle East. It has shorter fronds in a less dense head than *P. canariensis*. It is much taller when mature, up to 25 m high. Both *P. canariensis* and *P. dactylifera* will withstand -8°C when established but should not be exposed to hard frosts until they have a short trunk. *P. dactylifera* needs hot summers to grow well and is unlikely to produce edible dates in our climate.

A third species, the pygmy date palm (*P. roebelenii*), is considerably less hardy but it can be grown outdoors in frost-free areas. It is frequently used as a container plant as it only

Phoenix canariensis

Rhapis excelsa

Trachycarpus fortunei

grows to about 3 m high. There are several other species that would be suitable for growing in New Zealand gardens but they are rarely seen. Among those most likely to do well are *P. loureiri*, *P. rupicola* and *P. sylvestris*. All *Phoenix* palm seed germinates quickly and easily and all species make excellent houseplants when young.

RHAPIDOPHYLLUM

The needle palm (*R. hystrix*) is native to the south eastern United States. It is a hardy fan palm that remains low growing and bushy. The olive green fronds have sharp spines on the petioles and the tips of the leaflets are also sharp. It grows into a multi-trunked clump about 1.5 m high x 4 m wide and it makes a vicious, nearly impenetrable hedge. It is hardy to about -12°C but requires constant warm summer temperatures to grow well. It has 18 mm long, green, oval fruit, the seeds from which germinate erratically. Grow in full sun. Its spines make it unsuitable as a houseplant.

RHAPIS

The lady palms are multi-trunked fan palms that are hardy to about -3°C when established but require warm summers to grow well. Two very similar species are grown, lady palm (*R. excelsa*) and slender lady palm (*R. humilis*). They have small fronds on fibre-covered bamboo-like canes. They form dense bushy clumps to 4 m high with foliage to ground level. *R. excelsa* has 12 mm diameter green fruit and grows quickly and easily from seed. *R. humilis* does not produce seed and may

not be a true species. It is grown from basal suckers. Both species are excellent houseplants that tolerate low light levels and neglect.

RHOPALOSTYLIS

This genus is most commonly represented in gardens by our only native palm, the nikau (*R. sapida*), but also includes *R. baueri*, which is a similar species from Norfolk Island. Sometimes known as shaving brush palms because of the prominent bulge beneath the foliage head, both species are elegant feather palms that grow to about 8 m high under garden conditions, although *R. baueri* can reach 15 m high in the wild. Both species tolerate only light frosts. *R. sapida* grows well in cool climates provided they are nearly frost free, but *R. baueri* needs steady summer warmth. Both species have 18 mm diameter red fruit. Seed germinates reliably but may take over three months to sprout. Seedlings are slow growing and need shade. Good houseplants when young.

SABAL

The palmetto palms are native to the south eastern United States and Mexico. They are fan palms and often have large fronds. Two species are readily available: *S. minor* and *S. palmetto*. *S. minor* is bushy and often multi-trunked and grows to about 3.5 m high, while *S. palmetto* is more tree-like but rarely exceeds 7 m. *S. minor* has glaucous fronds. Both species

are hardy to about -6°C once established and both have black fruit. The seed germinates quickly and easily. There are several other species worth trying but they are seldom available. Of these *S. domingensis* is the most distinctive as it can grow to 25 m high. *S. mexicana* and *S. uresana* are also tree-sized. *S. uresana* has silver grey fronds and is very drought tolerant. These palms have high light requirements and are unlikely to be good houseplants except for conservatories.

SERENOA

The saw palmetto (*S. repens*) is a bushy fan palm native to Florida. It grows into a clump about 2.5 m high x 4 m wide, and is often multi-trunked. The fronds are silvery grey to glaucous with sharp tipped leaflets. It is hardy to about -4°C. Grow in full sun. The fruit is oval, about 18 mm long and black. The seed germinates well but may take a few months to sprout. This palm can also be grown from suckers. High light requirements would probably limit this species as a houseplant.

SYAGRUS

The queen palm (*S. roman-zoffiana* formerly *Arecastrum romanzoffiana*), is frequently seen as a street tree in tropical and subtropical cities. This Brazilian native has very long, finely divided, arching, plumose fronds that move in the slightest breeze. It has a slender trunk that can reach 18 m high but is

unlikely to exceed 10 m under New Zealand conditions. Hardy to -5°C when mature but needs protection from frosts until about 1.5 m high with a good crown. Also needs warm summers to grow well. Has yellow fruit about 25 mm in diameter and 18 mm long seeds that germinate quickly and easily. It makes a good houseplant when young but needs bright light and humidity.

TRACHYCARPUS

The Chinese fan palm (*T. fortunei*) is probably the hardiest of the tree-like palms. It will tolerate -12°C from a young age. The fronds are deep green and quite luxuriant on young plants grown in the shade but they rapidly deteriorate in full sun and strong wind. The trunk is covered in fibre and the bases of old fronds and may be up to 12 m high. The small 12 mm wide grape-like fruit are bluish with a grey bloom. The seed germinates quickly and easily. As this palm prefers shade when young, it makes a good houseplant. There are other species worth growing, such as the very dwarf *T. nanus*, but they are seldom available.

WASHINGTONIA

These palms are synonymous with Southern California. They are fan palms with very straight trunks. Two species are grown, one Californian (*W. filifera*) and the other Mexican (*W. robusta*). *W. filifera* can grow to 20 m high and is quite stocky. *W. robusta*, which is sometimes called sky duster, has a very narrow trunk and may reach 30 m high or more. Under New Zealand conditions they are slow growing and unlikely to reach such impressive dimensions. The fronds have long petioles for fan palms. These species will survive -6°C once established but need summer heat to grow well. Both species appreciate light shade when young and both have 18 mm diameter fruit that is reddish green when ripe. The seed germinates quickly and easily. Try growing as houseplants until too large to remain inside.

VEGETABLES

*Choosing the site; Soil quality;
Preparing the ground; Growing
vegetables from seed; Watering;
Fertilisers; Crop rotation;
Containers; Popular vegetables*

A well-ordered vegetable garden
with attractive supports for
climbing beans.

NOTHING CAN BEAT GROWING your own delicious vegetables. As well as reducing the grocery bill, home-grown vegetables usually have vastly superior flavour and their freshness is guaranteed. Most importantly you have control over what pesticides and fertilisers, if any, are used in growing them. The home gardener is also able to grow unusual vegetables that may not be freely available from stores or specific varieties to suit personal tastes. Such benefits more than make up for the regular upkeep and planning that are an essential part of any successful vegetable garden.

The home gardener is, of course, not concerned with high yields and uniformity as commercial growers are, but to grow good-quality produce requires a familiarity with local climatic conditions and soil types, both of which are quite variable in New Zealand and which will strongly influence the techniques employed and planting seasons. Most crops and cultivars are strongly seasonal in their cultural requirements and usually perform poorly when grown out of season. However, for some of the most widely grown crops, such as cabbages, early and late varieties will extend harvesting, and, of course, warm-season vegetables can be grown out of season in plastic or glass-covered cloches, tunnelhouses or glasshouses (see Section One: Gardening under cover).

CHOOSING THE SITE

Often little thought is given to choosing the best site for a vegetable garden. Many home owners hide the vegetable garden at the back of their section, yet a well-kept vegetable garden can be just as attractive as any ornamental planting. Selecting the best site is critical for success.

The site must receive full sun for as much of the day as possible, especially during winter; it should be sheltered from prevailing winds by hedges or fences, and the soil should be well-drained and must never become waterlogged. A site close to the kitchen for easy access is advantageous, as is proximity to a water tap, although an extension pipe-line can be laid if necessary. Avoid sites where trees and shrubs will compete for nutrients and water, and cast shade for part of the day.

Once you have decided on the best site, you will need to think about the size of the bed or beds. Think about the space available and the types of crops you want to grow. Some vegetables, such as potatoes and curcubits, take up a lot of room, while others provide a high yield within a small area. Another factor that may affect your decision is availability and cost of the vegetable. Some gardeners feel there is little to be gained from growing readily available, cheaper crops and look to grow the less common, more unusual vegetables. In New Zealand's mild climate we are able to grow a huge range of vegetables and fruit, and as more and more cultivars appear on the market this range increases.

When laying out your vegetable beds, be

Why hide your vegetable patch when it can make a decorative addition to your garden (above and right)

aware of the need for maintenance and easy access to harvest your crop. Don't make the beds so big that you can't get to the middle rows to weed and pick, and, if you wish to avoid a lot of bending over, consider growing your vegetables in raised beds.

SOIL QUALITY

Soil quality will determine the success or failure of the vegetables perhaps more than any other factor. The ideal soil should be friable, open-textured and moisture-retentive but well-drained. The preparation required will depend on the initial soil structure and texture (see Section One: Assessing and preparing your soil). However, incorporating organic material, such as compost, into any type of soil will improve the soil's structure and moisture-holding capacity and increase the volume of soil into which roots can penetrate.

Heavy soils are problematic for vegetables as they are poorly drained and aerated. In addition, they are slow to warm up in spring, which is important when growing early crops. However, alternate freezing and thawing or wetting and drying over winter will make them more workable and produce a fine tilth ideal for seed sowing in spring. To maintain this fine tilth in heavy soils and improve drainage, coarse organic material such as compost or

bulky straw mixtures are needed at rates of 5–8 kg or more per square metre every year. This can be dug into the soil in autumn.

With very sandy and volcanic soils, in which moisture and nutrient retention is poor, organic matter will improve the moisture-holding capacity and also supply valuable nutrients.

Soils in which root crops, such as carrots and parsnips, are to be grown should be free of large stones and fresh organic matter as these may cause the root to fork.

Subsoils vary greatly in their structure and texture, but it is rarely desirable to bring them

This very productive corner features a wide range of vegetables and fruit.

Raised beds allow you to provide the perfect soil for your crops and the compost bin (at back) supplies the all-important organic material.

If you want healthy vigorous vegetables, prepare the ground thoroughly before planting.

post and manure at least 20 cm deep over an area and plant or sow directly into this.

There are two methods of digging over an area: one is known as true or bastard trenching, and the other an inferior method known as single trenching.

SINGLE TRENCHING

When digging over an area for a vegetable garden, usually it is sufficient to dig to one spade's depth and the trench method is the most efficient way of doing this. Work across the area in orderly trenches, each about 30 cm wide. The soil from the first trench is left on top of the ground. As you dig the second trench, you back-fill the first trench, and so on. Continue in this way so that only the soil heaped on the surface – that removed from the first trench dug – is used to fill in the final trench.

Manure or compost can be dug in simultaneously as each successive trench is refilled. It should first be spread over the area before you begin trenching if it is to be mixed in well, otherwise it may end up in a lump at the bottom of each trench. This sort of trenching is especially suited to shallow or clay soils.

TRUE OR BASTARD TRENCHING

True trenching is of great value on all kinds of land and is especially beneficial during dry, hot periods. Working across the area, dig a trench

to the surface, except where compact layers near the soil surface have free-draining material below them. (This is best done by true trenching.) If the subsoil is very heavy and poorly drained, raising the beds is an alternative to installing a drainage system. The topsoil can be removed from paths and piled up on the area to be cultivated, or raised beds can be built using railway sleepers, boards, or ponga logs and filling them with either a good loam topsoil or pure compost.

PREPARING THE GROUND

Digging is not the most popular chore in the gardener's calendar, but it performs three important functions: it breaks up and aerates the soil; it helps to control annual weeds; and it enables fertilisers or compost to be worked into the ground. Usually digging is a once-a-year task for most gardeners and is normally tackled in autumn or early winter, leaving the soil in a rough condition to be weathered down over winter by rain and frosts. In districts that do not experience cold winters, gardens are often regularly dug or forked over. Thorough tilling of the soil is important for successfully growing vegetables and even when the soil is of a most undesirable nature, it will produce excellent results.

For digging to be most effective, keep the spade vertical. A slanting thrust achieves less depth and merely means the job will take much longer. Some gardeners advocate the 'no-digging' technique. This is usually practiced by organic gardeners who simply scatter com-

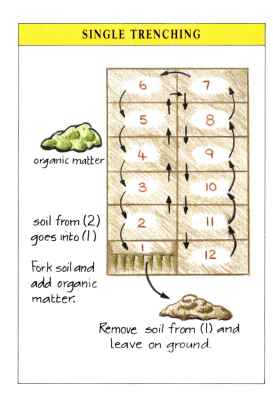

SINGLE TRENCHING

organic matter

soil from (2) goes into (1)

Fork soil and add organic matter.

Remove soil from (1) and leave on ground.

of the same width as that suggested for single trenching, but in this instance dig to two spade depths. Proceed to dig the adjoining ground, throwing the top spadeful of soil into the bottom of the open trench, and the second spadeful on top of this, thus reversing the original soil layers. At the same time, work in compost or farmyard manure. Repeat this until the final trench is filled with the soil removed from the first.

GROWING VEGETABLES FROM SEED

Seedlings of many vegetables are readily available from garden centres. However, growing your own vegetables from seed, although slower, enables more plants to be grown at significantly less expense.

It is important to sow crops in the correct seasons. Some are extremely frost-tender and should be sown outside only after all danger of frost is over. Such crops generally require a temperature of 20°C or more for germination. They are usually best germinated in seed trays, punnets or pots indoors or under plastic or glass, potted on, and gradually hardened off and planted out when temperatures have warmed up (see Chapter 24, Propagation). Most cool-season crops are best germinated at 15-20°C and can be sown in their final position. Most vegetables germinate quickly within 1-2 weeks. Slower germinating crops, such as asparagus, celery and parsnips, may take 4-5 weeks to emerge.

Sowing seed directly in the final position is essential for crops that dislike transplanting, such as peas, beans and root crops, and is also best for fine seeds. The soil is prepared as required and raked to a fine tilth. Any large stones or fresh organic material are removed and it is usually best to water the soil thoroughly prior to sowing rather than after.

Sowing in rows or drills is the usual method. A furrow is made in the soil using a draw hoe and a garden line as a guide. The depth varies with the crop. Fine seed is sown thinly along the drill (mixing the seed with fine sand may help) and seedlings are later thinned to the required final spacing. Larger seeds are more easily spaced. Some crops, such as cabbages, are commonly sown in groups or stations, three or four seeds per station, and later thinned to the strongest seedling at each station. After thinning, water with a fine spray to settle the soil.

If you have a small vegetable garden, plan the layout carefully, as there are some ways of increasing the yield over the same area. For example, the space between rows of taller-growing vegetables can be used for a rapidly maturing crop, such as radishes, which will be harvested before the taller crop nears maturity. Early and late cultivars can be grown to extend the season. Also, although some crops produce over a long period, consider small successive sowings rather than one large one to give a continuous supply of most crops rather than a huge amount all at once.

WATERING

An adequate and regular water supply is essential for optimal quality, growth and yield. Water requirements vary hugely between crops. Leafy crops, such as cabbage and lettuce, benefit from frequent watering from the seedling stage onwards provided that adequate nutrients are available. A reliable guide is to apply 9-12 litres per metre weekly during dry periods. Fruit crops, such as peas and some beans, produce leafy growth at the expense of flowers and pods if given too much water early on. Supplementary watering should not usually be necessary after they have become established, but applying 4-10 litres per metre in twice-weekly waterings at flowering and podding time will improve the crop. Root crops need an even water supply throughout their lives. For some crops the timing of watering is critical and is described under the crop concerned.

Water loss from the soil surface by evaporation can be significant, especially on hot windy days, and can be as much as 3 litres per metre on a sunny day. This does not mean, however, your crops will need drenching every day, as an excess of water may adversely affect growth by reducing soil aeration and promoting nutrient leaching, especially of nitrogen. It may also affect the produce's flavour.

Rather than watering every day, water less frequently but water deeply in the evening or early morning. A light sprinkling on the soil surface merely results in most of the water evaporating without reaching the roots and encourages shallow rooting.

Applying plenty of compost to the soil will greatly aid water retention and mulching with compost, straw or leaf mould will reduce water loss from the soil surface. The mulch should be applied after rain when the plants have become established. Competition between the roots of neighbouring plants and from weeds also affects water uptake.

If the soil is dry prior to sowing seed, water it thoroughly the day before sowing. Transplanted seedlings will also need a thorough water-

Sowing seed directly into the garden is important for root crops, like these carrots, as generally they dislike being transplanted.

Mulching performs a variety of functions in the vegetable garden: providing organic material to improve soil fertility and texture, suppressing weeds and helping to retain moisture.

Even a small urban courtyard can be productive – remember that many vegetables can be grown in containers.

ing after planting out and a feed with liquid blood and bone will prove beneficial. Each seedling will require at least 500 mls of water daily until it is established.

FERTILISERS

Intensive vegetable cultivation quickly reduces soil fertility unless measures are taken to replace what is lost. If starting a vegetable garden in virgin soil, 75% of the soil's humic content will be lost within one growing season and if this is not replenished a gradual reduction in soil fertility will result. Thus the addition of organic matter and fertilisers is essential whenever a new crop is planted.

Well-rotted farmyard manures and compost are commonly used as soil conditioners. They maintain soil structure and texture, improve the soil's moisture-holding capacity and provide the correct materials for soil microbes as well as earthworms. Organic material will supply some nutrients but usually not enough to support strong healthy growth and so it should be supplemented with other fertilisers.

Different crops have their own individual nutrient requirements. In general, leaf crops, such as cabbages and lettuce, require fertilisers with a high nitrogen content. Root and fruit crops need considerably less nitrogen, phosphorus and potassium are more critical. In fact, excessive nitrogen can be detrimental and hence a slow-acting form, such as blood and bone, or a slow-release fertiliser should be used. Commercial formulations containing essential nutrients at the optimal ratio are available for certain vegetables, such as potatoes and tomatoes, and these should be given preference.

Apply chemical fertilisers prior to planting out, but side-dressings can be applied as a top-up during the growing season. Liquid fertilisers are another effective means of feeding plants after planting out and ensuring that growth is rapid. Liquid blood and bone is an excellent general form, but formulations for specific crops, such as tomatoes, are also available.

CROP ROTATION

This is the practice of not growing similar types of vegetables in the same ground in successive years. It necessarily involves planning ahead, but a proper rotation of crops should be observed for the long-term health and productivity of your vegetable garden. It may be difficult to achieve in very small gardens but in larger gardens it is a sound cultural practice.

The main reason for adopting such a strategy is to help prevent the build-up of soil-borne pests and diseases. It is more likely to be effective against diseases than pests as they are less mobile, but some may remain dormant in the soil for several years. Brassicas are among the worst-affected crops that are likely to benefit from crop rotation.

Among the exceptions to rotation we may safely include leeks and onions, which grow well in the same ground year after year and revel in soil constantly enriched with generous dressings of manure.

CONTAINERS

You can still enjoy the best vegetables in town even if you do not have a garden. All you need is a sunny patio, verandah or concreted area. Many vegetables will grow well in pots, large tubs and troughs. Dwarf and early maturing cultivars and crops with compact root systems are the most suitable. This would include capsicums, lettuces, tomatoes, bush-type cucurbits, spring onions, radishes, and cress and mustard. A standard tub and shrub or potting mix is suitable, and inclusion of a suitable slow-release fertiliser is also advisable. Frequent liquid-feeding and watering are essential.

POPULAR VEGETABLES

THE FOLLOWING IS A GUIDE to the most widely grown vegetables, and a few others that deserve wider cultivation. The names of specific cultivars have not been included because the popularity of these changes year by year, and because there are so many new ones continually coming onto the market. It is, however, important to note that different cultivars can have widely varying sizes, maturing times, and growing seasons, so always choose the cultivar with care.

The vegetables are listed under their common name, as this is by far the most usual way to buy them, but their botanical names are also given. This indicates how various vegetables are related to one another, for example cauliflower, cabbage and broccoli are all *Brassica* species, which in turn gives clues to cultivation and likely pests and diseases, as they tend to have similar requirements and problems. The recommended spacing (e.g., 60 cm x 120 cm apart) refers to the distance between individual plants x the spacing between rows.

ARTICHOKE, GLOBE (CYNARA SCOLYMUS)

The globe artichoke is a tall-growing, thistle-like perennial that makes an attractive ornamental. The large flower buds are eaten. It is best propagated by rooted offsets as seeds do not grow true to type. Plant in spring 60 cm x 120 cm apart. Dig in compost and a complete fertiliser (100 g/m²) prior to planting. It is a three-year crop with each plant producing up to 10-12 heads annually. Harvest from December onwards when they are fleshy but while the scales are still green and shut tight; if the scales open they will be unpalatable. Cut the old stems down in autumn. It is a heavy feeder so incorporate plenty of compost in winter and water regularly. Good drainage is essential. It requires protection in frosty areas.

ARTICHOKE, JERUSALEM AND CHINESE (HELIANTHUS TUBEROSUS)

Both Jerusalem and Chinese artichokes are perennials grown for their edible tubers. The Jerusalem artichoke grows up to 3 m high, whereas the Chinese artichoke usually reaches about 1 m tall. Plant fairly large tubers during late August or September 10 cm deep and 40 cm x 1 m apart. The stems of Jerusalem

artichokes may need staking. Both tolerate a wide range of soils but dislike poorly drained and very acid soils. Poorer soils are best as they may produce excessive foliage and poor tubers if overfed. Earth up the plants when they are about 20 cm high as for potatoes. In autumn cut them back leaving about 12 cm of stem above ground. The tubers of both do not store well; Jerusalem artichokes can be left in the soil until required, but Chinese artichokes are more frost-tender and should be lifted when mature. Harvest carefully as they may become invasive.

ASPARAGUS (ASPARAGUS OFFICINALIS)

Asparagus is grown for its young succulent shoots, which are harvested in very early spring when other vegetables are scarce. It needs a deeply dug, well-manured and perfectly drained soil (pH 6.5). Plants are usually raised from purchased crowns, which can be 1-3 years old. Only male plants should be grown as they produce better spears. Plant in August, ensuring that the crowns do not dry out at any stage. Dig a trench 20 cm deep x 40 cm wide, fork over the subsoil and mix in compost or manure and blood and bone (100 g/m²). Form a mound in the trench, place the crowns 45 cm apart with the roots spread out, cover with 6 cm of

Asparagus shoot ready for harvest.

soil and water with liquid blood and bone. Allow the first year's growth to mature, cutting them down and discarding them in autumn. Harvest only a few spears in the second year. In the third year harvest from early August until early December, then leave the spears to mature. An annual mulch of seaweed in July is beneficial and in August apply a heavy dressing of complete fertiliser (160 g/m²). A top dressing of mushroom compost at least 10 cm deep is ideal because of its lime content, and a dressing of common salt (100 g/m²) is also beneficial. When cutting ceases apply another heavy dressing of fertiliser or manure. Slugs and snails love the young spears and thrips can also damage the stems. Phytophthora is the most serious problem.

AUBERGINE OR EGGPLANT (SOLANUM MELONGENA)

Aubergines are subtropical plants grown for their egg-

shaped fruits. The fruits are usually purple, but white-fruited types are also available. They do best in warm, sunny, humid conditions and are most successful in greenhouses. In the warmer areas of New Zealand they can be grown outdoors if temperatures do not fall below 16°C. They require well-drained, humus-rich soils. Sow in August or September in a warm position. The seedlings can be planted outdoors when about 3 cm high, spacing them 60 cm apart. When they are 15 cm high pinch out the shoot tips to encourage branching, but only allow three or four branches. Once the fruits have set, remove all but six fruits, remove any further flowers and pinch out any more side-shoots. Water them freely and feed with liquid blood and bone every second watering. The fruits should be ready in January while the skin is still shiny. If left too long the skin will thicken and the seeds become bitter. Handle carefully as they bruise easily. Fungal diseases can be controlled by spraying with copper at regular intervals. Caterpillars can be a problem.

BEANS, BROAD (VICIA FABA)

Easily grown throughout New Zealand, they require a rich well-manured soil (pH 6.5-7) and a heavy dressing of a complete fertiliser applied about two weeks before sowing. Sow from April to August, later in colder areas, but in warmer areas autumn is preferable. Make a trench 5-6 cm deep x 15 cm wide, sow the seed with the scar downwards in double, alternating rows 50 cm apart. Harvesting begins about 110

Aubergine (egg plant)

days from sowing. Taller varieties will need support, which can be done by placing stakes through the rows and intertwining string through and around the plants. Pinch out the shoot tips when the flowers have set, as this discourages aphids, gives you succulent tips for the table, and keeps the plant's height down. The beans are tastier if picked as soon as they are a useable size. The stalks can be cut off at ground level after harvesting, leaving the roots in the soil as a valuable source of nitrogen. Chocolate spot causes brown spots on the leaves; spray with cupric hydroxide as soon as it is noticed, and avoid overcrowding and overuse of nitrogenous fertilisers. Aphids and rust can also cause problems. Cold wet weather is often the cause of poor flower setting. Regular harvesting to prevent pods maturing and watering during dry weather is essential for all types of bean.

BEANS, FRENCH
(PHAESOLUS VULGARIS)

There are three kinds of French bean – dwarf, climbing and butter. All are sun-lovers and must have warmth to produce good crops. They are frost-tender and should not be sown until after the last frost – late October or early November is early enough. In winter fork in manure or compost and two weeks before sowing a complete fertiliser (50 g/m²) should be lightly worked into the soil. When the soil temperature is around 16°C, make a drill 3 cm deep x 12 cm wide and sow the seed 10 cm apart in a double, alternating row. Sow every four weeks for a continuous supply. Harvesting is around 50-55 days from sowing. Climbers will grow to about 2.5 m high and need a structure to grow up. Where space is limited dwarf types can be grown in pots or tubs using a tree and shrub potting mix.

BEANS, LIMA AND SOYA
(PHAESOLUS SPP.)

The lima bean is a climber and is treated the same as runner beans, but it needs a slightly longer growing season. It is more cold tender than other beans and will not mature in colder

areas of New Zealand. The soya bean grows to 1.8 m and needs similar conditions to the lima.

BEANS, SCARLET RUNNER
(PHAESOLUS COCCINEUS)

These are among the most prolific of all vegetables. They will grow to a height of 3 m and produce heavy crops for many years. Being perennials, extra soil preparation is required prior to sowing. In winter make a trench at least 50 cm deep, fork over the subsoil and add compost or manure as you refill it. When the soil has warmed up (to at least 10°C) sow the seed about 5 cm deep and 20 cm apart in a single row. Harvesting will begin about 75 days later. Aphids, red spider mites, looper caterpillars, green vegetable bugs and sometimes white fly all attack beans. Scarlet runner beans are insect pollinated so care should be taken with insecticides. Halo blight is a bacterial disease causing small angular spots surrounded by a wide yellowish-green 'halo' on the leaves. Cool damp weather is ideal for this disease. Only use certified disease-free seed or seed saved from plants known to be disease free. Burn affected plants and those beside them immediately. If halo blight has occurred, beans should not be grown in the same bed for at least two years. Rots can also occur, particularly during warm weather in late spring.

BEETROOT
(BETA VULGARIS)

Beetroot are easily grown biennials of which there are two main types – globe and cylindrical – and the flesh is either red or golden coloured. Beetroot are good for intercropping as a catch crop. In most parts of New Zealand they can be grown all year round. In mild climates they are particularly good winter crops. Do not grow them on freshly manured soil. The soil must be well-drained and only slightly acid (pH 6.5-7). Three weeks before sowing apply a general fertiliser (56-80 g/m). A sunny position is preferred as is even watering. Beetroot seed does not germinate well below 7°C. To improve germination, soak the

Scarlet runner beans

seeds for 1 hour or place them under running water before sowing. Place the seed 1.5 cm deep in stations 10 cm x 30 cm and later thin to one seedling per station. Beetroot will run to seed if temperatures fall below 10°C for several weeks, but bolt-resistant cultivars are more suitable for early sowing. Sow at monthly intervals for a continuous supply. Round varieties can be pulled as soon as they are large enough (around golf-ball size). Harvesting is likely 50-80 days after sowing. Twist rather than cut off the tops as beetroot bleed badly when cut. Rust may attack the foliage.

BROCCOLI AND CALABRESE
(BRASSICA OLERACCEA VAR. CYMOSA)

These hardy crops are useful in cold districts and poor soils where cauliflowers do not thrive. The small leafy flower heads are eaten. Sprouting broccoli matures all year round in most parts of New Zealand, but is best grown as a cool-season crop. Grow in a well-drained, heavily manured soil (pH 6.5-7). Sow in spring or autumn in a seed bed and transplant when the seedlings are about 7 cm high, planting them 20 cm x 50 cm apart. Harvest the main heads while they are still tightly packed. Side-shoots with smaller heads will then develop for two months or more and should be picked every few days. For pests and diseases refer to cabbages.

BRUSSELS SPROUTS
(BRASSICA OLERACEA VAR. GEMMIFERA)

These do better in colder districts and dislike high temperatures. They tolerate heavier soils, but avoid growing them in freshly manured soils as excessive nitrogen produces loose sprouts and reduces frost hardiness. Regular summer watering is required for strong growth. Sow in October and November in seed beds and transplant before January, planting them 60 cm x 60 cm apart. Frosts improve the flavour but if heavy may damage the sprouts. Harvesting begins in late autumn and winter. Pick the sprouts from the bottom upwards when they are about 2.5 cm in diameter and still hard. For pests and diseases refer to cabbages.

CABBAGE
(BRASSICA OLERACEA SPP.)

Cabbage is the most widely grown brassica and there are various types suitable for harvesting in different seasons. Work compost or manure and a general fertiliser (100 g/m²) into the soil (pH 6-6.5) prior to planting. Caterpillars of the cabbage white butterfly and aphids are the main pests. Club root is the major disease affecting brassicas. It is indicated by slow growth, wilting on hot days and eventual collapse of the plants. Once present it can remain in the soil for up to seven years. It is worse if the soil is acid and wet, and at temperatures between 18 and 25°C. Well-limed soil rarely supports this disease and a crop rotation of seven years should be practised if possible. Damping-off of young seedlings

Purple broccoli

Celery

Yellow capsicum

can also be a problem.

Chinese cabbage. These are not true cabbages. They are different flavoured and have a more upright habit. Sow seed in early spring in stations with a 10-15 cm x 30 cm spacing. Transplanting causes bolting, which can be a problem.

Spring cabbage. These are hardy and grown as an early green crop. Sow or plant out in March or April to mature in spring. Space plants 30-40 cm x 35 cm. Firm planting is important and a few weeks after planting draw up a little soil around the stems to give additional support and protection against frost-lifting in winter. In August, apply liquid blood and bone or a light dressing of nitrate of soda. The following cabbages can also be grown in this way.

Summer cabbage. Sow between August and October for harvesting from late January until autumn.

Winter cabbage. Sow in September or October and harvest from late autumn until late winter. They include the savoys, which are easily recognised by their wrinkled, dark green leaves.

Red cabbage. Sow in spring at the same time as summer cabbage, but it needs a longer growing season and is not harvested until the autumn.

CAPSICUM
(CAPSICUM ANNUUM)

Capsicums (sweet peppers and the smaller chilli types) are grown for their fruits, which are usually harvested green but turn red or orange if left to ripen on the plant. They should be sown under cover in spring and planted outdoors at least 45 cm apart from late October. The soil (pH 6-6.5) should contain well-rotted compost or manure and a general fertiliser (56 g/m²). Capsicums must have a warm, sunny position in well-drained soils, doing best in a 15-30°C temperature range. Some midday shade may be beneficial in hot areas. Water regularly and feed weekly with a foliar fertiliser. Pinch out the main shoot when the plants are about 12 cm high to encourage branching, and remove the first flower that forms as the resulting fruit may cause the stem to split. Some cultivars may need staking. Fruit set can be adversely affected by dry or cold weather. Pests include aphids and red spider mite. Grey mould may develop on fruit during dry conditions.

CARROT
(DAUCUS CAROTA)

Carrots are normally sown from early August to January, as except in very mild areas they tend to run to seed in winter. The best soils are deep, friable, well-drained loams that are slightly acid (pH 6.5). Dig the soil deeply in autumn and winter and apply a general fertiliser (70 g/m²) just before sowing. Choose an open sunny area that previously grew peas and beans. Do not add bulky compost unless it is well-rotted and worked into the top 15 cm of soil, as bulky manures and stony soils may cause forking of the root. Sow the seed thinly in drills about 1.5 cm deep and in rows 12 cm apart, or sow in a band in double rows about 16 cm wide. Radish seed can be sown with carrots as they grow more quickly and assist with thinning. When the first rough leaves appear, thin the seedlings to 5 cm apart and water lightly to settle the soil. When they are about 12 cm high draw up soil around the plants. Final thinning can be left until small carrots have formed, as these can be eaten and are very sweet and tender. Some gardeners broadcast a mixture of parsnip, carrot and radish seed over an area; no thinning is required and cropping will be over a long period. Carrot root fly is the major problem in Auckland and Waikato and in dry soils. The larvae burrow into the roots and cause wilting. Sprinkle diazinon along the rows when the plants are about 10 cm high and water in, and repeat in December and February. A better strategy is to cover the crop with mesh cloth (Enviromesh) after sowing to prevent the adult flies laying their eggs around the crowns. It also protects plants from aphids.

CAULIFLOWER (BRASSICA OLERACEA VAR. BOTRYTIS)

Different varieties mature over much of the year and can be divided into three groups: summer, autumn and winter cultivars. The latter are also known as heading broccoli. Cauliflowers have a more delicate flavour than broccoli. They must be grown quickly in a fertile, well-drained soil (pH 6.5-7) and kept well watered. They are gross feeders and need a plentiful supply of a balanced fertiliser. Sow and cultivate as for cabbages, although they need more space than cabbages. Summer and autumn cultivars should be planted 60-70 cm apart, and winter cultivars 75-80 cm apart. Depending on the variety, harvesting is 125-170 days from sowing. It pays to fold the leaves over the head to protect it from sunburn and frosts. For pests and disease refer to cabbages. Boron deficiency causes hollow stem and browning of the curd, and can be overcome by using borax (sodium borate) at 1-2 g/m².

CELERIAC
(APIUM GRAVEOLENS VAR. RAPACEUM)

The swollen basal stem of this plant has the typical celery flavour and is an excellent substitute for it. Celeriac is sown in spring as it needs a long growing season and the plants should have a 20 cm x 40 cm final spacing. Harvesting is about 140 days from sowing. For pests and diseases refer to celery.

CELERY (APIUM GRAVEOLENS VAR. DULCE)

Celery is grown for its distinctively flavoured leaf stalks. It requires a deep, fertile, well-drained soil (pH 6), warm temperatures and regular watering to do well. Sow it in seed trays in early spring. Germination is slow and erratic. Transplant when about 10 cm high, spacing plants 30 cm x 30 cm apart; this will ensure the plants shade each other, aiding blanching (which improves the flavour). Harvest by snapping off the stalks as soon as they are large enough. Protect from slugs and snails. Celery leaf spot is caused by a seed-borne fungus. Soak seed in thiram before sowing and spray affected plants with copper. An excess of nitrogen can lead to soft rot. The bacterium responsible enters through damaged tissue, so take care when transplanting. Bolting is caused by a check in growth from drought, cold temperatures, or if seedlings remain in the seed trays for too long before being planted out.

CHICORY AND ENDIVE
(CICHORIUM INTYBUS, C. ENDIVA)

Both are used in salads and resemble lettuce. Endive has a loose heart, whereas chicory leaves are larger and the heart is more compact. They are excellent winter crops, but excessive winter rain may cause rotting. Chicory is blanched (to remove the bitter taste) by covering with straw or black plastic for 2-3 weeks before harvest and is then called witloof. Endive is very frost hardy and loses bitterness when gradually exposed to cold temperatures. Prepare the soil (pH 6-6.5) as for lettuce. Sow in autumn as for lettuce and thin to 30 cm x 30 cm. Harvesting begins about 70 days from sowing.

CHOKO
(CHAYOTE) (SECHIUM EDULE)

Chokos are only suitable for the warmer parts of New Zealand. They are strong-growing perennial climbers and need strong supports on which to grow. The fruits are single seeded and pear-shaped and are produced in late summer and autumn. Chokos love a rich soil and each spring, before growth begins, work plenty of compost or manure into the soil. The vine will usually be cut back by light frosts but will shoot again the following spring. They are grown from sprouted fruit planted just below the soil surface in spring. Powdery mildew may attack and protect from slugs and snails in spring as the succulent shoots emerge.

COURGETTES AND MARROWS (CURCUBITA)

Large marrows are seldom grown now. Modern cultivars, known as courgettes and zucchinis, have been bred to produce fruit picked when only 10-20 cm long; if left to grow larger they will produce slender marrows. Both trailing and bush types are available. Well-drained soils (pH 5.5-6.5), full sun, and shelter from wind are required. Dig planting holes 40 cm deep and wide and fill with well-rotted manure or compost and replace the soil to form a mound with a depression made to take the plants and for watering. Space the mounds 90 cm apart for bush varieties and 150 cm for trailing cultivars. Seed can be sown directly into the planting site or seedlings transplanted. Sow two or three seeds 2 cm deep per site and retain the strongest plant. Late October is early enough for sowing. Regular watering and a weekly liquid feed will produce tender fruits. Harvesting begins in about 65 days. Hand pollination of flowers will ensure fruit set and regular harvesting is important for a continuous crop. For pests and diseases see pumpkins.

CRESS AND MUSTARD
(LEPIDIUM SATIVUM, SINAPSIS ALBA)

Cress and mustard are usually grown together and are excellent for salads, particularly in winter. Sow the seed thickly from September until the end of April. Press the seed into the soil, keep it moist, and it will germinate in two or three days. Mustard is faster germinating and can be sown four days after cress. When they are about 5 cm tall cut them at the base of the stem with a pair of scissors. They can be grown in the open ground or in pots.

CUCUMBERS AND GHERKINS
(CUCUMIS SATIVUS)

There are two main types of cucumber: white round (apple cucumbers) and long green varieties. Gherkins are made from immature fruit of the latter and should be harvested when no longer than 5 cm. Cucumbers are frost-tender and should be sown under cover and planted out when the threat of frosts is past. Labour Weekend in New Zealand is the traditional time for planting out. Prepare the ground well by digging out the soil to a depth of 40 cm and combining half of the original soil with compost, old mushroom compost or well-rotted manure. A neutral or slightly acid soil is best. It is important to place the seed on its edge to ensure it does not rot and do not sow it deeper than 2 cm. Space plants at least 50 cm x 60 cm apart. Alternatively they can be trained up netting or a similar support structure. When they have four to six leaves, pinch out the shoot tips to encourage branching. Cucumbers require plenty of water and must be grown rapidly. Feed with a liquid fertiliser weekly. Harvesting begins 60-75 days from sowing. Powdery mildew is the biggest problem, especially in summer.

GARLIC (ALLIUM SATIVUM)

Garlic is frost hardy and requires a warm sunny situation. Prepare the soil as for onions. It is grown from bulb segments or cloves. Split the bulbs into cloves and press them into the soil about 2 cm deep with the tops showing and 8 cm apart. Plant them from May until August. The bulbs can be lifted when the foliage has died off in February and left to

Golden courgette (zucchini)

dry in the sun for two or three days. Store in onion bags in a dry place. Elephant garlic is actually a type of leek that produces much larger bulbs and is considerably more frost hardy.

KALE (BRASSICA OLERACEA VAR. ACEPHALA)

Kale is a hardy perennial grown for its blanched leaf stems. If you like something a little different in the way of vegetables, kale is for you. For this crop the soil should be deeply worked and enriched with plenty of manure. Being a coastal plant, it benefits from an annual autumn dressing of seaweed lightly forked in or a light dressing of salt. Seed is sown in September in drills 2 cm deep and thinned to 15 cm apart. These seedlings are lifted in autumn and used as rootstocks for planting out the following season. Cuttings or thongs are made from the fleshy side-roots. They should be about 10 cm long and as thick as a pencil. Cut the lower end at an angle and the upper end straight across to indicate the polarity, tie into bundles and place in moist soil, moist sand or peat. In June or July plant them out 30 cm x 60 cm apart. After they sprout feed them weekly with liquid blood and bone and do not let the soil dry out. Only one shoot per crown should be allowed to develop. The new shoots will be ready for use in about four to five weeks. To blanch the crop outdoors, cover each plant with a 20 cm black plastic pot with the drainage holes covered to exclude all light. Alternatively cover the crowns with leaves or straw to a depth of 30 cm or black polythene can be draped over wire frames. When the blanched shoots are about 15-20 cm long harvesting can begin. Remove the shoots with a sharp knife and cut off any flower stems that appear. A well-tended bed will continue to produce for about five years. For indoor blanching lift the crowns in May or June, remove all side-roots and trim the main roots to about 15 cm long. Plant the crowns in a rich potting mix in 20 cm allowing three crowns per pot. Cover each pot with a pot of the same size placed upside down and keep them in complete darkness at 10-13°C. They should be ready for use within five weeks.

KOHLRABI (BRASSICA OLERACEA GONGLYOIDES)

Kohlrabi produces a swollen root-like stem that is pleasantly and distinctively flavoured. It can be grown all year round, although autumn and spring sowings are best. It has the same cultural requirements as other brassicas (see cabbages). A fertile, well-drained, humus-rich soil pH 6-6.5) is best. The plants require regular watering as the stems become woody and bitter if growth is checked. Sow in drills 2 cm deep and 30 cm apart. Sow in stations at 15 cm intervals and later thin to one seedling per station. For a continuous crop sow at monthly intervals. Harvest when the roots are about the size of tennis balls; beyond this they become woody and unpalatable. This will be about 60 days from sowing.

KUMARA, SWEET POTATO
(IPOMOEA BATATAS)

Kumara must have at least five frost-free months and both days and nights must be fairly warm. They will grow in acid soils (with pH as low as 5) but will not thrive in cold wet soils or where they are subject to cold winds. They are fairly drought tolerant once established. Kumara are sun-lovers and the hotter and sunnier the weather, the happier they are. For propagation purposes only select tubers that are well-shaped, undamaged and disease free. Dip them in benlate (half a sachet to 2 l of water) and place in a box on 6 cm of potting mix. Cover with another 6 cm of the mix, water well, and cover with a polythene sheet. Place in the hot water cupboard for 3-5 days then move to a sunny position where the tubers will sprout and the polythene should then be removed. The shoots are ready for planting out when they are 15-20 cm high and if gently pulled off the mother tuber should possess sufficient roots to sustain them. To prepare the soil work in plenty of well-rotted compost or mushroom compost in autumn. Dig the ground over in August leaving it in a rough state and in September bring it to a fine tilth with a rotary hoe or digging fork. Most growers apply a general fertiliser (100 g/m²) about 14 days before planting. Generally, planting begins in mid October, but some growers consider mid November is the best time. Plant the shoots 30 cm x 75 cm or more apart in raised ridges about 30 cm high and water with liquid blood and bone (1:100). Dry weather, coupled with early planting, will reduce yields. Prevent the stems from rooting by lifting them during tilling. Leave harvesting as late as possible but before any danger of frost. The tubers will not keep if damaged. Store them in dry sawdust and ensure tubers do not touch. Alternatively wrap them individually in newspaper. Pests include crickets, white-fringed weevils, grass grubs, cut worms, black beetles, slugs and caterpillars. Several diseases, such as black rot, scurf and pink rot, are carried over from tubers in store. Good hygiene and dipping the cuttings in benlate immediately before planting will help with disease prevention.

LEEK (ALLIUM PORRUM)

Leeks are frost hardy, will tolerate very severe conditions and have a long growing season. They grow best in very fertile, well-drained soils (pH 6-6.5) with plenty of compost or manure worked in at least two months before planting. Full sun is essential. Apply a complete fertiliser (120 g/m²) prior to sowing. Space seedlings 15 cm x 30 cm apart. As the plants grow, draw up soil around the stems to blanch them. Leeks are gross feeders and can be given liquid fertiliser every ten days. They mature about 25 weeks from sowing. For a continuous crop plant them through spring until autumn. Botrytis, downy mildew and white rot attack leeks.

LETTUCE
(LACTUCA SATIVA)

Lettuce is the salad plant for all seasons. By growing suitable varieties and with the correct growing conditions it is possible to harvest lettuce throughout the year. However, in some parts of the South Island the use of cloches is recommended in winter. There are four main types of lettuce: butterhead, crisphead, cos and looseleaf cultivars. It is important to grow the different cultivars in the correct season. The secret is to grow lettuce quickly and without any check in growth in relatively rich, moisture-retentive soil (pH 6-7). Work in well-rotted manure, peat or compost and apply dolomite lime (200 g/m²) and a general fertiliser (75 g/m²) two or three days before planting. Bitterness in lettuce is the result of slow growth or over-maturity. The seed can be sown where it is to mature or transplanted. In hot weather direct sowing is recommended as transplant shock may cause bolting and the seed should be refrigerated for a few days after dampening to break dormancy. Sow in trays and transplant when the leaves are 2-5 cm long. Take care when transplanting as the roots are easily damaged. Alternatively sow

Varieties of lettuce

in drills 1 cm deep with no more than 10 seeds per 30 cm long drill. The seeds require light to germinate so do not sow too deeply and keep them well watered. For a continuous crop sow at frequent intervals as once 'hearted' lettuce will soon bolt. Space plants about 35 cm x 40 cm apart. Harvest averages 60-90 days from sowing. Aphids, slugs and snails can be a problem and protect young plants from birds and white fly with Enviromesh. Grey mould, damping off, and stem rot are fungal diseases. Adequate plant spacing and benlate will provide good control. Slime or soft rot is a bacterial disease causing the central leaves to become slimy. Damage from frosts, heavy rains, or irregular watering may allow entry of the bacterium. Maintaining an even growth rate and copper oxychloride will control it. Lettuce drop is a fungal disease resulting in wilting of the outer leaves, yellowing and death of the whole head. Seedlings can be attacked just after transplanting. Good crop rotation is the best means of control.

MELONS (CUCUMIS SPP.)

Melons are sprawling vines bearing the sweet juicy fruits we all enjoy during the heat of summer. Muskmelons are round or oval, ribbed, with netting-like markings on the skin and orange or salmon-coloured flesh. Cantaloupes are a type of muskmelon. Honeydew melons are round or slightly elongated with smooth skin and light green flesh. They require a longer growing season. Melons dislike transplanting and need a long, hot growing season. They can be sown outdoors in late October in mounds as for courgettes. They grow well on a support system similar to tomatoes. Water them regularly until the fruit start to ripen. Allow 6-8 fruit to develop and pinch out the main runner and the laterals leaving one leaf beyond each fruit. Melons do not ripen off the vine. Harvest muskmelons when the fruit separates easily from the stem with slight pressure. Honeydew is picked when the skin turns yellow. Expect harvesting 100 days from sowing. For pests and diseases refer to pumpkins.

MUSHROOMS
(PSALLIOTA CAMPESTRIS)

Mushrooms are quite easily grown by the home gardener. Specially prepared mixes can be purchased or alternatively you can purchase mushroom spawn and prepare your own compost. The condition, quality and sterility of the compost is the key to success and it is hard for the home gardener to produce reliably uniform compost. Use fresh horse manure containing a large amount of wheat straw. Make a pile 1-2 m high, water it thoroughly and let it ferment for 14 days, then turn it over and water again. The temperature should reach 50-60°C; when it drops to 23°C after 7-12 days it is ready for use. It should be dark brown and friable without any smell of ammonia and open textured and spongy, but should not be waterlogged. Mushrooms can be grown in boxes or beds under greenhouse benches, in sheds, cellars or under the house. Boxes should be at least 30 cm deep and about 1 m long x 80 cm wide. Pack the compost firmly into the boxes leaving a 5 cm gap at the top. Break the mushroom spawn into walnut-sized pieces and scatter it evenly over the compost. Press it down firmly and cover with a sheet of newspaper. Do not water again unless the compost starts to dry out. After about two weeks, when thin white threads start to grow through the compost, remove the newspaper and cover the surface with 3 cm of moist sterile peat mixed equally with agricultural lime as a casing material. This retains moisture and prevents the compost from drying out. Try to maintain a temperature in the containers of about 16-18°C in a reasonably humid atmosphere. Water carefully, applying small quantities at regular intervals rather than heavy doses infrequently. Mushrooms should appear about three weeks after casing, but it will be another 7-10 days before they are ready to harvest. Each crop of mushrooms produces several flushes at about 2 week intervals over a 6-8 week period. To harvest gently twist and lift the mushrooms; do not cut them off. The favoured button mushrooms do not have as much flavour as the more open mature mushrooms. Never re-use mushroom compost as it is likely to contain harmful diseases. Use it as a mulch on the garden.

OKRA
(HIBISCUS ESCULENTUS)

Okra is grown for its long, green, finger-shaped seed pods. It is a tropical plant and thus very frost-tender. A well-drained, compost-enriched soil (pH 6-6.5) and a warm, sunny, sheltered situation are required. Soak the seeds in warm water for 24 hours before sowing in punnets or pots. A temperature of around 20°C is best for germination. Plant them 50 cm x 80 cm apart and when they are 20 cm high pinch out the shoot tip to encourage branching. Staking is necessary if

the site is windy. The pods are ready for harvesting a few days after the flowers have opened when they are about 7 cm long. Pick them daily for continued production. White fly and red spider mite can be troublesome in hot weather.

ONIONS (ALLIUM CEPA)

Onions can be planted in the same site year after year and silverbeet is a good alternate crop. To prepare the soil (pH 6.5-7), work in old stable manure or cow manure or, if this is unobtainable, compost in mid winter. In August scatter on wood ashes and a dressing of bone meal (100 g/m²). Avoid quick-acting nitrogenous fertilisers. Onions are easily grown from seed sown in March and April or mid August, but in cold areas only sow in spring. Work a general fertiliser (50 g/m²) into the soil prior to sowing. Sow in drills 1 cm deep in rows about 20 cm apart and later thin to 5-7 cm apart. Autumn-sown seedlings can be set out in mid winter in milder climates, spacing them 15 cm x 30 cm apart, and will produce larger, earlier-maturing onions. When transplanting, trim the tops and roots with scissors and ensure only the roots are buried. As onions reach maturity (usually 5-6 months from sowing), the tops begin to yellow and topple over and can be bent over by hand to assist bulb ripening. Lift the bulbs about two weeks later and leave them to dry in the hot sun for several days. One of the easiest ways to store them is in string onion bags. Downy mildew can attack the foliage, bulbs and seed and is most troublesome in wet weather. White rot is a serious fungal disease and once present it can infect plants for many years. Crop rotation is the best control method and burn any diseased plants. Neck rot may develop during storage. Ensure the foliage dries off thoroughly before harvesting and removing the tops. Aphids can also be bothersome.
Japanese Onion. These onions produce clusters of six to nine shallot-sized bulbs. The leaves and stalks are also eaten in salads.
Pickling Onion. These small

Pumpkin

onions are grown specifically for pickling. Sow the seed in September. Thinning is not necessary as the bulbs should not grow larger than the size of marbles. Lift in late January and dry in an airy room before pickling.
Potato and Tree Onions. These produce a cluster of small bulbs and are useful in areas where typical onions are difficult to grow. The tree onion also produces several small bulbs on the flower stem instead of normal seed. Both are grown from bulbs planted out in late autumn or winter using small bulbs saved from the previous season. They should be pushed into the soil until their tops are just covered. The bulbs mature in spring.
Salad or Spring Onions. Salad onions are grown from seed and are eaten while still immature. Sow as for typical onions. Sow thinly in rows 10 cm apart all year round. Harvest about 6-10 weeks after sowing as required.

ORACHE
(MOUNTAIN SPINACH)

Comparatively unknown in New Zealand, it is popular with those who have tried it. It is a hardy annual with arrow-shaped leaves that may be used like spinach. It requires a rich soil containing plenty of compost. The seeds are sown in spring in their final

position. Sow every 4-5 weeks until early February for a continuous supply. Sow the seed 2 cm deep and thin to 35 cm apart. To prevent the plants running to seed, pinch out the flower spikes as soon as they appear. Pick the leaves before they become too old.

PARSNIP (PASTINACEA SATIVA)

Parsnips have a long growing season, being among the first crops to be sown in spring and one of the last to be harvested. Grow them where a well-manured crop of lettuce or cabbage were previously grown. In August work the following fertiliser into the soil (150 g/m²): 5 parts blood and bone, 1 part sulphate of ammonia, and 2 parts reverted superphosphate. Ensure the soil (pH 6-6.5) has a fine tilth to prevent forking of the roots. As soon as the soil can be easily worked in early spring, soak the seed for 24 hours and sow in drills 2 cm deep. Sow fairly thickly as the germination percentage can be poor. Thin seedlings to 7-10 cm apart. The thinnings are delicious if steamed with a little butter. Apply another dressing (50 g/m²) of the above fertiliser in November. In warmer parts of the North Island another crop can be sown from January until March for late winter and spring harvesting. The flavour is

Spring onions

Parsnip

intensified by heavy frosts. Harvesting is 120-150 days from sowing. Lift as soon as the roots are large enough or wait until the foliage dies down. They can be left in the ground until required. Carrot root fly is the major pest (see carrots). Powdery mildew is the major disease but can be ignored if it occurs late in the season. Parsnip canker is a nasty fungal disease that carries over from crop to crop and is promoted by wet weather and poor drainage. Burn all diseased plants and only grow parsnips in the same area every three years.

PEA (PISUM SATIVUM)

Peas must have a well-drained, fertile soil (pH 6-7) and full sun. They grow best in deeply worked soils that remain cool. Dig in a 6 cm layer of manure in winter, however being legumes high-

nitrogen fertilisers are unnecessary. There are many cultivars classified by their height and growing season. In milder climates sowing should commence in May using 'William Massey' as your first early dwarf cultivar. In colder areas delay sowing until August. Sow every three weeks for a continuous crop. Sow the seed 2-5 cm deep and 6 cm apart in alternating, double rows in flat-bottomed drills. The distance between rows should be the same as the eventual height of the mature crop. A rapidly-maturing catch crop, such as radish, can be sown between the rows early in the season. The emerging pea seedlings should be protected from slugs, snails and birds. Peas grow best with some means of support. The simplest method is to place two stakes at either end of the row and secure 1 m high wire netting between them. If you have access to manuka, the bushy tops and twiggy branches are ideal. Harvesting will be about 65-80 days from sowing. When the seedlings are 6 cm tall, begin raking up soil around the plants for added support. Water peas thoroughly during dry weather. Pick as soon as the pods begin to fill out and regular picking is essential. Root diseases should not be a problem if the right conditions are provided and crops are rotated. However, mildew may occur during dry weather.

POTATO
(SOLANUM TUBEROSUM)

Potatoes are the most widely grown vegetable in temperate zones. They are propagated from specially grown, disease-free tubers (seed potatoes) saved from the previous season. It is not advisable for home gardeners to save their own seed tubers as potatoes are susceptible to viruses that adversely affect yields and quality. Always use small seed tubers producing only two or three shoots, as large tubers may result in overcrowding and reduced yields. Potatoes require a lot of space and unless you have a large vegetable garden only the early cropping varieties should be grown. Potatoes demand a warm sunny position

and prefer a deep, friable, well-drained soil containing plenty of organic material. Do not apply lime before planting as they grow best in a slightly acid soil (pH 6) and lime can promote scab disease. Soil in which peas have previously been grown is ideal. Before planting apply wood ashes and sulphate of potash (56 g/m²) or blood and bone (100 g/m²), with a side dressing of blood and bone at the final earthing up. For early crops in most areas of New Zealand, planting can commence around late August. Place them in seedling trays to sprout with the eye end upwards, place the trays in a sunny position sheltered from rain and strong shoots will soon appear. Plant the sprouted tubers 30 cm x 50 cm apart and 5 cm deep. When the shoots are about 12 cm high, commence spraying every 3 weeks with a suitable fungicide such as cupric hydroxide. This should prevent potato blight, which is the most serious disease. When they are 20 cm high rake up soil around the stems and repeat this every three weeks. Earthing up helps support the stems and prevents tubers from becoming green.

Watering during dry weather is important. They should be ready for harvesting when the flowers have fully opened or wait until the tops have died down naturally. Leave the tubers on the soil surface to dry for two or three hours before storing.

Discard any damaged, diseased or very small tubers and store in dry sacks or boxes in a dark, frost-free site. Darkness is essential to prevent greening. Greened tubers are poisonous and should not be eaten. Late blight may occur following two or three days of warm, humid conditions with temperatures of 21°C or above. Spray immediately with copper or with severe infections cut off the shoots 5 cm above ground level and burn them. Aphids can be troublesome, particularly in November and early December and sometimes in February. The larvae of the potato moth feeds on the tuber flesh. Keep plenty of soil over the developing tubers and keep it firm to prevent the moths from penetrating the soil and laying their eggs. Destroy infected

potatoes immediately. Blackleg is a bacterial disease that is usually only a problem in wet conditions. Infected stems will be black at ground level. All that can be done is to pull out infected stems. Avoid poorly drained soils and damaging underground parts of the plant when weeding. If infections occur avoid growing potatoes in that area for at least one full season.

PUMPKIN AND SQUASH
(CURCUBITA)

Pumpkins and winter squash are harvested when fully mature, whereas summer squash are picked when still immature and do not store well. Scallopinis are a type of summer squash best harvested when the fruit are about 7 cm in diameter. All types need four or five frost-free months with warm weather and are sensitive to wind damage. There are large trailing cultivars that require plenty of space and smaller bush forms. Smaller varieties may prove better value than the giant exhibition forms as they will produce eight to ten medium-sized fruits, whereas the latter yield only a few large fruit. Soil preparation is all important. Plenty of compost should be incorporated in early spring. As they are gross feeders, a heavy dressing of a general fertiliser (at least 150 g/m²) should be applied in the third week of September. A soil pH of 6-7 is best. Seedlings can be raised in peat pots and potted on into 15 cm pots. Labour Weekend (late October) is usually the best time for planting outdoors. Water them in well with liquid blood and bone and if the weather is hot, shade the plants for two or three days until they are growing strongly. Water regularly and feed with liquid blood and bone every 7-10 days. The large leaves are prone to wind damage so some form of shelter, such as a row of sweet corn sown several days before planting out, should be provided. Pinch out the tip of each runner when they are about 1 m long to encourage lateral growth. Many flowers on the laterals will be female and thus capable of bearing fruit. All cucurbits (pumpkins, marrows, cucumbers, etc.) bear separate male and female flowers and thus hand pollination will ensure flowers set. The fruit can be used once the skin begins to harden, but those required for storage should be left on the vines until the plants begin to die back. Always leave 5-7 cm of stalk attached to the fruit and avoid damaging the skin, otherwise the fruit may soon rot. As a precaution, paint the stems and surrounding skin with a mixture of equal parts acrylic paint and cupric hydroxide. The fruit should keep well if placed between layers of dry straw in a warm, but not draughty, shed. Examine every few weeks and remove those showing signs of deterioration. Rats and mice can damage stored fruit. White fly is a problem in hot weather. Powdery mildew is the most common disease.

RADISH
(RAPHANUS SATIVUS)

Radishes are one of the easiest of all root crops and are ready to use three to five weeks from sowing, depending on the variety grown. They must be grown quickly and respond to soil that has been manured for a previous crop. Many gardeners sow them as a catch crop. Good rich soil is essential for quick results and crisp, mild-flavoured roots. Sow seed thinly to avoid thinning. Each radish needs about 2 cm² of surface area. Deep watering during dry weather is essential. After each watering apply liquid blood and bone.

RHUBARB
(RHEUM RHABARBARUM)

Rhubarb is a hardy perennial grown for its delicately flavoured leaf-stalks. The leaf blades and roots are poisonous. It grows best in a sunny situation in a fairly heavy soil (pH 6), but dislikes wet conditions. The main requirements are plenty of manure and water. Rhubarb is usually propagated by dividing the rhizomes during late winter (see Chapter 24, Propagation, for the recommended technique), which should be done every four years. Choose only strong young pieces with healthy growth buds. Dig a large hole 1 m wide and as deep as possible. Fork over the subsoil

and add 1 kg of bone dust or bone meal. Mix equal parts of soil and manure (poultry manure is ideal) and replace to form a mound. Make a depression for holding water by forming a ridge around the perimeter of the mound. This site will take four new divisions. The divisions should be evenly spaced and planted with the strongest eye at soil level. Water in with liquid blood and bone. Only pull stems when the plants are growing strongly and always remove flower stalks. Each year in late August add poultry or cow manure and during dry weather flood the depression several times a week. To pick rhubarb, grasp the stem near the base and gently pull with an upwards, twisting motion. Downy mildew is the most troublesome disease. Burn affected leaves or spray if necessary.

SALSIFY AND SCORZONERA
(TRAGOPOGON PORRIFOLIUS)

Both are root crops widely grown in Europe, but only over the last few years have they become more popular in New Zealand. Salsify is commonly called the vegetable oyster on account of its flavour. Scorzonera roots are less strongly flavoured than salsify. The young shoots or chards of both are also eaten in salads in spring. Both vegetables should be cultivated in the same way. The soil (pH 6-6.5) must be deep, well-drained, and free of stones and fresh compost to ensure the long roots will not be obstructed. Apply a complete fertiliser (60 g/m²) 10 days before sowing. Sow seeds from September to November in drills 1 cm deep and 30 cm apart. Sow in groups of two or three seeds at 12 cm intervals and thin to one plant per station. Regular weeding is essential but take care as the roots may bleed if damaged. Plenty of water is essential for succulent roots. Mulching with compost will help retain moisture and smother weeds. Take care when lifting the roots as they snap easily. Some can be left in the ground until the following spring to provide chards. The old leaves should be cut off 2 cm above the soil and earth up the roots

to a depth of about 12 cm so that the chards are blanched as they develop in the following spring.

SHALLOT
(ALLIUM ASCALONICUM)

Shallots require a light soil containing well-rotted manure or old mushroom compost. Bring the soil (pH 6.5-7) to a fine tilth and before planting in July and August, rake in sulphate of potash (50 g/m²) and roll or tread to ensure a firm bed. Plant when the soil is not too wet. Simply press the small bulbs or sets into the surface to half their depth. Space them 15 cm apart and keep the soil moist. Feed fortnightly with liquid blood and bone. When the tops are about 20 cm high they can be picked for flavouring. The tops die down in January and February and the clusters of small bulbs are lifted and dried in the sun. Pickling should be done within a month of drying if their full flavour is to be preserved. Shallots are susceptible to white rot.

SILVERBEET, SWISS CHARD
(BETA VULGARIS VAR. CICLA)

Silverbeet is an evergreen relative of beetroot grown for its leaves. Consequently it needs more nitrogen than beetroot. It will thrive when manure, especially poultry manure, is worked into the soil (pH 6-6.5) about four weeks before sowing or planting. The leaves can be harvested all year round, even in colder areas, as it is very frost hardy. Make successional plantings every three months. Seed can be sown in drills 2 cm deep and when large enough to handle transplant 50 cm x 60 cm apart. Water in with liquid blood and bone and repeat at weekly intervals. Harvesting begins about 60 days from sowing. Like beetroot, it may bolt if planted too early in spring. September plantings will produce for many months if the leaves are picked regularly. Another sowing in late November will extend cropping through winter. The leaves are harvested as required, but never strip the plant right down to its heart, as this will severely check its growth. Rust is occasionally a

Shallots ready for harvesting

problem and, if it has been previously, dunk the plants in cupric hydroxide before planting.

SPINACH
(SPINACIA OLERACEA)

Spinach, made famous by Popeye, is an annual growing to 30 cm high with rosettes of broad, smooth or wrinkled leaves. It is a winter crop as in warm weather it tends to bolt. It requires a similar soil to silverbeet. Sow in late August in drills 1 cm deep and 45 cm apart and thin to 50 cm apart. Make regular sowings at three-week intervals. Leaves can be picked individually or the whole plant can be harvested. Pick the outside leaves while they are young and tender by breaking the stalk by hand. Do not tear the leaf stems away from the plant's base as this damages the plant. During summer give the plants a regular soaking (at least 18 litres per m² each week) to help prevent bolting. Harvesting will be 45-80 days from sowing. Downy mildew can be a problem.

SPINACH, NEW ZEALAND
(TETRAGONIA EXPANSA)

New Zealand spinach is a sprawling plant with fleshy leaves that thrives in hot dry climates and poor soils. Sow in early November after all danger of frost is over. The seed should be soaked overnight before sowing. Space plants at least 50 cm x 80 cm apart. Each plant will soon cover around 1 m². If space is limited grow them up wire netting. Harvesting should begin 6-8 weeks after sowing and will continue for several months.

SWEDE AND TURNIP
(BRASSICA CAMPESTRIS VAR. RUTABAGA, B. RAPA)

Turnips and swedes are biennials mainly grown for their edible roots, however the young leaves are also cut in August and September for use as a green vegetable. They are brassicas and so have similar requirements to cabbage. Swedes are usually grown for winter harvesting, but turnips may be grown all year round. The flavour of both is intensified by frosts. Main-crop turnips and swedes require much the same methods of cultivation, although sowing dates and plant spacings differ. Preparation of the soil (pH 6-6.5) is identical and both crops are sown in their final positions and not transplanted. The roots fork if they are grown in soil that contains fresh manure or compost. A site well-manured for a previous crop is preferable. The site is dug over and prepared as a seedbed. Before sowing rake in a balanced fertiliser (80 g/m²). Sow in drills 1 cm deep and 40 cm apart from August until January. Thin the seedlings to 20-25 cm apart when they are 4-5 cm high. Keep well weeded and feed with liquid blood and bone every three weeks. Harvesting is about 60 days from sowing. Club root attacks all brassicas, and turnips and swedes are no exception (see cabbages). Downy mildew sometimes attacks these crops.

SWEET CORN (ZEA MAYS)

This vegetable is a firm favourite with most New Zealanders. It is frost-tender and dislikes temperatures below 10°C. Short

Sweet corn

cobs are faster maturing than long cobs and are thus more suitable for colder areas. Sweet corn tolerates a range of soils so long as there is good drainage. Prepare the soil (pH 5.5-6.5) by digging in plenty of manure or compost in August. In early September rake the area over to bring it to a fine tilth and add blood and bone (250 g/m²) and Nitrophoska blue (100 g/m²). Sweet corn can be sown from late September at three-weekly intervals until January. Soak the seed for 2-4 hours before sowing. Sow the seed 5 cm deep and 7 cm apart in rows 1 m apart and later thin to 25 cm apart. Foliar feeding with liquid blood and bone improves the yield; apply initially when the plants are about 60 cm high and weekly thereafter. Take care when weeding as they dislike root disturbance. Sweet corn needs ample water for good quality, evenly matured cobs, particularly once the cobs start

New Zealand spinach

The ever-popular tomato

to fill. Expect each plant to produce at least two cobs and allow 85-100 days from sowing to harvest. Male flowers are produced at the top of the cob in tassels and the female flowers or 'ears' are enclosed by sheaths from which many silks emerge. The development of well-filled cobs depends on adequate pollination and, as sweet corn is wind pollinated, planting in several short rows or blocks is advisable for optimal pollination. Shaking the stalks on windless days will help release pollen. The cobs are best picked when the liquid exuded from a kernel changes from clear to milky. Some growers maintain that the cobs are ready when the tassels start to shrivel and turn brown, but this is unreliable. Remove the husks immediately, and if they are not cooked or frozen immediately, store the cobs in a plastic bag in the refrigerator. The main problem is corn earworm, a small caterpillar that feeds on the kernels. Once the caterpillar has moved inside the ear, control is difficult. Damaged cobs may still be eaten, but they are prone to rotting and attack from other insects. This caterpillar also attacks tomatoes, beans and strawberries. Dust with sumicidin or derris dust as the cobs start to form or spray

with carbaryl (1.25 g/l) every 7-10 days.

TOMATO (LYCOPERSICON ESCULENTUM)

Tomatoes are the most widely grown vegetable in New Zealand. Labour Weekend signals the tomato planting season in the North Island and early November in coastal Canterbury, but Central Otago and many parts of Southland prove too cold for tomatoes, except in greenhouses. Tomatoes require a warm friable soil (pH 6-6.5) well-enriched with manure or compost, a position in full sun and sheltered from wind, and regular watering. Frequent liquid feeding is also recommended. There is a plethora of cultivars bred for different traits. Determinate tomatoes grow to a certain height and thus often need no staking, and all the fruit sets within a relatively short time – usually about 7-10 days. For the home gardener indeterminate varieties are better as growth continues throughout the season and fruits set over a longer period. Indeterminate cultivars can grow for several years and still bear good crops in warmer areas or if they are grown by hydroponics or in a heated greenhouse.

TOMATO CULTIVATION

To prepare the site, sow a mixture of oats and mustard during April and in early August dig these in. Lupins are used by some gardeners, however they are susceptible to the fungus *Sclerotinia*, which can also attack tomatoes and potatoes and will sometimes kill them. Apply dolomite lime (200 g/m³) after digging in the green manure crop. In early October fork over the soil to at least 30 cm deep. Make a trench about 20 cm deep and apply a thin layer of a commercial fertiliser (e.g., with an NPK ratio of 5:10:10) and cover it with 5-6 cm of soil. Alternatively apply a deeper layer of organic fertiliser, such as dried animal or poultry manure or blood and bone, as well as additional organic matter including compost. Avoid quick-acting nitrogenous fertilisers.

Sow the seed in a tray or punnet in August so that plants are ready for planting outside in October and place in a warm situation. Prick them out as soon as they are large enough to handle and after several weeks harden them off before planting outdoors. Careful transplanting is essential. Mistakes, such as rushing your plants into the ground before they are properly hardened or roughing the roots when you're handling them, can set back the plants by weeks. Allow at least 90 cm between plants. To prevent your plants sprawling about, and to help them remain disease free, some system of support is needed. Staking individual plants saves space, keeps the plants and fruit off the ground, and the pruning that staked tomatoes require forces more of the plant's energy into ripening fruit, which thus matures earlier and is larger. However, the total yield of staked plants is often lower as all side-shoots or laterals must be removed. An alternative is to place 2 m high stakes every 4 m. Along their tops place some old galvanised water pipe and along the base tie wire very tightly. Stretch string or baler twine between the pipe and wire as close to each plant as possible and ensure it is reasonably taut. As the plants grow, secure them to the string every 20 cm. Nothing can better the single-stem method of training tomatoes. This involves removing all laterals as they appear as they will compete for nutrients with the main stem. If you want additional stems, allow them to develop from near the base. (Laterals make excellent cuttings.) When your plants reach the top of their support structure, pinch out the top just above a flower truss. Harvesting will begin 3-4 months from planting.

Temperature, rather than sunlight, is important for ripening. Fruit can be picked when they start to show colour and ripened indoors in a warm position or left to ripen on the plant.

Once plants are established it is advisable to remove the lower leaves to improve air circulation and reduce the risk of disease. Each leaf immediately above the lowest colouring fruit truss is also commonly removed, however the developing fruits could be scorched by strong sunlight if too many leaves are removed. White fly, caterpillars and aphids are among the most troublesome pests both outdoors and in greenhouses. Tomato stem borer can be a problem in summer. Wilting is often the first indication of trouble and an examination of the base of the stem will reveal the exit holes and general grub damage. Derris dust is excellent for control before the grubs burrow inside. Once inside the stem maldison will have to be used. Tomato russet mite may be present in large numbers on the undersurface of the leaf, on stems and on the fruit. The first symptom is usually the lower leaves becoming dull grey and smooth underneath and later brown and papery. The mites gradually move upwards, and with severe infestations blossom and fruit drop may occur. It attacks many plants, including tomatoes, peppers, eggplants, potatoes and petunias. Control is difficult. Do not plant tomatoes continually in the same site as mites can move from old leaves lying on the ground on to new plants. Spray immediately with maldison (1 ml/l). Late blight, which also attacks potatoes, can attack plants at any stage and is fostered by warm wet conditions. It appears first as greenish-brown to black areas on the leaves and stems. Eventually russet-brown mouldy areas develop on the fruit, which shrivels and turns brown. Stem rot is another common fungal disease indicated by dark lesions occurring near the base of the stem. Fruits can also be attacked, showing blackened areas around the calyx. Stringent hygiene is essential. Both late blight and stem rot can be controlled or prevented by spraying every 10-14 days with cupric hydroxide commencing before planting out. It is very important to cover every part of the plant with copper.

Numerous physiological disorders can also affect tomatoes. Catface is usually caused by low overnight temperatures or irregular watering. Blossom-end rot is caused by calcium deficiency, often as a result of inadequate watering or high levels of magnesium, sodium or potassium in the soil. Greenback is a failure of the fruit to colour properly. The change from green to red pigments is inhibited by temperatures above 30°C. Under direct sunlight, fruit temperatures can be up to 5°C above the air temperature, so ensure there is adequate foliage shading the fruits. The main cause of blotchy-ripening disorders seems to be overwatering.

Overwatering of 'non-greenback' or 'even-ripening' cultivars causes what is called 'waxiness', with the whole fruit appearing semi-transparent and the veins are clearly visible. Blossom drop, where many of the flowers on the first truss fall off without setting, is caused by overnight temperatures falling below 12°C or remaining above 32°C, or day temperatures consistently above 32°C.

YAM

Chinese yam. A member of the genus *Dioscorea*, these tuberous-rooted vegetables are rarely grown by home gardeners. The tubers are large and milky and are cooked like potatoes. Any well-drained soil in a sunny open position will suffice. Plant the small tubers 6 cm deep and 30 cm apart in September at the earliest. These plants need a structure to grow up. Avoid manures and fertilisers high in nitrogen as they are detrimental to tuber production.

Oka or New Zealand yam. One of the many vegetables grown commercially but rarely by home gardeners. Do not be put off by the fact it is an oxalis. They produce tubers of excellent quality and flavour and are used for roasting like parsnips, potatoes and kumaras. The tubers are a very light pink or red colour, cylindrical in shape and up to 15 cm long. They are smooth-skinned and shiny and the skin is pitted with eyes. Some tubers tend to be acidic, but leaving them to cure in the sun for a few days after harvesting will reduce the acidity. They are frost-tender and should not be planted until the end of October. Prepare the soil as for potatoes. Apply a well-balanced fertiliser (such as 8 parts blood and bone to 2 parts sulphate of potash) at planting time at 30 g/m² and repeat twice during the growing season. The longer the growing season, the greater the likely yield. The plant is vigorous and produces a mass of stems. Mound up with soil as for potatoes to encourage greater tuber production. Harvest when the tops die down naturally or are cut back by frosts. The tubers can be dug up and stored or left in the ground and lifted as required. Harvest carefully and lift every tuber as they can become invasive. Sometimes wireworm will attack the tubers, but they are otherwise free of pests and diseases.

THE PLANTS

HERBS

What is a herb? Preparing a herb garden; Popular herbs and their uses

HERBS MAKE AN IMPORTANT contribution to any garden. They consist of a range of undemanding annuals, biennials and perennials, shrubs and trees that with their differing habits of growth, leaf form and the colours of their leaves and flowers not only provide all the ornamental elements we expect from our garden plants, but serve a practical function as well. Herbs can be used to flavour our foods, they provide refreshing teas, their medicinal properties can soothe and heal and their aroma freshens and sweetens our air.

While prepared herbs are easy to find in shops, fresh herbs have a delicate, rich flavour often lost in drying. Herbs bought in shops are usually commercially grown and while being grown are saturated with poisonous insecticides, whilst those grown in your own garden can be free of these poisons. And with a constant supply on hand in the garden, herb growers can easily indulge in delicacies not available to others: cream cheese sandwiches on brown bread, packed with fresh marjoram leaves or mint and chives, or stimulating teas made from just-picked angelica, rosemary or sage.

The modern herb garden is the direct descendent of the apothecary's garden. However, many of the more colourful uses have passed into the realm of folklore. These days we're more likely to grow plants such as *Filipendula* and paeony for their beauty rather than for medicinal uses yet the value of a well-stocked herb garden is beyond dispute.

The emphasis in most modern herb gardens has shifted to the culinary herbs. There is, no doubt, an increasing interest in the medical and pharmaceutical value of herbs but by far the majority of herbs are sold for culinary use.

WHAT IS A HERB?

This question is bound to crop up in any discussion about herb gardens. The answer is, I'm afraid, fairly vague. The botanical definition is the same as that for a herbaceous perennial but in the gardening sense a herb is any plant that is commonly used for culinary, medical, pharmaceutical or cosmetic purposes.

That covers an extremely diverse range of plants many of which you would certainly not contemplate growing in your herb garden. Plants ranging from seaweed (carrageen) to the cinchona tree (quinine) fit this definition but the plants grown in domestic herb gardens tend to be culinary herbs, such as parsley and sage, or aromatic herbs, such as lavender. Keen herb growers will probably also have a few medicinal herbs, such as feverfew (*Tanacetum parthenium*) and *Verbascum*. Many common ornamental perennials also fit this definition although they are seldom used for anything other than decorative purposes.

PREPARING A HERB GARDEN

A herb garden can be as simple as a few pots on a kitchen windowsill or as complicated as an

Above: *Dipsacus fullonum*
Below: *Salvia sclarea*

elaborate Elizabethan knot garden. Yet however you choose to grow herbs their requirements are relatively few. In general, you should prepare the site just as you would a perennial border. Work in plenty of humus-containing material and give an all over dressing of a general purpose fertiliser. However, your exact method of preparation depends entirely on what you intend to grow.

The ideal herb garden will need to be able to provide a wide range of conditions to cover the wide range of plants that can be grown. There are herbs for all positions from shade (parsley and most mints) to full sun but the majority of herbs do best where they receive at least half a day's sun. Most herbs, especially rosemary, lavender and the chamomiles, need good drainage. Some, particularly those of Mediterranean origin, do best on light shingly soils while others, such as watercress, prefer boggy conditions.

Many herbs make effective additions to perennial borders and are often well worth growing for their ornamental merits alone. Others make useful container plants. Some, such as the carpeting thymes, can be used as ground covers or even lawn substitutes. Indeed if you put your mind to it there's a herb for just about every purpose.

Regular picking in spring and summer will keep the smaller shrubby herbs tidy and prevent them becoming too leggy. It also keeps

them steadily producing new growths, which are the best to use.

When planning a herb garden, or when using herbs in other parts of your garden, bear in mind the different sizes and habits of herbs, some are annual, some perennial.

Perennial herbs carry on growing from year to year as opposed to annuals, which have to be grown from seed sown each spring since they die off completely at the season's end. In comparison, many annual herbs have a comparatively short life. In little more than two months from the time they are growing strongly they can be spent. Luckily, all herbs can be grown from seed, with the exception of tarragon and mint. The seed is usually sown in spring.

If perennials are grown from seed, some time must be left, usually 18 months, before picking can start to allow the plants to become established. Many of these perennial herbs can be purchased as seedlings or established plants from better garden centres or from specialist nurseries, thus reducing the waiting period. Once you have a stock of these perennials, you can maintain or increase it by either taking small cuttings or by root division, according to the nature of the herb.

It is customary to group perennials of somewhat similar size and requiring roughly the same management and soil conditions in a special herb garden, preferably not far from the kitchen. The bigger and more impressive perennials might then form another group nearby or be dispersed individually among shrubs or in the perennial flower garden.

Low-growing herbs especially suited for borders are mint, chives, thyme and chervil. Mint can become invasive, so take preventative measures if this is a problem. These smaller bushier perennials and the medium sized ones are equally at home in window boxes, tubs and pots on a sunny patio growing in a commercially prepared potting mix. Tarragon, sweet basil, oregano, coriander, marjoram, winter savory and lemon balm are all of medium height.

Tall plants to use as background or a central feature include angelica, lovage, rosemary and dill, and borage is lovely if left to drift; a blue cloud in a corner of the garden.

Remember, too, that although herbs are generally grown together in an area set aside for them, they are ornamental plants in their own right and can be used in flower beds, borders, in lawns and 'meadows' as you would any flower or shrub.

A herb garden can provide a charming focal point for a vegetable garden.

POPULAR HERBS AND THEIR USES

THE FOLLOWING LIST provides special cultivation and propagation requirements of individual herb species. Most herbs have many varieties, but these have been listed separately only when their growing habits differ.

ALLIUM SCHOENOPRASUM

Chives belong to the onion family and are low-growing perennials with round spiky leaves and round mauve flowers. Pick the leaves on a regular basis and keep flowers from forming. The leaves have a mild onion flavour and die back in winter. Divide and replant bulbs in the autumn. Try also *A. tuberosum*, garlic chives, which have fat leaves and stay green and growing all year. Both need a rich well-drained soil and full sun with adequate moisture to do well.

ANETHUM GRAVEOLENS

Dill is an aromatic annual with bluish green feathery leaves and yellow flowers, borne in summer. It grows to at least 90 cm and is very hardy. Sow seed in a warm sunny position with rich well-drained soil in spring. The seeds have a pungent odour and are mainly used in pickles. Dill seeds are known for aiding digestion and both the seeds and leaves are good with cucumbers, potatoes, fish and seafood, cabbage, eggs and pork.

ANGELICA ARCHANGELICA

Angelica is a vigorous hardy biennial with large bright green leaves and umbels of small green or white flowers in late summer. It grows to 2 m. However, if you remove the seed heads before they flower, the plant keeps growing as a perennial. Old, established plants should be divided. If sowing, choose a moisture-retentive, well-drained site in light shade and protect from strong winds and use fresh seed, as it loses vitality quickly. The tender stems and leaf mid-ribs of angelica are used for flavouring confectionery and liqueurs.

ANTHRISCUS CEREFOLIUM

Chervil is an annual that should be grown from fresh seed. It also self-sows in some situations. Chervil prefers semi-shade in hot summer weather, and full sun in winter. It has white flowers and grows to about 40 cm high. Pick leaves from the outside and stop using once it has flowered. The flavour is fresh and spicy, with a hint of anise. It is a delicate alternative to parsley.

AMORACIA RUSTICANA

Horseradish is a very invasive perennial that needs to be kept contained. Every little piece of root will grow and these should be planted in spring. It likes a rich, well-drained soil in full sun or partial shade and the plant will last for years. The very hot roots are used in sauces for some meat dishes.

ARNICA MONTANA

Arnica is an extremely potent perennial herb that was once extensively used as an internal medicine. It is now regarded as being too dangerous to use internally without supervision but is still used externally in the treatment of bruises and inflammations. It has soft green stems and bright green leaves. The yellow daisy-like flowers appear in summer. Grow in moist well-drained soil in sun or light shade. Raise from seed or divide established clumps in late winter or early spring.

ARTEMISIA DRACUNCULUS

French tarragon is one of the most famous of all the culinary herbs. They are hardy bushy perennials that grow to around 1 m in warmer months, but die back in winter. They need a rich, moisture-retentive, well-drained soil in full sun. Propagate from root division and space them 50 cm apart. French tarragon is used in tarragon vinegar. Fresh tarragon leaves are used with other herbs to flavour omelettes and classical French sauces. Good with fish, poultry, eggs and salads. Although it does not dry well, it can be frozen in small plastic bags.

BORAGO OFFICINALIS

A very pretty annual herb that is grown from seed sown in late spring (September) or autumn (April). The beautiful blue flowers appear throughout winter and are enjoyed by bees for this reason. The plant grows to 80 cm and is hardy, requiring a light well-drained soil in full sun or partial shade. The leaves have a slight cucumber flavour and are used in cold drinks and salads. The blue flowers are edible and often used as garnish for salads, drinks and crystallised for cake decoration.

CALAMINTHA GRANDIFLORA

Calamint was once an important medicinal herb but is now mainly grown as an ornamental although some herbalists use it to make a tea, for which they use the whole plant. Several species are grown, all of which are perennials with oval, toothed leaves and spikes of pink or mauve flowers. Easily grown in any moist well-drained soil in sun or light shade. Propagate by the division of established clumps, basal cuttings or seed.

CARUM CARVI

Caraway is a hardy biennial grown from seed sown in spring or autumn in a light, well-drained soil in full sun. Caraway grows to about 90 cm and the lacy leaves, reminiscent of parsley, are followed in the second year by small white flowers. The seeds that develop are aromatic and known to aid digestion. They are used in breads (especially rye), cakes and pickles, and with meat and fish. The oil extracted from them is used in making the liqueur Kummel. The roots are also edible.

CHAMAEMELUM NOBILE

Chamomile is a well-known ground cover herb that is becoming increasingly popular as a herb lawn. There are flowering varieties, whose small white daisy-like flowers appear in spring through to autumn but if you wish to try it as a lawn use 'Treneague', a non-flowering variety. Chamomile is propagated by seed or root division of mature plants and it is hardy in moist well-drained soil in full sun. Chamomile is renowned as a relaxing herbal tea.

CORIANDRUM SATIVUM

Coriander is an annual grown for both its seeds and leaves. Sow from seed in spring in an open situation in full sun with a rich well-drained soil. Harvest leaves until the pink lacy flowers appear. It grows to about 60 cm high. Fresh leaves are a popular flavouring in Asian dishes and the seeds are also used for flavouring. Seeds shed easily so they need gathering when they are beginning to brown. Try both seeds and leaves in stews and curries, or with lamb, apples, marmalade and cakes.

CUMINUM CYMINUM

Cumin is an annual with finely cut leaves and heads of small white or pale pink flowers that resemble yarrow umbels. Although once regarded as a medicinal herb, the seeds are now used primarily for culinary purposes and are one of the main ingredients of curry powder. Grow in moist well-drained soil in a position sheltered from cold draughts. Raise from seed.

CYMBOPOGON CITRATUS

Lemon grass is widely grown as a culinary herb. The foliage has a strong lemon scent and flavour. It is a tropical plant that demands even moisture and warm temperatures to grow well and is usually treated as a summer annual in all but the mildest areas. It may be grown indoors but the flavour is a pale imitation of that of an outdoor

Foeniculum vulgare in flower.

Helichrysum angustifolium

Chamomile, lavender and *Santolina*.

cultivated plant. Raise from seed or divide established clumps.

DIPSACUS

Teasel (*D. fullonum*) and Fullers teasel (*D. sativus*) are nowadays primarily grown as ornamentals and for their seed heads, which are used as dried decorations. It was used as a medicinal herb in the Middle Ages, and the spiny seed heads were long used for combing wool. These species are hardy biennials with strong upright stems that grow to about 2 m high. They have small lavender flowers in rounded heads and it is these heads that develop into the characteristic seed heads. Grow in moist well-drained soil in sun and raise from seed.

ECHINACEA PURPUREA

Coneflower is most commonly seen as a garden ornamental but it is also used to make a herbal tonic. A similar species, *E. angustifolia* is supposedly more effective than the common perennial. Both species have deep green leaves and stiffly erect pinkish purple daisy-like flowers. Grow in light well-drained soil in full sun and propagate by division of well-established clumps or raise from seed.

ERUCA VESICARIA

Rocket is an annual or short-lived perennial with small yellow flowers and soft greyish-green leaves that are frequently added to salads. It reaches about 1 m high and is easily grown in any well-drained soil in full sun. Raise from seed.

FOENICULUM VULGARE

Common fennel is a hardy graceful perennial that grows to a height of 2 m. It has attractive grey-green leaves and yellow flowers that appear in summer. Bronze fennel (*F. vulgare* var. *azoricum*) is similar but has bronze green leaves and grows to around 1.5 m. Fennel will die back during winter in cooler climates and is sometimes grown as an annual. Propagate from seed sown in full sun in a well-drained alkaline soil in spring. The leaves are used for flavouring soups and as a sauce for fish dishes. The aniseed-like smell and flavour is very pleasant.
F. vulgare var. *dulce*, or Florence fennel, is often grown as an annual in the vegetable garden. Sow from seed in spring in colder areas and autumn in areas with mild winters. Florence fennel needs a rich well-drained soil in full sun and plenty of water in hot weather so the swollen oval leaf bases, that can be eaten raw or cooked, develop.

GALIUM

Lady's bedstraw (*G. verum*) and sweet woodruff (*G. odoratum*) are the most widely grown species of this genus. Both are low-growing perennials with narrow bright green leaves arranged in whorls around the stems. The small flowers are carried in loose heads. *G. odoratum* has white flowers reminiscent of candytuft (*Iberis*) while *G. verum* has golden yellow flowers. Both species are used for medicinal purposes and taken as infusions (teas). Grow in light well-drained soil in full sun or partial shade. Usually raised from seed.

HELICHRYSUM ANGUSTIFOLIUM

The curry plant is not one of the constituents of curry powder but it does have a strong curry scent and the leaves are edible. It is a perennial or sub-shrub with narrow silvery grey leaves and heads of small yellow flowers. Grow in light well-drained soil in full sun. May be raised from seed or semi-ripe cuttings.

HESPERIS MATRIONALIS

Sweet rocket is a short-lived perennial often found growing wild in waste areas and is also occasionally grown as an ornamental. The young leaves are used as a salad vegetable and it is occasionally used for medicinal purposes. The pink flowers are scented in the evening. Grow in moist well-drained soil in full sun. Raise from seed.

HYSSOPUS OFFICINALIS

Hyssop is a shrubby perennial that grows to 60 cm and has blue, pink or white flowers in summer. It is grown from seed in spring; by division of the roots in August; or from young soft tip cuttings in October/November. The leaves are narrow and aromatic and the young shoots and flowers infused in hot water are used as an expectorant. Plant in full sun in a light, alkaline, well-drained soil and prune after flowering to discourage leggy growth. Hyssop prefers cooler, drier regions.

LAURUS NOBILIS

A medium sized (7 m) ornamental tree, bay is slow growing and so is excellent for

growing in large tubs or pots. It is also an ideal focal point for a herb garden. It needs to be pruned heavily to produce new leaves and is a good topiary subject. However, it is only hardy to -10°C, and so may need to be brought inside in winter. Grow in a humus-enriched, well-drained soil and protect from dry winds and hot sun in very warm areas. The pungent and aromatic leaves can be used sparingly in stews, soups and other savoury dishes.

LEONURUS

Motherwort is a perennial with strongly upright stems that grows to about 1.2 m high. Long flower spikes with small pale pink flowers form at the tops of the stems. It is rather a coarse untidy plant that is seldom used for its medicinal purposes so only the most dedicated herb growers are likely to enthuse over it. May be grown from seed, by division or from semi-ripe cuttings.

LEPIDIUM SATIVUM

Cress is a rapidly germinating annual that is grown as a sprout and for the use of its young leaves as a salad vegetable. It takes about 5-7 days to germinate and can be used immediately. Wash the seed well and sprout on moist paper towels. When grown for its young leaves simply scatter the seed on the open ground and lightly rake in.

LEVISTICUM OFFICINALE

Lovage is a perennial, with yellow flowers in summer that will grow to at least 2 m in southern areas. Each plant will require at least 1 square metre. It is hardy, and indeed prefers cooler districts, doing best in a rich moisture-retentive soil in full sun. Propagate by seed sown in summer or by root division in spring. The leaves and stems have a pungent taste, rather like curry-flavoured celery. Add the leaves to stews and salads, and cook the fresh stems.

LIPPIA CITRIODORA

Lemon verbena is a delightfully scented small shrub which will grow to about 1.5 m in a warm, sheltered position in full sun. It prefers a humus-enriched well-drained soil, and needs watering in summer. Cut it back hard every spring to encourage new growth and prevent it becoming straggly. It is easily grown from cuttings taken anytime. Lemon verbena is grown for its leaves which have a strong lemon scent and can be used in teas, stuffings for poultry, fish and veal. It is also used in cakes and is an excellent pot pourri, either alone or in combination with other herbs.

MELISSA OFFICINALIS

Lemon balm is a perennial which grows to about 75 cm high. Its small white flowers appear in late summer and attract bees. It likes a rich moisture-retentive soil in light shade. Although it dies back in winter, it is very hardy and will shoot again in spring. It can be grown from seed or division. Its leaves have a distinct lemon taste and can be added fresh to cold drinks and fruit salads. Try also *M. officinalis* subsp. *altissima* or Turkish balm. This plant's arrival in this country is something of a mystery as it was first discovered growing wild. It is now cultivated for its wonderful scent. A tall-growing plant (1 m), the leaves are light green and slightly hairy. It does best in moist places in full sun. Cut back after flowering to avoid rampant self-sowing. Propagate by seed, cuttings or division.

MENTHA

There are many types of mints: *M. spicata* (spearmint) is the most popular mint for cooking; *M.* x *piperita* (peppermint) is grown for its fragrant foliage and

for cooking purposes; *M. puleguim* (pennyroyal) is a useful ground cover that can take some light foot traffic, but is not tolerant of drought; *M. suaveolens* (apple mint), another culinary mint; and *M.* x 'Citrata' (eau de cologne mint), which is too bitter for cooking but is grown for its fragrant leaves. Some are evergreen, some are deciduous and they vary in size from creeping ground covers to plants about 40 cm high. All are hardy perennials and all can be invasive in rich moist soils in full sun. They also need constant lifting and dividing to keep young new growths appearing. Grow from root cuttings.

MONARDA DIDYMA

Bergamot is a hardy perennial that grows to about 1 m in a moist, well-drained, slightly acid soil. It flowers well in sun or light shade and the scarlet flowers appear in late summer. The plant should be lifted every 2-3 years in spring and divided. Plants can also be trimmed back to shape regularly. Varieties bear differently coloured flowers including white and pink shades. The leaves are popular as a soothing tea.

MYRRHIS ODORATA

Sweet cicely is a culinary herb that has a mild aniseed flavour. It has bright green leaves and heads of white flowers and looks very much like the very poisonous hemlock (*Conium maculatum*). Although a herbaceous perennial, it is often treated as an annual and raised from seed each year. It may also be propagated by dividing established clumps in late winter.

NEPETA CATARIA

Catnip, or catmint as it is sometimes known, is a perennial with grey-green leaves that can grow to 1 m. The small flowers are white with reddish dots and can appear from late spring through summer. Plant in a light well-drained soil in full sun or light shade. Cats are often attracted to these plants and may lie on or even eat the leaves (they have been known to dig up the plants). It self-sows and

dies back in winter. Try making a refreshing tea from the leaves.

OCIMUM BASILICUM

Basil is a bushy annual with small white flowers that grows up to 60 cm. Nip out the tips to encourage a more bushy plant. Propagate from seed sown after the last frosts and sow in a moist well-drained soil in a warm sunny position. The leaves are pungent and aromatic, more so when fresh, and their flavour has an affinity with tomatoes, but is equally good with cheese, eggs and in dressings with vinegar. Young leaves are used to flavour salads and for cooked dishes.

ORIGANUM MARJORANA

Majoram is a neat, low, frost-tender, perennial bush, with mauve or white flowers, that grows to 60 cm. It is best sown annually in cooler climates. It is very susceptible to damping off when young and dying from wet feet in humid areas, so plant in a sunny well-drained position. Cut the stems before flowering and trim the foliage regularly. Its leaves are used in savoury foods and breads.

ORIGANUM

Oregano grows into a bushy perennial about 50 cm high. Flower colour can vary with the species, from purple, through pink to white, but all appear in summer. Plant in a rich well-drained soil in a sunny position and propagate from seed in spring or root division. The leaves are used both fresh and dried and give a pungent, hot flavour to many dishes. This herb is a must for Italian food like pizza and spaghetti, and is also good with tomatoes.

PETROSELINUM CRISPUM

I think parsley is one plant that is grown in every garden in New Zealand! It is a biennial herb that grows to around 30 cm. It must have rich, moist soil in which to grow and sow the seed, which is slow to germinate, in drills and then thin to 20 cm apart. One way to help germination is to mix a packet of seed with sufficient sand to fill three-quarters of a glass

Top: *Nepeta*
Above: Assorted forms of basil (*Ocimum*)

tumbler. Pour in some very hot water until the glass is full and then pour off the surplus water. Keep the moist mixture in a warm place and when the seeds start to sprout, set them out 15 cm apart in the garden. Maintain a good water supply and feed generously with liquid blood and bone. There are many varieties, the most common being the familiar curly-leafed type. Remember to use the leaves before the plant flowers.

PIMPINELLA ANISUM

Anise or aniseed is an annual that is strongly aromatic. It is primarily used as a culinary herb but also has some medicinal uses. The shape of the foliage varies with the maturity of the plant but at all stages is covered with fine hairs. The clusters of small white flowers are followed by seed pods that contain the strongly flavoured seeds. Easily grown in any sunny position. Raise from seed.

ROSMARINUS OFFICINALIS

Rosemary is a lovely garden plant with its pale mauve flowers and scented, aromatic foliage. It

Top: Ground cover thymes with purple sage and variegated sage in the background.
Above: *Rosmarinus officianalus* 'Prostratus'

is a shrub that grows to 1 m and can be grown outside in warmer areas. If grown in a container, take it indoors during cold winter (it doesn't like temperatures much below 0°C). It enjoys a light well-drained soil in full sun, and is good for coastal gardens as it withstands salt-laden winds well. Propagate from cuttings. The leaves, fresh or dried, are used to flavour lamb, veal, pork and corned beef dishes and are great in stews, soups and baked goods.

RUMEX ACETOSA

Sorrel and French sorrel (*R. scutatus*) are both very hardy perennials that prefer rich, moist, slightly acid, well-drained soils. They are easily grown from seed or division of the roots. Can be invasive and must be kept under control. The sour-tasting leaves can be used to flavour salads, soups and sauces – it is great in omelettes. *R. scutatus* has slightly smaller leaves than *R. acetosa*, and some say a better flavour.

RUTA GRAVEOLENS

Rue is a hardy perennial shrub that grows to 60 cm and has yellow flowers that appear in summer. It prefers a slightly alkaline well-drained soil in full

sun and is propagated by division or stem cuttings. The leaves have a strong rather bitter taste, and are used for medicinal rather than culinary purposes. They can even be dangerous if taken in large quantities. But the leaves are also very decorative in their own right.

SALVIA SCLAREA

Clary sage is a hardy biennial grown from seed which needs to be moist to germinate. It has bluish-white flowers in the second year and grows to about 35 cm high. It enjoys a light well-drained position in full sun. The leaves of clary sage are used for flavouring soups.

SALVIA

These popular plants are grown for both culinary and decorative purposes. *S. officinalis*, sage, is a hardy bushy perennial that will grow to about 60 cm. It has downy grey-green leaves and mauve flowers that appear during summer. Grown from cuttings, the plants should be replaced every three years. Grow in a well-drained soil in full sun or light shade. Propagate from cuttings. The pungent leaves are used in cheese dishes, stuffings for poultry, with pork, eggs, fish and tomatoes. *S. officinalis* var. *purpurea* (red sage) and *S. rutilans* (pineapple sage) are just some of the other species available for culinary purposes.

SANGUISORBA MINOR

The foliage of the common roadside perennial weed salad burnet is used as a salad vegetable. It is a rosette-forming plant with slightly glaucous leaves and small yellow flowers that grows in any light well-drained soil in sun. Raise from seed or by the division of established clumps.

SAPONARIA OFFICIANALIS

Soapwort is a spreading ground cover perennial with small oblong leaves and bright pink flowers. Often grown as an ornamental, particularly the large double flowered forms, it also has herbal uses. When rubbed between the hands with water it lathers well and can be used as a

soap substitute. It can be used for most cleaning purposes and has some medicinal uses. Plant in well-drained soil in sun. Usually propagated by cuttings or from self-layered pieces.

SATUREJA

Summer savory, *S. hortensis*, is a bushy annual grown from seed in spring. The seed takes about 10 days to germinate if soaked before sowing and should be sown in a sunny position. Thin the seedlings to 15 cm apart. The plant grows about 35 cm high and tends to be top-heavy. Its lavender flowers appear in late summer. The leaves are traditionally used with broad beans, runner bean and peas. Winter savory (*S. montana*) and *S. thymbra* are perennials and can be grown from seed but are usually grown from small cuttings, layers and root division. Creeping savory (*S. rependa*) is also grown from layers or division. These last three prefer a sunny site and poorer, stony soils – too rich a soil encourages sappy growth which does not stand up to winter weather. They should be cut back hard after flowering and dead wood removed in spring. All savorys have a hot, spicy flavour and should be used in small quantities. When it comes into flower, the whole plant should be cut off at the base and hung in a shady place to dry for winter use.

SYMPHYTUM OFFICINALE

Great care should be taken in growing comfrey as it is a very invasive perennial. If allowed to set seed, it will spread over large areas, so never let seed heads grow. It is usually propagated from seed or pieces of root. Grow in a humus-enriched well-drained soil in semi-shade. It may die back to the roots in colder areas. The mauve flowers appear in late spring or summer. It is an excellent additive in compost bins and a good companion plant. More popular for its medicinal properties than culinary ones as it is mildly poisonous in large quantities.

TANACETUM PARTHENIUM

Many gardens will already have the perennial feverfew growing

for decorative purposes. It self-sows easily in rich well-drained soil in sun or partial shade. The leaves are similar to chrysanthemum leaves and the small white daisy-like flowers appear in late spring and summer. It is grown from either seed, root division or small cuttings and should be cut back after flowering to prevent the plant becoming woody. Feverfew is being used increasingly to help with migraines and also as a relief for arthritis. Try one large leaf or several smaller leaves eaten with bread and butter every day.

TANACETUM VULGARE

Tansy is a hardy perennial propagated from root division or from seed sown in early spring. While it likes a well-drained soil it will thrive just about anywhere, but it does die back in winter. In summer it produces bright yellow flowers, that are popular in arrangements when dried. If you don't wish to use them as such, remove the flower spikes to encourage leaf growth. Care should be taken with this herb as it is considered dangerous if taken in large quantities. Dried or fresh tansy is used to freshen up stale smelling rooms.

TARAXACUM OFFICINALIS

Dandelion is well known in New Zealand as a weed, but the flowers make a very good wine and the roots, washed, sliced, dried and roasted, provide a caffeine-free dandelion 'coffee'. The leaves are used by tearing them rather than chopping and they can be added to salads, eaten with Marmite in sandwiches, or cooked lightly in butter.

THYMUS VULGARIS

The common thyme from Europe is the best known of this popular culinary genus. There are many more different thymes – orange, silver, golden, caraway, and lemon to mention just a few. All are perennials and grown from tiny tip cuttings taken in early spring. All thymes like a sunny, well-drained soil and are fairly hardy once established. Keep well trimmed. Use the leaves to flavour many different types of food.

0

0

0

0

0

0

0

0

0

0

0

0

0

0

0

0

0

0

0

0

THE PLANTS

FRUIT, NUTS, VINES AND BERRIES

*Canes and berries; Citrus; Pip
fruit; Nuts; Stone fruit;
Subtropical fruits; Vines;
Nutrient requirements;
Pruning and training;
Popular fruit for the home garden*

THE HOME ORCHARD is not as popular today as it was even 10 years ago, and the decline can be put down to three main factors: a growing trend away from purely functional to ornamental gardening; smaller gardens; and a general perception that producing good fruit is tricky and time consuming. However, many fruiting plants perform both an ornamental and functional role. Fruiting trees or plants can be grown in containers on patios, espaliered or used as ornamental plantings, hedges or shade trees. The introduction of dwarf or semi-dwarf varieties in most types of fruit trees has enabled a range of trees to be grown in a small area.

The view that fruit trees are difficult to cultivate is not so easy to counter, not because they are prone to any more pests and diseases than other plants but because anything that does go wrong inevitably affects the final crop. Very few gardeners strive to produce perfect flowers, but producing anything less than perfect fruit is considered disappointing. This, combined with the move away from extensive spraying, has lead many gardeners to remove their fruit trees, bushes or canes. In reality these are minor difficulties that are easily overcome; fresh fruit all year round is an achievable ambition for the home gardener.

Home fruit production falls into seven main categories: canes and berries, citrus, pip fruit, nuts, stone fruit, subtropical and less common fruit and vines. The cultivation requirements vary depending on the type of fruit so we will look at each category separately.

CANES AND BERRIES

The fruit considered here are true berries, such as gooseberries and currants, as well as those that are not berries in the botanical sense, e.g., blackberries and strawberries. The latter are actually aggregate fruit made up of numerous smaller fruit. Most are small shrubs or ramblers and are ideal for small gardens. The canes of ramblers, such as blackberries, are easily trained on fences, wires and other suitable structures. Shrubby plants, such as gooseberries and currants, can be grown as shrubs or in low hedges.

Strawberries have more unique requirements, which are covered under the listing for individual fruit.

CITRUS

Many parts of New Zealand are suitable for citrus cultivation. Regular winter frosts will limit the success of types such as grapefruit and oranges but the hardiest lemons and kumquats are able to produce good fruit in most districts. Careful siting and the provision of frost protection are very important and warm summers are important for thorough ripening. Smaller-fruited types normally crop well in tubs and this is one means of growing citrus in cooler climates as it allows you to move the plant indoors over winter.

Choosing the right cultivar and a healthy plant is very important; a low-quality young plant will not develop into a healthy, productive tree. So find out the requirements you

High bush blueberries grow to about 4 m and prosper in cool-summer areas.

While red currants don't have winter chilling requirements, they do crop better when winters are cold.

Fallen apples in a small domestic orchard.

The mild climate of Tauranga provides an ideal climate for sweet oranges, as shown by the healthy crop on this tree.

need and find a plant to match, then select your tree or bush carefully.

Citrus are heavy feeders so regular feeding with a commercial citrus fertiliser is advisable for good cropping; water it in well. Regular watering, particularly during dry spells, is essential and an annual mulch is beneficial.

A deep well-drained soil is best and, as citrus have a shallow feeder-root system, avoid digging around the tree and having weeds and grass growing around the plant, thereby competing with your tree for nutrients.

Citrus require no pruning at planting time and thereafter require only pruning to shape and to remove dead or diseased wood, suckers, watershoots and crossed branches. They may be attacked by a number of pests and diseases, including collar rot, leaf-roller caterpillars, lemon tree borer, scale insects and verrucosis.

PIP FRUIT

Pip fruit get their name from the so-called pips or seeds that are encased in a central core. Included here are apples, pears, the nashi or Asian pear, pomegranates and quinces. Pip fruits are the 'Jack of all trades' of the home orchard. They can be grown in most districts of New Zealand and can be trained to suit many situations where space is at a premium.

They can be planted any time from May to August. Pears and quinces prefer rather heavy soils but they will still suffer if drainage is poor and apples can cope with a wide range of soil types except very light or very heavy soils.

Pip fruits bear fruit on short spurs that remain productive for many years. Apples and pears are subject to numerous pests and diseases, but careful timing of spraying and atten-

tion to detail can control many problems without too many harsh environmental effects.

NUTS

Nut trees often take many years to crop heavily but once established they are relatively trouble free. Also, the wait is not so bad because most are attractive trees that are worth growing solely as ornamental specimens.

The ornamental value of nut trees has long been appreciated, especially in large English gardens where the 'nut walk', an avenue of nut trees that form a canopy, is a tradition thought to date back to at least the reign of Elizabeth I. Gertrude Jekyll's garden 'Munstead Wood' and Vita Sackville-West's 'Sissinghurst' both contain well-known nut walks.

Hazels are the nuts most commonly used for nut walks. The trees are trained as single-stemmed standards up to a height of about 80 cm to reduce any tendency towards bushiness. Over the years the area under the hazels develops into a rich woodland soil that is ideal for naturalising many of the smaller woodland perennials and bulbs.

STONE FRUIT

Now known as 'summer fruit' in the fruit and vegetable trade, the stone fruits have long been staples of the home orchard. However, gardeners frequently fail to get the best from their trees. Poor pollination, late frosts, bird damage, insects and diseases often conspire to lessen the crop. However, most of these trees are such heavy croppers that the losses are often tolerable even when quite severe.

Peaches and nectarines flower on young wood produced during the previous summer, so remove any branches more than two years old. Plums, apricots and cherries also fruit on older wood, which allows greater leeway when pruning. After the initial framework of the tree is established little pruning should be needed. Remove any watershoots as they appear as they are non-productive. Any pruning should be done as soon as possible after harvest to lessen the risk of silver leaf.

Stone fruit require a period of winter chilling for flower development and fruit set, but newer varieties with reduced chilling requirements have been developed.

Stonefruit are attacked by a range of pests and diseases, such as silver leaf, leaf curl, brown rot, bladder plum, black spot and pear slug. Refer to the pests and diseases chapter for information on identification and control.

SUBTROPICAL FRUITS

Although climatic limitations restrict the choice in many areas, a wide range of subtropical fruits are grown successfully outdoors in New Zealand, predominantly in Northland, Auckland, the Bay of Plenty and Hawke's Bay. Citrus are undoubtedly the best known, but a number, such as tamarillos and passionfruit, have always been popular and a host of others are yet to be discovered by gardeners. These plants require rich soils, abundant water, shelter from wind and frosts, and a warm, usually sunny situation. Some can be grown in containers indoors in cooler climates.

VINES

Fruiting vines are usually large plants so you will need to allow for plenty of growing space and provide a strong support structure. They can be used in the same manner as ornamental climbers and grapes in particular are often grown on pergolas to provide a cool shady area in summer.

Careful training and pruning is essential to produce good crops, and as most fruiting vines flower on new growth, they need to be cut back hard each winter. Leaving too many fruiting spurs will result in overcrowded and undersized fruit that may fail to ripen properly so be prepared to sacrifice some quantity to raise the quality.

The soil should be well prepared prior to planting and the young plants fed regularly to encourage strong growth and the development of a good framework of branches. However, once established, avoid overfeeding vines with nitrogenous fertilisers as this will encourage strong vegetative growth and poor flowering and fruiting.

NUTRIENT REQUIREMENTS

Fruit trees, like any plants, require certain nutrients to grow and develop flowers and fruit. The feeding needs of plants that produce harvested crops, especially, need to be met if the harvest is to be a good one.

If you provide a humus-enriched, fertile soil, including perhaps a slow-release fertiliser when you plant your fruit tree or vine, you will get the plant off to a good start. (Refer to the chapter on trees for details of planting and staking young trees.) However, most fruit trees will benefit greatly from regular feeding. What to feed and when depends on the individual fruit tree or vine. For example, citrus trees,

Even in a small area fruit trees can make an ornamental and productive contribution to the garden design.

bananas and peaches have high nitrogen requirements, whereas grapevines rarely need any extra; apples, pears and some berry fruits need plenty of potassium. On the other hand, too much of a specific element can also cause problems. Too much nitrogen will encourage leaf growth at the expense of fruit set and development.

Where applicable, specific nutrient requirements have been noted under the individual fruit.

Growing grapes against a wall gives added warmth to help in ripening.

PRUNING AND TRAINING

Pruning of fruits and nuts requires an understanding of the plant's growth habit and vigour and the age of the fruit-bearing wood. With the exception of espaliering, the methods are distinct from those used for ornamentals and so are discussed here rather than in the pruning chapter. There are a number of reasons why fruit trees need regular pruning:

- To keep the plant manageable by restricting its height and width.

Grape vines are popular
climbers and require little space
to produce wonderful fruit.

choose, always prune branches to an outward-facing bud and remove crossing or inward-growing branches.

CANES

Brambles and other berries are usually supported on a wire system. The simplest method is to extend two parallel wires between two posts. The lower wire should be at least 60 cm above the ground and the uppermost wire a further 60 cm above this. Since these plants fruit on two-year-old wood, the old canes that have fruited are cut out at ground level after harvesting and new canes are tied in to produce the following season's crop. Fruiting canes are tied to the upper wire and new canes to the lower wire.

STANDARD, CENTRAL LEADER OR PYRAMID

This method is commonly used for pip and stone fruits. The main stem is retained and a pyramid-shaped tree produced by training branches in tiers up the stem. It promotes early cropping and, after the initial training, the tree requires only minimal pruning after about the fourth year. However, they will eventually become too tall for small gardens and the central stem may need stopping at a suitable height.

After planting, stop the central stem at a height of about 50 cm to 1 m. The first tier of three or four branches are trained at about this height and all other shoots are removed. Keep the branches nearly horizontal and evenly spaced around the stem by using spreaders, coiled wire or tying the branches down with twine attached to a stake in the ground. This is best done in late spring. Do not leave them in place for more than 8 weeks or they may become embedded in the branches.

The following winter the central stem will have extended vertically and formation of the second tier is begun about 50 cm to 1 m above the first. If there are no suitable laterals, prune the main stem at the desired height to encourage branching at this point. This is repeated in subsequent years to produce successive tiers. To promote early and heavy cropping, pruning can be kept to a minimum, apart from thinning and removing poorly placed branches and maintaining the pyramid shape. Heavier pruning will encourage a stronger framework but delay heavy cropping.

CORDONS, ESPALIERS AND FANS

These techniques involve training the plant on a wire fence or against a wall. They are ideal for small gardens and enable more plants to be grown in a limited space. The end result

- To maintain productivity.
- To limit the number of fruit produced to prevent overbearing and so maximise fruit size and quality.
- To replace old unproductive wood with new productive growth.
- To remove dead or diseased wood.
- To improve light penetration and air circulation in the centre of the plant.

A number of different training systems have evolved for fruits. Some fruit, such as apples, can be trained in a variety of ways, so it is a matter of deciding which best suits your requirements. It is usually necessary to train the young plant from the planting stage, but once the basic framework of branches is established, pruning is simply a matter of maintaining the shape and keeping the plant manageable and productive. Whatever training method you

TWO METHODS OF TRAINING A VINE

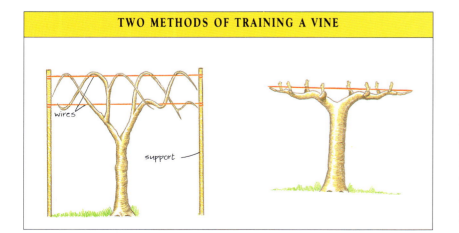

Above left: Rather than twine kiwifruit around a wire it is better to tie it.
Above right: Espalier is a useful technique for increasing productivity over a small area. Here apples are espaliered on wire supports.

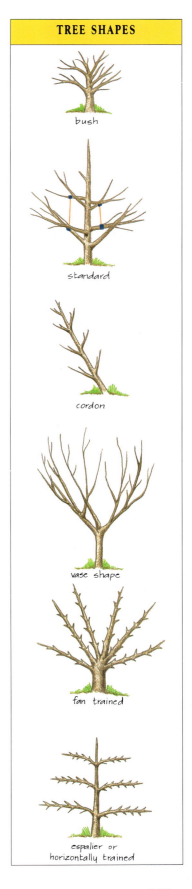

bush

standard

cordon

vase shape

fan trained

espalier or horizontally trained

can be most attractive and while they produce lower yields, the fruit quality is excellent.

Cordons have a single straight stem grown either erect or preferably obliquely at a 45–60° angle. Side shoots are pruned back to just a few buds to accelerate the formation of fruiting spurs and to maintain a narrow plant. After several years, thinning of the fruiting spurs to three or four per side shoot will become necessary. Plants should be spaced about 1 m apart depending on the type of plant. Apples and gooseberries are examples of fruit commonly trained as cordons.

It is also possible to train the cordon on two or more main stems. The original main stem is cut back to about 50 cm high and the desired number of shoots are trained accordingly. Multi-stemmed cordons must be planted at least 1–1.25 m apart.

Espaliers comprise a central, typically vertical, stem with several horizontal leaders trained along supporting wires about 50 cm apart. After the first growing season, prune the plant back to three buds. The two lowest shoots are trained horizontally along the wires and the third is trained vertically. The following winter the vertical shoot is pruned above two buds near the second wire and shoots are trained in the same manner as before. This is repeated in subsequent years. Many fruits, including pip fruits, are commonly trained as espaliers.

Fans are a variation in which the tree is trained with leaders radiating outwards from a central point. Several fruit trees, including stone fruits, can be trained as fans.

VASE SHAPE

The aim of this method is to keep the centre of the tree open while maintaining even outer growth. Training should begin as soon as the tree is planted. Fairly hard pruning is required for the first few years to build up a strong framework of branches. Pip and stone fruits are often trained in this manner.

At planting, select three or four strong laterals and remove all others as well as the central leader. Shorten the chosen branches to three or four buds from the base, always pruning to an outward-facing bud. The branches should be at least 50 cm above the ground and will form the main leaders. The following winter shorten the branches back hard to encourage a good branching structure in the lower portions of the leaders. In subsequent years, remove inward-growing, weak or poorly placed branches and thin out the uppermost branches to improve light penetration.

THE MAIN PARTS OF A FRUIT TREE

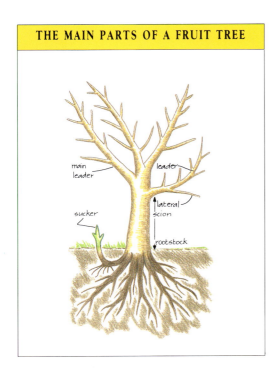

main leader

leader

sucker

lateral scion

rootstock

POPULAR FRUIT FOR THE HOME GARDEN

APPLES
(MALUS DOMESTICA)

Apples require well-drained, reasonably deep soil, but they are not very fussy about soil type. Shelter from wind is very important, however, as strong winds not only damage the tree directly but also cause the blossoms to drop prematurely and may damage the fruit through excessive rubbing against the branches.

Most areas of New Zealand are suitable for apple cultivation, although parts of Northland may not provide adequate winter chilling for some varieties. Those in areas subject to very late or very early frosts may also be limited in their choice.

Apple trees normally take several years to settle down to steady fruiting and while dwarf trees begin to fruit when very young, they still take some time to produce consistent crops.

Many modern gardens have room for only one apple tree, in which case a multiple-grafted tree is best. If you have room for several trees don't overcrowd them; a 5 m spacing is usual for regular trees but dwarf trees can be spaced about 2-2.5 m apart. Pruning is necessary to produce good crops that ripen evenly and this should be done in winter. Apples are adaptable to a wide range of training methods but training should begin as soon as a tree is planted. The traditional method is the vase shape, but they are also easily trained as espaliers, cordons, fans and central leader trees. Apples trained as cordons are grown on dwarf rootstocks whereas espaliers are grown on normal rootstocks. Dwarf apple trees are usually best trained as central leader trees.

After the initial training, pruning consists of the following: removing unwanted new growth, although this is the future fruiting wood so do not be too ruthless; removing old fruiting wood as it becomes exhausted; pruning long barren laterals to a healthy outward-facing bud; thinning clusters of old spurs; and thinning and shortening

Royal Gala apples are a popular New Zealand cultivar.

healthy fruiting wood to prevent overcrowding.

Black spot, fireblight, powdery mildew and codlin moth are the most common problems; mites, scale and leaf-roller caterpillars are occasional pests. Preventative spraying with fungicides during the growing season and a winter clean-up spray with oil and lime sulphur, or oil and a copper-based fungicide are recommended.

APRICOT
(PRUNUS ARMENIACA)

Apricots are cold hardy but they need warm summer conditions for the fruit to ripen properly. They are grown most successfully in Central Otago, Canterbury, Marlborough and Hawke's Bay. However, late frosts will damage the flowers and possibly ruin the crop.

Grow apricots in moist well-drained soil in full sun; they dislike heavy waterlogged soils. The main fertiliser requirement is nitrogen.

Apricots are spreading canopy-forming trees that grow to 3-4 m high. It is important to restrict the growth of young trees and to train them into a vase-shaped tree from the planting stage. Try to keep the growth as upright as possible as horizontal branches become very heavy with age and frequently break under their own weight.

Apricots are self-fertile, hence no pollinator is required. However, having more than one tree usually enhances pollination. Only harvest the fruit when it is fully ripe, which occurs from December to February depending on the cultivar. Apricots may be more prone to brown rot than other stone fruit.

ASIAN PEAR
(PYRUS PYRIFOLIA)

The nashi and other Asian pears are closely related to the European pears but have a distinctive appearance and texture. The fruit tends to be rounded and crisp, rather like a gritty cooking apple, and matures in autumn. Although they can be eaten raw, they are usually more palatable when cooked or preserved.

Nashis are vigorous small trees growing 4-8 m high and 3-5 m wide with a growth habit similar to apples. Nashi can be grown as

Although apricots are cold-hardy they need warm summers.

APPLE CULTIVARS

Early – December-February   Mid – February-March
Late – April-May

'Ballerina' – Very narrow upright growth. Ideal for small gardens. Requires little pruning.

'Braeburn' – Fast becoming the most popular apple. Russet to red-coloured fruit. Mid-late season. Good keeping quality.

'Cox's Orange Pippin' – Early maturing. Small fruit but good flavour. Requires a pollinator.

'Fuji' – Bright red fruit. Mid-late season. Very popular with orchardists because of its appearance.

'Gala' – Yellow fruit striped red. Matures mid-season. Good flavour.

'Golden Delicious' – Bright greenish-yellow fruit. Matures mid-season. Very crisp texture. Eating or cooking.

'Granny Smith' – Bright green fruit. Late maturing. Tart flavour. Primarily a cooking or sauce-making apple.

'Red Gravenstein' – Yellow fruit with deep red stripes and blush. Early to mid-season. Aromatic, almost spicy flavour. Good eating or sauce maker. Requires a pollinator.

'Irish Peach' – Yellow fruit with deep red blush. Very early maturing. Good flavour. Usually the first apple of the season.

'Jonathan' – Bright red fruit. Early to mid-season. Very crisp texture. Juicy.

'Red Delicious' – Fruit red or yellow striped and blushed red. Mid-late season. Good keeper. Requires a pollinator.

'Splendour' – Yellow to gold fruit with red stripes. Mid-season. Thin skinned. Good flavour.

a central leader tree, but because of the work involved in fruit thinning and harvesting, methods that keep most of the tree within easy reach of the ground are more suitable. The traditional Japanese form is a very large shallow vase-shaped tree with three primary leaders. Some cultivars are susceptible to black spot.

AVOCADO
(PERSEA AMERICANA)

Avocados are large rapid-growing evergreen trees that may reach 10 m or more tall and 7-10 m wide, and they can be untidy trees as they drop leaves constantly. The rough-surfaced pear-shaped fruit have a very high sugar and oil content. Frost-free winters and warm summers are preferred and avocados demand rich soil and perfect drainage, although they need adequate moisture when fruiting. The fruit can be had almost all year round by planting different cultivars.
Avocados can self-pollinate but it is beneficial to have plants that flower at different times, so more than one tree is required for pollination. Pests include aphids, leaf-roller caterpillars, scales and thrips, and *Phytophthora* can attack avocados.

BANANA
(MUSA PARADISIACA)

Commercial bananas are not suitable for the New Zealand climate, but the dwarf forms, for example the sugar banana 'Lady's Finger' (the main variety grown in New Zealand), and some 'red' bananas are more cold-tolerant and will crop well in mild northern areas. Grow them in rich, moist, well-drained soil in full sun. A warm sheltered situation and regular watering are essential. Under ideal conditions they will fruit in their second year. Cultivated bananas are seedless and must be propagated by suckers. Bunches will need protection with coloured plastic or hessian in cooler weather as the fruit is damaged below 12°C. After harvesting cut back the stem to 15 cm above the ground.

BLACKBERRY, BOYSENBERRY AND LOGANBERRY
(BRAMBLES, RUBUS SPP.)

The term brambles covers blackberry-type plants, excluding raspberries, and they can have a sprawling or erect growth habit. Many have prickly stems, however, there are now numerous thornless cultivars. They grow best in areas with cool winters and mild summers as a period of winter chilling is required. They are hardy to around -20°C but late frosts can damage the new spring growth. The boysenberry is the most heat-tolerant variety.
Brambles are happy with most soil types, except waterlogged conditions, and apart from regular watering over summer they are easily grown. Add plenty of compost to soil before planting and apply a mulch and a well-balanced fertiliser every August. Maximum sunlight is required to ripen the fruit.
Train the canes on wires or fences, spacing new plants 1-2 m apart for erect-growing cultivars and 2-2.5 m apart for sprawling types. Cut back the canes to 20-25 cm long after planting. The canes fruit in their second year. Cut out canes that have fruited after harvesting, tie in new canes for the following season's crop and pull out suckers. Harvesting is from mid summer to late autumn depending on the cultivar. Insects, such as leaf-roller

caterpillar, occasionally cause damage and fungal diseases such as botrytis are usually only a problem when wet weather coincides with the ripening period.

BLACK CURRANT
(RIBES NIGRUM)

Black currants require winter chilling and are not well-suited to mild northern areas; a cool moist climate suits them best and they need to be sheltered from hot drying winds. Plant them in a humus-enriched well-drained soil in full sun. As with all currants, black currants are sensitive to salt in the soil (especially chloride) so watch for salt build up.
After planting, young black currants should be cut back to just two buds above the ground and allowed to grow unpruned for two seasons.
They largely fruit on the new season's growth, so after fruiting cut back the old canes by at least one-third and remove any weak growth. Aim for a vase-shaped plant with well-spaced branches. Space the plants 1-2 m apart when grown in rows and 60 cm apart when grown as a hedge. They can also be trained on fences or wires. Water regularly in summer and each spring apply a mulch and a well-balanced fertiliser.

If you have a warm temperate climate, try growing bananas – they make a striking addition to the garden.

Boysenberries

BLUEBERRY AND CRANBERRY
(VACCINIUM SPP.)

Blueberries are hardy deciduous bushes that prefer a moist, well-drained, acid soil (pH 4.5-5) with a high humus content. There are two main types: highbush (growing to about 4 m tall) and rabbiteye (growing to about 6 m). The highbush types prosper in cool-summer areas and resist winter cold well. The rabbiteye tolerates summer heat and needs mild winters. Neither fare well in areas experiencing hot summers and cold winters. Regular watering is critical during the growing season. Mulching in August is also beneficial and if necessary apply an acidifying fertiliser in spring. Highbush cultivars can be planted 1 m apart in formal hedges or spaced 1.5 m apart, but space rabbiteye bushes 1.5 m apart in hedges and 2.4 m apart in open plantings. Prune at planting, retaining three or four strong canes 45-60 cm long. Pinch out the shoot tips when canes reach the desired height to promote branching. In subsequent pruning aim for a vase-shaped plant. Fruit are borne on the previous season's growth, so each year remove one or two old canes. Pruning can be done any time between harvesting and the following July; the preferred time is June (in milder areas) to mid July. Harvesting is mid November to mid March depending on the cultivar.
Cranberries are closely related to blueberries. They are creeping evergreen shrubs with slender ascending shoots. They are extremely hardy (withstanding -40°C) but in drier climates the flower buds and stems may be damaged by only mild frosts. Their requirements are very similar to blueberries, and they do especially well in acid peaty bog conditions.
They are relatively free of pests and diseases. Birds will probably be the biggest problem; botrytis, leaf spot and downy mildew may occur.

CHERRY (PRUNUS SPP.)

There are two main types of cherry – sweet (*P. avicum*) and sour (*P. cerasus*). The sweet cherries, which are the most popular, may be eaten raw or preserved as jams or bottled fruit. The sour cherries are seldom eaten raw but are better for pie fillings and other flavourings. Sweet cherries can grow to about 8 m tall x 6 m wide, whereas sour cherries are smaller and thus more suitable for home gardeners. Harvesting is from late November to early January depending on the cultivar.

Cherries need winter chilling in order to set good crops, so some northern areas are too mild for cherries. They do best in areas experiencing long cold winters, warm summers and dry weather at harvesting.

Good pollination is also essential. Cherries are somewhat self-fertile but always produce better crops with an appropriate pollinator.

They grow best in moist well-drained soil in full sun, but will grow in most soil types except heavy clay. Protect cherries from strong winds and late frosts, which can damage the flowers. They require plenty of nitrogen and potash to continue to crop well.

When growing a cherry as a free-standing tree, select several upright leaders after planting and prune them to outward-facing buds to build up a good branch structure. Thereafter any pruning should be kept to a minimum. The tip of any leader growing too strongly can be pinched out after harvesting. Sour cherries can also be grown as fans.

CHESTNUT
(CASTANEA SATIVA)

The edible chestnut, at 25 m high x 12 m wide or more, is not a tree for small city gardens. It grows well in most soils but benefits from regular summer watering when young. The young tree is pruned to a single trunk. Any lateral shoots lower down, as well as crossing and badly placed branches, are removed during the first 5 years. The similar Chinese chestnut (C. mollissima) is occasionally seen in large parks and gardens.

FEIJOA (F. SELLOWIANA)

Grown in small quantities as a commercial crop, the feijoa is still largely the domain of the home gardener. They are hardy evergreen trees that are often grown as hedges. They crop better in milder areas and early frosts may damage the fruit. For good pollination, two or more plants, preferably of different cultivars, should be grown. They will grow in any well-drained soil in full sun, but additional fertiliser and regular watering will improve the crop size and quality. Scale insects are the most common pest.

FIG (FICUS CARICA)

The fig is a large, hardy, deciduous shrub or tree that is often espaliered and it requires warm summer conditions to ripen the fleshy many-seeded fruit. When established it will withstand -10°C, but a mild frost-free climate is best. In areas with mild winters it is normal for two crops to set, one in autumn and another in late spring. Grow figs in moist well-drained soil in full sun. When growing they require plenty of nitrogen and water. The large deeply cut leaves make the fig an attractive tree even where the fruit fails to ripen properly. The fruit may require protecting from birds.

GOOSEBERRY
(RIBES GROSSULARIA)

Gooseberries are dense twiggy thorn-covered bushes growing about 2 m high. They should be trained to a strong upright stem at least 60 cm high before allowing branches to form. Subsequent pruning consists of thinning, removing spindly growth and shortening mature branches by about one-third. Prune immediately after harvesting. Fruit are borne on two-year and older wood. They can be trained in a variety of other ways, including as cordons and fans. The best crops are obtained where winters are cold and their requirements are very similar to black currants. Mildew-resistant cultivars are now available and are the only plants worth growing.

GRAPE (VITIS VINIFERA)

There are many cultivars of

Ripe cherries are irresistible!

grape; some are intended as table grapes, others as wine grapes and a few are dual purpose. Home wine production requires a greater area of vines than most domestic gardens can support so table grapes are the most suitable for small gardens. Grapes should be grown in light free-draining soil in a warm sunny situation and table grapes benefit from additional humus and summer moisture to produce the plumpest fruit. Mulching is also beneficial. Although hardy to at least -15°C, the new spring growth is easily damaged by late frosts. Thus in colder areas it is wise to train the vines against a warm sunny wall, but if necessary frost cloth can be used. Hot, dry, sunny autumns are optimal for fruit ripening.

Success with grapes lies in correct training and pruning. The exact method will depend on the type of support structure and the growth habit desired, but with all methods it is important to train the young vine on a single stem and develop a strong framework of branches. Fruit is borne on new growth from one or two-year-old wood and shoots arising from older wood are non-productive watershoots. All pruning should be completed by the end of July to avoid 'bleeding' of the stems. During the growing season the vines should be checked regularly as new buds are constantly appearing and will result in new shoots unless rubbed off.

In the home garden, vines are commonly trained on a wire system. The plants can be trained in many ways, including as cordons, fans or bushes. The young plant is initially allowed to grow unpruned. In the first winter after planting, prune the main shoot to two or three buds and remove all other shoots. In the second growing season only the strongest shoot is retained and is tied to a stake until it reaches the lowermost wire. At this point the shoot tip is pinched out to force the development of lateral shoots. All vines need regular attention during the growing season to ensure the plant puts its energy into producing a good crop of fruit. Thin the shoots to one per

A mild frost-free climate is best for figs.

spur, only retaining those with the best flower truss; cut back the unwanted laterals to one leaf rather than removing them completely. Pinch out the retained laterals at two leaves beyond the flower truss. Any sublaterals later produced are stopped at one leaf. Removal of some leaves will improve light penetration and assist with fruit ripening.

Thinning the number of bunches is also advisable to ensure a good-quality crop. The number retained will depend on the age and condition of the vine. As a guide, a well-matured vine should be able to carry one bunch every 25-30 cm along the leaders.

Overcropping and the removal of too many leaves in summer will depress fruit colour, sugar content and flavour.

In July apply a well-balanced fertiliser and a new mulch. Table grapes benefit from a liquid feed high in potassium from fruit set until the fruit begins to ripen. Water them well during dry spells.

A few pests can be serious if not controlled. Birds are the most damaging pest. Bird-proof netting can be used or individual bunches enclosed in bags made from muslin or old nylon stockings. Leaf-roller caterpillars, mites, mealy bug and scale can also cause problems. Downy and powdery mildew and botrytis are troublesome fungal diseases. Collecting the fallen leaves in autumn is a wise precaution as they may harbour pests and diseases over winter.

GRAPEFRUIT

The true grapefruit (*Citrus x paradisi*) will not grow in New Zealand, rather, we can grow the New Zealand grapefruit (thought to be a hybrid between a mandarin and a grapefruit). As it has a lower heat requirement than the true grapefruit, it is easily grown in mild areas, and can become a large tree, to 4 m or more, producing prolific crops. Shelter from strong wind is required or the heavy fruit may be damaged. Fruit is picked from August through to December.

'Golden Special' and 'Morrison's Seedless' are widely grown. The

Gooseberries

'Wheeny' grapefruit is a variety that ripens from November to March. The fruit is large, thin-skinned and more tart than New Zealand grapefruit and the tree, though vigorous, is not as hardy, requiring a warmer, more protected site. Refer to the section on citrus earlier in chapter for other cultivation requirements.

GUAVA (PSIDIUM SPP.)

The common guava is a subtropical fruit growing on small to medium sized trees 3-4 m tall. They are easily grown in warm frost-free areas on a wide range of free-draining soils. The tart pear-sized fruit ripen in autumn and winter. Regular watering and fertilising will encourage a heavy crop and light pruning will also encourage new growth and improve flowering and fruiting. Guavas are not troubled much by pests or diseases and generally do well without regular spraying.

HAZELNUT
(CORYLUS AVELLANA)

The hazelnut or filbert nut is the easiest of the nut trees to grow,

Strawberry guava

producing heavy crops particularly where summers are mild and humid. It is a deciduous tree that grows to about 5 m x 4 m and, while it needs protection from high winds, it is hardy and will grow on a wide range of fertile well-drained soils. The trees are drought-sensitive and as they have a shallow root system a mulch can be helpful.

If grown for their fruit, pollinators are required. The nuts are ripe when they fall in late summer or early autumn. Train each tree to have six main branches only, and once established prune them in March or April, removing shoots not less than two years old and shortening the previous year's growth by about one-third.

KIWIFRUIT
(ACTINIDIA CHINENSIS)

This vigorous deciduous vine is, despite setbacks, still among our most important export crops. It is too large for small gardens, especially as it is essential to have at least one male and one female plant for pollination, and although it is possible to buy

plants with both male and female stems grafted on the one rootstock, they are not common. A strong support structure is essential.

Plant them in moist humus-enriched well-drained soil in a sunny sheltered situation. The vines are hardy to about -15°C but as the fruit doesn't ripen until early winter and the flower buds develop in early spring, kiwifruit do best in areas not subject to early or late frosts. Feed them heavily and water well during the growing season. A single shoot on the young vine is trained up the support structure and the tip pinched out at the desired height. The required number of side shoots are then trained as leaders. The fruiting laterals develop from these. Fruit develop from the first three to five buds of new growth and the laterals will bear fruit for several years.

After harvesting in winter, prune out old or damaged wood and reduce the fruit-bearing laterals to two buds beyond the last fruit. Do not prune while in leaf as the stems will 'bleed'. However, the fruiting laterals are usually shortened in summer to seven or eight buds beyond the

A kiwifruit vine before annual pruning

Grapes, *Vitis vinifera* var. 'Albany Surprise'

last fruit to prevent over-crowding. Kiwifruit take six or more years to reach full productivity.

Leaf-roller caterpillar and scale are troublesome pests and botrytis may attack the fruit in wet conditions.

A. kolomikta, a closely related ornamental climber, is a slender-stemmed strong-growing climber that should be grown more in New Zealand. The attraction with this lovely creeper is the irregular variegations on the oval pointed leaves, which are blotched with cream and pink. The fruit is small but very sweet. Propagate from cuttings 10 cm long in midsummer.

KUMQUAT
(FORTUNELLA SPP.)

This member of the citrus family is very hardy and quite easily grown in most areas. They are small shrubs growing up to 1.5 m high and are often grown for ornamental purposes in containers. The small fruit are tart and not normally eaten fresh. It is worth growing for its ornamental foliage and form even in climates too cold for successful fruit production. Refer to the section on citrus earlier in chapter for other cultivation requirements.

LEMON (CITRUS LIMON)

Lemons are perhaps the most commonly seen fruit in gardens around the country as they are hardy, relatively free from disease and produce fruit over long periods. The most commonly grown is the 'Meyer' lemon, which is not a true lemon at all but thought to be a lemon-orange cross; the fruit is less tart than a true lemon and very juicy. It is the most frost-tolerant lemon and will grow and fruit over much of the country with minimal winter protection. It is a small shrub about 2.5 m tall and wide.

True lemons, such as 'Eureka', 'Lisbon' and 'Genoa' varieties, are larger, over 3 m, and are rather frost-tender.

The lemonade is a lemon hybrid with large sweet lemon-like fruit that can be eaten fresh. It is frost-tender but, in a suitably mild climate, heavy cropping. It may grow up to 3 m x 2 m.

Refer to the section on citrus earlier in chapter for other cultivation requirements.

LIME
(CITRUS AURANTIIFOLIA)

Limes are among the most frost-tender citrus trees. Two main types are grown – the Tahitian lime and West Indian lime. They are only suitable for warm frost-free areas and will produce one crop over an extended period, with fruit tending to drop when ripe. Refer to the section on citrus earlier in chapter for other cultivation requirements.

LOQUAT
(ERIOBOTRYA JAPONICA)

Loquats are large evergreen trees (5-6 m) with leathery deep green leaves up to 30 cm long. Although it is hardy to about -7°C, it fails to fruit well in cold areas. However, it is worth growing for its bold foliage alone. Loquats like coastal regions, but they will need some wind protection.

The small orange-yellow fruits ripen in late spring and early summer and it is worth thinning the fruit while small to only 3-4 fruit per cluster to produce a better sized crop. Plant in moist, humus-enriched, well-drained soil in full sun or partial shade.

MACADAMIA
(MACADAMIA SPP.)

There are 11 species of macadamia but only two are grown for their fruit: *M. integrifolia* and *M. tetraphylla* are similar and both grow to about 18 m high. Most commercial plants are hybrids between the two. The plants are hardy to about -6°C but require mild winters to produce good crops as the flowers are damaged by hard or repeated frosts. They are easily grown in moist well-drained soil in full sun and little pruning is necessary. However, to produce a good crop fertilise twice yearly. The best variety for home gardeners is 'Beaumont'.

MANDARIN
(CITRUS RETICULATA)

The fruit of mandarins are small

and sweet, like miniature oranges, and the tree forms a large shrub up to 3 m x 2 m. Their size makes them ideal citrus for home gardens. Although they require more heat than oranges, they are more frost resistant, particularly the satsuma varieties, and because of their ability to fruit even in relatively cool climates satsuma mandarins are fast replacing 'Clementine' and similar cultivars as the most popular types. The satsumas are cold hardy, slow growing and have a more open habit. They are worth growing for their foliage and form alone. Refer to the section on citrus earlier in chapter for other cultivation requirements.

MULBERRY (MORUS SPP.)

Two species of mulberry are grown, the black mulberry (*Morus nigra*) and the white mulberry (*M. alba*). They are hardy deciduous trees growing over 5 m tall with fruit rather like blackberries. The white mulberry has insipid but sweet fruit; the fruit of the black mulberry has more flavour and makes very good jam. The fallen fruit is very messy so unless the fruit is going to be harvested do not plant it near paths or driveways. They grow well in most well-drained soils in a sunny sheltered site and regular watering during dry spells is essential.

M. alba prefers a warm climate with mild humid summers. May reach 10 m tall, but it is not fast-growing and pruning, which should be done in winter, will control its size. *M. nigra* likes a cooler climate and has a higher chilling requirement. Mulberries can be espaliered or fan-trained on a wall or fence.

The fruit ripens gradually from mid summer into autumn. Birds are the only problem and will devastate a crop before it is ripe.

OLIVE (OLEA EUROPAEA)

The olive is an attractive evergreen tree growing 5 m or more tall. They grow best in areas with long hot summers and fairly light frosts. Olives will grow in most soils as long as drainage is good. Although drought tolerant, watering during flowering and over summer will increase the yield.

The fruit ripens in late autumn and winter and cannot be eaten fresh, requiring quite elaborate processing. Several cultivars, including some new commercial strains, are available. The gnarled trunk and semi-weeping habit make olives worth growing regardless of their fruit quality.

ORANGE (CITRUS SINENSIS)

The best known citrus crop, oranges require a mild climate to keep the skin thin. Plants survive in many parts of the country but fruit quality may be indifferent in cooler areas. Try one in a sunny sheltered spot.

Several cultivars of sweet orange are grown, including some navels, especially 'Washington Navel'. 'Harwood's Late' ('Valencia') is the most popular, with the fruit maturing from mid spring. It can be left on the tree until February, however, it does have a biennial fruiting habit. Seville (sour) oranges are occasionally grown. They are sometimes used for juicing but are mainly grown for marmalade. Blood oranges have very dark-coloured flesh and are often extremely juicy. 'Ruby Blood' is the most common cultivar of this type.

PASSIONFRUIT
(PASSIFLORA SPP.)

Several species of passionfruit are grown as ornamentals but few are commonly grown for their fruit. The most important is the black or purple passionfruit (*Passiflora edulis*), grown in temperate areas, and the subtropical golden or Hawaiian passionfruit (*P. edulis* var. *flavicarpa*), however the banana passionfruit (*P. mollissima*), which is hardier but less flavoursome is also grown. They are all strong-growing vines with showy flowers that climb by tendrils. They do not require formal training like other fruiting vines but are often trained on a trellis or wires. Give them a sunny position sheltered from wind and frosts and water and feed well during the growing season. Passionfruits have high nitrogen requirements and good drainage is essential to avoid problems with root rots.

The main insect pest is passion vine hopper.

PAWPAW
[CARICA PUBESCENS]

The tropical species of *Carica* are not really suitable for cultivation in New Zealand but the mountain pawpaw (*Carica pubescens*) is considerably hardier. It is very similar to the babaco and forms an upright-growing small tree to 3-4 m tall. It is easily grown in most soil types, but good drainage is essential to avoid root rots, and it tolerates very light frosts. A warm sunny situation is best.

PEACH AND NECTARINE
[PRUNUS PERSICA]

These two fruiting trees are very similar, the nectarine being essentially a smooth-skinned peach. They are available in a wide range of varieties. Naturally medium-sized round-headed trees up to 5 m in height and spread, they are also available on dwarfing rootstock. Natural dwarfs, such as 'Nectarina', are popular. They are very hardy, and indeed require winter chilling, but a warm dry summer is necessary to ripen the fruit properly.

Peaches and nectarines are described as either freestone or clingstone. The stones of freestones come away cleanly but the flesh adheres to clingstones. There is no difference in cultivation between the two. They must be grown in very well-drained soils in full sun. Feed them regularly with a general-purpose fertiliser and water well while the fruit is maturing.

Train into a vase-shaped tree from the planting stage. They fruit on the previous season's

Peanuts make an interesting crop if you have a frost-free climate and long warm summers.

Mulberry

growth so subsequent pruning should aim to remove previously fruited wood and thin out the new season's growth.

PEANUT
[ARACHIS HYPOGAEA]

Something of a novelty crop, peanuts are frost-tender and need a long warm summer to mature properly. The plants resemble small sweet peas but after flowering an unusual structure develops at the base of the flower. This 'peg' grows down into the soil. The subterranean tip develops into the peanut, which is ready for harvesting about 120 days after planting. Obviously this demands a reasonably loose soil, preferably one that is sandy. Peanuts may be grown from the raw peanuts available at any supermarket. They must be shelled before sowing in August or September. There are two types of peanut: bunch nuts or trailing nuts. The bunch type are best as the rows can be closer together. Sow 15-25 cm apart and 3 cm deep in rows 70-90 cm apart. Lift when the foliage turns yellow.

PEAR [PYRUS COMMUNIS]

Pears tolerate a wide range of soil types and climatic conditions but may be somewhat disappointing in very mild areas or those with very cold winters and regular late frosts. They do best in a sunny position with moist well-drained soil and shelter from strong winds.

Pears are naturally medium-sized upright pyramidal trees but dwarf forms are available. These are usually grafted onto low-

Olive tree with fruit

PEAR CULTIVARS

Early – February   Mid – March   Late – April

'Beurre Bosc' – Medium-sized green or yellow fruit. Mid season. Good flavour. Requires a pollinator.
'Doyenne du Comice' – Large thick-skinned greenish-yellow fruit with reddish blush. Mid to late season. Excellent flavour and texture. Slow to reach maturity but crops well once established. Requires a pollinator.
'Packham's Triumph' – Medium-sized yellow fruit. Mid season. Requires a pollinator.
'Williams' Bon Chretien' (syn. 'Bartlett') – Thin-skinned yellow fruit. Early maturing. Good fresh or preserved. Does not store well. Crops better with a pollinator.
'Winter Cole' – Medium-sized yellow fruit. Mid-late season. Good flavour. Good keeping quality.
'Winter Nelis' – Small to medium-sized, light green to yellow fruit. Good flavour. Not an attractive fruit but keeps very well.

PEACH AND NECTARINE CULTIVARS

Early - December-January   Mid - January-February
Late - February-March

PEACH

'Blackboy' – Medium to large fruit. Deep purplish-red skin and flesh. Late season. Best fresh. Freestone.
'Bonanza' – Natural dwarf. Medium-sized fruit. Yellow skin blushed red, yellow flesh. Good flavour. Freestone.
'Dixired' – Early to mid-season. Red skin with yellow flesh. Clingstone.
'Golden Queen' – Late season. Medium-sized fruit. Yellow skin and yellow flesh. Firm texture. Often bottled. Clingstone.
'Redhaven' – Ripens over a long season. Yellow skin blushed red, yellow flesh. Freestone.

NECTARINE

'Armking' – Early season. Yellow skin blushed red, yellow flesh. Clingstone.
'Fantasia' – Early season. Yellow skin blushed red, yellow and red flesh. Freestone. Low chilling requirement.
'Goldmine' – Mid to late season. Golden-yellow skin often blushed red, very pale yellow flesh. Freestone. Low chilling requirement.
'Nectarina' – Natural dwarf. Early to mid season. Red and yellow skin. Deep golden-yellow flesh. Freestone.
'Redgold' – Mid season. Red skin, yellow flesh. Freestone.

The popular pear 'Packham's Triumph'

growing quince rootstocks and can be grown as small trees or trained as espaliers, fans or cordons.

The pruning of pears is very similar to apples, however they are more vigorous and pose greater problems in training. Pears produce strong lateral growths and these should be tied to the horizontal or interlaced and shortened to 25 cm long during the following winter. The fruit is borne on long-lived spurs, making pears suitable for pruning and shaping without a major reduction in yield.

Pears are not generally self-fertile. The easiest way round this problem is to buy double-grafted trees. However, if you have the room to plant several trees, then compatible single variety trees will give good results. The bulk of the crop should be harvested before fully ripe as ripe fruit will not keep for long. A few can be left on the tree so that you can savour the delights of tree-ripened fruit. Pears are less prone to pests and diseases than apples and most of the common problems can be ignored, however fireblight can be particularly devastating.

PECAN (CARYA ILLINOINENSIS)

The pecan nut is a very hardy large deciduous tree. It is fast growing and makes an excellent shade tree. Several trees, preferably of differing cultivars, are required to ensure good pollination, however there are self-fertile cultivars. The cylindrical nuts are pointed at the end and taste rather like a strong walnut without the bitterness. Grow pecans in moist well-drained soil and water well

while the nuts are maturing. Climates with cool winters and long warm summers produce the best nuts. Harvesting is in March and April.

PERSIMMON (DIOSPYROS KAKI)

The Japanese persimmon is a hardy deciduous tree (12 m) that bears attractive golden-orange fruit the size of a small apple. Astringent and non-astringent cultivars are grown. Astringent persimmons must be very ripe before they lose their bitterness and can be eaten raw. The non-astringent types can be eaten while still firm.

Persimmons fruit on the new season's growth and the fruit is usually not ripe until winter. This leaves only a short period for pruning after harvest. The trees are trained to a vase shape or central leader system. Persimmons must have a well-drained soil and fruit best in temperate areas, though the tree itself is frost-hardy. If you have a cool climate, try an astringent cultivar. Birds often damage persimmons before they ripen so protection is nearly always necessary.

PINEAPPLE (ANANAS COMOSUS)

Pineapples, widely grown in the tropics, are also readily grown outdoors in protected sites in warmer areas of New Zealand. However they require a long warm growing season to produce good-quality well-ripened fruit and hence a glasshouse is often required.

Pineapples grow in any well-drained slightly acidic soil in a sunny sheltered frost-free situation and make good container plants. They are easily propagated by suckers and the top cuts from fruits.

PISTACHIO (PISTACIA VERA)

The pistachio is a large deciduous dry-climate tree somewhat hardier than the fig or olive. It is also one of the finest autumn-foliaged trees in New Zealand. The so-called nut is really the kernel of the fruit. Sexes are separate so both male and female trees are required; if they are not both present the

shells will still grow to about normal size but remain empty. Although hardy, late frosts may damage the new spring growth. Regular watering is required until the fruit approach maturity, with dry conditions preferred thereafter. Warm summers and autumns are also required. A vase-shaped tree is best.

PLUM (PRUNUS SPP.)

There are two distinct kinds of plum. Japanese plums (*P. salicina*) are slightly larger, more vigorous and pendulous in habit. European plums (*P. domestica*) are more upright, flower later in the season and are more suitable for areas that receive hard frosts. Both groups include cultivars that are self-fertile and some that require a pollinator. Japanese and European plums do not cross-pollinate, therefore it is necessary to plant two different cultivars from the same group to ensure good crops. Other types of plums are also grown, including cherry plums, damson plums and numerous hybrids.

Plums are the most easily grown of the stone fruits. They are subject to the same problems as the other types but are generally such heavy croppers that a few losses are tolerable.

Plums are vigorous trees growing to about 6 m high x 5 m wide. However, dwarfing rootstocks reduce the height to about 3-4 m. They grow best in fertile well-drained soils that have plenty of compost incorporated. An annual dressing of dolomite lime is of great benefit, especially on heavy soils.

European plums are unsuitable for areas that experience mild winters and warm wet summers; in these areas try Japanese plums. The vase shape is considered the best system to train plums. For smaller gardens, training as a fan or central leader tree is also suitable. Japanese plums bear their fruit on long-lived spurs located on all branches. Immediately after harvesting, thin out these spurs and work on a three-year pruning rotation to replace the older branches with new wood. European plums are not as vigorous and more

---

PLUM CULTIVARS

Early – December-January   Mid – January-February
Late – February-March

JAPANESE
'Burbank' – Mid season. Red skin, yellow flesh. Very hardy.
'Doris' – Mid season. Red skin, yellow flesh.
'Duff's Early Jewel' – Early season. Red skin, yellow flesh. Self-fertile. Good pollinator for other cultivars.
'Elephant Heart' – Large fruit. Mid to late season. Red skin, red flesh. Good flavour. Freestone.
'George Wilson' (syn. 'Omega') - Large fruit. Mid season. Red skin, red flesh. Self-fertile to some extent.
'Santa Rosa' – Medium to large fruit. Early season. Red skin with blue bloom. Yellow flesh turning red. Self-fertile. Good pollinator for other cultivars.
'Sultan' – Early to mid season. Red skin, red flesh.
'Wilson's Early' – Early season. Red skin, yellow flesh.

EUROPEAN
'Angelina' (syn. 'Angelina Burdett') – Early season. Light red skin, yellow flesh.
'Coe's Golden Drop' – Mid season. Yellow skin, yellow flesh.
'Damson' – Mid season. Purplish-blue skin, green flesh. Very tart flavour, usually a cooking or jam-making plum. Self-fertile.
'Greengage' – Mid season. Greenish-yellow skin, yellow flesh. Self-fertile to a large extent.
'President' – Large fruit. Mid to late season. Purplish-blue skin, yellow flesh.
'd'Agen' (French Prune) – Small fruit. Late season. Deep red to purple skin, dark brownish-red flesh. Very sweet. Dried to make prunes.

thought and care is needed when developing their framework, but thereafter pruning consists of shortening leading laterals by about 60 cm and removing all inward-facing and crossing shoots.

POMEGRANATE
(PUNICA GRANATUM)

This large deciduous shrub grows to 4-5 m tall and makes an attractive ornamental shrub with its large orange flowers, reddish new growth and autumn foliage. The very seedy globular fruit are about 75 mm in diameter. Although very frost hardy, the best fruiting forms require hot summers for the fruit to ripen properly and they are seldom successful except in the hottest areas. They withstand long summer droughts once established and make ideal tub plants for patios. The fruits are borne on short spurs that are at least two years old. Prune in winter, replacing older unproductive wood with younger growth.

RASPBERRY (RUBUS SPP.)

Raspberries are popular vigorous growers that require winter chilling and warm summers to ripen the fruit quickly. Cold wet summers will lead to fungal diseases. Plant them in a well-drained, humus-enriched, slightly acidic soil in full sun and feed them well during the establishment period. Then apply an annual mulch and balanced fertiliser in spring when growth commences. The canes fruit in their second year. Raspberry canes will require some support to stay upright; wires, trellis and fences are suitable. After harvesting, cut out canes that have fruited, tie in new canes for the following season's crop and remove damaged or weak wood. Plant canes in autumn 50 cm apart in rows. Shorten the cane to about 15 cm high and cut it out completely when new suckers appear.

RED AND WHITE CURRANT
(RIBES SATIVUM)

Currant bushes do not require much winter chilling but are generally better croppers in cold-

winter areas, however, as they flower early they are susceptible to spring frosts. The type of soil is not that important but good drainage is essential and they will need to be protected from winds as the shoots are brittle. Train them into a vase shape when young and thin out old wood and the centre of the bush once mature. Fruit forms on short lateral branches on two-year and older wood. The main branches should be cut back by about one-third to encourage lateral fruiting spurs to develop. Once established the oldest wood can be removed entirely each year. This will encourage new growth without adversely affecting fruiting. They can also be trained as cordons, fans or espaliers. Water them well as the fruit matures and feed annually with a well-balanced fertiliser.

STRAWBERRY
(FRAGARIA SPP.)

Undoubtedly strawberries are one of the delights of summer. They are usually grown as an annual crop in the North Island, though many are kept for second-year cropping, particularly in southern areas. In the South Island the plants are cropped for up to 3 years in Nelson and Canterbury and up to 5 years in Otago. Strawberries are best grown in broad mounds in moist well-drained soil in a warm sunny situation. The mounding is important because the fruit will rot if allowed to lie on wet soil. Weed mat, straw or some other dry mulch around the plants will also help prevent rotting. They will grow in a wide range of soil types and tolerate temporarily wet conditions better than most other crops. Add plenty of compost prior to planting. Space plants 15 cm apart in staggered double rows and remove any runners that appear.
Although strawberry plants are frost hardy, the flowers and young fruit are damaged by light frosts in spring, thus some protection may be needed. Flowering begins in early spring and is soon followed by the berries. Cultivars vary in their fruiting period and length of season and so fruit may be

Pomegranate

Ripe plums in early January.

Ever-popular strawberries

available from spring to autumn. Leaf-roller caterpillars may cause damage but by far the biggest pests are slugs, snails and birds. The entire crop will need to be covered with bird netting. Leaf spot and botrytis may also occur.

TAMARILLO
(CYPHOMANDRA BETACEA)

The tree tomato or tamarillo is a quick-growing soft-stemmed large shrub or small tree growing to about 3 m tall. It has large velvety leaves with a very distinctive smell and egg-shaped yellow, orange or red fruit. The fruit, which mature over winter and spring, are rather astringent and people seem to either love them or loathe them. Tamarillos are frost-tender and require good wind protection. Grow them in moist well-drained soil in full sun or partial shade and feed them regularly. They are short-lived and prone to aphids and white fly. Powdery mildew may occur during hot dry weather.

TANGELO

This is a hybrid between a grapefruit and mandarin and the tree is vigorous and productive. 'Seminole' is the most widely

grown; it has large juicy fruit with a thick skin and many seeds. 'Ugli' is somewhat sweeter with less seeds and has a very thick skin. Tangelos are reasonably fast-growing and may grow 3-4 m tall, but are fairly frost-tender. Refer to the section on citrus earlier in chapter for other cultivation requirements.

WALNUT (JUGLANS REGIA)

All walnuts are large deciduous trees exceeding 20 m high and wide, and so are suitable for large gardens only. The English walnut is a well-known fast-growing species that enjoys cold winters and mild dry summers. They tend to do well where apples are grown. However, the soft new spring growth is easily damaged by late frosts and strong winds.
Train the young plant to a single trunk with well-spaced branches. The nuts, which can take several years to appear, mature in late summer and autumn, and may be subject to fungal problems in areas with high summer humidity. Walnuts demand a moist well-drained soil and a warm position. They also need plenty of nitrogen and phosphate. Water well as the fruit matures.

243

Caring For Your Garden

CARING FOR YOUR GARDEN

PLANT NUTRITION

Nutrients – macronutrients; trace elements; Soil acidity; Fertilisers; Organic fertilisers; Chemical fertilisers; Efficient composting

Flowering shrubs, such as camellias and rhododendrons, provide plenty of leaf and petal fall to add to mulches and compost.

Plants are continually taking nutrients from the soil. When grown in containers, they can quickly exhaust the essential elements, so regular feeding is vital.

MOST PLANTS ARE composed of leaves and a system of stems above ground and a root system below ground. The leaves are the main food-producing organs. Through the process of photosynthesis, light energy is used to convert carbon dioxide and water to carbohydrates. This provides an energy source for plant growth. The root system is just as important to the plant as the leaves, being the major water and nutrient absorbing organ and also providing anchorage. Water is, of course, essential to all life forms, but plants must also obtain a number of mineral nutrients essential for plant growth from the soil.

Apart from the correct positioning in sun or shade, gardeners have little direct control over food production by plants. It is through the soil that gardeners have the greatest influence over plant growth. The importance of maintaining a friable fertile soil cannot be overemphasised, yet it is something many gardeners pay little attention to. It is essential for the long-term viability of any form of plant cultivation, and healthy plants are generally the most pest and disease resistant and aesthetically pleasing. Unfortunately very few gardeners are blessed with the 'perfect' soil and so some soil improvement is almost inevitable.

The best time to provide your plants with the basis of healthy strong growth is before planting. Preparation of vegetable and flower beds and planting holes is very important as many problems are difficult, if not impossible, to fix after a plant is in place.

Assessing and improving your soil, discussed in Section One, is a vital first step, but you will need to maintain the soil in peak condition for optimum results. Apart from needing the right pH level, plenty of humus for moisture retention and aeration and the presence of micro-organisms, plants need and extract numerous chemical elements from the soil. These need to be replaced regularly if the soil is to continue supporting viable plants. Understanding your plants' nutrient requirements will help you to maintain a suitable soil.

Indiscriminate and frequent application of general fertilisers can be wasteful and may cause toxicity problems. Different plants can have quite disparate requirements and to treat all plants the same is a recipe for disaster. Knowing what nutrients are important, and the best means of supplying them, to different types of plants will result in healthier plants and less soil leaching.

NUTRIENTS

Plant growth requires a regular supply of certain mineral nutrients from the soil. Those required in the greatest quantities are known as macronutrients. There are numerous other elements that are equally essential, but they are only required in minute quantities and are known as trace elements or micronutrients.

Plants absorb these elements in solution through the root system or by gas exchange through leaves. They do not 'feed' the plant, in the sense of providing the plant with energy, but are utilised in a wide range of vital metabolic processes and in the production of more complex chemical compounds, thus enabling growth to occur. A deficiency of just one element can have a serious effect on the plant.

Nitrogen, phosphorus and potassium are regarded as the 'big three' and are the most important for gardeners. The letters NPK on fertiliser packets refer to the percentage of these elements in the fertiliser blend. A fertiliser with an NPK ratio of 20:10:15 has 20% nitrogen, 10% phosphorus and 15% potassium. You will also find listed the types of compounds in which the nutrient is available, e.g., nitrogen in nitric or ammoniacal form, and potassium in nitrate, phosphate or chloride forms. This information is important in determining how quickly and for how long the nutrients will be available, as some forms are more readily available than others. Some plants have adapted to grow in soils that are deficient in particular elements. Most members of the Proteaceae, for example, have evolved on phosphorus-deficient soils and demand similar soils in cultivation. Other plants have evolved methods that enable them to make up for deficiencies. Leguminous plants, for example, are able to utilise atmospheric nitrogen, otherwise unavailable to plants, via symbiotic bacteria that live in special nodules on their roots, thus enabling them to grow in nitrogen-deficient soils.

Nevertheless, all plants need all of the essential elements. Some, such as iodine and zinc, are required in such minute quantities that you will probably never need to add them to your soil. Others, such as cobalt and molybdenum, are also only required in minute quantities, but may be absent in some New Zealand soils leading to stunted growth. However, most New Zealand soils are well-balanced.

Some fruit trees, such as the tamarillo shown here, are described as gross feeders and require regular feeding to obtain a good crop. Phosphorus and potassium in particular promote flowering and fruiting.

ESSENTIAL NUTRIENTS FOR PLANT GROWTH

MACRONUTRIENTS	TRACE ELEMENTS (Micronutrients)
Nitrogen	Iron
Phosphorus	Boron
Potassium	Molybdenum
Calcium	Manganese
Magnesium	Zinc
Sulphur	Copper
Carbon ⎤ obtained from	Chlorine
Hydrogen ⎬ the air and	
Oxygen ⎦ water	

MACRONUTRIENTS

NITROGEN is vital for many aspects of plant growth. It is absorbed through the root system in the form of nitrates or ammonia. It promotes vegetative growth and lush foliage at the expense of flowering and fruiting, so high-nitrogen fertilisers are recommended for lawns, leafy vegetables and ornamentals grown for their foliage. Low-nitrogen fertilisers are best for some flowering plants, e.g., bulbs. Sulphate of ammonia is a common source in chemical fertilisers, and manures and blood and bone are common organic sources. A general yellowing of the foliage and stunted growth is symptomatic of a deficiency.

PHOSPHORUS is generally applied to promote flowering, fruiting and root growth. Blood and bone or bone meal are excellent organic sources. Superphosphate is a common inorganic form, but is detrimental to soil micro-organisms. It is easily leached in acid soils but ground rock phosphate and organic sources are good choices. A deficiency leads to poor and stunted growth.

Some plants require less nutrients than others. *Clockwise from the top*: Kurume azalea 'Christmas Cheer'; *Rhododendron* 'Virginia Richards'; *Abies balsamea* 'Hudsonea', a conifer; and geraniums all come into this category.

plants, calcium sulphate or calcium nitrate are preferable, but light doses of dolomite lime provide calcium without excessively raising the soil pH. It is important not to add lime at the same time as nitrogenous fertilisers, as it may cause some loss of nitrogen as ammonia gas. Egg shells are a slow-acting source of calcium. Death of the growing point and general discoloration indicate a deficiency.

Soils are rarely deficient in MAGNESIUM, but a deficiency causes stunted and chlorotic foliage which eventually develops brown patches. This is probably best described as an 'autumn leaf' appearance. Magnesium is contained in dolomite lime; Epsom salts is another source.

SULPHUR is essential for normal root development and good foliage colour. It is only available to plants in the sulphate form, and is easily lost by leaching. Vegetables require more sulphur than other plants.

CARBON, HYDROGEN and OXYGEN are also essential elements, but they are obtained from water and by gas exchange.

TRACE ELEMENTS

A host of other nutrients are essential for plant growth, but are required in much smaller amounts than macronutrients. The most important are iron, boron, molybdenum, manganese, zinc, copper and chlorine. Only rarely are they deficient in New Zealand soils and so are usually of little concern for gardeners, particularly if organic matter is applied regularly.

'Lime-induced chlorosis' is an iron deficiency caused by too much lime and it affects various plants, including citrus, soft fruits and peas. Application of iron chelates will rectify it. Deficiencies may be more likely to occur with container plants.

A trace element mix can be applied if deficiencies do occur, and seaweed is a particularly good source of trace elements. It is important to realise an excess of any trace element may be just as damaging as a deficiency. Some trace elements are, in fact, used as weedkillers.

SOIL ACIDITY

The acidity or alkalinity of your soil can have a considerable bearing on the range of plants you will be able to grow and how they will need to be treated.

Acidity is measured by the pH (short for 'potential of hydrogen') scale. This is a logarithmic, 14 point scale based around the neutral mid-point of 7. Acidity increases as the pH

POTASSIUM (or potash) also promotes flowering and fruiting, as well as strengthening stems and woody tissues and may improve disease resistance. Several forms may be used in chemical fertilisers, and wood ash and seaweed are excellent organic sources. A deficiency may illicit numerous symptoms, but yellowing of the margins of older leaves is characteristic.

CALCIUM is usually applied as lime, which reduces soil acidity. However, all plants, including acid-loving plants, need calcium. For these

decreases (7–0), and the soil is increasingly alkaline as the pH increases (7–14). One pH unit represents a difference ten times more, or less than the next unit, e.g., 6 is ten times more acid than 7.

The pH range that will support plant growth is about 3.5 to 9. Progressively fewer plants will grow satisfactorily at either extreme. Most ornamentals prefer slightly acid soils, whereas most garden vegetables do best in neutral to slightly alkaline soils. Woodland plants often prefer quite acid soils as they have adapted to growing under trees with acidic foliage.

Knowing your soil's pH and planting accordingly can avoid a lot of problems later on. Simple soil-testing kits are available to give you an idea of your soil's pH.

Soil pH has an important influence on the availability of certain nutrients to plants. The solubility of nutrients such as iron, manganese and aluminium increases as acidity increases. In contrast, the solubility of potassium, calcium and magnesium increases as alkalinity increases. In general, trace element deficiencies will be more apparent on acid soils, but very few soils are so acid that the effect is greatly noticeable unless the soil is regularly cropped.

Bacterial activity is also affected by soil pH, being suppressed at both extremes.

Excessive acidity is easily corrected by adding lime but altering excessively alkaline soil is more difficult. Incorporating plenty of compost material and using acid-based fertilisers will help but planting in raised beds of specially prepared soil offers the best long-term solution. This is because lime is very soluble and will eventually seep back to neutralise any added acidity.

Some plants, known as calcicoles, will grow well in alkaline soils, for example bearded irises and *Pachystegia* species. However, a number of acid-loving plants, such as azaleas and rhododendrons, are quite intolerant of lime and require a soil pH of around 5–6.

FERTILISERS

There are two main groups of plant fertilisers, organic and chemical, or put another way, natural and artificial. Both forms are available in dry and liquid forms. Dry fertilisers are almost always worked into the soil or used as a soil dressing. Liquid fertilisers are often applied to the soil too, but many are intended to be applied to the foliage; these are known as foliar fertilisers or foliar feeds.

The use of organic fertilisers has increased enormously in recent years as gardeners move

away from using artificial chemicals. They are unquestionably the only means of maintaining the long-term fertility of your soil. A healthy fertile soil requires a high humus content and a thriving population of soil micro-organisms, which slowly break down the humus, releasing nutrients in forms that are available to plants. Regular addition of organic matter is necessary to replenish the humus content and keep the system going. Organic matter also improves the soil aeration and moisture retention.

Chemical fertilisers have no humus value and with prolonged use the soil humus becomes depleted; eventually you will be left with a proverbial 'dustbowl' and possibly toxicity problems. However, they are excellent for correcting deficiencies or satisfying the special needs of some plants.

Having extolled the virtues of organics, there are negatives. It is possible to overdo it; that is, apply too much organic material and make the soil extremely acid. In addition, many organic fertilisers are not 'complete', only supplying some of the essential elements.

Compost made from a range of materials should provide a well-balanced diet for your plants. However, blood and bone, for instance, only supplies nitrogen and phosphorus. Even nutrient-rich seaweed will not provide every essential element. The ideal solution for most gardens is probably a combination of organic

Top: The soil of vegetable gardens needs to be constantly enriched with organic matter and fertilisers, but watch out for a build up of acidity and remember to rotate your crops.

Above: Bearded irises, such as 'Orange Celebrity', grow well in alkaline soils.

Seaweed makes a valuable addition to the compost.

COMPOSITION (%) OF SOME INORGANIC FERTILISERS						
	N	P	K	S	Mg	Ca
Ammonium sulphate	21	0	0	24	0	0
Ammonium nitrate	34	0	0	0	0	0
Ammonium nitrate mixed with lime	26	0	0	0	0	8
Urea	46	0	0	0	0	0
Potassium nitrate	14	0	36	0	0	0
Diammonium phosphate	18	20	0	0	0	0
Superphosphate	0	9	0	11	0	20
Serpentine super	0	7	0	8	5	15
Triple super	0	20	0	2	0	40
Potassium chloride	0	0	50	0	0	0
Potassium sulphate	0	0	40	18	0	0

fertilisers, with chemical fertilisers to make up for any deficiencies or for plants with specific requirements.

ORGANIC FERTILISERS

Naturally occurring organic fertilisers tend to be relatively mild unless applied in large quantities. Many have the benefit of adding humus, but some are quite low in nutritive value and others supply only a few essential elements. You may need to supplement them with chemical fertilisers to ensure a well-balanced diet. They are particularly good for sandy or volcanic soils, which are naturally low in humus.

COMPOST

Compost is probably the best all-round product for adding nutrients and conditioning the soil. Any garden waste can be used to produce compost but the best materials are fallen leaves or conifer needles, kitchen waste and finely chopped plant trimmings. Compost is excellent for mulching and very important in improving all aspects of your soil.

ANIMAL MANURES

Animal manures should be well rotted before use. Fresh manure is very unpleasant to handle and is quite likely to burn fine surface roots. Animal manures frequently contain weed seeds but cow manure, which is the result of a very thorough digestive process, is usually almost weed-free. All are excellent sources of nitrogen, but the value of other nutrients varies between animals and the type of feed.

GREEN MANURES

Some crops, particularly the nitrogen-fixing legumes, are grown for the express purpose of digging in to the soil when mature. This adds humus to the soil but much of the nitrogen fixed by the crop is lost in the process of decomposition.

PROCESSED PRODUCTS

Organic products are frequently processed into more easily handled forms. Such pre-packaged fertilisers are often the best buy for those with small gardens as they require only a limited storage area and little or no preparation. Blood and bone is a slow-acting source of nitrogen and phosphorus, and is available in liquid form. Fish meal is a quicker-acting source of nitrogen and also provides various other nutrients.

CHEMICAL (INORGANIC) FERTILISERS

Chemical fertilisers are more suited to providing a balanced supply of nutrients and for correcting specific deficiencies. There appears to be no firm evidence to suggest that plants react any differently to, or are adversely affected by, direct chemical applications as opposed to the more subtle organic products. Chemical fertilisers come in two types – balanced mixes and more specific fertilisers.

GENERAL BLENDS

General fertilisers supply a balanced blend of nutrients. They are ideal as a dressing before planting and as a booster in general cultivation. Some mixes are intended for specific plant groups, such as acid-loving plants or orchids.

NUTRIENT-SPECIFIC FERTILISERS

These fertilisers supply one element or a specially selected group of elements, such as the trace elements, and are primarily intended to correct specific deficiencies. An example would be the use of iron sulphate or iron chelates to correct iron chlorosis.

The correct use of nutrient-specific fertilisers requires a good understanding of plant nutrition, but gives almost unlimited scope for making fine adjustments.

EFFICIENT COMPOSTING

Every garden and household produces garden and kitchen waste. Rather than burning it or putting it down the waste disposal unit, it can be turned into compost and is thus a wonderful source of nutrients and humus for the garden. There are many different ways of making compost, and as many different types of containers in which to make it. Nevertheless, for most gardeners good compost is the key to maintaining a fertile soil and healthy plants. Composting can be as simple or as technical as you care to make it, but it need never be a major drain on your time. For the most part it can be left to nature, but there are a few tricks to producing good quality compost.

WHAT IS COMPOST?

Compost is the end product derived from the breakdown of vegetable and animal matter into a form suitable for returning to the soil. Well-made compost can be used in any area of the garden, whether it be the vegetable garden, the orchard, for flowers or shrubs, or in the greenhouse for raising seedlings or potting.

Compost is both a fertiliser and soil conditioner and when well made the gardener will enjoy a number of benefits.

Good-quality compost should contain all the essential nutrients, thus raising the general soil fertility, and the physical structure of the soil is improved, making for easier cultivation. It increases the soil's humus content; benefiting soil fertility, improving aeration and helping the soil to warm up more quickly in the spring, permitting earlier plantings. Increased humus is also beneficial for earthworms and other soil organisms. Moisture retention is also improved (this is especially important for sandy and volcanic soils) and soil erosion and leaching will thus be reduced.

Many people think that by throwing together an accumulation of household refuse, waste materials and garden weeds, and leaving these to rot in a corner of the garden, they are making compost. They are certainly making (and destroying also) a lot of useful organic material that, provided it doesn't contain diseased plants or weed seeds, will add to the organic content of the soil. But this is not composting.

CREATING A GOOD COMPOST

The various organisms responsible for decomposition during composting have three essen-

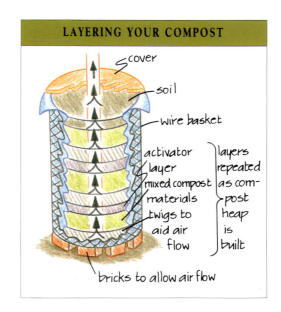

LAYERING YOUR COMPOST

cover
soil
wire basket
activator layer
mixed compost materials
twigs to aid air flow
layers repeated as compost heap is built
bricks to allow air flow

tial requirements; warmth, air and moisture.

Warmth is extremely important. Heat is generated within a compost heap through the activity of bacteria breaking down the moist vegetation. If the heat cannot easily escape, the temperature of the heap increases. This generation of heat is essential for bacterial activity during composting, and will mean that vegetation decomposes more rapidly. Activity slows down considerably as temperatures drop in autumn and winter. It is therefore important to insulate the heap to minimise heat loss.

Good aeration is also important, as the beneficial bacteria that promote the decomposition process during composting require oxygen, which they take from the air. They are known as aerobic bacteria to distinguish them from the type of bacteria that flourish in the absence of air, which are known as anaerobic bacteria. The effects of the latter type of bacteria are seen in decaying and putrefying matter where air is excluded. A typical example is a large heap of putrefying lawn clippings when the whole mass has compacted down, thus excluding air. Compare this with a properly made compost heap, which has little or no smell and is an open friable mass that is pleasant to handle. The properly made compost is also of greater nutritive value.

Moisture is also essential for bacterial activity. If the heap is too dry, activity is reduced or may not even start. If it is too wet, the chilling effect of the surplus moisture will prevent activity starting or continuing.

And, of course, if you are providing this ideal environment for the aerobic bacteria to do their job you must make sure they are pre-

Ensure there is enough room around your compost bins for a wheelbarrow to bring in organic materials and take out the compost.

COMPOST RATIOS

MATERIAL	CARBON-NITROGEN RATIO (WEIGHT:WEIGHT)
Lawn clippings	20:1
Weeds	19:1
Dead leaves	60:1
Paper	170:1
Fruit scraps	35:1
Other food scraps (not animal origin)	15:1
Untreated sawdust	500:1
Straw	100:1
Chicken manure	7:1
Chicken litter (from poultry farm)	10:1
Cattle manure	12:1
Sheep manure	8:1
Horse manure	8:1

sent to start the process. This can be done by mixing into the heap a small amount of fertile soil along with some animal or poultry manure or some organic material such as dried blood and bone. Alternatively, a commercially prepared compost activator is available from garden centres. The soil attached to plant roots is often sufficient for the purpose.

The big advantage of a well-made compost heap over decomposition on or within the soil is that the heap can preserve, even in winter, very high temperatures and so the rate of humus production is greatly accelerated. At its centre a compost heap may reach 70–76°C, which should kill most plant diseases and weed seeds. By turning the heap, it is possible to produce an almost sterile compost. In addition, good-quality compost is a balanced mixture of leafy and woody tissues (and hence of nitrogen and carbon compounds).

Composting problems usually arise because the heap has been poorly made or badly maintained. This leads to it failing to reach a high enough temperature through being too wet, too dry or inadequately aerated. Judging the correct moisture content is not difficult once the heap is up and running but it's important to avoid any problems before this stage by building the heap properly in the first place.

MATERIALS TO USE IN YOUR COMPOST

As a general rule, unless the materials have some preservative substance on them such as treated timber sawdust or creosoted wood, any organic material can be composted.

Such materials will include all kitchen waste, including tea or coffee grounds, fruit skins, peelings and other vegetable waste, urine, fish offal, egg shells (though be careful with animal food scraps as they can attract pests; it may be a good idea to restrict these to only very small amounts mixed well with other material), weathered sawdust from untreated timber, the contents of a vacuum cleaner, wood ashes, leaves, grass clippings, spent hay, straw, feathers, seaweed, soot, old sacks or woollen carpets, milk powder, any sugary liquids or solids, weeds, flowers, hair, old newspapers and cardboard, old potting mix, hedge trimmings, prunings and similar organic materials.

Woody material should be chopped up finely or put through a shredder to accelerate its decomposition. Be careful not to add too much woody material to your compost heap, as nitrogen is required for bacteria to break down woody tissues. The carbon/nitrogen ratio of the materials you add to your compost indicates the amount of nitrogen that will be

used in the decomposition process. The ideal is a ratio of around 30:1 and the table (below left) is a guide to help you achieve this. If you are worried that the ratio is too high, add a nitrogenous fertiliser to speed up the process and prevent nitrogen levels from becoming depleted. For the best results, aim for a balance between fine leafy materials and coarse woody materials.

Plant material affected by disease is best burnt and added to the compost heap as ash. Such material includes brassicas affected by club root, onions infected with white rot, potato foliage attacked by blight, or potato tubers from eelworm-attacked plants.

Deep litter poultry manure is ideal as an activator, as are most animal manures, but blood and bone and dried blood are excellent substitutes. Milk powder, sour milk or milk products, which are obtainable at a moderate cost, promote bacterial activity too.

MATERIALS TO AVOID

Such weeds as oxalis are better burnt, but if the heap is well-made the temperature will rise to 70°C or more and most weeds, including kikuyu, twitch, clover, and docks, will quickly break down at such temperatures.

Empty tins are useful in the heap as they quickly rust and add iron salts, and also because they create air pockets that assist in ventilation, but avoid them if they have contained harmful liquids. They can be used at the base of the heap in place of a grill.

Materials that interfere with decomposition in the heap include some water-soluble fertilisers (with the exception of natural products such as fish fertilisers and liquid blood and bone), coal and carbonate ashes, and plant material that has been sprayed with chemicals or weedkillers. In general, avoid plastics, detergents, glass, nylon and other synthetic materials, along with tarred, waxed or oiled papers and cardboard.

COMPOST BIN DESIGNS

There are various types of containers. Your choice will depend on cost, space availability, and the amount of material available for composting. The 'Southlander compost bin', made from timber formed into a square frame, is easy to make. The bin developed in England and called the 'Hotterotter' is made from insulated, heavy grade plastic with a lid and is stood on concrete blocks. A simple holding unit can be constructed from wire-netting encircling four stout stakes. Another type of bin is made of plastic and has panels that slide into place. These panels contain holes for air circulation. You will also need to decide whether you want to opt for a single heap or run a three-heap system; though your decision may be made by the available space.

BUILDING THE HEAP

Before placing it in the compost bin, it is desirable to cut the material into smaller pieces and to bruise large pieces, such as cabbage and corn stalks, as this increases the surface area for the bacteria to attack. Putting your material into a shredder is even better.

Best results are obtained by constructing the heap in a series of layers (see diagram on page 251). These can be added progressively over time, but it's better if you can fill a whole bin at once. A grill or layer of twigs at the base of the bin will assist with aeration. Each layer should be composed of a dry lower section, a moist centre, with a thin sprinkling of soil on top. Slightly drier materials, such as grass clippings, should be placed above the wetter materials. Each completed layer will be about 40–60 cm deep and composed of three or four materials. A dressing of lime on top of the soil layer will prevent overacidity and promote the activity of earthworms and micro-organisms.

To each layer may be added any animal manures at the rate of one-quarter of the whole bulk. If animal manure is not available, then add about 5 kg of blood and bone per cubic metre. Mix the materials thoroughly before placing in the compost bin, adding more water if necessary to keep it moist. Sea water can be added if you live near the coast, as it will contain valuable trace elements. The heap should be kept moist but not soggy – aim for the consistency of a squeezed-out sponge.

When the bin is full, top it off with a layer of garden soil and fit on the lid or cover it with a plastic sheet. The heap will begin to generate heat within a few hours and this process will continue for several weeks. The temperature will start to drop after about three weeks and it is an advantage to turn it over at this stage, when its temperature is little more than blood heat. The turning allows the heap to be moistened again, if necessary, and will ensure uniform decomposition throughout the heap. Decomposition will start again after this and after a further two to three weeks the heap will gradually cool off.

The completed compost will be ready for use after it has cooled or may be left to mature still further until needed. It should be ready for use after 2–5 months and should be dark brown and easily crumbled.

USES AND STORAGE

Compost can be applied to garden beds as a mulch, top-dressing or worked into the topsoil. Earthworms will incorporate it deeper into the soil. It is also suitable for potting purposes, but may require sieving.

Ideally compost should be used as soon as it is ready. If, however, there is the likelihood of leaching from heavy rain or if the soil is frost-bound or water-logged, storage may be preferable. This is best done under cover on an earth floor preferably, although concrete is acceptable. Compost so stored should be kept moist by covering.

Compost is essentially an intermediate stage in the breakdown of organic matter into simple chemicals. It is readily destroyed under hot dry conditions and so a soil needs constant replenishment of fresh organic matter in order to maintain the humic content.

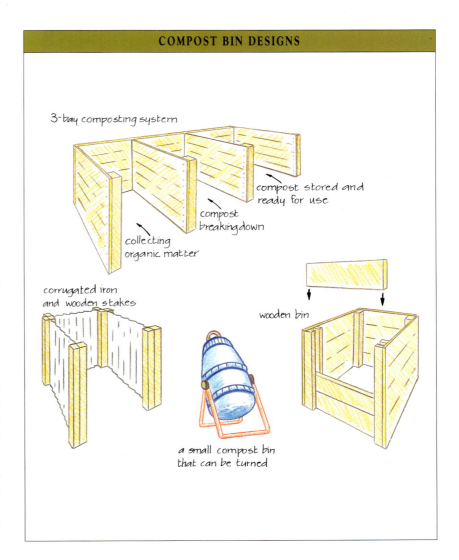

COMPOST BIN DESIGNS

3-bay composting system

collecting organic matter

compost breaking down

compost stored and ready for use

corrugated iron and wooden stakes

a small compost bin that can be turned

wooden bin

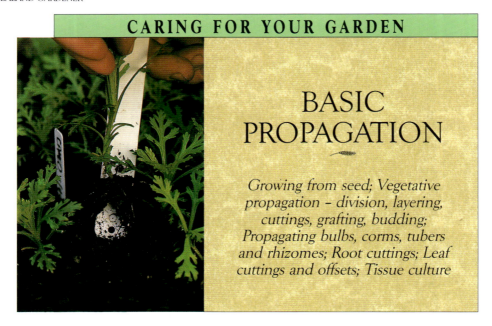

CARING FOR YOUR GARDEN

BASIC PROPAGATION

Growing from seed; Vegetative propagation – division, layering, cuttings, grafting, budding; Propagating bulbs, corms, tubers and rhizomes; Root cuttings; Leaf cuttings and offsets; Tissue culture

WHY BOTHER PROPAGATING your own plants when virtually any plant you may need can be bought at your local garden centre? Apart from the sense of satisfaction gained from producing your own plants, there are several reasons:

- The ability to produce large numbers of plants cheaply.
- The production of plants not normally available from garden centres or nurseries.
- The opportunity to produce your own hybrids.
- For profit – even small-scale propagation can provide a supplementary income.

- Because it is an enjoyable and relaxing pastime.

Plants can be propagated by sexual and asexual means. Sexual propagation involves the reproduction of plants from seed, and is the usual method used by plants in the wild. Asexual, or vegetative, propagation is where a new plant is produced from a part of an existing plant and includes techniques such as grafting and layering. Ferns are a special case and are propagated from spores. This is easily done by the keen home gardener and the method is described in detail in the chapter

Knowledge of the structure of plants and their flowers is vital for successful propagation, especially if you are growing from seed. At right, the flower parts of *Nanettia bicolor*; middle right, *Salix* spp. or pussy willow; far right, the floral structure of a tulip.

on ferns.

Vegetative propagation will always create an exact replica, or clone, of the parent plant, whereas sexual propagation can never produce clones. In general, seed-raised plants will be variable, especially if the parent is of hybrid origin, and a desirable characteristic of the parent may not be expressed in the seedlings. Some plants are sterile (e.g., triploids and plants with completely double flowers) and never set viable seed. So to perpetuate a cultivar or selected form, a vegetative technique is usually necessary, although some cultivars come relatively true from seed. Seed propagation is ideal for true species, which normally come true to type from seed, if you wish to select new forms, or if variation is immaterial.

GROWING FROM SEED

The plants most likely to be grown from seed are those available from commercial seed merchants, namely annual bedding plants and vegetables. They are among the easiest of plants to grow from seed, requiring minimal skill and quickly reaching maturity. However, you can collect seed from many different plants and store it in an airtight container with a desiccant, e.g., silica gel, in a cool, dry place until you want to use it. But bear in mind that seeds lose viability over time, some quite quickly.

PRE-GERMINATION TREATMENT AND DORMANCY

Germinating most seeds is simply a matter of providing the right moisture levels, light and temperatures. However, some seeds have dormancy mechanisms to prevent germination in unfavourable conditions. Knowledge of a plant's native environment will often provide vital clues to its germination requirements.

Plants from regions with very cold winters often have seed that require a period of moist-chilling to germinate. In the wild this means germination occurs in spring rather than in autumn, which would lead to the tender young plants being killed over winter.

Plants from arid regions would suffer a similar fate if they germinated with every passing shower. Consequently their seeds often have a hard coating that will not soften until thoroughly soaked, or they may contain certain germination-inhibiting chemicals that need to be washed away.

An understanding of the particular characteristics of a genus also helps. For example, most leguminous plants have seeds with hard coatings that need to be softened by soaking

If you are not concerned with variation, growing from seed is an easy method of propagation. Above are Iceland poppies.

While most of us buy our seeds in packets, you can collect and store your own seeds for propagation.

in water for up to 24 hours prior to sowing.

Apart from soaking, the two most common pre-germination treatments are STRATIFICATION and SCARIFICATION. Stratification is used to break dormancy for seeds that require winter chilling. The usual method is to place the seeds in a plastic bag containing moist potting mix, which is then stored in a refrigerator for several weeks. The exact period of stratification varies but it is usually from 4–12 weeks.

Scarification is the abrading of a hard seed coat, which is often sufficient in itself or it can be used in combination with soaking to initiate germination. The most common scarification method is to line a jar with sandpaper, put the seeds in the jar and shake it vigorously with the lid on. Large, very hard seeds may be dealt with individually by nicking the seed coat with a knife or by rubbing on sandpaper.

SOWING METHOD

Start with a soil mix of about 50% bark-based potting mix, 25% fine sphagnum moss and 25% perlite, thoroughly mixed and put through a 6 mm sieve. Commercial mixes are satisfactory but regular potting mix passed through a sieve, with the addition of sphagnum and perlite, often produces superior results. Whatever you use should be fresh and, if possible, sterilised.

Sphagnum moss and perlite lighten the mix and allow better oxygenation. Sphagnum moss also contains natural fungicides that may inhibit damping off and other fungal diseases. Blending the mix with a trowel in a wheelbarrow is the easiest way to make up small quantities.

After sieving, fill your tray to about two-thirds full. Shallow pans are better than deep pots, and perfect drainage is essential. Commercial propagating trays are ideal. If using a shallow tray this need be no more than 50 mm for all but the most vigorous seedlings. Many very fine seeds, such as begonias, require no more than 25 mm soil depth for initial germination.

It is important that you leave enough room for the seed leaves (cotyledons) to expand without touching the cover, or they will almost certainly rot. Having levelled the soil, moisten it thoroughly, but take care not to saturate the soil or compact it unnecessarily.

Now the seeds can be sown. Large seeds may be individually placed in position but most seeds are simply sprinkled evenly over the surface. Very fine seed is more easily sown if mixed with sand or icing sugar.

Many seeds require light to germinate and should not be covered. These are usually very fine seeds that do not have large food reserves. However, others must have darkness for successful germination. Knowing the needs of particular seeds usually requires experience and good references, but sometimes the information is on the seed packet. Use a very finely sieved mix that will not impede the cotyledons emergence. A good rule is to cover the seed to about the equivalent of its depth.

After moistening the covering soil, cover the tray with a pane of glass or plastic then place a sheet of newspaper over the cover. Panes of horticultural glass are ideal but plastic cling film or other plastic sheeting will do. However, condensation tends to form into large drops on plastic sheeting and this may damage young seedlings if it falls on them. The cover will stop the soil from overheating if the tray is inadvertently exposed to the sun, and also help prevent algae growing on the soil surface.

A heating pad or hot water cupboard can be an invaluable aid for seeds that need warm temperatures to germinate or if you are attempting to germinate seeds out of season, although heating pads rapidly dry the soil in the bottom of the trays and hot water cupboards are dark. When germinating temperate-climate seeds in

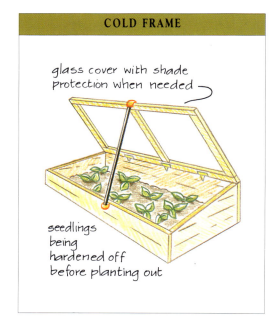

COLD FRAME

glass cover with shade protection when needed

seedlings being hardened off before planting out

Right: Sieve your seed raising mix through a 6 mm mesh sieve.
Far right: The soil level is below the lip of the tray to allow room for the seed leaves to grow under the cover.

spring or summer, all that is needed is to place the seed tray in a warm sheltered area away from direct sunlight.

The exact time required for germination varies enormously. Some seeds may only take a day or so, others several months. Commercial seeds often have information about germination percentage and time on the packet, otherwise it is a case of searching out the information or being vigilant.

Once the seeds have germinated, remove the newspaper and slowly, over several days, raise, then remove the glass or plastic cover to gradually harden off the seedlings. At this stage it is advisable to gently spray the young seedlings with a fungicide and dilute liquid fertiliser, but don't use strong chemicals or fertilisers that may damage the tender young plants.

To prick out the seedlings gently loosen them with a small dibbling tool (plastic labels are good), hold them by their seed leaves, not the tender stems, and pot them on. Very small seedlings may have to be transplanted in clumps and thinned further when they are easier to handle.

This procedure is the usual method for raising ornamentals, however many vegetable seeds are sown directly in the open ground.

VEGETATIVE PROPAGATION

Vegetative propagation techniques produce exact replicas of the parent plant and as the material used is generally from mature specimens the plants flower at a younger age than seedlings, often in the first year. They are also the only means of replicating sterile plants or self-sterile plants without a pollinator.

There are several methods of vegetative propagation – cuttings, layering, division, budding and grafting are the most common. Root cuttings, leaf cuttings and aerial layering are less widely used. A more technical method, tissue culture, is usually restricted to propagation laboratories due to its strict hygiene requirements and the need for specialised equipment. The most basic methods do not involve removing material from the parent plant until it has struck roots. The simplest of these methods are division and layering. Aerial layering is similar but slightly more complicated.

DIVISION

Division is the simplest method of vegetative propagation and is commonly used for clump-forming herbaceous perennials. It is usually

Above: Phlox has a fleshy crown with foliage at many points and distinct growth eyes, necessary for successful division.
Left: Libertias also require careful cutting to ensure there are enough roots on each division.

carried out when the plant is dormant or when it is just emerging from dormancy; this will vary between genera. There are no special tricks to dividing a plant; about the only question is knowing just how small the divisions can be yet still survive. This is largely a matter of experience but obviously each division must have some roots and a leaf bud. If in doubt err on the large side.

Plants suitable for division fall into three categories. First, those that form clumps of rosettes or offsets, like ajuga or saxifrages, which can be cut up or broken apart with a knife or spade and immediately regarded as new plants. In most cases, this sort of division can be done at any time of year.

Second, there are plants with distinct foliage clusters on fibrous crowns. Many of the lily family fall into this category, e.g., flax and libertia. They require more careful cutting and sometimes have only a few roots per division. The success rate for this form of division is highest in early spring.

Third, plants with fleshy crowns with foliage emerging at many points, e.g., astilbe, lythrum and phlox, can also be divided. They require careful cuttings too, and in many cases have distinct growth points or eyes. Each division needs at least one, and preferably two, of these to strike. This sort of division is best done when plants are just emerging from dormancy.

DIVISION

Clump-forming fibrous-rooted perennial.

Simply break or cut into rooted divisions, then replant.

Keep freshly planted divisions cool and moist until well established.

Dahlias and marguerite daisies (far right) are easy to strike from new shoots in spring.

Cuttings before and after preparation. Note there are fewer leaves and those remaining have been trimmed.

LAYERING

Layering is a very simple process and one that often occurs naturally with low spreading plants such as *Parahebe* or ground-cover azaleas. Such plants have a tendency to form roots at the points where their branches come in contact with the soil. Most plants are capable of doing this but an erect growth habit doesn't allow it to happen naturally.

Simple layering is just a matter of bending a branch down to the ground, pegging it in place and covering a section of it with soil. With time, roots will form on the buried section. The branch can then be separated from the parent plant and grown on. You will have more success if the branch or stem is wounded before you bury it. Make a shallow cut on the branch and dust with a little root-forming hormone.

The time it will take to strike varies with the season and plant involved, but it is typically between 9–12 months. Because of this, and the room required, it is usually only done on a small scale.

In some cases layering just isn't possible, so aerial layering is used instead. This takes the approach that if you can't bend the branch down to the soil, take the soil up to the branch. It is restricted to plants with fairly firm stems as it involves virtually ring-barking the stem.

Choose a short stem (45 cm) of the current

year's growth or work near the tip of a branch. Trim the foliage and split the bark around the stem, leaving just a small patch so as not to completely ring-bark the plant. The wound is then dusted with root-forming hormones, and tightly wadded sphagnum moss is packed around it. Cover the sphagnum carefully with black polythene, which both blocks out the light and raises the temperature. Thus the conditions of soil-based layering can be simulated above ground. Be careful that the moss doesn't dry out before the layer has taken.

AERIAL LAYERING

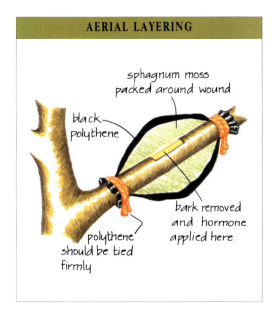

sphagnum moss packed around wound

black polythene

bark removed and hormone applied here

polythene should be tied firmly

CUTTINGS

Although layering gives satisfactory results, cuttings are one of the most common methods of vegetative propagation and certainly one of the easiest for gardeners. There are several types of cutting based on the ripeness of the material used.

SOFTWOOD AND SEMI-RIPE CUTTINGS

Both deciduous and evergreen shrubs can be grown from softwood cuttings. Softwood or tip cuttings are taken from the soft new tip growth and these cuttings usually strike quickly, but they can be difficult for home gardeners as they are inclined to wilt or rot before striking unless held under controlled conditions. Most nurseries use misting or fogging units to keep softwood cuttings turgid until they can look after themselves.

Softwood cuttings are usually taken in spring, while semi-ripe cuttings can be taken any time throughout the growing season, though usually in autumn.

LAYERING

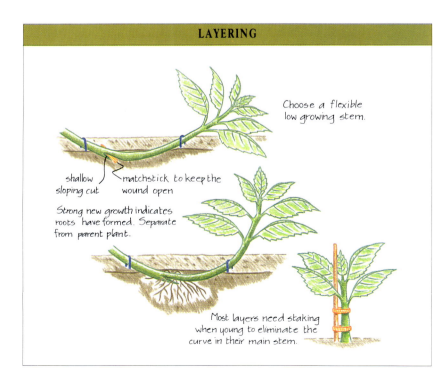

Choose a flexible low growing stem.

shallow sloping cut

matchstick to keep the wound open

Strong new growth indicates roots have formed. Separate from parent plant.

Most layers need staking when young to eliminate the curve in their main stem.

Semi-ripe or semi-hardwood cuttings are firm yet pliable pieces of stem wood. They are usually taken from tip growth but lateral shoots may also be used. The new growth of most plants is soft green wood that develops the characteristic brown bark as it ages and hardens. Softwood cuttings are still quite green and soft, whereas semi-ripe cuttings are taken from partially matured wood approaching the bark forming stage.

Softwood and semi-ripe cuttings are the most common types of cuttings in both nurseries and home gardens. They will nearly always perform better under mist but are usually firm enough to strike well in a cold frame or if kept in a cool sheltered place.

Taking cuttings is not a complicated procedure but the time it takes for the cuttings to strike and the success rate vary enormously depending on the species or variety. Experience will teach you which plants are the easiest but among them would be fuchsias, pelargoniums and marguerite daisies. Dahlias and delphiniums are also easy to strike from the fleshy new shoots that form in spring.

A good soil mix is important. A good quality bark-based potting mix blended at about three parts potting mix to one part perlite or fine pumice by volume gives good results. The mix should be passed through a 6 mm mesh sieve.

Fill a tray with cutting mix, use a board or some other straight edge to level the soil off with the top of the tray, then moisten the soil thoroughly. It is a good idea to add a fungicide to the water but do not use anti-wilting agents – these are usually oil based and can inhibit the cuttings' respiration.

Softwood and semi-ripe cuttings are prepared in the same way. The size of the cutting varies with the type of plant but is usually about three to four nodes long. Meristematic cells are present in large numbers at the nodes, the points at which the leaves are attached, so most cuttings are trimmed just below a node. Use secateurs to get a neat straight or slightly sloping cut. Carefully remove the lower leaves until only the top three to five leaves or leaf pairs remain. Sometimes the leaves come away easily but often you need to take care not to strip the bark away with the foliage. If the remaining leaves are large (over 40 mm long) cut them back to about one-half of their length to reduce moisture loss through transpiration. Some cuttings strike so easily this is unnecessary, others are so difficult that it makes little difference, but in most cases it is beneficial.

Gently push the cutting into the cutting mix to about one-third of its length. The cuttings can be packed quite tightly up to the point where their leaves are touching but not overlapping. Mist the cuttings and moisten the soil surface as you work.

Softwood and semi-hardwood cuttings should ideally be given high humidity to reduce water stress on the cuttings. The best way to achieve this is to use a misting or fogging unit but placing the tray in a clear plastic bag will be sufficient. Make sure the cuttings do not touch the plastic as they will probably begin to rot at any points of contact. Cuttings strike best when their tops can be kept cool and humid while the root zone is kept warm and moist. Ideally mist and some form of bottom heat, such as a heating pad or, even better, heating cables in moist sand, should be used. If you don't have access to such facilities, a warm sheltered position out of direct sun will usually suffice.

Top: Taking a fuchsia softwood tip cutting and (above) dipping the prepared cutting in root-forming hormone powder.

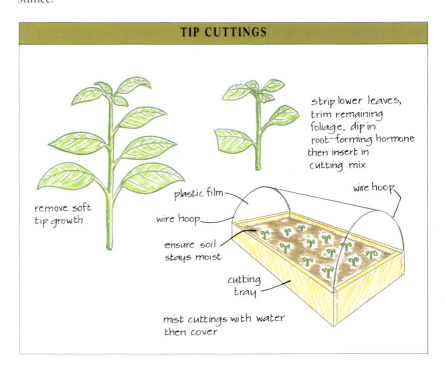

TIP CUTTINGS

remove soft tip growth

strip lower leaves, trim remaining foliage, dip in root-forming hormone then insert in cutting mix

plastic film

wire hoop

wire hoop

ensure soil stays moist

cutting tray

mist cuttings with water then cover

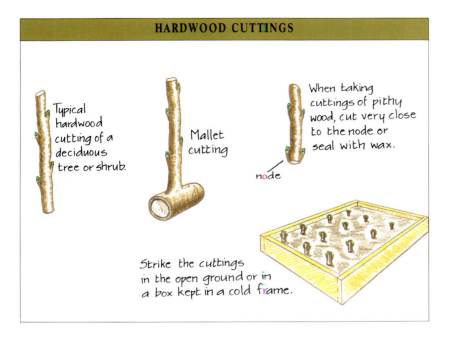

HARDWOOD CUTTINGS

Typical hardwood cutting of a deciduous tree or shrub.

Mallet cutting

When taking cuttings of pithy wood, cut very close to the node or seal with wax.

node

Strike the cuttings in the open ground or in a box kept in a cold frame.

inserted in the open ground outdoors, they can also be struck indoors in boxes of soil and may develop faster in spring if treated in this way.

Hardwood cuttings are treated less tenderly than other types of cuttings. They are fully matured pieces of stem of about 10–20 cm in length, depending on the plant, that are simply inserted into prepared garden beds. This is normally done in late autumn as the last of the foliage falls and the cuttings are left through the following growing season to be lifted when dormant in winter.

GRAFTING

Grafting is commonly used for propagating selected forms of ornamental trees, conifers and fruit trees. There are many types of grafting but all work on the same principle. Just below the bark is a layer of cells known as the cambium. This is a meristematic layer from which develop the plant's water- and nutrient-conducting tissues. When grafting, it is vital to match the cambium of the scion (the upper portion of the graft and the part that will produce the shape, foliage and flowers of the plant you wish to replicate) with that of the rootstock (the lower half of the graft, and the part that will provide the root system for your new plant); the better the match, the greater likelihood of the graft taking.

All grafting methods require the cutting and trimming of stock and scion into shapes that will enable them to be neatly joined, so a

Check your cuttings after about three weeks. Those that are easy to strike, such as marguerite daisies, should show some sign of growth in that time. More difficult plants could take several months and may form callus tissue before striking roots.

HARDWOOD CUTTINGS

Hardwood cuttings are generally used to propagate deciduous shrubs and trees and are taken from the fully hardened wood of the previous summer's growth. Although usually

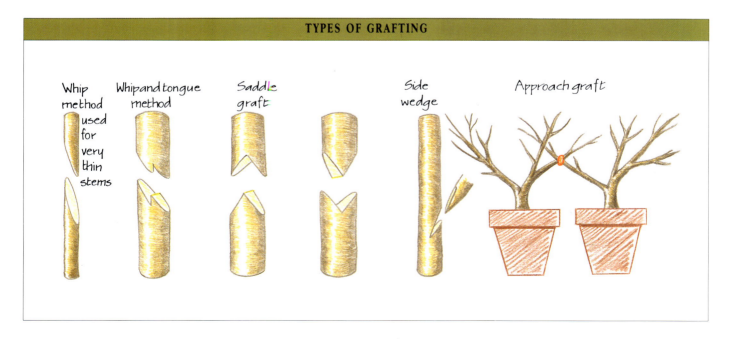

TYPES OF GRAFTING

Whip method used for very thin stems

Whip and tongue method

Saddle graft

Side wedge

Approach graft

sharp knife and steady hands are essential.

The stock and scion must be from reasonably closely related plants for a graft to be successful. They should be from within the same family but they don't necessarily have to be in the same genus. There are many examples of bi-generic grafts, such as lilacs on privet (*Syringa/Ligustrum*), and citrus on trifoliata rootstock (*Citrus/Ponciris*), but for simplicity keep your first grafts to members of the same genus.

Graftings of deciduous plants are normally made in late winter or early spring just as dormancy comes to an end. Grafting of evergreens can be made over a wider season but late winter is still a popular time.

Many methods of grafting have been developed to deal with different plants, but the most common are whip and tongue grafting, commonly used on small plants; side and cleft grafts, used on more substantial stock; bark grafts, used on established fruit trees; and approach grafts, used when other grafting methods are more difficult.

BUDDING

Budding is more advanced but still a straightforward procedure and is usually restricted to plants that are difficult to strike from cuttings or that grow poorly on their own roots. Due to the time, expense and uncertainty involved budding has never been a preferred method for mass production, the exceptions being roses and some trees.

There are two reliable methods of budding for inexperienced propagators; shield budding and chip budding. Shield is the more common and is the method most widely used for roses.

Budding requires a rootstock and scion, as in grafting, and where they are joined is called the bud union.

To bud, select a strong, non-suckering rootstock and train it to a single stem, removing the lower foliage. Buds can be inserted at any point on reasonably firm wood, but they are generally placed lower down to avoid regrowth of the rootstock below the bud union.

Make a T-shaped incision in the bark and peel back the two flaps.

Select a vigorous stem from the plant you want to replicate, this is called the scion, and look at the base of the leaves for a plump, healthy looking, active bud. Cut back the leaf, leaving a small stub as a handle.

Now remove the bud from the scion by making a shallow cut into the stem 10 mm below the bud, then cut under and past it

Above: A bark graft used on a new variety of apple tree.
Left: This tree shows the clear join of the rootstock (black walnut) and the scion (English walnut).

about 20 mm, gently lifting the sliver of stem and bud from the stem.

Insert the bud into the cut rootstock and gently replace the flaps. Trim the bark above the bud so it neatly fits the incision in the stock and wrap above and below the bud with tape. As soon as the bud shows signs of growth, trim the rootstock to 25 mm above the bud.

Chip budding is easier but less likely to succeed as there is less contact between the cambium layers of the two plants.

From the rootstock remove a wedge or chip of 50 mm in length and no more than a third into the stem. Now cut an identically shaped

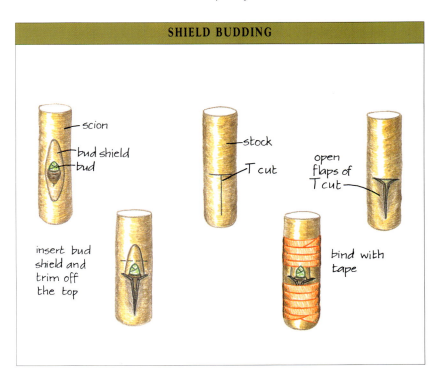

SHIELD BUDDING

scion
bud shield
bud

stock
T cut

open flaps of T cut

insert bud shield and trim off the top

bind with tape

A rose at the end of its first season after budding.

Below left: Bearded irises are rhizomatous perennials and so are grown from division.
Below right: *Narcissus* and *Muscari* on the other hand are bulbous plants and multiply easily by themselves, though the gardener can quicken the process.

chip, with the bud at its centre, from your scion. Insert the scion chip into the gap left on the stock, making sure that the cambium layers match. Then tape the chip into position.

The best time for budding is early summer, when the leaf axil buds first become obvious. At this time the bark of the stock plant should be at its most pliable, thus enabling easy insertion of the bud. There is also plenty of the growing season remaining for the wound to heal and the bud to take.

It is tempting to think that because budding is an early season job the results will be visible quickly. However, the bud will probably show no sign of development until the following spring, about 10 months after it was inserted.

PROPAGATING BULBS, CORMS, TUBERS AND RHIZOMES

Left alone these plants will often multiply by themselves but there are ways of speeding up the process and making it more reliable.

Typical rhizomatous plants, such as asparagus, often strike roots as they spread so propagation is simply a matter of division. In the instances where there are no roots already formed, roots will usually develop if a large

enough piece of rhizome is used.

Tubers can be lifted when dormant, cut into pieces, each with a growth point or 'eye', and replanted. Each cut surface should be dusted with a fungicide to prevent rotting.

Bulbous plants can be propagated by dividing established clumps which will contain offset bulbs, or produce bulbils in leaf axils, but if greater numbers are required other methods need to be used. Scaly bulbs, such as nerines, are propagated by separating the scales and growing them on as individual plants.

At the end of the growing season, when the bulbs are plump and fleshy, remove some scales from the outside of the bulb. The whole bulb can be stripped if you wish. Stir the bulbs up in some moist seed-rasing mix in a plastic bag and store in a warm moist place. Within 8–12 weeks there will be one or more small bulblets at the basal end of each scale. Do not separate them from the scale but simply pot up each scale as it is.

Tunicate bulbs, such as hyacinths, require a slightly more complex technique. This involves scraping out the base of the bulb, and storing it in a warm dark place, such as an airing cupboard. After about 8 weeks small bulblets will have formed on the cut surface. The original

bulb is then potted upside down and placed in a greenhouse or a sheltered position outdoors. Within a few weeks the young bulblets will start to grow.

Corms may be cut up in a similar manner to tubers, but the most common method is to lift the corms at the end of the season and remove the small cormels or offsets that have formed. Often there will be dozens of them. They are easily potted or replanted in the garden like mature corms.

ROOT CUTTINGS

Very few plants are grown from root cuttings. The problem is that there is often a lack of suitable roots. This means that the plants have to be lifted and root pruned the season before propagation to ensure the roots are in the right condition. This makes it an unpopular method with commercial nurseries except for certain plants, such as oriental poppies.

Once you have a plant with suitable roots it is a straightforward and reliable procedure. The plant is lifted in the dormant season and the roots washed clean of soil. Strong healthy roots are chosen and removed near the crown. The roots are then cut into pieces about 50 mm to 150 mm in length depending on the type of plant and the growing conditions. Larger pieces are used in outdoor beds whereas smaller pieces are better under controlled conditions. The cuttings are inserted vertically so that their tops are level with the soil surface. Cover them with a light layer of fine gravel or sand about 1 cm deep to prevent excessive drying. With time, leaves and roots develop and the plants can then be potted on. It is important not to insert root cuttings upside down. To ensure against this, the cut furthest from the crown can be made at an angle and this end is always pointed downwards.

LEAF CUTTINGS AND OFFSETS

Many plants can be grown from cuttings that utilise only the foliage or a leaf and a small portion of stem. Others produce young, ready-to-grow plantlets from the mature foliage.

Several plants, such as *Asplenium*, *Kalanchoe* and *Tolmiea* produce young plantlets at the base of the leaves or around the leaf margins. These may be carefully removed and grown on.

Many succulents produce offsets, or small plants with roots that are still attached to the parent plant. These may also be removed and grown on.

Some plants, particularly climbers, have long internodes. This makes it difficult to take normal stem cuttings as they are large and unwieldy. The answer is to use a single node – these are known as leaf-bud cuttings. This can be taken further where opposite leaf buds are present at each node by splitting the stem in half.

There are several different types of leaf cuttings, the most straightforward of which is the petiole cutting. Remove the whole leaf, including the petiole, and insert it into moist potting mix, petiole downwards. The petiole will develop roots and small plantlets or new growth will form at the base of the leaf.

Plants with long, thin, succulent leaves, such as *Sansevieria*, can be propagated from leaf sections. The leaf is cut into sections 6–8 cm long and these pieces are inserted into an appropriate mix in an upright position. The new plantlets develop at the base of the pieces.

Leaf slashing is only suitable for plants that have broad leaves with distinct veins, most notably the ornamental-foliaged begonias. Remove a healthy leaf and make several cuts through the prominent veins on the underside. Pin the leaf down flat on moist potting mix, preferably with the cut surface of the petiole in contact with the mix. After a few weeks small plantlets should start to appear at the points where the cuts were made. A variation of leaf slashing is to cut the leaf into pieces about 1.5 cm square. These leaf squares are pinned down and new plantlets eventually develop at the cut edges.

TISSUE CULTURE

Many plants that are otherwise difficult to propagate are now produced by tissue culture. This is a process whereby meristems or small pieces of plant tissue called explants are grown on nutrient-enriched agar jelly under strictly controlled laboratory conditions and induced to form new plantlets which can then be grown on as normal.

Regenerating from meristems has the advantage of producing virus-free plants, as meristems are normally unaffected by viruses. Since explants are normally derived from mature tissues, this advantage is lost unless the parent plant is known to be virus-free. Tissue culture also allows more rapid build-up of plant stocks than is possible with other propagation techniques. Because of its strict hygiene, temperature, nutrient and chemical requirements, the use of tissue culture is usually restricted to commercial propagation laboratories.

Some plants make propagation easy – *Kalanchoe* produces small plantlets which can be carefully removed and grown own.

CARING FOR YOUR GARDEN

PRUNING

*Theory; Tools; Techniques; When
to prune; Degree of pruning;
Special training methods; General
strategy*

PRUNING TO A BUD

Wrong – the cut is too high. The wood may die back to the bud.

Wrong – the cut is at the wrong angle to the bud.

Wrong – the cut is too close to the bud.

Correct – the cut is about 6mm above the bud and sloping away from it.

MANY GARDENERS NEVER prune their plants because they are scared of damaging them. The reason for this unfounded fear is that pruning has been made to appear more complicated than it really is. There is no great mystery to pruning, particularly pruning ornamentals, and there is really very little that can go wrong.

Pruning should not be seen as an essential chore. Most trees and shrubs, if grown well and sited correctly, will thrive without any attention. However, a little careful pruning can greatly enhance a plant's beauty, improve flowering and optimise fruit quality. Pruning also enables living sculptures to be created by manipulating a plant's growth habit. The basic rules are very simple – it is simply a matter of how they are applied.

THE THEORY OF PRUNING

The main reasons for pruning are to promote strong new growth that rejuvenates the plant, to produce a well-shaped plant, to limit a plant's size, to maintain plant health and to produce good crops of fruit or flowers. Pruning is also important in maintaining good air circulation, which reduces disease problems, and improving light penetration in the centre of the plant.

The essence of pruning can be summarised as follows. Removing the terminal growing tip of a shoot will force side shoots to develop. This is used to advantage for hedging, topiary and to encourage a more bushy habit. With many trees and shrubs the bud immediately below the cut will be the first to burst and will often suppress the growth of buds lower down. This is important as it enables you to determine the direction of a branch's growth. Shortening or removing side shoots will direct the plant's energy to the terminal shoot tip, thus encouraging extension growth and restricting lateral growth. This is exploited when training espaliers and standards.

The type of pruning will depend on the ultimate growth form you desire and the branching habit of the plant. If the plant's centre is to remain open you must cut to an outward-facing bud or shoot and remove any inward-growing branches. Leaving a few inward-facing buds will fill in the centre of an otherwise loose growing shrub.

Many plants are just too dense and twiggy to prune with precision. In these cases an all-over trimming and thinning will usually suffice. Many such plants produce a pair of buds at each leaf node and so pruning to an outward-facing bud is impossible. Some thinning is usually necessary to ensure the base of the plant does not become bare.

PRUNING TOOLS

The following tools are used for different pruning jobs:

- secateurs
- a sharp knife (to trim any rough edges from cuts)
- hedge clippers or hedgetrimmer
- long-handled pruners or loppers (will cut branches about 4 cm across)

- pruning saw (for larger branches)
- gloves (for pruning thorny or poisonous plants)

It is important for all tools to be sharp, clean and well maintained. Ragged cuts and dirty tools are an open invitation to diseases and pests.

PRUNING TECHNIQUES

Always prune to a leaf, dormant bud or another branch, otherwise die back may occur. If using scissor-type secateurs, ensure the blade is closest to the remaining portion of stem.

PRUNING TO A BUD

When pruning to a single bud, make the cut about 6 mm above the bud or leaf joint. The bud may not develop if cut any closer and cutting further away may lead to die back. The cut should be angled downwards and away from the bud so that moisture will drain away from the bud. If the plant produces a pair of buds at each node, the cut should be flat.

PRUNING BRANCHES

In the past, cuts were made flush with the trunk and the wound sealed with a pruning paste or paint. More is now known about the healing process and it is now considered better to leave a tub, or crown, and to leave the wound unsealed to encourage more rapid healing.

First shorten the branch to reduce its weight and prevent tearing when making the final cut. About 50 cm from the branch's base make an upward cut 2–3 cm deep on the underside with a pruning saw, then make a downward cut within 2 cm of the undercut. The branch separates easily if the cuts are fairly close.

The branch collar is a swollen area at the base of the branch. It is now known to be important in plant defence and should not be damaged or removed. The branch bark ridge runs diagonally behind the collar on the upper side of the branch-trunk junction. The final cut is made perpendicular to the branch bark ridge and just beyond the branch collar with an upward cut.

SHEARING

This is only performed regularly on hedges and topiary. Not all plants are responsive and it is best performed on plants that have a naturally dense habit and are able to re-shoot from leafless wood.

COPPICING

This involves cutting back a tree or shrub to near ground level to induce bushy regrowth.

Generally those plants that produce suckers or watershoots are responsive.

WHEN TO PRUNE

This depends on the type of plant and the severity of the winter. Hardy deciduous plants are usually best pruned in winter. They are unlikely to be damaged by the cold and the stems are less likely to bleed. However, deciduous plants that flower in spring and early summer should be pruned immediately after flowering, as they flower on previous seasons' growth; winter pruning will thus remove the flowering shoots.

Frost-tender plants are best left until spring; cutting back over winter only exposes the vulnerable cut stems to frost damage. Spring pruning will still allow for an entire season's growth before the next winter.

Top: This cherry laurel hedge is kept in shape with regular light trimming.
Above: The shape of a bush, in this case an azalea, 'Red Robin', can be greatly enhanced by regular pruning.

Top and above: Climbers tend to be very vigorous plants that need to be kept in check through regular pruning.

It is generally recommended that the best time to prune most hardy plants is late winter. This is mainly because the branch structure is more easily seen when the plants have few leaves, but there's no reason why you shouldn't trim and thin in summer if you wish. Don't cut back too early, as spring pruning can lead to cuts that refuse to heal properly.

Conifers can be pruned at any time, but winter and spring may be better, so that new growth quickly hides the pruning cuts.

Bare-rooted trees and shrubs should have one-third to one-half of the branches removed after planting to make up for the reduced root system. If training a plant into a special form, prune from the planting stage.

DEGREE OF PRUNING

How far to cut back? This question always leads to confusion. You can find all sorts of theories about how hard to cut back and why but it often comes down to the initial reasons for pruning, such as renewing vigour, maintaining health and shaping. Rejuvenation necessarily involves very hard pruning, whereas thinning and shaping only require pruning some branches back to old wood.

Some plants tolerate harder pruning than others. Whorl-branching conifers, such as *Abies* and *Pinus*, should only be lightly pruned back to two to four-year-old wood depending on the genus; random-branching conifers, such as *Cupressus* and *Juniperus*, can be pruned quite heavily along the leafy part of the stem. However, most conifers will not re-shoot from leafless wood (*Taxus* and *Podocarpus* are exceptions). In contrast, many flowering plants, such as rhododendrons and pohutukawa, re-shoot when cut back to bare wood.

Careful examination of the plant may give a clue. If a plant produces new growth from bare wood without any inducement or latent buds are evident, it should accordingly respond to heavy pruning.

The severity of pruning is important for plants that flower and fruit on previous seasons' growth. The harder the pruning, the more flower and fruit-bearing wood removed. Fast-growing plants require more frequent and harder pruning than slow-growing plants. Plants with a loose straggly habit also require severe pruning. Espaliers and standards are often pruned hard to keep growth compact and tidy. If severe pruning is necessary to keep a plant within its allotted space, you may destroy its beauty and replacing it with a smaller plant may be the best option.

SPECIAL TRAINING METHODS

Many plants can be trained into a variety of forms. This is especially so with fruit trees, where the aim is to maximise fruit yields and quality. Consult the chapter on fruit trees for further details on these techniques.

With regard to ornamentals, the emphasis is on enhancing a plant's inherent beauty or creating an artificial or sculptural growth form. This is taken to the extreme with topiary, but a few other techniques are easily practised by the home gardener.

ESPALIERS

Espaliered trees and shrubs are trained on wires, trellis or against a wall either for fruit production or decoration. Their advantage is the limited space required as well as enabling tender plants to be grown in colder climates by training against a north-facing wall. They can be trained in almost any shape but along horizontal wires is common.

It may take several years to complete the overall structure. Thereafter it is simply a mat-

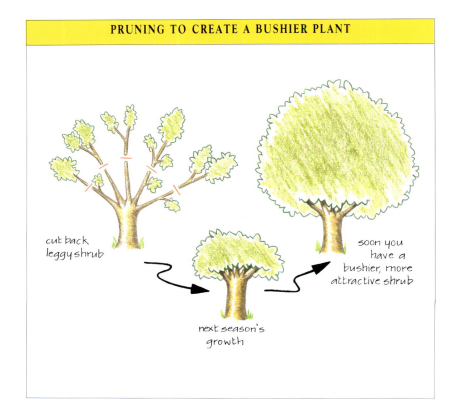

PRUNING TO CREATE A BUSHIER PLANT

cut back leggy shrub

next season's growth

soon you have a bushier, more attractive shrub

ter of maintaining the shape, pinching out shoots that grow towards or away from the wall during the growing season and shortening and thinning the side shoots during dormancy.

POLLARDING

One means of restricting the height of otherwise large trees is pollarding. The tree must initially be trained as a standard until 2.5–3 m tall, when it is headed. The resulting scaffold branches are headed when 0.5–1.5 m long. All new growth is cut out each winter, giving the trees a stunted and gnarled appearance. Suitable trees include chestnuts, elms, horse chestnuts, limes, plane trees, poplars, sycamores and willows.

STANDARDS

Trees and shrubs are often high grafted to produce standards, but many young plants are easily trained into the standard form. Simply tie the main stem to a stake and remove all side shoots that develop until the desired height is reached, when the shoot tip is pinched out to encourage branching at that point. The resulting shoots are pinched back to develop a cluster of branches. Once established, pruning involves cutting back the stems to leave a circle of strong well-spaced branches and removing any shoots developing on the trunk below the branches. Faster-growing plants will require harder and more frequent pruning than less vigorous plants.

GENERAL PRUNING STRATEGY

After the initial training of any plant, pruning will only be needed to maintain the plant's vigour, health and shape. When pruning shrubs and small trees there are a few simple rules. The primary objective is to keep the plant healthy and disease free, so firstly remove any dead, diseased or damaged wood. Examples of pests and diseases that cannot be controlled chemically and thus require pruning out include cankers, elm beetle, fireblight, silver leaf and stem borers.

Next take out any overlapping and spindly branches, watershoots and suckers. You will now have a healthy but unshaped plant.

You have the option of either maintaining the natural form or modifying it to suit your own taste. Each main branch should be cut back to an outward-facing bud accordingly and if necessary thin out some of the branches to avoid overcrowding. With some plants, such as roses and fruit trees, branches become less productive with age and should be removed to direct energy to younger growth.

The pruning of large trees can be difficult and is best left to a professional tree surgeon.

Always remove any fallen debris and spray with a fungicide after pruning, as the freshly cut stems are an open invitation to disease.

Above and below: While many trees require no pruning, some need to be kept to a certain size or shape to suit the needs of the gardener. Substantial trees may require the attention of a professional tree pruner.

PRUNING TO CLEAR OUT THE CENTRE OF A BUSH

cup shape bush

light and air are now able to enter the middle of the shrub

aim for a cup shape

prune out branches growing into the centre and remove old and diseased wood

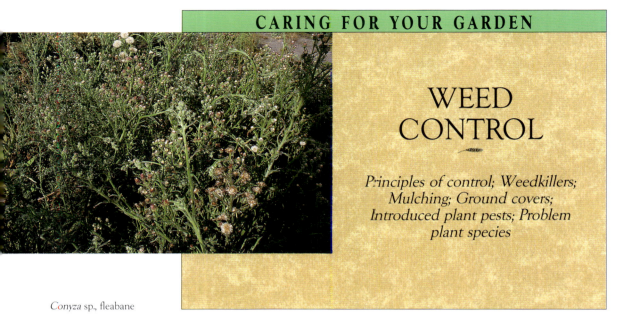

CARING FOR YOUR GARDEN

WEED CONTROL

Principles of control; Weedkillers; Mulching; Ground covers; Introduced plant pests; Problem plant species

Conyza sp., fleabane

TO SAY THAT a weed is just a plant in the wrong place will make you few friends among gardeners with weed problems. While nothing may be more satisfying than a freshly weeded border, there is nothing more demoralising than having to weed it again two weeks later. Effective weed control is not just about ridding your garden of weeds it's also about making your gardening more enjoyable – spending time in it a prospect to look forward to rather than one to dread.

As with the use of pesticides, the haphazard use of weedkillers (herbicides) is now frowned upon. However, new herbicides are far safer to use than their predecessors of only a few years ago: they break down faster and the active ingredients are usually safer. But these are not reasons to use them indiscriminately. Whatever claims made for their safety, they have to be handled with extreme care.

If, on the other hand, you intend to take the purely organic route, your primary means of weed control will be removal by hand and the use of mulches and ground covers. Whatever methods you use, a permanently weed-free garden is, in many cases, unobtainable. As with many pests and diseases, it is more a matter of control than eradication.

Weed control falls into three categories; clean up, control and prevention. Clearing a weed-infested site is a daunting prospect, but once the initial work is done the important thing is to keep the weeds under control. Once you have a measure of control, you should aim to actually prevent the worst weeds from reappearing. Each phase can be either organic or chemical, or a combination of the two.

PRINCIPLES OF CONTROL

Whether you are trying to clear a new garden of weeds, or deal with their habitual menace in an established one, there are many physical methods of weed control. Remember these basic principles:

- All green plants must have access to sunshine to survive. There are a variety of light-deprivation measures to control weeds including weed-mat, deep mulching and dense ground covers.
- Avoid areas of exposed soil by using densely planted borders in larger areas or sowing plants such as thymes and alyssum around paths and between paving stones to discourage weeds developing. This approach can enhance your garden, adding a 'rustic' informal look.
- Constant vigilance is important – remove weeds as soon as you see them. Regular hoeing will deny many weeds a foothold. The hoe is the most effective tool in your armoury; use it regularly, preferably in dry weather. For weeding, a Dutch or push hoe is best.
- Never let annual and biennial weeds flower or set seed and quickly cut back those, such as couch, kikuyu, convolvulus and oxalis, that spread by bulbs or runners.

WEEDKILLERS

Sometimes, you just have to use weedkillers, especially for large areas or particularly nasty weeds like oxalis and convolvulus. Remember to use them strictly according to the manufacturer's directions. Adding a little extra won't make it any more effective and may lead to residue problems.

Weedkillers come in four main types: those that defoliate the plant but are not taken into the sap stream; those that are systemic and which are translocated throughout the plant; those that work by rendering the soil unfit for any plant growth; and the pre-emergence weedkiller, which is applied to empty beds to prevent seeds from germinating.

Defoliating weedkillers work rapidly; often within a few hours of application the foliage is dry and brown. However, the roots of perennial weeds such as docks and dandelions are unaffected and will soon reshoot. This sort of weedkiller, which includes the fatty-acid-based organic sprays, is best used on patches of minor regrowth or as a regular clean-up spray.

Systemic sprays, which include glyphosate and hormone sprays such as 2,4-D, are more effective at clearing densely covered areas. They kill the entire plant by penetrating to all its extremities. This may take several weeks but is usually very effective. Such sprays tend to be residual in the soil for only short periods.

Long-term weedkillers that work by making the soil unsuitable for plant growth have little use in gardens but they are handy for paths and driveways. However, bear in mind the chemical can leach from the soil and may spread into your garden. They may be effective for a few months to several years.

Pre-emergence weedkillers work by coating the soil surface with a chemical that inhibits seed germination and damages any new growth that has to push up through the soil surface. Established garden plants are largely unaffected by these chemicals. Nurseries often use pre-emergence weedkillers on container-grown plants to prevent weed infestation. These weedkillers are very effective and relatively safe, but they are expensive.

Be careful when applying water-based weedkillers. It is all too easy to spray desirable plants along with the undesirables. Spray in the early morning or in the evening when the wind is least likely to be strong. If you have to spray near desirable plants, shield the spray nozzles with an old margarine pot or a similar container to prevent spray drift.

It is a very good idea to have a sprayer only for use with weedkillers. However, if your sprayer must do double duty, wash it thoroughly with a detergent and ammonia bleach solution then pump clean water through the system. This should remove or destroy most harmful residues but the risk of contamination will always be there.

When is a weed not a weed? Depending on the circumstances, some 'weeds' are considered to be useful plants; others are just a plain nuisance. From left: Dock, *Rumex obtusifolia*; elderberry, *Sambucus nigra*; chickweed, *Stellaria media*; willow herb, *Epilobium* sp.; hawksbeard, *Crepis capillaris*.

Other weeds are more serious: (below left) black nightshade, *Solanum nigrum*, and (below right) woolly nightshade, *S. mauritianum*.

It is imperative to wear the proper protective gear. Waterproof boots, leggings and jacket (with a hood) are the minimum. If you are spraying in an enclosed area you should also wear a gas mask or preferably a full-face hood with attached gas mask. Wash any residue from your protective clothing after spraying and regularly change the filters in your mask.

Weedkillers are very effective and convenient but don't use them to excess. Often it's just as easy to hand weed. Restrict your use of herbicides to the initial clean-up and any really troublesome maintenance areas. Mulches, hand weeding and ground covers can take care of most other weed problems.

MULCHING

As mentioned above, one of the ways to effectively kill weeds is to prevent light from reaching them. This can be done by mulching. It can also provide an environment where seeds cannot establish themselves, for example on stones or bark chips.

Mulches can do a great deal to reduce the amount of weeding and spraying required while at the same time improving soil texture and fertility, moderating extremes of soil temperature and conserving moisture. Regular mulching will also increase the stock of beneficial soil organisms, such as worms.

Mulches can also work by loosening the soil, which makes weed removal easier.

When using small bark chips or other fine mulches it is inevitable some of the material will be blown away or dug into the soil with new plantings. Annual mulching will replace the lost volume and further reduce the weed concentration.

Don't mound mulch too deeply around the trunks of trees and shrubs or it may lead to collar rots; gradually lessen the depth of mulch from the drip line back to the trunk to avoid great variations in soil level.

MULCHING MATERIALS

The best types of mulch are those that breathe and allow moisture through but not light. Natural products, such as bark chips and fine sterilised compost, look best but almost any material that is permeable to air and water can be used as a mulch. (Black polythene sheeting is now seldom used because of its lack of permeability.) Woven plastic products, usually sold as weed-mat, are very useful for laying around permanent plantings and can easily be disguised by a surface layer of bark chips.

Organic mulches should be at least partially composted before use. Fresh sawdust or grass clippings will rob the soil of nitrogen as they decompose and can create considerable heat, which may burn any nearby surface roots. If using sawdust add at least 1 kg of blood and bone with every barrow-load to provide the bacteria that break down the sawdust with enough nitrogen to prevent them depleting the soil. Be careful with grass clippings; if applied too thickly they will turn into a layer that no moisture can penetrate.

GROUND COVERS OR LIVING MULCHES

Weeds usually cannot grow where there is already a healthy plant taking up space, nutrients and light. In a closely planted herbaceous border weeds cannot get a look in as selected annuals and perennials prevent them being able to establish. Many difficulties with weeds arise when an area is left bare or there is sufficient space between plantings for them to get a hold. This is where ground covers can be used to perform a practical as well as an ornamental function. Throughout the plant lists within this book, plants suitable as ground covers are mentioned. But not all are ideal living mulches, as only some will have a sufficiently dense growth habit to suppress weeds.

Rapidly spreading ground weeds can be the most difficult to eradicate. Below, from left, are: barnyard grass, *Echinochloe crus-galli*, *Paspalum dilatatum* and couch or twitch grass, *Elytrigia repens*.

If you are wanting to cover a large open area but don't want a traditional grass lawn perhaps an alternative lawn would suit (see the lawns chapter); possibilities include chamomile, thyme, cotula and Mercury Bay weed. You need vigorous plants that can look after themselves.

However, for smaller areas in rockeries and borders you will need to use less invasive ground covers. Look for suitable plants in the annuals and perennials section of this book, or possibly also in shrubs. Many species now include prostrate cultivars that may be suitable for this task.

Whatever living mulch you use, be careful not to choose one that will end up causing more problems than it will solve.

Above: One of the nastiest weed species threatening our native forests is *Clematis vitalba* or old man's beard.

INTRODUCED PLANT PESTS

It may seem surprising that plants sold for the house or garden could become problems in the wild. However, many plants introduced for ornamental purposes have done so, such as broom (*Cytisus scoparius*) and old man's beard (*Clematis vitalba*), and at least two other *Clematis* species now present in New Zealand are suspected as potential problems: *C. flammula* and *C. maximowicziana* (Korean old man's beard). Cultivated forms of plants are often claimed to be harmless. In many cases this cannot be proved or is simply untrue. Many cultivars, such as those of wandering willie (*Tradescantia fluminensis*), readily revert to the hardier wild form of the species. Other cultivars, like those of Japanese honeysuckle, contribute to the species' spread or are also aggressive in the wild.

We can, however, learn from the mistakes of the past and develop an ecologically sensitive approach towards what is grown in New Zealand gardens. But this can only happen if the gardening public and plant suppliers acknowledge the potential effects of their actions on native communities.

Part of such a 'revolution' could also include the use of more native plants in our gardens instead of introduced ones. In suitable locations, natives generally require less maintenance than introduced species and they also attract native wildlife.

It is difficult to predict which plants will or won't become problems after their introduction to our country. Some wish to continue importing potential weeds unless it can be proved that they will become a major problem. Along with other conservation organisations and environmentalists, the Royal Forest and Bird

Protection Society advocates a cautious approach to further plant importations. A system is needed whereby no plant would be introduced unless there are strong indications that it will not become a problem. This is similar to the approach currently taken in New Zealand with regard to animal importations.

There are now about 25,000 introduced species of plants in New Zealand and more than 1900 of these have become naturalised (i.e., survive and reproduce in the wild). It is also estimated that four plants become naturalised every year in Auckland alone.

If our unique flora and fauna are to survive we urgently need to prevent more plants from becoming naturalised. The Royal Forest and Bird Protection Society, in conjunction with Noxious Plants Officers, is conducting a scheme to raise awareness and reduce the supply of 'problem plants'. Under the Forest Friendly Award scheme, plant suppliers agree not to stock a list of particularly undesirable plants (see table overleaf) and are presented with a 'Forest Friendly' certificate for public display. The list of plants addressed by the scheme was compiled through consultation with botanists, ecologists, conservationists, Noxious Plants Officers, plant suppliers and others throughout New Zealand. The scheme is supported by the Institute of Noxious Plants Officers, the Department of Conservation, Conservation Boards, Regional Councils, and the Queen Elizabeth II National Trust. However, while the Forest Friendly Award scheme is a significant step towards addressing the threats posed by introduced plants, it does not address the full range of plants which threaten our native communities.

Plants used as ornamentals overseas often ran riot when introduced into New Zealand's more temperate climate. Examples (from top) are the ubiquitous gorse, *Ulex europaeus*, *Bellis perennis* and broom, *Cytisus scoparius*.

PROBLEM PLANT SPECIES

The Forest Friendly Award scheme is merely a step towards addressing the problems of introduced plants. The major aim is to increase awareness that some introduced plants can threaten native communities. The scheme does not list *all* introduced plants in this category.

⊗ Indicates species should not be planted in this region.

Cortaderia selloana, also known as pampas grass, is a major problem throughout New Zealand.

NAME	REGION			THREAT
	NORTHERN	CENTRAL	SOUTHERN	
Climbing asparagus (*Asparagus scandens*)	⊗	⊗	⊗	Major invader of forest floor. Also sub-canopy killer. Kills host tree by strangulation. Spreads rapidly.
Smilax (*Asparagus asparagoides*)	⊗	⊗	⊗	Rapid invader of forest floor, bush and coastal fringes. Sub-canopy killer, can kill trees by strangulation.
Wandering willie (*Tradescantia fluminensis*)	⊗	⊗	⊗	Common invader of forest floor. Prevents regeneration of native seedlings.
Mexican daisy (*Erigeron karvinskianus*)	⊗	⊗	⊗	Rapid invader of stream sides, bluffs, bush edges and scrub. Replaces some rare ground cover species. Major weed potential, even in lawns.
Jasmine (*Jasminum polyanthum*)	⊗			Rampant vine, covers forest canopy killing all trees. Also smothers forest floor.
Japanese honeysuckle (*Lonicera japonica*)	⊗	⊗	⊗	Tenacious vine, smothers trees and shrubs. Very hard to kill.
Blue morning glory (*Ipomea indica*)	⊗			Prominent canopy invader of disturbed forest. Usually the terminal species in forest degradation.
Japanese spindle tree (*Euonymus japonicus*)	⊗	⊗		Forms dense colonies on bush margins, offshore islands, etc. Replaces native shrubs and small trees.
African club moss (*Selaginella kraussiana*)	⊗	⊗	⊗	Forms dense mats, preventing native regeneration.
Banana passionfruit (*Passiflora mollissima* & *P. mixta*)	⊗	⊗	⊗	Rampant vine, smothers forest canopy.
Italian buckthorn (*Rhamnus alaternus*)	⊗	⊗	⊗	Invades scrub and bush edges. Serious weed on offshore islands.
Chinese ladder fern (*Nephrolepis cordifolia*)	⊗	⊗	⊗	Serious weed of banks, rock outcrops and bush. Often mistaken as native. Completely smothers forest floor. Runners, tubers and spores equal an aggressive invader.
Lantana (*Lantana camara* var. *aculeata*)	⊗			Invades islands, seaside and bush margins, forms huge impenetrable masses. Poisonous.
Mile-a-minute (*Dipogon lignosus*)	⊗			Vigorous invader of scrub and regenerating bush. Name reflects growth rate.
Periwinkle (*Vinca major*)	⊗	⊗	⊗	Forms dense mats in shady areas, preventing forest regeneration. Long runners, roots at nodes. Very difficult to kill once established.
Cotoneaster (*Cotoneaster glaucophyllus*, *C. franchetti*)	⊗	⊗	⊗	Major invader of bush edges, sea cliffs, offshore islands, etc. Forms dense thickets, almost impossible to eradicate.

Himalayan honeysuckle, *Leycesteria formosa*, is a nasty invader in wetter areas of New Zealand.

Foxgloves, *Digitalis purpurea*, introduced to beautify colonial landscapes, have become a major plant pest in southern areas.

Lonicera japonica, Japanese honeysuckle, is a tenacious vine that is very hard to kill.

Hedychium gardnerianum is already classed as a noxious weed, and it is becoming apparent that many more introduced plant species also fall into this category.

NAME	REGION			THREAT
	NORTHERN	CENTRAL	SOUTHERN	
Port Jackson fig (*Ficus rubiginosa*)	⊗			Invades epiphyte niches and offshore islands. Major potential as serious weed.
Pampas (*Cortaderia selloana, C. jubata*)	⊗	⊗	⊗	Terrible weed of regenerating bush margins, seashore and islands. Forms dense thickets which pose extreme fire and vermin hazard.
Elaeagnus (*Elaeagnus* x *reflexa*)	⊗			Forms impenetrable thickets on bush and coast. Scrambles high into trees, ultimately killing them. Virtually impossible to eradicate.
Boneseed (*Chrysanthemoides monilifera*)	⊗	⊗	⊗	Major invader of coastal habitat and nearby islands.
Mothplant (*Araujia sericifera*)	⊗			Increasingly invading bush margins and offshore islands. Smothers bush canopy.
Mignonette vine (*Anredera cordifolia*)	⊗			Becomes massive canopy-covering vine. Aerial tubers break off and resprout in profusion.
German ivy (*Senecio mikanioides*)	⊗	⊗	⊗	Invades bush margins, rapid grower (mainly seasonally).
Tree privet (*Ligustrum lucidum*)	⊗	⊗		Nasty invader of disturbed bush. Forms permanent new forest shutting out almost all other species. Major human health hazard.
Chinese privet (*Ligustrum sinense*)	⊗	⊗	⊗	Significant invader of disturbed bush. Long-lived, forms dense stands. Major human health hazard.
Cathedral bells (*Cobaea scandens*)		⊗	⊗	Smothers bush and scrub. Capable of covering large areas.
Buddleia (*Buddleja davidii*)		⊗	⊗	Major invader of braided river systems. Causes flooding and destruction of habitat for wading birds. Also found in shrubland.
Heather (*Calluna vulgaris*)		⊗	⊗	Increasingly significant invader of scrub and tussock lands. Replacing many native species.
Himalayan honeysuckle (*Leycesteria formosa*)		⊗	⊗	Nasty invader of forest, shrubland and riversides in wetter areas of New Zealand.
Aluminium plant (*Galeoddolon luteum*)		⊗		Vigorous invader of shady areas and bush.
Cape ivy (*Senecio angulatus*)	⊗	⊗		Invades bush edges, especially on coastline.
Flowering currant (*Ribes sanguineum*)			⊗	Invader of dry areas in eastern and southern New Zealand. Competes with native shrubs.
Hieracium (*Hieracium* spp.)			⊗	Aggressive coloniser. Terrible weed of tussockland. Spreads quickly via rhizomes. Difficult to eradicate.

For further information about the Forest Friendly Awards, or any introduced plants that threaten native communities, contact: Royal Forest and Bird Protection Society Regional Office (Upper South Island), PO Box 2516, Christchurch.

CARING FOR YOUR GARDEN

PESTS AND DISEASES

Control methods; Organic controls; Companion planting; Synthetic controls; Pests; Diseases

Green leaf hopper

Top: Blackspot on a rose bush. Above: A rose badly infected with rust, a fungal disease.

MOST GARDENS ARE at some time attacked by insects or other pests and many plants are damaged or killed by fungal diseases or viruses. However, no gardening subject arouses more debate than the use of chemical sprays to control pests and diseases. There would now be very few gardeners unaware of the potentially damaging effects of garden chemicals on both their own health and that of the broader environment. Increasing awareness of the problems of chemical use has led to the banning of many of the most toxic sprays and a parallel acceleration in the development of safer alternatives.

CONTROL METHODS

Even if you opt for an entirely organic approach to pest and disease control, it is important to realise that most gardens are highly unnatural environments. The combinations of plants found in our gardens do not occur in nature and as long as we continue to grow large groups of attractive host plants in small gardens we are going to have pest and disease problems. Growing large numbers of the same plant in a single garden especially (creating a monoculture) is asking for trouble.

Also, practising good garden hygiene (for example, by removing dead or dying plant material such as prunings, lawn clippings and spent annuals) and keeping the garden as free of weeds as possible are both sensible preventative measures. Indeed, prevention and looking out for and dealing with potential problems ('nipping them in the bud' as it were) before they take over the garden can drastically reduce the damage caused by pests and diseases and the amount of spraying a gardener has to do.

ORGANIC CONTROLS

Over the years there have been many attempts at producing safe natural sprays but few could be said to be as immediately effective as synthetic chemical sprays. Nevertheless many organic sprays are capable of a level of control that is perfectly acceptable in a home garden.

Most safe insecticides work on one of three principles: suffocation, direct stomach poisoning or disease inoculation. Surface-coating sprays, such as fatty acids or soap-based sprays, smother the pest and prevent it breathing; stomach poisons kill by using naturally occurring poisons, usually pyrethrin or mild alkaloids; and disease inoculation works by infecting the pest with a fatal disease: the best known is the caterpillar-killing fungus *Bacillus thuringiensis*.

Another method is to trap the pests or interfere with their reproduction. Pheromone traps, which use sex lures, and other traps based on attractant colours and scents can reduce pest populations to manageable levels. Direct genetic controls that lead to mass sterility also appear promising but are beyond the scope of the home gardener.

Natural predator control is successful too. We are all familiar with the idea of using ladybirds to control aphids, but that is relatively unsophisticated. Modern predator control often involves using predators in combination with insecticides that are carefully targeted at specific points in the pest's life cycle. Considerable success has been achieved in commercial greenhouse whitefly control using such methods. Another popular predator insect is the mite *Phytoseilus persimilis*, used to control spider mites. It is often possible to buy these insects from garden centres or specialised organic gardening suppliers.

There are many naturally occurring insect predators in your garden and the use of chemical insecticides can kill those that can help you along with the pests, perhaps leading to worse problems later. If you are using an insecticide, make sure it is targeted to the specific insect you want to get rid of, or only sprayed where it is needed.

Remember that many 'safe' organic insecticides are every bit as lethal as chemical sprays. Black Leaf 40, for example, was an old-time spray based on naturally occurring nicotinic acid but it was eventually withdrawn from sale as it was just too toxic and quick-acting.

There are many homemade recipes to deal with pests and diseases, and their success varies from garden to garden. But in mild cases they may provide some measure of control. For example, some gardeners use a solution of baking soda to control powdery mildew. Try one teaspoon of baking soda to two litres of water combined with a commercial 'fixative' so that the solution sticks to the leaves.

A word must be said here for 'digital control', that is removing unwanted pests by hand. This easy method is often overlooked, and in gardens where some leaf damage is acceptable and the gardener is on the lookout for pests and spots them early, it can be a safe and effective means of control.

COMPANION PLANTING

Some plants show a natural resistance to certain pests and although this is often simply because the pest finds the plant unpalatable there are also many occasions when plants produce chemicals that actively repel harmful pests or attract beneficial insects. Companion planting attempts to capitalise on this by suggesting that growing insect-repellant or attractant plants among the susceptible crops will lessen the damage to the non-resistant plants. Plants can also be grown to encourage helpful predators such as ladybirds and hoverflies.

This is still a largely experimental area and probably the most common example, growing garlic among roses to lessen aphid damage, has proven largely ineffective as aphids will often infest the garlic. Other associations, such as marigold plants in the greenhouse to reduce whiteflies, have consistently proven more successful.

Diseases can be more difficult to control organically, and again the best method is prevention. As with pests, disease is less likely to attack healthy plants, so if you feed, water and weed your plants regularly they are less likely to succumb to fungal, bacterial and viral infections. Also, choosing the right plants for your site and climate can save a lot of heartache and money.

You can lessen the risk by adopting certain cultural practices, such as avoiding overhead watering so that foliage doesn't become wet, or if you do water overhead, watering in the morning so the foliage does not stay wet overnight. A humid environment is ideal for many fungal diseases, so avoid creating one if you can.

Organic prevention sprays can also stop the appearance of disease, and, depending on your plants, you may want to spray them with cupric hydroxide and lime sulphur to kill fungal spores. Both of these sprays are acceptable in organic gardening terms, but they are not to be overused and always follow the instructions for mixing and spraying.

SYNTHETIC CONTROLS

Careful use of synthetic chemicals definitely has a place in the garden, but do exercise moderation. It really comes down to a process of effective management and not overreacting to minor problems. Effective management means selecting healthy disease-resistant plants, growing them in the locations that best suit them, preparing the planting site and maintaining good growing conditions. Use only the sprays that most accurately target the pest, disease or weed and apply them at the most appropriate times.

Used responsibly, synthetic chemicals can save huge amounts of time and may, on occasion, save your plants. Their irresponsible use may eventually see them banned. Always follow the instructions for mixing and use carefully; this applies equally to organic sprays.

Consider your own protection too. Wear waterproof boots and clothing when spraying and if you are spraying plants above waist height wear a gas mask and protective hood. After spraying, always wash down your clothing, your equipment and yourself.

The two common mildews; downy mildew (left) and powdery mildew (right).

Severe thrip damage on a rhododendron – note the silvered foliage.

The larvae of the grass grub.

PESTS & DISEASES

The following tables describe most of the common pests and diseases found in New Zealand gardens. Many occur throughout the country, although some are more troublesome in particular areas. Crickets, for example, occasionally build up to plague proportions on the North Island's east coast but are rarely a great problem elsewhere.

PEST	DESCRIPTION	SYMPTOMS	CONTROL
APHIDS	Small sap-sucking insects. Usually present in large numbers. Often green but colour may vary. Some are subterranean root feeders.	Usually clearly visible. Sap sucking causes direct damage, leaf deformity and general debilitation. Subterranean types cause similar damage but are less obvious.	Washing off with a hose or soapy water gives temporary control. Most insecticides will give control. Use soil insecticides for root-feeding aphids.
BAGWORMS	The larvae of a moth. Caterpillars live within a case (bag) they construct from silk and plant material.	Leaves are chewed but the damage is seldom serious.	Removal by hand is generally the simplest means of control. Most insecticides are effective.
BRONZE BEETLE (Manuka Beetle)	A deep brown to bronze green beetle about 15 mm long.	Chewing of the leaves. The larvae live below ground and feed on roots.	Seldom a serious pest, the damage is usually tolerable. Most insecticides are effective.
CARROT RUST FLY	The small adult fly is no problem but the larvae eat into the carrots as they develop.	Carrots have small tunnels mined into them. The larvae may be present at harvest.	Soil insecticides should be sprinkled along the seed row at sowing. Delaying sowing until late November also helps.
CATERPILLARS	The larvae of moths and butterflies. Most are relatively harmless but some are serious pests.	Leaves chewed or rasped. The damage is usually very obvious.	If the numbers are small and the caterpillar is visible hand control may be enough, otherwise most insecticides are effective.
CENTIPEDES AND MILLIPEDES	Multi-legged arthropods that are usually active at night.	Centipedes are carnivorous but millipedes frequently destroy seedlings and may damage stems and roots.	Soil insecticides well watered in offer the best control as millipedes spend the day buried in the soil or leaf litter.
CICADAS	The chirping adult insects cause problems by laying their eggs on young branches.	Seldom obvious until too late. Weakened and distorted branches may give some indication of internal damage.	Only very rarely a major pest in New Zealand. Control is seldom necessary. Cut off badly affected branches.
CODLING MOTHS	A small moth whose larvae damages fruit, particularly apples.	Larvae tunnels into fruit causing tissue damage and rotting. Larvae may be present at harvest.	Pheromone traps are effective in many locations, otherwise spray with insecticide at petal fall and repeat at regular intervals until one month before harvest.
CRICKETS	The adult cricket is a small grasshopper-like insect that feeds on leaves and stems. The larvae are small burrowing grubs that feed on roots.	Adults are obvious when present. In large numbers they cause very significant damage, particularly to turf. Large patches may be entirely destroyed.	Only necessary in heavy infestations. Spray adults with insecticide and spread soil insecticide on the ground and water in well to kill the larvae.
CUTWORMS	The larvae of several large moths. The moths cause no damage but the nocturnal-feeding larvae are voracious feeders.	Obvious chewing of foliage, buds and flowers. If damage is occurring overnight and you find no indication of slugs or snails, suspect cutworms.	Hand picking at night with the aid of a flashlight is usually enough, otherwise sprinkle soil insecticides around the plant as the larvae bury themselves in the soil or leaf litter.
EELWORMS (Nematodes)	Very small worms that feed on stems, roots and tubers.	The plant will be stunted and weakened and there may be some sign of burrowing and tissue damage.	Soil insecticides offer some control but soil sterilisation is the only really effective control. Plant a less susceptible crop.

PEST	DESCRIPTION	SYMPTOMS	CONTROL
EUCALYPTUS TORTOISE BEETLES	The adult is an attractive light brown beetle, quite round and about 20 mm long. The larvae is yellowish-green to grey and slug-like. If disturbed it can eject a substance that smells of formalin.	The adults cause little damage. The larvae, which chew the foliage and are very destructive in large numbers, are usually obvious if present.	The damage is often tolerable. Removal by hand can be effective against minor infestations otherwise most insecticides will work.
GRASS GRUBS	The adult beetles, which feed on foliage, are on the wing from late October and are very obvious. The subterranean root-feeding larvae are present for most of the year.	Adult beetles cause chewing damage but are seldom present in large enough numbers to be very destructive. The larvae can kill off large patches of turf by destroying the roots. Look for yellow patches or dead areas.	Watering the turf will help birds to remove many of the larvae, otherwise soil insecticides are very effective. Adults are rarely a problem but are controlled by most insecticides.
GREEN VEGETABLE BUGS	A bright green shield-shaped insect that may be present in large numbers.	Insects are clearly present and cause obvious damage.	Minor damage is tolerable. Most insecticides are effective.
LEAF HOPPERS (Spittle Bug, Passionvine Hopper)	Any of a number of species of small hemipterid insects. The adults cause little damage but the larvae are sap sucking. Some have larvae that coat themselves in a protective foam, these are known as spittlebugs.	The foamy covering of the spittlebug or froghopper larvae is very visible. Other species may be less apparent. Damage is not usually visible but may lead to disease problems.	Unless large numbers are present removal by hand offers adequate control. In severe infestations, systemic insecticides provide the best control.
LEAF MINERS	Larvae of moths and flies that tunnel within leaves between the upper and lower layers.	The burrowing is usually very obvious as the leaf discolours where the tissue is destroyed.	As the larvae is within the leaf most surface-acting insecticides offer little control. Systemic or translaminar insecticides are required.
LEAF ROLLER CATERPILLARS	Moth larvae that use silk to tie foliage together to create shelters in which they live and feed.	New growth bunched and chewed, leaves tied together or leaf tips curled over. Severe infestations cause significant damage.	In minor cases removal by hand is adequate. The larvae are well protected inside their enclosures so systemic insecticides offer the best chemical control.
MEALY BUGS	Unusual white insects covered in a fine powder with fine filamentous outgrowths. Adults are up to 5 mm long.	Mealy bugs cause significant damage through sap sucking and tissue rasping. Usually obvious if present.	Hand picking will help but the eggs are laid in the soil. Soak pot plants in a bucket of insecticide or drench the soil around garden plants. Most insecticides will control the adults.
MITES	Various species, some very small, usually an orange colour. Some form small colonies that look like rust patches.	Generally poor growth, foliage yellows and drops. Examine the underside of the leaves with a magnifying glass.	Use a specialised mite killer, such as Dicofol. No truly effective organic control.
NARCISSUS FLY	The larvae of a small fly that lays its eggs on the crowns of *Narcissus* and related bulbs.	Bulbs produce stunted and deformed growth and have obvious burrowing and related tissue damage. Larvae may be present.	Soil and systemic insecticides are the most effective forms of control. Surface mulching will help too.
PEAR SLUGS (Saw Fly Larvae)	A black slug-like fly larvae, up to 10 mm long, that feeds primarily on the foliage of *Prunus* species.	Usually obvious if present. Causes rasping damage. Grubs and damage most often found on the upper surface of the leaf.	Often present in large numbers and quite debilitating. Most insecticides are effective.
PORINA CATERPILLARS	A large moth larvae that lives just below ground in tunnels. Feeds on roots and often emerges at night to feed above ground.	Mainly found in lawns and pastures and can cause considerable damage. May also feed on young seedlings.	Watering the turf will bring the caterpillars to the surface enabling birds to find them. Soil insecticides are very effective.

277

PEST	DESCRIPTION	SYMPTOMS	CONTROL
SCALE INSECTS	Sap-sucking insects that are usually covered in a protective outer case and which adhere tightly to plant stems and leaves.	Sap sucking causes debilitation and disfigurement. The honeydew secretions of scale insects often lead to the development of sooty mould.	The protective covering renders most contact insecticides ineffective. Systemic sprays in combination with spraying oil offer the best control. Squashing any visible scales will also help.
SLATERS (Woodlice)	Nocturnally active crustaceans with multi-segmented bodies and multiple legs.	Feed mainly on decaying vegetation but often damage or destroy seedlings. May also feed on tubers, such as potatoes.	Soil insecticides are usually the most effective means of control. Removing garden waste from growing areas lessens potential habitat.
SLUGS AND SNAILS	Well-known nocturnally active molluscs.	Cause significant damage to established plants and frequently seedlings.	Many homemade traps and remedies have been tried with varying degrees of success. Any of the commercially available baits are effective but the waterproof varieties are the longest lasting.
STEM BORERS	Larvae of various moths, sawflies, weevils and beetles that burrow into stems and feed on the plant from within.	The damage is usually not apparent until too late but may show as wilting foliage and broken branches with obvious tunnelling.	Seldom a significant problem. Systemic insecticides are the only really effective control.
THRIPS	Minute sap-sucking insects on the underside of leaves or in flower buds.	Silvery appearance to the foliage and sticky honeydew deposit, or damaged petals. Thrips may be observed with a low-power magnifying glass.	Most insecticides will give control. Good coverage essential with non-systemics.
WEEVILS	Beetle-like insects often with long 'snouts'. The larvae are subterranean or stem-boring grubs. A few have larvae that feed on foliage.	The adults chew the foliage and the larvae usually feed on the roots. Bad infestations can be devastating.	If readily apparent, the adults can be removed by hand, otherwise most insecticides are effective. Soil insecticides will control the larvae.
WHITE BUTTERFLY CATERPILLARS	The conspicuous white adult butterflies are nearly always present in summer. The green larvae, up to 30 mm long, are often found on brassica plants.	Very obvious and highly destructive; foliage is eaten. The presence of the larvae is usually very apparent.	Hand picking is seldom effective. Mild insecticides, such as derris dust, offer adequate control in most cases.
WHITEFLY	Small white flies that often congregate in large numbers on the underside of the foliage. The larvae do the damage.	Adults usually clearly visible. The larvae are tiny but visible. They damage the foliage and their honeydew deposits allows sooty mould to grow.	Adults are easily killed but the larvae and eggs are not. Pirimiphos methyl works well, it acts as both poison and fumigant. Whitefly traps are very effective in enclosed areas.
WIRE-WORMS	The subterranean larvae of several species of beetle. Usually white or cream and up to 20 mm long.	Feed on roots and tubers. Tissue damage to tubers is obvious and the larvae may be present.	Unless present in large numbers control is not usually necessary. Soil insecticides are very effective if watered in well.
WOOLLY APHIDS	Sap-sucking insects that live in small colonies and coat themselves with a protective white woolly covering.	Very obvious if present. Will damage and disfigure heavily infested plants.	Once a common problem but now largely controlled by an introduced parasite. Hand removal is adequate in minor cases otherwise most insecticides or oil sprays are effective.

DISEASE	DESCRIPTION	SYMPTOMS	CONTROL
BARK BLOTCH	A fungal disease seen mainly on citrus plants.	Starts as a slight discoloration, usually on the main trunk. Leads to corky tissue encircling the stem and eventually progressing to the heart wood thus killing the trunk or branch. Fruit becomes dry and brown.	Preventive spraying with copper-based fungicides offers the best control. If damage has already occurred, cut away any affected wood (do not ring bark the trunk) and apply a fungicide and pruning paste.
BLACK SPOT (Fungal Leaf Spot)	An extremely common fungal disease that affects all members of the rose family including apples and *Prunus*. Also found on citrus crops.	Irregular deep purplish-black spots up to about 6 mm in diameter on the upper surface of the foliage or on the fruit.	With certain plants some spotting is inevitable and must be tolerated but with other plants, such as roses and apples, control is vital. Many common fungicides offer effective control but good hygiene and ventilation are also important.
BLADDER PLUM	A fungal disease that affects the fruit of plums.	Japanese varieties swell and become spongy. European varieties become blotchy and hollow.	Apply a copper spray just as the spring buds begin to develop. Repeat after two weeks. If the tree is badly affected remove and burn any branches that have deformed fruit.
BLIGHT (Early and Late)	Fungal diseases that primarily affect tomatoes and potatoes.	New growth becomes distorted and the whole plant gradually withers, yellows and dies. Most prevalent in cool humid weather or when irregularities in the growing conditions cause fluctuations in the growth rate.	Almost impossible to eliminate once present. Preventive spraying with fungicides should eliminate any possibility of blight occurring.
BOTRYTIS (Grey Mould)	A fungal disease that is part of the natural process of decay. It may affect healthy plants particularly in humid weather.	Grey fluffy mould develops on fruit, leaves or stems. Damaged soft fruits, such as plums, often become botrytised as they rot and may spread the fungus if not removed.	Many fungicides give good control. Also consider the growing conditions. Good ventilation and hygiene greatly reduce the possibility of botrytis.
BROWN ROT	A fungal disease that affects many stone fruits.	Fruit develops soft brown patches that eventually lead to total decay then shrivelling.	Spray with an appropriate fungicide at bud break and repeat weekly until petal fall, then every 14-21 days until about a month before harvest.
BUD BLIGHT	A disease that destroys flower buds. Most often seen on rhododendrons and camellias.	Buds become brown and dry and fail to open. Can be distinguished from frost damage by the black fungal spores that develop in the final phase.	Seldom a major problem. Fungicides are effective but generally not necessary. Remove and destroy infected buds before they fall.
CITRUS BLAST	Primarily a disease of the foliage and fruit of grapefruits and oranges.	Leaves blacken from the stalks toward the tips and eventually fall leaving reddish-brown scabs. Fruit develops dark brown pitted areas.	The disease will often affect material already damaged so shelter from wind is important. Fungicides applied at petal fall are usually effective. Remove and destroy any infected material.
CLUBROOT	A fungal disease that attacks brassicas.	Plants develop swollen and distorted roots. The first sign above ground is wilting foliage, by which time the plant is already fatally diseased. Clubroot may occur at any time.	There is no cure, but preventative measures are effective. Before planting, work a dressing of lime into the soil. When planting, use a fungicide intended to control clubroot.
COLLAR ROT (Citrus Brown Rot)	A form of phytophthora usually seen on citrus plants. May occur on the stems or leaves. May badly damage or kill the plant.	On stems it first appears as a sap-oozing wound, which eventually dries. Foliage browns at the tip and eventually drops.	Very difficult to control. Most modern citrus are grafted on resistant stock. Systemic fungicides work but success depends on the problem being recognised early enough.

DISEASE	DESCRIPTION	SYMPTOMS	CONTROL
DAMPING OFF	A disease caused by several fungi that usually affects seedlings and very young plants.	The hypocotyl becomes soft and watery then collapses leading to the death of the seedling. In less severe instances the foliage dies back, becoming greyish-brown and dry.	Where the hypocotyl is affected there is no cure. If the foliage alone is affected and only slightly damaged spraying with an appropriate fungicide is effective. The use of soil fungicides in the seed mix and regular fungicide sprays are the best control measures.
FIREBLIGHT	A serious bacterial disease of many members of the rose family.	Flowers wilt and drop prematurely. New growth and branches blacken as if they have been burnt. Leaves dry out and brown.	Remove any infected growth and seal the wounds. Spraying with copper-based fungicides offers some control. Good hygiene and avoidance of over-feeding are important preventative measures.
FRUIT BLAST	A disease that causes improper development and premature decay of fruit.	Fruit fails to develop to its proper size and becomes brown and dry. Black fungal spores develop.	Copper-based fungicides applied at bud break, petal fall and during ripening will prevent this disease.
LEAF CURL (Curly Leaf)	A disease that mainly affects plums and peaches.	Leaves develop thickened and distorted pink patches. The whole leaf may eventually be affected. Leaves dry and fall prematurely.	Spray with fungicide at bud break and repeat in two weeks. If after the second spray the leaves are still not fully open repeat after a further week.
LEAF GALL	A fungal disease that mainly affects the foliage of evergreen azaleas. May also affect the flowers. Can also affect rhododendrons and camellias.	New growth becomes thickened and distorted and eventually coated in a white deposit.	Infected leaves should be removed and destroyed. Spray before bud break and as the new growth develops with a fungicide containing thiophanate methyl.
MELANOSE	A fungal disease that affects the soft tissues of citrus plants.	Watery spots develop into brown, yellow-edged patches that eventually cover large areas leading to the death of branches and leaves and the decay of the fruit.	Spray regularly with copper-based fungicides, particularly in cool moist spring and autumn weather and at petal fall. Remove and destroy any affected material.
MILDEW (Downy)	A fungal disease that affects many garden plants particularly fruit and vegetables.	Grey or pale purple streaking and blotching often accompanied by a downy deposit on the undersides of the leaves. Eventually the whole leaf may be covered.	Most fungicides will control downy mildew and can also be used as preventatives.
MILDEW (Powdery)	A fungal disease that may severely debilitate a plant if left unchecked. Mild cases do little damage but are unsightly.	The affected parts, usually tip growth and flower buds first, develop a silvery-white powder-like deposit. The foliage withers and drops.	Good ventilation helps prevent mildew but once it is prevalent control can be difficult. Many fungicides work but repeat spraying will be necessary.
MOSAIC VIRUS	A virus that is of particular concern on tomatoes and cucumbers.	The new growth is mottled and distorted. Eventually the whole plant collapses.	Incurable. Sterilise the soil between crops or repeated planting in the same area.
OVULINIA PETAL BLIGHT	A disease that causes the premature death of flowers. Mainly affects rhododendrons and camellias.	Watery spots develop on the petals and the flower quickly deteriorates to a slimy pulp. The flowers turn a light brown colour and dry out in the final phase.	Usually only a major problem when cool moist weather coincides with flowering or when plants are overcrowded. Good ventilation helps greatly. Spray with fungicides as the buds near maturity and start to open.
PHYTOPHTHORA AND PHOMOPSIS	Diseases that cause root rots and die-back of stems. Root-feeding larvae and stem-boring insects cause damage that can allow the spread of these diseases.	Often the first sign is complete wilting. This is because the plant's roots have died. With die-back, chlorosis usually develops, then the leaf edges brown and the stem dries out and dies back from the tip.	In cases of root rot there is no cure. Good drainage largely eliminates it but avoid replanting the same species until you have cured the problem. If not too advanced, die-back can be controlled by removing infected branches and spraying with a systemic fungicide.

DISEASE	DESCRIPTION	SYMPTOMS	CONTROL
RHIZOCTONIA BLIGHT	A disease that causes rotting and decay of the stems and foliage.	Similar to botrytis in appearance but the fluffy grey mould often forms a distinctive webbing. Affected tissues are watery at first but eventually become brown and dry.	Often caused by overcrowding, which leads to very high humidity and little air movement. Thin out plants or allow more space between container plants. Most fungicides are effective but remove any damaged material.
RUST	A fungal disease that affects many plants, particularly in autumn.	Orange deposits form on the undersides of the leaves and may cause blackening on the upper surfaces. Infected leaves eventually brown and die. White rust is a similar disease with white discoloration.	Good ventilation and avoidance of overcrowding will help prevent rust developing. Many fungicides give good control but achieving total coverage is important. Remove badly infected leaves and leaf litter.
SILVERLEAF	A serious disease that affects *Prunus* species.	Leaves become very dull or silvery. They hang limply and eventually the branch dies back. If untreated, entire limbs collapse and eventually, often after struggling on for many years, the plant dies.	There are no chemical control measures but the disease can sometimes be arrested if branches are cut back hard at the first signs of infection. *Prunus* species should not be pruned in winter or spring as this is when the spores of silverleaf are active. Instead prune immediately after harvest.
SOOTY MOULD	A very distinctive fungal disease that can affect almost any plant.	Black sooty deposits may affect any part of the plant and eventually entirely cover large areas of stem and foliage. The fungus, which does not damage the plant but restricts photosynthesis, grows on the honeydew secretions of sap-sucking insects such as scale and aphids.	Before the fungus can be controlled the insects that lead to the problem must be eliminated. This is usually done by using an insecticide and oil spray combination. The fungus will gradually weather away once its means of spreading have been removed. This process can be hastened by spraying with a fungicide.
TRISTEZA	A viral disease that primarily affects citrus plants. Fatal to non-grafted plants.	Causes root rot, wilting and collapse. In less severe forms it leads to pitting of the stems and severe chlorosis.	Incurable. Ensure that any citrus bought, other than 'Meyer' lemon, is grafted onto resistant rootstock.
VERRUCOSIS	A fungal diesease that can affect many fruits but is most commonly seen on citrus crops.	The fruit develop scaly blisters that become corky brown lesions. Once present this disease will also affect the foliage.	Preventive spraying with copper-based fungicides is the best control. Incurable once infection has occurred. Remove and destroy any damaged material.
VIRAL LEAF SPOT/VIRAL VARIEGATION	Various viral diseases cause foliage discoloration that may or may not badly affect the plant.	Irregular blackish-purple or red markings. Occasionally very distinctive patterns of concentric circles (ring spots). Viral variegation leads to yellow or white markings on the foliage.	Incurable. If the plant seems to perform more or less normally it can be left alone. If only one or two branches are affected, remove and destroy them. If the plant is obviously lacking vigour and in decline remove and destroy it.

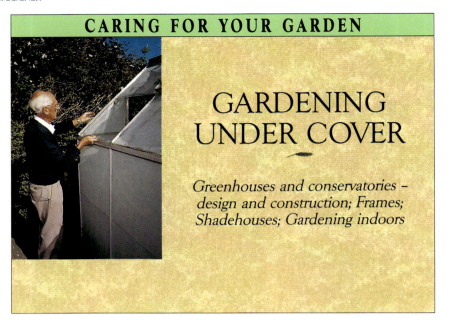

CARING FOR YOUR GARDEN

GARDENING UNDER COVER

*Greenhouses and conservatories –
design and construction; Frames;
Shadehouses; Gardening indoors*

THE COMBINED EFFECTS of sun, wind, rain and cold often make it difficult to grow your favourite plants outdoors. Equally, low light and low humidity frequently lead to house plants being disappointing. But a greenhouse, or even just a shadehouse, will greatly widen the range of plants that you can grow well. A conservatory, which is effectively a lean-to greenhouse attached to a dwelling, is also very useful. Other than considering how practices such as spraying and watering will affect your living environment, the information that follows applies equally to greenhouses and conservatories.

Simple controlled environments can't totally eliminate the vagaries of the weather but they can go a long way to lessening them. Reducing wind velocity alone will help enormously; and if the minimum temperature can be raised a few degrees so much the better.

New Zealand covers a wide latitude range so gardening under cover can vary considerably depending on where you live. Gardeners in Northland may find that a shadehouse is all that is required to successfully cultivate reasonably tough orchids, such as *Cattleya*, whereas in Southland a heated greenhouse is almost essential.

GREENHOUSES AND CONSERVATORIES

There are almost as many styles of greenhouse and conservatory as there are gardeners who use them. The details of the design are not all that important, what matters is that you create an efficient growing and working environment. If you have your greenhouse built professionally or buy a kitset, you will be choosing from a list of predefined options. If you build your own greenhouse or conservatory, there is a wider range of design and construction choices to make.

There are many different greenhouses, from the large Victorian-style glasshouse (below), to the smaller domestic types, such as the plastic greenhouse with a shadecloth cover and lean-to shelter (below middle) and the simple growing house (below right).

LOCATION

Choose a site that receives maximum light and is out of any prevailing cold winds. A lean-to greenhouse or conservatory will inevitably be shaded for part of the day as the sun moves behind the building, but this can be minimised by building with a northwest exposure if possible.

If you are intending to have water and electricity supplied to the greenhouse, you will need to ensure a reasonable proximity to the connection point. Most electrical authorities require domestic greenhouse cables to be run underground, which means digging a trench at least 60 cm deep. The novelty of ditch digging soon wears off, so try to keep the distance to a minimum.

GLASS OR PLASTIC?

For many years there was no choice, it was glass or nothing. And for many years after the introduction of suitable plastics, glass was still by far the superior material. Now plastics are at least equivalent, if not superior, to glass. You should consider:

- Cost. Per square metre glass is far more expensive than even the most sophisticated plastic film. This is mitigated to some extent by the superior durability and lower maintenance requirements of glass.
- Durability. The durability of glass is beyond question; it only deteriorates very slowly if at all. All plastics are affected by sunlight and will break down or discolour eventually. Modern films will last about five years (longer if shaded) before severe deterioration sets in. If you choose plastic, select the strongest and most ultraviolet resistant film you can afford. Even so, you should allow for its replacement when designing the greenhouse.

    Glass is very prone to damage. If the framework of the house moves, the glass may crack and, of course, any stones or other missiles can lead to breakages. Plastic is more resistant to impact but tears easily.
- Ease of use. This is where plastic has the greatest advantages. It is easy to handle and easily installed. Glass is heavy, dangerous to handle and requires special fastening. However, it is far easier to replace one broken pane of glass than to repair a long slit in a sheet of plastic.
- Insulation. A glass greenhouse will need to be lined to limit temperature fluctuations, as will a single-skinned plastic house. Lining can be time consuming and the finished results untidy, and double glazing is not very practical with greenhouses (although it is sometimes seen in conservatories). However, dou-

Conservatories can create wonderful garden environments right in your home, and allow you to create lush tropical effects whatever your climate.

ble-skinned plastic greenhouses are common. They are a neat and effective way of preventing frost damage, but require a power source to run the small fan that keeps the layers of plastic separated.
- Condensation. Not usually very significant in glass structures, but often a problem with plastic. Drips falling from the roof can damage young seedlings or cuttings.
- Alternatives. The only practical alternative to glass or plastic film is rigid fibreglass sheeting or a similar product. This material offers good long-term durability, especially if coated with an ultraviolet resistant product, but it is difficult to work with. It is hard to cut, tricky to install and lacks flexibility. It is also not the most attractive material.

In most cases, glass is the best material for small greenhouses, as its cost is not so important with houses less than 4 m x 3 m. However, if you are building your own framing you will almost certainly find it easier to work with plastic.

FRAMING

The framing material will, to a large extent, be determined by the type of covering you prefer. Glass requires a sturdy framework to support the weight of the glass and to lessen the risk of movement; plastic film can be stretched over very light framing; and sheeting only requires a frame solid enough to hold a screw.

Most home-built greenhouses have wooden framing. Aluminium or steel are longer-lasting materials, but not very practical for home construction. Use only dry treated timber (H3 above ground and H4 or H5 where in contact with the ground) or naturally rot-resistant timber. Painting the frame white will not only lengthen its life but also reflects light, making the house a little brighter.

If you are going to be using your greenhouse to grow ornamentals in pots rather than crops in the ground, then consider the half-solid wall. Bricks or weatherboarding are used to build solid walls up to about 1 m high; the rest of the walls and the roof are glazed. This makes for a more stable environment by lessening heat loss and slowing down heat build up. However, the reduction of light at ground level makes this method less than ideal for growing vegetable or fruit crops.

BASES AND FLOORING

The best base is a concrete pad with attaching brackets set in the concrete. A concrete surround is also very good. Strong wooden posts driven at least 60 cm into the ground are also very effective. If you choose to lay a solid concrete floor, make sure that any water or electrical lines are in place before laying the concrete. They will be difficult to install afterwards.

If your greenhouse is built on a concrete pad, then your floor is ready made. Other types of floor will leave exposed soil that will need to be covered. Sawdust or shingle retained by wooden boards is the cheapest choice, but concrete paving slabs are tidier and more durable.

Regular wetting of the path cools the greenhouse and raises the humidity. If you have a bench in your greenhouse, consider digging out some of the soil beneath it and filling the hole with shingle or even sawdust. Regular soaking of this area will have the same effect as wetting the path.

VENTILATION

This is the area that is most often overlooked in home-built greenhouses, yet it is all-important. The rule of thumb is that the area of venting should be roughly equal to 30% of the floor area of the house. Very few greenhouses measure up to this ideal, but it is well worth bearing in mind.

The type and positioning of vents is important too. Ridge vents are useful for clearing hot air that is trapped at the top of the house and end vents can be used to create a through draught that drops the temperature quickly. Consider having doors at both ends of the house to create a through draught.

Automatic vent openers, which usually work on hydraulic pressure, are useful labour-saving devices. They also eliminate the possibility of forgetting to open the vents.

SHADING

Even the best ventilated greenhouses will probably get too hot in summer. It is amazing how quickly even built-in decks and patios heat up to temperatures no plant can survive in, let alone people. Apart from the heat generated, hot sun through glass will quickly burn tender shoots. Shading is absolutely essential for all structures where glass is used, and it is beneficial with plastic too. The old method of applying whitewash or thinned white paint is perfectly adequate for glass, but totally unsuitable for plastic. Shadecloth strung on wires is the recommended method for shading plastic-covered houses and is equally effective for glasshouses.

Blinds are a more attractive alternative for conservatories. Roller blinds and outdoor venetian blinds in any suitable material are fine, but for maximum efficiency they need to be on the outside of the conservatory, which can cause problems with opening vents or windows. Lightweight awnings held above the conservatory is one way around this problem.

BENCHES

Unless your greenhouse is to be used solely for growing directly in the soil or in containers on the ground, you will need at least one bench. A simple timber bench is probably the easiest to construct. Make it high enough to be comfortable to stand at. If your bench is to be used for supporting plants or propagating equipment, as well as for working on, it will need to be sturdy enough to take the weight. Wet sand and potting mix are very heavy, so don't be skimpy with the construction.

WATER AND ELECTRICITY SUPPLIES

Having water and electricity supplied to your greenhouse makes many tasks easier. The installation is not difficult, but make sure that you use approved fittings and that the water and electrical suppliers are kept apart as much as possible. The work involved is well within the scope of most people, but have an electrician check your work and make the final electrical connections.

HEATING

There's no doubt about it, heating a greenhouse is expensive. For most plants, heating is not really necessary, but those that do need it are almost certain to die without some supple-

Half-solid walls, as in this alpine house, can create a more stable environment within your greenhouse, provided there is adequate light.

Hippeastrum cultivars on double-tiered staging.

mentary warmth. A love of tropical orchids is almost certain to lead to high power bills, but in most cases it is a matter of keeping the greenhouse frost-free rather than heating it to any great degree. Good insulation can help enormously. Double-skinned or double-glazed houses may not even need heating to keep them frost-free. Larger greenhouses and conservatories retain heat longer. Even in cold areas, a house with a floor area over 100 m² will need very little heating to keep the temperature above freezing.

Electric heating is the simplest to use, but you must, of course, have an electricity supply. Most conservatories will have power points or a lead can be run from the house, but many greenhouses are not so well endowed. Do not be tempted to run a power lead from your house to the greenhouse so that you can plug in a heater. **This is extremely dangerous**.

Kerosene or gas heaters can be used if there is no electricity supply, but they must be carefully set to avoid gassing the plants with the fumes. Also, they cannot be operated with a simple thermostat so they have to be left running, which leads to unnecessarily high fuel bills. Large greenhouses are often heated with hot water pipes connected to a coal-fired boiler. This is an excellent method of heating, but rarely practical for home greenhouses.

Whichever heating system you choose, install a maximum/minimum thermometer to make sure it is working effectively. A max/min thermometer is useful even in an unheated house. Keeping temperature records will provide you with a planting guide that becomes more reliable as the period of the record lengthens.

FRAMES

If you can't afford a full-size greenhouse, or don't have the space, frames are a sensible alternative. A cold frame is simply a box, usually wooden, that slopes towards the front, and a glazed or plastic-covered lid completes the unit. A few centimetres of gravel in the base of the box ensures good drainage. It is, in effect, a miniature greenhouse. Frames need insulating in winter and the usual method is a hessian cover that is rolled up when not in use during the day. Double-glazed or double-skinned lids are also helpful.

Portable growing frames, usually made of lightweight pipework covered with plastic film, are useful for giving crops an early start. They can be moved around the garden to wherever they are most needed. A portable frame is also

This shadehouse creates a wonderful area where the garden can extend into the living area of the home.

useful for keeping birds off tender young seedlings, such as lettuces.

Lightweight structures with a large surface area are very prone to wind damage, so make sure that any large frames are firmly tethered. Tying the corners of the frame to stakes driven into the ground is the usual method.

SHADEHOUSES

Many plants that do not need the fully protected environment of a greenhouse or conservatory may nevertheless be difficult to grow in the open garden. Such plants often benefit from some additional shading. Ferns, hostas and many tender woodland plants thrive in shadehouses. They may be grown in pots or planted directly into beds of specially prepared humus-rich soil.

While it is possible to buy shadehouses in kitset form based on the tunnel house design, most are home built. The construction certainly doesn't need to be elaborate, and since the introduction of woven plastic shadecloths the whole job is considerably easier. Before shadecloth was available, shadehouses were covered with thin wooden strips called laths, or with a permeable thatch of light twigs, such as manuka. Lath houses are still a very effective form of shadehouse but they are expensive and time

Below: Ferns and tender woodland plants often benefit from the additional protection provided by a shadehouse.

Tuberous begonias (top) and impatiens (above) are ideal plants for a more protected environment. The extent of that protection will be determined by your climate.

consuming to construct. Ready-made trellis can be substituted for individually placed laths, and this speeds up the job.

The framework for a shadehouse can be fairly light because it doesn't have to carry any great weight, but it should be strongly braced. The shadecloth will be pulled taut to eliminate excessive movement and it can act as a giant sail when exposed to strong wind.

Either steel pipe or wooden framing can be used. Wood has the advantage of being able to be easily nailed into place, but it may lack the durability and flexibility of piping. In areas subject to regular winter snows, it is important to get at least a shallow pitch to the roof. A flat-roofed shadehouse can collect an enormous weight of snow, under which it is almost certain to collapse. However, a roof with even a slight pitch will lessen the directly downward moments of inertia and allow the bracing to do its job.

The shadecloth is strung on wires connected to the frame. The cloth should be reasonably tight to eliminate excessive sagging when wet and to prevent movement, which will cause abrasion and the deterioration of the cloth. The shadecloth can be attached to the wires using special clips, hog-nose staples or by sewing.

It is usually easier to get the cloth tight by stringing up the wires first. Attaching the cloth while working across the frame usually causes the wires in the middle to be tighter than those at the edge, which leads to the whole structure bowing inwards.

Gardening under cover not only gives you something to do on a rainy day, it opens up new areas of gardening. Plant propagation in particular is far more successful in a protected environment. The extra protection allows a wide range of vegetables and fruit to be grown out of season or over a longer season. Many alpines, too, are easier to grow because they can be sheltered from damaging winter rains. And if you want to grow tender plants or prepare flowering potted plants for a colourful display, the greenhouse is almost essential. Once you start gardening under cover you may wonder how you ever managed before.

GARDENING INDOORS

The ultimate step in gardening under cover is to bring your garden right into your home or office. All of us, gardeners and non-gardeners, have grown houseplants, and while the idea is very appealing, it has to be admitted that the reality can be somewhat disappointing. To be successful with indoor plants you need to provide the correct conditions for survival, and it is important to realise that conditions that we find comfortable are not necessarily those that plants most appreciate. The main points to consider are light, humidity, soil moisture, temperature and feeding.

The environment within a house is one of the most difficult for a plant to survive in, let alone thrive, and there is a huge range of 'microclimates' within your home, (just as there are microclimates in your garden); such as the dark, damp bathroom, hot, dry sunroom, draughty hallway, steamy, sometimes smoky, kitchen. The office, too, is a tough place for a plant to live. Offices usually have very low levels of humidity, strong light, little ventilation and often there are fumes from photocopiers, computers and printers. Not to mention the fact that no one ever remembers to feed and water them regularly! But just as there is a plant for every garden situation, so there is a plant for every corner of your home or office; it is merely a matter of finding the right plant for the right place.

LIGHT

All plants need light for photosynthesis and even though most of the plants we use as houseplants can tolerate reasonably poor light, they will suffer if the light levels are too low. Plants suffering from inadequate light become leggy and lean towards the light. They will eventually become yellow and drop their foliage. Areas away from windows are often very dark and may require supplementary lighting.

Ordinary incandescent lights are not suitable for plant growth. Mercury vapour lamps, daylight fluorescent tubes (regular and compact) and the special plant growing fluorescent tubes (Grolux) all provide a more appropriate light for plants. One small spotlight or tube turned on for a few hours a day in the winter can make all the difference when trying to grow a plant in a dark corner.

TEMPERATURE

Modern houseplants generally thrive at normal room temperatures, but some prefer warmer or cooler conditions. Those that prefer cool temperatures and high humidity, such as maidenhair ferns, do best in bathrooms or rooms that are not regularly used or heated. Plants that prefer warmer conditions, such as *Fittonia*, are best grown in kitchens or living rooms.

Temperatures can vary markedly even within a heated room. Draughts from doors and windows can cause cold patches, and any plants near large areas of glass will be colder than those in the centre of the room.

SOIL MOISTURE

When to water is a question that faces every houseplant grower. There is no hard-and-fast rule, but bear in mind that more houseplants die through overwatering than any other cause.

Watering is best done in the morning. Fill the watering can the night before and allow it to stand in the room with the plants. This will ensure that the water is at the same temperature as the soil and allows any chlorine to evaporate.

How often you water and how much water you apply depends on the type of plant and is largely a matter of experience. The plant will give you a few signs, the most obvious is wilting, which indicates that water is needed immediately. The weight of the plant and its container is another indicator: a light pot plant is probably dry.

The best guide is to check the moisture level by poking your finger a centimetre or so into the soil. If the soil is moist it will feel cool and damp, if not, it will be dry and dusty. Most plants can be watered from above using a small watering can. However, a few, such as African violets, cyclamen and cinerarias, may rot if regularly watered from above. These plants are best stood in a bucket of water and left to soak until thoroughly moist.

HUMIDITY

Most houseplants come from the tropics and subtropics where the humidity can approach that of a sauna, whereas most houses have the humidity levels of a desert, especially in winter. Heating and air conditioning can dry the air to the point where few houseplants can survive. You can raise the humidity around your plants by sitting them in water and pebble-filled trays. Regular misting of the foliage will also help offset the effects of low humidity.

FEEDING

Well-fed plants look more luxuriant and are better able to resist variations in temperature and humidity than starved plants. Liquid fertilisers and slow-release pellets are the most convenient to use. It is a good practice to add a well-diluted liquid fertiliser every time you water.

POTS

Pots come in all manner of sizes and designs, so there are certain to be some that suit your decor. The design is up to you, but look at the functionality of the pot as well as its visual appeal.

To look this good, houseplants need the right temperature, humidity, food, water and light. But as this beautiful, healthy peace lily shows, the effort is worth it.

Make sure the pot has adequate drainage and can be fitted with a saucer to cope with the run-off. Ceramic pots are very heavy and prone to breakage. They are also very porous unless glazed. Plastic pots retain moisture but can be rather unattractive. Metal containers are best used as sleeves for other pots because they can corrode and may release toxins into the soil. Wooden containers are more commonly used outdoors, but if suitable they can be used indoors. Watch out for seepage and rotting with wooden containers.

POTTING MIXES

Most commercial potting mixes are perfectly satisfactory for a wide range of houseplants. Specific mixes are available for fussier plants like cacti, orchids and African violets. Potting mixes usually contain fertilisers, but the supply is often inadequate. Mix in additional slow-release granules and also add water-holding crystals and/or wetting agents if they are not already present.

PESTS

Other than soft rots caused by overwatering, houseplants do not seem to be greatly affected by diseases, but they are occasionally attacked by pests. The most common are aphids, mealy bugs, mites, scale insects, thrips and white flies. Mild insecticides or removal by hand are usually effective. Bad infestations, however, may need stronger sprays, and if mealy bugs are present the pot may have to be soaked in insecticide to kill the larvae.

CARING FOR YOUR GARDEN

GARDEN CALENDAR

July to June: Southern and northern regions; General; Shrubs, annuals, perennials and bulbs; Fruit; Vegetables; Under cover

WHENEVER YOU read gardening books it always seems there is so much to do. There are only so many hours in a day, so how can you find the time to prune, spray, weed, mow, water, sow, mulch and dig, let alone even think about harvesting or hybridising? Well, fortunately you don't have to do it all in one day. In fact, if you plan well there's plenty of time – and even some to spare. That is the object of this garden calendar. It is not an appointments diary that precisely plans your year, but a general approach to what to do when.

The gardener's year begins in July, so that is when our calendar starts. It also divides New Zealand into two climatic regions – Southern and Northern. Actual division is not that clear-cut, however. There are some parts of the South Island, for example parts of Marlborough and other sheltered coastal areas, that have a warm temperate climate typical of the north. Conversely, central North Island districts can have a climate more like that of the south and inland South Island. You will know best where your garden fits into this scheme, and it may be a good idea to personalise the calendar as you experiment with the optimum times for jobs around your garden.

JULY

SOUTHERN

GENERAL

The weather in July is usually unsuitable for most garden work. The soil is often too wet to work and the weather too cold to venture out for long. Make preparations for hotbeds by gathering manure and leaves. Plant hardy trees and shrubs when conditions are favourable. Repair and paint cold-frames ready for use. Prepare any areas of bare garden by working in plenty of compost.

SHRUBS, ANNUALS, PERENNIALS AND BULBS

Hardy shrubs, such as magnolias, rhodo-dendrons and heaths, can be layered. Roses can be pruned, but may be better left until early August in very cold areas.

Plant early sweet peas. Cut back any remaining dead top growth of perennials.

Very hardy perennials may be divided at the end of the month if the weather is reasonably mild.

FRUIT

Plant new fruit trees, vines and berries. Use copper oxychloride and oil as a winter clean-up spray. Prune fruit trees (including currants, raspberries and gooseberries). If you intend to do any grafting, now is the time to select suitable scion wood.

VEGETABLES

Clear ground of all exhausted crops. Manure and dig vacant ground. Put potatoes on end in shallow boxes to sprout. Sow cabbages, cauliflowers and peas (early types). Plant out early seedlings; also garlic, shallots, other winter onion crops, and asparagus. Rhubarb may be lifted and divided near the end of the month. Make up new beds of rhubarb and seakale.

UNDER COVER

Cut chrysanthemums down and put the plants in a cold frame close to the glass so as to obtain strong sturdy cuttings. Sow seed of lobelia, begonias, carnations, antirrhinum, nemesia, calendula and sweet pea, etc., for planting out in spring. Force rhubarb, asparagus and seakale. Ventilation and watering must have careful attention; only water when absolutely necessary.

NORTHERN

GENERAL

Make up hotbeds as required. Transplant trees, shrubs and climbers. Trim conifer hedges. Clean off spent crops, dig and manure vacant ground. Renovate lawns and re-sow towards the end of the month. Sharpen stakes, trim pea sticks and prepare labels during bad weather. Lay in scions ready for grafting.

SHRUBS, ANNUALS, PERENNIALS AND BULBS

Sow seed of lobelia and petunias (nothing too tender).

Before pruning roses, spray them and the ground around them with a fungicidal spray mixed with liquid manure. The spray will ensure any prunings not picked up and burnt will not infect new growth. Complete rose plantings.

Plant out begonia and dahlia tubers if the soil is not too wet. If it is, leave until August. Lift and divide dormant perennials and plant out new ones as they become available. Tidy up old foliage of perennials and spray with insecticide and fungicide to kill over-wintering larvae, eggs and spores. Plant an early batch of gladioli.

FRUIT
Plant fruit trees, vines and berries when the soil is dry enough to dig. Use copper oxychloride and oil as a winter clean-up spray. Prune apples and other winter-pruned crops.

VEGETABLES
Late sowings of broad beans, silverbeet, radishes and other hardy vegetables. Plant cabbages and cauliflowers; autumn-sown onions and shallots. Potatoes can be planted in frost-free areas, provided the soil is well-drained.

UNDER COVER
Sow seeds of cyclamen at 15°C and sow tuberous-rooted begonias, gloxinias and streptocarpus at 15°C. Insert cuttings of chrysanthemums and perpetual-flowering carnations. Fumigate on first signs of aphids, thrips and red spider mites.

AUGUST

SOUTHERN

GENERAL
It will probably be the middle of the month before the weather is suitable for gardening, but if the soil is workable, now it is a good time to dig in your compost ready for the coming season. Roll and repair lawns when the weather is fine and there is no frost. Plant out ornamental trees as they become available. Repair paths and drives and complete any maintenance.

SHRUBS, ANNUALS, PERENNIALS AND BULBS
Prepare the areas you intend to use for

summer annuals. Plant out new perennials and roses as they become available. Divide hardy perennials and add compost to the soil.
Prune roses.

FRUIT
Finish planting and pruning all fruit trees. Spray peaches and nectarines with cupric hydroxide before the buds start. Apply fertiliser ready for new season's growth.

VEGETABLES
Mulch asparagus. Lift and store parsnips. Sow peas, broad beans and other vegetables in a warm border. Plant onions and early potatoes in small quantities in a warm, sheltered area. Plant and divide chives. Sow celery, cabbage and cauliflower seed. Make hotbeds for cucumbers, melons and seed sowing.

UNDER COVER
Tuberous begonias and gloxinias should now be shaken out of their pots and placed in shallow boxes in light soil. Sow seed of begonias, gloxinias, streptocarpus, tender annuals and perennials. Increase the stock of bedding plants by striking cuttings. Sow seeds of nemesia, antirrhinums and dimorphotheca. Prune bouvardias, fuchsias and geraniums that have grown straggly. Sow celery, tomatoes, cucumbers and melons. Water and ventilation should be increased as the weather gets warmer.

NORTHERN

GENERAL
In a good year, August can be a good time to start serious spring planting, but sometimes it is safer to delay things until September. Trim edges of lawns and weed paths. Roll and mow lawns regularly, and sow new ones.

SHRUBS, ANNUALS, PERENNIALS AND BULBS
Plant out hollyhocks, carnations, antirrhinums and all herbaceous plants.
Prune early-flowering shrubs as soon as they have finished flowering. Prune *jackmanii*-type clematis (most other types are not pruned). Finish pruning roses, tie climbers and finish manuring and digging beds. Keep bulb beds free from weeds. Top-dress anemone and ranunculus beds with well-decayed manure. Plant more gladioli. Aphids will be apparent by the end of the month.

FRUIT
Prune and manure citrus trees. Transplant citrus. Prune autumn-fruiting raspberries. Keep strawberries clean by hoeing; do not

hoe too close to the plants; give a dressing of blood and bone. Finish pruning, digging and spraying in the orchard. Spray peach and nectarine trees at bud movement with a fungicide for leaf curl.

VEGETABLES
Continue planting autumn-sown onions. Sow or plant new asparagus beds. Manure rhubarb beds with any animal manures available; use blood and bone at 150 g per plant. Sow more peas if required; also leeks, cabbages, cauliflowers, beets, Brussels sprouts, lettuces, onions, radishes, carrots, parsnips, parsley and spinach. Plant main crop of Jerusalem artichokes and potatoes. Start kumaras on hotbed to provide plants for setting out in October.

UNDER COVER
Start gloxinia, begonia and achimenes corms by pushing them gently into an all-purpose potting mixture which should be kept damp until new growth emerges from the dormant corms. Repot paphiopedilum orchids if overcrowded. Pot ferns and permanent greenhouse plants. Continue taking cuttings of chrysanthemums and perpetual-flowering carnations. Bring in dahlia tubers if cuttings are required. Propagate soft-wooded plants for summer flowering. Sow more tomatoes, cucumbers, begonias, gloxinias, coleus and tender annuals. Take leaf cuttings of saintpaulias and peperomias and insert cuttings of philodendrons, begonias and coleus.

SEPTEMBER

SOUTHERN

GENERAL
This can be an extremely variable month, so proceed with caution. Late frosts may damage early plantings so there is very little advantage in trying to push things along too quickly. New lawns can be sown.

SHRUBS, ANNUALS, PERENNIALS AND BULBS
Complete pruning of roses.
Divide plants in herbaceous border and manure heavily. Plant violets and gladioli and sow hardy annuals.

FRUIT
If bud burst occurs, spray with a fungicide to prevent leaf curl and brown rot. Grafting can commence as the sap rises.

VEGETABLES
Sow main crop vegetables and plant early potatoes, cabbages and cauliflowers.

UNDER COVER
Feed hydrangeas in pots. Repot and pot on plants as necessary. Prick off seedlings. Start dahlia tubers into growth and take cuttings. Put bedding plants out into cold-frames to harden. Continue to sow seed of tender and half-hardy annuals. Pot off rooted chrysanthemum cuttings. Repot coleus cuttings. Repot ferns and palms. Sow vegetable marrow and pumpkin seed. Plant out tomatoes under glass early in the month, and pot those for planting outside, giving plenty of air and light. Vines in unheated houses should be starting into growth.

NORTHERN

GENERAL
Most spring plants will be well under way by the middle of the month and it is time to think about planning the summer garden. Mow and roll lawns regularly, and water with liquid manure. Finish tree and shrub planting.

SHRUBS, ANNUALS, PERENNIALS AND BULBS
Lift, divide and replant border chrysanthemums and dahlias. Plant more gladioli. Sow hardy and half-hardy annuals. Divide and replant primrose and polyanthus when flowering is finished. Plant violet and herbaceous plants. Fertilise cinerarias with liquid manure, and dust with derris dust if caterpillars appear.
Prune and plant bouvardias, bougainvilleas, poinsettias, luculias and other tender subjects.

FRUIT
When fruit has set, spray citrus with a fungicide to prevent melanose and verrucosis. When petals have fallen, spray stone fruits with lime sulphur or a fungicide to prevent brown rot. Graft fruit trees and keep surface soil loose with hoe. When buds show the flower clusters, spray apples and pears for blackspot and brown rot. Spray again when petals have fallen, add malathion or carbaryl for codling moth, or hang pheromone traps. Spray gooseberries and currants with a fungicide for leaf spot.

VEGETABLES
Plant main crop potatoes, spray and earth up earlier crops. Sow more peas, earth up

and stake those already up. Sow dwarf beans at end of month. Plant out cabbages, cauliflowers and lettuces.
Sow parsnips, cauliflowers, cabbages, leeks, parsley and most other vegetables. Plant or sow new asparagus beds. Finish onion planting and keep hoe going among crops.

UNDER COVER
Divide and repot permanent glasshouse plants, and repot where necessary any houseplants such as saintpaulias, philodendrons and peperomias. Pot on rooted cuttings of coleus, begonias and geranium. Make up hanging baskets and plant with fuchsias, begonias (tuberous hanging) and schizanthus. Pot begonias and gloxinias started last month; finish repotting ferns. Divide and repot aspidistras and other permanent greenhouse plants. Insert cuttings of winter-flowering begonias in heat. Pot and stop rooted cuttings of perpetual-flowering carnations. Sow half-hardy annuals and take dahlia cuttings. Complete taking of chrysanthemum cuttings. Fumigate for aphids and thrips and shade glass. Sow tomatoes, capsicums, cape gooseberries, eggplants, melons, cucumbers, vegetable marrows and pumpkins.

SOUTHERN

GENERAL
Spring is here. The bulbs will be at their best and it is time to think about summer planting. However, there is still a possibility of late frosts.

SHRUBS, ANNUALS, PERENNIALS AND BULBS
Thin out shoots of herbaceous plants; stake if necessary. Lift, divide and replant dahlias. Thin out old shoots of chrysanthemum plants and plant out new ones.

FRUIT
Rub off superfluous shoots on fruit trees and roses, especially where heavy pruning has to be done.

VEGETABLES
Sow peas, broad beans, French and runner beans, marrows and pumpkins. Plant pota-

toes, cabbages and cauliflowers. Thin out seedling crops when ready. Hoe regularly.

UNDER COVER
Continue potting and repotting plants as necessary. Harden off tender bedding plants. As azaleas finish flowering, pick off old flower spikes to prevent seeding. Syringe the plants and keep them in a warm moist atmosphere until growth is completed. Then place out of doors in a sheltered position. Watch for insect pests and fungal diseases, and spray or fumigate early. Increase ventilation and moisture as the temperature rises. Harden off tomato plants for planting outside. Disbud vines.

NORTHERN

GENERAL
By the end of October the summer garden should be taking shape, and now is the time to wage war on slugs, slaters and snails to avoid disappointment later on.

SHRUBS, ANNUALS, PERENNIALS AND BULBS
Plant fresh beds of violets. Plant fuchsias and more gladioli. Divide and plant dahlias. Sow annuals freely. Mulch roses, and water if dry weather.

FRUIT
Plant out passionfruit and cape gooseberries. When petals have fallen, spray apples and pears with carbaryl or malathion and lime sulphur, or a fungicide to prevent blackspot and codling moth. Alternatively, set pheromone traps. Remove ties from grafts as soon as the union swells. Rub off any buds appearing on the stocks. Mulch strawberries as the fruit begins to form.

VEGETABLES
Plant tomatoes and kumaras. Start tubers of kumaras to provide cuttings. Sow parsnips, carrots, dwarf and runner beans, tomatoes, melons, cucumbers, vegetable marrows, peas, silverbeet, savoy cabbage, winter and spring broccoli, and any others according to requirements.

UNDER COVER
Water, shade and ventilate greenhouses. Feed perpetual-flowering carnations and insert more cuttings. Insert cuttings of dahlias, fuchsias, heliotrope and coleus. Sow salvias and winter-flowering primulas. Repot begonias and gloxinias if necessary. Make up hanging baskets of ferns and fuchsias.

NOVEMBER

SOUTHERN

GENERAL
Although officially spring, the weather may have other ideas. Regular watering may be necessary this month in some areas but inland there is still the threat of very late frosts.

SHRUBS, ANNUALS, PERENNIALS AND BULBS
Plant out all bedding plants. Sow seed of biennials, e.g., Canterbury bells, sweet Williams, stocks and wallflowers, in prepared beds ready for autumn planting. Train and tie in climbing plants.
Mulch rhododendrons and azaleas.

FRUIT
Reduce excessive growth on fruit trees and thin out crops where they are too heavy.

VEGETABLES
Sow vegetable seeds to maintain a continuous supply. Plant out tomatoes, vegetable marrows, pumpkins and ridge cucumbers.

UNDER COVER
Sow seed of cineraria, primula and calceolaria. Pot on young plants as necessary. Repot amaryllis after flowering. Maintain ventilation and moisture as required. Shade if necessary. Cucumber and melons should be trained and stopped as necessary. Thin grapes and tie down shoots.

NORTHERN

GENERAL
November marks the transition from spring to summer, and summer annuals will be in full swing by the end of the month.

SHRUBS, ANNUALS, PERENNIALS AND BULBS
Complete dahlia and chrysanthemum planting, and stake those planted previously. Tie up herbaceous perennials. Take cuttings of pinks and rock plants. Mulch rhododendrons and azaleas, and pick off seed pods if the weather is dry. Keep sweet peas and roses well watered. Feed with liquid manure and remove faded flowers. Prune flowering shrubs as soon as the period of blooming is over: lilacs, philadelphus, shrubby spireas and deutzias.

FRUIT
Plant out cape gooseberries. Disbud fruit trees. Thin apricots, peaches and heavily cropped trees. Spray at 10-day intervals for codling moth. Check pheromone traps. Also spray with lime sulphur or a fungicide for blackspot and ripe rot.

VEGETABLES
Thin crops and hoe weeds. Sow sweet corn every 14 days. Sow haricot, runner, dwarf and Lima beans. Mound up and stake peas; water if weather is dry. Plant out cucumbers, tomatoes, vegetable marrow, capsicums, eggplants, kumaras, celery and melons of all kinds. Pinch out tips of early marrow and cucumber plants. Sow winter rhubarb, to grow without transplanting.

UNDER COVER
Thin grapes and tie down shoots. Maintain ventilation and moisture as required. Shade if necessary.
Feed ferns and plants in flower with liquid manure. Pot and stop perpetual-flowering carnations. Sow herbaceous calceolaria and Brompton stock in a cool position.

DECEMBER

SOUTHERN

GENERAL
The spring garden will largely be spent and warmer weather will be encouraging summer crops to make strong growth. Water as necessary and keep pests and diseases under control. Roll and mow lawns frequently.

SHRUBS, ANNUALS, PERENNIALS AND BULBS
Stake and tie up herbaceous plants. Plant bearded irises. Lift daffodils and other spring bulbs when foliage has turned yellow. Clean and replant, or store in a cool place. Line out wallflowers and sow forget-me-nots. Plant out tender bedding plants, e.g., salvias, cannas, zinnias. Put chrysanthemums into their flowering pots.

FRUIT
Continue tying and training canes and vines. Thin crop if very heavy. Early stone fruit will be ready this month.

VEGETABLES
Stop cutting asparagus. Sow more peas and beans, lettuce, etc., for succession. Plant main crop of celery, broccoli, Brussels sprouts, cabbage and leeks. Hoe constantly.

UNDER COVER
Ventilate plant houses. Pot on seedling begonias and gloxinias. Keep cinerarias, primulas, cyclamen and calceolarias in a cool frame facing south. Ventilate freely. After flowering, put pelargoniums outside in a sunny position and reduce watering. Tie up tomatoes and rub off lateral growths.

NORTHERN

GENERAL
Finish bedding out. Then it is mainly a month for keeping things progressing steadily. Water when necessary and keep pests and diseases under control.

SHRUBS, ANNUALS, PERENNIALS AND BULBS
Finish bedding out. Some short-lived annuals, e.g., nemesia, may need to be replaced. Sow portulaca and plant out salvias. Spray roses with lime sulphur and malathion for mildew, caterpillars and aphid. Water roses with clean water and spray with liquid manure afterwards.
Tie up chrysanthemums, dahlias and carnations. Layer clematis.
Divide and replant flag irises, plant autumn-flowering bulbs such as colchicum, belladonna lilies, hardy cyclamen, sternbergia.

FRUIT
Spray gooseberries with a fungicide for leaf spot. Thin fruits in their order of ripening and spray for codling moth and brown rot. Spray plums for cherry slug and grapes for mildew. Cut out branches of stone fruits showing silverleaf disease.

VEGETABLES
Make successional sowings of dwarf and runner beans and sweet corn. Prick out celery in beds of good soil. Spray potatoes and tomatoes. Finish cutting asparagus. Plant main crop of leeks, cabbages, cauliflowers and broccoli. Pinch lateral shoots from tomatoes and stop main vines of pumpkins, marrows and cucumbers, to encourage lateral growth.

UNDER COVER
Insert leaf cuttings of begonias, gloxinias and saintpaulias. Feed begonias with liquid manure. Sow seeds of cinerarias, primulas and calceolarias. Keep cool. Keep cyclamen growing in a cool position and

repot old corms. Stop and pot perpetual-flowering carnations. Finish grape thinning and allow more ventilation when berries start to colour.

Shade all glass, ventilate freely and keep moist.

JANUARY

SOUTHERN

GENERAL

If the weather is dry, watering and mulching will be necessary. Fruits and vegetables will be well under way and bedding displays will be approaching their best by the end of the month.

SHRUBS, ANNUALS, PERENNIALS AND BULBS

Plant belladonna lilies and autumn crocus. Line out wallflower seedlings in well-manured border. Layer carnations. Cut sweet pea flowers to prevent formation of seed pods.

FRUIT

Spray apples and pears for codling moth, and other fruit for fungal diseases. Prune stone fruit immediately after harvesting.

VEGETABLES

Sow beetroot and lettuce, and small sowings of carrots and onions. Plant leeks, celery, broccoli and cabbage.

UNDER COVER

Cut off decaying flowers and leaves. Give begonias and foliage plants applications of liquid manure. Pot on cinerarias, calceolarias and primulas, and keep growing in a cool frame. Cut back pelargoniums and keep slightly dry until growth starts. Put young cyclamen into their flowering pots. Prick out seedlings of polyanthus in boxes. Give chrysanthemums their final potting and put outside in full sun. When grapes are colouring, ventilate freely and water thoroughly, but avoid draughts.

NORTHERN

GENERAL

If the weather is dry, watering and mulching will be necessary. All summer fruits

and vegetables should be well under way and bedding displays will be approaching their best.

SHRUBS, ANNUALS, PERENNIALS AND BULBS

Mulch rhododendrons and azaleas. Bud roses and fruit trees. Thin out old flowering growths of rambler roses.

Commence bulb lifting; tulips should be lifted before the tops are quite dead.

Layer border carnations and prepare new bed. Stake and tie dahlias and chrysanthemums. Prepare ground for early-flowering sweet peas. Sow biennials, perennials and spring-flowering plants.

FRUIT

Feed tamarillos with liquid manure and keep moist. Tie in new canes of loganberries, marionberries, raspberries, etc. Spray for codling moth and brown rot, check pheromone traps. Thin fruit as required and summer prune fruit trees.

VEGETABLES

Plant cabbages, cauliflowers, broccoli and seakale for winter use. Sow lettuce in drills and thin out when ready. Sow radishes, dwarf beans, silverbeet, spinach and carrots. Spray tomatoes and trim and tie. Plant celery in prepared trenches.

UNDER COVER

Pot perpetual-flowering carnations. All final potting and stopping should be done this month. Sow calceolarias, cinerarias and primulas. Water and feed begonias, gloxinias and ferns. Pot on seedling cyclamen and keep cool. Pot freesias, lachenalias and other bulbs for early flowering.

FEBRUARY

SOUTHERN

GENERAL

By the end of February the first signs of autumn may be apparent, but liberal watering will still be necessary. Prune evergreen trees and cut hedges. Fungal diseases can become a problem this month.

SHRUBS, ANNUALS, PERENNIALS AND BULBS

Lift and replant *Lilium candidum*. Line out seedlings of sweet Williams, Canterbury

bells, forget-me-nots and double daisies.

FRUIT

Cut out old raspberry canes and tie up young canes. Apricots, peaches and nectarines will require attention with the removal of surplus new shoots.

VEGETABLES

Sow cabbages, onions, lettuces, prickly spinach and parsley. Onions as they ripen should be pulled, dried and stored. Earth up celery.

UNDER COVER

Shake out and repot cyclamen. Pot bulbs of freesias, hyacinths, early tulips and lachenalias. Keep the greenhouse bright and remove plants as they finish flowering. Watering and ventilation are very important.

NORTHERN

GENERAL

This can be the hottest month and many insect pests will reach their most active phase. Regular watering will almost certainly be essential. Sow vacant ground with lupin and barley or mustard for digging in later.

SHRUBS, ANNUALS, PERENNIALS AND BULBS

Layer carnations and prepare beds for them. Plant out perpetual-flowering carnations for winter flowering. Sow winter-flowering sweet peas. Insert cuttings of geraniums, pentstemons, antirrhinums, etc. Sow hollyhocks, aquilegias, Canterbury bells, primroses, anemones and ranunculus. Sow seeds of perennials and biennials. Feed dahlias and chrysanthemums. Keep them well staked and tied.

Lift early gladioli when foliage turns yellow. Plant daffodils and early-flowering bulbs. Spray roses for mildew.

FRUIT

Prepare ground for strawberry planting. Continue spraying for codling moth and cherry slug. Watch out for mildew on apples and botrytis on grapes. Gather fruit as it matures. Prune stone fruit immediately after harvest and cut out old canes of raspberries and similar fruit.

VEGETABLES

Plant cabbage and cauliflower when weather is favourable. Commence to earth up early-planted celery. Lift and dry shallots, onions and early crops of potatoes.

UNDER COVER

Sow cyclamen, cinerarias, primulas, schizanthus and calceolarias. Put in cuttings of hydrangeas for pot work. Hydrangeas in pots should be placed in full sun to ripen the wood. Sow winter-flowering stocks, Iceland poppies and *Primula malacoides*. Pot up perpetual-flowering carnations from the open ground. Pot bulbs of freesias and lachenalias and stand in cool frames. Pot up bulbs of *Lilium regale, L. longiglorum*, narcissi, hyacinths, tulips and plunge outside in pumice or scoria/gravel. Insert cuttings of tender bedding plants.

MARCH

SOUTHERN

GENERAL

By the end of March, autumn can no longer be ignored. Inland areas may experience their first frosts late in the month. Early March is a good time to sow lawns. It is also the most common time for fungal diseases, so spray if necessary.

SHRUBS, ANNUALS, PERENNIALS AND BULBS

Plant spring-flowering bulbs, e.g., daffodils. Sow sweet peas and hardy annuals. Plant out seedling biennials and perennials in their flowering positions towards the end of the month. Take cuttings of violas, pansies, aubretia, penstemons, geraniums and pelargoniums.

FRUIT

Pick and store apples and pears as they mature. Gather fallen fruit and destroy diseased specimens. Cut out old canes of raspberries and similar fruit.

VEGETABLES

Harvest onions. Earth up celery. Clear away exhausted crops. Sow onions, carrots, turnips, spinach, cabbages and lettuces.

UNDER COVER

Pot spring-flowering bulbs. e.g., daffodils, tulips, hyacinths. Bring chrysanthemums indoors as frosts appear. Repot pelargoniums and geraniums. Pot cinerarias into flowering pots. Slowly ripen off amaryllis, gloxinias and achimenes. Take cuttings of geraniums and other bedding plants. Sow schizanthus, clarkia and godetia seed for spring flowering. Pot bulbs in bowls for house decoration.

NORTHERN

GENERAL

By the end of the month the weather should have cooled enough to think about sowing new lawns. Fungal diseases can develop very quickly in warm, moist weather.

SHRUBS, ANNUALS, PERENNIALS AND BULBS

Plant *Lilium candidum*, anemone and ranunculus. Lift and plant rooted carnation layers. Sow 10-week and beauty stocks and early-flowering sweet peas. Replant narcissi and spring-flowering bulbs. Sow hardy annuals. Cut off faded blooms to prevent seed forming. Feed and disbud dahlias and chrysanthemums.

FRUIT

Cut out old canes of loganberries and raspberries. Thin out the outside growth of gooseberries and currants. Feed citrus trees and spray with a fungicide. Gather up fallen fruit.

VEGETABLES

Sow silverbeet, cabbage, early horn carrot, cauliflower, turnip, parsley, onion, spinach, broad beans and lettuce. Lift and store onions and potatoes. Earth up leeks and celery.

UNDER COVER

Propagate bedding plants by cuttings and layers. Pot primulas, cyclamen and cinerarias in flowering pots. Feed begonias with liquid manure. Pot bulbs for winter flowering. Cut back pelargoniums and keep fairly dry.

APRIL

SOUTHERN

GENERAL

The first light frosts will probably occur this month and most summer plants will be nearing the end of their lives. It is time to start clearing out the old plants and planting the new ones. Dig vacant land and sow with green manuring crops. Make a compost heap of all vegetable refuse and spent crops.

SHRUBS, ANNUALS, PERENNIALS AND BULBS

Plant out carnation layers and sow hardy annuals. Insert cuttings of roses, hardy trees and shrubs.

FRUIT

Prepare ground for planting fruit trees. Insert cuttings of currants and gooseberries. Root prune fruit trees if necessary. Gather and burn fallen fruit tree leaves.

VEGETABLES

Dig potatoes. Dig beetroot and carrots and store in dry earth or sand.

UNDER COVER

Box up bulbs of Spanish and English iris for early flower under cover and pot up clumps of varieties of astilbe for forcing. Chrysanthemums in pots should be brought indoors now. Put in cuttings of geraniums, penstemons and calceolarias and place in a cool frame. Check heating system to make sure it is in good working order for the forthcoming months.

NORTHERN

GENERAL

Lawns sown this month should make good growth before winter. Summer bedding plants may continue to be colourful but it is often better to replace them now to make sure of a good late winter and early spring display. Plant cuttings of evergreen and deciduous trees and shrubs.

SHRUBS, ANNUALS, PERENNIALS AND BULBS

Plant out antirrhinums, penstemons, pansies, aquilegias, Canterbury bells, Iceland poppies, nemesias, hollyhocks, gaillardias and myosotis. Finish planting narcissus, anemones and ranunculus. Sow summer-flowering sweet peas. Plant 10-week and beauty stocks.
Rose cuttings root well this month.

FRUIT

Prepare ground for strawberries and for new orchards. Gather fruit as it matures and pick up and destroy diseased fruit. Keep orchard clean and mark any unprofitable trees for removal.

VEGETABLES

Earth up celery and leeks. Give liquid manure. Lift late crops of potatoes and kumaras. Store pumpkins, marrows and melons.

UNDER COVER

Insert cuttings of penstemons, bedding calceolarias, zonal pelargoniums, verbenas and other tender bedding plants. Dry off begonias and gloxinias. Reduce water when weather is dull. Stake and tie perpetual-flowering carnations.

MAY

SOUTHERN

GENERAL

A month of fallen leaves and garden debris. Late April and May is when the compost bins get filled to overflowing. Lawns can be sprayed with broadleaf weedkiller and treated for moss. Small patches of lawn may be sown if the weather remains mild.

SHRUBS, ANNUALS, PERENNIALS AND BULBS

Lift dahlias and gladioli and store in a cool place. Trim back herbaceous perennials as they die off. Hardy perennials can be divided once dormant, but more tender plants are best left until they show some new growth in the spring. Insert cuttings of roses and hardy shrubs. If the ground is in good condition, fruit trees, ornamental trees and shrubs may be planted.

FRUIT

Insert cuttings of bush fruits. As soon as leaves have fallen, fruit trees may be pruned, except peaches and nectarines. (These are better pruned after picking the fruit, as wounds heal faster in the summer, thus preventing silverleaf disease.) Spray peaches, nectarines, apricots and any other trees that have been attacked by fungal diseases during the season.

VEGETABLES

Sow peas and broad beans at the beginning of the month. Cut off asparagus tops and mulch the bed lightly with half-rotted stable manure.

UNDER COVER

Plants will now require less water. Put calceolarias into their flowering pots and keep close to the glass in a cold house or frame. Bring in spring-flowering shrubs for forcing. Bulbs potted and plunged in sand or ashes should be watched and brought into the house to flower as fit. Hardier plants that have bloomed should be put in frames to make room for winter and spring-blooming plants.

NORTHERN

GENERAL

Light frosts may occur in exposed areas this month. However, sometimes it is mild enough to ripen late tomatoes and peppers. As the leaves fall and summer crops shrivel, it is the ideal time to make compost. Apply lime to land if needed and sterilise soil for ground pests. Plant evergreen trees and shrubs.

SHRUBS, ANNUALS, PERENNIALS AND BULBS

Insert cuttings of pansies, violas and bedding calceolarias. Plant English and Spanish iris and ixias. Shorten tops of dahlias in preparation for cutting down.

FRUIT

May is the best month to transplant citrus trees and to start planting new ones. Plant out strawberries as soon as plants are available. Put in cuttings of bush fruits, e.g., gooseberries, currants and blueberries. Start fruit tree pruning if not already done after picking fruit in the summer. Do any root pruning required.

VEGETABLES

Sow broad beans, earth up celery and leeks as necessary. Hoe and thin autumn sown crops. Plant cabbage, cauliflower and lettuce. Dig over and manure rhubarb beds. Cut down asparagus.

UNDER COVER

Take the chill off water before watering, and water carefully. Stake and tie perpetual-flowering carnations. Dry off begonias, gloxinias and achimenes. Keep a steady temperature; do not excite growth by heat. Give cinerarias, cyclamen and primulas manure water when the pots are full of roots. Clean greenhouse thoroughly and make repairs if necessary.

soil is in a suitable condition to work. However, a golden rule is to keep off the soil when it is sodden. Turn the soil up as roughly as possible to expose it to the sweetening influence of frost and air. Apply at least 100 g lime per square m and leave for the rain to wash down into the soil. Prune and spray unless it is likely to freeze soon after. During fine weather, planting can be started. Clean up all garden rubbish. Any that cannot be burned should be trenched in deeply or recycled through the compost bin. Carry out garden alterations, repair fences and pathways. Paint, clean and store stakes and labels. Check up on the year's successes and failures and make notes for next season. Make up the seed order and order new trees and shrubs. Inspect large tree and repair with tree surgery where necessary.

SHRUBS, ANNUALS, PERENNIALS AND BULBS

Tidy up old foliage of dormant perennials and spray with insecticide and fungicide to kill over-wintering larvae, eggs and spores. Hardy perennials like rudbeckia, asters and phlox can be lifted and divided. Mulch any tender perennials to protect them from soil-freezing frosts.

FRUIT

Prune stone fruit. Use a fungicide spray before and after pruning. Prune raspberries and other cane fruit, and spray with a copper-based fungicide. Plant new trees, vines and canes.

VEGETABLES

Earth up celery on dry days. Pick over onions in store. Keep them cool but protect from frost. Draw earth to the stems of beans and peas above ground. To protect from frost, part of the parsley bed should have a frame placed over it. Possibly sow a late crop of broad beans.

UNDER COVER

Bulbs that have been plunged in sand or ashes should now all be fit for bringing into the house. Sow sweet pea seed. Sow seeds of tomatoes for planting under glass. Ventilate freely when weather is bright and sunny, but keep cold winds out. Do not keep the temperature too high on dull days or at night; the day temperature should always be higher than the night temperature.

JUNE

SOUTHERN

GENERAL

Most tidying jobs should be completed by now and winter pruning is the main task. Dig and manure all vacant ground if the

NORTHERN

GENERAL

If the weather is suitable, this is a good time to clear overgrown areas and dig in compost. Trim hedges and plant new ones. Proceed with any alterations or reconstruction work. Inspect large trees and carry out any tree surgery that may be necessary. Check all mowing and spraying equipment. Repair and oil all tools.

Plant liliums in well-drained ground. Plant 10-week and beauty stocks. Lift and replant herbaceous perennials.
Prune climbing roses, ornamental trees and shrubs. Don't prune spring-flowering subjects until they have finished blooming.

Prune hydrangeas and thin out all weak growth. Start rose planting.

FRUIT
Plant strawberries and fruit trees. Prune and spray the orchard. Look over stored fruit and remove any that is damaged.

VEGETABLES
Plant or sow cabbages, cauliflowers, silverbeet and more winter lettuces. Sow a few dwarf early peas and plant a few early potatoes. Earth up celery and leeks as required. Prepare ground for new asparagus beds,

clean up old beds and give a dressing of manure.

UNDER COVER
Bring in freesias and other potted bulbs to force. Propagate bedding plants. Ventilate when the weather is favourable; be careful with watering. Remove shading from glass. Pot calceolarias, cinerarias and cyclamen. Start propagating perpetual-flowering carnations by cuttings. Prune greenhouse climbers; also vines under glass. Sow seeds of cyclamen.

GLOSSARY

Acaricide A chemical that kills mites and spiders.

Acerose Narrow with a sharp point.

Acid Any substance with a low pH. See also pH.

Acuminate Tapering to a point.

Acute Sharp pointed, without tapering.

Adpressed Tightly pressed against a surface. Usually refers to foliage that is held close to the stems.

Adventitious Occurring away from the usual place, e.g., aerial roots on stems.

Aerial layering A propagation process whereby roots are produced on a branch.

Aerial roots Those appearing above soil level, often from a branch, and used for both support and feeding.

Alkaline Any substance with a high pH. See also pH.

Alpine A habitat above the tree line and the plants that live there. Often refers to any small rockery plant of similar culture.

Alternate With leaves arranged singly on different sides of the stem and at different levels.

Angiosperm The flowering plants; the seeds of which are enclosed in an ovary.

Annual A plant that completes its life cycle from seed to maturity in one year.

Anther The pollen-bearing sac at the tip of a stamen.

Apex The tip of a leaf or organ.

Articulate A stem that is jointed or with nodes where it can be easily separated, *Schlumbergera*.

Asexual propagation To produce plants vegetatively, e.g., by cuttings, layering and tissue culture.

Attenuate Very gradually tapering.

Axil The upper angle between the stem and a leaf.

Bare rooted Trees and shrubs that are lifted from the open ground and sold with their roots wrapped in damp shredded newspaper, sphagnum moss etc.

Basal At the bottom.

Basal plate The flattened or conical stem within a bulb. Usually represented externally by a fleshy plate on the base of a bulb or corm.

Bicoloured Bearing two distinct colours at the same time.

Biennial A plant that completes its life cycle over two years.

Bigeneric hybrid A hybrid between two genera of plants.

Bipinnate A leaf that is doubly pinnate, the primary leaflets being again divided into secondary leaflets, e.g., *Jacaranda*.

Bisexual Having functional organs of both sexes in the same flower.

Bloom 1. A flower. 2. A fine powdery coating found on some leaves and fruit.

Bolt To flower and set seed prematurely.

Bottom heat Artificially heating the root zone of a cutting bed or pot, usually by electric heating pads or cables.

Bract A modified leaf or sepal at the base of a flower, often the most colourful part, e.g., *Poinsettia* and *Bougainvillea*.

Brassica Those members of the Cruciferae grown as edible vegetables, e.g., cabbage, cauliflower, Brussels sprouts and broccoli.

Broadcast To randomly scatter seeds by hand.

Bud break The period when new growth begins in spring.

Budding Grafting by inserting a stem-bud of one plant into the cambium layer of another similar plant.

Bulb An underground storage organ composed of fleshy scales.

Bulblets Small seedling bulbs or the small immature bulbs that often form around a larger parent bulb during the growing season. Those forming in the leaf axils of some bulbous plants are known as bulbils.

Bullate A puckered surface. A seersucker effect seen on some leaves, e.g., *Myrtus bullata*.

Calcareous Chalky, containing unusually high levels of calcium carbonate (lime).

Callus The protective tissue that forms over a wound and on the subterranean part of a cutting prior to root formation.

Calyx (pl. calyces) The outer, often decorative, covering of a flower bud, usually consisting of united sepals.

Cambium A layer of permanently meristematic cells found in roots and stems, but best known as the layer of cells immediately beneath the bark or skin of a stem.

Campanulate Bell shaped.

Canaliculate With upturned edges.

Cane 1. The jointed stem of large grassy plants, e.g., bamboo. 2. The long arching stems of some plant genera, e.g., orchids, raspberries and roses.

Capsule A dry, many-seeded fruit composed of two or more carpels.

Capillary action, capillarity The process whereby water is drawn up or down by the interaction of the forces of cohesion, adhesion and surface tension.

Carpel One of the units comprising the female part of the flower.

Catkin A scaly bracted, usually hanging, inflorescence. Also known informally as a tassel.

Chilling requirement A period of cold temperatures required by some plants, particularly fruit trees, to grow and flower well.

Chlorophyll The green pigment in plants essential for the process of photosynthesis.

Chlorosis An abnormal yellowing of a plant, most commonly due to a lack of iron.

Ciliate Fringed with small hairs.

Cladode A flattened, leaf-like stem performing the functions of a leaf. Also known as a cladophyll or phylloclade.

Clone An exact replica of an individual plant. Any plant propagated by vegetative means.

Companioning or companion planting A horticultural theory (by no means universally accepted) that certain plant genera grow better in proximity to certain others, each genus conferring some benefit on the other.

Compatible 1. When two or more chemicals can be mixed together without affecting the properties or activity of either. 2. A rootstock and scion that may be successfully joined by grafting or budding.

Compost Decomposed organic material used as a soil conditioner, mulch and fertiliser.

Composite Resembling a daisy, having dense flower heads composed of tiny disc florets in the centre surrounded by petal-like ray florets.

Compound 1. A leaf composed of two or more leaflets. 2. A flower composed of many small flowers or florets.

Cone The seed-bearing organs of conifers, composed of over-lapping scales on a central axis.

Conifer A plant that bears its seeds in cones.

Container grown Plants raised entirely in containers, as opposed to open ground or field grown.

Cordate Heart-shaped.

Corm An underground storage organ similar to a bulb but lacking scales, e.g., *Gladiolus*.

Cormlets Small seedling corms or the small immature corms that often form around a larger parent corm. Also known as cormels.

Corolla The petals of a flower.

Corona The crown or circle of appendages around the centre of a flower, usually between the petals and stamens, but it may be part of the corolla.

Corymb A more or less flat-topped inflorescence, the outer flowers opening first.

Cotyledon A seed leaf, part of the embryo within the seed. Cotyledons form the first leaf pair after germination in many dicotyledons and the initial leaf of many monocotyledons.

Crenate Having shallow, rounded teeth or scalloped edges.

Crenulate Finely crenate.

Crown 1. The corona. 2. The base of a plant where stem and root meet. 3. Part of a rhizome with a bud, suitable for propagation by dividing.

Cucurbit A plant belonging to the gourd family, such as pumpkins, marrows, cucumbers and squash.

Cultivar A botanical term for a variety that has arisen or is maintained in cultivation.

Cuneate Wedge shaped with a gradual, even taper to the base.

Cupressoid Resembling the genus *Cupressus*, especially the foliage.

Cutting An amputated section of a plant that will develop new roots and become self-sufficient.

Cyme A type of broad, flat-topped inflorescence in which the central flowers open first.

Damping off A disease resulting in the abrupt death of apparently healthy seedlings caused by fungi in the soil.

Deadheading The removal of faded flower heads to prevent the production of seed or to encourage heavier flowering.

Deciduous A plant that sheds all its leaves for part of the year.

Defoliant A chemical used to induce the leaves of a plant to fall.

Dentate With a serrated or toothed edge.

Denticulate Very finely toothed.

Desiccate To wilt and dry out.

Dicotyledons Flowering plants that produce two seed leaves.

Dieback A variety of fungal diseases that kill part or all of a plant by causing the tissues to die back from a shoot tip or cut branch.

Differentiation The process by which meristematic or cambial tissue becomes root, leaf, stem or flower tissue.

Digitate A leaf shape that resembles the arrangement of the fingers on a hand, e.g., *Schefflera*.

Dimorphic, dimorphous Occurring in two distinct but usually similar forms, often at the same time or within one growing season. Usually distinct from juvenile and adult forms that change over a long period.

Dioecious Having male and female reproductive organs borne on separate plants.

Diploid A plant with two complete sets of chromosomes.

Disbudding Removing lateral flower buds to concentrate growth on a single flower.

Dissected Deeply cut into numerous segments.

Divaricate Spreading widely.

Division The separation of a clump of perennial plants into smaller clumps.

Divided Describes a leaf that is separated nearly to the base or the mid rib.

Dolomite The mineral calcium magnesium carbonate, a form of lime used to add calcium to the soil without greatly altering the soil's pH.

Dominance A growth characteristic that assumes primary importance. Apical buds are dominant over those lower down the stem. Some plants have dominant flower colour pigments.

Dormancy A period of minimal growth, usually but not always occurring during winter. Seeds may also remain dormant until favourable conditions permit germination.

Drift 1. An informal planting. 2. The movement of air-borne particles of spray or dust away from the target area.

Drip line The circle around the outermost branch tips of a shrub or tree, the limit to which rainwater drips fall from the plant.

Drupe A pulpy fruit containing one (rarely two) seeds enclosed in a woody case (stone).

Embryo The young plant within the seed.

Endosperm The food storage tissue within a seed.

Endemic Native to a particular restricted area.

Epiphyte A plant growing on another tree or plant, using roots for support only and feeding

from nutrients in water and decaying plant or insect tissue, not from its host.

Espalier A shrub, tree or vine trained formally in two dimensions only, generally against a wall or fence.

Evergreen Retaining foliage throughout the year.

Exotic A plant originating in a foreign country and which is not native or endemic.

Exserted Protruding, as in the style or stamens of a flower.

Eye 1. An undeveloped growth bud on a storage organ such as a bulb, corm or tuber. 2. A contrasting colour spot in the centre of a flower.

F1 and F2 hybrids Respectively, the first and second generation offspring from a given parent plant or cross.

Family A group of related genera.

Fastigiate Narrow and upright with branches or stems erect and more or less parallel.

Fertilise 1. Apply nutrients, either to the soil or directly to the foliage of a plant. 2. Successfully pollinate flowers.

Filament A thread-like organ, especially of a stamen supporting an anther.

Floccose Covered in small woolly or hairy tufts.

Floret One of many small flowers in a compound head.

Forcing To artificially speed up maturation or flowering.

Friable Soil that is easily crumbled or reduced to a fine texture without being dry and dusty.

Frond The foliage of ferns. Also used to describe leaves of a similar appearance, such as the foliage of feather palms.

Fungicide A chemical that controls any type of fungus.

Genus (pl. genera) A grouping of closely related species.

Glabrous Without hairs of any kind.

Glaucous A distinct blue or grey tint, especially leaves.

Globose Globe shaped.

Grafting A propagation method whereby a bud or shoot is severed from its parent plant and joined to a rooted section of another.

Grex A group of seedlings from the same cross.

Growing-on line A newly propagated plant ready for potting on or planting out. Also known as a liner.

Gymnosperm A plant in which the seeds are not enclosed in an ovary, e.g., conifers and podocarps.

Half-hardy Plants damaged or killed in particularly severe or prolonged winters.

Harden off To acclimatise or prepare a young, tender plant for colder weather.

Hardwood cutting A cutting taken from wood of the previous season's growth.

Hardiness A measure of frost tolerance. The minimum temperature a particular plant can be expected to survive, perhaps with some damage. Should be used in conjunction with a rating, e.g., hardy to -10°C. Does not mean tough or disease resistant.

Haulm Stems and leaves of peas, beans, potatoes or grasses.

Heel A small strip of tissue from the main stem left on a side-shoot cutting.

Heeling in Temporarily covering a plant's roots with soil or other moisture-retentive material before final planting.

Herbaceous perennial A non-woody plant that dies back in winter, sending up new growth in spring.

Herbicide A chemical used to kill plants or weeds.

Honeydew The sticky secretion of many sap-sucking insects.

Hormone An imprecise term used for many synthetically produced growth-promoting or modifying agents, especially indolebutyric acid, a root-promoting hormone.

Hose-in-hose A flower with two corollas, one within the other.

Humus The rich debris resulting from the decomposition of vegetable and other organic material.

Hybrid The result of cross-fertilisation of different parent plants.

Indigenous Native to a particular country or area. See also endemic and exotic.

Indumentum See tomentum.

Inflorescence The flower-bearing part of a plant, irrespective of arrangement.

Insecticide A chemical used to kill insects.

Internode The length of stem between two nodes.

Invasive Said of a plant that grows quickly and spreads to occupy more than its allotted space, usually to the detriment of surrounding plants, e.g., couch grass, kikuyu grass, convolvulus and oxalis.

Juvenile A young or immature plant. Many plants display distinct differences between juvenile and adult foliage and growth habit.

Keel 1. The joined, lowermost petals in a pea-type flower. 2. A central ridge on the top part of a flower.

Laciniate Having fine lobes, giving the impression of being cut by hand.

Lanceolate Lance-shaped, long and gradually tapering.

Latent bud A normal bud that remains dormant.

Lateral On or at the side, e.g., a side-branch produced from a main stalk or trunk.

Layering Propagation by pinning a partly cut branch down to the ground until it produces roots. See also aerial layering.

Lax Loose, often semi-pendulous or trailing growth.

Leaching Movement sideways, downwards or outwards of any chemical or fertiliser in the soil as a result of rain or watering.

Leader The plant's dominant central shoot or one of several lateral shoots trained to produce a particular growth form.

Leaflet One of the smaller leaf-like parts of a compound leaf.

Leaf mould The fine compost created by the decomposition of fallen leaves.

Leaf scar The mark left after a leaf falls. Very noticeable on some plants, such as palms.

Leaf stage Growth stage of a crop or weed, usually expressed in number of leaves, e.g., second-leaf stage.

Legume A plant that produces pea-type seeds attached alternately to both sides of the pod and has root nodules that fix atmospheric nitrogen, e.g., peas, beans and lupins.

Lepidote Covered in small scales.

Lignotuber A subterranean, bulb-like storage chamber of many eucalypts and some members of the protea family that enables them to regenerate after fire.

Linear Narrow and short with sides almost parallel.

Loam A friable topsoil containing sand, clay and silt particles in certain proportions.

Lobulate Having small lobes.

Mature 1. A plant that has reached flowering age and is able to reproduce sexually. 2. A fully ripe fruit or seed.

Membranous Thin and flexible.

Miticide A chemical compound formulated to destroy mites.

Monoecious Having male and female reproductive organs in separate flowers on the one plant.

Monopodial A plant with a main stem that continues to grow indefinitely without branching.

Monotypic A genus containing only one species.

Mucronate With a sharply pointed tip.

Mulch A soil covering used to conserve moisture or prevent root damage by heat or frost.

Molluscicide A chemical used to kill or control snails and slugs.

Monocarpic A plant that dies after flowering. Such plants take longer than two years to reach maturity in contrast to annual and perennials.

Monocotyledon A plant that produces a single seedling leaf, e.g., grasses and cereals.

Mutant A spontaneous variant differing genetically and often visibly from its parent.

Mycorrhiza A beneficial association between a fungus and plant roots. Some plants, such as *Telopea*, rely on mycorrhizae for proper development.

Native A plant that occurs naturally in the area in which it is growing.

Natural cross A hybrid that occurs between two distinct, but usually related, plant species without human help.

Node A point on a stem which leaves, buds or branches are borne.

NPK A measure of the percentages of nitrogen (N), phosphorus (P) and potassium (K) in a fertiliser.

Obovate Egg shaped, with the broadest end at the top.

Offset A small division from the side of a mature clump-forming plant.

Open ground Plants raised in fields and lifted prior to sale, as opposed to container grown plants.

Opposite Leaves borne on both sides of the stem at the same node.

Orbicular A leaf that is almost circular and very flat.

Osmosis The process whereby water and sap is transported around a plant.

Ovary The structure at the base of the pistil in which the seeds of angiosperms develop.

Ovate Egg shaped, with the broadest end at the base.

Palmate Roughly hand-shaped, with three or more lobes radiating fan-like from the petiole.

Panicle A branching cluster of flowers.

Parasite A plant that lives off another plant and which is usually unable to survive without the host plant.

Pathogen An organism, especially a bacterium or fungus, capable of causing disease.

Pedicel The stalk of an individual floret within a compound head.

Peduncle The main stalk of an inflorescence or of a flower borne singly.

Peltate Shield shaped.

Perennial A plant that lives for more than two years and regrows from the same stem or root system each year.

Perianth A collective term for the entire floral envelope consisting of calyx, corolla, petals and sepals or the calyx and corolla separately.

Pericarp The outside layer or skin of a fruit.

Petaloid Resembling a petal. Usually a reference to modified stamens that have taken on a petal-like form.

Petiole The stalk of a leaf.

pH The degree of acidity or alkalinity measured on a scale from 0 (acid) to 14 (alkaline) with 7 as the neutral point.

Photosynthesis The process whereby plants use solar energy, through the catalytic action of chlorophyll, to convert water and carbon dioxide into carbohydrates.

Phylloclade See cladode.

Phytotoxic Harmful to plants.

Pilose Covered in a dense layer of soft hairs.

Pinna The individual leaflets of a pinnate leaf.

Pinnate A leaf form with leaflets arranged on both sides of the stalk, like a feather.

Pistil The female organ of a flower, comprising the stigma, style and ovary.

Pollen The spores or grains borne by an anther, containing the fertilising male gametes.

Pollination Applying pollen to the stigma.

Polymorphic Occurring in several forms, e.g., species with varying leaf forms.

Pricking out The initial transplanting of young seedlings or freshly struck cuttings.

Procumbent Said of trailing stems that do not form roots at regular intervals.

Prothallus The sexual regeneration stage of a fern.

Pseudobulb The thickened bulb-like storage organ produced by many orchids.

Pubescent Covered, often sparsely, in short hairs.

Raceme A stalk with flowers along its length, the individual blossoms with short stems.

Radicle The root of the embryo seedling, often covered in fine root hairs.

Ray 1. A stem of an umbel. 2. One of the outer florets of a compound head, especially of daisy flower heads.

Recurved Bent backwards and/or downwards.

Reflexed Sharply recurved.

Respiration A process similar to breathing whereby plants combine oxygen with carbohydrate molecules, releasing energy as carbon dioxide and water.

Reticulate A net-like structure or markings.

Rhizome Underground or surface-creeping stem that enables plants to spread. May also act as a storage organ.

Root hair The very fine hair-like growths at the tip of a root. The most active feeding and growing part of the root.

Rootstock A rooted section of plant used as the base onto which a scion from another plant is grafted.

Rosette An arrangement of leaves radiating from a crown or centre, usually close to the ground.

Run off The excess of a spray solution that runs off a surface after it has been thoroughly wetted.

Russet A rough brownish marking on leaves, fruits or tubers.

Sac A pouch-like structure, e.g., a pollen sac.

Scale 1. The protective covering of many so-called scale insects that suck vital fluids out of plant tissue. 2. A segment of bulb that may in some cases, e.g., lilies, be detached for propagation.

Scandent Having a climbing habit.

Scarify The method of weakening the covering of some hard-cased seeds to hasten germination.

Scion A bud or shoot that is grafted onto the stock of another plant.

Sepal The individual segment of a calyx.

Serrate Having a saw-toothed or serrate edge.

Sessile Without a stalk.

Softwood Unripened, immature tissue of any woody plant. Used for propagation in some species.

Spadix A fleshy spike or a small flower head.

Spatulate A oblong shape that gradually broadens towards the tip.

Species The basic or minor unit in binomial nomenclature.

Specific name A plant's second name, e.g., *Pinus* **radiata**.

Spike A series of stalkless flowers on a single stem. The lower flowers are the first to open.

Sporangia Spore clusters, usually found on the underside of a sporophyll.

Spore The asexual reproductive cell of ferns, mosses and fungi.

Sporophyll Modified leaves or fronds that bear sporangia, e.g., the 'fertile fronds' of ferns.

Sport A mutation showing distinct variations from the norm, e.g., a different foliage form or flower colour.

Spreader A substance that increases the area that a given volume of liquid will cover, usually by reducing surface tension.

Spur 1. A specialised flowering and fruiting side shoot found in many fruit trees. 2. The tubular structure seen on some flowers, e.g., larkspur and *Aquilegia*.

Stamen The pollen-bearing or male organ of a flower. Usually composed of a filament and an anther.

Standard 1. A plant grafted onto a tall, straight stock or trained to a bushy head at the top of a tall stem. 2. A more or less erect petal of a flower, e.g., *Iris*.

Stellate Star-like or star shaped.

Sticker A material added to a chemical to increase its adherence to a leaf surface.

Stigma A sticky pad at the end of the style that receives the pollen.

Stipe The petiole of a fern frond.

Stock 1. The rooted plant onto which the scion or cutting is grafted. 2. The parent plant from which cuttings are collected.

Stolon A shoot that grows along the soil surface, taking root at intervals and giving rise to new plants, e.g., couch or kikuyu grass.

Stomata The pores, largely on the underside of the leaves, through which a plant transpires and exchanges gases. Plants are able to regulate the flow of moisture through the stomata to help cope with water stress.

Stratify To treat dormant seeds by chilling under moist conditions to simulate winter and effect germination.

Strike To cause a cutting to take root.

Style The tubular part of the pistil between the ovary and stigma, often elongated.

Subshrub A permanently woody plant with soft pliable stems. Often green barked but woody at the base.

Succulent Leaves or stems that are juicy, fleshy and often thick.

Sucker An adventitious stem arising from the roots of a woody plant, often from the stock rather than the scion of a grafted plant.

Symbiosis Two plants or other organisms living together to their mutual benefit.

Systemic Any substance capable of permeating through the entire plant. Often said of insecticides and fungicides.

Taxonomy The science of plant classification.

Tender Intolerant of freezing conditions or prolonged exposure to low temperatures above freezing.

Tendril A twisting, thread-like extension by which a plant clings to a support. It may be a part of a leaf or stem.

Tepal The petal-like structures of a flower that does not have clearly defined sepals and petals, e.g., *Magnolia*.

Terminal bud The bud at the tip of the stem. Usually the first to burst into growth at bud break.

Ternate Arranged in threes.

Tetraploid A plant with four complete sets of chromosomes.

Thinning out 1. Pruning to reduce foliage density. 2. Removing some seedlings to allow more room for the remainder to grow.

Tip cutting A cutting of new growth used for the propagating many plants.

Tomentum The furry coating found on some leaves and stems, e.g., pohutukawa and many rhododendrons, hence tomentose. Also known as indumentum.

Topiary Trimming shrubs and trees to predetermined shapes for aesthetic appeal rather than growth restriction or function.

Transpiration Loss of moisture through the surface cells of the plant, primarily through the stomata.

Trifoliate A leaf that is divided into three leaflets, e.g., clover.

Triploid A plant with three complete sets of chromosomes.

Truncate Ending or cut off abruptly or at right angles.

Truss A compound terminal cluster of flowers borne on one stalk.

Tuber A modified root that acts as a storage organ. Similar to a rhizome but usually shorter and thicker and does not elongate greatly as it grows, e.g., potato.

Tuberous root An underground storage organ that resembles a tuber but is actually a root. Growth buds form from the point where the previous year's growth stems were, rather than from eyes, e.g., *Dahlia*.

Turgid Plant material at its normal moisture level. As opposed to wilted.

Umbel A group of flower heads growing from a common point on a stem, hence umbellate.

Undulate Having a wavy edge.

Union The join between a rootstock and scion.

Unisexual Flowers with either functional male or female organs but not both.

Varietal name see Cultivar.

Variety Strictly a subdivision of a species, but often refers to a recognisably different member of a plant species worthy of cultivation.

Vegetative 1. Those parts of the plant that are not involved with sexual reproduction. 2. A condition of growth in which flowering has not and is not about to occur.

Viability 1. The number of seeds in a group that are alive at any particular time. 2. The period of time after ripening in which a seed remains able to germinate.

Virus A minute acellular organism, only able to replicate within a living cell, that causes discolouration, malformation or death of infected tissues.

Verrucose Warty. Hence verrucosis, a disease that causes warty growths on the surface of fruit, especially citrus.

Voluble Twining, especially climbing by twining.

Water shoot Very vigorous, soft-wooded shoot that grows very rapidly. Usually non-productive and best removed.

Water stress When a plant is using more moisture than it can take in, usually leading to wilting.

Whorl A circle of three or more flowers or branches on a stem at the same level.

Wilt A viral disease characterised by wilted foliage, more properly known as verticillium wilt.

Xerophyte A plant adapted to growing in dry regions, hence xerophytic.

Zygomorphic Bilaterally symmetrical, i.e., capable of being divided into two equal halves in one plane only, as in many flowers.

INDEX

* Figures in italics refer to illustrations.